W9-BSS-198

the best of
Cooking Light

Tomato and
Roasted Pepper Salad
(page 250)

the best of
Cooking Light

compiled and edited by

Holley Contri Johnson, M.S., R.D.

©2004 by Oxmoor House, Inc.
Book Division of Southern Progress Corporation
P.O. Box 2463, Birmingham, Alabama 35201

All rights reserved. No part of this book may be reproduced in any form or by any means without the prior written permission of the publisher, excepting brief quotes in connection with reviews written specifically for inclusion in a magazine or newspaper.

Direct ISBN: 0-8487-3002-X
Retail ISBN: 0-8487-3061-5
Library of Congress Control Number: 2004111271

Printed in the United States of America
First printing 2004

Be sure to check with your health-care provider before making any changes in your diet.

Oxmoor House, Inc.

Editor in Chief: Nancy Fitzpatrick Wyatt
Executive Editor: Katherine M. Eakin
Art Director: Cynthia Rose Cooper
Copy Chief: Allison Long Lowery

The Best of Cooking Light®

Editor: Holley Contri Johnson, M.S., R.D.
Editorial Assistants: Terri Laschober, Dawn Russell
Publishing Systems Administrator: Rick Tucker
Director of Production: Phillip Lee
Production Manager: Terri Beste
Production Assistant: Faye Porter Bonner

Contributors:

Copy Editor: Lisa C. Bailey
Designer: Rita Yerby
Indexer: Mary Ann Laurens
Editorial Intern: Sheila Egts

To order additional publications, call 1-800-765-6400, or visit **oxmoorhouse.com**

Cover: *Strawberry-Almond Cream Tart* (page 373)

Cooking Light®

Editor in Chief: Mary Kay Culpepper
Executive Editor: Billy R. Sims
Managing Editor: Maelynn Cheung
Senior Food Editor: Alison Mann Ashton
Senior Editor: Anamary Pelayo
Editorial Coordinator: Carol C. Noe
Food Editor: Krista Ackerbloom Montgomery, M.S., R.D.
Associate Food Editor: Ann Taylor Pittman
Assistant Food Editor: Susan Stone, R.D.
Assistant Editor: Rachel Seligman
Senior Editor/Food Development Director:
    Ellen Templeton Carroll, M.S., R.D.
Art Director: Susan Waldrip Dendy
Assistant Art Director: Maya Metz Logue
Senior Designer: Fernande Bondarenko
Designer: J. Shay McNamee
Assistant Designer: Brigette Mayer
Senior Photographer: Becky Luigart-Stayner
Photographer: Randy Mayor
Senior Photo Stylist: Cindy Barr
Photo Stylists: Melanie J. Clarke, Jan Gautro
Digital Photo Stylist: Jan A. Smith
Studio Assistant: Celine Chenoweth
Test Kitchens Director: Vanessa Taylor Johnson
Food Stylist: Kellie Gerber Kelley
Assistant Food Stylist: M. Kathleen Kanen
Test Kitchens Staff: Sam Brannock, Kathryn Conrad,
    Jan Jacks Moon, Tiffany Vickers, Mike Wilson
Copy Chief: Maria Parker Hopkins
Senior Copy Editor: Susan Roberts
Copy Editor: Tara Trenary
Research Editor: Dani Leigh Clemmons
Production Manager: Liz Rhoades
Production Editors: Joanne McCrary Brasseal,
    Hazel R. Eddins
Office Manager: Rita K. Jackson
Editorial Assistants: Cindy Hatcher, Brandy Rushing
Correspondence Editor: Michelle Gibson Daniels
Interns: Virginia Gregory, Alicia Reece

CookingLight.com

Editor: Jennifer Middleton
Online Producer: Abigail Masters

contents

welcome

Most regular readers of *Cooking Light* turn to our

Greatest Hits column before they read anything else in the magazine. It's the box on the index page that lists our favorite recipes, the dishes we on the staff gravitate to when we're putting each issue together.

Mary Kay Culpepper
Editor, *Cooking Light*

To be sure, all *Cooking Light* recipes have to meet our high standards of great taste, balanced nutrition, and straightforward preparation. But a few each issue are so terrific that they stand out. Those Greatest Hits—plus a few other well-chosen recipes—comprise our annual Special Edition, *The Best of Cooking Light* available on newsstands and at bookstores. And because this book contains the first five volumes of *The Best of Cooking Light*, it offers over 500 of the best of our best recipes.

One thing that I've learned from editing America's foremost food and fitness magazine is that tastes are highly subjective; our Greatest Hits may not be what you fancy. Yet the range of recipes in this book is so broad, you're certain to find many that suit your tastes and the various occasions you have to cook for.

My own favorites over the years are all delicious and evoke happy memories in the making as well as the eating. **Here are some of my favorite recipes:**

Filet Mignon with Peppercorn-Mustard Sauce (page 169) is a glamorous New Year's Eve splurge.

Vegetable Lasagna (page 130) makes a terrific vegetarian dinner, especially in summer when produce is at its peak.

Vinegar-Braised Beef with Thyme, Carrots, and Onions (page 176) was a big hit for Christmas Eve dinner.

Anzac Bisuits (page 398) are incredible warm from the oven with a glass of cold milk.

Tiramisu Anacapri (page 392) is rich and sweet, and can conveniently be made ahead.

New Orleans Bread Pudding with Bourbon Sauce (page 382) is a fitting end to supper in front of the fireplace.

Plus, Miso-Glazed Salmon (page 81), a standby that's salty and savory, can be ready in minutes. Chicken Strudel (page 204)—an easy but showy entrée—works well for spring showers and brunches. And Buttermilk Pralines (page 404) are fun to make for holiday gifts.

If you like to eat smart, be fit, and live well, this is the cookbook for you. My colleagues and I hope you enjoy finding, cooking, and sharing your best in *The Best of Cooking Light*.

Mary Kay Culpepper

Appetizers and Beverages

Crostini with Gorgonzola, Caramelized
Onions, and Fig Jam, page 15

Baba Gha-Hummus

  1 large eggplant
  3 tablespoons tahini (sesame-seed paste)
  1½ teaspoons ground cumin
  1 teaspoon ground coriander
  ¾ teaspoon salt
  ⅛ teaspoon ground red pepper
  2 garlic cloves, chopped
  1 (15-ounce) can chickpeas (garbanzo beans), rinsed and drained

1. Preheat oven to 375°.
2. Pierce eggplant with a fork. Place eggplant on a jelly roll pan; bake at 375° for 30 minutes or until tender. Cool eggplant completely; peel. Cut eggplant into wedges.
3. Combine eggplant, tahini, and remaining ingredients in a food processor; process until smooth. Yield: 2 cups (serving size: ¼ cup).

CALORIES 114 (30% from fat); FAT 3.8g (sat 0.5g, mono 1.3g, poly 1.6g); PROTEIN 4.3g; CARB 17.3g; FIBER 5g; CHOL 0mg; IRON 1.5mg; SODIUM 368mg; CALC 51mg

Edamame Hummus with Pita Crisps

  6 (6-inch) pitas, split in half horizontally
  1½ cups frozen blanched shelled edamame (green soybeans)
  4 teaspoons extravirgin olive oil, divided
  ½ teaspoon salt
  ½ teaspoon ground cumin
  ¼ teaspoon ground coriander
  2 garlic cloves, peeled
  ½ cup fresh flat-leaf parsley leaves
  3 tablespoons tahini (sesame-seed paste)
  3 tablespoons water
  3 tablespoons fresh lemon juice
  ½ teaspoon paprika

1. Preheat oven to 350°.
2. Arrange pita halves in a single layer on oven rack. Bake pita halves at 350° for 15 minutes or until crisp, and cool completely on a wire rack. Break each pita half into about 6 chips.
3. Prepare edamame according to package directions, omitting salt. Place 1 tablespoon olive oil, salt, ground cumin, ground coriander, and garlic cloves in a food processor, and pulse 2 to 3 times or until coarsely chopped. Add edamame, parsley, tahini, water, and juice, and process 1 minute or

until smooth. Spoon hummus into a serving bowl. Drizzle with 1 teaspoon olive oil, and sprinkle with paprika. Serve with pita crisps. Yield: 12 servings (serving size: 2 tablespoons hummus and about 6 pita crisps).

CALORIES 147 (30% from fat); FAT 4.9g (sat 0.6g, mono 2.2g, poly 1.9g); PROTEIN 5.6g; CARB 20.3g; FIBER 2.2g; CHOL 0mg; IRON 1.5mg; SODIUM 268mg; CALC 48mg

Asian Peanut Dip

  ½ cup natural-style peanut butter
  ⅓ cup reduced-fat firm silken tofu
  3 tablespoons light brown sugar
  2 tablespoons fresh lime juice
  2 tablespoons low-sodium soy sauce
  ½ to ¾ teaspoon crushed red pepper
  2 garlic cloves, crushed

1. Place all ingredients in a blender, and process until smooth, scraping sides. Store in an airtight container in refrigerator up to 2 days. Yield: 1 cup (serving size: 2 tablespoons).

CALORIES 122 (57% from fat); FAT 7.7g (sat 1.5g, mono 3.8g, poly 2.5g); PROTEIN 5.4g; CARB 7.4g; FIBER 0.5g; CHOL 0mg; IRON 0.4mg; SODIUM 131mg; CALC 19mg

Salsa de Molcajete (Roasted Tomato and Green Chile Salsa)

  6 plum tomatoes (about 1 pound)
  3 garlic cloves, unpeeled
  2 jalapeño peppers
  ⅓ cup chopped fresh cilantro
  ¼ cup finely chopped onion
  1 teaspoon fresh lime juice
  ¼ teaspoon salt

1. Preheat broiler.
2. Place the tomatoes, garlic, and jalapeños on a foil-lined baking sheet. Broil for 16 minutes, turning after 8 minutes. Cool and peel tomatoes and garlic. Combine the garlic and peppers in a molcajete, mortar, or bowl; pound with a pestle or the back of a spoon to form a paste. Add tomatoes, and coarsely crush using the pestle or spoon. Combine the tomato mixture, cilantro, and remaining ingredients in a small bowl. Yield: 6 servings (serving size: ¼ cup).

CALORIES 23 (12% from fat); FAT 0.3g (sat 0g; mono 0.1g; poly 0.1g); PROTEIN 0.9g; CARB 5g; FIBER 1.2g; CHOL 0mg; IRON 0.5mg; SODIUM 106mg; CALC 10mg

above left: Roasted-Poblano Guacamole with Garlic and Parsley; right: Salsa de Molcajete

Roasted-Poblano Guacamole with Garlic and Parsley

Roasted poblano chiles work magic on the rich, almost nutty-tasting avocados.

2 poblano chiles (about 6 ounces)
2 plum tomatoes (about 6 ounces)
2 garlic cloves, unpeeled
1⅓ cups ripe peeled avocado, seeded and coarsely mashed (about 3)
3 tablespoons chopped fresh flat-leaf parsley
2 tablespoons fresh lime juice
¼ teaspoon salt
2 tablespoons grated Mexican añejo or fresh Parmesan cheese
2 tablespoons sliced radishes
7 ounces baked tortilla chips (about 7 cups)

1. Preheat broiler.
2. Cut poblano chiles in half lengthwise, and discard seeds and membranes. Place poblano halves, skin sides up, plum tomatoes, and garlic cloves on a foil-lined baking sheet. Broil for 12 minutes or until poblanos are blackened, turning tomatoes once. Place poblanos in a zip-top plastic bag, and seal. Let stand for 10 minutes. Peel poblanos, tomatoes, and garlic. Place poblanos and garlic in a food processor, and pulse until coarsely chopped. Combine poblano mixture, tomatoes, mashed avocado, chopped parsley, lime juice, and salt in bowl. Sprinkle with cheese and sliced radishes. Serve with tortilla chips. Yield: 8 servings (serving size: ¼ cup guacamole and about ¾ cup chips).

CALORIES 179 (38% from fat); FAT 7.5g (sat 1.3g, mono 4.1g, poly 1.5g); PROTEIN 3.6g; CARB 27g; FIBER 4.8g; CHOL 2mg; IRON 1mg; SODIUM 280mg; CALC 57mg

White Bean and Bacon Dip with Rosemary Pita Chips

The homemade rosemary-flecked chips are a great complement to the garlicky dip, but plain pita or bagel chips are a fine stand-in.

CHIPS:
- ½ teaspoon dried crushed rosemary
- ¼ teaspoon salt
- ¼ teaspoon garlic powder
- ⅛ teaspoon freshly ground black pepper
- 3 (6-inch) pitas, each cut into 8 wedges
- Cooking spray

DIP:
- 2 applewood-smoked bacon slices, chopped (such as Nueske's)
- 4 garlic cloves, minced
- ⅓ cup fat-free, less-sodium chicken broth
- 1 (19-ounce) can cannellini beans, drained
- ¼ cup chopped green onions
- 1 tablespoon fresh lemon juice
- ½ teaspoon hot sauce
- ⅛ teaspoon salt
- ⅛ teaspoon paprika

1. Preheat oven to 350°.

2. To prepare chips, combine first 4 ingredients. Arrange pita wedges in a single layer on a baking sheet. Lightly coat pita wedges with cooking spray, and sprinkle evenly with rosemary mixture. Lightly recoat pita wedges with cooking spray. Bake at 350° for 20 minutes or until golden.

3. To prepare dip, cook bacon in a small saucepan over medium heat until crisp. Remove bacon from pan with a slotted spoon, and set aside. Add garlic to drippings in pan, and cook 1 minute, stirring frequently. Add broth and beans; bring to a boil. Reduce heat, and simmer, uncovered, 10 minutes.

4. Combine bean mixture, onions, and remaining ingredients in a food processor, and process until smooth. Spoon mixture into a bowl; stir in 1 tablespoon reserved bacon. Sprinkle dip with remaining bacon just before serving. Serve with pita chips. Yield: 8 servings (serving size: 3 tablespoons dip and 3 pita chips).

CALORIES 137 (25% from fat); FAT 3.8g (sat 1.3g, mono 1.5g, poly 0.7g); PROTEIN 4.7g; CARB 20.5g; FIBER 2.6g; CHOL 3.8mg; IRON 1.4mg; SODIUM 397mg; CALC 39mg

Beet and Goat Cheese Crostini

Prepare the components of this recipe ahead of time, and assemble it at the last minute.

BEETS:
- ¾ pound beets (about 2 medium)
- 1 cup water
- 1 tablespoon balsamic vinegar
- 1 teaspoon grated lemon rind
- 1 teaspoon fresh lemon juice
- ¼ teaspoon sea salt
- ¼ teaspoon freshly ground black pepper

CHEESE SPREAD:
- 1 (5-ounce) package goat cheese
- 1 tablespoon light mayonnaise
- 2 teaspoons minced fresh or ½ teaspoon dried tarragon
- ⅛ teaspoon freshly ground black pepper
- 1 garlic clove, crushed
- 24 (½-inch-thick) slices diagonally cut French bread baguette, toasted

1. Preheat oven to 375°.

2. To prepare beets, leave root and 1 inch of stem on beets; scrub with a brush. Place beets in an 11 x 7-inch baking dish; add water. Cover and bake at 375° for 45 minutes or until tender. Drain and cool.

3. Trim off beet roots; rub off skins. Cut beets lengthwise into quarters; cut each quarter crosswise into 9 (⅛-inch) slices.

4. Combine vinegar, rind, juice, salt, and ¼ teaspoon pepper in a medium bowl. Add beets; toss gently to coat.

5. To prepare cheese spread, combine cheese, mayonnaise, tarragon, ⅛ teaspoon pepper, and garlic in a small bowl. Spread each baguette slice with 1 teaspoon cheese mixture; top with 3 slightly overlapping slices of beet. Yield: 12 servings (serving size: 2 crostini).

CALORIES 127 (27% from fat); FAT 3.8g (sat 2g, mono 0.9g, poly 0.3g); PROTEIN 5.2g; CARB 18g; FIBER 1.4g; CHOL 6mg; IRON 1.2mg; SODIUM 297mg; CALC 44mg

Muhammara

This pepper puree, originally from southeast Turkey, has become ubiquitous in Istanbul, where it's widely used as a condiment. You can also serve it as a dip with pita or flatbread.

2 red bell peppers
2 tablespoons water
1 tablespoon olive oil
1 teaspoon salt
1 teaspoon cumin seeds
2 teaspoons balsamic vinegar
2 teaspoons pomegranate molasses or molasses
¼ teaspoon crushed red pepper
3 garlic cloves
2 (2-ounce) slices whole-wheat nut bread
   (such as Arnold Health Nut)
1 habanero pepper, seeded
⅓ cup walnuts, toasted

1. Preheat broiler.
2. Cut bell peppers in half lengthwise; discard seeds and membranes. Place pepper halves, skin sides up, on a foil-lined baking sheet; flatten with hand. Broil 15 minutes or until blackened. Place in a zip-top plastic bag; seal. Let stand 20 minutes. Peel.
3. Place bell pepper and next 10 ingredients in a food processor, and process until mixture is smooth. Add walnuts, and pulse 5 times or until nuts are coarsely chopped. Yield: 2 cups (serving size: 2 tablespoons).

CALORIES 50 (49% from fat); FAT 2.7g (sat 0.3g, mono 1.1g, poly 1.2g); PROTEIN 1.5g; CARB 5.4g; FIBER 0.9g; CHOL 0mg; IRON 0.5mg; SODIUM 182mg; CALC 11mg

Pissaladière Tartlets

Present this classic French onion, anchovy, and olive pie in miniature form. They're an ideal make-ahead appetizer, and easy to take to a party or supper club. Prepare the tart shells and the filling a day in advance, and store separately in airtight containers—the shells at room temperature, and the filling in the refrigerator. Assemble at the party or dinner.

1 tablespoon olive oil
10 cups thinly vertically sliced onion (about 4 medium)
¼ teaspoon salt
3 canned anchovy fillets, chopped
¼ cup balsamic vinegar
1 teaspoon chopped fresh thyme
¼ cup niçoise olives, pitted and chopped
24 (½-ounce) slices very thin white bread (such as Pepperidge Farm)
Cooking spray
¼ teaspoon whole fresh thyme leaves

1. Heat olive oil in a large nonstick skillet over medium-high heat. Add onion; sauté 10 minutes. Stir in salt and anchovies, and sauté 10 minutes. Stir in vinegar and chopped thyme. Reduce heat to medium-low, and cook 3 minutes or until liquid is absorbed, stirring frequently. Stir in olives. Cool to room temperature.

2. Preheat oven to 375°.

3. Trim crusts from bread, and reserve crusts for another use. Lightly coat both sides of bread with cooking spray. Place 1 bread slice into each of 24 miniature muffin cups, pressing bread into pan to form cups (bread tips will stick up). Bake at 375° for 10 minutes or until dry and golden. Carefully remove bread cups from pan, and cool on a wire rack. Spoon 1 heaping tablespoon onion mixture into each bread cup. Sprinkle tartlets evenly with whole fresh thyme leaves. Yield: 12 servings (serving size: 2 tartlets).

CALORIES 122 (30% from fat); FAT 4g (sat 0.4g, mono 2.5g, poly 0.4g); PROTEIN 2.9g; CARB 18.3g; FIBER 1.8g; CHOL 1mg; IRON 0.8mg; SODIUM 281mg; CALC 39mg

Crostini with Gorgonzola, Caramelized Onions, and Fig Jam

(pictured on page 8)

The Gorgonzola is a great combo with the sweet fig jam, but feta or any other soft, pungent cheese will work.

JAM:
1 cup dried Black Mission figs (about 6 ounces)
1 teaspoon lemon juice
2 cups water
2 tablespoons maple syrup
Dash of salt

ONIONS:
Cooking spray
2 cups vertically sliced yellow onion
1 teaspoon balsamic vinegar
½ teaspoon chopped fresh thyme
¼ teaspoon salt
½ cup water

REMAINING INGREDIENTS:
½ cup (4 ounces) Gorgonzola cheese, softened
24 (1-inch-thick) slices diagonally cut French bread baguette, toasted (about 12 ounces)
1 teaspoon chopped fresh parsley

1. To prepare jam, remove stems from figs. Place figs and juice in a food processor, and process until figs are coarsely chopped. Place fig mixture, 2 cups water, syrup, and dash of salt in a medium saucepan, and bring to a boil. Reduce heat, and simmer 25 minutes or until thick. Cool completely.

2. To prepare onions, heat a large nonstick skillet coated with cooking spray over medium heat. Add onion, balsamic vinegar, thyme, and ¼ teaspoon salt; cover and cook 5 minutes. Uncover and cook 20 minutes or until onion is deep golden brown, stirring occasionally. While onion cooks, add ½ cup water, ¼ cup at a time, to keep onion from sticking to pan.

3. Spread 1 teaspoon Gorgonzola cheese over each baguette slice. Top each slice with about 1 teaspoon caramelized onions and 1 teaspoon jam. Sprinkle evenly with chopped parsley. Yield: 12 servings (serving size: 2 crostini).

CALORIES 106 (29% from fat); FAT 3.4g (sat 1.9g, mono 0.9g, poly 0.3g); PROTEIN 2.9g; CARB 16.3g; FIBER 2.4g; CHOL 8mg; IRON 0.6mg; SODIUM 82mg; CALC 85mg

Mushroom Duxelles on Bruschetta

Duxelles (dook-SEHL) is a mixture of finely chopped mushrooms cooked to the consistency of a pâté. This version uses shiitakes and creminis, but you can use any combination of mushrooms.

16 (½-inch-thick) slices diagonally cut French bread baguette
4 cups cremini mushrooms (about 8 ounces)
4 cups shiitake mushroom caps (about 8 ounces)
Cooking spray
3 garlic cloves, minced
2 tablespoons chopped fresh parsley
3 tablespoons whipping cream
2 teaspoons chopped fresh thyme
½ teaspoon kosher salt
¼ teaspoon ground black pepper

1. Prepare grill or broiler.
2. Place bread on a grill rack or baking sheet; cook 1 minute on each side or until toasted.
3. Place mushrooms in a food processor; pulse 10 times or until finely chopped.
4. Heat a large nonstick skillet coated with cooking spray over medium-high heat. Add mushrooms and garlic; sauté 10 minutes or until most of the liquid evaporates. Add parsley and remaining ingredients, and cook 2 minutes, stirring occasionally. Spoon 1 tablespoon duxelles onto each toasted bread slice. Serve immediately. Yield: 8 servings (serving size: 2 bread slices and 2 tablespoons duxelles).

CALORIES 117 (30% from fat); FAT 3.9g (sat 1.6g, mono 1.1g, poly 1g); PROTEIN 3.7g; CARB 16.4g; FIBER 2.1g; CHOL 8mg; IRON 1.1mg; SODIUM 244mg; CALC 12mg

Herbed Ricotta Won Tons with Spicy Tomato Sauce

The habanero pepper in the sauce is fiery, so wear gloves while chopping it. To tame the heat, substitute a jalapeño or poblano pepper. You can make the won tons ahead of time and freeze them. Bake them just before serving.

WON TONS:

- 1 cup part-skim ricotta cheese
- ¼ cup blanched almonds, toasted
- ½ teaspoon all-purpose flour
- ½ cup chopped fresh mint
- 2 tablespoons grated fresh Parmesan cheese
- 2 tablespoons fresh flat-leaf parsley leaves
- 2 tablespoons finely chopped fresh chives
- 1 tablespoon grated lemon rind
- ½ teaspoon fine sea salt
- ¼ teaspoon freshly ground black pepper
- 1 large egg white
- 1 garlic clove, chopped
- 30 won ton wrappers
  - Cooking spray
- 1 large egg white, lightly beaten

SAUCE:

- 1 (28-ounce) can whole tomatoes, drained
- 1 teaspoon olive oil
- ⅔ cup chopped onion
- 2 teaspoons finely grated orange rind
- 1 teaspoon sugar
- 1 habanero pepper, finely chopped
- 2 tablespoons chopped fresh basil

1. To prepare won tons, place colander in a 2-quart glass measure or bowl. Line colander with 2 layers of cheesecloth, allowing cheesecloth to extend over outside edges of bowl. Spoon ricotta into colander. Gather edges of cheesecloth together; tie securely. Refrigerate for 1 hour. Gently squeeze cheesecloth bag to remove excess liquid; discard liquid. Spoon ricotta into a food processor.

2. Preheat oven to 350°.

3. Place almonds and flour in a spice or coffee grinder; process until finely ground. Set aside 3 tablespoons of almond mixture; add remaining almond mixture, mint, and next 8 ingredients to ricotta in food processor. Process until mixture is smooth.

4. Working with 1 won ton wrapper at a time (cover remaining wrappers with a damp towel to keep from drying), spoon about 2 teaspoons ricotta mixture into center of each wrapper. Moisten edges of dough with water; bring 2 opposite corners together. Press edges together to seal, forming a triangle. Repeat procedure with remaining won ton wrappers and ricotta mixture.

5. Place won tons on 2 baking sheets lined with parchment paper and coated with cooking spray. Brush won tons with lightly beaten egg white; sprinkle with reserved almond mixture.

6. Bake at 350° for 15 minutes or until lightly browned. Cool won tons 5 minutes on a wire rack.

7. To prepare sauce, place tomatoes in food processor; process until finely chopped. Heat oil in a large nonstick skillet over medium-high heat. Add onion; sauté 3 minutes. Stir in orange rind, sugar, and habanero pepper; sauté 2 minutes. Reduce heat to medium. Stir in tomatoes and basil; cook 10 minutes, stirring occasionally. Serve with won tons. Yield: 15 servings (serving size: 2 won tons and about 1 tablespoon sauce).

CALORIES 120 (29% from fat); FAT 3.9g (sat 2.2g, mono 1g, poly 0.4g); PROTEIN 5.8g; CARB 15.5g; FIBER 1.9g; CHOL 10mg; IRON 1.3mg; SODIUM 456mg; CALC 111mg

Mini-Spanakopitas
(Greek Spinach Pies)

FILLING:
- 1 (10-ounce) package fresh spinach, coarsely chopped
- ⅓ cup (about 1½ ounces) feta cheese, crumbled
- ¼ cup 1% low-fat cottage cheese
- 2 tablespoons grated Parmesan cheese
- 2 teaspoons olive oil
- 1½ cups chopped green onions
- 1½ tablespoons chopped fresh or 1½ teaspoons dried dill
- 1 tablespoon fresh lemon juice
- ¼ teaspoon salt
- ¼ teaspoon black pepper
- 2 large egg whites, lightly beaten

REMAINING INGREDIENTS:
- 1 tablespoon olive oil
- ¼ teaspoon salt
- 1 large egg white
- 5 sheets frozen phyllo dough, thawed

1. Preheat oven to 350°.

2. To prepare filling, place spinach in a large skillet or Dutch oven. Place over medium heat; cook until spinach wilts. Place spinach in a colander and press until barely moist. Combine spinach and cheeses in a bowl, and set aside.

3. Heat 2 teaspoons oil in a nonstick skillet over medium-high heat. Add onions; sauté 2 minutes or until soft. Stir onions and next 5 ingredients into spinach mixture.

4. Combine 1 tablespoon olive oil, ¼ teaspoon salt, and 1 egg white in a small bowl, stirring mixture with a whisk. Working with 1 phyllo sheet at a time, cut each sheet lengthwise into 4 (3½-inch-wide) strips, and lightly brush with egg mixture (cover remaining phyllo dough to keep it from drying). Spoon about 1 tablespoon spinach mixture onto one end of each phyllo strip. Fold one corner of opposite end over mixture, forming a triangle, and keep folding back and forth into a triangle to end of phyllo strip.

5. Place triangles, seam sides down, on a baking sheet. Bake at 350° for 20 minutes or until golden. Yield: 20 appetizers (serving size: 1 triangle).

CALORIES 43 (44% from fat); FAT 2.1g (sat 0.6g, mono 1.1g, poly 0.3g); PROTEIN 2.3g; CARB 4g; FIBER 0.8g; CHOL 2mg; IRON 0.8mg; SODIUM 147mg; CALC 44mg

Grilled Clams with Sambuca and Italian Sausage

A vegetable grill grate can be used in place of the shellfish grate. Or you can buy bigger clams and set them directly on the grill rack. Adapted from Steven Raichlen's books *How to Grill* (Workman, 2001) and *BBQ USA* (Workman, 2003).

    4   ounces hot turkey Italian sausage (about ½ link)
    ¼   cup finely chopped onion
    ¼   cup finely chopped green bell pepper
    ¼   cup finely chopped red bell pepper
    ½   teaspoon butter
    1   garlic clove, minced
    1   (1-ounce) slice day-old white bread
    2   tablespoons Sambuca or Pernod
        (licorice-flavored liqueur)
    ½   teaspoon Worcestershire sauce
    ⅛   teaspoon black pepper
    Dash of salt
    36 littleneck clams, cleaned
    6   lemon wedges

1. Remove casings from sausage. Heat a large non-stick skillet over medium heat. Add sausage, and cook until browned, stirring to crumble. Add onion, peppers, butter, and garlic to pan; cook 5 minutes, stirring frequently.
2. Place the bread in a food processor, and pulse 5 times or until breadcrumbs form. Add breadcrumbs to sausage mixture; cook 3 minutes, stirring constantly. Pour Sambuca into one side of skillet. Ignite Sambuca with a long match; let flames die down. Stir in the Worcestershire sauce, pepper, and salt.
3. Prepare grill to high heat.
4. Shuck clams; discard any broken shells or shells that remain open. Place 12 clam halves on shellfish grate; discard top halves of shells. Top each with about 1 teaspoon breadcrumb mixture. Place grate on grill. Cover and cook 4 minutes or until clam juice in shells boils. Remove clams from grate; keep warm. Repeat procedure with remaining clams and breadcrumbs. Serve with lemon wedges. Yield: 6 servings (serving size: 6 clams and 1 lemon wedge).

CALORIES 120 (23% from fat); FAT 3.1g (sat 0.8g, mono 0.8g, poly 0.6g); PROTEIN 15g; CARB 6.2g; FIBER 0.4g; CHOL 44mg; IRON 5.9mg; SODIUM 221mg; CALC 38mg

Crab Salad with Corn Chips

Make the chips several days in advance; store them in a zip-top plastic bag to keep them crisp. It's best to make the crab salad the same day it will be served.

    6   (6-inch) corn tortillas
    1   teaspoon vegetable oil
    ¼   teaspoon kosher salt
    ¼   cup (2 ounces) ⅓-less-fat cream cheese
    2   tablespoons sliced green onions
    2   tablespoons low-fat mayonnaise
    1½   tablespoons fresh lime juice
    1   teaspoon taco seasoning
    1¾   cups lump crabmeat, shell pieces removed
         (about 6 ounces)
    ½   cup fresh corn kernels

1. Preheat oven to 400°.
2. Brush 1 side of each tortilla with oil; cut each tortilla into 8 wedges. Place wedges on a baking sheet; sprinkle with salt. Bake at 400° for 6 minutes or until lightly browned. Cool.
3. Combine cream cheese and next 4 ingredients in a bowl. Add crab and corn; stir gently. Cover and chill up to 4 hours. Serve with corn chips. Yield: 8 servings (serving size: 6 corn chips and ¼ cup crab salad).

CALORIES 103 (30% from fat); FAT 3.4g (sat 1.2g, mono 0.9g, poly 0.9g); PROTEIN 6.4g; CARB 12.3g; FIBER 1.2g; CHOL 27mg; IRON 0.6mg; SODIUM 252mg; CALC 60mg

Lemon-Macerated Okra and Olives

Try this zesty appetizer in place of peanuts or pretzels at your next party. Or combine with bread, cheese, artichokes, and cold shrimp for an antipasto platter.

3   cups small okra pods
½   cup kalamata olives
1   tablespoon grated lemon rind
¼   cup fresh lemon juice
2   tablespoons extravirgin olive oil
½   teaspoon kosher salt
½   teaspoon crushed red pepper
2   garlic cloves, thinly sliced
2   bay leaves
2   thyme sprigs

1. Combine all ingredients in a large zip-top plastic bag; seal. Marinate in refrigerator 48 to 72 hours, turning bag occasionally.
2. Strain through a sieve over a bowl, discarding marinade. Yield: 14 servings (serving size: ¼ cup).

CALORIES 29 (65% from fat); FAT 2.1g (sat 0.3g, mono 1.6g, poly 0.2g); PROTEIN 0.5g; CARB 2.4g; FIBER 0.8g; CHOL 0mg; IRON 0.2mg; SODIUM 105mg; CALC 20mg

Endive Stuffed
with Goat Cheese
and Walnuts

Endive Stuffed with Goat Cheese and Walnuts

The sweetness of the honeyed walnuts and oranges complements endive's natural bitterness, while the smooth cheese contrasts with crunchy greens and nuts.

⅓ cup coarsely chopped walnuts
2 tablespoons honey, divided
Cooking spray
¼ cup balsamic vinegar
3 tablespoons orange juice
16 Belgian endive leaves (about 2 heads)
16 small orange sections (about 2 navel oranges)
⅓ cup (1½ ounces) crumbled goat cheese or blue cheese
1 tablespoon minced fresh chives
¼ teaspoon cracked black pepper

1. Preheat oven to 350°.
2. Combine chopped walnuts and 1 tablespoon honey, and spread on a baking sheet coated with cooking spray. Bake at 350° for 10 minutes, and stir after 5 minutes.
3. Combine 1 tablespoon honey, balsamic vinegar, and orange juice in a small saucepan. Bring to a boil over high heat; cook until reduced to 3 tablespoons (about 5 minutes).
4. Fill each endive leaf with 1 orange section. Top each section with 1 teaspoon cheese and 1 teaspoon walnuts; arrange on a plate. Drizzle vinegar mixture evenly over leaves; sprinkle evenly with chives and pepper. Yield: 8 servings (serving size: 2 stuffed leaves).

CALORIES 92 (44% from fat); FAT 4.5g (sat 1.1g, mono 0.7g, poly 2.4g); PROTEIN 2.5g; CARB 11.9g; FIBER 2g; CHOL 3mg; IRON 0.6mg; SODIUM 29mg; CALC 43mg

Miso-Garlic Broiled Eggplant

¼ cup mirin (sweet rice wine)
3 tablespoons yellow miso (soybean paste)
2 teaspoons grated peeled fresh ginger
1 teaspoon dark sesame oil
½ teaspoon crushed red pepper
2 garlic cloves, minced
4 Japanese eggplants, cut diagonally into ½-inch-thick slices (about 1 pound)
Cooking spray
1 tablespoon sesame seeds
¼ cup thinly sliced green onions

1. Preheat broiler.
2. Combine first 6 ingredients, stirring with a whisk. Arrange eggplant slices on a baking sheet coated with cooking spray. Spread mirin mixture evenly over eggplant slices; sprinkle with sesame seeds. Broil 8 minutes or until topping is golden. Place eggplant slices on a platter; sprinkle with onions. Yield: 4 servings.

CALORIES 115 (26% from fat); FAT 3.3g (sat 0.5g, mono 1.1g, poly 1.5g); PROTEIN 3.3g; CARB 16.1g; FIBER 4g; CHOL 0mg; IRON 1.1mg; SODIUM 475mg; CALC 46mg

Mini Black Bean Cakes with Green Onion Cream and Avocado Salsa

Seasoned black beans lend a Southwestern kick.

CAKES:
½ cup bottled salsa
2 teaspoons ground cumin
2 (19-ounce) cans seasoned black beans, rinsed and drained (such as La Costeña)
1 cup dry breadcrumbs, divided
¼ cup thinly sliced green onions
½ teaspoon salt
Cooking spray
TOPPINGS:
½ cup reduced-fat sour cream
¼ cup thinly sliced green onions
¼ cup diced peeled avocado
¼ cup diced plum tomato
1 teaspoon fresh lime juice

1. Preheat oven to 375°.
2. To prepare cakes, combine first 3 ingredients in a food processor; process until smooth. Stir in ½ cup breadcrumbs, ¼ cup green onions, and salt.
3. Divide black bean mixture into 24 equal portions, shaping each into a ½-inch-thick patty. Place ½ cup breadcrumbs in a shallow dish. Dredge patties in breadcrumbs. Place patties on a baking sheet coated with cooking spray. Bake at 375° for 14 minutes, turning after 7 minutes.
4. To prepare toppings, combine sour cream and ¼ cup green onions. Combine avocado, tomato, and juice. Top each patty with 1 teaspoon green onion cream and 1 teaspoon avocado salsa. Yield: 12 servings (serving size: 2 cakes).

CALORIES 99 (25% from fat); FAT 2.8g (sat 1g, mono 0.5g, poly 0.2g); PROTEIN 3.8g; CARB 16.3g; FIBER 0.7g; CHOL 5mg; IRON 1.6mg; SODIUM 421mg; CALC 61mg

Buffalo-Style Catfish Strips with Ranch Dressing

The inspiration for this appetizer is Buffalo chicken wings. If you don't like spicy foods, omit the hot pepper sauce. Products labeled "hot sauce" generally have less heat and stronger vinegar flavor than those labeled "hot pepper sauce." Hot pepper sauce is extremely hot and should be used sparingly.

2 tablespoons all-purpose flour
1 teaspoon garlic powder
1 teaspoon paprika
½ teaspoon salt
½ teaspoon onion powder
⅛ teaspoon ground red pepper
2 large egg whites, lightly beaten
1½ cups coarsely crushed cornflakes
1 pound catfish fillets, cut into
  ½-inch-thick strips
Cooking spray
⅓ cup hot sauce (such as Crystal)
1 teaspoon hot pepper sauce
  (such as Tabasco)
½ teaspoon Worcestershire sauce
1 tablespoon butter
½ cup fat-free ranch dressing
4 celery stalks, cut into
  ¼ x 3-inch sticks
4 carrots, cut into ¼ x 3-inch sticks

1. Preheat oven to 400°.

2. Combine first 6 ingredients in a shallow dish, stirring with a whisk. Place egg whites in a shallow dish. Place cornflakes in a shallow dish. Working with 1 fish strip at a time, dredge in flour mixture. Dip in egg whites; dredge in cornflakes. Place on a baking sheet coated with cooking spray. Repeat procedure with remaining fish strips, flour mixture, egg whites, and cornflakes.

3. Lightly coat fish strips with cooking spray. Bake at 400° for 10 minutes or until done, turning once.

4. Combine hot sauce, hot pepper sauce, and Worcestershire in a small saucepan; bring to a boil. Reduce heat; simmer 1 minute. Remove from heat; stir in butter. Drizzle hot sauce mixture over fish. Serve with ranch dressing, celery, and carrots. Yield: 8 servings (serving size: about 2 ounces fish, ½ celery stalk, ½ carrot, and 1 tablespoon dressing).

CALORIES 183 (30% from fat); FAT 6.2g (sat 2g, mono 2.5g, poly 1.1g); PROTEIN 12.5g; CARB 19.2g; FIBER 2g; CHOL 31mg; IRON 3mg; SODIUM 618mg; CALC 34mg

Jalapeño Chile Poppers

Each pepper gets a double dip in the egg and breadcrumbs for an extracrisp coating. Use the tip of a paring knife to remove the membranes and seeds from the jalapeño peppers.

12   pickled whole jalapeño peppers (about 2 [12-ounce] jars)
½   cup (2 ounces) shredded reduced-fat sharp cheddar cheese
½   cup (4 ounces) ⅓-less-fat cream cheese, softened
½   cup egg substitute
2   tablespoons all-purpose flour
⅔   cup dry breadcrumbs
¾   teaspoon garlic powder
½   teaspoon salt
¼   teaspoon paprika
Cooking spray

1. Preheat oven to 400°.
2. Drain jalapeños. Cut ¼ inch off stem ends of peppers, reserving stem ends. Carefully remove seeds and membranes, leaving peppers intact.
3. Combine cheeses in a small bowl. Spoon cheese mixture into a zip-top plastic bag; seal. Carefully snip off 1 bottom corner of bag. Pipe cheese mixture evenly into peppers, and replace stem ends, pressing gently to seal.
4. Combine egg substitute and flour in a small bowl, stirring with a whisk. Combine breadcrumbs, garlic powder, salt, and paprika in a shallow bowl.
5. Working with 1 pepper at a time, dip in egg mixture, and dredge in breadcrumb mixture. Repeat procedure with remaining peppers, egg mixture, and breadcrumb mixture. Return peppers, 1 at a time, to egg mixture; dredge in breadcrumb mixture. Place peppers on a baking sheet coated with cooking spray. Lightly coat peppers with cooking spray.
6. Bake at 400° for 15 minutes or until lightly browned. Yield: 6 appetizer servings (serving size: 2 poppers).

CALORIES 153 (26% from fat); FAT 4.5g (sat 1.8g, mono 0.2g, poly 0.4g); PROTEIN 9g; CARB 18.8g; FIBER 1.9g; CHOL 14mg; IRON 1.4mg; SODIUM 532mg; CALC 216mg

Pearl Oyster Bar Crab Cakes with Sweet Corn Relish

Serve these quintessential crab cakes with a refreshing sweet corn relish.

CRAB CAKES:

1 tablespoon Dijon mustard
1 tablespoon fresh lemon juice
1 teaspoon dry mustard
2 teaspoons chopped fresh chives
½ teaspoon hot pepper sauce (such as Tabasco)
½ teaspoon Worcestershire sauce
¼ teaspoon salt
¼ teaspoon black pepper
2 large eggs
2 tablespoons finely chopped seeded plum tomato
1 pound lump crabmeat, drained and shell pieces removed
7 tablespoons dry breadcrumbs, divided
1½ teaspoons butter

RELISH:

¼ cup water
2¾ cups fresh corn kernels (about 4 ears)
¼ cup frozen green peas
1½ cups finely chopped seeded plum tomato (about 1 pound)
2 tablespoons chopped fresh basil
2 tablespoons chopped fresh chives
1 tablespoon butter
¼ teaspoon salt
⅛ teaspoon black pepper

1. To prepare crab cakes, combine the first 9 ingredients in a large bowl, stirring with a whisk. Add 2 tablespoons tomato and crabmeat, tossing gently to coat. Stir in 5 tablespoons breadcrumbs. Cover and chill 30 minutes.

2. Preheat oven to 450°.

3. Fill a ¼-cup measuring cup with crab mixture to form 1 patty. Remove from measuring cup; repeat procedure with remaining crab mixture to form 8 patties. Lightly dredge patties in 2 tablespoons breadcrumbs.

4. Melt 1½ teaspoons butter in a large ovenproof skillet over medium-high heat. Add patties, and cook 4 minutes. Turn patties, and wrap handle of pan with foil. Place pan in oven, and bake at 450° for 5 minutes or until the patties are golden brown and thoroughly heated.

5. To prepare relish, bring ¼ cup water to a boil in a medium saucepan. Add corn and peas; cook 2 minutes, stirring frequently. Remove from heat; stir in 1½ cups tomato and remaining ingredients. Serve relish with crab cakes. Yield: 8 servings (serving size: 1 crab cake and ⅓ cup relish).

CALORIES 173 (28% from fat); FAT 5.4g (sat 2g, mono 1.6g, poly 0.9g); PROTEIN 15.1g; CARB 17.5g; FIBER 2.3g; CHOL 103mg; IRON 1.7mg; SODIUM 462mg; CALC 81mg

Baked Grits with Country Ham, Wild Mushrooms, Fresh Thyme, and Parmesan

This is an adaptation of a signature appetizer at Highlands Bar and Grill in Birmingham, Alabama. The restaurant's owner and chef, Frank Stitt, has offered this on his menu for more than a decade.

GRITS:

  5 cups water
  1 teaspoon kosher salt
1¼ cups stone-ground yellow grits
  ¼ cup (1 ounce) grated Parmigiano-Reggiano cheese
  ¼ teaspoon white pepper
  1 large egg
Cooking spray

SAUCE:

  ½ cup finely chopped shallots
  ½ cup dry white wine
  ½ cup fat-free, less-sodium chicken broth, divided
  ¼ cup sherry vinegar
  1 bay leaf
  1 dried chile pepper, crushed
  1 teaspoon cornstarch
  2 tablespoons butter
  1 tablespoon whipping cream
  2 tablespoons grated Parmigiano-Reggiano cheese
  1 teaspoon fresh lemon juice
  ¼ teaspoon black pepper

REMAINING INGREDIENTS:

  1 ounce country ham, cut into julienne strips
2½ cups (½-inch) sliced shiitake mushroom caps
  1 tablespoon minced shallots
  1 teaspoon water
  3 thyme sprigs

1. Preheat oven to 325°.

2. To prepare grits, bring 5 cups water and salt to a boil in a large saucepan, and gradually stir in grits. Reduce heat; simmer 30 minutes or until thick, stirring constantly. Remove from heat; stir in ¼ cup cheese and white pepper. Stir in egg.

3. Spoon ½ cup grits mixture into each of 8 (4-ounce) ramekins or custard cups coated with cooking spray. Place ramekins in a 13 x 9-inch baking pan; add hot water to pan to a depth of 1 inch. Bake at 325° for 20 minutes. Remove ramekins from pan; cool completely on a wire rack.

4. To prepare sauce, bring ½ cup shallots, wine, ¼ cup broth, vinegar, bay leaf, and chile to a boil in a small saucepan over medium heat, and cook until reduced to 1 tablespoon liquid (about 6 minutes). Strain mixture through a sieve over a bowl; discard solids. Return liquid to pan.

5. Combine ¼ cup broth and cornstarch. Add cornstarch mixture to pan, and bring to a boil. Cook 1 minute, stirring constantly. Reduce heat to low, and add butter and cream, stirring with a whisk until well blended. Stir in 2 tablespoons cheese, lemon juice, and black pepper.

6. Cook the ham in a large nonstick skillet coated with cooking spray over medium heat 1 minute. Add mushroom, 1 tablespoon shallots, 1 teaspoon water, and 3 thyme sprigs; sauté 3 minutes or just until mushrooms are tender.

7. Loosen edges of grits with a knife or rubber spatula. Place a plate, upside down, on top of each ramekin; invert onto plates. Spoon 1 tablespoon sauce onto each plate; sprinkle ham mixture evenly among plates. Yield: 8 servings.

CALORIES 197 (29% from fat); FAT 6.3g (sat 3.9g, mono 1.1g, poly 0.2g); PROTEIN 7.1g; CARB 28.8g; FIBER 1.8g; CHOL 43mg; IRON 0.9mg; SODIUM 456mg; CALC 97mg

Grilled Stone Fruit Antipasto Plate

Black pepper and vanilla heighten the sweetness of the stone fruit. Firm fruit holds up best on the grill. You can also serve this as a salad course. If you can't find pluots (also known as plumcots), a hybrid of the plum and apricot, double up on peaches or plums.

DRESSING:
1 tablespoon brown sugar
3 tablespoons white balsamic vinegar
2 tablespoons extravirgin olive oil
2 tablespoons fresh lime juice
2 teaspoons vanilla extract
¼ teaspoon freshly ground black pepper
⅛ teaspoon salt
⅛ teaspoon hot sauce

FRUIT:
1 pound firm black plums, halved and pitted
1 pound firm peaches, halved and pitted
½ pound firm nectarines, halved and pitted
½ pound firm pluots, halved and pitted
Cooking spray
Chopped fresh mint (optional)

1. Prepare grill.
2. To prepare dressing, combine first 8 ingredients in a small bowl, stirring well with a whisk.
3. To prepare fruit, place fruit on grill rack coated with cooking spray; grill 3 minutes on each side. Remove from grill. Drizzle fruit with dressing. Garnish with chopped mint, if desired. Yield: 8 servings.

CALORIES 129 (29% from fat); FAT 4.1g (sat 0.5g, mono 2.9g, poly 0.4g); PROTEIN 1.4g; CARB 23.8g; FIBER 2.9g; CHOL 0mg; IRON 0.3mg; SODIUM 39mg; CALC 12mg

Mango-Mint-Rum Slush

3   cups coarsely chopped peeled mango
1   cup ice cubes
1   cup mango nectar
¾   cup white rum
¼   cup fresh lime juice
2   tablespoons sugar
1   tablespoon chopped fresh mint

1. Place mango in the freezer for 1 hour. Combine mango, ice cubes, and remaining ingredients in a blender; process until smooth. Serve immediately. Yield: 4 servings (serving size: about 1 cup).

CALORIES 242 (2% from fat); FAT 0.4g (sat 0.1g, mono 0.1g, poly 0.1g); PROTEIN 0.8g; CARB 34.8g; FIBER 2.4g; CHOL 0mg; IRON 0.3mg; SODIUM 5mg; CALC 17mg

Sangria

1   cup fresh orange juice (about 2 oranges)
⅓   cup sugar
1   (750-milliliter) bottle Merlot or other dry red wine
4   whole cloves
1   (8 x 1-inch) orange rind strip
2   (3-inch) cinnamon sticks
1   orange, thinly sliced and seeded
1   lemon, thinly sliced and seeded
2   cups club soda

1. Combine first 3 ingredients in a large pitcher; stir until sugar dissolves.
2. Press cloves into rind strip. Add strip, cinnamon, and fruit to wine mixture. Chill at least 30 minutes. Stir in club soda just before serving. Yield: 1½ quarts (serving size: 1 cup).

CALORIES 160 (0% from fat); FAT 0.1g (sat 0g, mono 0g, poly 0g); PROTEIN 1g; CARB 20.3g; FIBER 1.1g; CHOL 0mg; IRON 1.2mg; SODIUM 30mg; CALC 36mg

Cranberry Liqueur

Presented in small decanters or glass bottles, Cranberry Liqueur makes a memorable gift. Attach a gift tag and include the following: "Cranberry Cosmopolitans": ½ cup Cranberry Liqueur, ¼ cup Cointreau, 2 tablespoons lime juice. Mix with 1 cup crushed ice; strain into martini glass. Makes 2 cocktails."

2   cups sugar
1   cup water
1   (12-ounce) package fresh cranberries
3   cups vodka

1. Combine sugar and water in a medium saucepan; cook over medium heat 5 minutes or until sugar dissolves, stirring constantly. Cool completely.
2. Place cranberries in a food processor; process 2 minutes or until finely chopped. Combine sugar mixture and cranberries in a large bowl; stir in vodka.
3. Divide vodka mixture between clean jars; secure with lids. Let stand 3 weeks in a cool, dark place, shaking jars every other day.
4. Strain cranberry mixture through a cheesecloth-lined sieve into a bowl; discard solids. Carefully pour liqueur into decorative bottles or jars; store in refrigerator or at room temperature up to a year. Yield: 4½ cups (serving size: ¼ cup).

CALORIES 196 (0% from fat); FAT 0g (sat 0g, mono 0g, poly 0g); PROTEIN 0g; CARB 24.6g; FIBER 0.8g; CHOL 0mg; IRON 0 img; SODIUM 2mg; CALC 2mg

Breads

Buttered Sweet Potato
Knot Rolls, page 65

Angel Biscuits

The dough will keep for several weeks in the refrigerator. It's convenient to have on hand for company.

    1 package dry yeast (about 2¼ teaspoons)
    ½ cup warm water (100° to 110°)
    5 cups all-purpose flour
    ¼ cup sugar
    1 teaspoon baking powder
    1 teaspoon baking soda
    1 teaspoon salt
    ½ cup vegetable shortening
    2 cups low-fat buttermilk
  Cooking spray
    1 tablespoon butter or stick margarine, melted

1. Dissolve yeast in warm water in a small bowl, and let stand 5 minutes.

2. Lightly spoon flour into dry measuring cup; level with a knife. Combine flour and next 4 ingredients in a large bowl. Cut in the shortening with a pastry blender or 2 knives until mixture resembles coarse meal. Add yeast mixture and buttermilk, and stir just until moist. Cover and chill for 1 hour.

3. Preheat oven to 450°.

4. Turn dough out onto a heavily floured surface, and knead lightly 5 times. Roll dough to a ½-inch thickness, and cut with a 3-inch biscuit cutter. Place on a baking sheet coated with cooking spray. Brush melted butter over biscuit tops. Bake at 450° for 13 minutes or until golden. Yield: 2 dozen (serving size: 1 biscuit).

CALORIES 150 (28% from fat); FAT 4.6g (sat 1.2g, mono 1.5g, poly 1.3g); PROTEIN 3.6g; CARB 23.1g; FIBER 0.8g; CHOL 0mg; IRON 1.3mg; SODIUM 183mg; CALC 41mg

Drop Biscuits

These biscuits are dropped into muffin tins instead of onto a baking sheet, but their final shape is still free-form like that of traditional drop biscuits.

2 cups all-purpose flour
1 tablespoon baking powder
1 teaspoon sugar
½ teaspoon salt
¼ cup chilled butter or stick margarine, cut into small pieces
1 cup fat-free milk
Cooking spray

1. Preheat oven to 450°.
2. Lightly spoon flour into dry measuring cups; level with a knife. Combine flour, baking powder, sugar, and salt in a bowl; cut in butter with a pastry blender or 2 knives until mixture resembles coarse meal. Add milk; stir just until moist.
3. Spoon batter into 12 muffin cups coated with cooking spray. Bake at 450° for 12 minutes or until golden. Remove from pan immediately; place on a wire rack. Yield: 1 dozen (serving size: 1 biscuit).

CALORIES 119 (31% from fat); FAT 4.1g (sat 2.5g, mono 1.1g, poly 0.2g); PROTEIN 2.9g; CARB 17.6g; FIBER 0.6g; CHOL 11mg; IRON 1.1mg; SODIUM 270mg; CALC 97mg

Buttermilk Biscuits

Drizzle these biscuits with honey before serving.

2 cups all-purpose flour
2 teaspoons baking powder
¼ teaspoon baking soda
¼ teaspoon salt
3 tablespoons plus 1 teaspoon chilled stick margarine or butter, cut into small pieces
¾ cup 1% low-fat buttermilk

1. Preheat oven to 450°.
2. Lightly spoon flour into dry measuring cups, and level with a knife. Combine flour, baking powder, baking soda, and salt in a bowl; cut in margarine with a pastry blender or 2 knives until mixture resembles coarse meal. Add buttermilk, and stir just until moist (do not overstir).
3. Turn the dough out onto a floured surface, and knead 4 or 5 times (do not overknead). Roll the dough to a ½-inch thickness; cut with a 2½-inch biscuit cutter. Place biscuits on a baking sheet. Bake

at 450° for 12 minutes or until golden. Yield: 1 dozen (serving size: 1 biscuit).

CALORIES 112 (29% from fat); FAT 3.6g (sat 0.7g, mono 1.4g, poly 1.1g); PROTEIN 2.7g; CARB 16.8g; FIBER 0.6g; CHOL 0mg; IRON 1mg; SODIUM 161mg; CALC 59mg

Potato-and-Cheese Biscuits

For a crispier crust, try baking the biscuits in a 9-inch cast-iron skillet that has been preheated for 10 minutes. Bake same length of time.

1 cup (1-inch) cubed peeled Yukon gold or red potato
1½ cups all-purpose flour
2 teaspoons baking powder
½ teaspoon baking soda
¼ teaspoon salt
2 tablespoons chilled butter or stick margarine, cut into small pieces
¾ cup (3 ounces) shredded reduced-fat sharp cheddar cheese
½ cup plus 1 tablespoon low-fat buttermilk
¼ cup minced green onions
1 tablespoon cold water
1 large egg white, lightly beaten

1. Preheat oven to 425°.
2. Cook potato in boiling water 15 minutes or until very tender. Drain well; mash potato, and cool.
3. Lightly spoon flour into dry measuring cups; level with a knife. Combine flour, baking powder, baking soda, and salt in a bowl; cut in butter with a pastry blender or 2 knives until mixture resembles coarse meal. Add mashed potato, cheese, buttermilk, and green onions; stir just until moist.
4. Turn dough out onto a floured surface, and knead lightly 5 times. Roll the dough to a ¾-inch thickness, and cut with a 3-inch biscuit cutter. Place the biscuits on a baking sheet. Combine cold water and egg white, and brush over biscuits. Bake at 425° for 20 minutes or until golden. Yield: 9 servings (serving size: 1 biscuit).

CALORIES 151 (29% from fat); FAT 4.8g (sat 2.8g, mono 1.3g, poly 0.3g); PROTEIN 6.3g; CARB 20.6g; FIBER 0.9g; CHOL 13mg; IRON 1.3mg; SODIUM 353mg; CALC 170mg

Sun-dried Tomato Semolina Biscuits

Semolina is durum wheat that's more coarsely ground than all-purpose flour. (It's also what most dried pasta is made from.) It has the consistency of fine cornmeal, which will work as a substitute. This dough is sticky, but don't add more flour; it'll make the biscuits less tender.

2 cups boiling water
10 sun-dried tomatoes, packed without oil
2 cups all-purpose flour
¼ cup semolina flour or yellow cornmeal
1 tablespoon sugar
1½ teaspoons baking powder
¾ teaspoon salt
½ teaspoon baking soda
1 teaspoon dried basil
¼ teaspoon ground red pepper
¼ cup chilled butter or stick margarine, cut into small pieces
1 cup low-fat buttermilk
Cooking spray

1. Combine boiling water and sun-dried tomatoes in a bowl; let stand for 15 minutes. Drain and chop.

2. Preheat oven to 425°.

3. Lightly spoon flours into dry measuring cups; level with a knife. Combine flours and next 6 ingredients in a bowl; cut in butter with a pastry blender or 2 knives until mixture resembles coarse meal. (Flour mixture and butter can also be combined in a food processor; pulse until mixture resembles coarse meal.) Add tomatoes and buttermilk; stir just until moist.

4. Turn dough out onto a heavily floured surface; knead lightly 5 times. Roll the dough to a ½-inch thickness; cut with a 2½-inch biscuit cutter. Place on a baking sheet coated with cooking spray. Bake at 425° for 15 minutes or until golden. Yield: 1 dozen (serving size: 1 biscuit).

CALORIES 140 (29% from fat); FAT 4.5g (sat 2.6g, mono 1.3g, poly 0.3g); PROTEIN 3.4g; CARB 21.3g; FIBER 0.9g; CHOL 10mg; IRON 1.4mg; SODIUM 345mg; CALC 67mg

Coffee-Nut Scones

Cut through the circle of dough, but be careful not to separate the wedges—this will allow the wedges to bake as one large scone. The results will be scones much moister than those baked separately.

  ⅔ cup 1% low-fat milk
2½ tablespoons instant coffee
     granules
  1 teaspoon vanilla extract
  1 large egg, lightly beaten
2¼ cups all-purpose flour
  ⅓ cup sugar
2½ teaspoons baking powder
  ¾ teaspoon salt
  ¼ teaspoon ground cinnamon
  ¼ cup chilled butter or stick margarine,
     cut into small pieces
  3 tablespoons finely chopped walnuts
Cooking spray
  2 teaspoons 1% low-fat milk
  2 teaspoons sugar

1. Combine ⅔ cup milk and coffee granules in a microwave-safe bowl. Microwave at HIGH 1 minute, and stir until coffee dissolves. Cover and chill completely. Stir in vanilla and egg.
2. Preheat oven to 425°.
3. Lightly spoon the flour into dry measuring cups; level with a knife. Combine flour, sugar, baking powder, salt, and cinnamon in a bowl, and cut in butter with a pastry blender or 2 knives until mixture resembles coarse meal. (The flour mixture and butter can also be combined in a food processor; pulse until mixture resembles coarse meal.) Stir in walnuts. Add milk mixture, stirring just until moist (dough will be sticky).
4. Turn dough out onto a lightly floured surface, and knead lightly 4 times with floured hands. Pat the dough into an 8-inch circle on a baking sheet coated with cooking spray. Cut the dough into 10 wedges; do not separate. Brush the dough with 2 teaspoons milk, and sprinkle with 2 teaspoons sugar. Bake at 425° for 20 minutes or until lightly browned. Serve warm. Yield: 10 servings (serving size: 1 wedge).

CALORIES 207 (30% from fat); FAT 7g (sat 3.3g, mono 1.9g, poly 1.3g); PROTEIN 4.9g; CARB 31g; FIBER 1g; CHOL 35mg; IRON 1.7mg; SODIUM 361mg; CALC 101mg

Date and Maple Scones

You can substitute raisins or dried currants in place of dates, if desired.

  2 cups all-purpose flour
  ¼ cup packed brown sugar
1½ teaspoons baking powder
  ½ teaspoon baking soda
  ¼ teaspoon salt
  ⅓ cup chilled butter, cut into small pieces
  ½ cup chopped pitted dates
  ½ cup 1% low-fat milk
  3 tablespoons maple syrup
Cooking spray

1. Preheat oven to 400°.
2. Combine first 5 ingredients in a bowl; cut in butter with a pastry blender or 2 knives until mixture resembles coarse meal. Add dates; toss well. Combine milk and syrup. Add to flour mixture, stirring just until moist.
3. Turn the dough out onto a lightly floured surface, and knead 4 or 5 times. Pat the dough into an 8-inch circle on a baking sheet coated with cooking spray. Cut the dough into 12 wedges, cutting into, but not through, dough.
4. Bake at 400° for 15 minutes or until golden. Serve warm. Yield: 1 dozen (serving size: 1 scone).

CALORIES 176 (28% from fat); FAT 5.4g (sat 3.3g, mono 1.6g, poly 0.3g); PROTEIN 2.7g; CARB 29.8g; FIBER 1.1g; CHOL 14mg; IRON 1.3mg; SODIUM 173mg; CALC 61mg

Gingersnap Scones with Espresso Glaze

SCONES:

1¾ cups all-purpose flour
¼ cup gingersnap crumbs (about 6 cookies, finely crushed)
¼ cup sugar
1½ teaspoons baking powder
½ teaspoon baking soda
¼ teaspoon salt
¼ cup chilled butter or stick margarine, cut into small pieces
½ cup low-fat buttermilk
1 large egg, lightly beaten
Cooking spray

ESPRESSO GLAZE:

1 tablespoon hot water
1½ teaspoons instant coffee granules
¾ cup sifted powdered sugar
10 walnut halves

1. Preheat oven to 400°.

2. To prepare scones, lightly spoon flour into dry measuring cups, and level with a knife. Combine flour and next 5 ingredients in a bowl, and cut in butter with a pastry blender or 2 knives until mixture resembles coarse meal. Add the buttermilk and egg, stirring just until moist (dough will be sticky).

3. Turn dough out onto a lightly floured surface; with floured hands, knead lightly 4 times. Pat dough into a 10-inch circle on a baking sheet coated with cooking spray. Cut dough into 10 wedges, cutting into, but not through, dough. Bake at 400° for 15 minutes or until golden.

4. To prepare glaze, combine water and coffee granules in a medium bowl. Add powdered sugar, and stir well. Drizzle over scones. Cut into 10 wedges, and top each with 1 walnut half. Yield: 10 servings (serving size: 1 scone).

CALORIES 220 (30% from fat); FAT 7.4g (sat 1.4g, mono 2.8g, poly 2.5g); PROTEIN 4g; CARB 34.7g; FIBER 0.7g; CHOL 24mg; IRON 1.4mg; SODIUM 194mg; CALC 73mg

Ham and Cheese Scones

- 2 cups all-purpose flour
- 1 tablespoon baking powder
- 2 teaspoons sugar
- ¼ teaspoon salt
- ¼ teaspoon ground red pepper
- 3 tablespoons chilled butter, cut into small pieces
- ¾ cup (3 ounces) shredded reduced-fat extra-sharp cheddar cheese
- ¾ cup finely chopped 33%-less-sodium ham
- ¾ cup fat-free buttermilk
- 2 large egg whites

Cooking spray

1. Preheat oven to 400°.

2. Lightly spoon flour into dry measuring cups; level with a knife. Combine flour, baking powder, sugar, salt, and pepper in a large bowl; cut in butter with a pastry blender or 2 knives until mixture resembles coarse meal. Stir in cheese and ham. Combine buttermilk and egg whites, stirring with a whisk. Add to flour mixture, stirring just until moist.

3. Turn out onto a floured surface; knead 4 to 5 times with floured hands. Pat into an 8-inch circle on a baking sheet coated with cooking spray. Cut into 8 wedges, cutting into but not through dough. Bake at 400° for 20 minutes or until lightly browned. Yield: 8 servings (serving size: 1 wedge).

CALORIES 217 (30% from fat); FAT 7.2g (sat 4.1g, mono 1.6g, poly 0.4g); PROTEIN 10.4g; CARB 27.1g; FIBER 0.9g; CHOL 26mg; IRON 1.8mg; SODIUM 519mg; CALC 235mg

Blueberry-Lemon Muffins

If you're using frozen blueberries, there's no need to thaw them before adding them to the batter. In fact, they work best when still frozen.

- 1½ cups all-purpose flour
- ½ cup yellow cornmeal
- ½ cup sugar
- 1½ teaspoons baking powder
- ½ teaspoon baking soda
- ¼ teaspoon salt
- 1 cup blueberries
- 1 cup low-fat buttermilk
- 3 tablespoons butter or stick margarine, melted
- 1 tablespoon grated lemon rind
- 1 large egg, lightly beaten

Cooking spray

- 1 tablespoon sugar

1. Preheat oven to 400°.

2. Lightly spoon the flour into dry measuring cups; level with a knife. Combine flour and next 5 ingredients in a medium bowl. Stir in blueberries; make a well in center of mixture. Combine buttermilk, butter, rind, and egg; stir well with a whisk. Add to flour mixture; stir just until moist.

3. Spoon batter into 12 muffin cups coated with cooking spray; sprinkle evenly with 1 tablespoon sugar. Bake at 400° for 20 minutes or until a wooden pick inserted in center comes out clean. Remove the muffins from pans immediately; place on a wire rack. Yield: 1 dozen (serving size: 1 muffin).

CALORIES 164 (22% from fat); FAT 4g (sat 2.2g, mono 1.1g, poly 0.3g); PROTEIN 3.5g; CARB 28.8g; FIBER 1.1g; CHOL 26mg; IRON 1.1mg; SODIUM 209mg; CALC 66mg

Sugar Spot Banana Muffins

The brown spots on ripe bananas are called sugar spots; fruits that have them make the sweetest muffins.

- ⅔ cup packed light brown sugar
- ¼ cup vegetable oil
- 1 large egg
- 1 large egg white
- ¾ cup mashed ripe banana
- ⅓ cup fat-free milk
- 1⅓ cups all-purpose flour
- ⅔ cup honey-crunch wheat germ
- 1½ teaspoons baking powder
- ¼ teaspoon baking soda
- ¼ teaspoon salt

Cooking spray

1. Preheat oven to 350°.

2. Combine first 4 ingredients in a large bowl; beat with a mixer at medium speed until well blended. Add banana and milk; beat well.

3. Lightly spoon flour into dry measuring cups; level with a knife. Combine flour, wheat germ, baking powder, baking soda, and salt in a medium bowl, stirring well with a whisk. Add to sugar mixture; beat just until moist.

4. Spoon batter evenly into 12 muffin cups coated with cooking spray. Bake at 350° for 22 minutes or until muffins spring back when touched lightly in center. Cool in pan 5 minutes on a wire rack, and remove from pan. Place muffins on wire rack. Yield: 12 servings (serving size: 1 muffin).

CALORIES 183 (28% from fat); FAT 5.7g (sat 0.9g, mono 1.3g, poly 3.1g); PROTEIN 4.3g; CARB 30g; FIBER 1.4g; CHOL 18mg; IRON 1.6mg; SODIUM 155mg; CALC 61mg

Strawberry-Orange Muffins

1¼   cups halved strawberries
3   tablespoons butter or stick margarine, melted
2   teaspoons grated orange rind
2   large eggs
1½   cups all-purpose flour
1¼   cups sugar
1   teaspoon baking powder
½   teaspoon salt
Cooking spray
2   teaspoons sugar
½   cup strawberry jam or preserves (optional)

1. Preheat oven to 400°.
2. Combine the first 4 ingredients in a blender, and process just until mixture is blended. Lightly spoon flour into dry measuring cups, and level with a knife. Combine flour, 1¼ cups sugar, baking powder, and salt. Add strawberry mixture to flour mixture, stirring just until mixture is moist. Spoon the batter into 12 muffin cups coated with cooking spray. Sprinkle batter evenly with 2 teaspoons sugar. Bake at 400° for 20 minutes or until muffins spring back when touched lightly in center. Remove muffins from pan immediately. Serve muffins with jam, if desired. Yield: 1 dozen (serving size: 1 muffin and 2 teaspoons jam).

CALORIES 184 (20% from fat); FAT 4g (sat 2.1g, mono 1.2g, poly 0.3g); PROTEIN 2.8g; CARB 34.8g; FIBER 0.8g; CHOL 45mg; IRON 1mg; SODIUM 179mg; CALC 33mg

Maple-Walnut Muffins

2¼ cups all-purpose flour
  1 cup sugar
  1 teaspoon baking powder
  ½ teaspoon baking soda
  ¼ teaspoon salt
  ¼ cup chilled butter or stick margarine, cut
     into small pieces
  2 tablespoons maple syrup
  1 teaspoon imitation maple flavoring
  3 large egg whites, lightly beaten
  1 (8-ounce) carton plain fat-free yogurt
Cooking spray
  ¼ cup chopped walnuts

1. Preheat oven to 350°.
2. Lightly spoon flour into dry measuring cups; level with a knife. Combine flour and next 4 ingredients in a large bowl; cut in butter with a pastry blender or 2 knives until mixture resembles coarse meal. Combine maple syrup, maple flavoring, egg whites, and yogurt; add to flour mixture, stirring just until moist.
3. Divide the batter evenly among 18 muffin cups coated with cooking spray; sprinkle walnuts evenly over batter. Bake at 350° for 25 minutes or until muffins spring back when touched lightly in center. Remove muffins from pans immediately. Yield: 1½ dozen (serving size: 1 muffin).

CALORIES 149 (22% from fat); FAT 3.7g (sat 1.7g, mono 1g, poly 0.7g); PROTEIN 3.1g; CARB 25.8g; FIBER 0.5g; CHOL 7mg; IRON 0.8mg; SODIUM 140mg; CALC 46mg

Fresh Cranberry Muffins

Use your imagination with this basic muffin recipe by substituting other favorite fruits and flavors for the cranberries and orange rind.

  2 cups all-purpose flour
  ⅔ cup sugar
  2 teaspoons baking powder
  ¼ teaspoon salt
  1 cup chopped fresh cranberries
  ⅔ cup 2% reduced-fat milk
  ¼ cup butter or stick margarine,
     melted
  1 teaspoon grated orange rind
  ½ teaspoon vanilla extract
  1 large egg, lightly beaten
Cooking spray

1. Preheat oven to 400°.
2. Lightly spoon the flour into dry measuring cups; level with a knife. Combine the flour, sugar, baking powder, and salt in a large bowl; stir well with a whisk. Stir in cranberries; make a well in center of mixture. Combine milk, butter, rind, vanilla, and egg; add to flour mixture, stirring just until moist. Spoon the batter into 12 muffin cups coated with cooking spray. Bake at 400° for 18 minutes or until muffins spring back when touched lightly in center. Remove muffins from pan immediately; place on a wire rack. Yield: 12 servings (serving size: 1 muffin).
NOTE: These muffins freeze well. Bake them, cool completely, and store in freezer bags. To serve, thaw the muffins at room temperature. Reheat in aluminum foil at 300° for 10 to 15 minutes or until thoroughly heated.

CALORIES 174 (26% from fat); FAT 5g (sat 2.7g, mono 1.4g, poly 0.4g); PROTEIN 3.2g; CARB 29.2g; FIBER 0.7g; CHOL 30mg; IRON 1.2mg; SODIUM 182mg; CALC 69mg

Lemon-Glazed Cranberry Rolls

  1 (10-ounce) can refrigerated pizza
     crust dough
  ½ cup orange marmalade
  ⅔ cup sweetened dried cranberries
Cooking spray
  ½ cup sifted powdered sugar
1½ teaspoons lemon juice
  1 teaspoon hot water

1. Preheat oven to 375°.
2. Unroll pizza dough, and pat into a 12 x 9-inch rectangle. Spread orange marmalade over dough, leaving a ½-inch border. Sprinkle with cranberries, pressing gently into dough. Beginning with a long side, roll up jelly-roll fashion; pinch seam to seal (do not seal ends of roll). Cut roll into 12 (1-inch-thick) slices. Place slices, cut sides up, in muffin cups coated with cooking spray. Bake at 375° for 15 minutes or until golden. Remove rolls from pan, and place on a wire rack.
3. Combine powdered sugar, lemon juice, and hot water in a small bowl, stirring with a whisk until smooth. Drizzle the icing over warm rolls. Yield: 1 dozen (serving size: 1 roll).
NOTE: Substitute ⅓ cup apple jelly for the orange marmalade and ⅔ cup raisins for the cranberries, if desired.

CALORIES 137 (6% from fat); FAT 0.9g (sat 0.1g, mono 0.4g, poly 0.4g); PROTEIN 2.1g; CARB 30.6g; FIBER 0.3g; CHOL 0mg; IRON 0.6mg; SODIUM 166mg; CALC 5mg

White Chocolate-Apricot Muffins

Combining the chopped white chocolate with the flour mixture disperses it evenly and creates chocolate pockets throughout the muffins.

1¾ cups all-purpose flour
½ cup sugar
1½ teaspoons baking powder
½ teaspoon salt
2 ounces premium white baking chocolate, finely chopped
¾ cup 1% low-fat milk
3 tablespoons butter or stick margarine, melted
1 large egg, lightly beaten
Cooking spray
½ cup apricot preserves
1 tablespoon sugar

1. Preheat oven to 400°.
2. Lightly spoon the flour into dry measuring cups; level with a knife. Combine flour and next 4 ingredients in a medium bowl; stir well with a whisk. Make a well in center of mixture. Combine milk, butter, and egg; stir well with a whisk. Add to flour mixture, stirring just until moist.
3. Spoon about 1 tablespoon of the batter into each of 12 muffin cups coated with cooking spray. Spoon 2 teaspoons preserves into center of each muffin cup (do not spread over batter); top with remaining batter. Sprinkle evenly with 1 tablespoon sugar.
4. Bake at 400° for 22 minutes or until muffins spring back when touched lightly in center. Remove muffins from pan immediately; place on a wire rack. Yield: 1 dozen (serving size: 1 muffin).

CALORIES 199 (24% from fat); FAT 5.3g (sat 2.9g, mono 1.6g, poly 0.4g); PROTEIN 3.3g; CARB 35.3g; FIBER 0.7g; CHOL 27mg; IRON 1.2mg; SODIUM 212mg; CALC 72mg

Cinnamon-Apple Muffins

into 18 muffin cups coated with cooking spray.

3. Combine 3 tablespoons sugar and 2 teaspoons cinnamon, and sprinkle evenly over batter. Bake at 400° for 18 minutes or until done. Remove from pans immediately, and cool on a wire rack. Yield: 1½ dozen (serving size: 1 muffin).

CALORIES 153 (19% from fat); FAT 3.2g (sat 0.7g, mono 0.9g, poly 1.2g); PROTEIN 3.4g; CARB 27.6g; FIBER 0.8g; CHOL 13mg; IRON 1.0mg; SODIUM 133mg; CALC 67mg

Lemon-Glazed Zucchini Bread

Pat the zucchini dry with a paper towel after shredding it to ensure that the bread won't be soggy.

2⅓ cups all-purpose flour
¾ cup granulated sugar
2 teaspoons baking powder
1 teaspoon ground cinnamon
½ teaspoon baking soda
½ teaspoon salt
¼ teaspoon ground nutmeg
1 cup finely shredded zucchini
½ cup 1% low-fat milk
¼ cup vegetable oil
2 tablespoons grated lemon rind
1 large egg
Cooking spray
1 cup sifted powdered sugar
2 tablespoons fresh lemon juice

1. Preheat oven to 350°.
2. Lightly spoon the flour into dry measuring cups, and level with a knife. Combine flour and next 6 ingredients in a large bowl, and make a well in center of mixture. Combine the zucchini, milk, oil, rind, and egg in a bowl, and add to flour mixture. Stir just until moist.
3. Spoon batter into an 8 x 4-inch loaf pan coated with cooking spray. Bake at 350° for 1 hour or until a wooden pick inserted in center comes out clean. Cool 10 minutes in pan on a wire rack; remove from pan. Cool completely on wire rack.
4. Combine powdered sugar and lemon juice; stir with a whisk. Drizzle over loaf. Yield: 12 servings (serving size: 1 slice).

CALORIES 230 (21% from fat); FAT 5.4g (sat 1.1g, mono 1.6g, poly 2.4g); PROTEIN 3.5g; CARB 42.6g; FIBER 0.8g; CHOL 19mg; IRON 1.4mg; SODIUM 243mg; CALC 69mg

Cinnamon-Apple Muffins

2⅓ cups all-purpose flour
1 cup sugar
1 tablespoon baking powder
2 teaspoons ground cinnamon
1 teaspoon baking soda
½ teaspoon salt
1½ cups finely chopped peeled Granny Smith apple
1 cup low-fat buttermilk
⅓ cup 2% reduced-fat milk
⅓ cup light ricotta cheese
3 tablespoons vegetable oil
1 tablespoon vanilla extract
2 large egg whites
1 large egg
Cooking spray
3 tablespoons sugar
2 teaspoons ground cinnamon

1. Preheat oven to 400°.
2. Lightly spoon flour into dry measuring cups; level with a knife. Combine flour and next 5 ingredients in a large bowl. Stir in apple, and make a well in center of mixture. Combine buttermilk and next 6 ingredients, and stir well with a whisk. Add to flour mixture, stirring just until moist. Spoon batter

Jamaican Banana Bread

BREAD:

2 tablespoons butter or stick margarine, softened
2 tablespoons (1 ounce) ⅓-less-fat cream cheese, softened
1 cup granulated sugar
1 large egg
2 cups all-purpose flour
2 teaspoons baking powder
½ teaspoon baking soda
⅛ teaspoon salt
1 cup mashed ripe banana
½ cup fat-free milk
2 tablespoons dark rum or ¼ teaspoon imitation rum extract
½ teaspoon grated lime rind
2 teaspoons lime juice
1 teaspoon vanilla extract
¼ cup chopped pecans, toasted
¼ cup flaked sweetened coconut
Cooking spray

TOPPING:

¼ cup packed brown sugar
2 teaspoons butter or stick margarine
2 teaspoons lime juice
2 teaspoons dark rum or ⅛ teaspoon imitation rum extract
2 tablespoons chopped pecans, toasted
2 tablespoons flaked sweetened coconut

1. Preheat oven to 375°.

2. To prepare bread, beat 2 tablespoons butter and cheese at medium speed of a mixer; add granulated sugar, beating well. Add egg; beat well.

3. Lightly spoon flour into dry measuring cups; level with a knife. Combine flour, baking powder, baking soda, and salt. Combine banana and the next 5 ingredients. Add flour mixture to creamed mixture alternately with banana mixture, beginning and ending with flour mixture; mix after each addition. Stir in ¼ cup pecans and ¼ cup coconut.

4. Pour batter into an 8 x 4-inch loaf pan coated with cooking spray. Bake at 375° for 1 hour. Cool in pan 10 minutes, and remove from pan. Cool slightly on a wire rack.

5. To prepare topping, combine brown sugar and 2 teaspoons each butter, lime juice, and rum in a saucepan; bring to a simmer. Cook 1 minute, stirring constantly. Remove from heat. Stir in 2 tablespoons each pecans and coconut; spoon over loaf. Yield: 16 servings (serving size: 1 slice).

CALORIES 193 (26% from fat); FAT 5.5g (sat 2.4g, mono 1.9g, poly 0.7g); PROTEIN 2.9g; CARB 32.3g; FIBER 1.1g; CHOL 20mg; IRON 1mg; SODIUM 163mg; CALC 55mg

Marbled-Chocolate Banana Bread

Chocolate and bananas are a natural pair. Toast and top with a spoonful of peanut butter for breakfast.

2 cups all-purpose flour
¾ teaspoon baking soda
½ teaspoon salt
1 cup sugar
¼ cup butter, softened
1½ cups mashed ripe banana (about 3 bananas)
½ cup egg substitute
⅓ cup plain low-fat yogurt
½ cup semisweet chocolate chips
Cooking spray

1. Preheat oven to 350°.

2. Lightly spoon flour into dry measuring cups; level with a knife. Combine flour, baking soda, and salt, stirring with a whisk.

3. Place sugar and butter in a large bowl; beat with a mixer at medium speed until well blended (about 1 minute). Add banana, egg substitute, and yogurt; beat until blended. Add flour mixture; beat at low speed just until moist.

4. Place chocolate chips in a medium microwave-safe bowl; microwave at HIGH 1 minute or until almost melted, stirring until smooth. Cool slightly. Add 1 cup batter to chocolate, stirring until well combined. Spoon chocolate batter alternately with plain batter into an 8½ x 4½-inch loaf pan coated with cooking spray. Swirl batters together using a knife. Bake at 350° for 1 hour and 15 minutes or until a wooden pick inserted in center comes out clean. Cool 10 minutes in pan on a wire rack, and remove from pan. Cool completely on wire rack. Yield: 1 loaf, 16 servings (serving size: 1 slice).

CALORIES 183 (23% from fat); FAT 4.7g (sat 2.8g, mono 1.4g, poly 0.2g); PROTEIN 3.1g; CARB 33.4g; FIBER 1.3g; CHOL 8mg; IRON 1.1mg; SODIUM 180mg; CALC 18mg

Easy Banana Bread

Pure banana flavor—unmasked by spices—makes this bread delicious.

1 cup mashed ripe banana (about 2 medium)
⅔ cup sugar
¼ cup vegetable oil
1 large egg white
1 large egg
1¾ cups all-purpose flour
1¼ teaspoons cream of tartar
¾ teaspoon baking soda
½ teaspoon salt
Cooking spray

1. Preheat oven to 350°.

2. Combine first 5 ingredients in a large bowl; beat with a mixer at medium speed until smooth.

3. Lightly spoon the flour into dry measuring cups, and level with a knife. Combine the flour, cream of tartar, baking soda, and salt in a bowl, stirring with a whisk. Add flour mixture to banana mixture, stirring just until moist. Spoon batter into an 8 x 4-inch loaf pan coated with cooking spray.

4. Bake at 350° for 40 minutes or until a wooden pick inserted in center comes out clean. Cool 10 minutes in pan on a wire rack; remove from pan. Cool completely on rack. Yield: 12 servings (serving size: 1 slice).

NOTE: To freeze, wrap tightly in plastic wrap, and place in a heavy-duty zip-top plastic bag. Remove excess air from bag, and seal and freeze for up to 1 month. To thaw, unwrap bread and let stand at room temperature.

CALORIES 174 (27% from fat); FAT 5.3g (sat 1g, mono 1.5g, poly 2.4g); PROTEIN 3.1g; CARB 29.1g; FIBER 0.9g; CHOL 18mg; IRON 1.1mg; SODIUM 190mg; CALC 8mg

Pumpkin Streusel Bread

Be sure to buy canned pumpkin, not pumpkin-pie filling, for this recipe.

TOPPING:
¼ cup chopped pecans
2 tablespoons sugar
1½ tablespoons chilled butter or stick margarine, cut into small pieces
¼ teaspoon ground cinnamon

BREAD:
2 cups all-purpose flour
½ cup sugar
½ cup raisins
1 teaspoon baking soda
1 teaspoon salt
½ teaspoon ground cinnamon
½ teaspoon ground cloves
½ teaspoon ground nutmeg
1 cup canned pumpkin
½ cup plain low-fat yogurt
½ cup honey
¼ cup vegetable oil
1 teaspoon vanilla extract
2 large eggs
Cooking spray

1. Preheat oven to 350°.

2. To prepare topping, combine first 4 ingredients until crumbly. Set mixture aside.

3. To prepare bread, lightly spoon flour into dry measuring cups; level with a knife. Combine flour and next 7 ingredients in a large bowl; stir well with a whisk. Make a well in center of mixture. Combine pumpkin and next 5 ingredients in a bowl, and add to flour mixture. Stir just until moist. Spoon batter into a 9 x 5-inch loaf pan coated with cooking spray; sprinkle with topping. Bake at 350° for 1 hour or until a wooden pick inserted in center comes out clean. Cool in pan 10 minutes on a wire rack, and remove from pan. Cool completely on wire rack. Yield: 16 servings (serving size: 1 slice).

CALORIES 209 (30% from fat); FAT 6.9g (sat 1.7g, mono 2.4g, poly 2.2g); PROTEIN 3.4g; CARB 34.6g; FIBER 1.4g; CHOL 31mg; IRON 1.3mg; SODIUM 252mg; CALC 29mg

Spicy Pumpkin Bread

In our Test Kitchens we found that pumpkin-pie spice can be a tasty substitute for allspice, cinnamon, nutmeg, and cloves.

3½   cups all-purpose flour
  2   teaspoons baking powder
  1   teaspoon ground allspice
  1   teaspoon ground cinnamon
  1   teaspoon ground nutmeg
 ¾   teaspoon salt
 ½   teaspoon baking soda
 ½   teaspoon ground cloves
1⅓   cups packed brown sugar
 ¾   cup fat-free milk
 ⅓   cup vegetable oil
  2   teaspoons vanilla extract
  2   large eggs
  1   (15-ounce) can pumpkin
Cooking spray
 ⅓   cup chopped walnuts

1. Preheat oven to 350°.
2. Lightly spoon flour into dry measuring cups; level with a knife. Combine flour and the next 7 ingredients in a large bowl; make a well in center of mixture. Combine sugar and next 5 ingredients in a bowl, and stir well with a whisk until smooth. Add to flour mixture, stirring just until moist.
3. Spoon the batter into 2 (8 x 4-inch) loaf pans coated with cooking spray, and sprinkle with walnuts. Bake at 350° for 1 hour or until a wooden pick inserted in center comes out clean. Cool loaves in pans 10 minutes on a wire rack; remove from pans. Cool loaves completely. Yield: 2 loaves, 12 servings per loaf (serving size: 1 slice).

CALORIES 161 (26% from fat); FAT 4.7g (sat 0.8g, mono 1.3g, poly 2.3g); PROTEIN 3.1g; CARB 26.9g; FIBER 1.3g; CHOL 18mg; IRON 1.4mg; SODIUM 138mg; CALC 46mg

Pumpkin-Date Loaf with Cream Cheese Swirl

White pockets of cream cheese batter contrast with the orange pumpkin in this loaf.

 ½   cup (4 ounces) block-style ⅓-less-fat cream cheese
  2   tablespoons granulated sugar
  1   teaspoon vanilla extract
  1   large egg white, lightly beaten
  2   cups all-purpose flour
1½   teaspoons pumpkin-pie spice
  1   teaspoon baking powder
 ½   teaspoon salt
 ¼   teaspoon baking soda
  1   large egg, lightly beaten
  1   large egg yolk, lightly beaten
1¼   cups packed dark brown sugar
 ¾   cup canned pumpkin
  3   tablespoons vegetable oil
 ¾   cup whole pitted dates, chopped (about 5 ounces)
Cooking spray

1. Preheat oven to 350°.
2. Combine first 4 ingredients in a small bowl; beat with a mixer at medium speed until blended.
3. Lightly spoon flour into dry measuring cups; level with a knife. Combine flour and next 4 ingredients in a medium bowl; stir with a whisk. Combine egg, egg yolk, and brown sugar in a medium bowl; stir with a whisk until well blended. Add pumpkin and oil; stir well with a whisk. Stir in dates. Add to flour mixture, stirring just until moist.
4. Spoon batter into a 9 x 5-inch loaf pan coated with cooking spray. Spoon cream cheese mixture over batter, and swirl batters together using the tip of a knife. Bake at 350° for 1 hour and 10 minutes or until a wooden pick inserted in center comes out clean. Cool 10 minutes in pan on a wire rack, and remove from pan. Cool completely on wire rack. Yield: 16 servings (serving size: 1 slice).

CALORIES 208 (22% from fat); FAT 5.1g (sat 1.7g, mono 1.3g, poly 1.7g); PROTEIN 3.5g; CARB 38.1g; FIBER 1.6g; CHOL 32mg; IRON 1.4mg; SODIUM 167mg; CALC 50mg

Pumpkin-Date Loaf with
Cream Cheese Swirl

Vermont-Cheddar Spoon Bread

Cooking spray
2 teaspoons cornmeal
½ cup cornmeal
1½ cups fat-free milk
¼ teaspoon salt
⅛ teaspoon black pepper
1 large egg yolk, lightly beaten
2 large egg whites
½ cup (2 ounces) shredded Vermont sharp cheddar cheese

1. Preheat oven to 375°.

2. Coat a 1-quart soufflé dish with cooking spray; sprinkle with 2 teaspoons cornmeal, and set aside.

3. Combine ½ cup cornmeal, fat-free milk, salt, and pepper in a medium saucepan, and cook over medium heat 5 minutes or until thick, stirring constantly. Remove mixture from heat.

4. Gradually stir ½ cup hot cornmeal mixture into egg yolk, and add to remaining cornmeal mixture, stirring constantly. Pour the mixture into a large bowl, and cool completely.

5. Beat egg whites at high speed of a mixer until stiff peaks form. Gently fold egg whites and cheese into the cornmeal mixture. Spoon batter into the prepared dish. Bake at 375° for 1 hour or until puffy and browned. Serve immediately. Yield: 4 servings (serving size: 1 cup).

CALORIES 183 (32% from fat); FAT 6.6g (sat 3.6g, mono 2g, poly 0.5g); PROTEIN 10.6g; CARB 19.4g; FIBER 1g; CHOL 71mg; IRON 1.1mg; SODIUM 311mg; CALC 223mg

Cornmeal Cheese Twists

¼ cup water
4 large egg whites
1 cup yellow cornmeal
1 cup (4 ounces) grated Asiago cheese
1 cup (4 ounces) grated fresh Parmesan cheese
1 teaspoon paprika
Cooking spray
4 (11-ounce) cans refrigerated soft breadstick dough (such as Pillsbury)

1. Preheat oven to 375°.
2. Combine water and egg whites in a shallow bowl. Combine cornmeal, cheeses, and paprika in a shallow bowl. Coat 2 baking sheets with cooking spray.
3. Unroll breadstick dough, separating into strips. Roll each piece into a 7-inch-long strip. Dip 2 strips in egg white mixture, and dredge in cornmeal mixture. Twist strips together, pinching ends to seal, and place on baking sheet. Repeat procedure with remaining strips, egg white mixture, and cornmeal mixture. Bake at 375° for 15 minutes or until golden brown. Yield: 2 dozen twists (serving size: 1 twist).

CALORIES 202 (24% from fat); FAT 5.3g (sat 2.2g, mono 1.6g, poly 1.2g); PROTEIN 8.3g; CARB 29.9g; FIBER 0.3g; CHOL 8mg; IRON 1.7mg; SODIUM 521mg; CALC 107mg

Cajun Crawfish Corn Bread

Cooking spray
½ cup all-purpose flour
1½ cups yellow cornmeal
1 tablespoon baking powder
2 teaspoons All That Jazz Seasoning
½ teaspoon salt
1½ cups cooked crawfish tail meat, coarsely chopped (about 9 ounces)
1 cup (4 ounces) shredded sharp cheddar cheese
1 cup low-fat buttermilk
1 tablespoon butter, melted
1 large egg white, lightly beaten
1 large egg, lightly beaten
1 (8¾-ounce) can cream-style corn

1. Preheat oven to 375°.
2. Coat a 9-inch cast-iron skillet with cooking spray. Place in a 375° oven for 10 minutes.
3. Lightly spoon the flour into a dry measuring cup; level with a knife. Combine flour, cornmeal, baking powder, All That Jazz Seasoning, and salt in a large bowl. Combine crawfish meat and the remaining ingredients in a medium bowl; stir well with a whisk.
4. Add crawfish meat mixture to flour mixture, stirring until moist. Pour batter into preheated pan. Bake at 375° for 35 minutes or until a wooden pick inserted in the center comes out clean. Yield: 12 servings (serving size: 1 wedge).

(Totals include All That Jazz Seasoning) CALORIES 179 (27% from fat); FAT 5.3g (sat 2.6g, mono 0.6g, poly 0.4g); PROTEIN 9.9g; CARB 22.8g; FIBER 1.7g; CHOL 60mg; IRON 0.9mg; SODIUM 411mg; CALC 176mg

ALL THAT JAZZ SEASONING:

This spice blend has all the flavors of traditional Cajun seasoning, but with less salt than commercial brands.

¼ cup garlic powder
¼ cup onion powder
2 tablespoons paprika
1 tablespoon ground red pepper
1 tablespoon black pepper
1½ teaspoons celery seeds
1½ teaspoons chili powder
1 teaspoon salt
1 teaspoon lemon pepper
½ teaspoon ground nutmeg

1. Combine all ingredients. Yield: 1 cup (serving size: 1 tablespoon).

CALORIES 20 (14% from fat); FAT 0.3g (sat 0.1g, mono 0.1g, poly 0.1g); PROTEIN 0.8g; CARB 4.3g; FIBER 1.1g; CHOL 0mg; IRON 0.6mg; SODIUM 177mg; CALC 18mg

Jalapeño Corn Bread

    1   teaspoon vegetable oil
    Cooking spray
    1¼ cups all-purpose flour
    1¼ cups yellow cornmeal
    2   tablespoons sugar
    1   tablespoon baking powder
    1   teaspoon salt
    1   teaspoon ground cumin
    1   cup fat-free milk
    ½   cup chopped red bell pepper
    ¼ to ½ cup minced seeded jalapeño pepper
    3   tablespoons butter or stick margarine, melted
    2   tablespoons minced fresh cilantro
    2   large eggs, lightly beaten
    1   (7-ounce) can whole-kernel corn, drained

1. Preheat oven to 425°.

2. Coat a 10-inch cast-iron or heavy ovenproof skillet with oil and cooking spray. Place pan in a 425° oven for 7 minutes.

3. Lightly spoon flour into dry measuring cups; level with a knife. Combine flour and next 5 ingredients. Combine milk and remaining ingredients; add to cornmeal mixture. Stir just until moist. Pour into prepared pan. Bake at 425° for 25 minutes or until a wooden pick inserted in center comes out clean. Cool in pan 5 minutes on a wire rack. Remove from pan. Yield: 12 servings (serving size: 1 wedge).

CALORIES 174 (25% from fat); FAT 4.9g (sat 2.3g, mono 1.5g, poly 0.7g); PROTEIN 4.9g; CARB 28.1g; FIBER 1.4g; CHOL 45mg; IRON 1.8mg; SODIUM 416mg; CALC 105mg

Buttermilk Pancakes

    1   cup all-purpose flour
    1   teaspoon sugar
    1   teaspoon baking powder
    ½   teaspoon baking soda
    ¼   teaspoon salt
    1⅓ cups low-fat buttermilk
    1   tablespoon butter or stick margarine, melted
    1   large egg white
    Cooking spray
    ½   cup maple syrup

1. Lightly spoon flour into a dry measuring cup; level with a knife. Combine flour and the next 4 ingredients. Combine buttermilk, butter, and egg white. Add to flour mixture, stirring until smooth.

2. Spoon about ¼ cup pancake batter onto a hot nonstick griddle coated with cooking spray. Turn when top is covered with bubbles and edges look cooked. Serve with maple syrup. Yield: 4 servings (serving size: 3 pancakes and 2 tablespoons syrup).

CALORIES 293 (15% from fat); FAT 4.8g (sat 2.7g, mono 1.2g, poly 0.3g); PROTEIN 7.1g; CARB 55.7g; FIBER 0.8g; CHOL 8mg; IRON 1.9mg; SODIUM 489mg; CALC 185mg

Cheddar Pancakes with Sautéed Apples and Bacon

    1⅓ cups all-purpose flour
    1   tablespoon sugar
    1¼ teaspoons baking powder
    ¼   teaspoon salt
    ¼   teaspoon baking soda
    ¼   teaspoon ground nutmeg
    1⅓ cups plain low-fat yogurt
    1¼ cups (5 ounces) shredded reduced-fat
        extrasharp cheddar cheese
    2   tablespoons water
    2   tablespoons Dijon mustard
    2   teaspoons vegetable oil
    1   large egg
    1   large egg white
    Sautéed Apples and Bacon

1. Lightly spoon flour into dry measuring cups; level with a knife. Combine flour and next 5 ingredients in large bowl. Combine yogurt and next 6 ingredients; add to flour mixture, stirring until smooth.

2. Spoon ¼ cup batter onto a nonstick skillet. Turn when top is covered with bubbles and edges look cooked. Serve with Sautéed Apples and Bacon. Yield: 4 servings (serving size: 3 pancakes and ¾ cup topping).

(Totals include Sautéed Apples and Bacon) CALORIES 593 (30% from fat); FAT 19.8g (sat 8.2g, mono 6.8g, poly 2.8g); PROTEIN 22.8g; CARB 83.1g; FIBER 7.1g; CHOL 92mg; IRON 3mg; SODIUM 1,027mg; CALC 577mg

SAUTÉED APPLES AND BACON:

    2   bacon slices
    8   cups sliced, peeled Granny Smith apples
        (about 2 pounds)
    2   tablespoons sugar

1. Cook bacon in a nonstick skillet over medium heat until crisp. Remove bacon; reserve drippings. Crumble bacon; set aside. Add apples and sugar to pan. Sauté 10 minutes or until apples are golden. Stir in bacon. Yield: 4 servings (serving size: ¾ cup).

CALORIES 217 (30% from fat); FAT 7.3g (sat 2.5g, mono 3g, poly 1g); PROTEIN 1.4g; CARB 39.8g; FIBER 6g; CHOL 8mg; IRON 0.5mg; SODIUM 83mg; CALC 16mg

Waffles with Two-Berry Syrup

Wheat germ and flaxseed give these waffles a wonderfully nutty flavor and crunchy texture.
Frozen berries actually work better than fresh in this recipe.

WAFFLES:

  2 tablespoons flaxseed
  1 cup all-purpose flour
  ½ cup whole-wheat flour
  ¼ cup toasted wheat germ
  2 tablespoons sugar
1½ teaspoons baking powder
  ½ teaspoon salt
1½ cups fat-free milk
  ¾ cup egg substitute
1½ tablespoons vegetable oil
  1 teaspoon vanilla extract
Cooking spray

SYRUP:

1½ cups frozen blueberries
1½ cups frozen unsweetened raspberries
  ½ cup maple syrup
  ¼ teaspoon ground cinnamon

1. To prepare waffles, place flaxseed in a clean coffee grinder or blender; process until ground to measure ¼ cup flaxseed meal. Set flaxseed meal aside. Lightly spoon flours into dry measuring cups; level with a knife. Combine flaxseed meal, flours, wheat germ, sugar, baking powder, and salt in a large bowl; make a well in center of mixture. Combine milk, egg substitute, oil, and vanilla; add to flour mixture, stirring just until moist.

2. Coat a waffle iron with cooking spray; preheat. Spoon about ¼ cup batter per 4-inch waffle onto the hot waffle iron, spreading batter to edges. Cook 5 to 6 minutes or until steaming stops; repeat procedure with remaining batter.

3. To prepare syrup, combine berries, syrup, and cinnamon in a saucepan. Cook over medium heat until thoroughly heated. Serve warm over waffles. Yield: 6 servings (serving size: 2 waffles and ⅓ cup syrup).

NOTE: You can find flaxseed, a grain rich in heart-healthy omega-3 fats, in health-food stores or large supermarkets. Freeze leftover waffles individually on a cookie sheet and then transfer to a zip-top freezer bag for storage. To reheat, place frozen waffles in toaster. The yield on this recipe is based on a regular waffle iron, not a Belgian waffle maker.

CALORIES 332 (18% from fat); FAT 6.6g (sat 0.7g, mono 2.5g, poly 2.8g); PROTEIN 10.8g; CARB 60.5g; FIBER 6.5g; CHOL 1mg; IRON 3.3mg; SODIUM 400mg; CALC 199mg

Sweet Potato-Pecan Pancakes with
Vanilla-Maple Syrup

Sweet Potato-Pecan Pancakes

These pancakes go great with our Vanilla-Maple Syrup. You can use ¾ cup mashed winter squash instead of the sweet potatoes, if desired.

1¼ cups all-purpose flour
¼ cup chopped pecans, toasted and divided
2¼ teaspoons baking powder
1 teaspoon pumpkin-pie spice
¼ teaspoon salt
1 cup fat-free milk
¼ cup packed dark brown sugar
1 tablespoon vegetable oil
1 teaspoon vanilla extract
2 large eggs, lightly beaten
1 (16-ounce) can sweet potatoes or yams, drained and mashed (about ¾ cup)

1. Lightly spoon the flour into dry measuring cups, and level with a knife. Combine the flour, 2 tablespoons pecans, baking powder, pumpkin-pie spice, and salt in a large bowl. Combine the milk, brown sugar, vegetable oil, vanilla, and eggs; add to flour mixture, stirring until smooth. Stir in sweet potatoes or yams.
2. Spoon about ¼ cup batter per pancake onto a hot nonstick griddle or large nonstick skillet. Turn pancakes when tops are covered with bubbles and edges look cooked. Sprinkle pancakes with 2 tablespoons pecans. Yield: 6 servings (serving size: 2 pancakes and 1 teaspoon pecans).

CALORIES 270 (26% from fat); FAT 7.9g (sat 1.4g, mono 3.5g, poly 2.3g); PROTEIN 7.3g; CARB 42.6g; FIBER 2.3g; CHOL 74mg; IRON 2.2mg; SODIUM 333mg; CALC 185mg

Vanilla-Maple Syrup

Be sure to use pure maple syrup, not pancake syrup with imitation maple flavor, for this recipe.

1½ cups maple syrup
1 (3-inch) piece vanilla bean, split lengthwise or ¼ teaspoon vanilla extract

1. Pour the maple syrup into a medium saucepan. Scrape seeds from vanilla bean; add seeds and bean to syrup. Bring to a simmer over medium heat, and cook 5 minutes. Remove from heat; discard bean. Yield: 1½ cups (serving size: 1 tablespoon).

CALORIES 52 (0% from fat); FAT 0g (sat 0g, mono 0g, poly 0g); PROTEIN 0g; CARB 13.2g; FIBER 0g; CHOL 0mg; IRON 0.2mg; SODIUM 2mg; CALC 13mg

Crumb-Topped French Toast

Dredging the French bread slices in cornflake crumbs is a convenient way to add a crunchy coating to this melt-in-your-mouth breakfast.

½ cup skim milk
½ teaspoon vanilla extract
¼ teaspoon salt
2 large eggs
1 cup cornflake crumbs
8 (1-ounce) diagonally cut slices French bread (about 1 inch thick)
¼ cup butter, melted
½ cup maple syrup

1. Preheat oven to 450°.
2. Combine first 4 ingredients in a medium bowl, stirring with a whisk until well blended. Place cornflake crumbs in a shallow dish.
3. Dip bread slices in milk mixture, and dredge in cornflake crumbs. Place bread slices on a baking sheet, and drizzle with butter. Bake at 450° for 15 minutes or until golden brown. Serve with maple syrup. Yield: 8 servings (serving size: 1 toast slice and 1 tablespoon maple syrup).

CALORIES 212 (32% from fat); FAT 7.6g (sat 1.7g, mono 3.3g, poly 2.3g); PROTEIN 5.8g; CARB 29g; FIBER 0.8g; CHOL 56mg; IRON 1.7mg; SODIUM 468mg; CALC 40mg

French Toast Soufflé

A firm white bread produces the best texture in this make-ahead breakfast casserole.

- 10 cups (1-inch) cubed sturdy white bread (such as Pepperidge Farm Hearty White; about 16 [1-ounce] slices)
- Cooking spray
- 1 (8-ounce) block ⅓-less-fat-cream cheese, softened
- 8 large eggs
- 1½ cups 2% reduced-fat milk
- ⅔ cup half-and-half
- ½ cup maple syrup
- ½ teaspoon vanilla extract
- 2 tablespoons powdered sugar
- ¾ cup maple syrup

1. Place the bread cubes in a 13 x 9-inch baking dish coated with cooking spray. Beat cream cheese with a mixer at medium speed until smooth. Add eggs, 1 at a time, mixing well after each addition. Add milk, half-and-half, ½ cup maple syrup, and vanilla; mix until smooth. Pour cream cheese mixture over top of bread; cover and refrigerate overnight.

2. Preheat oven to 375°.

3. Remove bread mixture from refrigerator; let stand on counter for 30 minutes. Uncover; bake at 375° for 50 minutes or until set. Sprinkle soufflé with sugar; serve with ¾ cup syrup. Yield: 12 servings (serving size: 1 slice of soufflé and 1 tablespoon maple syrup).

CALORIES 346 (30% from fat); FAT 11.5g (sat 5.5g, mono 3.8g, poly 1g); PROTEIN 11.6g; CARB 51.7g; FIBER 2.7g; CHOL 169mg; IRON 1.9mg; SODIUM 396mg; CALC 131mg

French Toast Soufflé

Pear Dutch Baby

Serve this giant, soufflélike pancake right away.

- 4 Bartlett or Bosc pears, cored and thinly sliced (about 1 pound)
- ¼ cup packed brown sugar
- ¼ cup fresh lemon juice
- 1 cup all-purpose flour
- 1 cup 2% reduced-fat milk
- 3 tablespoons granulated sugar
- ¼ teaspoon salt
- 3 large eggs
- 2 teaspoons butter or stick margarine
- 1 tablespoon powdered sugar

1. Preheat oven to 425°.

2. Combine first 3 ingredients. Heat a 10-inch cast-iron or heavy ovenproof skillet over medium heat. Add the pear mixture, and sauté 5 minutes or until pears are golden. Remove pear mixture from pan, and keep warm.

3. Lightly spoon the flour into a dry measuring cup; level with a knife. Place flour in a large bowl. Combine milk, granulated sugar, salt, and eggs, stirring well with a whisk. Add milk mixture to flour, stirring with a whisk until well blended.

4. Melt butter in pan. Pour the batter into pan. Bake at 425° for 25 minutes or until puffy and golden. Spoon pear mixture into center of pancake, and sprinkle with powdered sugar. Cut into 6 wedges. Serve immediately. Yield: 6 servings.

CALORIES 253 (18% from fat); FAT 5.1g (sat 2.1g, mono 1.7g, poly 0.6g); PROTEIN 7.1g; CARB 46g; FIBER 2.3g; CHOL 117mg; IRON 1.7mg; SODIUM 168mg; CALC 82mg

Pear Dutch Baby

Homemade White Bread

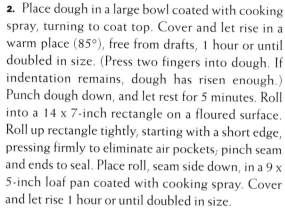

    1   package dry yeast (about 2¼ teaspoons)
    1   tablespoon sugar
1⅔   cups warm fat-free milk (100° to 110°)
    2   tablespoons butter or stick margarine, melted
4¾   cups all-purpose flour, divided
1½   teaspoons salt
        Cooking spray

1. Dissolve yeast and sugar in warm milk in a large bowl; let stand 5 minutes. Stir in butter. Lightly spoon flour into dry measuring cups; level with a knife. Add 4¼ cups flour and salt to yeast mixture; stir until blended. Turn dough out onto a floured surface. Knead until smooth and elastic (about 10 minutes); add enough of remaining flour, 1 tablespoon at a time, to prevent dough from sticking to hands (dough will feel sticky).

2. Place dough in a large bowl coated with cooking spray, turning to coat top. Cover and let rise in a warm place (85°), free from drafts, 1 hour or until doubled in size. (Press two fingers into dough. If indentation remains, dough has risen enough.) Punch dough down, and let rest for 5 minutes. Roll into a 14 x 7-inch rectangle on a floured surface. Roll up rectangle tightly, starting with a short edge, pressing firmly to eliminate air pockets; pinch seam and ends to seal. Place roll, seam side down, in a 9 x 5-inch loaf pan coated with cooking spray. Cover and let rise 1 hour or until doubled in size.

3. Preheat oven to 350°.

4. Uncover dough. Bake at 350° for 45 minutes or until loaf is browned on the bottom and sounds hollow when tapped. Remove loaf from pan, and cool on a wire rack. Yield: 1 loaf, 16 servings (serving size: 1 slice).

CALORIES 162 (11% from fat); FAT 1.9g (sat 0.4g, mono 0.7g, poly 0.6g); PROTEIN 4.9g; CARB 30.5g; FIBER 1.1g; CHOL 1mg; IRON 1.8mg; SODIUM 219mg; CALC 38mg

CHEESE-BREAD VARIATION:

You can use almost any kind of cheese in this bread; make sure it's one with a strong flavor. Parmesan and Romano are great choices.

Add 1 cup (4 ounces) shredded reduced-fat extrasharp cheddar cheese with the 4¼ cups flour and salt. Proceed with recipe.

CALORIES 176 (17% from fat); FAT 3.3g (sat 1.2g, mono 1.1g, poly 0.6g); PROTEIN 6.8g; CARB 30.5g; FIBER 1.1g; CHOL 5mg; IRON 2mg; SODIUM 301mg; CALC 100mg

HERB-BREAD VARIATION:

Add ½ cup grated Parmesan cheese, 1 teaspoon each of onion flakes, dried oregano, and dried basil, and ½ teaspoon each of garlic powder and coarsely ground black pepper in with the 4¼ cups flour and salt. Proceed with recipe.

CALORIES 175 (14% from fat); FAT 2.7g (sat 0.9g, mono 0.9g, poly 0.6g); PROTEIN 6g; CARB 30.9g; FIBER 1.2g; CHOL 2mg; IRON 2mg; SODIUM 297mg; CALC 76mg

Red Pepper-Cheese Bread

1 package dry yeast (about 2¼ teaspoons)
2 teaspoons sugar
1 cup warm water (100° to 110°)
3 cups bread flour, divided
2 teaspoons Dijon mustard
1 tablespoon vegetable oil
½ teaspoon salt
¼ to ½ teaspoon ground red pepper
¾ cup (3 ounces) shredded extrasharp
    cheddar cheese
Cooking spray

1. Dissolve yeast and sugar in warm water in a large bowl, and let stand 5 minutes. Lightly spoon flour into dry measuring cups, and level with a knife. Add 1 cup flour, mustard, oil, salt, and pepper to yeast mixture; stir until smooth. Add 1¾ cups flour and cheese; stir to form a soft dough. Turn the dough out onto a lightly floured surface. Knead the dough until smooth and elastic (about 10 minutes); add enough of the remaining flour, 1 tablespoon at a time, to prevent dough from sticking to hands.
2. Place dough in a large bowl coated with cooking spray, turning to coat top. Cover dough and let rise in a warm place (85°), free from drafts, 1 hour or until doubled in size. (Press two fingers into dough. If indentation remains, the dough has risen enough.) Punch dough down, and turn out onto a lightly floured surface. Roll dough into a 14 x 7-inch rectangle. Roll up rectangle tightly starting with a short edge, pressing firmly to eliminate air pockets; pinch seam and ends to seal. Place the roll, seam side down, in a 9 x 5-inch loaf pan coated with cooking spray. Cover dough and let rise 1 hour or until doubled in size.
3. Preheat oven to 375°.
4. Uncover dough; bake at 375° for 35 minutes or until loaf sounds hollow when tapped. Remove from pan immediately; cool on a wire rack. Yield: 16 servings (serving size: 1 slice).

CALORIES 126 (22% from fat); FAT 3.1g (sat 1.3g, mono 0.8g, poly 0.7g); PROTEIN 4.6g; CARB 19.4g; FIBER 0.1g; CHOL 6mg; IRON 1.2mg; SODIUM 125mg; CALC 42mg

BREAD MACHINE VARIATION: Follow manufacturer's instructions for placing all dough ingredients in bread pan. Select cycle, and start bread machine.

Beer-Cheese Bread

A beautiful dome forms as the bread bakes, but it tastes so good you'll want to cut into it anyway.

¾ cup beer
¼ cup butter or stick margarine
3½ cups bread flour, divided
1 tablespoon sugar
½ teaspoon salt
½ teaspoon dry mustard
¼ teaspoon ground red pepper
1 package dry yeast (about 2¼ teaspoons)
1 large egg, lightly beaten
1 cup (4 ounces) shredded reduced-fat sharp cheddar cheese
Cooking spray

1. Heat beer and butter in a small saucepan over medium-low heat until very warm (120° to 130°).
2. Lightly spoon flour into dry measuring cups; level with a knife. Combine 1½ cups flour, sugar, and next 4 ingredients in a large bowl. Add beer mixture and egg; beat at medium speed of a mixer for 2 minutes or until smooth. Stir in 1½ cups flour and cheddar cheese to form a soft dough.
3. Turn dough out onto a lightly floured surface. Knead dough until smooth and elastic (about 8 minutes); add enough of remaining flour, 1 tablespoon at a time, to prevent the dough from sticking to hands. Place dough in a large bowl coated with cooking spray, turning to coat top. Cover and let rise in a warm place (85°), free from drafts, 1 hour or until doubled in size. (Press two fingers into the dough. If an indentation remains, the dough has risen enough.)
4. Punch dough down; cover and let rest 10 minutes. Place in a 1-quart soufflé dish coated with cooking spray. Cover; let rise 40 minutes or until doubled in size.
5. Preheat oven to 375°.
6. Bake at 375° for 20 minutes. Cover loosely with foil; bake an additional 20 minutes or until loaf sounds hollow when tapped. Remove the loaf from dish; cool on a wire rack. Yield: 16 servings (serving size: 1 slice).

CALORIES 150 (29% from fat); FAT 4.8g (sat 1.5g, mono 1.8g, poly 1.1g); PROTEIN 5.3g; CARB 20.9g; FIBER 0.8g; CHOL 18mg; IRON 1.3mg; SODIUM 163mg; CALC 70mg

Basic Sponge

This is the foundation for the French Country Bread with Currants and Rosemary and the Ciabatta, so start the sponge a day ahead.

1 cup bread flour
2 teaspoons sugar
1 package dry yeast (about 2¼ teaspoons)
¾ cup very warm water (120° to 130°)

1. Lightly spoon flour into a dry measuring cup, and level with a knife.
2. Place the first 3 ingredients in a food processor; pulse 5 times. Add water; process for 1 minute or until well blended. Spoon mixture into a medium bowl; cover and chill sponge for 2 to 24 hours. Bring to room temperature before using.

French Country Bread with Currants and Rosemary

Make the Basic Sponge a day ahead. Chill and then bring to room temperature. Cover until ready to use.

1 cup bread flour
1 cup whole-wheat flour
Basic Sponge (at room temperature)
¾ cup water
½ cup rye flour
¼ cup regular oats
1½ teaspoons salt
¼ cup currants
2 tablespoons bread flour
2 tablespoons dried rosemary
Cooking spray

1. Lightly spoon 1 cup bread flour and the whole-wheat flour into dry measuring cups, and level flours with a knife.
2. Combine flours with Basic Sponge and the next 4 ingredients in a food processor, and process until dough forms a ball. Process dough 1 additional minute. Turn dough out onto a lightly floured surface, and knead in the currants, 2 tablespoons bread flour, and rosemary. Shape into a 9-inch round loaf, and place loaf on a baking sheet coated with cooking spray. Cover and let rise in a warm place (85°), free from drafts, 45 minutes or until doubled in size. (Press two fingers into dough. If indentation remains, dough has risen enough.)

3. Preheat oven to 375°.

4. Uncover loaf, and make a tic-tac-toe slash ¼-inch deep across top of loaf using a sharp knife. Bake at 375° for 40 minutes or until loaf sounds hollow when tapped. Remove loaf from pan, and cool on a wire rack. Yield: 16 servings (serving size: 1 [1½-ounce] slice).

CALORIES 115 (5% from fat); FAT 0.7g (sat 0.1g, mono 0.1g, poly 0.2g); PROTEIN 4g; CARB 23.4g; FIBER 1.9g; CHOL 0mg; IRON 1.5mg; SODIUM 221mg; CALC 13mg

4. Uncover the dough. Bake bread at 425° for 25 minutes or until the loaves sound hollow when tapped. Remove the ciabatta from the pan, and cool on a wire rack. Yield: 2 loaves, 24 servings (serving size: 1 slice).

NOTE: Serve one loaf now, and freeze the other loaf for a later use.

CALORIES 112 (4% from fat); FAT 0.5g (sat 0.1g, mono 0.1g, poly 0.2g); PROTEIN 3.8g; CARB 22.4g; FIBER 0.2g; CHOL 0mg; IRON 1.4mg; SODIUM 99mg; CALC 7mg

Ciabatta

    4 cups bread flour
Basic Sponge (at room temperature)
1¼ cups warm water (100° to 110°)
    2 teaspoons nonfat dry milk
    1 teaspoon salt
    1 package dry yeast (about 2¼ teaspoons)
    2 tablespoons cornmeal
    2 tablespoons bread flour

1. Lightly spoon 4 cups flour into dry measuring cups, and level with a knife. Combine with Basic Sponge and next 4 ingredients in a food processor; process until the dough forms a ball. Process 1 additional minute.

2. Turn the dough out onto a floured surface (dough will be sticky and soft), and divide dough in half. Working with one portion of the dough at a time (cover the remaining dough to keep it from drying), roll each portion into a 12 x 6-inch rectangle. Place dough on a parchment paper-lined baking sheet sprinkled with cornmeal. Taper the ends of dough to form a "slipper" shape. Sprinkle 2 tablespoons flour over the loaves. Cover and let rise 30 minutes or until doubled in size. (Press two fingers into dough. If indentation remains, the dough has risen enough.)

3. Preheat oven to 425°.

Ciabatta

Stout Chocolate-Cherry Bread

An overnight sponge made with stout creates a rich, complex flavor. Pearl sugar (available at gourmet stores and large supermarkets) adds texture.

4¼ cups bread flour, divided
1 (12-ounce) bottle Guinness Stout
1 package dry yeast (about 2¼ teaspoons)
1 tablespoon granulated sugar
1 teaspoon salt
½ cup dried tart cherries
4 ounces bittersweet chocolate, coarsely chopped
Cooking spray
1 teaspoon water
1 large egg white, lightly beaten
1 teaspoon pearl sugar (optional)

1. Lightly spoon flour into dry measuring cups; level with a knife. Combine 2 cups flour, beer, and yeast in a large bowl, stirring with a whisk. Cover and refrigerate 8 hours or overnight.

2. Remove from refrigerator; let stand 1 hour.

3. Add 2 cups flour, granulated sugar, and salt to yeast mixture; stir until a soft dough forms. Turn dough out onto a floured surface. Knead until smooth and elastic (about 8 minutes); add enough of remaining flour, 1 tablespoon at a time, to prevent dough from sticking to hands (dough will feel sticky). Knead in cherries and chocolate.

4. Place dough in a large bowl coated with cooking spray, turning to coat top. Cover and let rise in a warm place (85°), free from drafts, 1 hour or until doubled in size. (Gently press two fingers into dough. If indentation remains, dough has risen enough.)

5. Punch dough down; cover and let rest 5 minutes. Shape dough into a 9-inch round; place on a baking sheet lined with parchment paper. Lightly coat dough with cooking spray. Cover and let rise for 1 hour or until doubled in size.

6. Preheat oven to 350°.

7. Uncover dough. Combine water and egg white, stirring with a whisk; brush over dough. Sprinkle dough with pearl sugar, if desired. Make a ¼-inch-deep cut down center of dough using a sharp knife.

8. Bake at 350° for 30 minutes or until bread is browned on bottom and sounds hollow when tapped. Remove from pan; cool on a wire rack. Yield: 20 servings (serving size: 1 slice).

CALORIES 156 (14% from fat); FAT 2.4g (sat 1.3g, mono 0.2g, poly 0.2g); PROTEIN 4.3g; CARB 28.1g; FIBER 1.3g; CHOL 0mg; IRON 1.4mg; SODIUM 121mg; CALC 5mg

Baguette

One key to success is not adding too much flour to the dough. Let it rise long and slowly. Also, right before you put the loaves in the oven, throw ¼ cup water onto the oven floor (avoiding the heating element); this creates steam and gives the bread a crisp crust.

1 package dry yeast (about 2¼ teaspoons)
1 cup warm water (100° to 110°)
3 cups all-purpose flour, divided
1 tablespoon kosher or sea salt
2 teaspoons yellow cornmeal
¼ cup water

1. Dissolve yeast in warm water in a large bowl; let stand 5 minutes. Lightly spoon flour into dry measuring cups; level with a knife. Stir 2½ cups flour and salt into yeast mixture. Turn dough out onto a floured surface. Knead until smooth and elastic (about 10 minutes); add enough of remaining flour, 1 tablespoon at a time, to prevent dough from sticking to hands (dough will feel sticky).

2. Place dough in a large bowl. Cover and let rise in a warm place (85°), free from drafts, 45 minutes or until doubled in size. (Press two fingers into dough. If indentation remains, the dough has risen enough.) Punch dough down; cover and let rest 5 minutes. Divide in half. Working with 1 portion at a time (cover remaining dough to keep it from drying), roll each portion into a 16-inch rope on a floured surface. Place ropes on a large baking sheet sprinkled with cornmeal. Cover and let rise 30 minutes or until doubled in size. Uncover dough. Cut 3 slits in top of each loaf to allow steam to escape.

3. Preheat oven to 450°.

4. Throw ¼ cup water on oven floor (avoiding heating element). Place loaves in oven, and quickly close oven door. Bake at 450° for 20 minutes or until loaves are golden brown and sound hollow when tapped. Remove from pan; cool on wire racks. Cut each baguette into 12 slices. Yield: 2 loaves, 12 servings per loaf (serving size: 1 slice).

CALORIES 59 (4% from fat); FAT 0.3g (sat 0g, mono 0g, poly 0.1g); PROTEIN 1.7g; CARB 12.2g; FIBER 0.5g; CHOL 0mg; IRON 0.8mg; SODIUM 240mg; CALC 3mg

Saffron and Raisin Breakfast Bread

This recipe employs the technique of steeping saffron in hot liquid to release its color and aroma, which adds a wonderful, mellow flavor to the bread. Saffron breads are a tradition in southwestern England and throughout the Nordic countries, especially Sweden and Finland. Serve slices toasted or plain with honey for a special breakfast or weekend brunch.

1⅓ cups warm fat-free milk (100° to 110°)
¼ teaspoon saffron threads, crushed
1 package dry yeast (about 2¼ teaspoons)
1 teaspoon sugar
½ cup warm water (100° to 110°)
5¼ cups bread flour, divided
1½ cups raisins
¼ cup sugar
3 tablespoons butter, melted and cooled
1 teaspoon salt
Cooking spray

1. Combine milk and saffron; let stand 10 minutes.
2. Dissolve the yeast and 1 teaspoon sugar in warm water in a large bowl; let stand 5 minutes or until foamy. Stir in milk mixture. Lightly spoon flour into dry measuring cups; level with a knife. Add 5 cups flour, raisins, ¼ cup sugar, butter, and salt to milk mixture, stirring to form a soft dough. Turn dough out onto a floured surface. Knead until smooth and elastic (about 8 minutes); add enough of remaining flour, 1 tablespoon at a time, to prevent dough from sticking to hands (dough will feel sticky).

3. Place dough in a large bowl coated with cooking spray, turning to coat top. Cover and let rise in a warm place (85°), free from drafts, for 1½ hours or until doubled in size. (Gently press two fingers into dough. If indentation remains, dough has risen enough.) Punch dough down; cover and let rest 5 minutes. Divide in half. Shape each portion into a 5-inch round loaf. Place loaves, 3 inches apart, on a large baking sheet coated with cooking spray. Make 2 diagonal ¼-inch-deep cuts across top of each loaf using a sharp knife. Cover and let rise 30 minutes or until doubled in size.
4. Preheat oven to 375°.
5. Uncover dough. Bake at 375° for 30 minutes or until loaves are browned on bottom and sound hollow when tapped. Remove from pan; cool on wire racks. Yield: 2 loaves, 10 servings per loaf (serving size: 1 slice).

CALORIES 199 (11% from fat); FAT 2.4g (sat 1.2g, mono 0.6g, poly 0.3g); PROTEIN 5.4g; CARB 39.5g; FIBER 1.4g; CHOL 5mg; IRON 1.9mg; SODIUM 145mg; CALC 33mg

Raisin-Rosemary Rye Bread

Because rye flour produces a soft dough, we added whole-wheat flour, bread flour, and cornmeal to give the loaf body.

  1   tablespoon sugar
  1   package dry yeast (about 2¼ teaspoons)
1½   cups warm water (100° to 110°)
  1   teaspoon olive oil
2⅓   cups bread flour, divided
  1   cup whole-wheat flour
½   cup rye flour
⅓   cup nonfat dry milk
¼   cup yellow cornmeal
  1   teaspoon salt
¾   teaspoon coarsely ground black pepper
  1   cup raisins
½   cup chopped walnuts
1½   tablespoons dried rosemary
      Cooking spray

1. Dissolve sugar and yeast in warm water in a large bowl; let stand 5 minutes. Stir in oil. Lightly spoon flours into dry measuring cups, and level with a knife. Combine 2 cups bread flour, whole-wheat flour, and next 5 ingredients in a bowl. Add flour mixture to yeast mixture. Turn dough out onto a lightly floured surface. Knead until smooth and elastic (about 10 minutes); add enough of remaining bread flour, 1 tablespoon at a time, to prevent dough from sticking to hands. Knead in raisins, chopped walnuts, and rosemary.
2. Place dough in a large bowl coated with cooking spray, turning to coat top. Cover and let rise in a warm place (85°), free from drafts, 45 minutes or until doubled in size. (Press two fingers into dough. If an indentation remains, the dough has risen enough.) Punch dough down; cover and let rest 10 minutes. Form dough into a ball; place in a 9-inch pie plate coated with cooking spray. Cover and let rise 30 minutes or until doubled in size.
3. Preheat oven to 400°.
4. Uncover dough. Score top of loaf in a diamond pattern using a sharp knife. Bake at 400° for 50 minutes or until loaf sounds hollow when tapped. Remove from pan; cool on a wire rack.
5. Cut loaf in half lengthwise. Place cut sides down; cut each half into slices. Yield: 1 loaf, 20 slices (serving size: 1 slice).

CALORIES 149 (16% from fat); FAT 2.6g (sat 0.3g, mono 0.6g, poly 1.4g); PROTEIN 5g; CARB 27.7g; FIBER 1.9g; CHOL 0mg; IRON 1.5mg; SODIUM 130mg; CALC 39mg

Walnut and Rosemary Loaves

  2   cups warm 1% low-fat milk (100° to 110°)
¼   cup warm water (100° to 110°)
  3   tablespoons sugar
  2   tablespoons butter, melted
  2   teaspoons salt
  2   packages dry yeast (about 4½ teaspoons)
5½   cups all-purpose flour, divided
  1   cup chopped walnuts
  3   tablespoons coarsely chopped fresh rosemary
  1   large egg, lightly beaten
      Cooking spray
  1   tablespoon yellow cornmeal
  1   tablespoon 1% low-fat milk
  1   large egg, lightly beaten

1. Combine first 5 ingredients in a large bowl, stirring with a whisk. Add yeast, stirring with a whisk; let stand 5 minutes.
2. Lightly spoon flour into dry measuring cups; level with a knife. Add 2 cups flour to yeast mixture, stirring with a whisk. Cover and let rise in a warm place (85°), free from drafts, 15 minutes.
3. Add 2½ cups flour, walnuts, rosemary, and 1 egg, stirring with a whisk. Turn dough out onto a lightly floured surface. Knead until smooth and elastic (about 10 minutes), adding enough of the remaining flour, ¼ cup at a time, to prevent dough from sticking to hands.
4. Place dough in a large bowl coated with cooking spray, turning to coat top. Cover; let rise in a warm place (85°), free from drafts, 1 hour or until doubled in size. (Lightly press two fingers into dough. If an indentation remains, the dough has risen enough.)
5. Preheat oven to 400°.
6. Punch dough down, and turn dough out onto a lightly floured surface. Divide dough in half, shaping each portion into a round. Place loaves on a baking sheet dusted with yellow cornmeal. Cover and let rise 30 minutes or until doubled in size.
7. Combine 1 tablespoon milk and 1 egg, stirring with a whisk, and brush over loaves. Make 3 diagonal cuts ¼-inch deep across top of each loaf using a sharp knife.
8. Place loaves in oven; reduce oven temperature to 375°, and bake 40 minutes or until bottom of each loaf sounds hollow when tapped. Let the loaves stand 20 minutes before slicing. Yield: 2 loaves, 12 servings per loaf (serving size: 1 piece).

CALORIES 170 (28% from fat); FAT 5.2g (sat 1.2g, mono 1g, poly 2.6g); PROTEIN 5.2g; CARB 25.7g; FIBER 1.3g; CHOL 21mg; IRON 1.7mg; SODIUM 222mg; CALC 39mg

Walnut and Rosemary Loaves

Caramelized Onion and Roasted Red Pepper Tart

You can make the onion topping and roasted peppers a day ahead or during the dough's first rising.

CRUST:

1 package dry yeast (about 2¼ teaspoons)
1 teaspoon honey
¾ cup warm water (100° to 110°)
1½ cups bread flour, divided
¼ cup whole-wheat flour
1 tablespoon olive oil
1 teaspoon sea salt
Cooking spray

TOPPING:

1 tablespoon olive oil
6 cups vertically sliced onion
1 teaspoon sea salt
3 thyme sprigs
3 garlic cloves, minced
2 bay leaves
3 large red bell peppers
¼ teaspoon freshly ground black pepper
1 tablespoon chopped fresh thyme

1. To prepare crust, dissolve yeast and honey in warm water in a large bowl; let stand 5 minutes. Lightly spoon flours into dry measuring cups; level with a knife. Stir 1 cup bread flour and 1 tablespoon oil into yeast mixture. Cover and let rise in a warm place (85°), free from drafts, 1½ hours or until bubbly. Stir in ½ cup bread flour, whole-wheat flour, and 1 teaspoon salt.

2. Turn dough out onto a floured surface. Knead until smooth and elastic (about 10 minutes; dough will feel sticky). Place dough in a large bowl coated with cooking spray, turning to coat top. Cover and let rise in a warm place (85°), free from drafts, 1 hour or until doubled in size. (Press two fingers into dough. If indentation remains, the dough has risen enough.) Punch the dough down; cover and let rest 10 minutes.

3. To prepare topping, heat 1 tablespoon oil in a 12-inch nonstick skillet coated with cooking spray over medium-high heat. Add onion; cook 5 minutes, stirring frequently. Stir in 1 teaspoon salt, 3 thyme sprigs, garlic, and bay leaves; cook 15 minutes or until deep golden brown, stirring frequently. Remove mixture from heat. Discard the thyme sprigs and bay leaves.

4. Preheat broiler.

5. While onion is cooking, cut bell peppers in half lengthwise, discarding seeds and membranes. Place pepper halves, skin sides up, on a foil-lined baking sheet; flatten with hand. Broil 15 minutes or until blackened. Place in a zip-top plastic bag; seal. Let stand 15 minutes. Peel and coarsely chop.

6. Preheat oven to 425°.

7. Roll dough into a 12 x 8-inch rectangle. Place dough on a baking sheet coated with cooking spray. Top with onion mixture and chopped bell pepper. Sprinkle with black pepper. Bake at 425° for 25 minutes or until crust is golden brown. Cool slightly. Sprinkle with chopped thyme. Cut into 8 squares; cut each square in half diagonally. Yield: 8 servings.

CALORIES 192 (20% from fat); FAT 4.2g (sat 0.6g, mono 2.6g, poly 0.6g); PROTEIN 5.6g; CARB 34.3g; FIBER 4.1g; CHOL 0mg; IRON 2mg; SODIUM 581mg; CALC 32mg

Spicy Peppercorn and Pecorino Breadsticks

Spicy Peppercorn and Pecorino Breadsticks

With black and red pepper, these breadsticks pack some heat. If you don't have semolina, use cornmeal.

   1   package dry yeast (about 2¼ teaspoons)
1⅓   cups warm water (100° to 110°)
3½   cups bread flour, divided
   2   tablespoons extravirgin olive oil
   2   teaspoons coarsely ground black pepper
1¾   teaspoons salt
   ¾   teaspoon crushed red pepper
   1   cup (4 ounces) grated fresh pecorino Romano
        cheese
   Cooking spray
   2   tablespoons ground semolina

1. Dissolve yeast in warm water in a large bowl; let stand 5 minutes. Lightly spoon flour into dry measuring cups; level with a knife. Add ½ cup flour to yeast mixture, stirring with a whisk. Let stand 30 minutes. Add remaining 3 cups flour, oil, black pepper, salt, and red pepper to yeast mixture; stir until a soft dough forms. Turn dough out onto a lightly floured surface. Knead until smooth and elastic (about 8 minutes); cover and let rest 10 minutes. Knead in half of cheese; cover and let rest 5 minutes. Knead in remaining cheese.
2. Place dough in a large bowl coated with cooking spray, turning to coat top. Cover; let rise in a warm place (85°), free from drafts, 45 minutes or until doubled in size. (Gently press two fingers into dough. If indentation remains, dough has risen enough.) Punch dough down. Turn out onto a lightly floured surface. Roll into a 12 x 8-inch rectangle.
3. Preheat oven to 450°.
4. Sprinkle 1 tablespoon semolina onto each of 2 baking sheets. Cut dough in half lengthwise to form 2 (12 x 4-inch) rectangles. Cut each rectangle crosswise into 12 (1-inch-wide) strips. Working with 1 strip at a time (cover remaining dough to prevent drying), gently roll into a 15-inch-long rope. Place rope on prepared pan; repeat procedure with remaining strips, placing 12 on each pan. Cover and let dough rise 20 minutes.
5. Uncover dough; bake each pan at 450° for 12 minutes. Remove breadsticks from pans; cool completely on wire racks. Yield: 2 dozen breadsticks (serving size: 1 breadstick).

CALORIES 99 (22% from fat); FAT 2.4g (sat 1g, mono 1.2g, poly 0.1g); PROTEIN 4.4g; CARB 15.7g; FIBER 0.7g; CHOL 5mg; IRON 1.1mg; SODIUM 228mg; CALC 52mg

Spanish Toast

Spanish Toast

Rubbing ripe tomatoes over garlic toast may seem unusual, but it's a tradition in Spain, where it's common to find a plate of tomatoes and garlic on the table, waiting for the toast to arrive. The crisp toast almost melts the garlic and the tomatoes, which complement the crunchy kosher salt. Very ripe tomatoes and a hearty, dense bread work best.

   8   (2-ounce) slices sourdough bread
   4   garlic cloves, halved
   4   small tomatoes, each cut in half crosswise
        (about ¾ pound)
   4   teaspoons extravirgin olive oil
   ¼   teaspoon kosher salt or sea salt
   ¼   teaspoon freshly ground black pepper

1. Prepare grill or broiler.
2. Place bread slices on grill rack or broiler pan, and cook 2 minutes on each side or until lightly browned. Rub 1 side of each bread slice with 1 garlic clove half and 1 tomato half (tomato pulp will rub off onto bread). Discard tomato peels. Drizzle ½ teaspoon olive oil over each bread slice; sprinkle evenly with salt and pepper. Yield: 8 servings.

CALORIES 168 (19% from fat); FAT 3.5g (sat 0.6g, mono 2.1g, poly 0.5g); PROTEIN 5.5g; CARB 29.3g; FIBER 1.4g; CHOL 0mg; IRON 1.6mg; SODIUM 351mg; CALC 60mg

Buttermilk-Oat Rolls

¾ cup regular oats
½ cup boiling water
1 tablespoon sugar
1 package dry yeast (about 2¼ teaspoons)
1½ teaspoons sugar
¼ cup warm water (100° to 110°)
2¼ cups bread flour or all-purpose flour, divided
¼ cup low-fat buttermilk
1 tablespoon butter or stick margarine, melted
¾ teaspoon salt
Cooking spray
1 tablespoon water
1 large egg white, lightly beaten
1 tablespoon regular oats

1. Combine the first 3 ingredients in a small bowl, stirring until well blended. Let stand 5 minutes.
2. Dissolve yeast and 1½ teaspoons sugar in warm water in a large bowl, and let stand for 5 minutes. Lightly spoon the flour into dry measuring cups, and level with a knife. Add oat mixture, 1¾ cups flour, buttermilk, butter, and salt to yeast mixture, stirring to form a soft dough. Turn the dough out onto a lightly floured surface. Knead dough until smooth and elastic (about 8 minutes), adding enough of the remaining flour, 1 tablespoon at a time, to prevent the dough from sticking to hands. (Dough will be slightly sticky.)
3. Place dough in a large bowl coated with cooking spray, turning to coat top. Cover and let rise in a warm place (85°), free from drafts, 45 minutes or until doubled in size. (Press two fingers into dough. If indentation remains, dough has risen enough.) Punch dough down; cover and let rest for 5 minutes. Divide dough into 12 equal portions. Working with 1 portion at a time (cover the remaining dough to keep from drying), shape each into a ball. Place balls in a 9-inch square baking pan coated with cooking spray. Cover and let rise 30 minutes or until doubled in size.
4. Preheat oven to 375°.
5. Uncover rolls. Combine 1 tablespoon water and egg white, and brush over rolls. Sprinkle the rolls with 1 tablespoon oats. Bake at 375° for 25 minutes or until lightly browned. Serve warm. Yield: 1 dozen (serving size: 1 roll).

CALORIES 120 (13% from fat); FAT 1.7g (sat 0.3g, mono 0.6g, poly 0.5g); PROTEIN 3.8g; CARB 22.2g; FIBER 1.3g; CHOL 0mg; IRON 1.4mg; SODIUM 165mg; CALC 13mg

Buttered Sweet Potato Knot Rolls

(pictured on page 28)

  1 package dry yeast (about 2¼ teaspoons)
  1 cup warm 2% reduced-fat milk (100° to 110°)
  ¾ cup canned mashed sweet potatoes
  3 tablespoons butter, melted and divided
1¼ teaspoons salt
  2 large egg yolks, lightly beaten
  5 cups bread flour, divided
    Cooking spray

1. Dissolve yeast in warm milk in a large bowl; let stand 5 minutes.

2. Add the sweet potatoes, 1 tablespoon butter, salt, and egg yolks to yeast mixture, stirring with a whisk.

3. Lightly spoon flour into dry measuring cups, and level with a knife. Add 4½ cups flour to sweet potato mixture; stir until a soft dough forms.

4. Turn dough out onto a floured surface. Knead until smooth and elastic (about 8 minutes); add enough of remaining flour, 1 tablespoon at a time, to prevent dough from sticking to hands (dough will feel soft and sticky).

5. Place dough in a large bowl coated with cooking spray, turning to coat top. Cover and let rise in a warm place (85°), free from drafts, for 45 minutes or until dough has doubled in size. (Press two fingers into dough. If indentation remains, dough has risen enough.) Punch dough down. Cover and let rest for 5 minutes.

6. Line 2 baking sheets with parchment paper. Divide dough into 24 equal portions. Working with 1 portion at a time (cover remaining dough to prevent drying), shape each portion into a 9-inch rope. Carefully shape rope into a knot; tuck top end of knot under roll. Place roll on prepared pan.

7. Repeat procedure with remaining dough, placing 12 rolls on each pan. Lightly coat rolls with cooking spray; cover and let rise 30 minutes or until doubled in size.

8. Preheat oven to 400°.

9. Uncover rolls. Bake at 400° for 8 minutes with 1 pan on bottom rack and 1 pan on second rack from top. Rotate pans; bake an additional 7 minutes or until golden brown and sound hollow when tapped.

10. Remove from pans; place on wire racks. Brush with 2 tablespoons butter. Serve warm or at room temperature. Yield: 2 dozen (serving size: 1 roll).

CALORIES 134 (17% from fat); FAT 2.6g (sat 1.2g, mono 0.7g, poly 0.3g); PROTEIN 4.3g; CARB 23g; FIBER 0.9g; CHOL 22mg; IRON 1.4mg; SODIUM 147mg; CALC 21mg

English Muffins

These freeze well or can be stored for a day at room temperature in an airtight container.

  1 cup 2% reduced-fat milk
  3 tablespoons vegetable oil
  2 tablespoons sugar
1¼ teaspoons salt
  1 package dry yeast (about 2¼ teaspoons)
  ¼ cup warm water (100° to 110°)
3½ cups all-purpose flour, divided
  1 large egg, lightly beaten
    Cooking spray

1. Cook milk in a heavy saucepan over medium-high heat to 180° or until tiny bubbles form around edge (do not boil). Remove from heat. Pour milk into a large bowl. Stir in oil, sugar, and salt. Cool mixture to about 90°.

2. Dissolve yeast in warm water in a small bowl; let stand 5 minutes. Lightly spoon flour into dry measuring cups; level with a knife. Add yeast mixture, 3 cups flour, and egg to milk mixture, stirring well. Turn the dough out onto a lightly floured surface. Knead until smooth and elastic (about 10 minutes); add enough of remaining flour, 1 tablespoon at a time, to prevent the dough from sticking to hands (dough will feel sticky). Place dough in a large bowl coated with cooking spray, turning to coat top. Cover and let rise in a warm place (85°), free from drafts, 45 minutes or until doubled in size. (Press two fingers into dough. If indentation remains, the dough has risen enough.)

3. Punch dough down, and divide in half. Working with one portion at a time (cover remaining dough to keep from drying), roll each portion to ¼-inch thickness. Let dough rest about 5 minutes. Cut with a 4-inch biscuit cutter into 8 muffins. Place muffins on a large baking sheet. Repeat procedure with the remaining dough. Cover and let rise 30 minutes or until doubled in size.

4. Preheat oven to 350°.

5. Bake at 350° for 7 minutes. Turn muffins over, and bake an additional 7 minutes or until lightly browned. Yield: 16 servings (serving size: 1 muffin).

NOTE: To freeze, place in heavy-duty zip-top plastic bags. Remove excess air from bags; seal and freeze for up to 1 month. To thaw, unwrap and let stand at room temperature.

CALORIES 142 (22% from fat); FAT 3.5g (sat 0.8g, mono 1g, poly 1.4g); PROTEIN 3.9g; CARB 23.4g; FIBER 0.9g; CHOL 15mg; IRON 1.4mg; SODIUM 195mg; CALC 25mg

Pennsylvania Dutch Tea Rolls

a time, to prevent dough from sticking to hands (dough will feel sticky).

3. Place dough in a large bowl coated with cooking spray, turning to coat top. Cover dough and let rise in a warm place (85°), free from drafts, 1½ hours or until doubled in size. (Lightly press two fingers into dough. If indentation remains, the dough has risen enough.)

4. Turn dough out onto a lightly floured surface; lightly dust with flour and pat into a 10 x 8-inch rectangle. Divide dough by making 3 lengthwise cuts and 4 crosswise cuts to form 20 equal pieces; shape each piece into a ball. Place balls in a 13 x 9-inch baking pan coated with cooking spray.

5. Lightly coat the dough with cooking spray. Cover with plastic wrap, and let rise in a warm place (85°), free from drafts, 1 hour or until doubled in size.

6. Preheat oven to 375°.

7. Brush 3 tablespoons milk lightly over dough; sprinkle with poppy seeds. Bake at 375° for 20 minutes or until browned. Cool rolls in pan 5 minutes. Serve warm, or cool completely on a wire rack. Yield: 20 servings (serving size: 1 roll).

CALORIES 173 (17% from fat); FAT 3.2g (sat 1.7g, mono 0.9g, poly 0.3g); PROTEIN 4.6g; CARB 31.3g; FIBER 1.0g; CHOL 18mg; IRON 1.7mg; SODIUM 154mg; CALC 31mg

Pennsylvania Dutch Tea Rolls

These sweet, buttery rolls were historically served with afternoon tea, but they're just as at home with Sunday night's chicken dinner.

5¼ cups all-purpose flour, divided
1⅓ cups warm 1% low-fat milk (100° to 110°)
 1 package quick-rise yeast (about 2¼ teaspoons)
 ½ cup sugar
 ¼ cup butter, melted and cooled to room
   temperature
 1 teaspoon salt
 1 large egg
Cooking spray
 3 tablespoons 1% low-fat milk
1½ teaspoons poppy seeds

1. Lightly spoon flour into dry measuring cups; level with a knife. Combine 2 cups flour, warm milk, and yeast in a large bowl. Cover with plastic wrap; let stand 1½ hours (batter should become very bubbly and almost triple in size).

2. Add 3 cups flour, sugar, butter, salt, and egg; stir with a wooden spoon 3 minutes or until well combined. Turn dough out onto a lightly floured surface. Knead dough until smooth and elastic (about 8 minutes); add enough of remaining flour, 1 tablespoon at

Pumpkin-Cinnamon Streusel Buns

BUNS:
 1 package dry yeast (about 2¼ teaspoons)
 ¼ cup warm water (100° to 110°)
3¾ cups all-purpose flour, divided
 ½ cup canned pumpkin
 ½ cup 1% low-fat milk
 ¼ cup butter, melted
 1 tablespoon granulated sugar
1¼ teaspoons salt
 ¼ teaspoon ground nutmeg
Cooking spray
 3 tablespoons granulated sugar
 3 tablespoons brown sugar
 2 tablespoons all-purpose flour
1½ teaspoons ground cinnamon
 2 tablespoons chilled butter, cut into small pieces
GLAZE:
 ¾ cup sifted powdered sugar
 1 tablespoon hot water
 ¼ teaspoon vanilla extract

1. Dissolve yeast in warm water in a large bowl, and let stand for 5 minutes. Lightly spoon 3¾ cups flour into dry measuring cups, and level with a knife. Add 3 cups flour, canned pumpkin, and next 5 ingredients to yeast mixture, and beat with a mixer at medium speed until smooth. Turn the dough out onto a floured surface. Knead the dough until smooth and elastic (about 10 minutes), and add enough of remaining flour, 1 tablespoon at a time, to prevent the dough from sticking to hands (dough will feel sticky).

2. Place dough in a large bowl coated with cooking spray, turning to coat top. Cover and let rise in a warm place (85°), free from drafts, 45 minutes or until dough is doubled in size. (Press two fingers into dough. If an indentation remains, the dough has risen enough.)

3. Combine 3 tablespoons granulated sugar, brown sugar, 2 tablespoons flour, and ground cinnamon in a small bowl. Cut in chilled butter pieces with a pastry blender or 2 knives until mixture resembles coarse meal.

4. Punch dough down; cover and let rest 5 minutes. Roll dough into a 12 x 10-inch rectangle on a floured surface. Sprinkle with brown sugar mixture. Roll up rectangle tightly starting with a long edge, pressing firmly to eliminate air pockets; pinch seam and ends to seal. Cut roll into 12 (1-inch) slices; place in a 9-inch square baking pan coated with cooking spray. Cover and let rise for 25 minutes or until doubled in size.

5. Preheat oven to 375°.

6. Bake at 375° for 20 minutes or until golden. Cool 15 minutes in pan on a wire rack.

7. Combine powdered sugar, 1 tablespoon water, and vanilla in a small bowl, stirring with a whisk until smooth. Drizzle glaze over buns. Serve warm. Yield: 12 servings (serving size: 1 bun).

CALORIES 262 (22% from fat); FAT 6.3g (sat 3.7g, mono 1.8g, poly 0.4g); PROTEIN 5g; CARB 46.3g; FIBER 1.8g; CHOL 16mg; IRON 2.2mg; SODIUM 311mg; CALC 31mg

Pumpkin-Cinnamon
Streusel Buns

Cinnamon-Bun Bread

BREAD:

- 1 package dry yeast (about 2¼ teaspoons)
- ¼ cup granulated sugar, divided
- 1⅔ cups warm fat-free milk (100° to 110°)
- ¼ cup butter or stick margarine, melted
- 4 teaspoons vanilla extract
- 2 large egg yolks
- 5 cups all-purpose flour, divided
- 2 teaspoons salt
- Cooking spray
- ⅔ cup packed brown sugar
- 2 teaspoons ground cinnamon
- ½ cup apricot preserves, melted

GLAZE:

- 1 tablespoon butter or stick margarine, softened
- 1 cup sifted powdered sugar
- 1 tablespoon fat-free milk
- ½ teaspoon vanilla extract

1. To prepare the bread, dissolve yeast and 1 tablespoon granulated sugar in warm milk in a large bowl; let stand 5 minutes. Stir in ¼ cup butter, 4 teaspoons vanilla, and egg yolks. Lightly spoon flour into dry measuring cups, and level with a knife. Add 4½ cups flour, remaining 3 tablespoons granulated sugar, and salt to yeast mixture; stir to form a soft dough. Turn dough out onto a floured surface. Knead until smooth and elastic (about 10 minutes); add enough of remaining flour, 1 tablespoon at a time, to prevent dough from sticking to hands (dough will feel sticky).

2. Place dough in a large bowl coated with cooking spray, turning to coat top. Cover and let rise in a warm place (85°), free from drafts, 1 hour or until doubled in size. (Press two fingers into dough. If indentation remains, dough has risen enough.) Punch dough down, and let rest 5 minutes. Divide in half. Working with one portion at a time (cover the remaining dough to keep from drying), roll each portion into a 14 x 7-inch rectangle on a floured surface. Combine brown sugar and cinnamon. Sprinkle each dough portion with half of brown sugar mixture, leaving a ½-inch border. Roll up each dough rectangle tightly, starting with a short edge, pressing firmly to eliminate air pockets, and pinch seams and ends to seal. Cut each dough roll crosswise into 3 pieces. Place 3 pieces, cut sides up, into each of 2 (8 x 4-inch) loaf pans coated with cooking spray. Cover dough and let rise 30 minutes or until doubled in size.

3. Preheat oven to 350°.

4. Uncover the dough, and bake at 350° for 35 minutes or until the loaves are browned on bottoms and sound hollow when tapped. Cool in pans 10 minutes on a wire rack, and remove from pans. Brush the tops of loaves with the melted preserves. Cool loaves on rack.

5. To prepare the glaze, beat 1 tablespoon butter at low speed of a mixer until creamy. Add remaining ingredients, beating just until blended. Spread over tops of loaves. Yield: 2 loaves, 12 servings per loaf (serving size: 1 slice).

CALORIES 198 (15% from fat); FAT 3.2g (sat 0.7g, mono 1.3g, poly 0.9g); PROTEIN 3.7g; CARB 38.5g; FIBER 0.9g; CHOL 19mg; IRON 1.5mg; SODIUM 239mg; CALC 38mg

Triple-Play Cinnamon Rolls

Three sugars go into these rolls: Granulated sweetens the dough, brown adds a light molasses flavor to the filling, and powdered sweetens the glaze. Use dental floss to make easy work of cutting the dough.

DOUGH:
 1 package dry yeast (about 2¼ teaspoons)
 ¼ cup warm water (100° to 110°)
 ½ cup warm 1% low-fat milk (100° to 110°)
 ⅓ cup granulated sugar
 ¼ cup butter, softened
 1 teaspoon vanilla extract
 ¾ teaspoon salt
 1 large egg, lightly beaten
 3½ cups all-purpose flour, divided
 Cooking spray
FILLING:
 ¾ cup raisins
 ⅔ cup packed brown sugar
 1 tablespoon ground cinnamon
 2 tablespoons butter, melted
GLAZE:
 1 cup powdered sugar
 2 tablespoons 1% low-fat milk
 ½ teaspoon vanilla extract

1. To prepare dough, dissolve yeast in warm water in a large bowl; let stand 5 minutes. Add ½ cup warm milk, granulated sugar, ¼ cup butter, 1 teaspoon vanilla, salt, and egg, and stir with a wooden spoon until combined (batter will not be completely smooth).

2. Lightly spoon flour into dry measuring cups, and level with a knife. Add 3 cups flour to yeast mixture, and stir until a soft dough forms. Turn the dough out onto a lightly floured surface. Knead the dough until smooth and elastic (about 8 minutes), and add enough of the remaining flour, 1 tablespoon at a time, to prevent dough from sticking to hands (dough will feel sticky).

3. Place dough in a large bowl coated with cooking spray; turn to coat top. Cover and let rise in a warm place (85°), free from drafts, 1 hour or until dough has doubled in size. (Press two fingers into dough. If indentation remains, dough has risen enough.)

4. To prepare filling, combine raisins, brown sugar, and cinnamon. Roll dough into a 15 x 10-inch rectangle, and brush with 2 tablespoons melted butter. Sprinkle the filling over the dough, leaving a ½-inch border. Beginning with a short side,
roll up dough jelly-roll fashion, and pinch seam to seal (do not seal ends of roll). Wrap roll in plastic wrap, and chill 20 minutes.

5. Unwrap roll, and cut into 20 (½-inch) slices. Arrange slices, cut sides up, 1 inch apart on a jelly roll pan coated with cooking spray. Cover and let rise in a warm place (85°), free from drafts, 1 hour and 15 minutes or until doubled in size.

6. Preheat oven to 350°.

7. Uncover dough. Bake at 350° for 20 minutes or until rolls are golden brown. Remove from pan; place on wire racks.

8. To prepare glaze, combine powdered sugar, 2 tablespoons milk, and ½ teaspoon vanilla, stirring well with a whisk. Drizzle glaze over warm rolls. Yield: 20 servings (serving size: 1 roll).

CALORIES 200 (18% from fat); FAT 4g (sat 2.3g, mono 1.1g, poly 0.3g); PROTEIN 3.2g; CARB 38.3g; FIBER 1.1g; CHOL 20mg; IRON 1.5mg; SODIUM 134mg; CALC 28mg

Monkey Bread

 1¼ cups granulated sugar, divided
 ¼ cup packed brown sugar
 ¼ cup 1% low-fat milk
 1 tablespoon butter
 1¾ teaspoons ground cinnamon, divided
 2 (1-pound) loaves frozen white bread dough, thawed
 Cooking spray

1. Combine 1 cup granulated sugar, brown sugar, milk, butter, and 1¼ teaspoons cinnamon in a small saucepan. Bring to a boil; cook 1 minute. Remove sugar syrup from heat; cool 10 minutes.

2. Combine ¼ cup granulated sugar and ½ teaspoon cinnamon in a shallow dish; stir well. Cut each loaf of dough into 24 equal portions. Roll each portion in sugar mixture; layer dough balls in a 12-cup Bundt pan coated with cooking spray. Pour sugar syrup over dough; cover and let rise in a warm place (85°), free from drafts, 35 minutes or until dough has doubled in size.

3. Preheat oven to 350°.

4. Uncover dough, and bake at 350° for 25 minutes or until lightly browned. Immediately loosen edges of bread with a knife. Place a plate upside down on top of pan, and invert bread onto plate. Drizzle any remaining syrup over bread. Yield: 24 servings (serving size: 2 rolls).

CALORIES 159 (13% from fat); FAT 2.3g (sat 0.5g, mono 0.8g, poly 0.8g); PROTEIN 4.1g; CARB 32.4g; FIBER 1.3g; CHOL 1mg; IRON 1.5mg; SODIUM 218mg; CALC 16mg

Apricot-Cream Cheese Braid

All the good stuff from a cream cheese Danish is rolled into this bread, which was a favorite in our Test Kitchens. The finished braids can be covered in plastic wrap and refrigerated for a couple of days or frozen for up to a month.

DOUGH:

½ cup granulated sugar
⅓ cup butter
½ teaspoon salt
1 (8-ounce) carton low-fat sour cream
2 packages dry yeast (about 4½ teaspoons)
½ cup warm water (100° to 110°)
2 large eggs, lightly beaten
4 cups all-purpose flour

FILLING:

⅔ cup apricot preserves
¼ cup granulated sugar
1 teaspoon vanilla extract
2 (8-ounce) blocks ⅓-less-fat cream cheese, softened
1 large egg, lightly beaten
Cooking spray

GLAZE:

1½ cups sifted powdered sugar
2 tablespoons fat-free milk
1 teaspoon vanilla extract

1. To prepare dough, combine the first 4 ingredients in a saucepan over medium heat, stirring until sugar dissolves. Remove from heat, and cool. Dissolve the yeast in warm water in a large bowl, and let stand 5 minutes. Stir in sour cream mixture and 2 eggs. Lightly spoon flour into dry measuring cups, and level with a knife. Gradually stir flour into sour cream mixture (dough will be soft and sticky). Cover dough, and chill 8 hours or overnight.

2. To prepare filling, combine preserves and next 4 ingredients in a medium bowl; beat with a mixer at medium speed until mixture is well blended.

3. Divide dough into 4 equal portions. Turn each portion out onto a lightly floured surface, and knead lightly 4 or 5 times. Roll each portion into a 12 x 8-inch rectangle. Spread one-fourth of filling over each portion, leaving a ½-inch border. Starting at a long side, carefully roll up each portion jelly-roll fashion, and pinch seam and ends to seal.

4. Place 2 loaves on each of 2 baking sheets coated with cooking spray. Cut 4 (¼-inch-deep) "X"s in top of each loaf with scissors. Cover and let rise in a warm place (85°), free from drafts, 25 minutes or until doubled in size.

5. Preheat oven to 375°.

6. Place 1 baking sheet in oven (cover remaining loaves to keep from drying). Bake at 375° for 15 minutes or until lightly browned. Repeat procedure with remaining loaves. Cool loaves slightly.

7. To prepare glaze, combine powdered sugar, milk, and 1 teaspoon vanilla, stirring with a whisk. Drizzle warm loaves with glaze. Yield: 4 loaves, 10 slices per loaf (serving size: 1 slice).

CALORIES 145 (31% from fat); FAT 5g (sat 3g, mono 1.5g, poly 0.3g); PROTEIN 3.3g; CARB 21.6g; FIBER 0.5g; CHOL 30mg; IRON 0.8mg; SODIUM 102mg; CALC 26mg

Fig-Swirl Coffeecake

Figs and other dried fruits are excellent sources of fiber. The whole-wheat flour in the dough also boosts the fiber content. This high-nutrition recipe proves that "good for you" and "great to eat" do go together: It received our Test Kitchens' highest rating.

    1   package dry yeast (about 2¼ teaspoons)
    ½   teaspoon granulated sugar
    ¼   cup warm water (100° to 110°)
    ⅓   cup fat-free milk
    2   teaspoons vanilla extract, divided
    1   large egg
 1½   cups all-purpose flour
 1¼   cups whole-wheat flour
    ⅓   cup granulated sugar
    3   tablespoons chilled butter or stick margarine,
        cut into small pieces
    ¾   teaspoon salt
 Cooking spray
 1½   cups dried Calimyrna or Black Mission figs
        (about 12 ounces)
    ½   cup fresh orange juice (about 1 orange)
    1   cup powdered sugar
    2   tablespoons fresh lemon juice

1. Dissolve yeast and ½ teaspoon granulated sugar in warm water in a small bowl; let stand 5 minutes. Stir in milk, 1 teaspoon vanilla, and egg. Lightly spoon flours into dry measuring cups; level with a knife. Place flours, ⅓ cup granulated sugar, butter, and salt in a food processor; pulse 5 times or until blended. With processor on, slowly add yeast mixture through food chute; process until dough forms a ball. Process 1 additional minute. Turn dough out onto a floured surface; knead lightly 4 to 5 times (dough will feel sticky).

2. Place dough in a large bowl coated with cooking spray, turning to coat top. Cover and let rise in a warm place (85°), free from drafts, 1 hour or until dough is almost doubled in size. (Press two fingers into dough. If indentation remains, the dough has risen enough.)

3. Trim stems off figs. Combine 1 teaspoon vanilla, figs, and orange juice in food processor, and process until finely chopped. Set aside.

4. Punch the dough down; cover and let rest 5 minutes. Roll dough into a 15 x 10-inch rectangle on a floured surface. Spread the fig mixture evenly over the dough, leaving a 1-inch margin along one long edge. Roll up rectangle tightly, starting with the opposite long edge, pressing firmly to eliminate air pockets; pinch seam to seal. Place roll, seam side down, on floured surface; split roll in half lengthwise using a serrated knife. Working on a 12-inch pizza pan coated with cooking spray, coil one half of the dough, cut side up, around itself in a spiral pattern. Place other half of dough, cut side up, at the end of the first strip, pinching ends together to seal; continue coiling the dough to form a circle. Cover and let rise 1 hour or until doubled in size.

5. Preheat oven to 350°.

6. Bake cake at 350° for 30 minutes or until golden. Place cake on a plate. Combine the powdered sugar and lemon juice in a small bowl; drizzle over hot cake. Serve warm or at room temperature. Yield: 16 servings (serving size: 1 wedge).

NOTE: The coffeecake dough can be made ahead of time. Follow the recipe as directed through step 2. Punch dough down, and return to bowl. Cover the dough with plastic wrap, and chill 8 hours. When ready to use, shape and bake according to recipe instructions.

CALORIES 208 (13% from fat); FAT 3.1g (sat 1.6g, mono 0.9g, poly 0.4g); PROTEIN 4g; CARB 43g; FIBER 4.2g; CHOL 20mg; IRON 1.5mg; SODIUM 142mg; CALC 45mg

How to Roll a Fig-Swirl Coffeecake

Coil dough, cut side up, around itself in a spiral pattern.

Kalamata Olive Bread

Kalamata Olive Bread

1 (1-pound) loaf frozen white bread dough
½ cup pitted kalamata olives
3 tablespoons capers
3 tablespoons fresh lemon juice
1 teaspoon dried thyme
4 canned anchovy fillets
2 garlic cloves, peeled
Cooking spray

1. Thaw dough in refrigerator 12 hours.
2. Combine pitted kalamata olives and next 5 ingredients in a food processor, and process until the mixture is well blended.
3. Roll dough into a 12 x 8-inch rectangle on a lightly floured surface. Spread olive mixture onto dough, leaving a ½-inch border. Starting from short end, roll up jelly-roll fashion; pinch seam and ends to seal. Place roll, seam side down, in an 8 x 4-inch loaf pan coated with cooking spray. Cover and let rise in a warm place (85°), free from drafts, 2½ hours or until doubled in size. (Press two fingers into dough. If indentation remains, the dough has risen enough.)
4. Preheat oven to 375°.
5. Uncover and bake at 375° for 25 minutes or until lightly browned. Cool in pan 10 minutes on a wire rack, and remove from pan. Cool the loaf completely on wire rack. Yield: 1 loaf, 12 slices (serving size: 1 slice).

CALORIES 163 (17% from fat); FAT 3g (sat 0.5g, mono 1g, poly 1.3g); PROTEIN 5.7g; CARB 28.4g; FIBER 1.1g; CHOL 1mg; IRON 1.7mg; SODIUM 423mg; CALC 46mg

Rosemary-Olive Bread

1 (1-pound) loaf frozen white bread dough
½ cup chopped pitted kalamata olives
1½ teaspoons dried rosemary
Cooking spray
1 large egg white, lightly beaten

1. Thaw dough in refrigerator 12 hours.
2. Sprinkle olives and rosemary over dough; gently knead on a lightly floured surface 4 or 5 times or just until olives are incorporated into dough. Cover dough; let rest 10 minutes.
3. Uncover and roll dough into a 10 x 8-inch rectangle. Beginning with long side, roll up jelly-roll fashion; pinch seam to seal. Place roll, seam side down, on a baking sheet coated with cooking spray. Cover and let rise in a warm place (85°), free from drafts, 1 hour or until doubled in size.
4. Preheat oven to 375°.
5. Uncover dough; cut several 2-inch diagonal slits into top of dough using a sharp knife. Brush dough with egg white. Bake at 375° for 40 minutes or until loaf sounds hollow when tapped. Remove loaf from baking sheet; cool on a wire rack. Yield: 1 loaf, 12 servings (serving size: 1 slice).

CALORIES 96 (18% from fat); FAT 1.9g (sat 0.5g, mono 0.9g, poly 0.5g); PROTEIN 3.3g; CARB 16.4g; FIBER 0.2g; CHOL 0mg; IRON 1mg; SODIUM 226mg; CALC 27mg

Rosemary-Olive Bread

Good-for-Toast Wheat Bread

Place ingredients in your bread machine and start. What could be easier for breakfast?

1⅔ cups bread flour
1½ cups whole-wheat flour
1 cup water
3 tablespoons sugar
1 tablespoon vegetable oil
1½ teaspoons dry yeast
1¼ teaspoons salt

1. Lightly spoon flours into dry measuring cups; level with a knife. Follow manufacturer's instructions for placing flours and remaining ingredients into bread pan; select bake cycle, and start bread machine. Yield: 1 (1½-pound) loaf, 12 servings.

CALORIES 143 (11% from fat); FAT 1.8g (sat 0.3g, mono 0.4g, poly 0.8g); PROTEIN 4.5g; CARB 28g; FIBER 2g; CHOL 0mg; IRON 1.5mg; SODIUM 245mg; CALC 8mg

Orange Bubble Bread

Tender Yeast Rolls

In this recipe, the bread machine simply mixes the dough and allows it to rise in anticipation of your final shaping and baking.

 4 cups bread flour
 1 cup water
 6 tablespoons sugar
 3 tablespoons vegetable oil
 1¼ teaspoons salt
 1 large egg, lightly beaten
 1 package dry yeast (about 2¼ teaspoons)
Cooking spray

1. Lightly spoon flour into dry measuring cups; level with a knife. Follow manufacturer's instructions for placing flour and remaining ingredients except cooking spray into bread pan; select dough cycle; start bread machine. Remove the dough from machine (do not bake).
2. Turn dough out onto a lightly floured surface, and knead for 30 seconds. Cover dough, and let rest for 10 minutes. Punch dough down, and divide into 18 equal portions. Shape each portion into a ball, and place on baking sheets coated with cooking spray. Cover dough and let rise in a warm place (85°), free from drafts, for 20 minutes or until doubled in size.
3. Preheat oven to 400°.
4. Uncover dough and bake at 400° for 13 minutes or until browned. Remove rolls from pans, and serve warm or at room temperature. Yield: 1½ dozen (serving size: 1 roll).

CALORIES 152 (18% from fat); FAT 3.1g (sat 0.6g, mono 0.8g, poly 1.4g); PROTEIN 4.1g; CARB 26.4g; FIBER 0.1g; CHOL 12mg; IRON 1.5mg; SODIUM 167mg; CALC 6mg

Anadama Bread

 1 cup boiling water
 ½ cup yellow cornmeal
 ¼ cup molasses
 3 tablespoons butter or stick margarine, melted
 2 tablespoons sugar
 1 large egg, lightly beaten
 3 cups bread flour
 ½ teaspoon salt
 1 teaspoon dry yeast

1. Combine the first 5 ingredients in a bowl. Cool slightly, and stir in egg. Lightly spoon flour into dry measuring cups, and level with a knife. Follow manufacturer's instructions for placing cornmeal mixture, flour, salt, and yeast into bread pan; select bake cycle, and start bread machine. Yield: 1 (1¾-pound) loaf, 14 servings.

CALORIES 174 (18% from fat); FAT 3.4g (sat 0.7g, mono 1.3g, poly 1.1g); PROTEIN 4.5g; CARB 31g; FIBER 0.3g; CHOL 16mg; IRON 1.9mg; SODIUM 120mg; CALC 19mg

Orange Bubble Bread

 1 cup 2% reduced-fat milk
 ¼ cup butter
 ¼ cup granulated sugar
 ¼ cup water
 1 teaspoon salt
 4 cups bread flour
 2½ teaspoons bread machine yeast
 1 large egg, lightly beaten
 ½ cup granulated sugar
 2 tablespoons grated orange rind
 ¼ cup butter, melted
Cooking spray
 ½ cup powdered sugar
 1 tablespoon orange juice

1. Combine first 5 ingredients in a 2-cup glass measure; microwave at HIGH 3 minutes. Cool 5 minutes. Lightly spoon flour into dry measuring cups, and level with a knife. Follow manufacturer's instructions for placing milk mixture, flour, yeast, and egg into bread pan; select the dough cycle. Start bread machine, and allow dough to complete cycle. Remove dough from machine (do not bake).
2. Turn dough out onto a floured surface; knead 30 seconds. Cover dough; let rest 10 minutes. Divide dough into 24 equal portions, shaping each into a ball (cover remaining dough to keep from drying). Combine ½ cup granulated sugar and rind. Dip each ball into ¼ cup melted butter; roll in sugar mixture. Place balls in bottom of a 10-inch tube pan coated with cooking spray. Cover and let rise in a warm place (85°), free from drafts, 45 minutes or until doubled in size.
3. Preheat oven to 350°.
4. Bake at 350° for 35 minutes. Cool in pan 5 minutes on a wire rack; remove bread from pan. Cool bread 15 minutes on wire rack.
5. Combine ½ cup powdered sugar and orange juice. Drizzle over loaf; serve warm. Yield: 24 servings (serving size: 1 roll).

CALORIES 161 (26% from fat); FAT 4.7g (sat 2.6g, mono 1.3g, poly 0.4g); PROTEIN 3.6g; CARB 26.2g; FIBER 0.1g; CHOL 20mg; IRON 1.1mg; SODIUM 145mg; CALC 19mg

Prosciutto-Wrapped Shrimp
on Artichoke, Fennel, and
Tomato Salad, page 97

Fish and Shellfish

Oven-Fried Catfish

We used Louisiana brand hot sauce here because of its mild heat. If you prefer a spicier sauce (such as Tabasco), decrease the amount to ¼ cup or to your taste.

½ cup light beer
½ cup hot sauce
4 (6-ounce) farm-raised catfish fillets
½ cup yellow cornmeal
2 tablespoons cornstarch
⅛ teaspoon salt
⅛ teaspoon black pepper
Cooking spray

1. Combine first 3 ingredients in a large zip-top plastic bag; seal and marinate in refrigerator 30 minutes. Remove fish from bag; pat dry with paper towels. Discard marinade.
2. Preheat oven to 450°.
3. Combine cornmeal, cornstarch, salt, and pepper in a shallow dish. Dredge fish in cornmeal mixture.
4. Lightly coat fish with cooking spray. Place fish on a baking sheet coated with cooking spray; bake at 450° for 15 minutes or until fish flakes easily when tested with a fork. Yield: 4 servings (serving size: 1 fillet).

CALORIES 296 (27% from fat); FAT 8.8g (sat 1.9g, mono 3.1g, poly 2.5g); PROTEIN 32.8g; CARB 17.7g; FIBER 1.1g; CHOL 99mg; IRON 2.8mg; SODIUM 361mg; CALC 74mg

Gingered Flounder

Add a side of somen noodles or vermicelli tossed with a little sesame oil and soy sauce.

⅔ cup coarsely grated peeled ginger
2 tablespoons low-sodium soy sauce
2 tablespoons dry sherry
2 tablespoons lemon juice
2 teaspoons sugar
4 (6-ounce) flounder fillets
Cooking spray
1 teaspoon dark sesame oil

1. Place ginger on several layers of damp cheesecloth. Gather edges of cheesecloth together, and squeeze cheesecloth bag over a small bowl. Set aside 3 tablespoons ginger juice; reserve remaining ginger juice for another use.
2. Combine 2 tablespoons ginger juice, soy sauce, and next 3 ingredients in a shallow dish; add fish,

turning to coat. Cover and marinate in refrigerator 20 minutes, turning fish occasionally. Remove fish from marinade; discard marinade.
3. Preheat broiler.
4. Place fish on a broiler pan coated with cooking spray, and broil 3 minutes or until lightly browned (do not turn). Brush oil over fish, and broil an additional minute or until fish flakes easily when tested with a fork. Place fish on each of 4 plates, and drizzle 1 tablespoon ginger juice over fish. Yield: 4 servings (serving size: 1 fillet).

CALORIES 191 (19% from fat); FAT 4g (sat 0.7g, mono 1.1g, poly 1.2g); PROTEIN 31g; CARB 5g; FIBER 0g; CHOL 87mg; IRON 0.5mg; SODIUM 427mg; CALC 25mg

Baked Flounder with Fresh Lemon Pepper

Use fresh lemon, good olive oil, freshly ground peppercorns, and garlic, and you'll never look at packaged lemon pepper the same way again. Serve with steamed asparagus.

2 tablespoons grated lemon rind
   (about 3 lemons)
1 tablespoon extravirgin olive oil
1¼ teaspoons black peppercorns, crushed
½ teaspoon salt
2 garlic cloves, minced
4 (6-ounce) flounder fillets
Cooking spray
Lemon wedges (optional)

1. Preheat oven to 425°.
2. Combine first 5 ingredients. Place fillets on a jelly roll pan coated with cooking spray. Rub garlic mixture evenly over fillets. Bake at 425° for 8 minutes or until fish flakes easily when tested with a fork. Serve fish with lemon wedges, if desired. Yield: 4 servings.

CALORIES 189 (26% from fat); FAT 5.4g (sat 0.9g, mono 2.9g, poly 0.9g); PROTEIN 32.2g; CARB 1.2g; FIBER 0.4g; CHOL 82mg; IRON 0.8mg; SODIUM 432mg; CALC 39mg

Arctic Char with Bouillabaisse Broth

Bouillabaisse, a popular seafood stew in Provence, is the inspiration for this flavorful broth.
Try this recipe with salmon if you can't find arctic char.

2 teaspoons olive oil, divided
1 cup finely chopped onion
1 cup finely chopped fennel bulb
3 tablespoons finely chopped shallots
¾ teaspoon saffron threads, crushed
½ teaspoon chopped fresh thyme
½ teaspoon aniseed
2 garlic cloves, minced
2 cups water
2 tablespoons tomato paste
1 (8-ounce) bottle clam juice
2 cups cubed peeled Yukon gold potato
(about 12 ounces)
1 (½-pound) fennel bulb, cut into 8 wedges
4 (6-ounce) arctic char or salmon fillets
½ teaspoon salt
¼ teaspoon freshly ground black pepper

1. Heat 1 teaspoon oil in a large saucepan over medium heat. Add onion and next 6 ingredients; cook 7 minutes or until tender, stirring frequently. Stir in water, tomato paste, and clam juice; bring to a boil. Reduce heat; simmer 45 minutes.

2. Strain mixture through a sieve over a bowl; discard solids. Return mixture to pan; bring to a boil. Add potato; cook 5 minutes. Add fennel; cook 4 minutes. Remove from heat; keep warm.

3. Heat 1 teaspoon oil in a large nonstick skillet over medium-high heat. Sprinkle fish with salt and pepper. Add fish to pan; cook 3 minutes on each side or until fish flakes easily when tested with a fork. Yield: 4 servings (serving size: 1 fillet, ½ cup potatoes, 2 fennel wedges, and ¼ cup broth).

CALORIES 371 (33% from fat); FAT 13.4g (sat 2.2g, mono 7g, poly 2.7g); PROTEIN 37.5g; CARB 24.7g; FIBER 4.3g; CHOL 96mg; IRON 4.1mg; SODIUM 607mg; CALC 128mg

Grilled Halibut and
Fresh Mango Salsa

Grilled Halibut and Fresh Mango Salsa

2 cups diced seeded plum tomatoes
1½ cups diced peeled ripe mango
½ cup diced onion
½ cup chopped fresh cilantro
2 tablespoons fresh lime juice
1 tablespoon cider vinegar
1 teaspoon sugar
1 teaspoon salt, divided
1 teaspoon black pepper, divided
2 garlic cloves, minced
4 (6-ounce) halibut fillets
1 tablespoon olive oil

1. Prepare grill.
2. Combine first 7 ingredients. Stir in ½ teaspoon salt, ½ teaspoon pepper, and minced garlic.
3. Rub fish with oil; sprinkle with ½ teaspoon salt and ½ teaspoon pepper. Place fish on grill rack; grill 3 minutes on each side or until fish flakes easily when tested with a fork. Serve with mango salsa. Yield: 4 servings (serving size: 1 fillet and ¾ cup salsa).

CALORIES 295 (24% from fat); FAT 7.8g (sat 1.1g, mono 3.9g, poly 1.7g); PROTEIN 37g; CARB 19.5g; FIBER 2.8g; CHOL 54mg; IRON 2.3mg; SODIUM 687mg; CALC 105mg

Easy Pesto Salmon

2 cups fresh spinach leaves
½ cup basil leaves
¼ cup fat-free, less-sodium chicken broth
1 tablespoon olive oil
¼ teaspoon salt
3 garlic cloves, peeled
Cooking spray
2 (6-ounce) salmon fillets, skinned
⅔ cup hot cooked brown rice

1. Preheat oven to 400°.
2. Place the first 6 ingredients in a food processor or blender, and process until the mixture is smooth. Spoon 3 tablespoons pesto into bottom of an 8-inch square baking dish coated with cooking spray. Top with salmon fillets, and spread fillets with remaining pesto.
3. Bake at 400° for 20 minutes or until fish flakes easily when tested with a fork. Yield: 2 servings (serving size: 1 fillet and ⅓ cup rice).

CALORIES 443 (45% from fat); FAT 22.1g (sat 3.5g, mono 12g, poly 4.4g); PROTEIN 38.7g; CARB 20.6g; FIBER 3.1g; CHOL 111mg; IRON 3.2mg; SODIUM 483mg; CALC 96mg

Maple-Glazed Salmon

Look for hoisin sauce and five-spice powder in the Asian food sections of large supermarkets.

2 tablespoons maple syrup
1½ tablespoons apple juice
1½ tablespoons fresh lemon juice
2 teaspoons hoisin sauce
1½ teaspoons grated peeled fresh ginger
1½ teaspoons country-style Dijon mustard
¼ teaspoon five-spice powder
4 (6-ounce) salmon fillets (about 1 inch thick)
Cooking spray

1. Preheat broiler.
2. Combine the first 7 ingredients in a large zip-top plastic bag. Add fillets to bag, and seal. Marinate in refrigerator 15 minutes.
3. Remove fillets from bag, reserving the marinade. Place fillets, skin sides down, on a broiler rack coated with cooking spray. Broil for 12 minutes or until fish flakes easily when tested with a fork; baste fillets occasionally with reserved marinade. Yield: 4 servings (serving size: 1 fillet).

CALORIES 316 (41% from fat); FAT 14.4g (sat 2.5g, mono 6.9g, poly 3.2g); PROTEIN 35g; CARB 9.3g; FIBER 0.1g; CHOL 111mg; IRON 0.9mg; SODIUM 184mg; CALC 18mg

Miso-Glazed Salmon

¼ cup packed brown sugar
2 tablespoons hot water
2 tablespoons low-sodium soy sauce
2 tablespoons miso (soybean paste)
4 (6-ounce) salmon fillets (about 1 inch thick)
Cooking spray
1 tablespoon chopped fresh chives

1. Preheat broiler.
2. Combine first 4 ingredients, stirring with a whisk. Arrange fish in a shallow baking dish coated with cooking spray. Spoon miso mixture evenly over fish.
3. Broil 10 minutes or until fish flakes easily when tested with a fork, basting twice with miso mixture. Sprinkle with chives. Yield: 4 servings (serving size: 1 salmon fillet).

CALORIES 297 (33% from fat); FAT 10.9g (sat 2.5g, mono 4.7g, poly 2.8g); PROTEIN 32.4g; CARB 15.7g; FIBER 0.3g; CHOL 80mg; IRON 1mg; SODIUM 742mg; CALC 29mg

Sherry-Glazed Salmon with Collard Greens

This sauce is slightly sweet and is balanced nicely by the bitter collard greens. Line your pan with foil for easy cleanup.

¼ cup dry sherry
2 tablespoons brown sugar
1 tablespoon low-sodium soy sauce
⅛ teaspoon five-spice powder
1 teaspoon cider vinegar
4 (6-ounce) salmon fillets, skinned (about 1 inch thick)
Cooking spray
½ cup water
½ cup fat-free, less-sodium chicken broth
1½ teaspoons olive oil
½ teaspoon fresh lemon juice
½ teaspoon bottled minced garlic
¼ teaspoon salt
⅛ teaspoon black pepper
1 (1-pound) bag chopped collard greens

1. Preheat oven to 375°.
2. Combine first 4 ingredients in a small saucepan, and bring to a boil, stirring occasionally. Cook until mixture is reduced to 3 tablespoons (about 5 minutes). Remove from heat; stir in vinegar.
3. Arrange fish on a broiler pan coated with cooking spray. Brush fish with half of sherry mixture. Bake at 375° for 5 minutes; brush fish with remaining sherry mixture. Bake an additional 5 minutes or until fish flakes easily when tested with a fork.
4. While fish bakes, combine water and the next 6 ingredients in a large skillet over medium-high heat, and bring to a simmer. Add greens; cover, reduce heat to medium, and cook 10 minutes or until tender. Yield: 4 servings (serving size: 1 salmon fillet and ¾ cup greens).

CALORIES 354 (39% from fat); FAT 15.2g (sat 3.4g, mono 6.9g, poly 3.5g); PROTEIN 39.6g; CARB 11.9g; FIBER 4.1g; CHOL 87mg; IRON 1.1mg; SODIUM 442mg; CALC 193mg

Alder-Planked Salmon in an Asian-Style Marinade

Grilling over indirect heat allows the fish to stay moist and take on a subtle smokiness from the plank.

1 (15 x 6½ x ⅜-inch) alder grilling plank
½ cup rice vinegar
½ cup low-sodium soy sauce
2 tablespoons honey
1 teaspoon ground ginger
½ teaspoon freshly ground black pepper
3 garlic cloves, minced
1 lemon, thinly sliced
1 (3½-pound) salmon fillet
¼ cup chopped green onions
1 tablespoon sesame seeds, toasted

1. Immerse and soak the alder plank in water for 1 hour, and drain.
2. To prepare grill for indirect grilling, heat one side of grill to high heat.
3. Combine vinegar and next 6 ingredients in a large zip-top plastic bag; seal. Shake to combine. Add fish; seal. Marinate in refrigerator 30 minutes, turning once.
4. Place plank on grill rack over high heat; grill 5 minutes or until lightly charred. Carefully turn plank over; move to cool side of grill. Remove fish from marinade; discard marinade. Place fish, skin side down, on charred side of plank. Cover and grill 15 minutes or until fish flakes easily when tested with a fork. Sprinkle with onions and sesame seeds. Yield: 9 servings (serving size: 5 ounces).

CALORIES 306 (41% from fat); FAT 14.1g (sat 3.3g, mono 6.1g, poly 3.5g); PROTEIN 38.3g; CARB 4.6g; FIBER 0.5g; CHOL 90mg; IRON 0.9mg; SODIUM 353mg; CALC 36mg

Alder-Planked Salmon in an
Asian-Style Marinade

Baked Fish with Roasted Potatoes, Tomatoes, and Salmoriglio Sauce

Here's a one-dish main course that you can serve directly from the dish in which it's baked. You can make the roasted-potato mixture and tomato topping up to an hour ahead. Just cover them with foil and keep warm while finishing the dish.

    6   cups peeled red potatoes, cut into 1/8-inch slices (about 2 pounds)
    4   cups thinly sliced fennel bulb (about 2 small bulbs)
    1   tablespoon olive oil, divided
    3/4 teaspoon kosher salt, divided
    1/2 teaspoon black pepper, divided
    1   teaspoon fennel seeds
    3   garlic cloves, minced
    3/4 cup dry white wine
    6   tablespoons chopped fresh flat-leaf parsley, divided
    1   tablespoon grated orange rind
    1 1/2 teaspoons dried oregano
    1   (28-ounce) can whole tomatoes, drained and chopped
    6   (6-ounce) sea bass fillets or other firm white fish fillets
  Lemon rind strips (optional)
  Salmoriglio Sauce

1. Preheat oven to 450°.
2. Combine potatoes, sliced fennel, 2 teaspoons oil, 1/4 teaspoon salt, and 1/4 teaspoon pepper in a 13 x 9-inch baking dish; toss gently to coat. Bake at 450° for 30 minutes.
3. Heat 1 teaspoon oil in a medium nonstick skillet. Add fennel seeds and garlic; sauté for 1 minute. Add 1/4 teaspoon salt, 1/8 teaspoon pepper, wine, 4 tablespoons parsley, orange rind, oregano, and tomatoes; bring to a boil. Reduce heat; simmer 8 minutes.
4. Sprinkle fillets with 1/4 teaspoon salt and 1/8 teaspoon pepper. Arrange fillets over potato mixture; spread tomato mixture over fillets. Bake at 450° for 20 minutes or until the fish flakes easily when tested with a fork. Sprinkle with 2 tablespoons parsley, and garnish with lemon rind strips, if desired. Serve with Salmoriglio Sauce. Yield: 6 servings (serving size: 1 fillet, about 1 cup potato mixture, and 2 teaspoons Salmoriglio Sauce).

(Totals include Salmoriglio Sauce) CALORIES 379 (26% from fat); FAT 10.9g (sat 1.9g, mono 5.8g, poly 2g); PROTEIN 37.2g; CARB 34.2g; FIBER 3.6g; CHOL 70mg; IRON 4.6mg; SODIUM 892mg; CALC 145mg

SALMORIGLIO SAUCE:
Salmoriglio (sahl-moh-REE-lyee-o) is a pungent Italian sauce of olive oil, lemon, garlic, and oregano. Pass it around the table for drizzling over the fish. Freshness is key for this vibrant sauce, so make it as close to serving time as possible.

    2   tablespoons fresh lemon juice
    2   tablespoons extravirgin olive oil
    1 1/2 teaspoons chopped fresh or 1/2 teaspoon dried oregano
    1   teaspoon kosher salt
    1   teaspoon grated lemon rind
    2   garlic cloves, minced
  Dash of freshly ground black pepper

1. Combine all the ingredients, stirring well with a whisk. Yield: 1/4 cup (serving size: 2 teaspoons).

CALORIES 44 (92% from fat); FAT 4.5g (sat 0.6g, mono 3.3g, poly 0.4g); PROTEIN 0.1g; CARB 1.1g; FIBER 0.1g; CHOL 0mg; IRON 0.2mg; SODIUM 320mg; CALC 9mg

Broiled Sea Bass with Pineapple-Chili-Basil Glaze

Serve with a spinach and mushroom salad and basmati rice with toasted pecans.

    3   tablespoons pineapple preserves
    2   tablespoons rice vinegar
    1   teaspoon chopped fresh or 1/4 teaspoon dried basil
    1/8 teaspoon crushed red pepper
    1   garlic clove, minced
    3/4 teaspoon salt, divided
    4   (6-ounce) sea bass or other firm white fish fillets (about 1 inch thick)
    1/4 teaspoon black pepper
  Cooking spray

1. Preheat broiler.
2. Combine first 5 ingredients and 1/4 teaspoon salt in a small bowl.
3. Sprinkle fillets with 1/2 teaspoon salt and black pepper. Place fillets on a broiler pan coated with cooking spray; broil 5 minutes. Remove from oven; brush fillets evenly with glaze. Return to oven; broil an additional 5 minutes or until fish flakes easily when tested with a fork. Yield: 4 servings (serving size: 1 fillet).

CALORIES 208 (15% from fat); FAT 3.4g (sat 0.9g, mono 0.7g, poly 1.3g); PROTEIN 31.4g; CARB 10.7g; FIBER 0.2g; CHOL 70mg; IRON 0.6mg; SODIUM 487mg; CALC 23mg

Potato Cod Cakes with Dijon Tartar Sauce

Shape the cakes up to 8 hours ahead; cover and refrigerate until you are ready to cook them. Have the cod steamed at the market to save time. If you can't find panko, substitute fresh breadcrumbs.

SAUCE:
- ½ cup fat-free mayonnaise
- 3 tablespoons finely chopped onion
- 3 tablespoons sweet pickle relish
- 2 teaspoons fresh lemon juice
- 4 teaspoons Dijon mustard

CAKES:
- 1 cup cubed peeled baking potato
- 1½ cups panko (Japanese breadcrumbs)
- ½ cup thinly sliced green onions
- ⅓ cup finely chopped red bell pepper
- 3 tablespoons chopped fresh parsley
- 1 teaspoon salt
- 1 teaspoon dried oregano
- ¼ teaspoon freshly ground black pepper
- 2 large eggs, lightly beaten
- 1½ pounds cod fillets, cooked
- 1 garlic clove, minced
- 2 tablespoons vegetable oil, divided
- Cooking spray

GARNISH:
- Flat-leaf parsley sprigs (optional)

1. Preheat oven to 350°.

2. To prepare sauce, combine first 5 ingredients in a small bowl. Cover and refrigerate.

3. Place potato in a large glass bowl, and cover with plastic wrap. Microwave at HIGH 5 minutes or until tender. Mash the potato with a potato masher, and cool.

4. Add panko and the next 9 ingredients to potato; stir well. Divide mixture into 12 equal portions, shaping each into a ½-inch-thick patty.

5. Heat 1 tablespoon vegetable oil in a large non-stick skillet over medium-high heat. Add 6 patties, and cook for 2 minutes on each side. Place patties on a baking sheet coated with cooking spray. Repeat the procedure with remaining vegetable oil and patties.

6. Bake patties at 350° for 10 minutes. Serve potato cod cakes with Dijon tartar sauce. Garnish with parsley sprigs, if desired. Yield: 6 servings (serving size: 2 potato cod cakes and 2 tablespoons sauce).

CALORIES 254 (28% from fat); FAT 7.8g (sat 1g, mono 3.9g, poly 2.2g); PROTEIN 24.5g; CARB 21.3g; FIBER 1.7g; CHOL 113mg; IRON 1.4mg; SODIUM 869mg; CALC 43mg

Chile and Lime-Marinated Snapper with Roasted Corn and Black-Eyed Pea Salsa

Grouper, tilapia, and different varieties of snapper all work in this recipe. For a great snack, double the salsa and eat it with baked tortilla chips. You can serve the salsa chilled or at room temperature.

SALSA:

- 1 cup fresh black-eyed peas
- 1 cup water
- 1 (14-ounce) can fat-free, less-sodium chicken broth
- 2 ears corn, husks removed

Cooking spray

- ½ cup diced red onion
- ⅓ cup chopped fresh cilantro
- 2 tablespoons apple cider vinegar
- 1 tablespoon olive oil
- ½ teaspoon salt
- 2 jalapeño peppers, seeded and minced
- 1 garlic clove, minced

FISH:

- ½ cup chopped red onion
- ½ cup fresh lime juice (about 4 limes)
- 2 tablespoons honey
- 1 tablespoon olive oil
- 2 jalapeño peppers, seeded and minced
- 4 (6-ounce) red snapper fillets
- ¾ teaspoon salt
- ¼ teaspoon black pepper

Lime twists (optional)

1. To prepare salsa, combine first 3 ingredients in a small saucepan, and bring to a boil. Reduce heat, and simmer, partially covered, 30 minutes or until tender. Drain.

2. Place corn on a broiler pan coated with cooking spray, and broil 6 minutes or until lightly browned, turning every 2 minutes. Cool. Cut kernels from ears of corn to measure 2 cups. Combine corn, peas, ½ cup onion, and next 6 ingredients in a medium bowl; chill.

3. To prepare fish, combine ½ cup onion and next 4 ingredients in a large zip-top plastic bag; add fish. Seal and marinate in refrigerator 20 minutes, turning bag once. Remove fish from bag, and discard marinade.

4. Preheat broiler.

5. Sprinkle ¾ teaspoon salt and black pepper evenly over fish. Place fish on a broiler pan coated with cooking spray; cook 10 minutes or until fish flakes easily when tested with a fork. Serve with salsa; garnish with a lime twist, if desired. Yield: 4 servings (serving size: 1 fillet and 1 cup salsa).

CALORIES 323 (23% from fat); FAT 8.2g (sat 1.4g, mono 4.3g, poly 1.6g); PROTEIN 38.2g; CARB 24.5g; FIBER 2g; CHOL 63mg; IRON 1.2mg; SODIUM 860mg; CALC 114mg

Oven-Roasted Sea Bass with Couscous and Warm Tomato Vinaigrette

While the fish is roasting, prepare the couscous so you can serve it as soon as the fish comes out of the oven. We used a bit more liquid in our couscous than the package calls for to get extra moistness.

- 1   green onion
- 2   tablespoons olive oil
- 2   garlic cloves, minced
- 1   cup chopped tomato
- 3   tablespoons fresh lemon juice, divided
- 1   tablespoon sherry vinegar
- 1   teaspoon kosher salt, divided
- 1¼   cups fat-free, less-sodium chicken broth
- ⅔   cup uncooked couscous
- ¼   cup chopped fresh chives
- 4   (6-ounce) sea bass or halibut fillets (about 1½ inches thick)
- ¼   teaspoon freshly ground black pepper
- Cooking spray
- 8   (¼-inch-thick) slices lemon, halved (about 1 lemon)

1. Preheat oven to 350°.

2. Cut onion into 3-inch pieces; cut pieces into julienne strips.

3. Heat oil in a large nonstick skillet over medium-high heat. Add garlic; sauté 30 seconds or until garlic begins to brown. Add tomato and onion; reduce heat to medium; cook 1 minute. Remove from heat; stir in 2 tablespoons juice, vinegar, and ½ teaspoon salt. Keep warm.

4. Combine 1 tablespoon juice, ¼ teaspoon salt, and broth in a medium saucepan, and bring to a boil. Gradually stir in couscous and chopped chives. Remove from heat; cover and let stand 5 minutes. Fluff with a fork. Cover and keep warm.

5. Sprinkle fish with ¼ teaspoon salt and pepper. Place fillets in an 11 x 7-inch baking dish coated with cooking spray. Place 4 halved lemon slices on each fillet. Bake at 350° for 20 minutes or until fish flakes easily when tested with a fork. Serve over couscous; top with vinaigrette. Yield: 4 servings (serving size: 1 fillet, ½ cup couscous, and ¼ cup vinaigrette).

NOTE: Try the vinaigrette over grilled fish or chicken for a change.

CALORIES 346 (29% from fat); FAT 11.2g (sat 1.9g, mono 5.8g, poly 2.2g); PROTEIN 36.5g; CARB 25.2g; FIBER 1.9g; CHOL 70mg; IRON 1.6mg; SODIUM 777mg; CALC 49mg

Snapper Tacos with Chipotle Cream

The fish cooks on top of the vegetables in the same skillet. Break the fish into chunks to finish the filling.

- ½   cup fat-free sour cream
- ⅛   teaspoon salt
- 1   canned chipotle chile in adobo sauce, seeded and minced
- 1½   cups chopped onion, divided
- 1½   cups chopped tomato, divided
- 2   tablespoons butter
- 1   teaspoon ground cumin
- ½   teaspoon salt
- ½   teaspoon ground cinnamon
- 4   garlic cloves, minced
- 3   tablespoons chopped fresh cilantro
- 1   pound red snapper fillets, skinned
- 1   teaspoon grated lime rind
- 2   tablespoons fresh lime juice
- 4   (8-inch) fat-free flour tortillas

1. Combine sour cream, ⅛ teaspoon salt, and chile, and set aside. Combine ½ cup onion and ½ cup tomato, and set aside.

2. Melt butter in a large nonstick skillet over medium heat. Add 1 cup onion, 1 cup tomato, cumin, ½ teaspoon salt, cinnamon, and garlic; cook 5 minutes, stirring frequently. Stir in cilantro. Arrange fish over onion mixture in pan; cover and cook 3 minutes. Turn fish; cover and cook 2 minutes. Break fish into chunks. Stir in rind and juice; cook 2 minutes. Remove from heat.

3. Warm tortillas according to package directions. Fill each tortilla with ½ cup fish mixture and ¼ cup reserved onion mixture, and top each serving with 2 tablespoons reserved chipotle cream. Fold in half or roll up. Yield: 4 servings (serving size: 1 taco).

CALORIES 340 (21% from fat); FAT 7.8g (sat 4g, mono 2g, poly 0.9g); PROTEIN 28.1g; CARB 38.1g; FIBER 3.3g; CHOL 56mg; IRON 2mg; SODIUM 896mg; CALC 108mg

French West Indian Grilled Snapper with Caper Sauce

The marinade features four essential seasonings used in traditional French West Indian cooking: lime juice, garlic, thyme, and Scotch bonnet chile peppers. We left the seeds in the pepper, but you can remove them for a milder flavor.

MARINADE:
- ¼ cup fresh lime juice
- 1 teaspoon salt
- 1 teaspoon fresh or ¼ teaspoon dried thyme
- 1 teaspoon black pepper
- 3 garlic cloves, chopped
- 1 to 2 Scotch bonnet or habanero peppers, minced
- 4 (6-ounce) red snapper or other firm white fish fillets

CAPER SAUCE:
- 2 tablespoons chopped fresh cilantro
- 2 tablespoons fresh lime juice
- 2 tablespoons water
- 2 tablespoons extravirgin olive oil
- 1 tablespoon capers
- 1 tablespoon red wine vinegar
- 1½ teaspoons minced Scotch bonnet or habanero pepper
- ¼ teaspoon salt
- ¼ teaspoon freshly ground black pepper
- 1 garlic clove, chopped
- 1 large shallot, chopped
- Cooking spray

1. To prepare marinade, place first 6 ingredients in a blender; process until smooth. Combine marinade and fish in a large zip-top plastic bag; seal. Marinate in refrigerator 2 to 4 hours, turning bag occasionally.
2. Prepare grill.
3. To prepare caper sauce, place cilantro and next 10 ingredients in a blender or food processor; process until smooth.
4. Remove fish from marinade; discard marinade. Place fish on grill rack coated with cooking spray; grill 3 minutes on each side or until fish flakes easily when tested with a fork. Serve with caper sauce. Yield: 4 servings (serving size: 1 fillet and 2 tablespoons sauce).

CALORIES 246 (35% from fat); FAT 9.6g (sat 1.5g, mono 5.5g, poly 1.6g); PROTEIN 35.4g; CARB 2.8g; FIBER 0.2g; CHOL 63mg; IRON 0.6mg; SODIUM 425mg; CALC 63mg

Curry-Chutney Snapper

- 2 tablespoons all-purpose flour
- 2 teaspoons curry powder
- ¼ teaspoon salt
- 4 (6-ounce) red snapper or mahimahi fillets
- 1 tablespoon butter or stick margarine
- ½ cup fat-free, less-sodium chicken broth
- ¼ cup mango chutney
- ¼ teaspoon hot sauce
- 2 tablespoons minced fresh cilantro

1. Combine first 3 ingredients in a shallow dish. Dredge fish in flour mixture. Melt butter in a nonstick skillet over medium-high heat. Add fish; cook 3 minutes on each side or until fish flakes easily when tested with a fork. Remove from pan; keep warm.
2. Add chicken broth, chutney, and hot sauce to pan; bring to a boil. Cook 1 minute, stirring constantly. Spoon sauce over fish, and sprinkle with cilantro. Yield: 4 servings (serving size: 1 fillet and 2 tablespoons sauce).

CALORIES 257 (19% from fat); FAT 5.3g (sat 1.1g, mono 1.8g, poly 1.7g); PROTEIN 36.1g; CARB 14.4g; FIBER 0.5g; CHOL 63mg; IRON 1.1mg; SODIUM 386mg; CALC 69mg

Ginger-Lime Swordfish

- 2 teaspoons grated lime rind
- ½ cup fresh lime juice (about 2 limes)
- ¼ cup honey
- 2 tablespoons minced green onions
- 1 tablespoon low-sodium soy sauce
- 2 tablespoons bottled fresh ground ginger
- 2 teaspoons bottled minced garlic
- 4 (6-ounce) swordfish steaks (about ¾ inch thick)
- Cooking spray
- ¼ teaspoon salt
- ¼ teaspoon black pepper

1. Preheat broiler.
2. Combine first 7 ingredients in a small saucepan. Dip each steak into lime mixture to coat.
3. Place fish on broiler pan coated with cooking spray. Sprinkle with salt and pepper. Broil 10 minutes or until fish flakes easily when tested with a fork.
4. While fish cooks, place remaining lime mixture over medium heat; cook until reduced by half. Serve sauce with fish. Yield: 4 servings (serving size: 1 swordfish steak and 2 tablespoons sauce).

CALORIES 235 (20% from fat); FAT 5.2g (sat 1.4g, mono 2g, poly 1.2g); PROTEIN 25.8g; CARB 22g; FIBER 0.6g; CHOL 50mg; IRON 1.3mg; SODIUM 397mg; CALC 15mg

Seafood Fettuccine

The sauce is like a traditional Alfredo, with no flour or other thickener. Don't worry if it looks thin.
It's the perfect consistency for coating the pasta. Pat the shrimp and scallops dry with paper towels
before cooking so they don't dilute the sauce.

1½ tablespoons butter
1   cup chopped green onions
4   garlic cloves, minced
1   pound medium shrimp,
    peeled
1   pound sea scallops
2   cups half-and-half
½   teaspoon salt
¼   teaspoon black pepper
½   pound lump crabmeat, shell
    pieces removed
¾   cup (3 ounces) grated fresh
    Parmesan cheese, divided
8   cups hot cooked fettuccine (about
    1 pound uncooked pasta)
¼   cup chopped fresh parsley

1. Melt butter in 12-inch nonstick skillet over medium-high heat. Add onions and garlic; sauté 1 minute or until tender. Add shrimp and scallops; sauté 3 minutes or until done. Reduce heat to medium-low.

2. Add half-and-half, salt, pepper, and crabmeat; cook 3 minutes or until thoroughly heated, stirring constantly (do not boil). Gradually sprinkle ½ cup cheese over seafood mixture, stirring constantly; cook 1 minute, stirring constantly.

3. Remove from heat. Combine pasta and seafood mixture in a large bowl. Top each serving with 1½ teaspoons cheese and 1½ teaspoons parsley. Yield: 8 servings (serving size: 1½ cups).

CALORIES 438 (30% from fat); FAT 14.8g (sat 7.7g, mono 3.6g, poly 0.9g); PROTEIN 38.5g; CARB 38g; FIBER 2.2g; CHOL 160mg; IRON 3.4mg; SODIUM 747mg; CALC 257mg

Grilled Sesame Swordfish with Monterey Bay Pesto

The pesto can be made up to a day ahead and refrigerated. Bring to room temperature before serving.

PESTO:

½ cup chopped fresh parsley
¼ cup chopped fresh basil
2½ tablespoons fat-free, less-sodium chicken broth
2 tablespoons fresh lemon juice
1 tablespoon extravirgin olive oil
1 tablespoon water
⅛ teaspoon salt
⅛ teaspoon freshly ground black pepper
3 garlic cloves

FISH:

6 (6-ounce) swordfish steaks (about 1 inch thick)
1 teaspoon extravirgin olive oil
1½ teaspoons sesame seeds
1 teaspoon coarse sea salt
Cooking spray

1. Prepare grill.
2. To prepare pesto, combine first 9 ingredients in a food processor; process until minced.
3. To prepare fish, rub fish with 1 teaspoon olive oil. Rub sesame seeds and sea salt evenly over fish. Place fish on grill rack coated with cooking spray, and grill 4 minutes on each side or until fish flakes easily when tested with a fork. Serve with pesto. Yield: 6 servings (serving size: 1 steak and about 1 tablespoon pesto).

CALORIES 236 (37% from fat); FAT 9.6g (sat 2.2g, mono 4.8g, poly 1.8g); PROTEIN 32.8g; CARB 1.4g; FIBER 0.3g; CHOL 64mg; IRON 2.8mg; SODIUM 594mg; CALC 21mg

Tuna Puttanesca

¼ cup chopped pimiento-stuffed olives
1 tablespoon capers
2 teaspoons bottled minced garlic
1 teaspoon fresh lemon juice
1 teaspoon anchovy paste
⅛ teaspoon crushed red pepper
1 (14.5-ounce) can diced tomatoes, drained
1 tablespoon olive oil
4 (6-ounce) tuna steaks
½ teaspoon salt
¼ teaspoon black pepper
¼ cup chopped fresh parsley

1. Combine first 7 ingredients.
2. Heat oil in a large nonstick skillet over medium-high heat. Sprinkle tuna with salt and pepper. Add fish to pan, and cook 2 minutes on each side or until desired degree of doneness. Remove fish from pan; keep warm.
3. Add tomato mixture to pan; cook until thoroughly heated (about 2 minutes). Stir in parsley. Pour sauce over fish. Yield: 4 servings (serving size: 1 tuna steak and ¼ cup sauce).

CALORIES 236 (23% from fat); FAT 6.1g (sat 1.2g, mono 3.5g, poly 0.9g); PROTEIN 38.6g; CARB 5.1g; FIBER 1.7g; CHOL 81mg; IRON 3.1mg; SODIUM 801mg; CALC 85mg

Tuna "London Broil" with Wasabi Cream

From the Pacific Rim, here's a "London broil" with piquant Asian influences. Adapted from Steven Raichlen's books *How to Grill* (Workman, 2001) and *BBQ USA* (Workman, 2003).

2 teaspoons sesame seeds, toasted
2 teaspoons wasabi powder (dried Japanese horseradish)
2 teaspoons cracked black pepper
1 teaspoon garlic powder
¼ teaspoon salt
4 (6-ounce) tuna steaks (about ¾ inch thick)
1 tablespoon wasabi powder
1 tablespoon water
¼ cup low-fat mayonnaise
¼ cup fat-free sour cream
1 tablespoon fresh lemon juice
1 tablespoon low-sodium soy sauce
Cooking spray
2 tablespoons sliced green onions

1. Combine first 5 ingredients; rub over tuna. Cover and chill 30 minutes. Combine wasabi and water. Let stand 5 minutes. Stir in mayonnaise, sour cream, juice, and soy sauce.
2. Prepare grill to high heat.
3. Place the tuna steaks on grill rack coated with cooking spray, and grill for 5 minutes on each side or until steaks are desired degree of doneness. Serve steaks with wasabi cream, and sprinkle with onions. Yield: 4 servings (serving size: 1 steak, 2 tablespoons wasabi cream, and 1½ teaspoons onions).

CALORIES 308 (30% from fat); FAT 10.3g (sat 2.4g, mono 3g, poly 3g); PROTEIN 41.3g; CARB 9.7g; FIBER 0.9g; CHOL 66mg; IRON 4.4mg; SODIUM 500mg; CALC 47mg

Grilled Tuna with Basil Butter and Fresh Tomato Sauce

BASIL BUTTER:
- ¾ cup fresh basil leaves
- 2 tablespoons butter, softened
- 1 tablespoon fresh lemon juice
- ¼ teaspoon salt
- 2 garlic cloves, minced

TOMATO SAUCE:
- 2 teaspoons olive oil
- ½ cup finely chopped red onion
- 2 garlic cloves, minced
- 3 cups grape or cherry tomatoes, halved
- ½ cup dry white wine
- 3 tablespoons capers
- 2 tablespoons balsamic vinegar
- ¼ teaspoon sugar
- ¼ cup chopped fresh flat-leaf parsley

TUNA:
- 4 (6-ounce) tuna steaks (about 1 inch thick)
- ½ teaspoon salt
- ¼ teaspoon black pepper
- Cooking spray
- 4 basil leaves (optional)

1. Prepare grill or broiler.

2. To prepare basil butter, combine first 5 ingredients in a food processor; process until smooth, scraping sides as needed.

3. To prepare sauce, heat oil in a saucepan over medium-high heat. Add onion and 2 garlic cloves; sauté 3 minutes. Add tomatoes; sauté 2 minutes. Stir in wine, capers, vinegar, and sugar; bring to a boil. Reduce heat; simmer 5 minutes, stirring occasionally. Stir in parsley.

4. To prepare tuna, sprinkle tuna with ½ teaspoon salt and pepper. Place tuna on grill rack or broiler pan coated with cooking spray. Cook 5 minutes on each side or until desired degree of doneness. Serve with basil butter and sauce. Garnish with basil leaves, if desired. Yield: 4 servings (serving size: 1 tuna steak, ¾ cup sauce, and about 1 tablespoon basil butter).

CALORIES 323 (28% from fat); FAT 10.2g (sat 4.4g, mono 3.7g, poly 1.1g); PROTEIN 41.8g; CARB 10.9g; FIBER 2.4g; CHOL 92mg; IRON 2.7mg; SODIUM 770mg; CALC 72mg

Soft-Shell Crabs with Fresh Thai Green Curry

The heat of this dish depends on the number of chiles that you use.

CURRY:

    2 cups fresh cilantro sprigs
    ½ cup coarsely chopped shallots
    1 tablespoon grated lime rind
    8 to 12 serrano chiles, seeded
    3 garlic cloves, peeled
    1 (3-inch) piece fresh ginger, peeled
    1 teaspoon vegetable oil
    2 cups sliced red bell pepper
    1½ cups (1-inch) cubed Japanese eggplant
    1½ cups water
    ½ cup diagonally cut carrot
    2 tablespoons brown sugar
    1 (13.5-ounce) can light coconut milk
    2 tablespoons fresh lime juice
    1 teaspoon salt

CRABS:

    ¼ cup cornstarch
    ¼ teaspoon salt
    6 (5- to 6-ounce) soft-shell crabs, cleaned
    4 teaspoons vegetable oil, divided
    3 cups hot cooked jasmine rice

1. To prepare curry, combine first 6 ingredients in a food processor, and process for 3 minutes or until a paste forms.

2. Heat 1 teaspoon oil in a large Dutch oven over medium-high heat. Add chile mixture; sauté 3 minutes. Add bell pepper and next 5 ingredients; bring to a boil. Cover, reduce heat, and simmer 10 minutes. Uncover and simmer 10 minutes. Stir in lime juice and 1 teaspoon salt; keep warm.

3. To prepare crabs, combine cornstarch and ¼ teaspoon salt in a shallow dish. Dredge crabs in cornstarch mixture.

4. Heat 2 teaspoons oil in a large nonstick skillet over medium-high heat. Place 3 crabs in pan, top sides down; cook 3 minutes, gently pressing body and legs against pan. Turn crabs; cook 2 minutes. Remove from heat. Repeat procedure with remaining oil and crabs.

5. Place ½ cup jasmine rice in each of 6 shallow bowls; spoon ¾ cup curry mixture over each serving. Top each serving with 1 crab. Yield: 6 servings.

CALORIES 406 (22% from fat); FAT 9.8g (sat 3.1g, mono 1.5g, poly 3.3g); PROTEIN 30.5g; CARB 49.2g; FIBER 3.3g; CHOL 0mg; IRON 4.9mg; SODIUM 519mg; CALC 43mg

Crab Quiche Florentine

Open the can of breadstick dough, cover, and allow to reach room temperature before using.

    1 (7-ounce) can refrigerated breadstick dough
    Cooking spray
    ¾ cup (3 ounces) grated Gruyère cheese
    8 ounces lump crabmeat, drained and shell pieces removed
    ½ cup chopped onion
    4 cups coarsely chopped spinach
    ⅛ teaspoon dried tarragon
    ⅛ teaspoon Old Bay seasoning
    ⅛ teaspoon ground nutmeg
    ⅛ teaspoon black pepper
    1 cup evaporated fat-free milk
    ½ cup egg substitute
    Cherry tomatoes, quartered (optional)

1. Unroll dough, separating into strips. Working on a flat surface, coil one strip of dough around itself in a spiral pattern. Add second strip of dough to the end of the first strip, pinching ends together to seal; continue coiling dough. Repeat procedure with remaining dough strips. Cover dough with a towel; let rest 20 minutes. Roll dough into a 13-inch circle; fit into a 9-inch pie plate coated with cooking spray. Fold edges under, and flute. Sprinkle grated cheese over bottom of crust. Top with crabmeat, and set aside.

2. Preheat oven to 375°.

3. Place a large nonstick skillet coated with cooking spray over medium-high heat. Add onion, and sauté 4 minutes. Add spinach and next 4 ingredients; cook 2 minutes or until spinach wilts. Arrange spinach mixture over crabmeat.

4. Combine milk and egg substitute, and stir well with a whisk. Pour milk mixture over spinach mixture. Bake at 375° for 45 minutes or until a knife inserted in the center comes out clean, and let stand 10 minutes. Garnish quiche with cherry tomatoes, if desired. Yield: 6 servings.

NOTE: Place the pie plate on a baking sheet in case the filling bubbles over.

CALORIES 248 (29% from fat); FAT 7.7g (sat 3.7g, mono 2.1g, poly 1.4g); PROTEIN 20.8g; CARB 23.2g; FIBER 2.6g; CHOL 55mg; IRON 1.9mg; SODIUM 556mg; CALC 354mg

Seafood Lasagna

We've managed to incorporate lots of rich flavor into this indulgent, cheesy lasagna, just right for when you want to impress guests. You can always splurge on fresh crabmeat, but we liked canned Chicken of the Sea lump crabmeat.

　2　teaspoons olive oil
　5　cups finely chopped mushrooms (about
　　　1 pound)
1½　cups chopped onion
　2　tablespoons chopped fresh thyme
　2　garlic cloves, minced
　¼　cup dry white wine
　2　(6.5-ounce) cans lump crabmeat
　1　pound uncooked large shrimp
　2　cups water
1½　teaspoons celery salt
　1　teaspoon fennel seeds
1¼　cups (5 ounces) crumbled goat or feta cheese
　1　cup 2% reduced-fat cottage cheese
　¼　cup finely chopped fresh basil
　1　tablespoon fresh lemon juice
　1　garlic clove, minced
　¼　cup all-purpose flour
　1　cup 1% low-fat milk
　¼　cup (1 ounce) grated
　　　fresh Parmesan
　　　cheese
Cooking spray
　1　(8-ounce) package
　　　precooked lasagna
　　　noodles
　2　cups (8 ounces)
　　　shredded part-skim
　　　mozzarella cheese
　¼　cup chopped fresh
　　　flat-leaf parsley

1. Preheat oven to 375°.
2. Heat oil in a large non-stick skillet over medium heat. Add chopped mushrooms, onion, thyme, and 2 garlic cloves; cook 10 minutes, stirring occasionally. Add wine. Bring to a boil; cook 1½ minutes or until liquid almost evaporates. Remove from heat; stir in crabmeat. Set aside.

3. Peel and devein shrimp, reserving shells. Cut each shrimp in half lengthwise, and cover and refrigerate. Combine reserved shells, 2 cups water, celery salt, and fennel seeds in a small saucepan. Bring to a boil; cook until reduced to 1½ cups shrimp stock (about 15 minutes). Strain stock through a sieve into a bowl; discard solids. Set stock aside.

4. Combine goat cheese, cottage cheese, basil, juice, and 1 garlic clove; set aside.

5. Lightly spoon flour into a dry measuring cup; level with a knife. Place flour in a small saucepan; gradually add milk, stirring with a whisk. Stir in shrimp stock; bring to a boil. Reduce heat; simmer 5 minutes or until thick. Remove from heat; stir in Parmesan cheese.

6. Spread ½ cup sauce in bottom of a 13 x 9-inch baking dish coated with cooking spray. Arrange 4 noodles, slightly overlapping, over sauce; top with one-third goat cheese mixture, one-third crab mixture, one-third shrimp, ⅔ cup sauce, and ⅔ cup mozzarella. Repeat layers twice, ending with mozzarella. Bake at 375° for 40 minutes or until golden. Let stand 15 minutes. Sprinkle with parsley. Yield: 8 servings (serving size: 1 [3-inch] square).

CALORIES 428 (29% from fat); FAT 13.9g (sat 7.7g, mono 2.5g, poly 1.1g); PROTEIN 40.1g; CARB 33.6g; FIBER 3.6g; CHOL 143mg; IRON 4.1mg; SODIUM 934mg; CALC 414mg

Thai-Style Mussels with Pickled Ginger

Serve over hot cooked rice or rice noodles for a delicious entrée. Or cut the serving size in half to make it an appetizer for an Asian meal.

    2   teaspoons vegetable oil
    ½   cup minced shallots
    1   tablespoon chile paste with garlic
    1   garlic clove, minced
    ½   cup light coconut milk
    ¼   teaspoon lime rind
    ¼   cup fresh lime juice
    ¼   cup minced pickled ginger
    ¼   cup chopped fresh parsley
    2   pounds mussels, scrubbed and debearded
        (about 40 mussels)
    Parsley sprigs (optional)

1. Heat oil in a large Dutch oven over medium-high heat. Add the minced shallots, chile paste, and garlic; cook 2 minutes or until tender, stirring constantly. Add the coconut milk and next 5 ingredients; bring to a boil. Cover and cook 5 minutes or until the shells open. Remove from heat, and discard any unopened shells. Garnish with parsley sprigs, if desired. Yield: 4 servings (serving size: about 10 mussels and ¼ cup sauce).

CALORIES 160 (32% from fat); FAT 5.6g (sat 1.8g, mono 1.2g, poly 1.6g); PROTEIN 10.6g; CARB 16.2g; FIBER 0.4g; CHOL 24mg; IRON 4mg; SODIUM 368mg; CALC 76mg

Bourbon-Bacon Scallops

Serve these scallops over rice with a side of snow peas and broccoli.

    3   tablespoons minced green onions
    2   tablespoons bourbon
    2   tablespoons maple syrup
    1   tablespoon low-sodium soy sauce
    1   tablespoon Dijon mustard
    ¼   teaspoon black pepper
    24 large sea scallops (about 1½ pounds)
    6   low-sodium bacon slices (4 ounces)
    Cooking spray

1. Combine first 6 ingredients in a bowl. Add scallops, stirring gently to coat. Cover and marinate in refrigerator 1 hour, stirring occasionally.
2. Remove scallops from bowl; reserve marinade.

Cut each bacon slice into 4 pieces. Wrap 1 bacon piece around each scallop (bacon might only wrap halfway around scallops if they are very large). Thread scallops onto 4 (12-inch) skewers, leaving some space between scallops so bacon will cook.
3. Preheat broiler.
4. Place skewers on a broiler pan coated with cooking spray; broil 8 minutes or until bacon is crisp and scallops are done, basting occasionally with reserved marinade (cooking time will vary greatly with size of scallops). Yield: 4 servings (serving size: 6 scallops).

CALORIES 245 (26% from fat); FAT 7g (sat 2g, mono 2.5g, poly 1.1g); PROTEIN 32.4g; CARB 11.3g; FIBER 0.1g; CHOL 68mg; IRON 0.7mg; SODIUM 642mg; CALC 51mg

Simple Seared Scallops

These scallops are crisp and glazed outside, tender and moist inside. Serve with orzo tossed with chopped tomato, feta, basil, salt, and black pepper.

    3   tablespoons all-purpose flour
    ½   teaspoon salt
    ½   teaspoon dried marjoram
    1½   pounds sea scallops
    2   teaspoons olive oil
    ½   cup dry white wine
    1   tablespoon balsamic vinegar
    Fresh parsley sprigs (optional)

1. Combine first 3 ingredients in a large zip-top plastic bag, and add scallops. Seal bag, and shake to coat scallops.
2. Heat oil in a large nonstick skillet over medium-high heat. Add scallops; cook 3 minutes on each side or until done. Remove from pan; keep warm.
3. Add wine and vinegar to pan; cook 3 minutes or until slightly thick, stirring with a whisk. Stir in scallops; remove from heat. Garnish with parsley sprigs, if desired. Yield: 4 servings (serving size: about 5 ounces scallops).

CALORIES 211 (15% from fat); FAT 3.6g (sat 0.4g, mono 1.7g, poly 0.6g); PROTEIN 29.2g; CARB 9.2g; FIBER 0.2g; CHOL 56mg; IRON 1mg; SODIUM 567mg; CALC 46mg

Simple Seared Scallops

Pan-Seared Scallops on Linguine with Tomato-Cream Sauce

A touch of cream gives the slightly tangy sauce a silky-smooth finish. Be sure to serve this dish with bread so you can savor every drop of sauce.

 1 cup dry white wine
¼ cup minced shallots
 2 tablespoons fresh lime juice
 1 tablespoon grated peeled fresh ginger
 2 tablespoons whipping cream
 1 tablespoon butter, cut into small pieces
⅔ cup chopped seeded plum tomato
 2 tablespoons chopped fresh cilantro
¼ teaspoon salt
⅛ teaspoon black pepper
1½ cups hot cooked linguine
Cooking spray
¾ pound large sea scallops
⅛ teaspoon salt
Chopped fresh cilantro (optional)

1. Combine first 4 ingredients in a medium skillet; bring to a boil. Cook until reduced to ½ cup (about 5 minutes). Drain mixture through a fine sieve into a bowl, reserving liquid; discard solids.

2. Return wine mixture to skillet. Add cream, and cook over medium heat for 1 minute. Add butter, stirring until butter melts. Stir in chopped tomato, 2 tablespoons chopped cilantro, ¼ teaspoon salt, and pepper. Add linguine, and toss well. Cover and keep warm.

3. Heat a large nonstick skillet coated with cooking spray over medium-high heat. Sprinkle scallops with ⅛ teaspoon salt. Arrange scallops in pan; cook 2 minutes on each side or until done. Add scallops to pasta mixture; toss gently to combine. Garnish with chopped cilantro, if desired. Yield: 2 servings (serving size: about ¾ cup pasta mixture and about 5 ounces scallops).

CALORIES 426 (29% from fat); FAT 13.5g (sat 7.3g, mono 3.5g, poly 1.2g); PROTEIN 34.8g; CARB 40.6g; FIBER 2.6g; CHOL 92mg; IRON 2.8mg; SODIUM 794mg; CALC 75mg

Prosciutto-Wrapped Shrimp on Artichoke, Fennel, and Tomato Salad

(pictured on page 76)

Suitable for a dinner party, this recipe can be started early by preparing the dressing and salad in advance and finished quickly by cooking the shrimp at the last minute.

DRESSING:

- 1 teaspoon grated lemon rind
- 1 tablespoon fresh lemon juice
- 1 tablespoon fresh lime juice
- 1 tablespoon extravirgin olive oil
- 1 teaspoon paprika
- ¼ teaspoon sugar
- ⅛ teaspoon freshly ground black pepper
- 1 garlic clove, minced

SALAD:

- 4 cups water
- ⅓ cup fresh lemon juice
- 8 medium artichokes (about 8 ounces each)
- 1 cup thinly sliced fennel bulb
- 1 cup grape or cherry tomatoes, halved
- ½ cup sliced bottled roasted red bell peppers
- 2 tablespoons thinly sliced fresh basil
- 1 tablespoon large capers

SHRIMP:

- 1½ tablespoons butter
- 2 garlic cloves, minced
- 1 teaspoon grated lemon rind
- 1 tablespoon fresh lemon juice
- 1½ teaspoons Dijon mustard
- 1 teaspoon Worcestershire sauce
- ½ teaspoon hot sauce
- 3 ounces very thin slices prosciutto
- 1 pound jumbo shrimp, peeled and deveined
Cooking spray

1. To prepare dressing, combine first 8 ingredients, stirring with a whisk; set aside.

2. To prepare salad, combine water and ⅓ cup lemon juice in a Dutch oven. Cut off stem of each artichoke to within ½ inch of base, and peel stem. Cut 1 inch off tops of artichokes. Remove bottom leaves and tough outer leaves, leaving tender heart and bottom. Cut artichokes lengthwise into quarters; place in lemon water. Bring to a boil, reduce heat, and simmer 20 minutes or until tender. Drain and plunge into cold water. Drain well. Remove fuzzy thistles from bottoms with a spoon.

3. Combine artichokes, fennel, and next 4 ingredients in a large bowl. Drizzle with dressing; toss gently to coat. Set aside.

4. To prepare shrimp, melt butter in a small saucepan over low heat. Add 2 garlic cloves; cook 1 minute, stirring frequently. Add rind and next 4 ingredients, stirring with a whisk.

5. Preheat broiler.

6. Cut prosciutto slices lengthwise into ½-inch strips. Wrap prosciutto strips around the shrimp. Arrange shrimp on a broiler pan coated with cooking spray. Brush shrimp with half of butter mixture, and broil 3 minutes. Remove pan from oven. Turn shrimp; brush with remaining butter mixture. Broil an additional 3 minutes or until shrimp are done.

7. Arrange 1½ cups salad on each of 4 plates. Top each serving with prosciutto-wrapped shrimp, dividing evenly. Yield: 4 servings.

CALORIES 384 (29% from fat); FAT 12.5g (sat 4.3g, mono 5.1g, poly 1.9g); PROTEIN 37.7g; CARB 36.1g; FIBER 6.5g; CHOL 196mg; IRON 7.2mg; SODIUM 975mg; CALC 207mg

Jalapeño-Lime Shrimp

- 4 pounds large shrimp, peeled, deveined, and butterflied
- 1 cup thawed orange juice concentrate, undiluted
- 2 teaspoons grated lime rind
- ½ cup fresh lime juice
- ½ cup honey
- 4 teaspoons ground cumin
- ½ teaspoon salt
- 6 garlic cloves, minced
- 4 jalapenos, seeded and chopped
Cooking spray

1. Combine first 9 ingredients in a large zip-top plastic bag; seal and marinate in refrigerator 30 minutes. Remove shrimp from bag, reserving marinade. Thread shrimp onto 12 skewers.

2. Prepare grill or broiler.

3. Place the skewers on a grill rack or broiler pan coated with cooking spray, and cook 4 minutes on each side or until shrimp are done, basting frequently with the marinade. Yield: 12 servings (serving size: 1 kebab).

NOTE: You can substitute 3 pounds of skinned, boned chicken breast or pork tenderloin, cut into 1-inch cubes, for the shrimp, if preferred.

CALORIES 210 (9% from fat); FAT 2.2g (sat 0.4g, mono 0.4g, poly 0.8g); PROTEIN 24g; CARB 23.8g; FIBER 0.3g; CHOL 172mg; IRON 3.4mg; SODIUM 268mg; CALC 78mg

Barbecue Shrimp

In this signature Creole-Sicilian favorite from New Orleans, the peels are left on the shrimp
so they can add flavor to the lush, buttery-peppery sauce. The bread means no sauce goes to waste.
Be sure to have plenty of napkins available.

½ cup fat-free Caesar dressing
⅓ cup Worcestershire sauce
2 tablespoons butter or stick margarine
1 tablespoon dried oregano
1 tablespoon paprika
1 tablespoon dried rosemary
1 tablespoon dried thyme
1½ teaspoons black pepper
1 teaspoon hot pepper sauce
5 bay leaves
3 garlic cloves, minced
2 pounds large shrimp
⅓ cup dry white wine
10 (1-ounce) slices French bread baguette
10 lemon wedges

1. Combine the first 11 ingredients in a large non-stick skillet, and bring to a boil. Add the shrimp, and cook for 7 minutes, stirring occasionally. Add the wine, and cook for 1 minute or until the shrimp are done. Serve with bread and lemon wedges. Yield: 5 servings (serving size: 5 ounces shrimp with sauce, 2 bread slices, and 2 lemon wedges).

CALORIES 403 (20% from fat); FAT 9.1g (sat 3.8g, mono 2.4g, poly 1.7g); PROTEIN 34.4g;
CARB 41.7g; FIBER 2.8g; CHOL 219mg; IRON 7mg; SODIUM 1,021mg; CALC 211mg

Prosciutto-Wrapped Shrimp with Lemon Couscous

The sweet maple syrup and salty prosciutto contrast well with the lemony couscous.

    3 tablespoons maple syrup
    2 tablespoons bourbon
    1 tablespoon teriyaki sauce
    2 teaspoons Dijon mustard
    ½ teaspoon chili powder
   24 jumbo shrimp (about 1½ pounds)
    6 very thin slices prosciutto or ham
       (about 3½ ounces)
   Cooking spray
   Lemon Couscous

1. Preheat broiler.
2. Combine the first 5 ingredients in a bowl, and stir with a whisk. Peel shrimp, leaving tails intact. Add shrimp to the maple mixture, tossing to coat. Remove the shrimp from bowl, and discard marinade. Cut each prosciutto slice lengthwise into 4 strips. Wrap 1 prosciutto strip around each shrimp. Thread shrimp onto 4 (8-inch) skewers. Place skewers on broiler pan coated with cooking spray, and broil for 3 minutes on each side or until done. Serve shrimp over Lemon Couscous. Yield: 4 servings (serving size: 6 shrimp and ½ cup couscous).

(Totals include Lemon Couscous) CALORIES 305 (12% from fat); FAT 4.2g (sat 1.2g, mono 1.4g, poly 0.9g); PROTEIN 36.1g; CARB 27.2g; FIBER 1.4g; CHOL 263mg; IRON 5.2mg; SODIUM 927mg; CALC 67mg

LEMON COUSCOUS:

   1¼ cups water
    ¾ cup uncooked couscous
    ¼ cup sliced green onions
    2 tablespoons finely chopped fresh parsley
    2 tablespoons orange juice
    1 teaspoon grated lemon rind
    1 tablespoon fresh lemon juice
    ¼ teaspoon salt
    ⅛ teaspoon black pepper

1. Bring water to a boil in a medium saucepan, and gradually stir in couscous. Remove couscous from heat, and cover and let stand for 5 minutes. Fluff couscous with a fork. Stir in sliced green onions and the remaining ingredients. Yield: 4 servings (serving size: ½ cup).

CALORIES 102 (3% from fat); FAT 0.3g (sat 0g, mono 0g, poly 0g); PROTEIN 3.7g; CARB 21.8g; FIBER 1.3g; CHOL 0mg; IRON 0.8mg; SODIUM 151mg; CALC 9mg

Shrimp on Sugarcane with Rum Glaze

This Caribbean-influenced dish relies on high heat to caramelize the glaze and infuse the shrimp from the inside out with the cane's mild sweetness. Look for sugarcane swizzle sticks in the produce section, or order them from www.melissas.com. If you can't find sugarcane, bamboo skewers will do. Adapted from Steven Raichlen's books *How to Grill* (Workman, 2001) and *BBQ USA* (Workman, 2003).

    1 tablespoon vegetable oil
    1 tablespoon fresh lemon juice
    ¼ teaspoon black pepper
    ⅛ teaspoon salt
    1 garlic clove, minced
   24 jumbo shrimp, peeled and deveined (about
       1½ pounds)
    8 sugarcane swizzle sticks, each cut into
       3 pieces
    ¼ cup packed dark brown sugar
    ¼ cup dark rum
    ¼ cup corn syrup
    3 tablespoons Dijon mustard
    1 tablespoon white vinegar
    1 tablespoon butter
    ¼ teaspoon salt
    ¼ teaspoon ground cinnamon
    ¼ teaspoon black pepper
   Cooking spray

1. Prepare grill to high heat.
2. Combine first 5 ingredients in a large bowl. Add shrimp; toss to coat. Cover and chill 15 minutes.
3. Cut one end of each swizzle stick piece at a sharp angle. Thread 1 shrimp onto each skewer.
4. Combine brown sugar and next 8 ingredients in a saucepan; bring to a boil. Reduce heat; simmer 5 minutes or until syrupy.
5. Place shrimp on grill rack coated with cooking spray. Grill 3 minutes on each side or until done, basting generously with glaze. Yield: 6 servings (serving size: 4 shrimp).

CALORIES 273 (22% from fat); FAT 6.8g (sat 1.9g, mono 1.6g, poly 2.3g); PROTEIN 23.6g; CARB 23.3g; FIBER 0.2g; CHOL 177mg; IRON 3.5mg; SODIUM 541mg; CALC 83mg

Orange-Ginger Shrimp Skewers

½ cup fresh orange juice (about 2 oranges)
2 tablespoons minced green onions
1 tablespoon minced peeled fresh ginger
1 tablespoon minced fresh cilantro
2 tablespoons rice vinegar
2 tablespoons low-sodium soy sauce
1 tablespoon vegetable oil
2 teaspoons grated orange rind
1 pound large shrimp, peeled and deveined
2 oranges, peeled, cut in half, and quartered
Cooking spray

1. Combine first 8 ingredients in a bowl. Add shrimp; toss to coat. Cover and marinate in refrigerator 15 minutes.
2. Remove shrimp from dish, reserving marinade. Thread shrimp and orange quarters alternately onto each of 8 (8-inch) skewers.
3. Heat a large grill pan coated with cooking spray over medium-high heat. Cook skewers 4 minutes on each side or until done, basting with reserved marinade. Yield: 8 servings (serving size: 1 skewer).

CALORIES 104 (24% from fat); FAT 2.8g (sat 0.4g, mono 0.6g, poly 1.4g); PROTEIN 12.2g; CARB 7.4g; FIBER 1g; CHOL 86mg; IRON 1.5mg; SODIUM 218mg; CALC 46mg

Crusted Shrimp with Spicy Black Beans and Saffron Sauce

1 tablespoon cumin seeds
1½ teaspoons fennel seeds
½ cup sunflower seed kernels
1 teaspoon dried orange peel
1 teaspoon black peppercorns
3 tablespoons golden cane syrup or light-colored corn syrup
2 large egg whites, lightly beaten
1½ pounds large shrimp, peeled and deveined
1 teaspoon olive oil
Cooking spray
Spicy Black Beans
Saffron Sauce

1. Heat a nonstick skillet over medium-high heat. Add the cumin and fennel seeds, and cook for 1 minute or until cumin seeds are browned. Place the seed mixture in a spice or coffee grinder. Add the sunflower kernels, orange peel, and peppercorns, and process until ground. Place the seed mixture in a shallow dish.

2. Combine the corn syrup and beaten egg whites. Dip shrimp in syrup mixture, and dredge one side of shrimp in seed mixture. Set shrimp aside, coated sides up.
3. Heat oil in a nonstick skillet coated with cooking spray over medium-high heat. Place shrimp, coated sides down, in pan, and sauté for 3 minutes on each side. Serve the shrimp immediately with the Spicy Black Beans and Saffron Sauce. Yield: 4 servings (serving size: 5 ounces shrimp, ½ cup black beans, and 2 tablespoons sauce).

(Totals include Spicy Black Beans and Saffron Sauce) CALORIES 498 (27% from fat); FAT 15.1g (sat 1.9g, mono 3.4g, poly 7.8g); PROTEIN 39.3g; CARB 54g; FIBER 5.5g; CHOL 195mg; IRON 8mg; SODIUM 587mg; CALC 156mg

SPICY BLACK BEANS:

½ cup water
¼ to ½ teaspoon crushed red pepper
⅛ teaspoon salt
⅛ teaspoon black pepper
1 (15-ounce) can black beans, undrained
1 dried ancho chile (about 1 ounce), seeded
½ teaspoon butter or stick margarine
Cooking spray
⅔ cup chopped onion
1 garlic clove, minced
⅓ cup thinly sliced green onions

1. Combine the first 6 ingredients in a medium saucepan; bring to a boil. Reduce heat; simmer 15 minutes. Discard ancho.
2. Melt the butter in a large nonstick skillet coated with cooking spray over medium-high heat. Add the chopped onion and garlic; sauté 5 minutes or until onion begins to brown. Add onion mixture to bean mixture. Stir in green onions. Yield: 2 cups (serving size: ½ cup).

CALORIES 114 (9% from fat); FAT 1.2g (sat 0.2g, mono 0.2g, poly 0.4g); PROTEIN 6.8g; CARB 20.4g; FIBER 3.8g; CHOL 0mg; IRON 1.8mg; SODIUM 270mg; CALC 34mg

SAFFRON SAUCE:

1 (9-ounce) bottle hot mango chutney
2 tablespoons water
1 tablespoon light mayonnaise
¾ teaspoon saffron threads, crushed

1. Strain chutney through a fine sieve over a bowl to equal 6 tablespoons, discarding solids. Combine chutney liquid with remaining ingredients. Yield: ½ cup (serving size: 2 tablespoons).

CALORIES 72 (6% from fat); FAT 1g (sat 0.2g, mono 0g, poly 0.6g); PROTEIN 0.4g; CARB 16.1g; FIBER 0g; CHOL 1mg; IRON 0.3mg; SODIUM 79mg; CALC 8mg

Crusted Shrimp with Spicy Black
Beans and Saffron Sauce

Coconut Shrimp with Pineapple Salsa

SHRIMP:

28 large shrimp (about 1½ pounds)
⅓ cup cornstarch
¾ teaspoon salt
½ to ¾ teaspoon ground red pepper
3 large egg whites
1½ cups flaked sweetened coconut
Cooking spray

SALSA:

1 cup finely chopped fresh pineapple
⅓ cup finely chopped red onion
¼ cup finely chopped fresh cilantro
¼ cup pineapple preserves
1½ tablespoons fresh lime juice
1 tablespoon finely chopped seeded jalapeño
   pepper
¼ teaspoon black pepper

1. Preheat oven to 400°.

2. To prepare shrimp, peel and devein shrimp, leaving tails intact. Rinse shrimp in cold water; drain on paper towels until dry.

3. Combine cornstarch, salt, and red pepper in a shallow dish; stir with a whisk. Place egg whites in a medium bowl; beat with a mixer at medium-high speed until frothy (about 2 minutes). Place coconut in a shallow dish.

4. Working with 1 shrimp at a time, dredge in cornstarch mixture. Dip in egg white, and dredge in coconut, pressing gently with fingers. Place the shrimp on a baking sheet coated with cooking spray. Repeat procedure with remaining shrimp, cornstarch mixture, egg white, and coconut. Lightly coat the shrimp with cooking spray. Bake at 400° for 20 minutes or until shrimp are done, turning after 10 minutes.

5. To prepare salsa, combine chopped pineapple and remaining ingredients in a medium bowl; stir to combine. Yield: 4 servings (serving size: 7 shrimp and about ¼ cup salsa).

CALORIES 397 (26% from fat); FAT 11.4g (sat 8.4g, mono 0.7g, poly 1g); PROTEIN 29.9g; CARB 45g; FIBER 2.2g; CHOL 194mg; IRON 3.9mg; SODIUM 753mg; CALC 80mg

Spice-Crusted Shrimp with Rémoulade Sauce

SAUCE:

¼ cup low-fat mayonnaise
¼ cup plain fat-free yogurt
1½ tablespoons fresh lime juice
1 teaspoon grated lime rind
1 teaspoon capers, chopped
Dash of ground red pepper

SHRIMP:

2 teaspoons ground cumin
2 teaspoons paprika
1 teaspoon ground coriander
½ teaspoon garlic powder
¼ teaspoon salt
⅛ teaspoon black pepper
48 large shrimp, peeled and deveined
   (about 1½ pounds)
1 tablespoon olive oil, divided
Cilantro sprigs (optional)

1. To prepare sauce, combine first 6 ingredients in a bowl; stir with a whisk.

2. To prepare shrimp, combine cumin and next 5 ingredients. Add shrimp; toss well. Heat 1½ teaspoons oil in a large nonstick skillet over medium-high heat; add half of shrimp. Cook 3 minutes on each side or until done. Remove shrimp; keep warm. Repeat procedure with remaining oil and shrimp. Serve shrimp with sauce. Garnish with cilantro, if desired. Yield: 8 servings (serving size: 6 shrimp and about 1 tablespoon sauce).

CALORIES 100 (28% from fat); FAT 3.1g (sat 0.4g, mono 1.4g, poly 0.5g); PROTEIN 13.7g; CARB 3.7g; FIBER 0.5g; CHOL 121mg; IRON 2.3mg; SODIUM 300mg; CALC 48mg

Grilled-Shrimp and Plum Skewers with Sweet Hoisin Sauce

The ginger gives these kebabs a spicy, peppery bite that's mellowed by the sweet sauce.

12 jumbo shrimp, peeled and deveined (about
     1 pound)
3   plums, quartered
2   tablespoons minced peeled fresh ginger
1   tablespoon olive oil
½   teaspoon kosher salt
½   teaspoon white or black pepper
Sweet Hoisin Sauce
Cooking spray
¼   cup (1½-inch) julienne-cut green onions
     (optional)
1   lime, quartered (optional)

1. Prepare grill.
2. Toss shrimp, plums, ginger, oil, salt, and pepper in a large bowl. Thread 3 shrimp and 3 plum sections alternately onto each of 4 (10-inch) skewers.
3. Spoon ½ cup Sweet Hoisin Sauce into a measuring cup, and place remaining sauce in a serving bowl. Place kebabs on grill rack coated with cooking spray, and cook 4 minutes. Turn kebabs; brush with about ¼ cup sauce. Cook 4 minutes. Turn kebabs, and brush with about ¼ cup sauce. Cook 2 minutes, turning once. Serve remaining ½ cup sauce as a dipping sauce. Garnish with onions and lime wedges, if desired. Yield: 4 servings (serving size: 1 kebab and about 2 tablespoons sauce).

(Totals include Sweet Hoisin Sauce) CALORIES 220 (26% from fat); FAT 6.4g (sat 0.9g, mono 3.2g, poly 1.6g); PROTEIN 18.6g; CARB 21.5g; FIBER 1.5g; CHOL 130mg; IRON 2.6mg; SODIUM 800mg; CALC 60mg

SWEET HOISIN SAUCE:

Hoisin is a blend of soybeans, garlic, chile peppers, and spices; it serves as the base for this Chinese-inspired barbecue sauce. Five-spice powder, also used extensively in Chinese cooking, is a pungent mixture of ground cinnamon, cloves, fennel, star anise, and peppercorns.

⅓   cup bottled hoisin sauce
¼   cup rice vinegar
2   tablespoons sherry
2   tablespoons ketchup
1   tablespoon brown sugar
½   teaspoon five-spice powder

1. Combine all ingredients in a small bowl. Yield: about 1 cup (serving size: 1 tablespoon).

CALORIES 17 (11% from fat); FAT 0.2g (sat 0g, mono 0.1g, poly 0.1g); PROTEIN 0.2g; CARB 3.5g; FIBER 0.2g; CHOL 0mg; IRON 0.1mg; SODIUM 108mg; CALC 3mg

Traditional Spanish Paella

Vibrant in color and flavor, paella has held a place of honor in Spanish homes for centuries. Making it is well worth the effort. Simplify the recipe by preparing ingredients the day before serving; this makes the final dish come together much quicker. To round out the meal, choose a good red wine from Spain's Rioja region, a crusty baguette, and a light salad.

HERB BLEND:
- 1 cup chopped fresh parsley
- ¼ cup fresh lemon juice
- 1 tablespoon olive oil
- 2 large garlic cloves, minced

PAELLA:
- 1 cup water
- 1 teaspoon saffron threads
- 3 (15.75-ounce) cans fat-free, less-sodium chicken broth
- 8 unpeeled jumbo shrimp (about ½ pound)
- 1 tablespoon olive oil
- 4 skinned, boned chicken thighs, cut in half
- 2 links Spanish chorizo sausage (about 6½ ounces) or turkey kielbasa, cut into ½-inch-thick slices
- 1 (4-ounce) slice prosciutto or 33%-less-sodium ham, cut into 1-inch pieces
- 2 cups finely chopped onion
- 1 cup finely chopped red bell pepper
- 1 cup canned diced tomatoes, undrained
- 1 teaspoon sweet paprika
- 3 large garlic cloves, minced
- 3 cups uncooked Arborio rice or other short-grain rice
- 1 cup frozen green peas
- 8 mussels, scrubbed and debearded
- ¼ cup fresh lemon juice
- Lemon wedges (optional)

1. To prepare herb blend, combine first 4 ingredients; set aside.

2. To prepare paella, combine water, saffron, and broth in a large saucepan. Bring to a simmer (do not boil). Keep warm over low heat. Peel and devein shrimp, leaving tails intact; set aside.

3. Heat 1 tablespoon oil in a large paella pan or very large skillet over medium-high heat. Add chicken; sauté 2 minutes on each side. Remove from pan. Add sausage and prosciutto; sauté for 2 minutes. Remove from pan. Add reserved shrimp, and sauté for 2 minutes. Remove from pan. Reduce heat to medium-low. Add onion and bell pepper; sauté 15 minutes, stirring occasionally. Add tomatoes, paprika, and 3 garlic cloves; cook 5 minutes. Add rice; cook for 1 minute, stirring constantly. Stir in herb blend, broth mixture, chicken, sausage mixture, and peas. Bring to a low boil; cook 10 minutes, stirring frequently. Add mussels to pan, nestling them into rice mixture. Cook 5 minutes or until shells open, and discard any unopened shells. Arrange shrimp, heads down, in rice mixture, and cook for 5 minutes or until shrimp are done. Sprinkle with ¼ cup lemon juice. Remove from heat; cover with a towel, and let stand 10 minutes. Serve with lemon wedges, if desired. Yield: 8 servings (serving size: 1½ cups paella, 1 shrimp, and 1 mussel).

CALORIES 521 (23% from fat); FAT 13.3g (sat 3.7g, mono 6.8g, poly 2g); PROTEIN 25.5g; CARB 72.1g; FIBER 3.6g; CHOL 80mg; IRON 6mg; SODIUM 871mg; CALC 60mg

Greek-Style Scampi

Feel free to use fewer garlic cloves if you aren't really a garlic lover.

- 1 teaspoon olive oil
- 5 garlic cloves, minced
- 3 (28-ounce) cans whole tomatoes, drained and coarsely chopped
- ½ cup chopped fresh parsley, divided
- 1¼ pounds large shrimp, peeled and deveined
- 1 cup (4 ounces) crumbled feta cheese
- 2 tablespoons fresh lemon juice
- ¼ teaspoon freshly ground black pepper

1. Preheat oven to 400°.

2. Heat oil in a large Dutch oven over medium heat. Add minced garlic, and sauté 30 seconds. Add tomatoes and ¼ cup parsley; reduce heat, and simmer 10 minutes. Add shrimp; cook for 5 minutes. Pour mixture into a 13 x 9-inch baking dish, and sprinkle with feta cheese. Bake at 400° for 10 minutes. Sprinkle with ¼ cup parsley, lemon juice, and pepper. Yield: 6 servings.

CALORIES 191 (31% from fat); FAT 6.5g (sat 3.2g, mono 1.7g, poly 1g); PROTEIN 19.9g; CARB 14.4g; FIBER 2.1g; CHOL 125mg; IRON 3.8mg; SODIUM 752g; CALC 211mg

Greek-Style Scampi

Bell Pepper-Feta
Pasta Toss, page 127

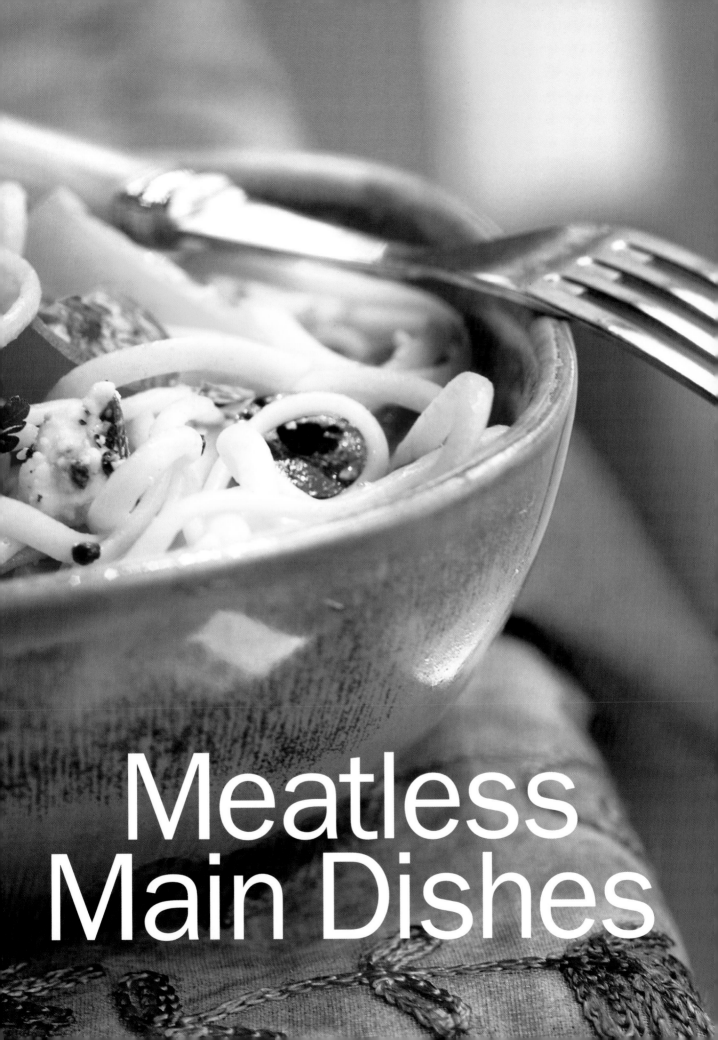

Meatless
Main Dishes

Buttercrust Corn Pie with Fresh-Tomato Salsa

SALSA:
2½ cups chopped tomato
½ cup thinly sliced green onions
2 tablespoons chopped seeded jalapeño pepper
2 tablespoons fresh lemon juice
½ teaspoon salt
½ teaspoon dried oregano
⅛ teaspoon black pepper

PIE:
1¼ cups crushed fat-free saltine crackers (about 35 crackers)
3 tablespoons grated fresh Parmesan cheese
3 tablespoons butter, melted
1 large egg white, lightly beaten
Cooking spray
1¼ cups fat-free milk, divided
2¾ cups fresh corn kernels (about 5 ears)
1 teaspoon sugar
½ teaspoon onion salt
2 tablespoons all-purpose flour
½ cup thinly sliced green onions
3 tablespoons chopped ripe olives
2 large egg whites, lightly beaten
1 large egg, lightly beaten
⅛ teaspoon paprika

1. Preheat oven to 400°.
2. To prepare salsa, combine first 7 ingredients in a medium bowl.
3. To prepare pie, combine crackers, cheese, butter, and 1 egg white in a medium bowl. Toss with a fork until moist; reserve 2 tablespoons. Press remaining cracker mixture into bottom and up sides of a 9-inch pie plate coated with cooking spray. Bake at 400° for 5 minutes; cool on a wire rack.
4. Combine 1 cup milk, corn, sugar, and onion salt in a medium saucepan. Bring to a boil over medium heat. Reduce heat; simmer 3 minutes. Combine ¼ cup milk and flour in a small bowl; gradually add to corn mixture. Cook until thick (about 1 minute), and remove from heat. Stir in ½ cup onions and olives. Combine 2 egg whites and egg in a small bowl; gradually add to corn mixture. Pour into prepared crust; sprinkle with reserved 2 tablespoons cracker mixture and paprika.
5. Bake at 400° for 20 minutes or until set. Yield: 6 servings (serving size: 1 wedge and ½ cup salsa).

CALORIES 277 (30% from fat); FAT 9.6g (sat 4.8g, mono 3g, poly 0.9g); PROTEIN 11.1g; CARB 40.2g; FIBER 3.9g; CHOL 54mg; IRON 2.3mg; SODIUM 758mg; CALC 140mg

Hollandaise-Asparagus Tart

The crust for the Hollandaise-Asparagus Tart may be baked, cooled, and stored in an airtight container a day ahead.

CRUST:
1 cup all-purpose flour
2 tablespoons sugar
3 tablespoons vegetable shortening
3½ tablespoons ice water
Cooking spray

FILLING:
1 pound asparagus spears, trimmed
⅔ cup evaporated fat-free milk
½ teaspoon grated lemon rind
2 tablespoons fresh lemon juice
½ teaspoon dried tarragon
¼ teaspoon salt
1 large egg
1 large egg white
½ cup (2 ounces) grated fresh Parmesan cheese

1. Preheat oven to 450°.
2. To prepare crust, lightly spoon flour into a dry measuring cup, and level with a knife. Place flour and sugar in a food processor, and pulse 3 times or until combined. Add shortening, and pulse 6 times or until mixture resembles coarse meal. With the processor on, add ice water through food chute, processing just until combined. Gently press mixture into a 6-inch circle on a lightly floured surface, and roll dough into a 12-inch circle. Fit dough into a 9-inch pie plate coated with cooking spray; fold edges under, and flute. Pierce bottom and sides of dough with a fork, and bake at 450° for 10 minutes or until crust is lightly browned. Cool crust on a wire rack.
3. Reduce oven temperature to 375°.
4. To prepare filling, snap off tough ends of asparagus. Steam asparagus, covered, for 3 minutes or until crisp-tender. Rinse asparagus under cold water; drain well. Arrange asparagus spokelike in prepared crust with the tips toward inside of crust. Combine milk, lemon rind, lemon juice, tarragon, salt, egg, and egg white; stir well with a whisk. Pour over asparagus; sprinkle with cheese. Bake at 375° for 30 minutes or until puffy and lightly browned. Serve warm. Yield: 6 servings.

CALORIES 212 (33% from fat); FAT 7.9g (sat 2.4g, mono 3g, poly 1.7g); PROTEIN 9.5g; CARB 26.2g; FIBER 1g; CHOL 41mg; IRON 1.6mg; SODIUM 240mg; CALC 158mg

Florentine Frittata

2 tablespoons water
½ teaspoon dried basil
½ teaspoon freshly ground
  black pepper
¼ teaspoon salt
¼ teaspoon dried oregano
1 (16-ounce) carton egg substitute
1 (10-ounce) package frozen chopped spinach,
  thawed, drained, and squeezed dry
2 teaspoons butter
2 cups thinly sliced Vidalia or other
  sweet onion
2 cups frozen shredded hash brown potatoes
1 (7-ounce) bottle roasted red bell peppers,
  drained and sliced
¾ cup (3 ounces) crumbled feta cheese

1. Combine first 7 ingredients in a medium bowl; set aside.

2. Melt butter in a 10-inch cast-iron or nonstick skillet over medium heat. Add onion; sauté 5 minutes. Add hash brown potatoes; cook 9 minutes or until lightly browned, stirring occasionally. Pour egg mixture over onion mixture. Arrange roasted bell pepper slices on top of frittata. Cook 7 minutes or until set.

3. Preheat broiler.

4. Sprinkle frittata with cheese. Wrap handle of pan with foil. Broil frittata 5 minutes or until cheese is lightly browned (feta will not melt). Cut into 4 wedges. Yield: 4 servings (serving size: 1 wedge).

CALORIES 265 (26% from fat); FAT 7.6g (sat 4.6g, mono 1.6g, poly 0.7g); PROTEIN 19.6g; CARB 31.3g; FIBER 5.7g; CHOL 24mg; IRON 5.1mg; SODIUM 800mg; CALC 251mg

Cheese Soufflé with Fresh Corn

This soufflé is fairly easy to make and can be ready for the oven sooner than you might think. The pureed ingredients give it a rich, creamy consistency.

1½ cups fresh corn kernels (about 3 ears)
 1 cup fat-free milk
 ½ cup all-purpose flour
 ½ cup fat-free cottage cheese
 ½ teaspoon salt
 ¼ teaspoon ground red pepper
 ⅛ teaspoon ground nutmeg
 2 large egg yolks
 1 cup (4 ounces) shredded reduced-fat extrasharp cheddar cheese
 4 large egg whites
 ½ teaspoon cream of tartar
 Cooking spray

1. Preheat oven to 400°.
2. Place first 8 ingredients in a food processor or blender, and process until blended, scraping sides of bowl once. Add the cheddar cheese, and pulse 2 times or until well blended. Spoon corn mixture into a large bowl.
3. Beat the egg whites and cream of tartar at high speed of a mixer until stiff peaks form. Stir one-fourth of egg white mixture into corn mixture, and gently fold in remaining egg white mixture. Pour mixture into a 2½-quart soufflé dish coated with cooking spray.
4. Place soufflé in a 400° oven; immediately reduce oven temperature to 375°, and bake 45 minutes or until puffy and golden. Yield: 6 servings (serving size: 1 cup).

CALORIES 187 (29% from fat); FAT 6.1g (sat 2.8g, mono 1.8g, poly 0.6g); PROTEIN 14.9g; CARB 19.1g; FIBER 1.5g; CHOL 87mg; IRON 1mg; SODIUM 467mg; CALC 239mg

Spinach, Caramelized-Onion, and Feta Quiche

To decrease fat without sacrificing creaminess, we've used two egg yolks and five egg whites in the filling. You can refrigerate the leftover yolks for up to three days in an airtight container (add a tablespoon of water so the yolks don't develop a film).

 2 teaspoons olive oil
 3 cups chopped onion
 1 teaspoon sugar
 ½ teaspoon salt
 2 cups frozen Southern-style hash brown potatoes, thawed
 1 (11-ounce) can refrigerated soft breadstick dough (such as Pillsbury)
 Cooking spray
 1 (10-ounce) package frozen chopped spinach, thawed, drained, and squeezed dry
 1 cup fat-free milk
 5 large egg whites
 2 large egg yolks
1¼ cups (5 ounces) crumbled feta cheese

1. Heat oil in a large nonstick skillet over medium heat. Add onion, sugar, and salt; cook for 30 minutes or until golden brown, stirring occasionally. Stir in potatoes; cook for 5 minutes or until lightly browned. Remove from heat.
2. Preheat oven to 350°.
3. Unroll dough, separating into strips. Working on a flat surface, coil one strip of dough around itself in a spiral pattern. Add second strip of dough to the end of the first strip; pinch ends together to seal. Continue coiling the dough. Repeat procedure with the remaining dough strips. Cover and let the dough rest for 10 minutes. Roll the dough into a 12-inch circle; fit into a 10-inch deep-dish pie plate coated with cooking spray.
4. Spread potato mixture in bottom of prepared crust, and top with chopped spinach. Combine the milk, egg whites, egg yolks, and feta cheese; pour milk mixture over spinach. Bake at 350° for 1 hour or until quiche is set, shielding crust with foil after 50 minutes. Let stand for 10 minutes before serving. Yield: 8 servings.
NOTE: If Southern-style hash browns are not available in your supermarket's freezer section, you can substitute any frozen hash browns.

CALORIES 262 (29% from fat); FAT 8.4g (sat 3.7g, mono 2.8g, poly 1.3g); PROTEIN 11.7g; CARB 35.3g; FIBER 2.4g; CHOL 72mg; IRON 2.5mg; SODIUM 713mg; CALC 188mg

Spinach, Caramelized-Onion, and
Feta Quiche

Onion Bread Pudding

The nutty flavor of Gruyère pairs nicely with the sweet onion. Or you can substitute fontina or Monterey Jack.

1 Vidalia or other sweet onion, cut into ¼-inch slices
2 cups 2% reduced-fat milk
½ teaspoon salt
½ teaspoon dried thyme
⅛ teaspoon freshly ground black pepper
2 large eggs, lightly beaten
8 cups cubed French bread (about 8 ounces)
¾ cup (3 ounces) shredded Gruyère cheese, divided
Cooking spray

1. Preheat oven to 425°.

2. Heat a large nonstick skillet over medium-high heat. Add onion slices (keep slices intact); cook 3 minutes on each side or until browned.

3. Combine milk, salt, thyme, pepper, and eggs in a large bowl, stirring with a whisk. Add bread cubes and ½ cup cheese; toss well. Place bread mixture in an 8-inch square baking dish coated with cooking spray. Arrange onion slices on top of bread mixture. Sprinkle with ¼ cup cheese. Bake at 425° for 25 minutes or until set and golden. Yield: 4 servings (serving size: about 1½ cups).

CALORIES 364 (30% from fat); FAT 12.2g (sat 5.7g, mono 3.7g, poly 1.1g); PROTEIN 19.7g; CARB 43.8g; FIBER 3.4g; CHOL 136mg; IRON 2.1mg; SODIUM 806mg; CALC 294mg

Double-Mushroom Bread Pudding

3 cups fat-free milk,
  divided
8 cups (2-inch) cubed country or
  peasant bread (about 12 ounces)
2 (4-ounce) portobello
  mushrooms
2 teaspoons vegetable oil
6 cups quartered cremini mushrooms
  (about 12 ounces)
½ cup chopped fresh parsley
2 teaspoons chopped fresh or
  ½ teaspoon dried rosemary
¼ teaspoon salt
¼ teaspoon black pepper
1 garlic clove, minced
3 large eggs
1 large egg white
Cooking spray
1 cup (4 ounces) shredded
  Gruyère cheese, divided

1. Combine 2 cups milk and bread. Cover and chill for 30 minutes, stirring occasionally. Remove brown gills from the undersides of portobello mushrooms using a spoon, and discard gills and stems. Cut mushroom caps in half, and cut halves crosswise into ½-inch slices.

2. Preheat oven to 375°.

3. Heat oil in a large nonstick skillet over medium-high heat. Add portobello and cremini mushrooms, and sauté 4 minutes. Stir in parsley, rosemary, salt, pepper, and garlic; sauté 1 minute.

4. Combine 1 cup milk, eggs, and egg white, and stir with a whisk. Spoon 2 cups bread mixture into a 2-quart casserole coated with cooking spray. Top with the mushroom mixture; sprinkle with ⅓ cup cheese. Top with the remaining bread mixture and ⅔ cup cheese. Pour egg mixture over top. Bake at 375° for 45 minutes or until set. Yield: 6 servings.

CALORIES 368 (30% from fat); FAT 12.1g (sat 5.2g, mono 4g, poly 2.2g); PROTEIN 20.9g; CARB 42.8g; FIBER 2.8g; CHOL 135mg; IRON 3.2mg; SODIUM 602mg; CALC 394mg

Mushroom and Caramelized-Shallot Strudel

This recipe makes two strudels. For an eye-catching centerpiece, place them on a large platter, and surround them with fresh thyme sprigs.

   1   teaspoon olive oil
1½   cups sliced shallots (about 8 ounces)
   ⅛   teaspoon sugar
   1   tablespoon water
   4   (8-ounce) packages presliced mushrooms
   2   tablespoons dry Marsala or Madeira
   ⅔   cup low-fat sour cream
   ¼   cup chopped fresh parsley
   ½   teaspoon salt
   ½   teaspoon minced fresh thyme
   ¼   teaspoon freshly ground black pepper
   8   sheets frozen phyllo dough, thawed
      Cooking spray
   ⅓   cup dry breadcrumbs, divided
   1   tablespoon butter, melted

1. Preheat oven to 400°.
2. Heat olive oil in a large skillet over medium heat. Add shallots and sugar; cook for 2 minutes, stirring constantly. Sprinkle with water; cover, reduce heat to medium-low, and cook for 10 minutes, stirring occasionally until shallots are soft. Add mushrooms; cook, uncovered, over medium-high heat 20 minutes or until liquid evaporates, stirring frequently. Add Marsala; cook 1 minute. Remove from heat; cool. Stir in sour cream, parsley, salt, thyme, and pepper.
3. Place 1 phyllo sheet on a large cutting board or work surface (cover remaining dough to keep from drying), and lightly coat with cooking spray. Sprinkle with about 2 teaspoons breadcrumbs. Repeat layers with 3 phyllo sheets, cooking spray, and breadcrumbs, ending with phyllo. Spoon 1¾ cups mushroom mixture along 1 long edge of phyllo, leaving a 1-inch border. Starting at the long edge with the 1-inch border, roll up jelly-roll fashion. Place strudel, seam side down, on a baking sheet coated with cooking spray. Tuck ends under. Repeat procedure with remaining phyllo sheets, cooking spray, breadcrumbs, and mushroom mixture. Brush strudels with butter; bake at 400° for 20 minutes. Let stand 5 minutes. Cut each strudel into 4 slices. Yield: 2 strudels, 8 servings (serving size: 1 slice).

CALORIES 176 (28% from fat); FAT 5.5g (sat 2.7g, mono 1.6g, poly 0.5g); PROTEIN 7.4g; CARB 24.9g; FIBER 2.1g; CHOL 11mg; IRON 2.6mg; SODIUM 314mg; CALC 60mg

Pear and Roquefort Strata

Other cheeses, such as Gouda or Gruyère, could stand in for the Roquefort.

      Cooking spray
   10   (1¾-ounce) slices sturdy white bread
   2   cups Riesling or other slightly sweet white wine
   ¼   teaspoon salt
   ¼   teaspoon black pepper
1½   cups (6 ounces) crumbled Roquefort or other blue cheese
   3   Bartlett pears, peeled, cored, and cut lengthwise into ¼-inch-thick slices (about 4 cups)
   3   cups fat-free milk
   4   large eggs

1. Coat a 13 x 9-inch baking dish with cooking spray. Arrange 5 bread slices in bottom of dish in a single layer. Pour 1 cup wine over bread. Sprinkle with ⅛ teaspoon salt and ⅛ teaspoon pepper. Top with ¾ cup cheese. Arrange the pear slices over cheese; top with remaining bread, wine, salt, pepper, and cheese.
2. Combine milk and eggs in a bowl; stir well with a whisk. Pour milk mixture over bread mixture. Let stand 20 minutes.
3. Preheat oven to 425°.
4. Cover and bake at 425° for 30 minutes. Uncover and bake an additional 25 minutes or until golden. Let stand 10 minutes. Yield: 10 servings (serving size: 1 piece).

CALORIES 319 (30% from fat); FAT 10.6g (sat 4g, mono 3.3g, poly 0.6g); PROTEIN 13g; CARB 40.6g; FIBER 1.6g; CHOL 102mg; IRON 2.2mg; SODIUM 701mg; CALC 264mg

Pear and Roquefort Strata

Fresh Tomato and Zucchini Tart with Mozzarella and Basil

Fresh Tomato and Zucchini Tart with Mozzarella and Basil

1 tablespoon yellow cornmeal
1 (10-ounce) can refrigerated pizza crust dough
1 cup (⅛-inch-thick) diagonally sliced zucchini
4 plum tomatoes, seeded and cut into ¼-inch-thick slices (about ½ pound)
¼ teaspoon kosher salt
¼ teaspoon freshly ground black pepper
4 ounces fresh mozzarella cheese, sliced
1 teaspoon extravirgin olive oil
½ cup torn fresh basil leaves

1. Preheat oven to 400°.
2. Line a baking sheet with parchment paper; secure with masking tape. Sprinkle paper with cornmeal. Unroll dough onto paper; let stand 5 minutes. Pat dough into a 12-inch square. Arrange zucchini and tomato over dough, leaving a 1-inch border. Sprinkle evenly with salt and pepper. Fold edges of dough over zucchini and tomato (dough won't completely cover zucchini and tomato).
3. Bake at 400° for 15 minutes or until dough is lightly browned. Top with cheese; bake 5 minutes or until cheese melts. Drizzle with oil; sprinkle with basil. Cool on baking sheet 10 minutes on a wire rack. Yield: 4 servings.

CALORIES 304 (30% from fat); FAT 10.1g (sat 4.3g, mono 3.8g, poly 1.4g); PROTEIN 12.9g; CARB 40.1g; FIBER 2.5g; CHOL 22mg; IRON 2.5mg; SODIUM 702mg; CALC 164mg

Roasted-Onion Tart with Maytag Blue Cheese

Using a touch of honey yields supersweet, buttery-soft roasted garlic, onions, and shallots that contrast well with the pungent cheese. If you're not a fan of blue cheese, try goat cheese, feta, or another sharp-flavored cheese.

1 medium Vidalia or other sweet onion, peeled
10 shallots, peeled and halved (about ½ pound)
10 large garlic cloves, peeled and halved
3 tablespoons balsamic vinegar
1 tablespoon butter, melted
2 teaspoons honey
¼ teaspoon dried thyme
1 tablespoon yellow cornmeal
1 (10-ounce) can refrigerated pizza crust dough
¼ teaspoon kosher salt
½ teaspoon freshly ground black pepper
⅔ cup (about 2½ ounces) crumbled Maytag blue cheese
1 tablespoon chopped fresh parsley

1. Preheat oven to 425°.
2. Cut onion into 8 wedges, leaving root intact. Place the onion wedges, shallot halves, and garlic halves in a 13 x 9-inch baking dish. Combine balsamic vinegar, butter, honey, and dried thyme in a small bowl; drizzle over onion mixture, tossing to coat. Bake at 425° for 30 minutes or until tender, stirring occasionally.
3. Line a baking sheet with parchment paper, and secure with masking tape. Sprinkle the paper with cornmeal. Unroll dough onto paper; let stand 5 minutes. Pat dough into a 14 x 12-inch rectangle. Arrange onion mixture over dough, leaving a 1-inch border. Sprinkle evenly with salt and pepper. Fold edges of dough over onion mixture (dough will not completely cover onion mixture). Sprinkle with cheese.
4. Bake at 425° for 15 minutes or until lightly browned. Cool on baking sheet 10 minutes on a wire rack. Sprinkle with parsley. Yield: 4 servings.

CALORIES 358 (28% from fat); FAT 11.1g (sat 5.7g, mono 3.4g, poly 1.3g); PROTEIN 12.6g; CARB 51.9g; FIBER 2.9g; CHOL 22mg; IRON 2.8mg; SODIUM 892mg; CALC 145mg

Tomato, Basil, and Parmesan Flatbreads

Flatbread Dough
- 2 yellow tomatoes, each cut in half and thinly sliced crosswise (about 8 ounces)
- 3 cups thinly sliced plum tomato (about 8 ounces)
- ½ cup minced fresh basil
- 4 teaspoons olive oil
- ¼ teaspoon salt
- ⅛ teaspoon black pepper
- 4 garlic cloves, minced
- 1 cup (4 ounces) grated fresh Parmesan cheese

1. Prepare Flatbread Dough; let rise, and shape into 4 ovals on baking sheets as directed. Cover.

2. Preheat oven to 475°.

3. Divide the tomatoes evenly among 4 flatbread dough ovals. Bake at 475° for 13 minutes. Combine basil and next 4 ingredients in a small bowl; spread evenly over tomatoes. Sprinkle evenly with cheese. Bake at 475° for 2 minutes or until cheese melts. Yield: 4 servings (serving size: 1 flatbread).

(Totals include Flatbread Dough) CALORIES 497 (29% from fat); FAT 15.8g (sat 5.8g, mono 7.4g, poly 1.4g); PROTEIN 20.2g; CARB 69.1g; FIBER 4.8g; CHOL 19mg; IRON 4.9mg; SODIUM 911mg; CALC 370mg

FLATBREAD DOUGH:

- 1 cup boiling water
- ⅓ cup yellow cornmeal
- 1 package dry yeast (about 2¼ teaspoons)
- ¼ cup warm water (100° to 110°)
- 2 cups all-purpose flour
- ½ teaspoon salt
- 2 teaspoons olive oil
- Cooking spray
- 1 tablespoon yellow cornmeal, divided

1. Combine boiling water and ⅓ cup cornmeal in a bowl; let stand 20 minutes, stirring occasionally. Dissolve yeast in warm water in a small bowl, and let stand 5 minutes. Lightly spoon flour into dry measuring cups, and level with a knife. Combine cornmeal mixture, flour, and salt in a food processor, and pulse 4 times or until blended. With processor on, slowly add yeast mixture and oil through food chute; process until dough forms a ball. Process 1 additional minute. (To prepare dough by hand, combine the cornmeal mixture, flour, and salt in a bowl, and stir until well blended. Add yeast mixture and oil, stirring well.) Turn dough out onto a floured surface, and knead lightly 4 or 5 times (dough will feel sticky).

2. Place the dough in a bowl coated with cooking spray, turning to coat top. Cover, and let rise in a warm place (85°), free from drafts, 1 hour or until doubled in size. (Press two fingers into dough. If indentation remains, the dough has risen enough.)

3. Punch dough down; cover and let rest 5 minutes. Divide the dough into 4 equal portions, shaping each into a ball (cover remaining dough to prevent it from drying).

4. Roll each ball into a 10 x 6-inch oval. Place 2 ovals on a baking sheet lightly dusted with 1½ teaspoons cornmeal. Repeat procedure with remaining 2 ovals on an additional baking sheet lightly dusted with 1½ teaspoons cornmeal. Add toppings and bake according to recipe directions. Yield: 4 servings (serving size: 1 flatbread).

NOTE: If you use whole-grain cornmeal, which still contains some of the hull and germ of the dried corn kernel, increase the flour to 2¼ cups.

CALORIES 304 (10% from fat); FAT 3.3g (sat 0.4g, mono 1.8g, poly 0.5g); PROTEIN 8.3g; CARB 59g; FIBER 2.9g; CHOL 0mg; IRON 3.8mg; SODIUM 295mg;

Caramelized-Onion Pizza with Gorgonzola and Arugula

You can substitute blue cheese or feta for the Gorgonzola.

2 teaspoons olive oil
12 cups thinly sliced onion (about 3 pounds)
2 teaspoons chopped fresh or ½ teaspoon dried rosemary, divided
½ teaspoon salt
¼ teaspoon black pepper
½ recipe Whole-Wheat Pizza Dough (recipe on page 121)
Cooking spray
1 tablespoon yellow cornmeal
½ cup (2 ounces) crumbled Gorgonzola
2 tablespoons coarsely chopped walnuts
1 cup trimmed arugula

1. Heat oil in a cast-iron or nonstick skillet over medium-high heat. Add onion, and sauté for 5 minutes, stirring frequently. Stir in 1 teaspoon rosemary, salt, and pepper. Continue cooking 15 to 20 minutes or until onion is a deep golden brown, stirring frequently.

2. Preheat oven to 500°.

3. Roll the dough into a 12-inch circle on a lightly floured surface. Place the dough on a 12-inch pizza pan or baking sheet coated with cooking spray and sprinkled with cornmeal. Crimp the edges of dough with fingers to form a rim. Top with onion mixture. Bake at 500° for 10 minutes. Add cheese and walnuts; bake an additional 3 minutes or until cheese melts. Remove from oven, and top with 1 teaspoon rosemary and arugula. Cut the pizza into 4 wedges. Yield: 4 servings (serving size: 1 wedge).

(Totals include half-recipe of Whole-Wheat Pizza Dough) CALORIES 449 (24% from fat); FAT 11.8g (sat 3.6g, mono 4.7g, poly 2.6g); PROTEIN 14.8g; CARB 73.8g; FIBER 10.1g; CHOL 11mg; IRON 3.7mg; SODIUM 944mg; CALC 172mg

Whole-Wheat Pizza Dough

- 1 package dry yeast (about 2¼ teaspoons)
- ¼ teaspoon sugar
- 1½ cups warm water (100° to 110°)
- 2½ to 2¾ cups all-purpose flour, divided
- 1 cup whole-wheat flour
- 1 tablespoon olive oil
- 1½ teaspoons salt
- Cooking spray

1. Dissolve yeast and sugar in warm water in a large bowl; let stand 5 minutes. Lightly spoon flours into dry measuring cups, and level with a knife. Add 2¼ cups all-purpose flour, whole-wheat flour, oil, and salt to yeast mixture, stirring until well blended. Turn dough out onto a floured surface. Knead until smooth and elastic (about 10 minutes); add enough of the remaining flour, 1 tablespoon at a time, to prevent the dough from sticking to hands (dough will feel sticky).

2. Place dough in a large bowl coated with cooking spray, turning to coat top. Cover and let rise in a warm place (85°), free from drafts, for 45 minutes or until doubled in size. (Press two fingers into the dough. If indentation remains, the dough has risen enough.) Punch dough down; cover and let rest 5 minutes. Divide dough in half; roll each half into a 12-inch circle on a floured surface. Top and bake according to recipe directions. Yield: 2 (12-inch) pizza crusts.

NOTE: This dough may be frozen. Follow directions for kneading dough, and shape dough into 2 balls. Coat balls with cooking spray and place into a zip-top plastic freezer bag; freeze. Thaw the dough overnight in the refrigerator. Cover and let rise in a warm place (85°), free from drafts, for 1½ hours or until doubled in size. (Press two fingers into dough. If indentation remains, the dough has risen enough.) Shape as instructed.

(Totals are for 1 [12-inch] pizza crust) CALORIES 847 (11% from fat); FAT 9.9g (sat 1.4g, mono 5.4g, poly 1.9g); PROTEIN 25.7g; CARB 164.6g; FIBER 12.7g; CHOL 0mg; IRON 10.2mg; SODIUM 1,764mg; CALC 47mg

PLAIN PIZZA DOUGH VARIATION:

Whole-wheat flour may be omitted; replace it with 1 cup all-purpose flour.

(Totals are for 1 [12-inch] pizza crust) CALORIES 871 (10% from fat); FAT 9.4g (sat 1.3g, mono 5.3g, poly 1.7g); PROTEIN 23.9g; CARB 168.8g; FIBER 6.9g; CHOL 0mg; IRON 10.8mg; SODIUM 1,762mg; CALC 36mg

Leek, Ricotta, and Walnut Pizza

Leeks and ricotta share a natural sweetness that contrasts with the richness of toasted walnuts. You can also use pine nuts or pecans.

- ½ recipe Plain Pizza Dough Variation
- Cooking spray
- 1 tablespoon cornmeal
- 1 teaspoon olive oil
- 4 cups thinly sliced leek (about 3 large)
- ½ cup part-skim ricotta cheese
- ¼ cup (1 ounce) grated fresh Parmesan cheese
- ¼ teaspoon salt
- ¼ teaspoon black pepper
- 1 garlic clove, minced
- 2 tablespoons coarsely chopped walnuts

1. Preheat oven to 450°.

2. Roll dough into a 12-inch circle on a lightly floured surface. Place dough on a 12-inch pizza pan or baking sheet coated with cooking spray and sprinkled with cornmeal. Crimp edges of dough with fingers to form a rim.

3. Heat oil in a large nonstick skillet over medium heat. Add leek; sauté 10 minutes. Cool to room temperature.

4. Combine cheeses, salt, pepper, and garlic in a bowl. Spread cheese mixture over dough, leaving a 1-inch border. Top with leek mixture; sprinkle with walnuts. Bake at 450° for 15 minutes or until lightly browned. Cut into 8 wedges. Yield: 4 servings (serving size: 2 wedges).

(Totals include half-recipe of Plain Pizza Dough) CALORIES 359 (26% from fat); FAT 10.3g (sat 3.4g, mono 3.7g, poly 2.5g); PROTEIN 13.4g; CARB 53.6g; FIBER 3.5g; CHOL 14mg; IRON 4.6mg; SODIUM 611mg; CALC 234mg

Smoked Gouda Macaroni and Cheese

This American classic has been updated here for heightened flavor. You can use regular Gouda, Swiss, or any other cheese that melts well.

1 (1-ounce) slice whole-wheat bread
1 tablespoon butter
¼ cup thinly sliced green onions
2 garlic cloves, minced
2 tablespoons all-purpose flour
2 cups fat-free milk
½ teaspoon salt
¼ teaspoon black pepper
½ cup (2 ounces) shredded smoked Gouda cheese
⅓ cup (about 1½ ounces) grated fresh Parmesan cheese
5 cups coarsely chopped fresh spinach
4 cups hot cooked elbow macaroni (about 2 cups uncooked)
Cooking spray

1. Preheat oven to 350°.

2. Place bread in a food processor; pulse 10 times or until coarse crumbs measure ½ cup.

3. Melt butter in a large saucepan over medium heat. Add sliced onions and minced garlic, and cook 1 minute. Add flour; cook 1 minute, stirring constantly. Gradually add milk, salt, and pepper, stirring constantly with a whisk until blended. Bring to a boil, and cook until thick (about 2 minutes). Remove from heat, and add cheeses, stirring until melted.

4. Add spinach and macaroni to cheese sauce, stirring until well blended. Spoon mixture into a 2-quart baking dish coated with cooking spray. Sprinkle with breadcrumbs. Bake at 350° for 15 minutes or until bubbly. Yield: 4 servings (serving size: 1¼ cups).

CALORIES 399 (25% from fat); FAT 10.9g (sat 6.2g, mono 3g, poly 0.8g); PROTEIN 20.1g; CARB 54.9g; FIBER 3.7g; CHOL 33mg; IRON 3.6mg; SODIUM 725mg; CALC 421mg

Cavatappi With Spinach, Beans, and Asiago Cheese

The warm cavatappi slightly wilts the spinach and softens the cheese during tossing.

    8   cups coarsely chopped spinach
    4   cups hot cooked cavatappi (about 6 ounces
        uncooked spiral-shaped pasta)
    2   tablespoons olive oil
    ¼   teaspoon salt
    ¼   teaspoon black pepper
    1   (19-ounce) can cannellini beans or other
        white beans, drained
    2   garlic cloves, crushed
    ½   cup (2 ounces) shredded Asiago cheese
  Freshly ground black pepper (optional)

1. Combine first 8 ingredients in a large bowl; toss well. Sprinkle with freshly ground black pepper, if desired. Yield: 4 servings (serving size: 2 cups).

CALORIES 401 (27% from fat); FAT 12g (sat 3.4g, mono 6.2g, poly 1.2g); PROTEIN 18.8g; CARB 54.7g; FIBER 6.7g; CHOL 10mg; IRON 6.4mg; SODIUM 464mg; CALC 306mg

Penne with Roasted-Pepper Marinara Sauce

      Cooking spray
  1½ cups finely chopped onion
    4 garlic cloves, minced
    2 cups coarsely chopped bottled roasted red
       bell peppers
    1 tablespoon dried basil
    ¾ teaspoon sugar
    ¼ teaspoon crushed red pepper
    ¼ teaspoon salt
    2 (14.5-ounce) cans diced tomatoes, undrained
    2 tablespoons extravirgin olive oil
    6 cups hot cooked penne (about 3 cups
       uncooked tube shaped pasta)

1. Heat a large nonstick skillet coated with cooking spray over medium-high heat. Add onion and garlic; sauté for 6 minutes or until tender. Add bell peppers and the next 5 ingredients, and bring to a boil.
2. Reduce heat, and simmer for 20 minutes, stirring occasionally. Remove from heat; stir in oil. Serve over pasta. Yield: 6 servings (serving size: ¾ cup sauce and 1 cup pasta).

CALORIES 315 (18% from fat); FAT 6.4g (sat 0.9g, mono 3.6g, poly 1.4g); PROTEIN 9.6g; CARB 55.9g; FIBER 3.7g; CHOL 0mg; IRON 3.6mg; SODIUM 330mg; CALC 76mg

Fettuccine with Cashew Cream

Delicious, easy, and fast—and much better for you than a creamy sauce like Alfredo. Cashew cream (a mixture of water and cashew nut butter) replaces the traditional heavy cream in this recipe, with no loss of richness and an improved fat profile.

    ½   cup roasted cashews
  1¼   cups water
      Cooking spray
    3   garlic cloves, minced
    4   cups hot cooked fettuccine (about 8 ounces
        uncooked pasta)
    ¼   cup (1 ounce) grated fresh Parmesan
        cheese
    ¼   teaspoon freshly ground black pepper
    ⅛   teaspoon salt

1. Place cashews in a food processor, and process until smooth (about 2 minutes), scraping sides of bowl once. With processor on, slowly pour water through food chute; process until smooth, scraping sides of bowl once.
2. Place cashew cream in a small saucepan over medium-high heat. Bring to a boil, stirring occasionally with a whisk. Reduce heat, and simmer 1 minute or until cream is thick.
3. Heat a large nonstick skillet coated with cooking spray over medium-high heat. Add garlic; sauté 30 seconds. Stir in cashew cream, pasta, cheese, pepper, and salt; cook until thoroughly heated. Yield: 4 servings (serving size: about 1⅓ cups).

CALORIES 378 (35% from fat); FAT 14.7g (sat 3.6g, mono 7g, poly 1.9g); PROTEIN 14.7g; CARB 51g; FIBER 2.7g; CHOL 6mg; IRON 3.5mg; SODIUM 388mg; CALC 128mg

125

Eggplant Parmesan Lasagna

2 large egg whites
1 large egg
1 (1-pound) eggplant, cut crosswise into
   ¼-inch-thick slices
3 tablespoons all-purpose flour
1 cup Italian-seasoned breadcrumbs
Cooking spray
2 cups (8 ounces) shredded part-skim
   mozzarella cheese, divided
5 tablespoons (1¼ ounces) grated fresh
   Parmesan cheese, divided
1 teaspoon dried oregano
1 teaspoon dried basil
1 (15-ounce) carton part-skim ricotta cheese
1 (12-ounce) carton 1% low-fat cottage cheese
1 large egg white
1 (26-ounce) bottle fat-free tomato-basil pasta
   sauce
12 cooked lasagna noodles

1. Preheat oven to 450°.
2. Combine 2 egg whites and egg in a small bowl, stirring with a whisk. Dredge 1 eggplant slice in flour. Dip in egg mixture; dredge in breadcrumbs. Repeat procedure with remaining eggplant, flour, egg mixture, and breadcrumbs. Place slices in a single layer on a baking sheet coated with cooking spray. Coat tops of slices with cooking spray. Bake at 450° for 20 minutes, turning eggplant after 10 minutes. Remove from baking sheet; cool. Reduce oven temperature to 375°.
3. Combine 1 cup shredded mozzarella, 3 tablespoons Parmesan, oregano, basil, ricotta, cottage cheese, and 1 egg white in a large bowl.
4. Spread ¼ cup pasta sauce in the bottom of a 13 x 9-inch baking dish coated with cooking spray. Arrange 4 lasagna noodles over pasta sauce (noodles should overlap slightly); top with half of cheese mixture, half of eggplant slices, and ¾ cup pasta sauce. Repeat layers, ending with noodles. Spread remaining pasta sauce over noodles. Sprinkle with 1 cup mozzarella and 2 tablespoons Parmesan. Cover and bake at 375° for 15 minutes. Uncover and bake an additional 35 minutes or until cheeses melt. Let stand 5 minutes. Yield: 9 servings.

CALORIES 432 (23% from fat); FAT 11g (sat 6.2g, mono 3.1g, poly 0.9g); PROTEIN 28.3g; CARB 53.8g; FIBER 3.7g; CHOL 58mg; IRON 3.2mg; SODIUM 976mg; CALC 460mg

Vegetable Lasagna

For easy cleanup, you can assemble in a disposable 8-inch aluminum-foil pan. Make it ahead and deliver to a friend uncooked with baking instructions.

1 teaspoon olive oil
¾ cup sliced mushrooms
¾ cup chopped zucchini
½ cup sliced carrot
½ cup chopped red bell pepper
½ cup thinly sliced red onion
1 (26-ounce) bottle fat-free tomato
   basil pasta sauce
2 tablespoons commercial pesto
1 (15-ounce) carton part-skim ricotta cheese
Cooking spray
6 hot cooked lasagna noodles (about 6 ounces
   uncooked), cut in half
¾ cup (3 ounces) shredded part-skim mozzarella
   cheese
Basil leaves (optional)

1. Preheat oven to 375°.
2. Heat oil in a medium saucepan over medium heat. Add mushrooms and next 4 ingredients; cook for 5 minutes, stirring frequently. Add pasta sauce; bring to a boil. Reduce heat; simmer 10 minutes.
3. Combine pesto and ricotta in a small bowl. Spread ½ cup tomato mixture in the bottom of a 8-inch square baking dish or pan coated with cooking spray. Arrange 4 noodle halves over tomato mixture. Top noodles with half of ricotta mixture and 1 cup tomato mixture. Repeat layers, ending with noodles. Spread remaining tomato mixture over noodles; sprinkle with mozzarella.
4. Cover and bake at 375° for 30 minutes. Uncover and bake an additional 20 minutes. Let stand 10 minutes. Garnish with basil leaves, if desired. Yield: 6 servings.
NOTE: To make ahead, assemble as directed; stop before baking. Cover and refrigerate overnight. Let stand 30 minutes at room temperature, and bake as directed.

CALORIES 328 (30% from fat); FAT 10.9g; (sat. 5.4g, mono. 3.8g, poly. 0.9g); PROTEIN 18.2g; CARB 39g; FIBER 3.7g; CHOL 31mg; IRON 2.9mg; SODIUM 491mg; CALC 418mg

Vegetable
Lasagna

Lasagna with Grilled Summer Vegetables

To save time, substitute three (8-ounce) cans of tomato puree for the homemade tomato puree and use a grill pan to prepare the vegetables indoors.

GRILLED VEGETABLES:

3　large red or yellow bell peppers, seeded and each cut lengthwise into quarters
　Cooking spray
3　medium yellow squash, each cut lengthwise into ¼-inch slices
1　large red onion, cut into ¼-inch slices

TOMATO PUREE:

4　pounds tomatoes, cut lengthwise into quarters
⅓　cup vodka
1½　teaspoons salt

WHITE SAUCE:

2½　tablespoons all-purpose flour
¼　teaspoon salt
¼　teaspoon ground nutmeg
2　cups fat-free milk

REMAINING INGREDIENTS:

4　quarts water
12　uncooked lasagna noodles
1　cup chopped fresh basil
¾　teaspoon freshly ground black pepper
1　cup (4 ounces) finely shredded Gruyère cheese
½　cup (2 ounces) grated fresh Parmesan cheese

1. Prepare grill or grill pan.
2. To prepare grilled vegetables, place bell peppers, skin sides down, on a grill rack or grill pan coated with cooking spray; cook 15 minutes or until blackened. Place in a zip-top plastic bag; seal. Let stand 15 minutes. Peel and cut into strips.
3. Place squash and onion on rack or grill pan; cook 5 minutes on each side or until tender.
4. To prepare the tomato puree, place tomatoes in a large Dutch oven. Cover and cook over medium heat 30 minutes or until tender, stirring occasionally. Place tomatoes in a blender or food processor, and process until smooth. Return to pan. Stir in the vodka, and bring to a boil. Reduce heat, and simmer, uncovered, 10 minutes, stirring occasionally. Stir in 1½ teaspoons salt. (You will have 5 cups puree.)
5. To prepare white sauce, combine flour, ¼ teaspoon salt, and nutmeg in a medium saucepan; gradually add milk, stirring with a whisk. Cook over medium-high heat until thick (about 7 minutes), stirring constantly. Set aside.
6. Bring water to a boil in a large stockpot. Add noodles; return to a boil. Cook, uncovered, 10 minutes or until noodles are done; stir occasionally. Drain.
7. Preheat oven to 375°.
8. Spread ⅓ cup white sauce in bottom of a 13 x 9-inch baking dish coated with cooking spray. Arrange 3 noodles over white sauce, and top with one-third of grilled vegetables, ⅓ cup chopped basil, ⅓ cup white sauce, and ½ cup tomato puree. Sprinkle with ¼ teaspoon black pepper, ¼ cup Gruyère, and 2 tablespoons Parmesan. Repeat layers twice, ending with noodles. Spread the remaining white sauce, 1½ cups tomato puree, ¼ cup Gruyère, and 2 tablespoons Parmesan over noodles. Bake at 375° for 45 minutes or until bubbly and browned. Remove from oven, and let stand 15 minutes. Yield: 8 servings (serving size: 1 piece).
NOTE: You will have 2 cups leftover tomato puree. Refrigerate for 1 week, or freeze up to 3 months.

CALORIES 347 (22% from fat); FAT 8.4g (sat 4.3g, mono 2.3g, poly 1g); PROTEIN 17.4g; CARB 51.8g; FIBER 4.7g; CHOL 22mg; IRON 3.3mg; SODIUM 567mg; CALC 358mg

Pasta Quattro Formaggio

1　tablespoon butter or stick margarine
1　tablespoon all-purpose flour
½　teaspoon black pepper
¼　teaspoon salt
1　(12-ounce) can evaporated fat-free milk
¼　cup (1 ounce) shredded fontina cheese
¼　cup (1 ounce) crumbled Gorgonzola or other blue cheese
¼　cup (1 ounce) diced Camembert cheese
6　cups hot cooked rigatoni (about 9 ounces uncooked pasta)
2　tablespoons chopped fresh or 2 teaspoons dried basil
¼　cup (1 ounce) finely grated fresh Parmesan cheese

1. Melt butter in a large saucepan over medium heat. Add flour, and cook for 30 seconds, stirring constantly with a whisk. Add pepper, salt, and milk; bring to a simmer, stirring frequently. Remove from heat; add fontina, Gorgonzola, and Camembert cheeses, stirring until cheeses melt. Stir in pasta and basil, and spoon into each of 4 bowls. Sprinkle with Parmesan cheese. Yield: 4 servings (serving size: 1¼ cups pasta and 1 tablespoon Parmesan).

CALORIES 485 (23% from fat); FAT 12.2g (sat 7g, mono 3.3g, poly 0.9g); PROTEIN 23.6g; CARB 68.9g; FIBER 3.3g; CHOL 35mg; IRON 3.3mg; SODIUM 548mg; CALC 453mg

Linguine with Two Sauces

Both of these sauces can be made a day ahead. Store separately in airtight containers in the refrigerator.
Then start with step 4 to finish the recipe.

2 teaspoons olive oil
2 garlic cloves, minced
1 tablespoon chopped fresh or 1 teaspoon
    dried basil
¾ teaspoon black pepper, divided
½ teaspoon salt, divided
2 (14.5-ounce) cans Italian-style diced
    tomatoes, undrained
Cooking spray
4 cups sliced cremini or button mushrooms
    (about 12 ounces)
½ cup all-purpose flour
2 cups 1% low-fat milk
1 cup (4 ounces) shredded reduced-fat,
    reduced-sodium Swiss cheese
    (such as Alpine Lace)
½ cup dry white wine
8 cups hot cooked linguine
    (about 1 pound uncooked pasta)
¼ cup (1 ounce) grated fresh Parmesan cheese
Oregano sprigs (optional)

1. Preheat oven to 350°.
2. Heat the oil in a nonstick skillet over medium
heat. Add garlic, and sauté 30 seconds. Add basil,
¼ teaspoon pepper, ¼ teaspoon salt, and tomatoes;
cook over low heat 20 minutes, stirring occasionally. Set aside.
3. Place a large saucepan coated with cooking
spray over medium-high heat until hot. Add the
sliced mushrooms, and cook for 5 minutes. Remove
the mushrooms from saucepan, and set aside.
Lightly spoon the flour into a dry measuring cup,
and level with a knife. Add flour to saucepan. Gradually add milk, stirring with a whisk until blended.
Place the flour mixture over medium heat, and cook
until mixture is thick (about 3 minutes), stirring
constantly. Stir in Swiss cheese, wine, ½ teaspoon
pepper, and ¼ teaspoon salt. Cook mixture until
the cheese melts (about 1 minute), stirring constantly. Remove mixture from heat, and stir in
cooked mushrooms.
4. Combine linguine and mushroom sauce in a
large bowl. Spoon linguine mixture into a 13 x 9-
inch baking dish coated with cooking spray. Spread
tomato sauce evenly over linguine mixture, and
sprinkle with Parmesan cheese. Cover and bake at
350° for 20 minutes. Uncover and bake an additional 5 minutes. Garnish with oregano, if desired.
Yield: 8 servings (serving size: 1¼ cups).

CALORIES 349 (19% from fat); FAT 7.2g (sat 3.4g, mono 1.4g, poly 0.6g); PROTEIN 16.3g;
CARB 54.8g; FIBER 3.2g; CHOL 15mg; IRON 3.3mg; SODIUM 527mg; CALC 172mg

Pasta with Roasted
Butternut Squash and
Shallots

Pasta with Roasted Butternut Squash and Shallots

- 3 cups (1-inch) cubed peeled butternut squash
- 1 tablespoon dark brown sugar
- 1½ tablespoons olive oil, divided
- 1 teaspoon salt
- ½ teaspoon black pepper
- 8 shallots, peeled and halved lengthwise (about ½ pound)
- 1 tablespoon chopped fresh or 1 teaspoon dried rubbed sage
- 4 ounces uncooked pappardelle (wide ribbon pasta) or fettuccine
- ¼ cup (1 ounce) grated fresh Parmesan cheese

1. Preheat oven to 475º.

2. Combine squash, sugar, 2½ teaspoons oil, salt, pepper, and shallots in a jelly roll pan; toss well. Bake at 475º for 20 minutes or until tender, stirring occasionally. Stir in sage.

3. While squash mixture bakes, cook pasta according to package directions, omitting salt and fat. Drain. Place cooked pasta in a bowl. Add 2 teaspoons oil; toss well. Serve squash mixture over pasta; sprinkle with cheese. Yield: 4 servings (serving size: ¾ cup pasta, ¾ cup squash mixture, and 1 tablespoon cheese).

CALORIES 248 (29% from fat); FAT 7.9g (sat 2g, mono 4.5g, poly 0.8g); PROTEIN 7.1g; CARB 39.4g; FIBER 5.2g; CHOL 5mg; IRON 1.4mg; SODIUM 713mg; CALC 137mg

Rigatoni Caprese

This dish is based on the classic salad hailing from the island of Capri—hence the name "Caprese." It consists of tomatoes, fresh mozzarella, and basil.

- 6 cups hot cooked rigatoni, penne, or ziti (about ¾ pound uncooked pasta)
- 4 cups chopped plum tomato (about 2½ pounds)
- 1½ cups fresh basil leaves, thinly sliced
- 1 cup (4 ounces) diced fresh mozzarella cheese
- 2 tablespoons extravirgin olive oil
- 1 tablespoon capers
- 1 teaspoon salt
- ½ teaspoon freshly ground black pepper
- 1 garlic clove, crushed
- ⅓ cup (1½ ounces) grated fresh Parmesan or Romano cheese

1. Combine the first 4 ingredients in a large bowl. Combine oil, capers, salt, pepper, and crushed garlic in a small bowl, stirring well with a whisk. Pour over pasta mixture, and toss gently. Sprinkle with Parmesan cheese; toss well. Yield: 5 servings (serving size: 2 cups).

CALORIES 390 (29% from fat); FAT 12.5g (sat 5g, mono 5.3g, poly 1.2g); PROTEIN 16g; CARB 54g; FIBER 4.5g; CHOL 25mg; IRON 3mg; SODIUM 553mg; CALC 233mg

Pasta with Sautéed Tomatoes, Olives, and Artichokes

Because this Italian-style main dish cooks quickly, assemble all the ingredients before you begin. Add more freshly ground pepper at the table, if you wish.

- 1 teaspoon olive oil
- 2 cups halved cherry tomatoes
- ½ cup thinly sliced pitted kalamata olives
- 1 (14-ounce) can quartered artichoke hearts, drained
- 4 cups hot cooked ziti (short tube-shaped pasta)
- ½ cup chopped fresh basil
- ⅓ cup (1¼ ounces) shredded Asiago cheese
- ¼ teaspoon salt
- ¼ teaspoon freshly ground black pepper

1. Heat oil in a large nonstick skillet over medium-high heat. Add tomatoes, olives, and artichokes; cook 5 minutes or until thoroughly heated. Place pasta in a large bowl. Add tomato mixture, basil, cheese, salt, and freshly ground pepper; toss well. Yield: 6 servings (serving size: 1 cup).

CALORIES 287 (17% from fat); FAT 5.4g (sat 1.6g, mono 2.1g, poly 1g); PROTEIN 12.5g; CARB 48.2g; FIBER 6.1g; CHOL 55mg; IRON 2.5mg; SODIUM 626mg; CALC 85mg

Pesto

When storing, cover the surface of the pesto with plastic wrap to prevent discoloration. The pesto should keep for two weeks in the refrigerator. It works beautifully stirred into pasta or soup, or on grilled meat and vegetables. Another way to enjoy it is in Eggplant Torte with Pesto and Sun-Dried Tomatoes (page 136).

     4   garlic cloves, peeled
     4   cups packed basil leaves (about 2½ ounces)
    ¼   cup pine nuts
    ½   cup (2 ounces) grated fresh Parmesan cheese
    ¾   teaspoon salt
    ½   teaspoon freshly ground black pepper
    ½   cup warm water
     6   tablespoons extravirgin olive oil

1. Drop garlic through food chute with food processor on, and process until minced. Place basil and next 4 ingredients in processor, and process 10 seconds. Combine water and oil in a measuring cup. With processor on, slowly pour oil mixture through food chute, processing just until blended. Yield: 1¼ cups (serving size: 1 tablespoon).

CALORIES 59 (87% from fat); FAT 5.7g (sat 1.2g, mono 3.5g, poly 0.7g); PROTEIN 1.6g; CARB 0.7g; FIBER 0.2g; CHOL 2mg; IRON 0.3mg; SODIUM 134mg; CALC 41mg

Pesto

Spinach Ravioli with Tomato Sauce

RAVIOLI:

    ½   cup part-skim ricotta cheese
    ⅓   cup (1⅓ ounces) grated fresh Romano cheese
    ¼   teaspoon salt
    ⅛   teaspoon ground nutmeg
     1   (10-ounce) package frozen chopped spinach, thawed, drained, and squeezed dry
     1   large egg white, lightly beaten
    32   won ton wrappers
     1   large egg white, lightly beaten
     1   tablespoon cornstarch

SAUCE:

     2   teaspoons olive oil
     4   garlic cloves, chopped
     1   teaspoon sugar
    ¼   teaspoon salt
    ¼   teaspoon crushed red pepper
     2   (14.5-ounce) cans no-salt-added diced tomatoes, drained
    ¼   cup chopped fresh basil
    ¼   cup (1 ounce) grated fresh Romano cheese

1. Combine the first 6 ingredients in a bowl.
2. Working with 1 won ton wrapper at a time (cover remaining wrappers with a damp towel to keep them from drying), spoon about 1 level tablespoon spinach mixture into the center of each of 16 wrappers. Brush edges of wrappers with remaining egg white, and top each with another wrapper, stretching the top slightly to meet edges of bottom wrapper. Press edges together firmly with fingers. Cut ravioli into rounds with a 3-inch biscuit cutter, and discard edges. Place ravioli on a large baking sheet sprinkled with cornstarch. Fill a large Dutch oven with water, and bring to a simmer; add half of the ravioli to pan (cover the remaining ravioli with a damp towel to keep them from drying). Cook for 4 to 5 minutes or until ravioli are done (do not boil). Remove ravioli with a slotted spoon. Keep warm. Repeat the procedure with remaining ravioli.
3. Heat oil in a saucepan over medium heat. Add garlic, and sauté 1 minute. Stir in sugar, salt, red pepper, and tomatoes; bring to a boil. Reduce heat, and simmer for 2 minutes. Remove from heat; stir in basil. Spoon sauce over ravioli, and top with ¼ cup Romano cheese. Yield: 4 servings (serving size: 4 ravioli, ½ cup sauce, and 1 tablespoon cheese).

CALORIES 298 (30% from fat); FAT 9.9g (sat 4.8g, mono 3.7g, poly 0.7g); PROTEIN 17.3g; CARB 35.9g; FIBER 2.2g; CHOL 30mg; IRON 3.4mg; SODIUM 830mg; CALC 406mg

Spinach Ravioli with
Tomato Sauce

Pesto with Penne

4 cups fresh basil leaves
2 tablespoons pine nuts
2 tablespoons extravirgin olive oil
¼ teaspoon salt
2 garlic cloves, peeled
½ cup (2 ounces) grated fresh Parmesan cheese
2 tablespoons grated fresh Romano cheese
2 teaspoons butter, softened
2 cups uncooked penne (about 8 ounces)

1. Combine first 5 ingredients in a food processor; process until finely minced. Place in a large bowl. Stir in cheeses and butter until blended.
2. Cook pasta according to package directions, omitting salt and fat. Drain in a colander over a bowl, reserving 3 tablespoons cooking liquid. Add pasta and reserved cooking liquid to pesto, tossing to coat. Yield: 4 servings (serving size: about 1 cup).

CALORIES 390 (39% from fat); FAT 17g (sat 5.4g, mono 6.5g, poly 2.1g); PROTEIN 14.5g; CARB 45.3g; FIBER 3.2g; CHOL 18mg; IRON 4mg; SODIUM 352mg; CALC 281mg

Orecchiette with Broccoli Rabe and Smoked Cheese

Broccoli rabe resembles little clusters of broccoli florets amid bunches of leaves. Substitute kale or spinach, if you'd like.

1 teaspoon olive oil
¼ teaspoon crushed red pepper
4 garlic cloves, minced
4 cups chopped broccoli rabe
½ cup vegetable broth
¼ teaspoon salt
4 cups hot cooked orecchiette (about 8 ounces uncooked small ear-shaped pasta)
½ cup (2 ounces) shredded smoked mozzarella or smoked gouda cheese

1. Heat oil in a large nonstick skillet over medium heat. Add pepper and garlic, and cook 1 minute or until garlic begins to brown. Stir in broccoli rabe, and cook for 1 minute. Add broth and salt; cover and cook for 5 minutes or until tender. Stir in pasta and cheese. Serve immediately. Yield: 4 servings (serving size: 1 cup).

CALORIES 283 (17% from fat); FAT 5.4g (sat 2.2g, mono 1.9g, poly 0.7g); PROTEIN 11.9g; CARB 47.1g; FIBER 3.2g; CHOL 11mg; IRON 2.8mg; SODIUM 334mg; CALC 116mg

Eggplant Torte with Pesto and Sun-Dried Tomatoes

If you don't have a spare loaf pan to weigh down the torte, cut a piece of cardboard the size of the pan, and wrap it in foil.

¼ teaspoon salt
2 medium eggplant, cut lengthwise into ½-inch-thick slices
Cooking spray
1 cup boiling water
2 ounces sun-dried tomatoes, packed without oil (about ½ cup)
5 cooked lasagna noodles, cut into thirds
4 ounces thinly sliced provolone cheese
¼ cup Pesto (recipe on page 134)
32 (½-inch-thick) slices diagonally cut French bread baguette, toasted (about 8 ounces)

1. Preheat broiler.
2. Sprinkle salt over 9 eggplant slices; reserve any remaining slices for another use. Place eggplant on a baking sheet coated with cooking spray; broil 10 minutes on each side or until lightly browned. Cool and halve slices crosswise.
3. Combine boiling water and tomatoes; let stand 10 minutes or until soft. Drain and finely chop.
4. Coat an 8½ x 4½-inch baking dish with cooking spray; line dish with plastic wrap. Lightly coat plastic wrap with cooking spray. Arrange 5 noodle pieces in bottom of dish, and top with half of cheese slices. Spread half of Pesto over cheese, and top with 9 eggplant pieces. Sprinkle half of tomato over eggplant. Repeat layers, ending with noodles. Cover with plastic wrap, allowing plastic wrap to extend over edges of dish. Place an empty 8½ x 4½-inch baking dish on top of the torte. Place 2 (15-ounce) canned goods upright in dish. Refrigerate overnight.
5. Remove cans, empty baking dish, and top sheet of plastic wrap. Invert torte onto a platter; remove remaining plastic wrap. Cut torte crosswise into 8 slices. Serve at room temperature with bread slices. Yield: 8 servings (serving size: 1 torte slice and 4 bread slices).

CALORIES 246 (30% from fat); FAT 8.3g (sat 3.1g, mono 2.2g, poly 0.8g); PROTEIN 10.3g; CARB 34.6g; FIBER 4.7g; CHOL 11mg; IRON 2.2mg; SODIUM 577mg; CALC 158mg

Grits Casserole with White Beans and Rosemary

Fresh breadcrumbs and Parmesan cheese create a savory crumb topping.

4   (1-ounce) slices French bread or other firm white bread, cubed
½   cup (2 ounces) grated fresh Parmesan cheese
2   tablespoons finely chopped fresh parsley
7   cups boiling water, divided
3   ounces sun-dried tomatoes, packed without oil, chopped
1   tablespoon olive oil
2   cups vertically sliced red onion
1   tablespoon chopped fresh rosemary
⅛   teaspoon crushed red pepper
2   garlic cloves, minced
1½ teaspoons sea salt, divided
¼   teaspoon black pepper
1   (19-ounce) can cannellini beans or other white beans, drained
1½ cups uncooked regular grits
2   tablespoons butter
    Cooking spray

1. Place bread in a food processor; pulse 10 times or until coarse crumbs measure 1 cup. Combine breadcrumbs, cheese, and parsley in a small bowl, and set aside.

2. Combine 3 cups boiling water and sun-dried tomatoes in a bowl; let stand 10 minutes or until soft. Drain tomatoes over a bowl, reserving 1 cup liquid.

3. Preheat oven to 400°.

4. Heat oil in a nonstick skillet over medium-high heat. Add onion, rosemary, red pepper, and garlic; sauté 3 minutes. Add tomatoes and reserved 1 cup liquid. Bring to a boil; cook 7 minutes or until most of liquid evaporates. Add ½ teaspoon salt, black pepper, and beans.

5. Combine 4 cups boiling water, 1 teaspoon salt, grits, and butter in a large saucepan. Cook for 8 minutes over medium heat, stirring constantly. Pour grits mixture into an 11 x 7-inch baking dish coated with cooking spray. Spoon tomato mixture evenly over grits, and top with breadcrumb mixture. Bake at 400° for 20 minutes or until top is golden. Yield: 8 servings.

CALORIES 303 (22% from fat); FAT 7.4g (sat 3.4g, mono 2.9g, poly 0.9g); PROTEIN 10.2g; CARB 47.2g; FIBER 5.2g; CHOL 13mg; IRON 2.5mg; SODIUM 781mg; CALC 146mg

Roasted Squash Stuffed with Corn Bread Dressing

You can make the Maple Corn Bread recipe and toast it ahead of time. Roast the squash and refrigerate it up to two days.

7½ cups (½-inch) cubed Maple Corn Bread
    Cooking spray
 5 acorn squash (about 1 pound each)
 4 cups boiling water, divided
 1 cup dried cranberries
¼ cup dried currants
 2 teaspoons olive oil
 1 cup finely chopped onion
 1 cup finely chopped celery
 1 cup finely chopped carrot
 2 tablespoons chopped fresh sage
 3 garlic cloves, minced
 1 cup vegetable broth
¼ cup chopped pecans, toasted
 2 tablespoons finely chopped fresh parsley
¾ teaspoon fine sea salt
¼ teaspoon black pepper

1. Preheat oven to 400°.
2. Arrange corn bread cubes in a single layer on a jelly roll pan coated with cooking spray. Bake at 400° for 30 minutes or until corn bread is toasted, stirring twice. Set aside.
3. Decrease oven temperature to 350°.
4. Cut each squash in half lengthwise; discard seeds and membranes. Place squash, cut sides down, in a 13 x 9-inch baking pan. Coat squash with cooking spray. Pour 2 cups water over squash. Cover; bake at 350° for 20 minutes. Remove squash from pan.
5. Place cranberries, currants, and 2 cups water in a bowl. Cover and let stand 30 minutes. Drain.
6. Heat oil in a large nonstick skillet over medium-high heat. Add onion; sauté 5 minutes. Add celery, carrot, sage, and garlic; sauté 3 minutes.
7. Combine toasted corn bread cubes, cranberry mixture, onion mixture, broth, and the remaining ingredients in a bowl, tossing to coat.
8. Spoon about 1½ cups dressing into each squash half. Place squash halves in baking pan, cut sides up.
9. Bake at 350° for 30 minutes or until the tip of a knife pierces squash easily. Yield: 10 servings (serving size: 1 stuffed squash half).

(Totals include Maple Corn Bread) CALORIES 398 (23% from fat); FAT 10.2g (sat 4.1g, mono 3.8g, poly 1.6g); PROTEIN 6.5g; CARB 74.2g; FIBER 7.7g; CHOL 16mg; IRON 3.8mg; SODIUM 732mg; CALC 198mg

MAPLE CORN BREAD:
 1 teaspoon vegetable oil
1½ cups all-purpose flour
¾ cup masa harina
¾ cup yellow cornmeal
 1 tablespoon baking powder
 1 teaspoon fine sea salt
1½ cups water
⅓ cup maple syrup
 5 tablespoons butter, melted
 1 jalapeño pepper, finely chopped

1. Preheat oven to 350°.
2. Coat a 9-inch cast-iron skillet with oil. Place in oven for 10 minutes.
3. Lightly spoon flour and masa harina into dry measuring cups; level with a knife. Combine flour, masa harina, cornmeal, baking powder, and salt in a large bowl, stirring well with a whisk.
4. Combine water and remaining ingredients in a small bowl, stirring with a whisk. Add water mixture to flour mixture, stirring until moist. Spoon batter into preheated pan.
5. Bake at 350° for 25 minutes or until a wooden pick inserted in center comes out clean. Remove corn bread from pan; cool completely on a wire rack. Yield: 12 servings.

CALORIES 184 (27% from fat); FAT 5.6g (sat 3.1g, mono 1.6g, poly 0.6g); PROTEIN 3g; CARB 31.5g; FIBER 1.2g; CHOL 13mg; IRON 1.4mg; SODIUM 342mg; CALC 62mg

Falafel with Yogurt-Tahini Dip

1½ cups dried chickpeas (garbanzo beans; about 12 ounces)
 2 cups chopped fresh cilantro (about 1 large bunch)
 1 teaspoon ground cumin
 1 teaspoon ground allspice
 ¼ teaspoon salt
 ¼ teaspoon black pepper
 ⅛ teaspoon ground red pepper
 5 garlic cloves, peeled
 1 onion, quartered
 1 leek, trimmed and cut into 3 pieces
 6 tablespoons olive oil, divided
Yogurt-Tahini Dip
 8 (6-inch) pitas, cut in half

1. Sort and wash chickpeas; place in a large bowl. Cover with water to 2 inches above beans. Cover; let stand 8 hours. Drain.

2. Combine chickpeas, cilantro, and next 8 ingredients in a food processor, and process until mixture resembles coarse meal. Divide chickpea mixture into 16 equal portions, shaping each into a ½-inch-thick patty.

3. Heat 2 tablespoons oil in a large nonstick skillet. Add 5 patties; cook 3 minutes on each side or until golden. Repeat procedure twice with remaining oil and patties.

4. Spread 1 tablespoon Yogurt-Tahini Dip in each pita half; fill with 1 patty. Yield: 8 servings (serving size: 2 pita halves).

(Totals include Yogurt-Tahini Dip) CALORIES 430 (29% from fat); FAT 13.9g (sat 1.8g, mono 8.3g, poly 2.5g); PROTEIN 14.6g; CARB 63.3g; FIBER 5.3g; CHOL 0mg; IRON 5.7mg; SODIUM 398mg; CALC 140mg

YOGURT-TAHINI DIP:

 1 cup plain low-fat yogurt
 3 tablespoons tahini (sesame-seed paste)
 2 tablespoons fresh lemon juice
 1 tablespoon chopped flat-leaf parsley
 ½ teaspoon salt
 1 garlic clove, crushed

1. Combine all ingredients in a large bowl; cover and refrigerate for 30 minutes. Yield: 1 cup (serving size: 1 tablespoon).

CALORIES 27 (60% from fat); FAT 1.8g (sat 0.4g, mono 0.6g, poly 0.6g); PROTEIN 1.3g; CARB 1.9g; FIBER 0.3g; CHOL 1mg; IRON 0.3mg; SODIUM 87mg; CALC 41mg

Navy Bean-and-Artichoke Casserole with Goat Cheese

 2 (1-ounce) slices whole-wheat bread
 2 (15-ounce) cans navy beans, undrained
 2 teaspoons chopped fresh or ½ teaspoon dried thyme
 2 teaspoons chopped fresh or ½ teaspoon dried rubbed sage
 ¼ teaspoon black pepper
 4 garlic cloves, minced and divided
 2 tablespoons olive oil, divided
 3 cups chopped leek (about 3 large)
 2 teaspoons chopped fresh or ½ teaspoon dried rosemary
 ⅛ teaspoon salt
 1 (14-ounce) can artichoke bottoms, drained and each cut into 8 wedges
Olive oil-flavored cooking spray
1¼ cups (5 ounces) crumbled goat cheese
Rosemary sprig (optional)

1. Place bread in a food processor; pulse 10 times or until coarse crumbs form to measure 1 cup.

2. Preheat oven to 400°.

3. Drain beans in a colander over a bowl, reserving liquid. Add enough water to bean liquid to measure 1 cup. Combine beans, thyme, sage, pepper, and 1 garlic clove.

4. Heat 1 tablespoon oil in a large nonstick skillet over medium-high heat. Add 3 garlic cloves, leek, rosemary, salt, and artichokes; sauté 4 minutes. Stir in bean liquid mixture. Cover, reduce heat, and simmer 10 minutes, stirring occasionally. Remove from heat. Spread half of bean mixture in an 11 x 7-inch baking dish coated with cooking spray, and top with half of goat cheese. Spread artichoke mixture over goat cheese; top with remaining bean mixture and remaining goat cheese. Combine breadcrumbs and 1 tablespoon oil; sprinkle over goat cheese. Bake at 400° for 25 minutes or until lightly browned. Garnish with rosemary, if desired. Yield: 6 servings (serving size: about 1 cup).

CALORIES 349 (28% from fat); FAT 10.8g (sat 4.4g, mono 4.7g, poly 1.1g); PROTEIN 17.3g; CARB 47.2g; FIBER 8.7g; CHOL 21mg; IRON 5.1mg; SODIUM 926mg; CALC 252mg

Navy Bean-and-Artichoke
Casserole with Goat
Cheese

Rice and Feta-Stuffed Baby Eggplant

2 cups chopped tomato
¼ cup dry white wine
½ teaspoon sugar
1 teaspoon sea salt, divided
6 baby eggplants (about 1¼ pounds), cut in half lengthwise
2 teaspoons olive oil
1 cup finely chopped onion
1 cup finely chopped yellow bell pepper
2 garlic cloves, minced
2 tablespoons finely chopped fresh basil
1 jalapeño pepper, seeded and finely chopped
1 cup cooked brown basmati rice
½ cup (2 ounces) crumbled feta cheese
1 tablespoon finely chopped fresh parsley
Parsley sprigs (optional)

1. Preheat oven to 375°.
2. Combine tomato, wine, sugar, and ¼ teaspoon salt in a 13 x 9-inch baking dish; spread evenly.
3. Scoop the pulp from eggplant halves, leaving ¼-inch-thick shells. Chop pulp. Sprinkle inside surfaces of eggplant shells with ¼ teaspoon salt.
4. Heat oil in a large nonstick skillet over medium-high heat. Add onion, bell pepper, garlic, and ½ teaspoon salt; sauté 3 minutes. Stir in eggplant pulp, basil, and jalapeño.
5. Cover, reduce heat, and cook over low heat 10 minutes or until eggplant is tender. Remove from heat; stir in rice, cheese, and parsley.
6. Spoon about ¼ cup eggplant mixture into each eggplant shell, pressing gently; place shells, cut sides up, over tomato mixture in dish. Cover and bake at 375° for 15 minutes.
7. Uncover, and bake for an additional 15 minutes or until the eggplant shells are tender. Spoon about 1½ tablespoons tomato mixture over each eggplant half. Garnish the eggplant halves with parsley sprigs, if desired. Yield: 4 servings (serving size: 3 eggplant halves).

CALORIES 256 (28% from fat); FAT 8.1g (sat 3.5g, mono 3g, poly 0.9g); PROTEIN 7.9g; CARB 40.1g; FIBER 3.7g; CHOL 17mg; IRON 1.6mg; SODIUM 810mg; CALC 132mg

Butternut Squash Risotto

Here's a perfect example of a traditional Italian dish and cooking technique adapted to an American ingredient. Where the recipe originated in Italy, the Italian pumpkin is used. Butternut squash is a suitable substitute. Adapted from *Every Night Italian* by Giuliano Hazan (Scribner, 2000).

  2 cups water, divided
  2 (14¼-ounce) cans low-salt beef broth
  2 teaspoons olive oil
  ½ cup finely chopped yellow onion
  3 cups (¾-inch) cubed peeled butternut squash
      (about 1 pound)
  ½ teaspoon salt
  ¼ teaspoon freshly ground black pepper
1½ cups Arborio rice or other short-grain rice
  ½ cup (2 ounces) grated Parmigiano-Reggiano
      cheese
  3 tablespoons unsalted butter
  2 tablespoons finely chopped fresh parsley

1. Bring 1½ cups water and beef broth to a simmer in a large saucepan (do not boil). Keep mixture warm over low heat.
2. Heat oil in a Dutch oven over medium heat. Add onion, and cook 8 minutes or until golden, stirring frequently. Add ½ cup water, squash, salt, and pepper; cook 10 minutes or until squash is tender and water has almost evaporated. Add rice, and stir until mixture is combined. Stir in ½ cup broth mixture, and cook until liquid is nearly absorbed, stirring constantly. Add remaining broth mixture, ½ cup at a time, stirring constantly until each portion of broth is absorbed before adding the next (about 30 minutes total). Stir in cheese, butter, and chopped parsley. Serve immediately. Yield: 6 servings (serving size: ¾ cup).

CALORIES 361 (25% from fat); FAT 10.1g (sat 5.3g, mono 3.7g, poly 0.7g); PROTEIN 10.5g; CARB 55.1g; FIBER 3.7g; CHOL 20mg; IRON 1mg; SODIUM 366mg; CALC 158mg

Monterey Jack, Corn, and Roasted-Red Pepper Risotto

We never seem to run out of ways to make risotto. Here, the creamy rice dish takes on a Southwestern flavor with corn, Monterey Jack cheese, and cumin. Monterey Jack, Corn, and Roasted-Red Pepper Risotto calls for several common ingredients from your pantry.

1¾ cups water
  2 (14½-ounce) cans vegetable broth
  2 teaspoons olive oil
  1 cup uncooked Arborio or short-grain rice
  1 teaspoon ground cumin
  1 teaspoon ground coriander (optional)
  4 garlic cloves, minced
  1 cup thinly sliced green onions
  ¾ cup (3 ounces) shredded Monterey Jack
      cheese with jalapeño peppers
  ¼ to ½ teaspoon hot sauce
  2 cups frozen whole-kernel corn
  ¾ cup chopped bottled roasted red bell peppers

1. Combine the water and broth in a medium saucepan; bring to a simmer (do not boil). Keep broth mixture warm over low heat.
2. Heat oil in a large saucepan over medium-high heat. Add rice, cumin, coriander (if desired), and garlic; sauté 1 minute. Stir in ½ cup broth mixture; cook 2 minutes or until liquid is nearly absorbed, stirring constantly. Add remaining broth mixture, ½ cup at a time, stirring constantly until each portion of liquid is absorbed before adding the next (about 20 minutes total). Stir in onions, cheese, hot sauce, corn, and bell peppers; cook 3 minutes or until thoroughly heated. Yield: 4 servings (serving size: 1 cup).

CALORIES 383 (24% from fat); FAT 10.4g (sat 4.6g, mono 3.9g, poly 0.9g); PROTEIN 12g; CARB 63.3g; FIBER 3.8g; CHOL 17mg; IRON 3.6mg; SODIUM 583mg; CALC 198mg

Sesame-Crusted Tofu Sticks with Vegetable Sauté

TOFU:
- ½ teaspoon salt
- ¼ teaspoon black pepper
- 1 large egg
- 1 large egg white
- 1 cup dry breadcrumbs
- ¼ cup all-purpose flour
- 2 tablespoons sesame seeds
- 1 (15-ounce) package extrafirm tofu, drained and cut into 18 sticks
- 2 tablespoons dark sesame oil, divided

VEGETABLES:
- 1 (6-ounce) can pineapple juice
- Cooking spray
- ½ cup chopped shallots
- 1 garlic clove, minced
- ½ pound shiitake mushroom caps (about 10 mushrooms)
- 2 cups (2-inch) sliced green onions
- 1 cup cherry tomatoes, halved
- 1 tablespoon chopped fresh thyme
- 2 tablespoons balsamic vinegar
- 1 tablespoon Japanese sweet and sour sauce (such as abc sauce; optional)

1. To prepare tofu, combine first 4 ingredients in a shallow dish. Combine breadcrumbs, flour, and sesame seeds in a shallow dish.

2. Dip tofu, 1 piece at a time, in egg mixture; dredge in breadcrumb mixture. Return tofu to egg mixture; dredge in breadcrumb mixture. Repeat procedure with remaining tofu, egg mixture, and breadcrumb mixture.

3. Heat 1 tablespoon oil in a large nonstick skillet over medium-high heat. Add half of tofu; cook 4 minutes, turning to brown all sides. Remove from pan. Repeat procedure with remaining oil and tofu. Keep warm.

4. To prepare the vegetables, pour the pineapple juice into the pan. Bring to a boil, and cook until the juice is reduced to ¼ cup (about 5 minutes). Remove from pan.

5. Heat pan coated with cooking spray over medium-high heat. Add chopped shallots, minced garlic, and mushrooms, and sauté for 4 minutes, stirring occasionally. Add sliced green onions, cherry tomatoes, and thyme; cook 1 minute. Stir in pineapple juice and balsamic vinegar, and cook for 30 seconds.

6. Arrange about ½ cup vegetable mixture on each of 6 plates; top each serving with 3 tofu sticks. Drizzle with ½ teaspoon sweet and sour sauce, if desired. Serve immediately. Yield: 6 servings.

CALORIES 253 (29% from fat); FAT 8.1g (sat 1.4g, mono 3g, poly 3.1g); PROTEIN 12.5g; CARB 32.9g; FIBER 3g; CHOL 36mg; IRON 3.5mg; SODIUM 846mg; CALC 119mg

Tofu with Red Curry Paste, Peas, and Yellow Tomatoes

You can find red curry paste in the ethnic or gourmet sections of most large supermarkets. The paste is a blend of clarified butter (ghee), curry powder, vinegar, and other seasonings. Use either Indian or Asian curry paste; it comes in mild and hot versions, so adjust the heat to suit your preference.

- 1 (14-ounce) package firm tofu, drained and cut into 1-inch cubes
- 2 tablespoons fresh lime juice
- 1 teaspoon ground turmeric
- ¼ teaspoon salt
- ⅛ teaspoon black pepper
- 2 teaspoons olive oil
- 2 cups thinly sliced onion
- 1 cup light coconut milk
- 1 to 2 tablespoons red curry paste
- 1 cup shelled green peas (about 1 pound unshelled) or frozen green peas, thawed
- ½ cup chopped yellow tomato
- 4 cups hot cooked long-grain rice

1. Place a large nonstick skillet over medium-high heat. Add tofu; cook until liquid from tofu evaporates (about 3 minutes). Remove the tofu from pan; sprinkle with lime juice, turmeric, salt, and pepper. Keep tofu mixture warm.

2. Heat the olive oil in pan over medium-high heat. Add sliced onion; sauté for 5 minutes. Add tofu, and cook mixture for 7 minutes or until golden. Combine coconut milk and curry paste; add to pan. Reduce heat, and simmer for 3 minutes. Add the green peas and tomato; cook 2 minutes. Serve tofu mixture over rice. Yield: 4 servings (serving size: 1 cup tofu mixture and 1 cup rice).

CALORIES 421 (23% from fat); FAT 10.6g (sat 3.1g, mono 2.9g, poly 3.1g); PROTEIN 15.5g; CARB 66.9g; FIBER 5.3g; CHOL 0mg; IRON 8.7mg; SODIUM 344mg; CALC 154mg

Vietnamese Lettuce Rolls with Spicy Grilled Tofu

1   (16-ounce) package water-packed firm tofu, drained
½   cup fresh lime juice
½   cup honey
¼   cup thinly sliced peeled fresh lemongrass
2   tablespoons low-sodium soy sauce
¾   teaspoon chile paste with garlic
¼   teaspoon freshly ground black pepper
3   garlic cloves, minced
Cooking spray
1   head romaine lettuce
½   cup cilantro leaves
3   tablespoons chopped dry-roasted peanuts
36   small mint leaves
36   (2-inch) strips julienne-cut carrot
12   basil leaves

1. Cut tofu crosswise into 12 (½-inch) slices. Place tofu slices on several layers of heavy-duty paper towels, and cover with additional paper towels. Place a cutting board on top of tofu, and place a cast-iron skillet on top of cutting board. Let tofu stand 30 minutes to 1 hour. (Tofu is ready when a slice bends easily without tearing or crumbling.)

Arrange tofu slices in a single layer in a 13 x 9-inch baking dish.

2. Combine lime juice and next 6 ingredients in a small saucepan; bring to a boil. Cook 1 minute, stirring until honey dissolves. Pour over tofu slices. Cover and let stand at room temperature 1 hour.

3. Prepare grill.

4. Remove tofu slices from dish, and reserve marinade for sauce. Coat tofu slices with cooking spray. Place the tofu on a grill rack coated with cooking spray. Grill tofu slices for 3 minutes on each side or until browned.

5. Remove 12 large outer leaves from lettuce head, and reserve remaining lettuce for another use. Remove bottom half of each lettuce leaf, and reserve for another use. Place 1 tofu slice on each lettuce leaf top. Top each lettuce leaf top with 2 teaspoons cilantro leaves, ¾ teaspoon chopped peanuts, 3 mint leaves, 3 carrot strips, and 1 basil leaf. Wrap lettuce leaf around toppings. Serve with reserved marinade. Yield: 4 servings (serving size: 3 lettuce rolls and about ¼ cup sauce).

CALORIES 294 (29% from fat); FAT 9.5g (sat 1.5g, mono 2.5g, poly 4.9g); PROTEIN 14.8g; CARB 44.9g; FIBER 2.8g; CHOL 0mg; IRON 3.5mg; SODIUM 334mg; CALC 157mg

Stir-fried Vegetables and Tofu

A julienne cut is made by slicing vegetables into 2-inch-long by ¼-inch-thick sticks. Uniformity in size helps ensure that the vegetables cook evenly.

2	tablespoons olive oil, divided
⅔	cup julienne-cut carrot
2	garlic cloves, minced
¼	cup dry white wine, divided
2	cups julienne-cut zucchini
1½	cups julienne-cut yellow squash
2½	cups quartered cremini mushrooms (about 8 ounces)
1	(8-ounce) package button mushrooms, quartered
1	(12.3-ounce) package reduced-fat extrafirm tofu, drained and cut into cubes
3	tablespoons low-sodium soy sauce
2	cups fresh bean sprouts
¼	teaspoon salt
¼	teaspoon black pepper
3	cups hot cooked jasmine or other long-grain rice

1. Heat 1 tablespoon oil in a nonstick skillet over medium-high heat. Add carrot; stir-fry 4 minutes. Add garlic and 2 tablespoons wine; stir-fry 3 minutes. Add zucchini and squash; stir-fry 5 minutes. Add 2 tablespoons wine and mushrooms; stir-fry 5 minutes. Remove from heat.

2. Heat 1 tablespoon oil in a medium nonstick skillet over medium-high heat. Add tofu; sauté 7 minutes, browning on all sides. Add soy sauce; cook for 1 minute. Stir in sprouts, salt, and pepper. Add tofu mixture to vegetable mixture, and heat thoroughly. Serve over rice. Yield: 6 servings (serving size: 1 cup stir-fry and ½ cup rice).

CALORIES 225 (22% from fat); FAT 5.5g (sat 0.8g, mono 3.4g, poly 0.9g); PROTEIN 10.1g; CARB 36g; FIBER 2.6g; CHOL 0mg; IRON 3.4mg; SODIUM 418mg; CALC 58mg

Fettuccine and Tofu with Finger-Licking Peanut Sauce

This dish has many variations: Substitute chicken, pork, or shrimp for the tofu and almost any kind of pasta for the fettuccine. Or add some snow peas, bell pepper strips, or other vegetables.

½ cup fat-free, less-sodium chicken broth
¼ cup chunky peanut butter
¼ cup low-sodium soy sauce
3 tablespoons brown sugar
2 tablespoons rice vinegar
2 teaspoons grated peeled fresh ginger
2 teaspoons chile paste with garlic
4 garlic cloves, minced
8 ounces uncooked fettuccine
1 pound firm tofu, drained and cubed
1 cup (2-inch) sliced green onions
1 cup shredded carrot

1. Combine chicken broth, peanut butter, and next 6 ingredients in a small saucepan. Cook over medium heat 5 minutes or until smooth, stirring frequently. Remove from heat.
2. Cook pasta in boiling water 8 minutes, omitting salt and fat. Add tofu, onions, and carrot; drain. Place pasta mixture in a large bowl. Add peanut butter mixture; toss gently. Yield: 4 servings (serving size: 2 cups).

CALORIES 465 (29% from fat); FAT 14.5g (sat 2.3g, mono 5.3g, poly 6g); PROTEIN 23g; CARB 60.8g; FIBER 4.5g; CHOL 1mg; IRON 9.6mg; SODIUM 713mg; CALC 174mg

Asian Noodle, Tofu, and Vegetable Stir-fry

Stir-fries feel so easy and undemanding. This one is even more so because it has cellophane noodles right in it, making it a one-dish meal. Also known as glass noodles or bean threads, cellophane noodles aren't flour-based but are instead made from the starch of green mung beans.

2 ounces uncooked bean threads
    (cellophane noodles)
½ ounce dried wood ear mushrooms (about 6)
1 cup boiling water
2 teaspoons peanut oil or vegetable oil
1 cup coarsely chopped onion
1 tablespoon minced seeded jalapeño pepper
2 teaspoons minced peeled fresh ginger
2 garlic cloves, minced
3 cups (¼-inch) diagonally sliced carrot
    (about 1 pound)
¼ teaspoon salt
7 cups (1-inch) sliced bok choy
2 tablespoons low-sodium soy sauce
1 (12.3-ounce) package reduced-fat firm tofu,
    cubed
3 tablespoons water
2 teaspoons cornstarch
1 teaspoon dark sesame oil or chili oil

1. Place noodles in a large bowl; cover with warm water. Let stand 20 minutes. Drain; set aside.
2. Combine the mushrooms and boiling water in a bowl, and let stand for 20 minutes. Strain through a sieve into a bowl, reserving the mushroom liquid. Cut mushrooms into strips.
3. Heat peanut oil in a wok or nonstick Dutch oven over medium-high heat. Add chopped onion, minced jalapeño, ginger, and garlic; stir-fry for 1 minute. Add mushrooms, sliced carrot, and salt, and stir-fry 2 minutes. Stir in ¼ cup reserved mushroom liquid; cover and cook 3 minutes or until carrots are crisp-tender and liquid evaporates.
4. Add bok choy; stir-fry 1 minute. Stir in noodles, remaining mushroom liquid, soy sauce, and tofu; cook for 2 minutes.
5. Combine 3 tablespoons water and cornstarch; pour into pan. Bring to a boil, and cook 2 minutes or until slightly thick. Drizzle with sesame oil. Yield: 4 servings (serving size: 2 cups).

CALORIES 195 (29% from fat); FAT 6.4g (sat 1g, mono 1.9g, poly 2.8g); PROTEIN 10.3g; CARB 27.4g; FIBER 6.1g; CHOL 0mg; IRON 2.6mg; SODIUM 539mg; CALC 206mg

Soba with Sesame and Tofu

If you cook these noodles ahead of time, make sure you rinse them well. We used rice vinegar in this dish because it has a milder flavor than most other vinegars.

⅓ cup low-sodium soy sauce
2 tablespoons rice vinegar
1 tablespoon minced peeled fresh ginger
1 teaspoon sugar
1½ teaspoons dark sesame oil
½ teaspoon chili oil or vegetable oil
1½ tablespoons sesame seeds
4 cups cooked soba (about 8 ounces uncooked buckwheat noodles)
2 cups sliced peeled cucumber
1 cup thinly sliced green onions
2 cups cubed firm tofu (about 12 ounces)

1. Combine the first 6 ingredients in a small bowl, and set aside.
2. Cook the sesame seeds in a small saucepan over medium heat 1 minute or until toasted.
3. Combine sesame seeds, noodles, cucumber, and onions in a large bowl; toss gently.
4. Divide noodle mixture evenly among 4 bowls; top with tofu and sauce. Yield: 4 servings (serving size: 1 cup noodles, ½ cup tofu, and 2 tablespoons sauce).

CALORIES 310 (24% from fat); FAT 8.4g (sat 1.2g, mono 2.4g, poly 4.2g); PROTEIN 18.3g; CARB 46.3g; FIBER 2.2g; CHOL 0mg; IRON 6.8mg; SODIUM 844mg; CALC 159mg

Tofu Vegetable Hot Pot

1 teaspoon vegetable oil
Cooking spray
1 cup thinly sliced shallots
1 tablespoon matchstick-cut peeled fresh ginger
1 teaspoon ground turmeric
1 serrano chile, thinly sliced
1 garlic clove, minced
1½ cups shredded green cabbage
1 cup sliced shiitake mushroom caps (about 3 ounces)
½ cup (¼-inch-thick) diagonally cut carrot
1 cup water
¼ cup low-sodium soy sauce
½ teaspoon sea salt
1 (14-ounce) can light coconut milk
1 pound water-packed firm tofu, drained and cut into 1-inch cubes
2 tomatoes, cut into 1-inch-thick wedges
½ cup torn fresh basil leaves
¼ cup (1-inch) sliced green onions
2 cups hot cooked jasmine rice
4 lime wedges

1. Heat oil in a large nonstick saucepan coated with cooking spray over medium-high heat. Add shallots; sauté 2 minutes. Reduce heat to medium. Add ginger, turmeric, chile, and garlic; cook 1 minute, stirring constantly. Add cabbage, mushroom, and carrot; cook 2 minutes, stirring occasionally.
2. Stir in water, soy sauce, salt, and coconut milk; bring to a boil. Add tofu. Reduce heat; simmer 5 minutes. Add tomato; simmer 3 minutes. Stir in basil and onions. Serve over rice with lime wedges. Yield: 4 servings (serving size: 2 cups soup, ½ cup rice, and 1 lime wedge).

CALORIES 407 (23% from fat); FAT 10.2g (sat 4.3g, mono 1.2g, poly 2.7g) PROTEIN 14.5g; CARB 63.3g; FIBER 4.8g; CHOL 0mg; IRON 4.4mg; SODIUM 933mg; CALC 87mg

Tofu Vegetable Hot Pot

Stir-Fried Tempeh with Spinach and Thai Basil

Thai basil has small purple leaves and a stronger taste than sweet basil; if unavailable, use the latter. The longer you marinate the tempeh, the more flavorful it will be. We liked this dish best with soy tempeh, but any variety (five-grain, three-grain, soy-rice) will work.

TEMPEH:
- 3 tablespoons low-sodium soy sauce
- 1½ tablespoons sake (rice wine)
- 2 tablespoons minced shallots
- 1 teaspoon dark sesame oil
- 1 pound soy tempeh, cut into bite-sized pieces
- 1½ tablespoons olive oil

SPINACH:
- 1½ teaspoons olive oil
- 1½ tablespoons sake (rice wine)
- ½ teaspoon salt
- 1 (10-ounce) package fresh spinach

REMAINING INGREDIENTS:
- 2 tablespoons sugar
- 3 tablespoons water
- 3 tablespoons low-sodium soy sauce
- 2 teaspoons fresh lime juice
- 1 tablespoon olive oil
- 3½ cups thinly, vertically sliced red onion (about 3 medium)
- 3 tablespoons chopped fresh garlic
- 2 cups loosely packed fresh Thai basil leaves or coarsely chopped sweet basil
- 4½ cups hot cooked basmati rice

1. To prepare tempeh, combine first 4 ingredients, stirring with whisk. Add tempeh, turning to coat. Let stand at room temperature 20 minutes to 4 hours, turning once. Remove tempeh from marinade; discard marinade.

2. Heat 1½ tablespoons oil in a wok or large non-stick skillet over medium-high heat. Add tempeh; sauté 2 minutes. Remove tempeh from pan.

3. To prepare spinach, heat 1½ teaspoons oil in pan over medium-high heat. Add 1½ tablespoons sake, salt, and spinach; stir-fry 1 minute or until spinach wilts. Remove spinach from pan with a slotted spoon; set aside.

4. Combine sugar, water, 3 tablespoons soy sauce, and juice, and set aside. Heat 1 tablespoon olive oil in pan over medium-high heat. Add onion and garlic; stir-fry for 3 minutes or until onions are tender. Add tempeh, sugar mixture, and basil, stirring to combine. Cook 2 minutes or until heated, stirring frequently. Spoon the tempeh mixture into center of a serving platter; arrange spinach around tempeh. Serve with rice. Yield: 6 servings (serving size: about ¾ cup tempeh mixture, ⅓ cup spinach, and ¾ cup rice).

CALORIES 416 (26% from fat); FAT 11.9g (sat 2.4g, mono 6.1g, poly 2.7g); PROTEIN 22.6g; CARB 54.7g; FIBER 7.5g; CHOL 0mg; IRON 5.8mg; SODIUM 646mg; CALC 218mg

Pad Thai with Tofu

This vegetarian version of Thailand's classic dish is spicy. If you prefer the dish mild, use only ½ teaspoon of hot sauce.

SAUCE:
- ¼ cup low-sodium soy sauce
- 2 tablespoons rice vinegar
- 1 to 2 tablespoons hot sauce
- 1 tablespoon mirin (sweet rice wine)
- 1 tablespoon maple syrup

NOODLES:
- 1 teaspoon vegetable oil
- 2 cups thinly sliced shiitake mushroom caps (about 5 ounces)
- 1 cup grated carrot
- 1 garlic clove, minced
- 8 ounces extrafirm tofu, drained and cut into ½-inch cubes
- 1 cup light coconut milk
- 2 cups shredded romaine lettuce
- 1 cup fresh bean sprouts
- 1 cup (1-inch) sliced green onion tops
- 1 cup chopped fresh cilantro
- ⅓ cup dry-roasted peanuts
- 8 ounces uncooked wide rice stick noodles (Banh Pho), cooked and drained
- 5 lime wedges

1. To prepare sauce, combine first 5 ingredients, stirring with a whisk.

2. To prepare noodles, heat oil in a large nonstick skillet over medium-high heat. Add mushroom, carrot, and garlic; sauté 2 minutes. Add sauce and tofu; cook 1 minute.

3. Stir in coconut milk, and cook 2 minutes. Stir in lettuce and next 5 ingredients; cook 1 minute. Serve with lime wedges. Yield: 5 servings (serving size: 2 cups).

CALORIES 385 (29% from fat); FAT 12.5g (sat 3g, mono 4g, poly 4.2g); PROTEIN 13.5g; CARB 55.8g; FIBER 4.6g; CHOL 0mg; IRON 7.1mg; SODIUM 868mg; CALC 365mg

149

Meats

Tenderloin with Grilled
Antipasto Vegetables,
page 172

Drunken Stir-fried
Beef with Green Beans

Drunken Stir-fried Beef with Green Beans

Most Thai dishes are named after the main ingredients or cooking techniques. But occasionally, a dish has a playful name, such as this one.

PASTE:
- ½ teaspoon kosher salt
- 7 garlic cloves, minced
- 2½ teaspoons minced serrano chile
- 2 teaspoons coarsely chopped peeled fresh ginger
- 1 tablespoon chopped peeled fresh lemon grass
- 1 teaspoon grated lime rind

STIR-FRY:
- Cooking spray
- 1 (1-pound) flank steak, trimmed and cut into ¼-inch strips
- 2 cups (1-inch) diagonally cut green beans
- 1 cup quartered cherry tomatoes
- 1 tablespoon sugar
- 3 tablespoons Thai fish sauce
- 1 teaspoon cider vinegar
- 1 cup basil leaves

1. To prepare paste, combine salt and garlic in a mortar and pestle; pound to form a paste. Add chile, ginger, lemon grass, and lime rind, 1 at a time, until each ingredient is incorporated into paste.

2. To prepare stir-fry, heat a wok or large nonstick skillet coated with cooking spray over medium-high heat. Add paste; stir-fry 30 seconds (fumes may cause eyes and throat to burn slightly). Add beef; stir-fry 3 minutes. Add beans, and stir-fry 1 minute. Add tomatoes, sugar, fish sauce, and vinegar; stir-fry 1 minute or until beef reaches desired degree of doneness. Stir in basil. Yield: 5 servings (serving size: ¾ cup).

CALORIES 202 (41% from fat); FAT 9.2g (sat 3.7g, mono 3.5g, poly 0.5g); PROTEIN 20.2g; CARB 10g; FIBER 1.4g; CHOL 45mg; IRON 2.7mg; SODIUM 1,100mg; CALC 50mg

Bourbon and Brown Sugar Flank Steak with Garlic-Chive Mashed Potatoes

STEAK:
- ¼ cup packed dark brown sugar
- ¼ cup minced green onions
- ¼ cup bourbon
- ¼ cup low-sodium soy sauce
- ¼ cup Dijon mustard
- ½ teaspoon freshly ground black pepper
- ¼ teaspoon Worcestershire sauce
- 1 (2-pound) flank steak, trimmed
- Cooking spray
- ½ teaspoon cornstarch

POTATOES:
- 3 pounds small red potatoes
- 6 garlic cloves, peeled
- ½ cup reduced-fat sour cream
- ⅓ cup 2% reduced-fat milk
- 2½ tablespoons butter
- 1 teaspoon salt
- ¼ teaspoon freshly ground black pepper
- ¼ cup chopped fresh chives

1. Combine first 7 ingredients in a large zip-top plastic bag; add steak. Seal and marinate in refrigerator 8 hours or overnight, turning bag occasionally. Remove steak from bag, reserving marinade.

2. Prepare grill.

3. Place steak on grill rack coated with cooking spray; grill 5 minutes on each side or until desired degree of doneness. Let stand 10 minutes. Cut diagonally across grain into thin slices.

4. Combine reserved marinade and cornstarch in a saucepan. Bring to a boil, and cook 1 minute, stirring constantly.

5. Place potatoes and garlic in a large Dutch oven; cover with water. Bring to a boil. Reduce heat, and simmer 30 minutes or until tender. Drain.

6. Return potatoes and garlic to pan; place over medium heat. Add sour cream, milk, butter, salt, and ¼ teaspoon pepper. Mash potato mixture to desired consistency with a potato masher. Stir in chopped chives. Mound ¾ cup potatoes on each of 8 plates; arrange 3 ounces steak around each serving of potatoes. Drizzle 1 tablespoon sauce on each plate. Yield: 8 servings.

CALORIES 456 (30% from fat); FAT 15.4g (sat 7.4g, mono 4.9g, poly 0.8g); PROTEIN 29.1g; CARB 45.9g; FIBER 3.7g; CHOL 77mg; IRON 4.8mg; SODIUM 887mg; CALC 84mg

Flank Steak with Cilantro-Almond Pesto

Ground almonds thicken this lively herb sauce. The pesto is also good as a spread for burgers and sandwiches, or as a pizza sauce.

 ¾ cup fresh cilantro
 2 tablespoons slivered almonds, toasted
 1 tablespoon chopped seeded jalapeño pepper
 ⅛ teaspoon salt
 ⅛ teaspoon black pepper
 1 garlic clove, chopped
 3 tablespoons plain fat-free yogurt
 1½ teaspoons fresh lime juice
 1 (1-pound) flank steak, trimmed
 Cilantro sprigs (optional)

1. Prepare grill.
2. Combine first 6 ingredients in a blender, and process until finely chopped (about 15 seconds). Add yogurt and juice; process until smooth.
3. Grill flank steak 6 minutes on each side or until desired degree of doneness. Cut steak diagonally across grain into thin slices. Serve steak with pesto. Garnish with cilantro sprigs, if desired. Yield: 4 servings (serving size: 3 ounces steak and about 1 tablespoon pesto).

CALORIES 209 (47% from fat); FAT 10.8g (sat 3.9g, mono 4.9g, poly 0.8g); PROTEIN 24.6g; CARB 2.4g; FIBER 0.6g; CHOL 57mg; IRON 2.5mg; SODIUM 152mg; CALC 36mg

Beef-Broccoli Lo Mein

 4 cups hot cooked spaghetti (about 8 ounces uncooked pasta)
 1 teaspoon dark sesame oil
 1 tablespoon peanut oil
 1 tablespoon minced peeled fresh ginger
 4 garlic cloves, minced
 3 cups chopped broccoli
 1½ cups vertically sliced onion
 1 (1-pound) flank steak, trimmed and cut across the grain into long, thin strips
 3 tablespoons low-sodium soy sauce
 2 tablespoons brown sugar
 1 tablespoon oyster sauce
 1 tablespoon chile paste with garlic

1. Combine pasta and sesame oil, tossing well to coat; set aside.
2. Heat peanut oil in a large nonstick skillet over medium-high heat. Add ginger and garlic; sauté 30 seconds. Add broccoli and onion; sauté 3 minutes. Add steak; sauté 5 minutes or until done. Add pasta mixture, soy sauce, and remaining ingredients; cook 1 minute or until thoroughly heated, stirring constantly. Yield: 6 servings (serving size: 1⅓ cups).

CALORIES 327 (26% from fat); FAT 9.3g (sat 3g, mono 3.6g, poly 1.6g); PROTEIN 21.7g; CARB 39.1g; FIBER 2.9g; CHOL 36mg; IRON 3.6mg; SODIUM 382mg; CALC 47mg

Grilled Flank Steak with Green Onion-Ginger Chimichurri

Mint, rice vinegar, ginger, and green onions add an Asian twist to *chimichurri*, the Latin condiment that is a pungent cross between vinaigrette and pesto, and a must with grilled meats.

 ¾ cup (1-inch) sliced green onions
 ⅓ cup chopped fresh parsley
 ¼ cup fresh mint leaves
 3 tablespoons rice vinegar
 2 tablespoons finely chopped peeled fresh ginger
 2 tablespoons olive oil
 1 tablespoon water
 ½ teaspoon salt
 ½ teaspoon black pepper
 2 garlic cloves, peeled
 1 (1½-pound) flank steak, trimmed
 ½ teaspoon salt
 ½ teaspoon black pepper
 Cooking spray

1. Prepare grill.
2. Place first 10 ingredients in a blender or food processor; process until smooth.
3. Sprinkle steak with ½ teaspoon salt and ½ teaspoon pepper. Place steak on grill rack coated with cooking spray; grill 8 minutes on each side or until desired degree of doneness. Let stand 5 minutes. Cut steak diagonally across grain into thin slices. Serve with sauce. Yield: 6 servings (serving size: 3 ounces meat and about 2 tablespoons sauce).

CALORIES 218 (54% from fat); FAT 13g (sat 4.2g, mono 6.7g, poly 0.9g); PROTEIN 22.1g; CARB 2g; FIBER 0.6g; CHOL 54mg; IRON 2.6mg; SODIUM 462mg; CALC 24mg

Oriental Flank Steak with Asparagus and Wild-Rice Pilaf

Omit the red pepper from this recipe if you prefer a less spicy entrée.

16 asparagus spears
⅓ cup low-sodium soy sauce
¼ cup dry sherry
½ teaspoon black pepper
⅛ teaspoon ground red pepper
1 garlic clove, minced
1 (1-pound) flank steak
4 cups sliced spinach
2 cups cooked wild rice
⅔ cup chopped green onions
½ cup finely chopped celery
2 teaspoons dark sesame oil

1. Snap off tough ends of asparagus spears. Cook asparagus in boiling water for 2 minutes or until crisp-tender. Drain well, and chill.

2. Combine soy sauce and the next 4 ingredients, reserving ⅓ cup soy sauce mixture. Set aside. Place remaining soy sauce mixture, asparagus spears, and steak in a heavy-duty zip-top plastic bag, and seal.

Marinate in refrigerator 1 hour, turning the bag occasionally.

3. Remove the asparagus and steak from bag, and discard the marinade. Heat a grill pan or skillet over medium-high heat. Add the asparagus and steak, and cook steak for 3 minutes on each side or until desired degree of doneness, turning asparagus as needed. Place steak on a platter and asparagus on a plate, and cover both with foil. Let stand for 5 minutes. Cut the steak diagonally across the grain into thin slices.

4. Combine ⅓ cup of reserved soy sauce mixture, sliced spinach, cooked wild rice, chopped green onions, chopped celery, and sesame oil, and toss to coat. Divide asparagus spears, steak, and wild-rice pilaf evenly among 4 plates. Yield: 4 servings (serving size: 4 asparagus spears, 3 ounces steak, and 1 cup wild-rice pilaf).

CALORIES 362 (39% from fat); FAT 15.5g (sat 5.9g, mono 6.3g, poly 1.6g); PROTEIN 28.9g; CARB 26.7g; FIBER 5.5g; CHOL 60mg; IRON 5mg; SODIUM 427mg; CALC 97mg

Spaghetti Pie

Though it's really a deep-dish casserole, many Midwesterners lovingly refer to this as Spaghetti Pie. Substitute plain tomato sauce plus ¼ teaspoon garlic powder, if desired, for the canned sauce in the recipe.

1 pound ground round
¼ teaspoon salt
¼ teaspoon black pepper
2 (8-ounce) cans tomato sauce with garlic
1½ cups low-fat sour cream
½ cup chopped green onions
¼ cup (2 ounces) ⅓-less-fat cream cheese, softened
4 cups hot cooked spaghetti (about 8 ounces uncooked pasta)
Cooking spray
1⅓ cups (about 5 ounces) shredded reduced-fat extrasharp cheddar cheese

1. Preheat oven to 350°.

2. Cook meat in a large nonstick skillet over medium heat until browned, stirring to crumble. Drain well, and return meat to pan. Stir in salt, pepper, and tomato sauce. Bring to a boil; reduce heat, and simmer for 20 minutes. Combine the sour cream, onions, and cream cheese in a small bowl; set aside. Place spaghetti noodles in a 2-quart casserole dish coated with cooking spray. Spread sour cream mixture over spaghetti noodles. Top with meat mixture. Sprinkle with cheddar cheese. Cover and bake at 350° for 25 minutes. Uncover; bake an additional 5 minutes or until cheese is bubbly. Yield: 6 servings.

CALORIES 408 (30% from fat); FAT 13.7g (sat 7.3g, mono 4.2g, poly 0.8g); PROTEIN 28.4g; CARB 39.9g; FIBER 2.9g; CHOL 67mg; IRON 3.4mg; SODIUM 849mg; CALC 376mg

Beef-and-Chicken Fajitas with Peppers and Onions

The meat and vegetables for these colorful wraps are marinated in a zesty mixture of lime, garlic, and other seasonings.

MARINADE:
¼ cup olive oil
1 teaspoon grated lime rind
2½ tablespoons fresh lime juice
2 tablespoons Worcestershire sauce
1½ teaspoons ground cumin
1 teaspoon salt
½ teaspoon dried oregano
½ teaspoon coarsely ground black pepper
2 garlic cloves, minced
1 (14.25-ounce) can low-salt beef broth

FAJITAS:
1 (1-pound) flank steak
1 pound skinned, boned chicken breast
2 red bell peppers, each cut into 12 wedges
2 green bell peppers, each cut into 12 wedges
1 large Vidalia or other sweet onion, cut into 16 wedges
Cooking spray
16 (6-inch) fat-free flour tortillas
1 cup bottled salsa
⅓ cup low-fat sour cream
½ cup chopped fresh cilantro
Fresh cilantro sprigs (optional)

1. To prepare marinade, combine first 10 ingredients in a large bowl; set aside.
2. To prepare fajitas, trim fat from flank steak. Score a diamond pattern on both sides of flank steak. Combine 1½ cups marinade, steak, and chicken in a large zip-top plastic bag. Seal and marinate in refrigerator 4 hours or overnight, turning occasionally. Combine remaining marinade, bell peppers, and onion in a zip-top plastic bag. Seal and marinate in refrigerator for 4 hours or overnight, turning occasionally.
3. Prepare grill or broiler.
4. Remove steak and chicken from bag, discarding marinade. Remove vegetables from bag, reserving the marinade. Place the reserved marinade in a small saucepan, and set aside. Place steak, chicken, and vegetables on grill rack or broiler pan coated with cooking spray; cook 8 minutes on each side or until desired degree of doneness.
5. Wrap tortillas tightly in foil; place tortilla packet on grill rack for the last 2 minutes of grilling time. Bring reserved marinade to a boil. Cut steak and chicken diagonally across the grain into thin slices. Place the steak, chicken, and vegetables on a serving platter, and drizzle with the reserved marinade.
6. Arrange about 1 ounce steak slices, about 1 ounce chicken, 3 bell pepper wedges, and 1 onion wedge in a tortilla; top with 1 tablespoon salsa, about 1 teaspoon sour cream, and 1½ teaspoons cilantro. Fold sides of tortilla over the filling, and garnish with cilantro sprigs, if desired. Serve immediately. Yield: 8 servings (serving size: 2 fajitas).

CALORIES 407 (31% from fat); FAT 14.2g (sat 4.3g, mono 7.1g, poly 1.4g); PROTEIN 31.1g; CARB 40.6g; FIBER 5.3g; CHOL 64mg; IRON 3.9mg; SODIUM 841mg; CALC 79mg

Barbecued Flank Steak with Chutney-Bourbon Glaze

1 (1-pound) flank steak
⅓ cup peach or mango chutney
⅓ cup pineapple juice
3 tablespoons bourbon or apple juice
1½ tablespoons rice wine vinegar
1½ tablespoons hot pepper sauce
¼ teaspoon salt
2 garlic cloves, minced

1. Prepare grill or broiler.
2. Trim fat from steak. Combine the flank steak and remaining ingredients in a large zip-top plastic bag. Seal and marinate in refrigerator 15 minutes. Remove steak from bag, reserving marinade.
3. Place steak on a grill rack or broiler pan. Cook 8 minutes on each side or until desired degree of doneness. Cut steak diagonally across grain into thin slices. Keep warm.
4. Pour reserved marinade into a small saucepan. Bring to a boil; cook 1 minute, stirring occasionally. Serve with steak. Yield: 4 servings (serving size: 3 ounces steak and 2 tablespoons glaze).

CALORIES 254 (39% from fat); FAT 11.1g (sat 4.6g, mono 4.3g, poly 0.4g); PROTEIN 22.8g; CARB 13.9g; FIBER 0.7g; CHOL 57mg; IRON 2.4mg; SODIUM 308mg; CALC 12mg

Italian Meat Loaf with Fresh
Basil and Provolone

Italian Meat Loaf with Fresh Basil and Provolone

Even though the sun-dried tomatoes, basil, and pro-volone add a sophisticated flair to this meat loaf, it's still homey enough to serve with your favorite mashed-potato recipe.

```
 1   cup boiling water
 ½   cup sun-dried tomatoes, packed without oil
 ½   cup ketchup
 1   cup seasoned breadcrumbs
 ¾   cup finely chopped onion
 ¾   cup chopped fresh basil
 ½   cup (2 ounces) shredded sharp provolone
     cheese
 2   large egg whites
 2   garlic cloves, minced
 1   pound ground round
     Cooking spray
 ⅓   cup ketchup
```

1. Combine boiling water and tomatoes in a bowl; let stand 30 minutes or until soft. Drain and finely chop tomatoes.

2. Preheat oven to 350°.

3. Combine chopped tomatoes, ½ cup ketchup, and next 7 ingredients in a large bowl. Shape meat mixture into a 9 x 5-inch loaf on a broiler pan coated with cooking spray. Spread ⅓ cup ketchup over meat loaf. Insert a meat thermometer into loaf. Bake at 350° for 1 hour or until thermometer registers 160°. Let stand 10 minutes before slicing. Cut into 12 slices. Yield: 6 servings (serving size: 2 slices).

CALORIES 294 (27% from fat); FAT 8.7g (sat 3.6g, mono 3.2g, poly 0.7g); PROTEIN 24.3g; CARB 30.8g; FIBER 2.5g; CHOL 53mg; IRON 3.9mg; SODIUM 893mg; CALC 149mg

Superfast Salisbury Steak

We used two kinds of ground meats for the patties: ground round for moistness and flavor, and ground turkey breast to bring down the total fat. Serve with roasted vegetables, such as potatoes and carrots.

```
 ¾   pound ground round
 ¾   pound ground turkey breast
 ⅓   cup dry breadcrumbs
 2   large egg whites
     Cooking spray
 ¾   cup water
 3   tablespoons tomato paste
 2   tablespoons Madeira wine or dry sherry
1½   teaspoons Worcestershire sauce
 ¼   teaspoon freshly ground black pepper
 1   (10½-ounce) can condensed French onion
     soup (such as Campbell's)
```

1. Combine first 4 ingredients. Divide meat mixture into 6 equal portions, shaping each into a ½-inch-thick patty. Heat a large nonstick skillet coated with cooking spray over medium-high heat. Add patties; cook 6 minutes or until browned, turning after 3 minutes. Remove patties from pan; keep warm. Stir in water and remaining ingredients. Bring to a boil; add patties. Cover, reduce heat, and simmer 10 minutes. Uncover and cook until wine mixture is reduced to ¾ cup (about 10 minutes). Yield: 6 servings (serving size: 1 patty and 2 tablespoons sauce).

CALORIES 210 (25% from fat); FAT 5.9g (sat 2g, mono 1.9g, poly 0.8g); PROTEIN 27.4g; CARB 10g; FIBER 0.9g; CHOL 64mg; IRON 2.4mg; SODIUM 621mg; CALC 38mg

Sesame Beef and Asian Vegetable Stir-fry

Purchase Chinese black vinegar at Asian markets, or order it from www.ethnicgrocer.com. It has a sweet flavor and a rich, dark color that sets it apart from commonly used clear rice vinegars.

- ¼ cup low-sodium soy sauce, divided
- ¼ cup Chinese black (Chinkiang) vinegar or rice vinegar, divided
- 4 teaspoons dark sesame oil
- ½ teaspoon five-spice powder
- ¾ pound top round, cut into ¼-inch strips
- ⅓ cup water
- 1 teaspoon cornstarch
- 2 teaspoons peanut oil, divided
- 3 tablespoons sesame seeds, toasted and divided
- 1 tablespoon minced peeled fresh ginger
- 2 garlic cloves, minced
- 2 cups red bell pepper strips
- 1½ cups frozen blanched shelled edamame (green soybeans), thawed
- 1 cup sliced shiitake mushroom caps
- 1 (15-ounce) can whole baby corn, drained
- ½ cup diagonally cut green onions
- 3 cups hot cooked jasmine rice

1. Combine 2 tablespoons soy sauce, 2 tablespoons dark vinegar, sesame oil, and five-spice powder in a medium bowl, stirring with a whisk. Add beef; toss to coat. Let stand 10 minutes. Remove beef from bowl; discard marinade.

2. Combine 2 tablespoons soy sauce, 2 tablespoons black vinegar, water, and cornstarch, stirring mixture with a whisk.

3. Heat 1 teaspoon peanut oil in a large nonstick skillet over medium-high heat. Add beef; stir-fry 1 minute. Remove beef from pan. Add 1 teaspoon peanut oil, 2 tablespoons sesame seeds, ginger, and garlic to pan; stir-fry 30 seconds. Add bell pepper, edamame, mushrooms, and corn; stir-fry 2 minutes. Add beef and cornstarch mixture, and stir-fry 3 minutes or until sauce thickens. Remove from heat; stir in 1 tablespoon sesame seeds and onions. Serve over rice. Yield: 6 servings (serving size: 1 cup stir-fry and ½ cup rice).

CALORIES 434 (30% from fat); FAT 14.4g (sat 3.3g, mono 4.8g, poly 3.5g); PROTEIN 21.7g; CARB 55.9g; FIBER 6.3g; CHOL 36mg; IRON 3.7mg; SODIUM 318mg; CALC 62mg

Country-Fried Steak with Mashed Potatoes and Mushroom Gravy

You may know country-fried steak as chicken-fried steak, depending on where you live. We call for cubed steak, but you can buy regular sirloin steak and pound it with a rolling pin. For the mashed potatoes, you can't beat the frozen variety for speed.

- 3 tablespoons fat-free milk
- 2 large egg whites
- ⅓ cup all-purpose flour
- ½ teaspoon onion powder
- ½ teaspoon salt
- ¼ teaspoon garlic powder
- ¼ teaspoon black pepper
- 4 (4-ounce) sirloin cubed steaks
- 2 teaspoons vegetable oil
- 2⅔ cups frozen mashed potatoes (such as Ore-Ida)
- 1⅓ cups fat-free milk
- 2 cups mushrooms, quartered
- 2½ tablespoons all-purpose flour
- ¼ teaspoon salt
- 1 (14-ounce) can fat-free, low-salt beef broth
Parsley sprig (optional)

1. Combine 3 tablespoons milk and egg whites in a shallow dish, stirring with a whisk. Combine ⅓ cup flour and next 4 ingredients (⅓ cup flour through pepper) in a shallow dish. Working with 1 steak at a time, dip in egg mixture; dredge in flour mixture. Repeat procedure with remaining steaks, egg mixture, and flour mixture.

2. Heat oil in a nonstick skillet over medium-high heat. Add steaks, and cook 3 minutes on each side or until browned. Remove steaks from pan, and keep warm.

3. While steaks cook, prepare the mashed potatoes according to package directions, using 1⅓ cups milk. Keep warm.

4. Add mushrooms to pan, and sauté 3 minutes. Combine 2½ tablespoons flour, ¼ teaspoon salt, and broth, stirring with a whisk. Add broth mixture to pan. Bring to a boil, and cook 1 minute, stirring constantly. Spoon over steaks. Serve with mashed potatoes. Garnish with a parsley sprig, if desired. Yield: 4 servings (serving size: 1 steak, about ⅓ cup gravy, and about 1 cup mashed potatoes).

CALORIES 436 (30% from fat); FAT 14.7g (sat 5.1g, mono 4.8g, poly 2.2g); PROTEIN 38.2g; CARB 34.7g; FIBER 1.9g; CHOL 189mg; IRON 4.6mg; SODIUM 759mg; CALC 147mg

Country-Fried Steak with
Mashed Potatoes and
Mushroom Gravy

Bulgogi
(Korean Beef Barbecue)

Serve the beef over lettuce and rice for an attractive presentation.

1   pound top sirloin steak, trimmed
1   tablespoon brown sugar
3   tablespoons low-sodium soy sauce
1   tablespoon mirin (sweet rice wine)
1   teaspoon minced peeled fresh ginger
1   teaspoon dark sesame oil
3   garlic cloves, minced
Cooking spray

1. Wrap beef in plastic wrap; freeze 1 hour or until firm. Remove plastic wrap; cut beef diagonally across grain into $\frac{1}{16}$-inch-thick slices.

2. Combine beef, brown sugar, and next 5 ingredients in a large zip-top plastic bag. Seal and marinate in refrigerator 1 hour, turning bag occasionally.
3. Prepare grill.
4. Place a wire grilling basket on grill rack. Remove beef from bag, and discard marinade. Place beef on grilling basket coated with cooking spray, and grill for 5 minutes or until beef is desired degree of doneness, turning frequently. Yield: 4 servings (serving size: 3 ounces).

CALORIES 208 (33% from fat); FAT 7.6g (sat 2.7g, mono 3.2g, poly 0.7g); PROTEIN 26.1g; CARB 6.4g; FIBER 0.2g; CHOL 76mg; IRON 3.1mg; SODIUM 457mg; CALC 19mg

Saucy Sirloin Steak

This 20-minute entrée is bound to be a weekly staple since it uses ingredients you probably have on hand.

½   teaspoon salt
½   teaspoon garlic powder
¼   teaspoon black pepper
1   pound boneless sirloin steak, trimmed
Cooking spray
1   teaspoon olive oil
2   garlic cloves, minced
½   cup beef broth
¼   cup hoisin sauce
2   teaspoons Dijon mustard
1   teaspoon tomato paste
3   teaspoons red wine vinegar

1. Preheat broiler.
2. Combine first 3 ingredients in a small bowl; sprinkle over steak. Place steak on broiler rack coated with cooking spray. Broil 6 minutes on each side or until desired degree of doneness. Let stand for 5 minutes.
3. While steak is standing, heat oil in a small saucepan over medium heat. Add garlic; cook 30 seconds, stirring constantly. Add broth and remaining ingredients. Bring to a boil; reduce heat, and simmer 5 minutes or until thick, stirring with a whisk. Cut steak diagonally across grain into thin slices; serve with sauce. Yield: 4 servings (serving size: 3 ounces steak and 3 tablespoons sauce).

CALORIES 227 (35% from fat); FAT 8.8g (sat 2.9g, mono 4g, poly 0.7g); PROTEIN 27.1g; CARB 8.5g; FIBER 0.7g; CHOL 76mg; IRON 3.2mg; SODIUM 765mg; CALC 24mg

Smothered Sirloin Steak with Adobo Gravy

1   pound ground sirloin
1   (7-ounce) can chipotle chiles in adobo sauce
Cooking spray
2   cups thinly sliced onion
⅓   cup beef consommé
1   teaspoon low-sodium soy sauce
½   teaspoon cornstarch

1. Divide sirloin into 4 equal portions, shaping each into a ½-inch-thick patty.
2. Drain chipotles in a colander over a bowl, reserving ¼ cup adobo sauce. Reserve chiles for another use.
3. Heat a large nonstick skillet coated with cooking

spray over medium-high heat. Add patties and onion; cook 5 minutes on each side. Add adobo sauce and consommé; bring to a boil. Cover, reduce heat, and simmer 10 minutes. Combine soy sauce and cornstarch; stir well. Add to pan; bring to a boil. Cook 1 minute or until thick. Yield: 4 servings (serving size: 1 steak and 3 tablespoons sauce).

CALORIES 203 (33% from fat); FAT 7.4g (sat 2.5g, mono 3g, poly 0.6g); PROTEIN 26g; CARB 6.8g; FIBER 1.3g; CHOL 70mg; IRON 2.6mg; SODIUM 294mg; CALC 20mg

Beef with Rosemary-Mushroom Sauce

There's plenty of sauce to serve with the steak and spoon over the mashed potatoes. Complete the menu with steamed broccoli and French bread.

1   (8-ounce) package presliced mushrooms
1   cup dry red wine
1   pound boneless top sirloin steak (about ¾ inch thick)
Cooking spray
1   cup chopped green onions
¼   cup chopped fresh parsley, divided
1½ teaspoons chopped fresh or ½ teaspoon dried rosemary
1   teaspoon balsamic vinegar
4   garlic cloves, minced
1   (10½-ounce) can beef consommé
1   (8-ounce) can no-salt-added tomato sauce

1. Combine mushrooms, wine, and steak in a large zip-top plastic bag; seal. Marinate in refrigerator 30 minutes, turning occasionally.
2. Remove steak from bag, reserving marinade. Place a large nonstick skillet coated with cooking spray over medium-high heat. Add steak; cook 6 minutes or until desired degree of doneness, turning after 3 minutes. Remove from pan.
3. Combine onions, 2 tablespoons parsley, rosemary, and remaining ingredients. Add onion mixture and reserved marinade to pan. Bring to a boil; cook until reduced to 2 cups (about 15 minutes), stirring frequently.
4. Cut beef diagonally across grain into thin slices. Place beef on a serving platter. Serve mushroom sauce with beef. Sprinkle with 2 tablespoons parsley. Yield: 4 servings (serving size: 3 ounces beef and ½ cup sauce).

CALORIES 229 (26% from fat); FAT 6.6g (sat 2.3g, mono 2.5g, poly 0.7g); PROTEIN 30g; CARB 12.4g; FIBER 1.7g; CHOL 69mg; IRON 5.1mg; SODIUM 479mg; CALC 55mg

Vietnamese Summer Rolls

SAUCE:
¼ cup rice vinegar
1 tablespoon water
1½ teaspoons sugar
1 teaspoon dark sesame oil
1 teaspoon chile paste with garlic
½ teaspoon salt

ROLLS:
8 (8-inch) round sheets rice paper
8 Boston lettuce leaves
½ cup cooked bean threads (cellophane noodles)
½ cup fresh bean sprouts
½ cup julienne-cut seeded peeled cucumber
½ cup julienne-cut carrot
½ cup fresh mint leaves
½ cup fresh cilantro leaves
6 ounces Lemon Grass Beef, cut into
   16 (1-inch-thick) strips

1. To prepare sauce, combine first 6 ingredients in a small bowl, stirring well with a whisk.
2. To prepare rolls, add cold water to a large, shallow dish to a depth of 1 inch. Place 1 rice paper sheet in dish of water; let stand 2 minutes or until soft.
3. Place softened rice paper sheet on a flat surface. Place 1 lettuce leaf on bottom third of sheet. Top with 1 tablespoon each of noodles, sprouts, cucumber, carrot, mint, and cilantro; add 2 beef strips.
4. Fold sides of rice paper sheet over filling; roll up. Gently press seam to seal; place, seam side down, on a serving platter (cover with a damp cloth to keep from drying). Repeat procedure to make 8 rolls. Serve with sauce. Yield: 4 servings (serving size: 2 summer rolls and 1½ tablespoons sauce).

(Totals include Lemon Grass Beef) CALORIES 230 (16% from fat); FAT 4g (sat 1g, mono 1.5g, poly 0.7g); PROTEIN 14.8g; CARB 34g; FIBER 1.1g; CHOL 34mg; IRON 2.3mg; SODIUM 443mg; CALC 43mg

Lemon Grass Beef

Freezing the beef makes slicing it easy. Reserve a quarter of the cooked beef for Vietnamese Summer Rolls.

2 pounds sirloin tip roast
½ cup chopped peeled fresh lemon grass
⅓ cup chopped shallots
3 tablespoons fish sauce
1½ tablespoons sugar
1 teaspoon dark sesame oil
1 teaspoon peanut oil
¼ teaspoon salt
6 garlic cloves, crushed
2 serrano chiles, seeded and chopped
Cooking spray

1. Cover roast with plastic wrap; freeze 30 minutes. Remove beef from freezer; cut beef horizontally into ⅛-inch-thick slices.
2. Combine lemon grass and remaining ingredients except cooking spray in a food processor; process until smooth (about 1 minute). Combine beef and lemon grass mixture in a large zip-top plastic bag. Seal and marinate in refrigerator 2 to 4 hours.
3. Prepare grill.
4. Remove beef from bag; discard marinade. Place beef on grill rack coated with cooking spray; grill 1 minute on each side or until desired degree of doneness. Yield: 8 servings (serving size: 3 ounces).
NOTE: Store cooked beef in an airtight container in the refrigerator for up to 2 days.

CALORIES 158 (29% from fat); FAT 5.1g (sat 1.7g, mono 2g, poly 0.4g); PROTEIN 24.8g; CARB 2g; FIBER 0.1g; CHOL 69mg; IRON 2.8mg; SODIUM 353mg; CALC 10mg

Grilled Steak with Charred Tomato Salsa

The high heat used in grilling quickly caramelizes the tomatoes' natural sugars, producing slightly charred, juicy vegetables with rich flavor. To make your own basil oil, heat ¼ cup chopped basil and ¼ cup olive oil in a small saucepan over low heat just until the oil sizzles. Remove from heat, and let stand about an hour or until cool. Strain and discard the basil. The basil oil will keep in the refrigerator for up to two weeks.

1 pound large tomatoes, cored, cut in half horizontally, and seeded (about 2 medium)
Cooking spray
½ cup thinly sliced red onion
1 tablespoon red wine vinegar
1 teaspoon basil-flavored olive oil
¼ teaspoon salt, divided
¼ teaspoon freshly ground black pepper, divided
6 basil leaves, thinly sliced
1 (1-pound) boneless sirloin steak

1. Place tomato halves, cut sides down, on paper towels. Let stand 30 minutes.

2. Heat a grill pan coated with cooking spray over medium-high heat. Place tomato halves, cut sides down, in pan; grill 5 minutes. Turn tomato halves over, and grill 1 minute or until skin is blackened. Remove from pan, and cool 5 minutes. Cut the tomato halves into 1-inch pieces. Combine tomato pieces, onion, vinegar, oil, ⅛ teaspoon salt, ⅛ teaspoon pepper, and basil.

3. Sprinkle steak with ⅛ teaspoon salt and ⅛ teaspoon pepper. Place steak in pan coated with cooking spray, and grill 6 minutes on each side or until desired degree of doneness. Let stand 5 minutes. Cut steak diagonally across the grain into thin slices. Serve with tomato salsa. Yield: 4 servings (serving size: 3 ounces steak and about ¼ cup tomato salsa).

CALORIES 206 (35% from fat); FAT 8g (sat 2.8g, mono 3.7g, poly 0.5g); PROTEIN 26.4g; CARB 6.6g; FIBER 1.6g; CHOL 76mg; IRON 3.4mg; SODIUM 213mg; CALC 20mg

Churrasco with Chimichurri
Sauce

Churrasco with Chimichurri Sauce

1 (1½-pound) boned sirloin steak
1½ cups cilantro sprigs
1 cup white vinegar
¾ cup chopped onion
2 teaspoons ground cumin
2 teaspoons dried oregano
2 teaspoons dried thyme
2 teaspoons black pepper
1 teaspoon salt
6 garlic cloves, chopped (about ¼ cup)
3 bay leaves
Cooking spray
Chimichurri Sauce

1. Trim fat from steak; set aside. Combine cilantro and next 9 ingredients in a large zip-top plastic bag. Add steak to bag, and seal. Marinate in refrigerator for 3 hours, turning occasionally. Remove steak from bag, and discard marinade.
2. Prepare grill or broiler.
3. Place the steak on grill rack or broiler pan coated with cooking spray; cook 8 minutes on each side or until desired degree of doneness. Let stand 3 minutes. Cut steak diagonally across grain into thin slices. Serve with Chimichurri Sauce. Yield: 6 servings (serving size: 3 ounces steak and about 2½ tablespoons sauce).

(Totals include Chimichurri Sauce) CALORIES 239 (43% from fat); FAT 11.5g (sat 3.3g, mono 6.2g, poly 0.8g); PROTEIN 26.6g; CARB 7.5g; FIBER 1.7g; CHOL 76mg; IRON 5.4mg; SODIUM 459mg; CALC 79mg

CHIMICHURRI SAUCE:

¼ cup white vinegar
2 tablespoons extravirgin olive oil
½ teaspoon salt
6 garlic cloves, peeled
3 bay leaves
2 jalapeño peppers, stems removed
1 cup minced fresh parsley
¼ cup minced fresh oregano

1. Place the first 6 ingredients in a blender, and process until smooth. Add parsley and oregano, stirring well with a whisk. Yield: 1 cup (serving size: about 2½ tablespoons).

CALORIES 55 (77% from fat); FAT 4.7g (sat 0.7g, mono 3.4g, poly 0.5g); PROTEIN 0.7g; CARB 3.5g; FIBER 0.8g; CHOL 0mg; IRON 1.4mg; SODIUM 202mg; CALC 40mg

Filet Mignon with Peppercorn-Orange Sauce

SAUCE:

2 teaspoons grated orange rind
¼ cup fresh orange juice
¼ cup low-sodium soy sauce
2 tablespoons brown sugar
2 tablespoons fresh lemon juice
2 tablespoons balsamic vinegar
2 teaspoons honey
½ cup coarsely chopped green onions
½ cup coarsely chopped fresh cilantro
2 tablespoons drained brine-packed green peppercorns
1 garlic clove, peeled
2 teaspoons extravirgin olive oil
2 teaspoons sesame seeds, toasted
½ teaspoon salt

STEAKS:

12 (4-ounce) beef tenderloin steaks, trimmed (1 inch thick)
½ teaspoon salt
½ teaspoon black pepper
Cooking spray
Cilantro sprigs (optional)

1. Prepare grill.
2. To prepare sauce, combine first 7 ingredients in a small saucepan; bring to a boil. Cook until reduced to ⅓ cup (about 6 minutes). Cool.
3. Place green onions, chopped cilantro, peppercorns, garlic clove, and oil in a food processor; process until finely chopped. Add orange juice mixture, sesame seeds, and ½ teaspoon salt; pulse to combine. Set aside.
4. To prepare steaks, sprinkle beef with ½ teaspoon salt and black pepper. Place steaks on a grill rack coated with cooking spray; grill 3 minutes on each side or until desired degree of doneness. Serve steaks with sauce. Garnish with cilantro sprigs, if desired. Yield: 12 servings (serving size: 1 steak and about 1 tablespoon sauce).

CALORIES 208 (39% from fat); FAT 9.1g (sat 3.1g, mono 3.6g, poly 0.4g); PROTEIN 24.4g; CARB 5.7g; FIBER 0.5g; CHOL 71mg; IRON 3.3mg; SODIUM 497mg; CALC 18mg

Filet Mignon with
Peppercorn-Mustard Sauce

Filet Mignon with Peppercorn-Mustard Sauce

4 (4-ounce) beef tenderloin steaks (1½ inches thick)
¼ teaspoon salt
¼ teaspoon coarsely ground or cracked black pepper
1 teaspoon vegetable oil
⅓ cup minced shallots
½ cup cognac
½ cup fat-free beef broth
¼ cup Dijon mustard

1. Sprinkle steaks with salt and pepper. Heat oil in a 9-inch cast-iron skillet over medium-high heat. Add steaks, and cook 5 minutes on each side or until desired degree of doneness. Remove steaks from pan, and keep warm. Add shallots to pan, and sauté 30 seconds. Add cognac; cook 10 seconds. Add broth and mustard; stir well. Reduce heat; cook 2 minutes, stirring constantly. Serve steaks with sauce. Yield: 4 servings (serving size: 1 steak and 2 tablespoons sauce).

CALORIES 279 (31% from fat); FAT 9.6g (sat 3.5g, mono 3.7g, poly 1g); PROTEIN 24g; CARB 3.8g; FIBER 0.1g; CHOL 70mg; IRON 3.3mg; SODIUM 656mg; CALC 13mg

Spiced Pepper-Crusted Filet Mignon with Asparagus

Brandy and spices create a flavorful paste for rubbing on the beef.

1 teaspoon bottled minced garlic
½ teaspoon olive oil
½ teaspoon salt, divided
12 ounces fresh asparagus, trimmed
1 tablespoon cracked black pepper
2 teaspoons brandy
½ teaspoon garlic powder
4 (4-ounce) beef tenderloin steaks (about 1 inch thick)
Cooking spray

1. Preheat broiler.
2. Combine minced garlic, oil, ¼ teaspoon salt, and asparagus in a large bowl, tossing gently to coat.
3. Combine ¼ teaspoon salt, pepper, brandy, and garlic powder; rub evenly over steaks. Place steaks on a broiler pan coated with cooking spray; broil 6 minutes. Turn the steaks over, and add asparagus to pan. Broil 5 minutes or until desired degree of doneness. Yield: 4 servings (serving size: 1 steak and 3 ounces asparagus).

CALORIES 269 (39% from fat); FAT 11.6g (sat 4.1g, mono 4.5g, poly 0.5g); PROTEIN 34.9g; CARB 4.7g; FIBER 1.2g; CHOL 95mg; IRON 5.1mg; SODIUM 367mg; CALC 36mg

Pepper-Crusted Filet Mignon with Horseradish Cream

Roasted new potatoes and asparagus make easy sides for an elegant dinner for two.

2 (4-ounce) beef tenderloin steaks, trimmed (about ¾ inch thick)
½ teaspoon sea salt
¼ teaspoon freshly ground black pepper
1 teaspoon butter
Cooking spray
1 garlic clove, minced
¼ cup fat-free sour cream
½ teaspoon prepared horseradish

1. Sprinkle both sides of steaks with salt and pepper.
2. Melt butter in a nonstick skillet coated with cooking spray over medium heat. Add the steaks, and cook for 3 minutes on each side or until desired degree of doneness. Sprinkle the steaks with minced garlic, and cook over medium-low heat for 1 minute on each side.
3. Combine sour cream and horseradish; serve with steaks. Yield: 2 servings (serving size: 1 steak and 2 tablespoons horseradish cream).

CALORIES 231 (44% from fat); FAT 11.3g (sat 4.8g, mono 4g, poly 0.5g); PROTEIN 25.2g; CARB 5.6g; FIBER 0.1g; CHOL 78mg; IRON 3.3mg; SODIUM 684mg; CALC 58mg

Easy Savory Gravy

This gravy is thickened with a lightly browned roux to add richness. Soy sauce gives it a hearty flavor.

  2   tablespoons olive oil
  6   tablespoons all-purpose flour
  2   (14½-ounce) cans vegetable broth
  ¼   cup low-sodium soy sauce
  ½   teaspoon black pepper

1. Heat oil in a saucepan over medium heat. Add flour; cook 5 minutes or until lightly browned and fragrant, stirring constantly with a whisk. (If flour browns too quickly, remove pan from heat; stir constantly until it cools.)
2. Gradually add vegetable broth to pan, stirring constantly with a whisk. Stir in soy sauce and pepper, and cook until mixture is thick (about 15 minutes), stirring frequently. Yield: 3 cups (serving size: about ¼ cup).

CALORIES 42 (54% from fat); FAT 2.5g (sat 0.3g, mono 1.7g, poly 0.2g); PROTEIN 1.3g; CARB 4.1g; FIBER 0.1g; CHOL 0mg; IRON 0.2mg; SODIUM 493mg; CALC 0mg

Pepper Steak with Port-Wine Mushroom Sauce

The deeply flavored Port-Wine Mushroom Sauce is reminiscent of a classic bordelaise sauce but made in a fraction of the time. It's virtually fat-free—another plus. It also garnered our highest rating in the Test Kitchens.

Port-Wine Mushroom Sauce
  4   (4-ounce) beef tenderloin steaks
       (about 1 inch thick)
  1   tablespoon black peppercorns, crushed
  ½   teaspoon kosher salt

1. Prepare the Port-Wine Mushroom Sauce; set aside, and keep warm.
2. Sprinkle tenderloin steaks with crushed peppercorns and kosher salt. Heat a nonstick skillet over medium-high heat. Add steaks, and cook for 3 minutes on each side or until steaks are desired degree of doneness. Serve steaks with Port-Wine Mushroom Sauce. Yield: 4 servings (serving size: 1 steak and ¼ cup sauce).

(Totals include Port-Wine Mushroom Sauce) CALORIES 241 (29% from fat); FAT 7.7g (sat 3g, mono 2.9g, poly 0.4g); PROTEIN 27.5g; CARB 9.4g; FIBER 1g; CHOL 70mg; IRON 4.6mg; SODIUM 722mg; CALC 28mg

PORT-WINE MUSHROOM SAUCE:

  1½   cups sliced shiitake mushroom caps (about
         3½ ounces)
    1   tablespoon all-purpose flour
   ⅓   cup port or other sweet red wine
   ¼   cup minced shallots
    1   tablespoon balsamic vinegar
    1   cup beef broth
    2   teaspoons Worcestershire sauce
    1   teaspoon tomato paste
   ⅛   teaspoon dried rosemary
   ½   teaspoon Dijon mustard

1. Combine mushrooms and flour in a bowl; toss.
2. Combine the wine, shallots, and balsamic vinegar in a skillet. Bring to a boil; cook until thick (about 3 minutes).
3. Reduce heat to medium. Add broth, Worcestershire, tomato paste, and rosemary; cook 1 minute. Add mushroom mixture, and cook 3 minutes, stirring constantly.
4. Stir in mustard. Yield: 1 cup (serving size: ¼ cup).

CALORIES 69 (3% from fat); FAT 0.2g (sat 0g, mono 0g, poly 0.1g); PROTEIN 3.8g; CARB 8.4g; FIBER 0.5g; CHOL 0mg; IRON 1mg; SODIUM 367mg; CALC 14mg

How to Prepare Port-Wine Mushroom Sauce

Combine wine, shallots, and balsamic vinegar. Boil. Cook until thick.

Stir in mustard.

Pepper Steak with Port-Wine
Mushroom Sauce

Onion-Smothered Roast Brisket and Vegetables

A meat-and-three classic, this dish places meat and potatoes squarely in the center of the plate, yet leaves room for more.

 1 (2½-pound) beef brisket
 6 cups thinly sliced onion, separated into rings
 1 cup bottled chili sauce
 ½ cup beer
 1 tablespoon brown sugar
 1 tablespoon Worcestershire sauce
 1 pound carrots, cut into 1½-inch-thick pieces (about 2 cups)
 1½ pounds red potatoes (about 6), quartered
 ½ teaspoon seasoned salt
 ½ teaspoon garlic pepper (such as Lawry's)

1. Preheat oven to 325°.
2. Trim fat from brisket. Place brisket in a large roasting pan; top with onion. Combine chili sauce, beer, sugar, and Worcestershire sauce; pour over onion. Cover and bake at 325° for 1½ hours.
3. Stir onion into cooking liquid. Arrange the carrots and potatoes around brisket, and spoon cooking liquid over vegetables. Sprinkle the seasoned salt and garlic pepper over meat and vegetables. Cover and bake an additional 1½ hours or until vegetables are tender.
4. Cut brisket diagonally across the grain into thin slices. Arrange the beef and vegetables in each of 8 shallow bowls, and serve with sauce. Yield: 8 servings (serving size: 3 ounces beef, 1 cup vegetables, and ⅓ cup sauce).
NOTE: If you don't have a large roasting pan, cut brisket in half, and place in a large Dutch oven.

CALORIES 361 (28% from fat); FAT 11.3g (sat 4.1g, mono 5g, poly 0.5g); PROTEIN 29.2g; CARB 35.8g; FIBER 4g; CHOL 79mg; IRON 4.2mg; SODIUM 682mg; CALC 55mg

Standing Rib Roast with Madeira Sauce and Herbed Yorkshire Puddings

Yorkshire pudding, a popover, derives its name from the Yorkshire region of northern England, where it's been a holiday classic for generations. Let the roast sit while you finish the sauce and make the popovers; it will be easier to carve.

ROAST:
 1 (5-pound) French-cut rib-eye roast, trimmed
 1 garlic clove, halved
 ½ teaspoon salt
 ½ teaspoon freshly ground black pepper
Cooking spray
SAUCE:
 1 cup water
 2 tablespoons all-purpose flour
 ½ cup Madeira wine
 ½ cup beef broth
 ½ teaspoon black pepper
PUDDINGS:
 1½ cups all-purpose flour
 1 teaspoon salt
 ¾ teaspoon freshly ground black pepper
 1½ cups 1% low-fat milk
 1 tablespoon chopped fresh or 1 teaspoon dried thyme
 1 tablespoon chopped fresh parsley
 1 teaspoon grated lemon rind
 5 large egg whites
 2 large eggs

1. Preheat oven to 450°.
2. To prepare roast, rub roast on all sides with garlic. Sprinkle with ½ teaspoon salt and ½ teaspoon pepper. Place roast, fat side up, on a broiler pan coated with cooking spray. Insert meat thermometer into thickest portion of roast. Bake roast at 450° for 25 minutes. Reduce oven temperature to 300° (do not remove the roast from oven), and bake an additional 1½ hours or until thermometer registers 145° (medium) or desired degree of doneness. Place roast on a platter, and let stand while finishing the sauce and Yorkshire puddings. Reserve 1½ tablespoons drippings from pan for puddings, and set aside.
3. To prepare sauce, wipe remaining drippings from pan with paper towels, leaving browned bits on bottom of pan. Combine water and 2 tablespoons flour in a small bowl. Add Madeira to pan;

Standing Rib Roast with
Madeira Sauce and
Herbed Yorkshire Puddings

bring to a boil over medium-high heat, scraping bottom of pan with a wooden spoon to loosen browned bits. Add flour mixture; cook 1 minute or until slightly thick. Stir in broth and ½ teaspoon pepper; cook 2 minutes. Keep warm.

4. Preheat oven to 450°.

5. To prepare puddings, coat 12 muffin cups with reserved pan drippings. Lightly spoon 1½ cups flour into dry measuring cups, and level with a knife. Combine 1½ cups flour, 1 teaspoon salt, and ¾ teaspoon pepper in a medium bowl. Gradually add the milk, stirring with a whisk until smooth. Add chopped thyme and remaining ingredients, stirring with a whisk until smooth. Spoon batter into prepared cups. Bake at 450° for 15 minutes. Reduce oven temperature to 375° (do not remove puddings from oven), and bake for an additional 15 minutes or until golden. Yield: 12 servings (serving size: 3 ounces beef, 2 tablespoons Madeira sauce, and 1 pudding).

CALORIES 304 (38% from fat); FAT 12.8g (sat 5g, mono 5.2g, poly 0.6g); PROTEIN 29g; CARB 16.1g; FIBER 0.6g; CHOL 106mg; IRON 3.5mg; SODIUM 410mg; CALC 58mg

Vinegar-Braised Beef with Thyme, Carrots, and Onions

To start a day ahead, prepare the recipe up to draining the cooking liquid in Step 4. Return the drained liquid and beef to the pan, refrigerate for up to a day, skim the solidified fat from the surface, and continue with Step 5.

1 tablespoon minced fresh thyme
1 large garlic clove, minced
1 (3½-pound) beef brisket, trimmed
2 teaspoons olive oil, divided
¾ teaspoon salt, divided
¼ teaspoon freshly ground black pepper
1½ cups chopped onion
1 cup chopped carrot
1 cup chopped celery
3 cups low-salt beef broth
½ cup Merlot or other fruity red wine
½ cup red wine vinegar
1 bay leaf
1 pound baby carrots with tops
1 pound cipollini or pearl onions, peeled
2 tablespoons chopped fresh parsley
1 teaspoon chopped fresh thyme

1. Preheat oven to 350°.

2. Combine 1 tablespoon thyme and garlic. Make 12 slits on outside of beef; stuff each with ¼ teaspoon garlic mixture. Rub beef with 1 teaspoon oil. Sprinkle with ¼ teaspoon salt and pepper.

3. Heat a large ovenproof nonstick skillet over medium-high heat. Add beef; cook 2 minutes on all sides or until browned. Remove from pan. Add chopped onion, chopped carrot, and celery to pan; sauté 6 minutes. Add ½ teaspoon salt, broth, wine, vinegar, and bay leaf; bring to a boil. Return beef to pan. Cover and place pan in oven. Bake at 350° for 1 hour. Reduce heat to 325°; turn beef. Cover and bake an additional 90 minutes or until tender, turning beef twice. Remove beef from pan.

4. Drain cooking liquid through a sieve into a bowl; press down on vegetables to extract liquid. Discard solids. Place a zip-top plastic bag inside a 2-cup glass measure. Pour drippings into bag; let stand 10 minutes (fat will rise to top). Seal bag; snip off 1 bottom corner of bag. Drain drippings into a bowl, stopping before fat layer reaches opening; discard fat.

5. Trim all but 1 inch from tops of baby carrots. Heat 1 teaspoon oil in a nonstick skillet over medium-high heat. Add cipollini onions, and sauté 3 minutes or until browned. Add beef, cooking liquid, and baby carrots; bring to a boil. Cover, and bake at 350° for 1 hour, turning once. Sprinkle with parsley and 1 teaspoon thyme. Serve with vegetables and sauce. Yield: 8 servings (serving size: about 3 ounces beef, about 5 onions, about 4 carrots, and about 1½ tablespoons sauce).

CALORIES 327 (26% from fat); FAT 9.3g (sat 2.8g, mono 4.4g, poly 0.6g); PROTEIN 41.5g; CARB 16.4g; FIBER 3.9g; CHOL 113mg; IRON 4.2mg; SODIUM 375mg; CALC 57mg

Cinnamon-Beef Noodles

In this Chinese classic, beef simmers in a soy sauce mixture. Ginger, garlic, and cinnamon add extra flavor.

5 cups water
1½ cups rice wine or sake
¾ cup low-sodium soy sauce
¼ cup sugar
2 teaspoons vegetable oil
2 pounds beef stew meat, cut into
1½-inch cubes
8 green onions, cut into 1-inch
pieces
6 garlic cloves, crushed
2 cinnamon sticks
1 (1-inch) piece peeled fresh ginger, thinly
sliced
1 (10-ounce) package fresh spinach, chopped
4 cups hot cooked wide lo mein noodles or
vermicelli (about 8 ounces uncooked pasta)

1. Combine first 4 ingredients in a large bowl; stir with a whisk. Set aside.
2. Heat 1 teaspoon oil in a large Dutch oven over medium-high heat, and add half of beef, browning on all sides. Remove beef from pan. Repeat procedure with remaining oil and beef. Return beef to pan, and add water mixture, green onions, garlic, cinnamon sticks, and ginger. Bring to a boil; cover, reduce heat, and simmer for 2 hours or until beef is tender. Discard ginger and cinnamon. Stir in spinach, and cook for 3 minutes or until wilted. Serve over lo mein noodles. Yield: 8 servings (serving size: 1 cup beef mixture and ½ cup lo mein noodles).

CALORIES 403 (14% from fat); FAT 6.2g (sat 2.3g, mono 3.3g, poly 1.3g); PROTEIN 30.5g; CARB 50.4g; FIBER 2.9g; CHOL 44mg; IRON 5.2mg; SODIUM 1,080mg; CALC 80mg

Beef Curry with Toasted Spices

You can also prepare this recipe with cubed leg of lamb. Fenugreek seed is a common spice in Indian food. Find it at an ethnic grocery such as World Market, or order online at www.americanspice.com. Serve this dish over rice.

BEEF:

1 tablespoon Homemade Curry Powder
1½ teaspoons salt
2 teaspoons freshly ground black pepper
3½ pounds beef stew meat, trimmed and cut into bite-sized pieces

TOASTED SPICES:

2 tablespoons coriander seeds
1 tablespoon cumin seeds
2 teaspoons fenugreek seeds
3 whole cloves
1 (1-inch) cinnamon stick, broken
2 dried hot red chiles
3 bay leaves
2 tablespoons sugar
½ teaspoon ground cardamom
¼ teaspoon salt

REMAINING INGREDIENTS:

1 tablespoon olive oil, divided
3 cups vertically sliced onion
3 tablespoons minced peeled fresh ginger
¼ cup minced garlic
2 tablespoons Hungarian sweet paprika
2 cups plain low-fat yogurt
1½ cups low-salt beef broth
1 cup chopped red bell pepper
½ cup minced fresh cilantro stems
½ cup tomato puree

1. To prepare beef, combine first 3 ingredients, and rub over beef. Cover and marinate in refrigerator 2 hours, tossing occasionally.

2. To prepare toasted spices, heat a nonstick skillet over medium-high heat. Add coriander and next 6 ingredients, and cook 1 minute or until fragrant, shaking pan constantly. Place coriander mixture, sugar, cardamom, and ¼ teaspoon salt in a spice or coffee grinder; process until finely ground.

3. Heat 1½ teaspoons oil in a Dutch oven over medium-high heat. Add half of beef mixture; sauté 5 minutes on all sides or until browned. Remove from pan with a slotted spoon. Repeat procedure with remaining oil and beef mixture; remove from

pan. Reduce heat to medium. Add onion and ginger to pan; cook 6 minutes or until onion is tender, stirring occasionally. Add toasted spice mixture, garlic, and paprika; cook 1 minute, stirring constantly. Add beef, yogurt, and remaining ingredients; bring to a boil. Cover, reduce heat, and simmer 1 hour and 30 minutes or until beef is tender. Yield: 12 servings (serving size: about 1 cup).

(Totals include Homemade Curry Powder) CALORIES 262 (38% from fat); FAT 11g (sat 3.9g, mono 5g, poly 0.5g); PROTEIN 27.6g; CARB 12.9g; FIBER 2.1g; CHOL 79mg; IRON 4.1mg; SODIUM 440mg; CALC 118mg

HOMEMADE CURRY POWDER:

In a pinch, use Patak's Original Garam Masala Curry Paste, which we believe is a better substitute than a commercial curry powder.

3 tablespoons Hungarian sweet paprika
2 teaspoons ground cumin
2 teaspoons ground fennel seed
2 teaspoons ground yellow or brown mustard
2 teaspoons ground red pepper
1 tablespoon ground coriander
1 tablespoon ground turmeric
1 teaspoon ground cardamom
½ teaspoon ground cinnamon
½ teaspoon ground cloves

1. Combine all ingredients. Yield: ½ cup (serving size: 1 teaspoon).
NOTE: Store in an airtight container in a cool, dark place for up to 2 months.

CALORIES 6 (45% from fat); FAT 0.3g (sat 0g, mono 0.1g, poly 0g); PROTEIN 0.2g; CARB 0.8g; FIBER 0.5g; CHOL 0mg; IRON 0.3mg; SODIUM 1mg; CALC 8mg

Corned Beef and Cabbage Dinner

1 (4-pound) cured corned beef brisket, trimmed
16 cups water
2 cups chopped onion
1 cup chopped celery
1 cup chopped carrot
1½ teaspoons pickling spice
3 garlic cloves, peeled
Cooking spray
1 tablespoon caraway seeds
1 (2½-pound) head green cabbage, cored and
cut into 1-inch strips
4 pounds small red potatoes, quartered
2 tablespoons chopped fresh parsley
2 teaspoons butter
2 teaspoons grated lemon rind
2 teaspoons fresh lemon juice
⅛ teaspoon black pepper
½ cup dry breadcrumbs
1 (5-ounce) jar prepared horseradish, drained
and squeezed dry
3 tablespoons Dijon mustard

1. Place beef brisket in a large stockpot, and add water and next 5 ingredients. Bring mixture to a boil. Cover, reduce heat, and simmer for 3 hours. Remove brisket from pot.

2. Place beef brisket on rack of a broiler pan or roasting pan coated with cooking spray, and place rack in pan. Strain cooking liquid through a colander into 2 large bowls, and discard solids. Return liquid to pot. Add caraway seeds and cabbage, and bring to a boil. Reduce heat, and simmer for 20 minutes. Drain.

3. While cabbage is cooking, place potatoes in a large Dutch oven. Cover with water. Bring to a boil, and cook 20 minutes or until tender. Drain. Return potatoes to pan. Stir in parsley, butter, rind, juice, and pepper; toss to coat.

4. Preheat broiler.

5. Combine breadcrumbs and horseradish. Spread mustard over one side of brisket. Press breadcrumb mixture onto mustard. Broil for 3 minutes or until lightly browned. Serve brisket with cabbage and potatoes. Yield: 8 servings (serving size: 3 ounces corned beef, about 1½ cups cabbage, and about 1⅓ cups potatoes).

CALORIES 321 (41% from fat); FAT 14.5g (sat 4.6g, mono 6.5g, poly 0.8g); PROTEIN 22.8g; CARB 27.6g; FIBER 10g; CHOL 86mg; IRON 4.3mg; SODIUM 927mg; CALC 11mg

179

Lamb Shanks on
Cannellini Beans

Lamb Shanks
on Cannellini Beans

Cooking the beans and the lamb at the same time frees you to work on other dishes for your meal. We loved using dry beans, but for a quicker approach, substitute drained canned beans. Just stir them in along with the bacon.

    6   (¾-pound) lamb shanks, trimmed
    ½   teaspoon salt
    ¼   teaspoon black pepper
    2   cups finely chopped carrot
    1   cup finely chopped onion
    1   cup finely chopped celery
    1   cup dry red wine
    ½   cup beef broth
 1 ½   teaspoons dried rosemary
    2   (14½-ounce) cans diced tomatoes
    2   bay leaves
    1   cup dried cannellini beans or other white
        beans
    4   bacon slices
    4   garlic cloves, sliced
 Rosemary sprigs (optional)

1. Heat a large nonstick skillet over medium-high heat. Sprinkle lamb with salt and pepper. Add lamb to pan, and cook 12 minutes, browning on all sides. Remove from pan. Add carrot, onion, and celery to pan; sauté 3 minutes. Add wine. Bring to a boil, and cook 5 minutes. Stir in broth, rosemary, tomatoes, and bay leaves. Return lamb to pan (pan will be very full).
2. Cover, reduce heat, and simmer for 2 hours or until the lamb is very tender, turning lamb once. Remove lamb from pan; bring liquid to a boil; cook 5 minutes. Discard bay leaves.
3. Sort and wash beans; place in a large Dutch oven. Cover with water to 2 inches above beans; bring to a boil, and cook 2 minutes. Remove from heat; cover and let stand 1 hour.
4. Drain the beans, and return them to Dutch oven. Cover with water to 2 inches above beans, and bring to a boil. Reduce heat; simmer 1 hour or until tender. Drain.
5. Cook bacon in Dutch oven over medium-high heat until crisp. Remove bacon from pan, reserving 2 teaspoons drippings. Crumble bacon. Heat the reserved drippings over medium-high heat. Add garlic; sauté 2 minutes or until golden. Stir in beans and bacon; remove from heat.

6. Divide bean mixture evenly among 6 plates; arrange lamb on beans. Spoon sauce over lamb. Garnish with rosemary sprigs, if desired. Yield: 6 servings (serving size: 1 lamb shank, ⅔ cup beans, and 1⅓ cups sauce).

CALORIES 506 (26% from fat); FAT 14.5g (sat 5.1g, mono 5.9g, poly 1.7g); PROTEIN 60.2g; CARB 32.9g; FIBER 6.3g; CHOL 156mg; IRON 8.3mg; SODIUM 791mg; CALC 130mg

Lamb Stew with
Hazelnut Butter and Dates

    ⅔   cup coarsely chopped hazelnuts, toasted
 Cooking spray
 1 ½   pounds lean lamb stew meat, cubed
 2 ½   cups chopped onion
    ¾   teaspoon salt
    ¼   teaspoon ground cinnamon
    ¼   teaspoon ground allspice
    ¼   teaspoon crushed red pepper
    3   garlic cloves, crushed
    2   (14½-ounce) cans fat-free, less-sodium
        chicken broth
 2 ½   cups (½-inch) cubed peeled turnips (about
        1 pound)
 2 ½   cups small red potatoes, halved (about
        1 pound)
    2   cups water
 1 ½   cups baby carrots, peeled
    ½   cup whole pitted dates, chopped
 1 ½   cups frozen green peas

1. Place the hazelnuts in a food processor; process until smooth (about 2½ minutes), scraping the sides of the bowl once.
2. Heat a large Dutch oven coated with cooking spray over high heat. Add lamb; cook 5 minutes, browning on all sides.
3. Reduce heat to medium-high. Add onion, salt, cinnamon, allspice, red pepper, and garlic; sauté 7 minutes or until the onion is lightly browned.
4. Add hazelnut butter and broth to pan; stir well, scraping the pan to loosen browned bits. Stir in turnips, potatoes, water, carrots, and dates; bring to a boil. Cover, reduce heat to medium, and simmer 15 minutes.
5. Uncover and simmer 1 hour and 20 minutes, or until lamb is tender and sauce has thickened. Stir in peas; simmer 5 minutes. Yield: 8 servings (serving size: about 1 cup).

CALORIES 361 (29% from fat); FAT 11.8g (sat 2.5g, mono 6.7g, poly 1.4g); PROTEIN 28.4g; CARB 36.7g; FIBER 608g; CHOL 69mg; IRON 3.8mg; SODIUM 518mg; CALC 65mg

Garlic and Herb-Crusted Lamb

4 whole garlic heads
1 tablespoon Dijon mustard
1 tablespoon olive oil
1 tablespoon thinly sliced fresh chives
1 tablespoon fresh thyme leaves, coarsely chopped
1 (8-pound) leg of lamb
12 fresh garlic slices
1¼ teaspoons salt, divided
½ teaspoon freshly ground black pepper
2 cups fresh French breadcrumbs (about 4 ounces)
2¼ cups low-salt beef broth
½ cup Merlot or other dry red wine
2½ tablespoons cornstarch
Fresh thyme sprigs (optional)

1. Preheat oven to 350°.
2. Remove white papery skin from garlic heads (do not peel or separate the cloves). Cut off top portions of garlic heads. Wrap garlic heads in foil. Bake at 350° for 1 hour, and cool for 10 minutes. Squeeze garlic heads to extract pulp. Discard skins. Place the garlic pulp, mustard, and oil in a food processor, and process until smooth. Stir in chives and thyme leaves.
3. Increase oven temperature to 425°.

4. Trim fat from lamb. Cut 12 (¾-inch) slits in lamb, and place a fresh garlic slice in each slit. Sprinkle surface of lamb with ½ teaspoon salt and pepper; rub with roasted garlic paste mixture. Press breadcrumbs over surface of lamb. Place the lamb on a broiler pan. Insert a meat thermometer into thickest part of lamb, making sure not to touch bone.
5. Bake at 425° for 10 minutes. Decrease oven temperature to 325°. Bake for an additional 2 hours and 10 minutes or until the thermometer registers 140° (medium-rare) to 155° (medium). Remove lamb from rack; place on a shallow serving platter. Lightly cover with foil; let stand 15 minutes.
6. Drain fat from bottom of pan (do not scrape pan). Place broiler pan on stovetop over medium-high heat. Add broth; bring to a boil, scraping pan to loosen browned bits.
7. Combine red wine and cornstarch; stir with a whisk until blended. Add to beef broth; return to boiling. Cook 1 minute or until mixture is slightly thick, stirring constantly. Stir in remaining ¾ teaspoon salt. Serve warm with lamb. Garnish with fresh thyme sprigs, if desired. Yield: 20 servings (serving size: about 3 ounces lamb and 2 tablespoons sauce).

CALORIES 211 (28% from fat); FAT 6.6g (sat 2.1g, mono 2.9g, poly 0.7g); PROTEIN 25.4g; CARB 9.9g; FIBER 0.4g; CHOL 73mg; IRON 2.9mg; SODIUM 337mg; CALC 40mg

Pistachio-Crusted Rack of Lamb

You can prepare the mustard mixture and breadcrumb mixture (minus the lemon juice) earlier in the day. Just remember to add the juice before patting the pistachio crust onto the lamb.

 3 (1-ounce) slices day-old white bread
⅓ cup finely chopped pistachios
1¼ teaspoons grated lemon rind
2½ tablespoons finely chopped fresh parsley
¼ cup lemon juice
¾ teaspoon salt, divided
¼ cup finely chopped fresh chives
¼ cup finely chopped fresh mint
2½ tablespoons Dijon mustard
 2 garlic cloves, minced
 2 (1½-pound) French-cut racks of lamb (8 ribs each), trimmed
 Cooking spray
 Mint sprigs (optional)

1. Preheat oven to 425°.
2. Place bread in a food processor; pulse 10 times or until coarse crumbs measure about 1¼ cups.
3. Combine breadcrumbs, nuts, rind, parsley, juice, and ½ teaspoon salt in a small bowl.
4. Combine chives, mint, mustard, and garlic in a small bowl.
5. Sprinkle lamb with ¼ teaspoon salt. Heat a large nonstick skillet coated with cooking spray over medium-high heat. Add lamb; cook 2 minutes on each side or until browned. Spread half of mustard mixture over meaty portion of each rack. Carefully pat half of breadcrumb mixture into mustard mixture on each rack.
6. Place lamb on a broiler pan coated with cooking spray. Bake at 425° for 35 minutes or until meat thermometer registers 140° (medium-rare) to 155° (medium). Place lamb on platter; cover with foil. Let stand 10 minutes before serving (temperature will increase 5° upon standing). Slice each rack into 4 pieces (2 ribs per piece). Garnish with mint sprigs, if desired. Yield: 8 servings (serving size: 1 piece, 2 ribs).

CALORIES 206 (47% from fat); FAT 10.8g (sat 3.1g, mono 4.6g, poly 1.5g); PROTEIN 18.5g; CARB 8.5g; FIBER 0.9g; CHOL 52mg; IRON 2.1mg; SODIUM 472mg; CALC 37mg

Turkish Lamb, Fig, and Mint Kebabs

Serve this with a side of bulgur tossed with a little olive oil and feta cheese. Beef or pork also will taste great in place of the lamb.

 2 pounds lean boned leg of lamb
 3 tablespoons chopped fresh or
 1 tablespoon dried mint
 2 teaspoons olive oil
 1 teaspoon ground cumin
½ teaspoon salt
½ teaspoon ground cinnamon
½ teaspoon paprika
¼ teaspoon ground nutmeg
¼ teaspoon black pepper
 3 garlic cloves, minced
 1 cup boiling water
24 dried figs
 2 red onions
 Cooking spray

1. Trim fat from lamb. Cut lamb into 48 (1-inch) pieces; set aside.
2. Combine mint and next 8 ingredients in a large zip-top plastic bag. Add lamb; seal and marinate in refrigerator 20 minutes, turning bag occasionally. Remove lamb from bag, and discard marinade.
3. Combine boiling water and figs in a large bowl; cover and let stand 10 minutes or until soft. Drain well, and cut in half. Cut each onion into 6 wedges, and cut each wedge in half crosswise (for a total of 24 pieces).
4. Thread 4 lamb pieces, 2 figs, and 2 onion pieces alternately onto each of 12 (10-inch) skewers.
5. Prepare grill or broiler.
6. Place kebabs on a grill rack or broiler pan coated with cooking spray; cook 4 minutes on each side or until desired degree of doneness. Yield: 6 servings (serving size: 2 kebabs).

CALORIES 441 (23% from fat); FAT 11.3g (sat 3.4g, mono 4.6g, poly 1.1g); PROTEIN 35g; CARB 53.4g; FIBER 10.1g; CHOL 101mg; IRON 4.4mg; SODIUM 185mg; CALC 131mg

Pork Saltimbocca with Polenta

Traditional saltimbocca is made with thin slices of pounded veal, but lean pork chops update the recipe and provide more flavor. The butternut overtone of fontina cheese is also a pleasant addition. Top with a whole sage leaf for a handsome presentation.

PORK:

6 (4-ounce) boneless center-cut loin pork chops, trimmed

6 very thin slices prosciutto (about 2 ounces)

6 large fresh sage leaves

⅓ cup (about 1½ ounces) shredded fontina cheese

¼ teaspoon freshly ground black pepper

⅛ teaspoon salt

2 tablespoons all-purpose flour

1 tablespoon olive oil

½ cup dry white wine

1 cup fat-free, less-sodium chicken broth

1 tablespoon thinly sliced fresh sage

POLENTA:

2 cups 2% reduced-fat milk

1 (14-ounce) can fat-free, less-sodium chicken broth

1 cup instant polenta

½ teaspoon salt

1. To prepare pork, place each chop between 2 sheets of heavy-duty plastic wrap; pound to ¼-inch thickness using a meat mallet or rolling pin. Arrange 1 prosciutto slice over each chop; top with 1 sage leaf and about 1 tablespoon cheese. Fold chops in half to sandwich filling; secure with wooden picks. Sprinkle both sides of pork chops with pepper and ⅛ teaspoon salt. Place flour in a shallow dish; dredge stuffed chops in flour.

2. Heat olive oil in a large nonstick skillet over medium-high heat. Add chops; cook 3 minutes on each side or until browned. Remove chops from pan; cover and set aside.

3. Add wine to pan, scraping pan to loosen browned bits; cook until reduced to ¼ cup (about 2 minutes). Add 1 cup broth, and bring to a boil. Cook until reduced to ½ cup (about 5 minutes). Stir in 1 tablespoon sliced sage. Reduce heat to medium. Return chops to pan; cook 2 minutes or until thoroughly heated, turning once. Remove wooden picks from chops.

4. To prepare polenta, bring milk and 1 can broth to a boil. Gradually stir in polenta and ½ teaspoon salt. Cover, reduce heat to medium-low, and cook 2 minutes. Arrange ½ cup polenta on each serving plate. Top with a chop and drizzle with 4 teaspoons sauce. Serve immediately. Yield: 6 servings.

CALORIES 404 (30% from fat); FAT 13.3g (sat 5.3g, mono 6g, poly 1g); PROTEIN 34.9g; CARB 30.8g; FIBER 2.8g; CHOL 85mg; IRON 1.6mg; SODIUM 733mg; CALC 172mg

Peach-Glazed Barbecue Pork Chops and Peaches

The cooking time for the peaches will vary depending on their ripeness. The glaze also works well on chicken.

  3 cups chopped peeled peaches (about 1½ pounds)
  1 cup dry white wine
  ¼ cup sugar
  1 teaspoon salt, divided
  ¼ teaspoon black pepper, divided
  2 tablespoons white wine vinegar
  2 tablespoons molasses
  1 teaspoon chili powder
  ½ teaspoon paprika
  ¼ teaspoon ground red pepper
  6 (6-ounce) bone-in center-cut pork chops (about ½ inch thick), trimmed
  6 peaches, halved and pitted
Cooking spray

1. Combine first 3 ingredients in a small saucepan; bring to a boil. Cover, reduce heat, and simmer 25 minutes. Uncover and simmer 5 minutes. Place peach mixture in a food processor, and process until smooth. Add ¾ teaspoon salt, ⅛ teaspoon black pepper, vinegar, and next 4 ingredients; pulse to combine. Let stand 5 minutes. Place half of peach mixture in a large heavy-duty zip-top plastic bag, and reserve other half for basting. Add chops to bag; seal and marinate in refrigerator 30 minutes to 4 hours.

2. Preheat grill.

3. Remove pork from bag; discard marinade. Sprinkle pork with ¼ teaspoon salt and ⅛ teaspoon black pepper. Place pork and peach halves on grill rack coated with cooking spray; grill 10 minutes or until pork is done and peaches are tender, turning once. Baste pork and peach halves with reserved peach mixture every 2 minutes during first 6 minutes of cooking. Yield: 6 servings (serving size: 1 chop and 2 peach halves).

CALORIES 301 (23% from fat); FAT 7.6g (sat 2.6g, mono 3.4g, poly 0.9g); PROTEIN 26.1g; CARB 33.1g; FIBER 3.5g; CHOL 62mg; IRON 1.7mg; SODIUM 449mg; CALC 34mg

One-Pan Whiskey-Flavored Pork Chops

  ⅔ cup fat-free sour cream
  ½ cup water
  2 tablespoons all-purpose flour
  ½ teaspoon salt
  ½ teaspoon dried rubbed sage
  ¼ teaspoon black pepper
  4 (6-ounce) bone-in center-cut pork chops, trimmed
  ¼ teaspoon salt
  ⅛ teaspoon black pepper
  1 teaspoon olive oil
  ½ cup chopped onion
  1 (8-ounce) package presliced mushrooms
  ½ cup whiskey

1. Preheat oven to 300°.

2. Combine first 6 ingredients in a small bowl.

3. Sprinkle pork with ¼ teaspoon salt and ⅛ teaspoon pepper. Heat oil in a large nonstick skillet over medium-high heat. Add pork; sauté 5 minutes on each side or until golden. Remove pork from pan. Add onion and mushrooms to pan; sauté 3 minutes. Carefully add whiskey to pan, and cook 1 minute or until liquid almost evaporates. Stir sour cream mixture into pan. Return pork to pan; spoon sauce over pork.

4. Wrap the handle of the skillet with foil. Cover and bake at 300° for 1 hour. Serve immediately. Yield: 4 servings (serving size: 1 pork chop and about ⅓ cup sauce).

CALORIES 310 (28% from fat); FAT 9.6g (sat 3g, mono 4.5g, poly 1.1g); PROTEIN 29.5g; CARB 24.3g; FIBER 1.3g; CHOL 71mg; IRON 2mg; SODIUM 546mg; CALC 16mg

Barbecued Pork Chops with Sautéed Apples

Pork paired with apples is a traditional favorite, and no wonder—the flavor combination is satisfying and comforting. Here, the tart sweetness of the barbecue sauce complements that of the apples.

SAUCE:

¼ cup packed brown sugar
¼ cup ketchup
1 tablespoon Worcestershire sauce
1 tablespoon low-sodium soy sauce

REMAINING INGREDIENTS:

6 (6-ounce) bone-in center-cut pork chops (about ½ inch thick)
1 teaspoon dried thyme
1 teaspoon garlic salt
¼ teaspoon ground red pepper
Cooking spray
Sautéed Apples
Parsley sprigs (optional)

1. Prepare grill or broiler.
2. To prepare the sauce, combine brown sugar and next 3 ingredients in a small bowl (makes about ½ cup). Place ¼ cup of the brown sugar sauce in another small bowl, and set aside.
3. Trim fat from pork chops. Combine thyme, garlic salt, and ground red pepper; sprinkle pork chops with the thyme mixture. Place pork chops on a grill rack or broiler pan coated with cooking spray, and cook 6 minutes on each side, basting with ¼ cup brown sugar sauce. Serve pork chops with Sautéed Apples and reserved ¼ cup sauce. Garnish with parsley sprigs, if desired. Yield: 6 servings (serving size: 1 pork chop, ⅔ cup Sautéed Apples, and about 1½ tablespoons brown sugar sauce).

(Totals include Sautéed Apples) CALORIES 425 (37% from fat); FAT 17.4g (sat 7.5g, mono 6.7g, poly 1.7g); PROTEIN 24.8g; CARB 43.7g; FIBER 2.3g; CHOL 93mg; IRON 2mg; SODIUM 699mg; CALC 44mg

SAUTÉED APPLES:

3 tablespoons butter or stick margarine
6 cups sliced peeled Granny Smith apples (about 2 pounds)
½ cup packed brown sugar
⅛ teaspoon ground cinnamon

1. Melt butter in a large skillet over medium-high heat. Add apples; sauté 6 minutes or until apples are just tender. Stir in brown sugar and ground cinnamon. Cook for 1 minute or until sugar melts. Yield: 6 servings (serving size: ⅔ cup).

CALORIES 183 (30% from fat); FAT 6.1g (sat 3.7g, mono 1.7g, poly 0.3g); PROTEIN 0.2g; CARB 34.2g; FIBER 2.1g; CHOL 16mg; IRON 0.5mg; SODIUM 66mg; CALC 22mg

Hoisin-Marinated Pork Chops

Because the chops need to marinate for at least 8 hours, this is a choice make-ahead dinner.

¼ cup low-sodium soy sauce
¼ cup hoisin sauce
¼ cup honey
1 teaspoon crushed red pepper
2 garlic cloves, minced
8 (4-ounce) boneless center-cut loin pork chops (about ¾ inch thick)
Cooking spray

1. Combine soy sauce and next 4 ingredients in a large zip-top plastic bag; add pork chops. Seal and marinate in refrigerator 8 hours or overnight.
2. Prepare grill.
3. Remove pork from bag; discard marinade. Place pork on grill rack coated with cooking spray; grill 3 minutes on each side or until done. Yield: 8 servings (serving size: 1 pork chop).
NOTE: Store cooked pork in an airtight container in the refrigerator for up to 2 days.

CALORIES 188 (30% from fat); FAT 6.2g (sat 2.1g, mono 2.8g, poly 0.7g); PROTEIN 25.1g; CARB 6.7g; FIBER 0.2g; CHOL 62mg; IRON 1mg; SODIUM 249mg; CALC 27mg

Pork Medallions with Olive-Caper Sauce

1	pound pork tenderloin, trimmed
½	teaspoon salt
½	teaspoon black pepper
¼	cup all-purpose flour
1	tablespoon olive oil
½	cup dry white wine
½	cup fat-free, less-sodium chicken broth
½	cup coarsely chopped pitted kalamata olives
2	tablespoons capers
2	tablespoons chopped fresh flat-leaf parsley

1. Cut pork crosswise into 8 pieces. Place each pork piece between 2 sheets of heavy-duty plastic wrap, and pound to ¼-inch thickness using a meat mallet or rolling pin. Sprinkle both sides of pork with salt and pepper. Place flour in a shallow bowl. Dredge pork in flour, turning to coat; shake off excess flour. Heat 1½ teaspoons olive oil in a nonstick skillet over medium-high heat. Add half of pork; cook 2 minutes on each side or until done. Remove pork mixture from pan; keep warm. Repeat procedure with remaining oil and pork. Return pork to pan. Add wine and broth; bring to a boil. Stir in olives and capers; cook 4 minutes. Sprinkle with parsley. Yield: 4 servings (serving size: 2 medallions and 2 tablespoons sauce).

CALORIES 212 (34% from fat); FAT 8.1g (sat 1.8g, mono 5.1g, poly 0.9g); PROTEIN 25.5g; CARB 8.1g; FIBER 0.9g; CHOL 74mg; IRON 2.7mg; SODIUM 894mg; CALC 30mg

Maple-Mustard Pork Tenderloin with Caramelized Apples

2   (½-pound) pork tenderloins
Cooking spray
¼   cup Dijon mustard
6   tablespoons maple syrup, divided
1   tablespoon chopped fresh rosemary
½   teaspoon salt
¼   teaspoon black pepper
4   medium Granny Smith apples, each peeled
    and cut into 16 wedges (about 2½ pounds)

1. Preheat oven to 425°.
2. Trim fat from pork. Place the pork on a broiler pan coated with cooking spray. Combine mustard, 2 tablespoons syrup, rosemary, salt, and pepper in a small bowl, and brush over pork. Insert a meat thermometer into thickest part of pork. Bake at 425° for 25 minutes or until thermometer registers 160° (slightly pink).
3. While pork is baking, heat a nonstick skillet over medium-high heat. Add apples, and sauté 5 minutes or until lightly browned. Reduce heat to low, and add ¼ cup maple syrup. Simmer 10 minutes or until apples are tender, stirring occasionally. Cut pork crosswise into slices; spoon cooked apples over pork. Yield: 4 servings (serving size: 3 ounces pork and ½ cup apples).

CALORIES 301 (13% from fat); FAT 4.3g (sat 1.1g, mono 1.8g, poly 0.5g); PROTEIN 24.1g; CARB 44.6g; FIBER 4.5g; CHOL 74mg; IRON 2.1mg; SODIUM 351mg; CALC 39mg

Glazed Pork

1   pound pork tenderloin, trimmed
1   tablespoon all-purpose flour
2   tablespoons brown sugar, divided
½   teaspoon salt
½   teaspoon ground cumin
¼   teaspoon ground cardamom
⅛   teaspoon ground red pepper
¼   cup raisins
¼   cup orange juice
3   tablespoons balsamic vinegar
2   tablespoons capers
1   tablespoon olive oil

1. Cut pork crosswise into 16 pieces.
2. Combine flour, 1 tablespoon sugar, salt, cumin, cardamom, and pepper; rub evenly over pork.
3. Combine 1 tablespoon sugar, raisins, orange juice,

vinegar, and capers, stirring until sugar dissolves.
4. Heat oil in a large nonstick skillet over medium-high heat. Add pork; cook 2 minutes. Turn pork over; cook 1 minute. Add vinegar mixture; cook 1 minute or until sauce thickens and pork is done. Yield: 4 servings (serving size: 4 pork pieces and 2 tablespoons sauce).

CALORIES 234 (25% from fat); FAT 6.5g (sat 1.5g, mono 3.8g, poly 0.6g); PROTEIN 27.9g; CARB 15.5g; FIBER 1g; CHOL 67mg; IRON 2.1mg; SODIUM 482mg; CALC 20mg

Jamaican Jerk Pork Tenderloin

Use one pepper for mild heat or four for a very spicy dish. Here, butterflying the pork increases the surface area for the marinade to penetrate.

2   cups coarsely chopped green onions
½   cup coarsely chopped onion
2   tablespoons white vinegar
1   tablespoon soy sauce
1   tablespoon vegetable oil
2   teaspoons kosher salt
2   teaspoons fresh thyme
2   teaspoons brown sugar
2   teaspoons chopped peeled fresh ginger
1   teaspoon ground allspice
¼   teaspoon ground nutmeg
¼   teaspoon black pepper
⅛   teaspoon ground cinnamon
2   garlic cloves, minced
1   to 4 Scotch bonnet or habanero peppers,
    seeded and chopped
1   (1½-pound) pork tenderloin, trimmed
Cooking spray

1. Place first 15 ingredients in a blender or food processor; process until smooth.
2. Slice the pork lengthwise, cutting to, but not through, other side. Open halves, laying each side flat. Slice each half lengthwise, cutting to, but not through, other side; open flat. Combine pork and green onion mixture in a large zip-top plastic bag. Seal; marinate in refrigerator 3 to 24 hours. Remove pork from bag; discard remaining marinade.
3. Prepare grill.
4. Place pork on grill rack coated with cooking spray; grill 8 minutes on each side or until meat thermometer registers 160° (slightly pink). Yield: 4 servings (serving size: 3 ounces pork).

CALORIES 248 (27% from fat); FAT 7.5g (sat 2g, mono 2.8g, poly 2g); PROTEIN 36.9g; CARB 7.1g; FIBER 1.5g; CHOL 111mg; IRON 3.1mg; SODIUM 1,126mg; CALC 52mg

Almond-Crusted Pork Tenderloin with Dried Cranberry-Apple Conserve

2   (1-pound) pork tenderloins
2   (1-ounce) slices white bread
3   tablespoons sliced almonds, finely chopped
1   tablespoon dried rosemary
1   teaspoon coarsely ground black pepper
½   teaspoon salt
2   large egg whites, lightly beaten
Cooking spray
Dried Cranberry-Apple Conserve
Rosemary sprig (optional)

1. Preheat oven to 425°.
2. Trim fat from pork. Place bread in a food processor; pulse 10 times or until crumbs measure 2 cups. Combine breadcrumbs and next 4 ingredients in a shallow dish. Dip pork in egg whites; dredge in breadcrumb mixture. Place pork on a broiler pan coated with cooking spray. Insert a meat thermometer into thickest part of pork. Bake at 425° for 30 minutes or until thermometer registers 160° (slightly pink). Cover with foil; let stand 10 minutes. Cut into ¼-inch-thick slices. Serve pork with Dried Cranberry-Apple Conserve. Garnish with a rosemary sprig, if desired. Yield: 8 servings (serving size: 3 ounces pork and ¼ cup conserve).

(Totals include Dried Cranberry-Apple Conserve) CALORIES 316 (13% from fat); FAT 4.7g (sat 1.3g, mono 2.2g, poly 0.8g); PROTEIN 27.2g; CARB 45g; FIBER 2.4g; CHOL 74mg; IRON 2.8mg; SODIUM 285mg; CALC 47mg

DRIED CRANBERRY-APPLE CONSERVE:

2   cups sweetened dried cranberries
1½ cups boiling water
⅓   cup diced dried apple
¼   cup raisins
1   tablespoon minced crystallized ginger
⅓   cup white wine vinegar
3   tablespoons sugar
⅛   teaspoon ground red pepper
Dash of ground allspice
Dash of ground cinnamon
Dash of ground ginger
¼   cup red plum or raspberry jam

1. Combine the first 5 ingredients; cover, and let stand 30 minutes.
2. Combine vinegar and next 5 ingredients in a small saucepan, and bring to a boil, stirring mixture frequently. Add the fruit mixture. Bring to a boil; reduce heat, and simmer for 5 minutes. Stir in jam. Remove from heat, and cool to room temperature. Yield: 2½ cups (serving size: ¼ cup).

CALORIES 139 (1% from fat); FAT 0.2g (sat 0.1g, mono 0g, poly 0.1g); PROTEIN 1.1g; CARB 38.4g; FIBER 1.8g; CHOL 0mg; IRON 0.8mg; SODIUM 12mg; CALC 18mg

Red Chile Pork Tacos with Caramelized Onions

1 tablespoon ancho chile powder
1 teaspoon brown sugar
½ teaspoon salt
1 pound pork tenderloin, trimmed
Cooking spray
1 teaspoon vegetable oil
3 cups thinly sliced onion
8 hard taco shells
½ cup chopped tomato
8 teaspoons chopped green onions

1. Preheat oven to 425°.
2. Combine first 3 ingredients; rub over pork. Place pork on a broiler pan coated with cooking spray. Bake at 425° for 20 minutes or until a thermometer registers 160° (slightly pink). Remove pork from oven; let sit 5 minutes before slicing.
3. While pork cooks, heat oil in a large nonstick skillet coated with cooking spray over medium heat. Add sliced onion; cover and cook 10 minutes or until golden brown, stirring frequently. Uncover and cook 1 minute, stirring constantly.
4. Fill each taco shell with about 2 ounces pork, 3 tablespoons sautéed onion, 1 tablespoon chopped tomato, and 1 teaspoon green onions. Yield: 4 servings (serving size: 2 tacos).

CALORIES 304 (30% from fat); FAT 10.2g (sat 2.2g, mono 5.4g, poly 1.8g); PROTEIN 26.9g; CARB 25g; FIBER 4.5g; CHOL 74mg; IRON 2.1mg; SODIUM 444mg; CALC 46mg

Barbecued Pork Tenderloin

This combination of marinade, dry rub, and barbecue sauce provides the tenderloin with a flavor that's reminiscent of delicious slow-smoked Kansas City ribs.

½ cup strong brewed coffee
2 tablespoons cider vinegar
1 tablespoon spicy brown mustard
1 tablespoon dark molasses
2 (1-pound) pork tenderloins, trimmed
¼ cup finely ground coffee
2 tablespoons sugar
2 tablespoons paprika
2 tablespoons coarsely ground black pepper
1½ teaspoons sea or kosher salt
¼ cup barbecue sauce
1 tablespoon cider vinegar
Cooking spray

1. Combine first 4 ingredients in a large zip-top plastic bag, and add pork. Seal and marinate in refrigerator 2 to 12 hours, turning bag occasionally. Remove pork from bag; discard marinade.
2. Prepare grill, heating one side to medium and one side to high heat.
3. Combine ground coffee and next 4 ingredients, and rub over pork. Let stand at room temperature for 15 minutes.
4. Combine ¼ cup barbecue sauce and 1 tablespoon cider vinegar. Reserve 2 tablespoons of the barbecue sauce mixture; set aside.
5. Place the pork on grill rack coated with cooking spray over high heat; grill 3 minutes, turning pork on all sides. Place pork over medium heat; grill 15 minutes, turning pork occasionally. Baste with 3 tablespoons barbecue sauce mixture; grill 5 minutes or until thermometer registers 160° (slightly pink), turning pork occasionally.
6. Place pork on a platter, and brush with reserved 2 tablespoons barbecue sauce mixture. Cover with foil; let stand 5 minutes before slicing. Yield: 8 servings (serving size: about 3 ounces).

CALORIES 196 (21% from fat); FAT 4.5g (sat 1.5g, mono 1.8g, poly 0.6g); PROTEIN 28.9g; CARB 8.4g; FIBER 1.3g; CHOL 80mg; IRON 2.4mg; SODIUM 566mg; CALC

Korean-Style Pork Tenderloin

⅓ cup low-sodium soy sauce
2 tablespoons sugar
1 tablespoon minced peeled fresh ginger
3 tablespoons rice vinegar
1 tablespoon dark sesame oil
¼ teaspoon crushed red pepper
4 garlic cloves, minced
1½ pounds pork tenderloin, trimmed
Cooking spray

1. Combine the first 7 ingredients in a large zip-top plastic bag, and add pork. Seal and marinate in refrigerator for 8 hours or overnight, turning bag occasionally.
2. Preheat oven to 425°.
3. Heat a large ovenproof skillet coated with cooking spray over medium-high heat. Remove pork from bag, reserving marinade. Add pork to pan; cook 6 minutes, browning on all sides.
4. Place pan in oven, and bake at 425° for 15 minutes or until meat thermometer registers 160° (medium) or until desired degree of doneness. Let stand 5 minutes before slicing.

5. Bring reserved marinade to a boil in a small saucepan. Reduce heat, and simmer 5 minutes.

6. Cut pork into ¼-inch-thick slices; serve with sauce. Yield: 6 servings (serving size: 3 ounces pork and about 1 tablespoon sauce).

CALORIES 184 (30% from fat); FAT 6.2g (sat 1.7g, mono 2.7g, poly 1.4g); PROTEIN 24.7g; CARB 6.2g; FIBER 0.2g; CHOL 74mg; IRON 1.7mg; SODIUM 531mg; CALC 12mg

Lombo di Maiale Coi Porri
(Pan-Roasted Pork Loin with Leeks)

Leeks, a mild, sweet member of the onion family, are cooked slowly along with the pork until they form a rich, delectable sauce for this supereasy pan roast.

  4 large leeks (about 2¼ pounds)
  ½ cup water
  1 tablespoon butter, divided
  ½ teaspoon salt, divided
  ½ teaspoon black pepper, divided
  1 (2-pound) boneless pork loin, trimmed
  ½ cup dry white wine
Chopped fresh parsley (optional)

1. Remove roots and tough upper leaves from leeks. Cut each leek in half lengthwise. Cut each half crosswise into ½-inch-thick slices (you should have about 6 cups). Soak in cold water to loosen dirt.

2. Put leeks, ½ cup water, 1 teaspoon butter, ¼ teaspoon salt, and ¼ teaspoon pepper in a large Dutch oven or deep sauté pan; place over medium-high heat. Cook 10 minutes or until leeks have wilted. Pour leeks into a bowl.

3. Heat 2 teaspoons butter in pan over medium-high heat. Add pork; cook 5 minutes, browning on all sides. Add ¼ teaspoon salt, ¼ teaspoon pepper, and wine, and cook 15 seconds, scraping pan to loosen browned bits. Return leeks to pan. Cover, reduce heat, and simmer 2 hours or until pork is tender. Remove pork from pan; increase heat to reduce sauce if too watery. Cut pork into ¼-inch-thick slices. Serve with sauce; garnish with parsley, if desired. Yield: 6 servings (serving size: about 3 ounces pork and about 2½ tablespoons leek mixture).

CALORIES 246 (39% from fat); FAT 10.7g (sat 4.2g, mono 4.4g, poly 1.1g); PROTEIN 24.8g; CARB 12.1g; FIBER 1g; CHOL 73mg; IRON 2.8mg; SODIUM 306mg; CALC 60mg

How to Cook Pan-Roasted Pork Loin with Leeks

Cook the leeks in water and butter to preserve their delicate flavor.

Brown the pork on all sides to develop a deep, rich taste.

Vietnamese Caramelized Pork with Pickled Bean Sprouts

SPROUTS:

- 4 cups warm water
- ⅓ cup white vinegar
- ¾ teaspoon salt
- 1 pound fresh bean sprouts
- ½ cup (1½-inch) julienne-cut green onions
- ¼ cup chopped fresh cilantro
- 1 teaspoon dark sesame oil

PORK:

- 1 (2-pound) boned pork loin roast
- ⅓ cup sugar
- 3 tablespoons fish sauce
- 2 cups thinly sliced shallots
- ¼ teaspoon black pepper
- ½ cup fat-free, less-sodium chicken broth
- 5 (⅛-inch) slices peeled fresh ginger
- 2 garlic cloves, sliced
- 6 cups hot cooked long-grain rice

1. To prepare sprouts, combine the first 3 ingredients. Add sprouts and onions, and toss well. Cover and refrigerate for 1½ hours. Drain well. Toss with cilantro and oil.

2. Immerse top and bottom of a 3-quart clay cooking pot in water for 10 minutes. Empty and drain well.

3. To prepare pork, trim fat from pork; cut into ½-inch slices. Set aside. Place sugar in a small, heavy saucepan over medium heat; cook until sugar dissolves, stirring as needed to dissolve the sugar evenly. Cook until golden (for about 5 minutes). Remove from heat; carefully stir in fish sauce (mixture will splatter). Stir in the shallots and pepper. Place pan over low heat, and cook for 5 minutes or until shallots are soft.

4. Pour into a large bowl. Add the pork, broth, ginger, and garlic, tossing to coat. Place pork mixture in prepared clay pot. Place clay pot in cold oven, and set to 450°. Bake 1 hour. Carefully remove clay pot from oven; remove top. Stir the pork mixture. Cover, return to oven, and bake an additional 30 minutes. Place pork on a serving platter; drizzle caramel sauce over pork. Serve with sprouts and rice. Yield: 6 servings (serving size: 3 ounces pork, about 1½ tablespoons sauce, 1 cup pickled sprouts, and 1 cup rice).

CALORIES 569 (19% from fat); FAT 11.9g (sat 3.9g, mono 5.2g, poly 1.6g); PROTEIN 38.1g; CARB 76.6g; FIBER 2.6g; CHOL 85mg; IRON 4.7mg; SODIUM 944mg; CALC 73mg

Roasted Pork and Autumn Vegetables

- 2 fennel bulbs (about 1½ pounds)
- 2 small onions
- 1 tablespoon olive oil, divided
- 4 cups (1-inch) cubed peeled rutabaga
- 16 baby carrots (about ¾ pound)
- 1 (2¼-pound) boneless pork loin roast, trimmed
- Cooking spray
- 2 tablespoons chopped fresh sage
- ¾ teaspoon kosher salt, divided
- ¾ teaspoon freshly ground black pepper, divided
- ¾ cup fat-free, less-sodium chicken broth
- ½ cup dry white wine
- 2 teaspoons Dijon mustard

1. Preheat oven to 400°.

2. Trim stalks from fennel; discard. Cut each fennel bulb into 8 wedges. Peel onions, leaving root intact; cut each onion into 8 wedges.

3. Heat 1½ teaspoons oil in a large nonstick skillet over medium-high heat. Add fennel and onion, and sauté 8 minutes or until lightly browned, stirring frequently. Remove from pan. Add remaining oil, rutabaga, and carrots to pan, and sauté 5 minutes or until lightly browned, stirring frequently.

4. Preheat oven to 400°.

5. Place pork on a rack coated with cooking spray; place rack in a shallow roasting pan. Sprinkle pork with sage, ½ teaspoon salt, and ½ teaspoon pepper. Arrange vegetables around pork; sprinkle with ¼ teaspoon salt and ¼ teaspoon pepper.

6. Bake at 400° for 50 minutes or until thermometer registers 160° (slightly pink). Remove the pork and vegetables from pan, and cover loosely with foil. Remove rack. Place pan over medium heat; stir in broth, wine, and mustard, scraping pan to loosen browned bits. Bring to a boil; reduce heat, and simmer 4 minutes, stirring occasionally. Serve with pork and vegetables. Yield: 8 servings (serving size: 3 ounces pork, about ⅔ cup vegetables, and 2 tablespoons sauce).

CALORIES 282 (37% from fat); FAT 11.5g (sat 3.6g, mono 5.5g, poly 1g); PROTEIN 29.9g; CARB 14.6g; FIBER 4.5g; CHOL 78mg; IRON 2.2mg; SODIUM 359mg; CALC 96mg

Roasted Pork and
Autumn Vegetables

Spaghetti with Parmesan and Bacon

The eggs and milk create a rich, creamy sauce that coats the pasta. The key to the creaminess is tempering the eggs—heating them gently so they don't cook too fast and curdle. Do this by slowly whisking in the hot water in which the pasta cooked.

    1   pound uncooked spaghetti
    12   bacon slices, chopped
    3   garlic cloves, minced
    1   cup 2% reduced-fat milk
    1   teaspoon salt
    1   teaspoon freshly ground black pepper
    3   large eggs
    1   cup frozen petite green peas, thawed
    1½   cups (6 ounces) grated fresh Parmesan cheese

1. Cook pasta according to package directions. Drain in a colander over a bowl, reserving ½ cup hot cooking liquid.

2. While pasta cooks, cook bacon in a large nonstick skillet over medium heat until crisp. Remove bacon from pan, reserving 1 tablespoon drippings in pan. Discard remaining drippings, and set bacon aside. Add garlic to drippings in pan; cook 30 seconds, stirring constantly.

3. Combine milk, salt, pepper, and eggs, stirring with a whisk. Gradually add reserved hot cooking liquid to milk mixture, stirring constantly with a whisk. Add pasta, milk mixture, and peas to pan; cook over low heat 3 minutes or until sauce thickens. Add bacon and cheese; stir to combine. Yield: 8 servings (serving size: 1¼ cups).

CALORIES 359 (28% from fat); FAT 11.2g (sat 5.6g, mono 3.6g, poly 1g); PROTEIN 18.9g; CARB 44.6g; FIBER 3.3g; CHOL 99mg; IRON 2.8mg; SODIUM 721mg; CALC 315mg

Spaghetti with Parmesan and Bacon

Sweet Potato and Canadian Bacon Hash

Sweet potatoes and Canadian bacon update classic New England hash. To avoid mushy hash, don't boil the potatoes too long; remove them from the water while they're still al dente.

    4   cups (¾-inch) diced peeled sweet potato
         (about 1 pound)
    2   cups (¾-inch) diced red potato (about
         8 ounces)
    2   tablespoons vegetable oil
    1   cup diced Canadian bacon (about 8 ounces)
    1   cup chopped green bell pepper
    ⅔   cup chopped green onions
    ¾   teaspoon salt
    ½   teaspoon celery seed
    ½   teaspoon freshly ground black pepper
    ⅛   teaspoon grated whole nutmeg
    ¼   cup fat-free, less-sodium chicken broth
    1   tablespoon cider vinegar

1. Place potatoes in a saucepan; cover with water. Bring to a boil. Reduce heat, and simmer 5 minutes. Drain and set aside.

2. Heat vegetable oil in a large nonstick skillet over medium heat. Add bacon, and cook 4 minutes, stirring frequently. Add bell pepper and green onions, and cook 2 minutes, stirring frequently. Add potatoes, salt, celery seed, pepper, and nutmeg, and cook 4 minutes, gently stirring occasionally. Stir in broth and vinegar. Toss gently until the liquid is absorbed. Yield: 6 servings (serving size: about 1 cup).

CALORIES 207 (30% from fat); FAT 6.8g (sat 1.4g, mono 2.1g, poly 3g); PROTEIN 8.8g; CARB 28g; FIBER 3g; CHOL 19mg; IRON 1.4mg; SODIUM 711mg; CALC 32mg

Asparagus, Ham, and Fontina Bread Puddings

These savory bread puddings are baked and served in individual custard cups.

    1 pound asparagus
    1 teaspoon olive oil
    1 cup chopped onion
    Cooking spray
    5 (1.4-ounce) slices firm white sandwich bread
       (such as Pepperidge Farm Farmhouse hearty
       white bread), cut into ½-inch cubes
    ½ cup chopped reduced-fat ham
    ¾ cup (3 ounces) shredded fontina cheese
    1⅔ cups fat-free milk
    ¾ cup egg substitute
    2 teaspoons Dijon mustard
    ½ teaspoon dried basil
    ¼ teaspoon salt
    ¼ teaspoon black pepper

1. Preheat oven to 375°.
2. Cut a 3-inch tip from each asparagus spear; reserve stalks for another use. Cut tips into ½-inch pieces.
3. Heat oil in a nonstick skillet over medium-high heat. Add onion; sauté 5 minutes or until tender, stirring frequently. Add asparagus; cover and cook 4 minutes, stirring once. Remove from heat; set aside.
4. Coat 6 (10-ounce) custard cups or ramekins with cooking spray; place in a large baking pan. Place bread cubes evenly into custard cups. Top evenly with asparagus mixture, ham, and cheese. Combine milk and remaining ingredients, stirring with a whisk. Pour evenly into custard cups; let stand 20 minutes. Add hot water to pan to a depth of 1 inch. Cover and bake at 375° for 30 minutes. Uncover and bake an additional 15 minutes. Let stand 10 minutes before serving. Yield: 6 servings.

CALORIES 237 (30% from fat); FAT 7.9g (sat 3.3g, mono 2.4g, poly 0.9g); PROTEIN 16.4g; CARB 26.2g; FIBER 3.9g; CHOL 23mg; IRON 2mg; SODIUM 624mg; CALC 223mg

Ham with Vanilla and Champagne Glaze

Much of the flavor from the Champagne and vanilla bean seeds ends up in the pan drippings, which are used to create a simple sauce.

    1 (11-pound) 33%-less-sodium smoked, fully
       cooked bone-in ham
   24 whole cloves
    Cooking spray
    1½ cups Champagne or sparkling wine, divided
    1 (2-inch) piece vanilla bean, split lengthwise
    1 cup apple jelly

1. Preheat oven to 350°.
2. Trim fat and rind from ham. Score outside of ham in a diamond pattern, and stud with cloves. Place ham, bone end up, in a roasting pan coated with cooking spray. Pour 1 cup Champagne over ham. Bake at 350° for 45 minutes.
3. Scrape seeds from vanilla bean into a small saucepan. Add bean and ½ cup Champagne to pan. Bring to a boil; cook 2 minutes. Stir in jelly; cook 3 minutes or until jelly dissolves, stirring constantly. Remove from heat. Discard vanilla bean. Pour half of Champagne mixture over ham. Bake 30 minutes; pour remaining Champagne mixture over ham. Bake an additional 30 minutes or until ham is thoroughly heated. Place ham on a platter; cover loosely with foil. Let stand 15 minutes.
4. Place a zip-top plastic bag inside a 2-cup glass measure or bowl. Pour drippings into bag; let stand 10 minutes (fat will rise to the top). Seal bag, and carefully snip off 1 bottom corner of bag. Drain drippings into a bowl, stopping before fat layer reaches opening; discard fat. Serve sauce with ham. Yield: 30 servings (serving size: 3 ounces ham and about 1½ teaspoons sauce).

CALORIES 154 (28% from fat); FAT 4.7g (sat 1.5g, mono 2.2g, poly 0.5g); PROTEIN 17.8g; CARB 8.4g; FIBER 0g; CHOL 45mg; IRON 1.3mg; SODIUM 830mg; CALC 8mg

Gingersnap-Crusted Ham with
Apricot-Mustard Sauce

Gingersnap-Crusted Ham with Apricot-Mustard Sauce

Whole hams usually weigh at least 15 pounds; ham halves, which are labeled either "shank" or "butt end," are more manageable. A bone-in shank is easier to carve than the butt end, which contains part of the hipbone.

HAM:
- 1 (8-pound) 33%-less-sodium smoked, fully cooked ham half
- 2 tablespoons apricot preserves
- 2 tablespoons Dijon mustard
- ½ cup brown sugar
- ½ cup gingersnap crumbs (about 9 cookies, finely crushed)

SAUCE:
- 1½ cups apricot preserves
- ½ cup dry Marsala wine
- 3 tablespoons Dijon mustard
- ½ teaspoon ground allspice

1. Preheat oven to 325°.

2. To prepare ham, line a broiler pan with foil. Trim fat and rind from ham. Score outside of ham in a diamond pattern. Place ham on prepared pan. Bake at 325° for 1 hour. Remove ham from oven; cool slightly. Increase oven temperature to 375°.

3. Combine 2 tablespoons preserves and 2 table-spoons mustard, stirring with a whisk. Combine sugar and crumbs. Brush preserves mixture over ham. Carefully press crumb mixture onto preserves mixture (some crumb mixture will fall onto pan). Bake at 375° for 45 minutes or until a thermometer registers 145°. Place ham on a platter; let stand 15 minutes before slicing.

4. To prepare sauce, combine 1½ cups preserves and the remaining ingredients in a small saucepan. Bring to a boil; cook for 5 minutes. Serve sauce with ham. Yield: 24 servings (serving size: about 3 ounces ham and 2 teaspoons sauce).

CALORIES 233 (24% from fat); FAT 6.3g (sat 1.9g, mono 2.9g, poly 0.7g); PROTEIN 21.2g; CARB 22.4g; FIBER 0.4g; CHOL 53mg; IRON 1.9mg; SODIUM 1,076mg; CALC 23mg

Butternut Squash Ravioli with Pancetta and Sage

- ¼ cup dried porcini mushrooms (about ¼ ounce)
- 1½ tablespoons olive oil
- ⅔ cup chopped pancetta (about 2½ ounces)
- 1 cup mashed cooked butternut squash (about 1 pound uncooked)
- 5 tablespoons dry breadcrumbs
- ¼ cup (1 ounce) grated fresh Parmesan cheese
- 2 teaspoons grated lemon rind
- ¼ teaspoon salt
- ⅛ teaspoon ground nutmeg
- 1 large egg, lightly beaten
- 40 won ton wrappers
- 2 teaspoons chopped fresh sage
- ¼ teaspoon freshly ground black pepper

1. Pour boiling water over mushrooms in a bowl. Cover and let stand 30 minutes or until tender; drain. Squeeze to remove excess moisture; chop.

2. Heat oil in a medium saucepan over medium-high heat. Add pancetta; cook until crisp. Remove half of pancetta from pan with a slotted spoon; place in a bowl, reserving remaining pancetta and drippings. Add mushrooms, squash, and the next 6 ingredients, stirring to combine.

3. Working with 1 won ton wrapper at a time (cover remaining wrappers with a damp towel to keep from drying), spoon about 1 tablespoon squash mixture into center of each wrapper. Brush edges of wrapper with water; top with another wrapper, stretching top wrapper slightly to meet edges of bottom wrapper. Press edges together firmly with fingers, and cut edges with a 2½-inch round cutter. Repeat procedure with remaining won ton wrappers and squash mixture.

4. Fill a large Dutch oven with water; bring to a simmer. Add half of ravioli; cook 3 minutes or until done (do not boil). Remove with a slotted spoon; keep warm. Repeat procedure with remaining ravioli.

5. Reheat remaining pancetta and drippings over medium-low heat, and drizzle over ravioli. Sprinkle with sage and pepper. Yield: 4 servings (serving size: 5 ravioli).

CALORIES 389 (27% from fat); FAT 11.6g (sat 3.1g, mono 6g, poly 1.5g); PROTEIN 18.4g; CARB 52.5g; FIBER 4.6g; CHOL 74mg; IRON 5.3mg; SODIUM 961mg; CALC 171mg

197

Lumberjack Hash

Frozen hash browns make this version of the popular diner dish quick and easy.

2 teaspoons vegetable oil
2 teaspoons butter
1 cup chopped onion
1 cup chopped green bell pepper
2 garlic cloves, minced
8 cups frozen shredded hash brown potatoes, thawed (about 1 pound)
½ teaspoon salt
½ teaspoon black pepper
4 ounces 33%-less-sodium ham, diced
¾ cup (3 ounces) reduced-fat shredded cheddar cheese

1. Heat the vegetable oil and butter in a large non-stick skillet over medium heat. Add the chopped onion, and cook for 5 minutes. Add the bell pepper and minced garlic cloves, and cook for 3 minutes. Add the hash brown potatoes, salt, black pepper, and diced ham to pan, and cook 16 minutes or until the potatoes are golden brown, stirring occasionally. Top the potato mixture with cheese, and cook 2 minutes or until the cheese melts. Yield: 4 servings (serving size: 1¼ cups).

CALORIES 276 (30% from fat); FAT 9.1g (sat 4.2g, mono 1.6g, poly 1.6g); PROTEIN 16.5g; CARB 33.7g; FIBER 3.5g; CHOL 33mg; IRON 0.8mg; SODIUM 738mg; CALC 208mg

Linguine with Pancetta and Parmesan

1 (9-ounce) package fresh linguine
Cooking spray
1 cup chopped onion
⅔ cup chopped pancetta or ham (about 2 ounces)
½ teaspoon bottled minced garlic
1 (26-ounce) bottle fat-free Italian herb pasta sauce
¼ cup chopped ripe olives
1 tablespoon capers, drained
¼ cup (1 ounce) shredded fresh Parmesan cheese

1. Cook pasta according to package directions, omitting salt and fat.
2. While pasta cooks, heat a large nonstick skillet coated with cooking spray over medium-high heat. Add onion, pancetta, and garlic, and sauté 5 minutes. Add pasta sauce; cook 5 minutes. Stir in olives and capers. Add pasta; toss to combine. Sprinkle with cheese. Yield: 4 servings (serving size: 1½ cups pasta mixture and 1 tablespoon cheese).

CALORIES 381 (30% from fat); FAT 12.5g (sat 4.5g, mono 5.1g, poly 1.7g); PROTEIN 14.1g; CARB 53g; FIBER 5.2g; CHOL 61mg; IRON 3.5mg; SODIUM 626mg; CALC 237mg

Pasta with Prosciutto and Peas

Cooking spray
3 ounces very thin slices prosciutto, chopped
3 tablespoons extravirgin olive oil
2 garlic cloves, thinly sliced
6 cups hot cooked fusilli (about 12 ounces uncooked short twisted spaghetti)
1 cup (4 ounces) shaved Parmigiano-Reggiano cheese
⅓ cup chopped fresh parsley
1 tablespoon fresh lemon juice
½ teaspoon kosher salt
½ teaspoon freshly ground black pepper
1 (10-ounce) package frozen peas, cooked and drained

1. Heat a large nonstick skillet coated with cooking spray over medium heat. Add prosciutto; cook 3 minutes or until lightly browned. Remove from pan. Add oil and garlic; cook 1 minute or until garlic begins to brown. Combine prosciutto, oil mixture, pasta, and remaining ingredients in a large bowl; toss to coat. Yield: 8 servings (serving size: 1 cup).

CALORIES 312 (30% from fat); FAT 10.6g (sat 3.5g, mono 5.4g, poly 1.1g); PROTEIN 14.9g; CARB 37.8g; FIBER 1.2g; CHOL 16mg; IRON 2.7mg; SODIUM 554mg; CALC 189mg

Pasta with Prosciutto and Peas

Roasted Pepper, Kalamata, and
Prosciutto Pasta

Roasted Pepper, Kalamata, and Prosciutto Pasta

Wide, flat pappardelle pasta's cascading quality gives the dish height. If you can't find it, substitute a short pasta, such as cavatappi or penne. You can complete steps 1 through 3 up to a day ahead.

   3 red bell peppers (about 1½ pounds)
   1 yellow bell pepper
   ⅓ cup pitted kalamata olives, quartered
   2 tablespoons capers
   2 tablespoons extravirgin olive oil
   ½ teaspoon grated lemon rind
   1½ teaspoons fresh lemon juice
   ¼ teaspoon salt
   ⅛ teaspoon freshly ground black pepper
   ⅓ cup chopped fresh flat-leaf parsley
   4 ounces prosciutto, sliced into ⅛-inch strips
   6 cups hot cooked pappardelle pasta (about 12 ounces uncooked pasta)
   6 tablespoons (1½ ounces) shaved Parmigiano-Reggiano cheese

1. Preheat broiler.
2. Cut bell peppers in half lengthwise; discard seeds and membranes. Place pepper halves, skin sides up, on a foil-lined baking sheet; flatten with hand. Broil 10 minutes or until blackened. Place in a zip-top plastic bag; seal. Let stand 10 minutes. Peel and cut into thin strips.
3. Combine olives and next 6 ingredients in a bowl. Add bell pepper strips and chopped parsley; toss gently to combine.
4. Cook prosciutto in a large nonstick skillet over medium heat 3 minutes or until crisp; remove from pan. Add bell pepper mixture to pan; cook over low heat 3 minutes or until heated.
5. Place pasta in a large bowl. Add the bell pepper mixture and prosciutto; toss gently to combine. Sprinkle with cheese. Yield: 6 servings (serving size: 1¼ cups pasta mixture and 1 tablespoon cheese).

CALORIES 343 (29% from fat); FAT 11.2g (sat 2.8g, mono 6.3g, poly 1.4g); PROTEIN 14.5g; CARB 46.2g; FIBER 4.3g; CHOL 16mg; IRON 3mg; SODIUM 707mg; CALC 111mg

Tomato-Basil Lasagna with Prosciutto

After assembling the lasagna, you can cover it with heavy-duty foil and freeze it for up to three months. Thaw in the refrigerator, and bake as directed.

   5 garlic cloves, peeled
   1 (16-ounce) carton 1% low-fat cottage cheese
   ½ cup (4 ounces) block-style fat-free cream cheese
   ¼ cup (1 ounce) grated fresh Romano cheese, divided
   2½ teaspoons dried basil
   ½ teaspoon crushed red pepper
   1 large egg
   1 (26-ounce) bottle fat-free tomato-basil pasta sauce
Cooking spray
   12 cooked lasagna noodles
   1 cup (4 ounces) chopped prosciutto or ham
   1 cup (4 ounces) shredded part-skim mozzarella cheese

1. Preheat oven to 375°.
2. Drop garlic cloves through food chute with food processor on, and process until minced. Add cottage cheese; process for 2 minutes or until smooth. Add cream cheese, 2 tablespoons Romano, basil, pepper, and egg; process until well blended.
3. Spread ½ cup pasta sauce in bottom of a 13 x 9-inch baking dish coated with cooking spray. Arrange 3 noodles over pasta sauce; top with 1 cup cheese mixture, ⅓ cup prosciutto, and ¾ cup pasta sauce. Repeat the layers two times, ending with noodles. Spread remaining pasta sauce over noodles. Sprinkle with 2 tablespoons Romano and mozzarella.
4. Cover and bake at 375° for 45 minutes or until sauce is bubbly. Uncover and bake at 375° an additional 15 minutes. Let lasagna stand 5 minutes. Yield: 9 servings.

CALORIES 272 (19% from fat); FAT 5.6g (sat 2.8g, mono 1.8g, poly 0.6g); PROTEIN 20.8g; CARB 33g; FIBER 2.1g; CHOL 47mg; IRON 2.3mg; SODIUM 775mg; CALC 213mg

Poultry

Chicken Cacciatore
"Pronto," page 216

Chicken Strudel

Cooking spray
1 cup chopped onion
1 (10-ounce) package fresh spinach, chopped (about 8 cups)
4 cups chopped cooked chicken breast (about 1¼ pounds)
¾ cup (3 ounces) shredded Swiss cheese
¼ cup egg substitute
2 tablespoons dry white wine
¼ teaspoon salt
⅛ teaspoon black pepper
2 garlic cloves, minced
8 sheets frozen phyllo dough, thawed
½ cup dry breadcrumbs
1 tablespoon butter, melted
¼ teaspoon paprika

1. Heat a large nonstick skillet coated with cooking spray over medium heat. Add onion, and sauté for 6 minutes or until tender. Stir in spinach, and cook 2 minutes or until the spinach wilts, stirring constantly. Remove from heat. Stir in chicken and next 6 ingredients.
2. Lightly coat 1 phyllo sheet with cooking spray (cover the remaining dough to keep from drying). Sprinkle with 1 tablespoon breadcrumbs. Repeat the layers with 3 sheets phyllo dough, cooking spray, and 3 tablespoons breadcrumbs.
3. Gently press layers together. Place about 2½ cups chicken mixture along 1 long edge of top phyllo sheet, leaving a ½-inch border. Starting at long edge with ½-inch border, roll up jelly-roll fashion. Place strudel, seam side down, on a baking sheet coated with cooking spray. Tuck ends under. Repeat with remaining phyllo, cooking spray, ¼ cup breadcrumbs, and 2½ cups chicken mixture. Brush strudels evenly with butter; sprinkle each with ⅛ teaspoon paprika.
4. Preheat oven to 375°.
5. Bake strudels at 375° for 20 minutes or until brown. Let stand 5 minutes before slicing. Cut each into 4 slices. Serve immediately. Yield: 2 strudels, 4 servings per strudel (serving size: 1 slice).

CALORIES 248 (30% from fat); FAT 8.2g (sat 3.6g, mono 2.3g, poly 1.5g); PROTEIN 23.8g; CARB 18.8g; FIBER 2g; CHOL 59mg; IRON 2.8mg; SODIUM 345mg; CALC 172mg

Barbecued-Chicken Potpie

Use this no-fuss recipe for quick weeknight meals or casual entertaining. Just add a salad or coleslaw.

1 teaspoon butter or stick margarine
Cooking spray
2 cups chopped onion
½ cup chopped green bell pepper
⅓ cup diced, seeded poblano chile or 1 (4.5-ounce) can chopped green chiles, drained
1 small garlic clove, minced
1½ teaspoons cumin seeds
1 teaspoon ground coriander
¼ cup cider vinegar
4 cups shredded cooked chicken breast (about 1½ pounds)
1¼ cups fat-free, less-sodium chicken broth
2 tablespoons brown sugar
1 ounce unsweetened chocolate, grated
1 (12-ounce) bottle chili sauce
1 (11.5-ounce) can refrigerated corn bread twists or 1 (11-ounce) can refrigerated soft breadsticks

1. Preheat oven to 375°.
2. Melt butter in a large nonstick skillet coated with cooking spray over medium-high heat. Add onion, pepper, chile, and garlic; sauté 5 minutes. Stir in cumin and coriander; cook 2 minutes. Stir in vinegar, scraping skillet to loosen browned bits. Add the chicken and the next 4 ingredients, and cook until thick (about 15 minutes), stirring occasionally. Spoon chicken mixture into an 11 x 7-inch baking dish coated with cooking spray.
3. Unroll corn bread dough, separating into strips. Place dough strips in a lattice fashion over chicken mixture. Bake at 375° for 25 minutes or until golden brown, and let stand 15 minutes before serving. Yield: 8 servings.

CALORIES 387 (27% from fat); FAT 11.8g (sat 3.9g, mono 5.1g, poly 1.6g); PROTEIN 32.1g; CARB 38.6g; FIBER 1.4g; CHOL 74mg; IRON 3.2mg; SODIUM 1,046mg; CALC 43mg

Barbecued-Chicken Potpie

Boka Dushi
(Dutch West Indian Chicken Kebabs)

¼ cup kejap manis or 2 tablespoons soy sauce
plus 2 tablespoons molasses
1 tablespoon fresh lime juice
1 teaspoon ground cumin
2 teaspoons grated peeled fresh ginger
1 teaspoon sambal ulek or Thai chile paste
½ teaspoon ground turmeric
1½ pounds skinless, boneless chicken breast, cut
into ½-inch-wide strips, or 1½ pounds
chicken tenders
Cooking spray
Dutch West Indian Peanut Sauce

1. Combine first 7 ingredients in a large zip-top plastic bag; seal and marinate in refrigerator 30 minutes.
2. Prepare grill.
3. Remove chicken from bag; discard marinade. Thread chicken strips onto 18 (8-inch) skewers.
4. Place kebabs on grill rack coated with cooking spray; grill 2 minutes on each side or until done. Serve with Dutch West Indian Peanut Sauce. Yield: 6 servings (serving size: 3 kebabs and 2 tablespoons Dutch West Indian Peanut Sauce).

(Totals include Dutch West Indian Peanut Sauce) CALORIES 212 (26% from fat); FAT 6.1g (sat 1.1g, mono 2.5g, poly 1.8g); PROTEIN 29.5g; CARB 9.5g; FIBER .9g; CHOL 66mg; IRON 1.9mg; SODIUM 676mg; CALC 40mg

DUTCH WEST INDIAN PEANUT SAUCE:
⅓ cup fat-free, less-sodium chicken broth
3 tablespoons creamy peanut butter
½ cup chopped seeded tomato
2 tablespoons minced green onions
2 tablespoons chopped fresh cilantro
1 tablespoon fish sauce
1 tablespoon fresh lime juice
1 teaspoon grated peeled fresh ginger
1 teaspoon minced seeded Thai chile
1 teaspoon honey
1 garlic clove, crushed

1. Combine broth and peanut butter in a small saucepan; cook over low heat 5 minutes or until smooth, stirring with a whisk. Pour into a bowl; stir in remaining ingredients. Serve at room temperature. Yield: ¾ cup (serving size: 2 tablespoons).

CALORIES 60 (63% from fat); FAT 4.2g (sat 0.7g, mono 2g, poly 1.3g); PROTEIN 2.9g; CARB 3.8g; FIBER 0.8g; CHOL 0mg; IRON 0.4mg; SODIUM 301mg; CALC 9mg

Lasagna-Chicken Florentine

1½ tablespoons butter or stick margarine
3 tablespoons all-purpose flour
2 (12-ounce) cans evaporated fat-free milk
½ teaspoon salt
⅛ teaspoon ground nutmeg
Cooking spray
6 oven-ready lasagna noodles (such as Ranco or Pasta Vigo)
1½ cups shredded cooked chicken breast (about 6 ounces)
1 (10-ounce) package frozen chopped spinach, thawed, drained, and squeezed dry
½ teaspoon freshly ground black pepper, divided
¾ cup (3 ounces) preshredded reduced-fat pizza-blend cheese or cheddar cheese

1. Preheat oven to 450°.
2. Melt butter in a medium saucepan over medium heat. Add flour; cook 30 seconds, stirring constantly. Gradually add the milk, stirring with a whisk until blended. Stir in salt and nutmeg; cook until thick, stirring constantly (about 3 minutes).
3. Spread ½ cup sauce in the bottom of an 8-inch square baking dish coated with cooking spray. Arrange 2 noodles over sauce, and top with half of chicken and half of spinach. Sprinkle with ¼ teaspoon pepper; top with ¾ cup sauce. Repeat layers, ending with noodles. Spread remaining sauce over noodles. Cover, and bake at 450° for 25 minutes or until noodles are tender and sauce is bubbly. Uncover and top with cheese; bake an additional 5 minutes. Let stand 5 minutes. Yield: 4 servings.
NOTE: If using an 8-inch metal baking pan, increase baking time by 5 minutes.

CALORIES 450 (22% from fat); FAT 11g (sat 4g, mono 4.1g, poly 2.1g); PROTEIN 38.7g; CARB 48.4g; FIBER 3.2g; CHOL 57mg; IRON 3.9mg; SODIUM 782mg; CALC 755mg

Chicken-Orange Stir-fry

1 (11-ounce) can mandarin oranges in light syrup, undrained
⅓ cup thawed orange juice concentrate, undiluted
2 tablespoons low-sodium soy sauce
1 tablespoon minced peeled fresh ginger
1½ teaspoons apricot preserves
½ teaspoon dark sesame oil
⅛ teaspoon chili oil (optional)
1 garlic clove, minced
½ pound skinless, boneless chicken breasts, cut into bite-size pieces
1½ teaspoons vegetable oil
1 cup (1-inch) diagonally sliced asparagus (about 4 ounces)
½ cup (3-inch) julienne-cut red bell pepper
½ cup (3-inch) julienne-cut zucchini (about 1 small)
½ cup (3-inch) julienne-cut carrot (about 1 medium)
½ cup snow peas
½ cup diagonally sliced celery
½ pound green beans, trimmed and diagonally sliced
1 (8-ounce) package presliced mushrooms
1½ teaspoons cornstarch
3 cups hot cooked rice
2 tablespoons slivered almonds, toasted

1. Drain oranges in a colander over a bowl, reserving syrup.
2. Combine juice concentrate and next 6 ingredients in a bowl, stirring with a whisk. Add chicken; cover and marinate in refrigerator 1 hour.
3. Heat vegetable oil in a stir-fry pan or wok over medium-high heat. Add sliced asparagus and next 6 ingredients, and stir-fry for 6 minutes or until crisp-tender. Add mushrooms, and stir-fry for 2 minutes. Remove vegetable mixture from pan. Add chicken mixture to pan; stir-fry for 4 minutes or until chicken is done. Return vegetable mixture to pan. Combine reserved syrup and cornstarch in a small bowl, stirring well with a whisk. Add syrup mixture to pan; bring to a boil, and cook for 1 minute or until slightly thick. Stir in oranges. Serve over hot rice and slivered almonds. Yield: 4 servings (serving size: 1½ cups chicken mixture, ¾ cup rice, and 1½ teaspoons almonds).

CALORIES 434 (11% from fat); FAT 5.5g (sat 0.7g, mono 2g, poly 2.1g); PROTEIN 21.9g; CARB 76g; FIBER 5.5g; CHOL 33mg; IRON 4.6mg; SODIUM 313mg; CALC 94mg

Sichuan-Style Stir-fried Chicken with Peanuts

Also known as kung pao chicken, this Sichuan classic reflects the regional style.

MARINADE:
- 2 tablespoons low-sodium soy sauce
- 2 tablespoons rice wine or sake
- 1 teaspoon cornstarch
- 1 teaspoon dark sesame oil
- 1½ pounds skinless, boneless chicken breasts, cut into bite-sized pieces

STIR-FRYING OIL:
- 2 tablespoons vegetable oil, divided

SAUCE:
- ½ cup fat-free, less-sodium chicken broth
- 2 tablespoons sugar
- 2½ tablespoons low-sodium soy sauce
- 2 tablespoons rice wine or sake
- 1 tablespoon Chinese black vinegar or Worcestershire sauce
- 1¼ teaspoons cornstarch
- 1 teaspoon dark sesame oil
- 2 tablespoons minced green onions
- 1½ tablespoons minced peeled fresh ginger
- 1½ tablespoons minced garlic (about 7 cloves)
- 1 teaspoon chile paste with garlic

REMAINING INGREDIENTS:
- 1½ cups drained, sliced water chestnuts
- 1 cup (½-inch) sliced green onion tops
- ¾ cup unsalted, dry-roasted peanuts
- 6 cups hot cooked long-grain rice

1. To prepare marinade, combine first 5 ingredients in a medium bowl; cover and chill 20 minutes.

2. Heat 1 tablespoon vegetable oil in a wok or large nonstick skillet over medium-high heat. Add the chicken mixture; stir-fry 4 minutes or until chicken is done. Remove from pan; set aside.

3. To prepare sauce, combine broth and the next 6 ingredients; stir well with a whisk. Heat 1 tablespoon vegetable oil in pan. Add 2 tablespoons onions, ginger, garlic, and chile paste; stir-fry 15 seconds. Add the broth mixture; cook 1 minute or until sauce is thick, stirring constantly.

4. Stir in chicken, water chestnuts, sliced onion tops, and peanuts; cook 1 minute or until thoroughly heated. Serve over rice. Yield: 6 servings (serving size: ¾ cup stir-fry and 1 cup rice).

CALORIES 590 (25% from fat); FAT 16.7g (sat 2.7g, mono 6.8g, poly 6g); PROTEIN 36.9g; CARB 71.4g; FIBER 3.3g; CHOL 66mg; IRON 3.8mg; SODIUM 591mg; CALC 75mg

Buffalo Chicken with Blue Cheese Fondue

To keep the cheeses creamy and smooth, stir the dippers in a figure-eight motion. A heavy enamel fondue pot helps prevent the cheeses from burning on the bottom. You can find wing sauce with other hot sauces in the condiment section of your grocery store.

DIPPERS:
- 4 (4-ounce) skinless, boneless chicken breast halves
- Cooking spray
- ¼ cup bottled wing sauce, divided
- 2 cups green beans, trimmed (about 8 ounces)
- 2 cups (3 x ½-inch) carrot sticks
- 2 cups (3-inch) celery sticks
- 2 cups red bell pepper strips
- 12 ounces French bread, toasted and cut into 1-inch cubes

FONDUE:
- 2 cups (8 ounces) crumbled blue cheese
- 1 tablespoon cornstarch
- 1 cup dry white wine
- ⅔ cup 1% low-fat milk
- 1 (8-ounce) block fat-free cream cheese, softened

1. Preheat oven to 400°.

2. Place each chicken breast half between 2 sheets of heavy-duty plastic wrap, and flatten to a ½-inch thickness using a meat mallet or rolling pin. Place chicken on a baking sheet coated with cooking spray. Brush with 2 tablespoons wing sauce. Bake at 400° for 5 minutes. Turn chicken over, and brush with 2 tablespoons wing sauce. Bake an additional 5 minutes or until done. Cut chicken into 1-inch pieces.

3. Cook beans in boiling water for 1 minute or until crisp-tender; drain. Rinse with cold water; drain well. Place beans on a platter with carrot, celery, bell pepper, and bread; set aside.

4. Combine blue cheese and cornstarch in a large saucepan. Stir in wine, milk, and cream cheese. Bring to a boil over medium heat; cook for 1 minute, stirring constantly with a whisk. Reduce heat to medium-low; cook 8 minutes or until mixture is smooth, stirring frequently. Pour into a fondue pot. Keep warm over low flame. Serve with dippers. Yield: 8 servings (serving size: 1½ ounces chicken, ¼ cup beans, ¼ cup carrots, ¼ cup celery, ¼ cup bell pepper, 1½ ounces bread, and about ⅓ cup fondue).

CALORIES 352 (27% from fat); FAT 10.5g (sat 5.9g, mono 3g, poly 0.8g); PROTEIN 28.7g; CARB 34.1g; FIBER 3.3g; CHOL 60mg; IRON 2.5mg; SODIUM 991mg; CALC 319mg

"Fried" Chicken with Cucumber and Fennel Raita

A raita (RI-tah) is a yogurt-based salad popular in India.

1 cup plain fat-free yogurt
½ cup (½-inch) diced cucumber
½ cup (½-inch) diced fennel bulb
1 teaspoon finely chopped
    fresh mint
¼ teaspoon salt
¼ teaspoon coarsely ground
    black pepper
4 (6-ounce) skinless, boneless
    chicken breast halves
⅛ teaspoon salt
Cooking spray
⅓ cup Italian-seasoned breadcrumbs
1 tablespoon olive oil
Fresh mint sprigs (optional)

1. Combine first 6 ingredients in a medium bowl. Cover and chill.

2. Place each chicken breast half between 2 sheets of heavy-duty plastic wrap, and pound to ¼-inch thickness using a meat mallet or rolling pin. Sprinkle chicken with ⅛ teaspoon salt, and lightly coat both sides of chicken with cooking spray. Dredge chicken in breadcrumbs.

3. Heat oil in a large nonstick skillet over medium-high heat. Add chicken; cook 2 minutes on each side or until done. Serve with raita. Garnish with mint sprigs, if desired. Yield: 4 servings (serving size: 1 chicken breast half and about ⅓ cup raita).

CALORIES 213 (26% from fat); FAT 6.1g (sat 1.5g, mono 3.3g, poly 0.7g); PROTEIN 30g; CARB 7.9g; FIBER 0.6g; CHOL 70mg; IRON 1.1mg; SODIUM 358mg; CALC 140mg

Champion Chicken Parmesan

Champion Chicken Parmesan

To add punch to this recipe, try more pungent Asiago or provolone cheese in place of the mozzarella.

TOMATO SAUCE:
- 1 cup boiling water
- ¼ cup sun-dried tomatoes, packed without oil
- 1 teaspoon olive oil
- 2 cups chopped red bell pepper
- 1 cup chopped onion
- 2 (14.5-ounce) cans diced tomatoes, undrained
- ¼ cup chopped fresh parsley
- 2 tablespoons chopped fresh basil
- 1 tablespoon balsamic vinegar
- ¼ teaspoon black pepper
- 2 garlic cloves, minced

CHICKEN:
- ¼ cup all-purpose flour
- ¼ cup grated Parmesan cheese
- ¼ teaspoon black pepper
- 4 (4-ounce) skinless, boneless chicken breast halves
- 1 large egg white, lightly beaten
- 1 tablespoon olive oil
- Cooking spray
- 1 cup (4 ounces) shredded part-skim mozzarella cheese
- 3 cups hot cooked linguine (about 6 ounces uncooked pasta)

1. To prepare the tomato sauce, combine the water and sun-dried tomatoes in a bowl; cover and let stand for 30 minutes or until soft. Drain and finely chop tomatoes.

2. Heat 1 teaspoon olive oil in a large saucepan over medium-high heat. Add the sun-dried tomatoes, bell pepper, and onion; sauté for 7 minutes. Stir in the canned tomatoes, and bring to a boil. Cover, reduce heat, and simmer 10 minutes. Remove from heat; stir in parsley, basil, vinegar, ¼ teaspoon black pepper, and garlic.

3. Preheat oven to 350°.

4. To prepare chicken, lightly spoon flour into a dry measuring cup; level with a knife. Combine the flour, Parmesan, and ¼ teaspoon black pepper in a shallow dish. Place each breast half between 2 sheets of heavy-duty plastic wrap; flatten to ¼-inch thickness using a meat mallet or rolling pin. Dip each breast half in egg white, and dredge in flour mixture. Heat 1 tablespoon olive oil in a large nonstick skillet over medium-high heat. Add chicken; cook 5 minutes on each side or until golden. Arrange in a 13 x 9-inch baking dish coated with cooking spray. Pour tomato sauce over chicken. Sprinkle with mozzarella. Bake at 350° for 15 minutes. Serve over linguine. Yield: 4 servings (serving size: 1 chicken breast half, 1 cup sauce, ¼ cup cheese, and ¾ cup pasta).

CALORIES 559 (26% from fat); FAT 15.9g (sat 5.6g, mono 6.3g, poly 2g); PROTEIN 46.3g; CARB 58.1g; FIBER 6.4g; CHOL 93mg; IRON 6.1mg; SODIUM 792mg; CALC 359mg

Chicken with Italian Vegetables

- 1 teaspoon garlic powder
- ½ teaspoon salt, divided
- ¼ teaspoon black pepper, divided
- 4 (4-ounce) skinless, boneless chicken breast halves
- Cooking spray
- 1 tablespoon olive oil
- 1 (8-ounce) package presliced mushrooms
- 1 small zucchini, quartered lengthwise and sliced (about 5 ounces)
- 4 garlic cloves, minced
- 1 cup chopped plum tomato
- ½ cup chopped red onion
- ½ cup chopped fresh basil
- 4 teaspoons balsamic vinegar
- ¼ cup (1 ounce) grated fresh Parmesan cheese

1. Preheat broiler.

2. Combine garlic powder, ¼ teaspoon salt, and ⅛ teaspoon pepper in a small bowl; sprinkle chicken with the garlic powder mixture. Place chicken on a broiler pan coated with cooking spray; broil 6 minutes on each side or until done. Remove chicken from pan; keep warm.

3. Heat oil in a large nonstick skillet over medium-high heat. Add ¼ teaspoon salt, sliced mushrooms, zucchini, and minced garlic; sauté 2 minutes. Add ⅛ teaspoon pepper, tomato, onion, basil, and vinegar; sauté for 3 minutes. Serve vegetable mixture over chicken, and sprinkle with cheese. Yield: 4 servings (serving size: 1 chicken breast half, ½ cup vegetables, and 1 tablespoon cheese).

CALORIES 229 (29% from fat); FAT 7.3g (sat 2.1g, mono 3.5g, poly 1g); PROTEIN 31.4g; CARB 9.7g; FIBER 2.1g; CHOL 71mg; IRON 2.3mg; SODIUM 489mg; CALC 126mg

Chicken with Rosemary Sauce

Chicken breasts are enveloped in an herb sauce that is enriched with wine and half-and-half in this dish.

    1   teaspoon olive oil
    4   (4-ounce) skinless, boneless chicken breast
        halves
    ¼   teaspoon salt
    ⅛   teaspoon black pepper
    ½   cup chopped green onions
    ¼   cup dry white wine
    1   teaspoon minced fresh rosemary
    ½   cup fat-free, less-sodium chicken broth
    ½   cup half-and-half

1. Heat oil in a nonstick skillet over medium-high heat. Sprinkle chicken with salt and pepper. Add to pan; cook 3 minutes on each side. Add green onions, wine, and rosemary; cook 30 seconds. Stir in broth; cook 2 minutes. Add half-and-half; cook 2 minutes. Yield: 4 servings (serving size: 1 chicken breast half and about 3 tablespoons sauce).

CALORIES 183 (30% from fat); FAT 6g (sat 2.7g, mono 2.2g, poly 0.5g); PROTEIN 27.5g; CARB 2.7g; FIBER 0.5g; CHOL 77mg; IRON 0.9mg; SODIUM 293mg; CALC 46mg

Chicken Parmesan

This recipe can be put together in a 13 x 9-inch baking dish, if desired.

    4   (4-ounce) skinless, boneless chicken breast
        halves
    ½   cup seasoned breadcrumbs
    ¼   cup grated Parmesan cheese
    ½   teaspoon dried Italian seasoning
    ⅛   teaspoon black pepper
    ⅓   cup all-purpose flour
    2   large egg whites, lightly beaten
    2   teaspoons olive oil
    4   cups hot cooked spaghetti
        (about 8 ounces uncooked pasta)
    3   cups Quick-and-Easy Pasta Sauce,
        heated
    1   cup (4 ounces) shredded part-skim
        mozzarella cheese
    Basil sprigs (optional)

1. Place each chicken breast half between 2 sheets of heavy-duty plastic wrap; flatten to ¼-inch thickness using a meat mallet or rolling pin.

2. Combine breadcrumbs, Parmesan cheese, Italian seasoning, and pepper in a shallow dish. Dredge 1 chicken breast half in flour. Dip in egg whites, and dredge in breadcrumb mixture. Repeat procedure with the remaining chicken, flour, egg whites, and breadcrumb mixture.

3. Heat oil in a large nonstick skillet over medium-high heat. Add chicken; cook 5 minutes on each side or until done.

4. Place 1 cup spaghetti in each of 4 gratin dishes. Spoon ½ cup Quick-and-Easy Pasta Sauce over each serving. Top each with 1 chicken breast half. Spoon ¼ cup sauce over each serving. Sprinkle each serving with ¼ cup mozzarella cheese.

5. Preheat broiler.

6. Place gratin dishes on a baking sheet; broil 3 minutes or until cheese melts. Garnish with basil sprigs, if desired. Yield: 4 servings.

(Totals include Quick-and-Easy Pasta Sauce) CALORIES 614 (19% from fat); FAT 12.8g (sat 5g, mono 4.8g, poly 1.5g); PROTEIN 49.1g; CARB 74.8g; FIBER 5.4g; CHOL 86mg; IRON 6.1mg; SODIUM 937mg; CALC 375mg

QUICK-AND-EASY PASTA SAUCE:

This sauce is also delicious served over a simple dish of your favorite pasta.

    1   teaspoon olive oil
    1   cup chopped onion
    4   garlic cloves, minced
    ½   cup dry red wine or 2 tablespoons
        balsamic vinegar
    1   tablespoon sugar
    1   tablespoon chopped fresh or 1 teaspoon
        dried basil
    2   tablespoons tomato paste
    ½   teaspoon dried Italian seasoning
    ¼   teaspoon black pepper
    2   (14.5-ounce) cans diced tomatoes, undrained
    2   tablespoons chopped fresh parsley

1. Heat olive oil in a saucepan or large skillet over medium-high heat. Add onion and garlic; sauté 5 minutes. Stir in wine and next 6 ingredients, and bring to a boil. Reduce heat to medium, and cook about 15 minutes to thicken. Stir in parsley. Yield: 3 cups (serving size: 1 cup).

CALORIES 126 (16% from fat); FAT 2.3g (sat 0.4g, mono 1.3g, poly 0.5g); PROTEIN 4.1g; CARB 25.2g; FIBER 3.7g; CHOL 0mg; IRON 2.8mg; SODIUM 461mg; CALC 110mg

Chicken Breasts Stuffed with Artichokes, Lemon, and Goat Cheese

2½ tablespoons Italian-seasoned breadcrumbs
  2 teaspoons grated lemon rind
  ¼ teaspoon salt
  ¼ teaspoon freshly ground black pepper
  1 (6-ounce) jar marinated artichoke hearts, drained and chopped
  1 (3-ounce) package herbed goat cheese, softened
  4 (6-ounce) skinless, boneless chicken breast halves
  Cooking spray

1. Preheat oven to 375°.

2. Combine first 6 ingredients; stir well.

3. Place each chicken breast half between 2 sheets of heavy-duty plastic wrap; pound to ¼-inch thickness using a meat mallet or rolling pin. Top each breast half with 2 tablespoons cheese mixture; roll up jelly-roll fashion. Tuck in sides, and secure each roll with wooden picks.

4. Heat a large nonstick skillet coated with cooking spray over medium-high heat. Add chicken to pan, and cook for 3 minutes on each side or until browned. Wrap handle of pan with foil, and bake at 375° for 15 minutes or until chicken is done. Yield: 4 servings.

CALORIES 234 (30% from fat); FAT 7.8g (sat 3.5g, mono 1.4g, poly 0.5g); PROTEIN 33g; CARB 7.2g; FIBER 1.5g; CHOL 78mg; IRON 1.6mg; SODIUM 545mg; CALC 49mg

Gruyère, Arugula, and Prosciutto-Stuffed Chicken Breasts with Caramelized Shallot Sauce

CHICKEN:
- 6 (4-ounce) skinless, boneless chicken breast halves
- 6 (½-ounce) slices prosciutto
- 6 (½-ounce) slices Gruyère cheese
- 1½ cups trimmed arugula
- ½ teaspoon salt
- ½ teaspoon black pepper
- 3 tablespoons all-purpose flour
- 1 tablespoon olive oil

SAUCE:
- 1 cup thinly sliced shallots
- 2 teaspoons tomato paste
- 2 cups dry white wine
- 2¼ cups fat-free, less-sodium chicken broth
- 1½ teaspoons water
- 1 teaspoon cornstarch

1. Preheat oven to 350°.

2. Place each chicken breast half between 2 sheets of heavy-duty plastic wrap; pound to ¼-inch thickness using a meat mallet or rolling pin. Top each chicken breast half with 1 slice prosciutto, 1 slice cheese, and ¼ cup arugula, leaving a ¼-inch border around edges. Fold in half, pinching edges together to seal, and sprinkle with salt and pepper. (The chicken can be prepared up to a day ahead and refrigerated at this point.)

3. Dredge chicken in flour, shaking off excess. Heat oil in a nonstick skillet over medium-high heat. Add chicken; cook 5 minutes on each side. Place chicken in a shallow baking pan, and bake at 350° for 5 minutes or until done. Keep warm.

4. Add shallots to skillet; sauté 4 minutes over medium-high heat or until browned. Add tomato paste; cook 1 minute, stirring constantly. Stir in wine; bring to a boil over high heat. Cook until reduced to 1 cup (about 6 minutes). Add broth; bring to a boil. Cook until reduced by half (about 8 minutes).

5. Combine water and cornstarch in a small bowl, stirring with a fork until smooth. Add cornstarch mixture to sauce; bring to a boil. Cook 1 minute, stirring constantly. Yield: 6 servings (serving size: 1 chicken breast half and about ¼ cup sauce).

CALORIES 300 (29% from fat); FAT 9.8g (sat 4g, mono 4g, poly 0.9g); PROTEIN 29.7g; CARB 9.7g; FIBER 0.5g; CHOL 75mg; IRON 1.7mg; SODIUM 562mg; CALC 189mg

Brie-and-Caramelized Onion-Stuffed Chicken Breasts

- 1 teaspoon olive oil, divided
- 1½ cups sliced onion
- 4 garlic cloves, thinly sliced
- ⅔ cup dry white wine, divided
- 2 ounces Brie or Camembert cheese, rind removed and cut into small pieces (about 2 tablespoons)
- ⅛ teaspoon salt
- ⅛ teaspoon black pepper
- 4 (4-ounce) skinless, boneless chicken breast halves
- 2 tablespoons minced fresh onion
- 1 tablespoon chopped fresh or ¾ teaspoon dried rubbed sage
- 2 garlic cloves, minced
- 1¼ cups fat-free, less-sodium chicken broth
- Sage sprigs (optional)

1. Heat ½ teaspoon oil in a large nonstick skillet over medium heat. Add sliced onion; sauté 30 minutes or until golden brown. Add sliced garlic, and sauté 5 minutes. Stir in ⅓ cup wine, and cook 5 minutes or until liquid almost evaporates. Spoon the onion mixture into a bowl, and cool. Stir in cheese, salt, and pepper.

2. Cut a horizontal slit through the thickest portion of each chicken breast half to form a pocket. Stuff about 1½ tablespoons of the onion mixture into each pocket.

3. Heat ½ teaspoon oil in pan over medium-high heat. Add chicken; sauté 6 minutes on each side or until chicken is done. Remove chicken from skillet. Set aside; keep warm.

4. Add ⅓ cup wine, minced onion, chopped sage, and minced garlic to pan. Cook over medium-high heat for 2 minutes. Stir in chicken broth. Bring to a boil, and cook until reduced to ¾ cup (about 7 minutes). Return chicken to pan; cover and simmer 2 minutes or until thoroughly heated. Serve sauce with chicken. Garnish with sage sprigs, if desired. Yield: 4 servings (serving size: 1 chicken breast half and 3 tablespoons sauce).

CALORIES 216 (28% from fat); FAT 6.6g (sat 3g, mono 2.3g, poly 0.6g); PROTEIN 31g; CARB 6.7g; FIBER 1g; CHOL 80mg; IRON 1.3mg; SODIUM 389mg; CALC 62mg

Enchiladas de Pollo
(*Chicken Enchiladas*)

FILLING:

- 3 cups water
- ¼ teaspoon salt
- 8 black peppercorns
- 1 onion, quartered
- 1 bay leaf
- 1 pound skinless chicken breast halves
- ¾ cup (3 ounces) shredded Monterey Jack cheese, divided
- ¾ cup (3 ounces) shredded reduced-fat extrasharp cheddar cheese, divided
- ½ cup chopped onion

SAUCE:

- ⅔ cup 2% reduced-fat milk
- ¼ cup chopped fresh cilantro
- ¼ cup egg substitute
- ⅛ teaspoon salt
- 1 (11-ounce) can tomatillos, drained
- 1 (4.5-ounce) can chopped green chiles, undrained

REMAINING INGREDIENTS:

- 8 (6-inch) corn tortillas
- ⅔ cup fat-free sour cream

1. To prepare filling, place first 6 ingredients in a Dutch oven; bring to a boil. Cover, reduce heat, and simmer 45 minutes. Remove chicken from pan; cool. Remove chicken from bones; shred with 2 forks. Discard bones. Reserve broth for another use.

2. Preheat oven to 375°.

3. Combine chicken, ½ cup each Monterey Jack and cheddar cheeses, and ½ cup chopped onion in a bowl, and set aside.

4. To prepare sauce, place milk and next 5 ingredients in a food processor; process until smooth.

5. To prepare tortillas, fill a medium skillet with 1 inch of water; bring to a simmer. Dip 1 tortilla in water using tongs. Spoon ½ cup filling in center of tortilla. Roll tightly, and place in an 11 x 7-inch baking dish. Repeat procedure with remaining tortillas and filling.

6. Pour sauce over enchiladas. Cover and bake at 375° for 20 minutes. Uncover; sprinkle with ¼ cup each Monterey Jack and cheddar. Bake an additional 5 minutes or until cheeses melt. Top with sour cream. Yield: 4 servings (serving size: 2 enchiladas and about 2½ tablespoons sour cream).

CALORIES 502 (30% from fat); FAT 16.6g (sat 8.4g, mono 3.7g, poly 2g); PROTEIN 47.6g; CARB 40g; FIBER 4.6g; CHOL 114mg; IRON 3mg; SODIUM 725mg; CALC 598mg

Grilled Chicken with White Barbecue Sauce

CHICKEN:

8 (8-ounce) bone-in chicken breast halves
1 teaspoon salt
1 teaspoon onion powder
1 teaspoon garlic powder
1 teaspoon paprika
1 teaspoon chipotle chile powder
Cooking spray

SAUCE:

½ cup light mayonnaise
⅓ cup white vinegar
1 tablespoon coarsely ground black pepper
½ teaspoon ground red pepper
1½ teaspoons fresh lemon juice

1. Preheat grill to medium-hot using both burners.
2. Loosen skin from breasts by inserting fingers, gently pushing between skin and meat. Combine salt and next 4 ingredients; rub under loosened skin.
3. Turn left burner off (leave right burner on). Coat grill rack with cooking spray. Place chicken on grill rack over right burner; grill 5 minutes on each side or until browned. Move chicken to rack over left burner. Cover and cook 35 minutes or until done, turning once. Remove from grill; discard skin.
4. Combine mayonnaise and remaining ingredients, stirring with a whisk. Serve with chicken. Yield: 8 servings (serving size: 1 breast half and about 2 tablespoons sauce).

CALORIES 252 (25% from fat); FAT 6.9g (sat 1.3g, mono 1.4g, poly 3.4g); PROTEIN 34.4g; CARB 10.9g; FIBER 0.6g; CHOL 91mg; IRON 1.5mg; SODIUM 536mg; CALC 26mg

Blueberry-Balsamic Barbecue Sauce

2 cups fresh blueberries
¼ cup balsamic vinegar
3 tablespoons sugar
3 tablespoons ketchup
½ teaspoon garlic powder
¼ teaspoon salt

1. Place all ingredients in a saucepan. Bring mixture to a boil, and reduce heat. Simmer for 15 minutes or until mixture is slightly thick, stirring occasionally. Remove pan from heat, and cool. Place blueberry mixture in a blender; cover with top, and process until smooth.

2. Place sauce in an airtight container; cover and chill. Yield: 1½ cups (serving size: about ¼ cup).

CALORIES 67 (3% from fat); FAT 0.2g (sat 0g, mono 0g, poly 0.1g); PROTEIN 0.5g; CARB 16.9g; FIBER 1.4g; CHOL 0mg; IRON 0.2mg; SODIUM 194mg; CALC 8mg

Chicken Cacciatore "Pronto"

(pictured on page 202)

Adapted from *Michael Chiarello's Casual Cooking*, by Michael Chiarello (Chronicle Books, 2002). Serve with cavatappi pasta and green beans.

1 (½-ounce) package dried porcini mushrooms
1 cup hot water
2 teaspoons olive oil
8 skinless, boneless chicken thighs
1 teaspoon salt
½ teaspoon freshly ground black pepper
3 garlic cloves, minced
3 tablespoons minced fresh parsley, divided
¾ cup canned crushed tomatoes
½ cup fat-free, less-sodium chicken broth
½ cup water

1. Combine mushrooms and hot water in a bowl; cover and let stand 30 minutes. Remove mushrooms with slotted spoon. Finely chop mushrooms; set aside. Strain soaking liquid into a bowl through a sieve lined with cheesecloth or paper towels. Discard solids; reserve soaking liquid.
2. Heat oil in a large nonstick skillet over medium-high heat. Sprinkle chicken with salt and pepper. Add chicken to pan; cook 4 minutes on each side or until browned. Remove chicken from pan. Reduce heat to medium. Add garlic, and cook 2 minutes or until golden, stirring constantly. Add 2 tablespoons parsley; cook 30 seconds, stirring constantly. Add mushrooms; cook 30 seconds, stirring constantly. Stir in reserved soaking liquid, tomatoes, broth, and water; bring to a simmer. Return chicken to pan, and reduce heat to low. Cover and cook 10 minutes or until chicken is done.
3. Remove chicken; keep warm. Increase heat to medium-high; cook until sauce is reduced to 1 cup (about 5 minutes). Spoon sauce over chicken, and sprinkle with 1 tablespoon parsley. Yield: 4 servings (serving size: 2 thighs and ¼ cup sauce).

CALORIES 263 (29% from fat); FAT 8.5g (sat 1.7g, mono 3.7g, poly 1.8g); PROTEIN 33.6g; CARB 11.7g; FIBER 3.5g; CHOL 115mg; IRON 5.7mg; SODIUM 771mg; CALC 31.6mg

Cilantro Rice with Chicken

A sauce of fresh cilantro, green onions, ginger, and garlic is stirred into cooked rice to lend intense fragrance and flavor. Shiitake mushrooms provide an earthy, smoky flavor.

RICE:

1 tablespoon olive oil
2 cups quartered shiitake mushroom caps (about 6 ounces)
¼ cup chopped green onion bottoms
1 (½-inch) piece peeled fresh ginger
1 garlic clove, crushed
2 cups uncooked long-grain rice
2 teaspoons ground cumin
6 skinless, boneless chicken thighs (about 1¾ pounds), cut into bite-sized pieces
3 cups fat-free, less-sodium chicken broth

SAUCE:

2 cups loosely packed cilantro leaves
½ cup fat-free, less-sodium chicken broth
2 tablespoons chopped green onion tops
1 teaspoon chopped peeled fresh ginger
½ teaspoon kosher salt
1 garlic clove, peeled

TOPPING:

1 teaspoon olive oil
2 cups grape or cherry tomatoes, halved
2 tablespoons chopped green onion tops
Cilantro sprigs (optional)

1. Preheat oven to 350°.

2. To prepare rice, heat 1 tablespoon olive oil in a Dutch oven over medium heat. Add mushrooms, green onion bottoms, ginger piece, and crushed garlic, and cook 5 minutes, stirring frequently. Stir in rice, cumin, and chicken; cook 1 minute. Stir in broth; bring to a boil. Cover and bake at 350° for 25 minutes. Remove from oven, and let stand, covered, for 10 minutes.

3. To prepare sauce, place cilantro leaves and the next 5 ingredients in a food processor or blender, and process until smooth. Stir into rice mixture. Discard ginger piece.

4. To prepare the topping, heat 1 teaspoon olive oil in a medium skillet over medium-low heat. Add the grape tomatoes, and cook for 2 minutes. Stir in 2 tablespoons chopped green onion tops. Place the rice mixture in a large bowl, and spoon the tomato topping over the rice. Garnish with cilantro sprigs, if desired. Yield: 8 servings (serving size: about 1 cup rice mixture and about ¼ cup tomato topping).

CALORIES 339 (18% from fat); FAT 6.8g (sat 1.4g, mono 3g, poly 1.3g); PROTEIN 25.3g; CARB 41.5g; FIBER 1.8g; CHOL 82mg; IRON 3.9mg; SODIUM 416mg; CALC 44mg

Asian Barbecue Chicken

Asian Barbecue Chicken

¼ cup packed brown sugar
¼ cup low-sodium soy sauce
 1 tablespoon fresh lime juice
½ teaspoon crushed red pepper
¼ teaspoon curry powder
 3 garlic cloves, minced
 8 (6-ounce) chicken thighs, skinned
Cooking spray
Lime wedges (optional)
Green onion tops (optional)

1. Combine first 6 ingredients in a large zip-top plastic bag; add chicken. Seal and marinate in refrigerator 4 hours or overnight, turning occasionally.
2. Prepare grill.
3. Remove chicken from bag, reserving marinade. Place marinade in a small saucepan. Bring to a boil; cook 1 minute.
4. Place chicken on grill rack coated with cooking spray; grill 20 minutes or until done, turning and basting frequently with cooked marinade. Garnish with lime wedges and green onion tops, if desired. Yield: 4 servings (serving size: 2 thighs).

CALORIES 297 (23% from fat); FAT 7.7g (sat 2g, mono 2.4g, poly 1.9g); PROTEIN 39.2g; CARB 16.1g; FIBER 0.4g; CHOL 161mg; IRON 2.7mg; SODIUM 706mg; CALC 39mg

Oven-Fried Chicken Thighs with Mustard-Buttermilk Sauce

Preheating the baking sheet helps crisp the chicken on the bottom. Serve with mashed potatoes.

¼ cup low-fat buttermilk
 4 teaspoons Dijon mustard
 1 tablespoon honey
¼ teaspoon salt
¼ teaspoon freshly ground black pepper
⅛ teaspoon dried rosemary
¼ cup dry breadcrumbs
1½ tablespoons grated fresh Parmesan cheese
 4 (6-ounce) chicken thighs, skinned
Cooking spray

1. Preheat oven to 425°.
2. Combine the first 6 ingredients in a small microwave-safe bowl. Spoon 3 tablespoons buttermilk mixture into a shallow bowl; reserve the remaining mixture.
3. Combine breadcrumbs and cheese in a small bowl. Dip the chicken in 3 tablespoons buttermilk mixture; dredge in breadcrumb mixture. Chill 15 minutes. Lightly coat a baking sheet with cooking spray; place in oven 5 minutes.
4. Place chicken on baking sheet. Bake at 425° for 24 minutes or until thermometer registers 180°, turning chicken after 12 minutes. Microwave the reserved buttermilk mixture at HIGH for 20 seconds or until warm. Drizzle sauce over chicken. Yield: 2 servings (serving size: 2 chicken thighs and 2 table-spoons sauce).

CALORIES 376 (29% from fat); FAT 12g (sat 3.5g, mono 4g, poly 2.8g); PROTEIN 43.6g; CARB 20.4g; FIBER 0.4g; CHOL 168mg; IRON 3mg; SODIUM 971mg; CALC 152mg

Chicken Thighs with Tomatoes, Olives, and Capers

 8 skinless, boneless chicken thighs
½ teaspoon salt
¼ teaspoon black pepper
 1 teaspoon vegetable oil
 1 tablespoon bottled minced garlic
 1 cup chopped fresh parsley
¼ cup chopped pitted kalamata olives
 2 teaspoons capers
 1 (14.5-ounce) can no-salt-added diced tomatoes, undrained

1. Sprinkle chicken with salt and pepper. Heat oil in a large nonstick skillet over medium-high heat. Add chicken; cook 4 minutes on each side. Remove chicken from pan; keep warm.
2. Add garlic to pan, and sauté 30 seconds. Add remaining ingredients; scrape pan to loosen browned bits. Return chicken to pan. Reduce heat; simmer 5 minutes or until chicken is done. Yield: 4 servings (serving size: 2 thighs and about ¼ cup sauce).

CALORIES 174 (28% from fat); FAT 5.5g (sat 1.2g, mono 2.1g, poly 1.2g); PROTEIN 23.9g; CARB 7.2g; FIBER 2.5g; CHOL 94mg; IRON 2.8mg; SODIUM 566mg; CALC 61mg

Braised Root Vegetables
and Chicken Thighs

Braised Root Vegetables and Chicken Thighs

¼   cup all-purpose flour
8   chicken thighs (about 2 pounds), skinned
5   teaspoons olive oil, divided
2   cups chopped onion
2   cups (¾-inch) cubed peeled rutabaga
2   cups (¾-inch) cubed peeled turnip (about 1 pound)
2   cups (¾-inch) cubed peeled butternut squash
1   cup (¼-inch-thick) slices parsnip
1   garlic clove, minced
½   cup fat-free, less-sodium chicken broth
1   teaspoon chopped fresh or ¼ teaspoon dried thyme
1   teaspoon chopped fresh or ¼ teaspoon dried rubbed sage
½   teaspoon salt
¼   teaspoon black pepper
1   bay leaf
Sage sprigs (optional)

1. Place flour in a shallow dish, and dredge chicken in the flour.
2. Heat 1 tablespoon oil in a large nonstick skillet over medium-high heat. Add chicken; sauté 5 minutes, turning once. Remove from pan; keep warm.
3. Heat 2 teaspoons oil in pan. Add onion; sauté 3 minutes. Add rutabaga, turnip, squash, parsnip, and garlic; sauté 3 minutes. Stir in broth and next 5 ingredients; nestle chicken into vegetable mixture. Bring to a boil. Cover, reduce heat, and simmer 20 minutes or until chicken is done. Uncover and simmer 3 minutes or until thick. Discard bay leaf. Garnish with sage sprigs, if desired. Yield: 4 servings (serving size: 2 chicken thighs and 1¼ cups vegetable mixture).

CALORIES 355 (29% from fat); FAT 11.3g (sat 2.2g, mono 5.8g, poly 2g); PROTEIN 30.2g; CARB 34g; FIBER 7.5g; CHOL 107mg; IRON 3.1mg; SODIUM 522mg; CALC 114mg

Chicken Thighs with Garlic and Lime

After the chicken is baked, it's removed from the pan, and the drippings are reduced on the stovetop to a slightly syrupy sauce. The recipe can easily be doubled; use a larger skillet.

1   tablespoon minced garlic
1½   teaspoons ground cumin
½   teaspoon dried oregano
¼   teaspoon salt
⅛   teaspoon black pepper
2   tablespoons fresh lime juice, divided
4   (6-ounce) chicken thighs, skinned
3   tablespoons fat-free, less-sodium chicken broth
1   tablespoon white vinegar
2   teaspoons chopped fresh cilantro
2   lime wedges

1. Preheat oven to 350°.
2. Combine the first 5 ingredients in a small bowl, and stir in 1 tablespoon lime juice. Rub garlic mixture over chicken. Place chicken in a medium nonstick skillet.
3. Combine 1 tablespoon juice, broth, and vinegar; pour over chicken. Place over medium-high heat; bring to a boil. Remove from heat. Wrap handle of pan with foil. Cover and bake at 350° for 30 minutes or until thermometer registers 180°.
4. Remove chicken from pan; keep warm. Place pan over medium-high heat. Bring to a boil; cook until liquid is reduced to ¼ cup (about 3 minutes). Spoon over chicken. Sprinkle with cilantro; serve with lime wedges. Yield: 2 servings (serving size: 2 thighs and 2 tablespoons sauce).

CALORIES 326 (29% from fat); FAT 10.4g (sat 2.6g, mono 3.3g, poly 2.6g); PROTEIN 51.1g; CARB 4.8g; FIBER 0.5g; CHOL 212mg; IRON 4mg; SODIUM 517mg; CALC 59mg

Chicken with Olives and Lemon

Add couscous and steamed green beans for a Mediterranean-inspired menu.

½ cup chopped fresh cilantro
1 tablespoon ground cumin
2 teaspoons paprika
1 teaspoon ground ginger
1 teaspoon ground turmeric
1 teaspoon ground red pepper
¼ teaspoon salt
4 garlic cloves, minced
8 chicken thighs (about 2 pounds), skinned
Cooking spray
½ cup all-purpose flour
¼ cup fresh lemon juice
1 (14-ounce) can fat-free, less-sodium chicken broth
24 pimiento-stuffed olives, coarsely chopped
8 lemon wedges

1. Preheat oven to 325°.
2. Combine the first 8 ingredients in a large bowl, stirring well. Add the chicken thighs, and toss to coat. Arrange chicken in a single layer in a 13 x 9-inch baking dish coated with cooking spray. Lightly spoon flour into a dry measuring cup, and level with a knife.
3. Combine flour, lemon juice, and chicken broth, stirring with a whisk until smooth. Sprinkle flour mixture over chicken, tossing to coat. Top chicken with chopped olives and lemon. Bake at 325° for 1 hour or until a thermometer registers 180°. Yield: 4 servings (serving size: 2 chicken thighs and about ⅓ cup sauce).

CALORIES 297 (30% from fat); FAT 10g (sat 1.4g, mono 3.7g, poly 3.4g); PROTEIN 30.8g; CARB 18.9g; FIBER 2.1g; CHOL 115mg; IRON 3.2mg; SODIUM 941mg; CALC 43mg

Stewed Chicken with Okra and Tomatoes

Canned tomatoes form the savory base for this dish. Soaking the okra gives it a better texture.

 4 cups water
 3 cups okra pods, trimmed (about ¾ pound)
 ¼ cup fresh lemon juice
1¼ teaspoons salt, divided
 1 tablespoon olive oil
 2 chicken breast halves (about 1¾ pounds), skinned
 2 chicken leg quarters (about 1¾ pounds), skinned
 ¼ teaspoon freshly ground black pepper
 ½ cup thinly sliced red onion
 ½ cup fat-free, less-sodium chicken broth
 ½ cup dry white wine
 ½ teaspoon dried thyme
 1 teaspoon ground cumin
 2 whole cloves
 1 (14.5-ounce) can diced tomatoes, undrained
 1 garlic clove, minced
 2 tablespoons chopped fresh flat-leaf parsley
 ½ teaspoon red wine vinegar

1. Combine first 3 ingredients and 1 teaspoon salt in a large bowl. Let mixture stand 1 hour. Drain well; pat dry with paper towels.
2. Heat oil in a large nonstick skillet over medium-high heat. Sprinkle chicken with ¼ teaspoon salt and pepper. Add chicken to pan, and cook 4 minutes on each side or until browned. Remove from pan. Add okra and onion; sauté 3 minutes or until lightly browned. Add broth and next 6 ingredients, stirring to combine.
3. Return chicken to pan, and bring to a boil. Cover, reduce heat, and simmer 25 minutes or until chicken is done. Remove chicken from pan; keep warm. Bring tomato mixture to a boil; cook until reduced to 2 cups (about 5 minutes), stirring frequently. Discard cloves. Stir in parsley and vinegar. Serve with chicken. Yield: 4 servings (serving size: about 4 ounces chicken and ½ cup sauce).

CALORIES 311 (30% from fat); FAT 10.3g (sat 1.6g, mono 4g, poly 1.3g); PROTEIN 34.8g; CARB 18.9g; FIBER 4.8g; CHOL 64mg; IRON 2.9mg; SODIUM 681mg; CALC 148mg

Chicken with 40 Cloves of Garlic

Though this is a lot of garlic, the flavor mellows while imparting a rich taste to the chicken.

2½ cups chopped onion
 1 teaspoon dried tarragon
 6 parsley sprigs
 4 celery stalks, each cut into 3 pieces
 8 chicken thighs, skinned (about 2¾ pounds)
 8 chicken drumsticks, skinned (about 1¾ pounds)
 ½ cup dry vermouth
1½ teaspoons salt
 ¼ teaspoon black pepper
 Dash of ground nutmeg
 40 unpeeled garlic cloves (about 4 heads)
 Tarragon sprigs (optional)
 French bread (optional)

1. Preheat oven to 375°.
2. Combine first 4 ingredients in a 4-quart casserole. Arrange chicken over vegetables. Drizzle with vermouth, and sprinkle with salt, pepper, and nutmeg. Nestle garlic around chicken. Cover casserole with foil and casserole lid. Bake at 375° for 1½ hours. Garnish with tarragon sprigs and serve with French bread, if desired. Yield: 8 servings (serving size: 1 thigh, 1 drumstick, ¼ cup vegetable mixture, and 5 garlic cloves).

CALORIES 294 (24% from fat); FAT 7.8g (sat 2g, mono 2.4g, poly 2g); PROTEIN 43.1g; CARB 11g; FIBER 1.6g; CHOL 165mg; IRON 2.7mg; SODIUM 641mg; CALC 73mg

Cajun Oven-Fried Chicken

⅓ cup low-fat buttermilk
1 tablespoon salt-free Cajun seasoning (such as Spice Hunter)
½ teaspoon salt
1 cup panko (Japanese breadcrumbs)
2 chicken breast halves (about 1 pound), skinned
2 chicken drumsticks (about ½ pound), skinned
2 chicken thighs (about ½ pound), skinned
Cooking spray

1. Preheat oven to 400°.
2. Combine first 3 ingredients in a shallow dish. Place panko in a shallow dish. Dip chicken, 1 piece at a time, into buttermilk mixture; dredge in panko.
3. Place chicken on a baking sheet lined with parchment paper. Lightly coat chicken with cooking spray. Bake at 400° for 40 minutes or until done, turning after 20 minutes. Yield: 4 servings (serving size: 1 breast half or 1 thigh and 1 drumstick).

CALORIES 206 (16% from fat); FAT 3.7g (sat 1g, mono 1g, poly 0.8g); PROTEIN 31.7g; CARB 9g; FIBER 0.3g; CHOL 95mg; IRON 1.2mg; SODIUM 439mg; CALC 39mg

Senegalese Lemon Chicken

6 cups sliced onion (about 3 pounds)
⅓ cup fresh lemon juice
1 teaspoon salt
½ teaspoon black pepper
1 jalapeño pepper, seeded and minced
4 chicken breast halves (about 2 pounds), skinned
4 chicken leg quarters (about 2 pounds), skinned
Cooking spray
1½ tablespoons peanut oil
2 cups thinly sliced carrot
1½ cups less-sodium, fat-free chicken broth
½ cup pimiento-stuffed olives
½ cup water
1 tablespoon Dijon mustard
1 Scotch bonnet pepper, pierced with a fork
4 cups hot cooked long-grain rice

1. Combine first 5 ingredients, and divide evenly between 2 (1-gallon) heavy-duty zip-top plastic bags. Divide chicken evenly between bags, and seal bags. Toss each bag well to coat. Refrigerate 3 hours, turning bags occasionally.
2. Preheat broiler.

3. Remove chicken from bags, reserving marinade. Place chicken on broiler rack coated with cooking spray, and broil 6 minutes on each side or until lightly browned.
4. Strain marinade through a colander over a bowl, and reserve marinade and onion. Heat oil in a Dutch oven over medium-high heat. Add onion to pan; sauté 5 minutes. Add reserved marinade; bring to a boil. Cook 1 minute; add chicken, carrot, broth, olives, water, mustard, and Scotch bonnet pepper. Bring to a boil; cover, reduce heat, and simmer 1 hour or until chicken is done. Discard Scotch bonnet. Serve over rice. Yield: 8 servings (serving size: about 4 ounces chicken, ⅔ cup stew, and ½ cup rice).

CALORIES 422 (29% from fat); FAT 13.6g (sat 3g, mono 5.5g, poly 3.6g); PROTEIN 32.7g; CARB 40.4g; FIBER 3.6g; CHOL 99mg; IRON 3mg; SODIUM 704mg; CALC 48mg

Jerk Chicken

This version of jerk chicken starts out with bottled jerk sauce, which simplifies the preparation.

½ cup jerk sauce, divided
1 cup vertically sliced onion
¼ cup fresh lemon juice
¼ teaspoon salt
¼ teaspoon black pepper
3 garlic cloves, chopped
4 chicken breast halves (about 1½ pounds), skinned
4 chicken thighs (about 1 pound), skinned
½ cup light beer
3 tablespoons ketchup
1 tablespoon hot sauce
Cooking spray
Julienne-cut green onions (optional)

1. Combine ¼ cup jerk sauce and next 5 ingredients in a large zip-top plastic bag. Add chicken; seal. Marinate in refrigerator overnight; turn occasionally. Remove chicken; discard marinade.
2. Prepare grill to medium-high heat.
3. Combine ¼ cup jerk sauce, beer, ketchup, and hot sauce.
4. Place chicken on grill rack coated with cooking spray; grill 20 minutes or until done, turning and basting frequently with beer mixture. Garnish chicken with green onions, if desired. Yield: 6 servings (serving size: about 4 ounces chicken).

CALORIES 245 (20% from fat); FAT 5.4g (sat 1.1g, mono 1.3g, poly 1.1g); PROTEIN 42.4g; CARB 6g; FIBER 1.3g; CHOL 129mg; IRON 1.9mg; SODIUM 589mg; CALC 26mg

Jerk Chicken

Coq au Vin

2 large leeks
12 thyme sprigs
12 parsley stems
4 bay leaves
1 (4-pound) roasting chicken
¾ teaspoon kosher or sea salt, divided
¾ teaspoon black pepper, divided
3 tablespoons unsalted butter, divided
1 bacon slice, cut into 1-inch pieces
½ cup Calvados (apple brandy) or brandy
4 cups fat-free, less-sodium chicken broth, divided
1 (750-milliliter) bottle hearty dry red wine (such as Pinot Noir or Burgundy)
2 garlic cloves, halved
3 (8-ounce) packages mushrooms, stemmed
3 tablespoons all-purpose flour

1. Remove and reserve 8 leek leaves; remove white portion of leaves (reserve the leeks and remaining leaves for another use). Flatten the leaves. Place 3 thyme sprigs, 3 parsley sprigs, and 1 bay leaf lengthwise in each of 4 leek leaves. Top each filled leaf with 1 of the remaining leaves. Tie with twine at 2-inch intervals.

2. Rinse chicken with cold water, and pat dry. Trim excess fat. Remove and reserve giblets; discard neck. Remove skin; cut chicken into quarters. Mince giblets; set aside. Sprinkle chicken pieces with ½ teaspoon salt and ½ teaspoon pepper. Heat 1 tablespoon butter in a large Dutch oven over medium heat. Add chicken to pan; cook 10 minutes, browning on all sides. Remove from pan. Add bacon, and cook until crisp. Return chicken to pan. Add filled leek leaves, giblets, Calvados, 2 cups broth, wine, and garlic; bring to a boil. Cover, reduce heat, and simmer 1½ hours.

3. Remove chicken from wine mixture; cover and refrigerate. Cover and chill wine mixture 8 to 24 hours. Discard filled leek leaves. Skim solidified fat from surface; discard.

4. Combine mushrooms and 2 cups broth in a large nonstick skillet, and bring to a boil. Partially cover, reduce heat, and simmer 30 minutes. Uncover and cook 10 minutes or until liquid almost evaporates. Sprinkle with ¼ teaspoon salt and ¼ teaspoon pepper. Set aside.

5. Bring wine mixture to a boil. Reduce heat, and simmer 20 minutes. Combine 2 tablespoons butter and flour in a small bowl, and work into a paste with fingers or a fork. Add ¼ cup wine mixture, stirring with a whisk until well blended. Add butter mixture to wine mixture, and bring to a boil. Reduce heat, and simmer for 10 minutes. Return the chicken pieces and mushrooms to pan. Bring to a boil; reduce heat, and simmer 10 minutes or until thoroughly heated. Yield: 4 servings (serving size: 1 chicken quarter and 1 cup broth mixture).

CALORIES 470 (32% from fat); FAT 16.5g (sat 7g, mono 4.6g, poly 2.5g); PROTEIN 48g; CARB 36.6g; FIBER 2.5g; CHOL 267mg; IRON 7.8mg; SODIUM 1,109mg; CALC 54mg

Baked Chicken with Lemon

Soaking the chicken in brine overnight allows for uniform salting and produces a very moist bird.

4 quarts water
⅔ cup kosher salt
1 (4- to 5-pound) roasting chicken
4 (⅛-inch-thick) slices lemon
¼ teaspoon black pepper
4 lemon wedges
4 flat-leaf parsley sprigs
2 garlic cloves, cut in half
1 shallot, peeled and quartered

1. Combine 4 quarts water and salt in a Dutch oven, stirring until the salt dissolves. Remove and discard giblets and neck from chicken. Rinse chicken with cold water, and pat dry. Trim excess fat. Add the chicken to the salt mixture; cover and refrigerate 8 hours or overnight.

2. Preheat oven to 400°.

3. Remove chicken from brine; discard brine. Pat chicken dry with paper towels. Starting at the neck cavity, loosen skin from breast and drumsticks by inserting fingers, gently pushing between skin and meat. Place the lemon slices under loosened skin. Sprinkle cavity with pepper; place lemon wedges, parsley, garlic, and shallot into cavity. Lift wing tips up and over back, and tuck under chicken. Place on a broiler pan. Insert a meat thermometer into meaty part of thigh, making sure not to touch bone. Bake at 400° for 1 hour and 10 minutes or until thermometer registers 180°. Discard skin. Yield: 8 servings (serving size: 3 ounces chicken).

CALORIES 164 (35% from fat); FAT 6.3g (sat 1.7g, mono 2.3g, poly 1.5g); PROTEIN 24.7g; CARB 1g; FIBER 0.1g; CHOL 76mg; IRON 1.1mg; SODIUM 494mg; CALC 18mg

Beer-Can Chicken with Cola Barbecue Sauce

There are a variety of beer-can roasters that hold the can in place and stabilize the chicken. Aluminum cans bend easily under the pressure, so when piercing holes, it's a good idea to use a can-holding gadget. Adapted from Steven Raichlen's books *How to Grill* (Workman, 2001) and *BBQ USA* (Workman, 2003).

CHICKEN:
- 1 (12-ounce) can beer
- 1 cup hickory wood chips
- 2 teaspoons kosher or sea salt
- 2 teaspoons brown sugar
- 2 teaspoons sweet paprika
- 1 teaspoon coarsely ground black pepper
- 1 (4-pound) whole chicken
- Cooking spray

SAUCE:
- ½ cup cola
- ½ cup ketchup
- 2 tablespoons Worcestershire sauce
- ½ teaspoon instant onion flakes
- ½ teaspoon instant minced garlic
- 1½ teaspoons steak sauce (such as A-1)
- ½ teaspoon liquid smoke
- ¼ teaspoon black pepper

1. To prepare chicken, pour out half of beer into a glass for another use. Carefully pierce top of can with "church-key" can opener several times; set aside. Soak wood chips in water for 1 hour. Combine salt, sugar, paprika, and 1 teaspoon pepper, and set aside.

2. To prepare grill for indirect grilling, place a disposable aluminum foil pan in center of grill. Arrange charcoal around foil pan; heat to medium heat.

3. Remove and discard giblets and neck from chicken. Rinse chicken with cold water, and pat dry. Trim excess fat. Starting at neck cavity, loosen skin from breast and drumsticks by inserting fingers, gently pushing between skin and meat.

4. Rub 2 teaspoons spice mixture under loosened skin. Rub 2 teaspoons spice mixture in body cavity. Rub 2 teaspoons spice mixture over skin. Slowly add remaining spice mixture to can (beer will foam). Holding chicken upright with body cavity facing down, insert can into cavity.

5. Drain wood chips. Place half of wood chips on hot coals. Coat grill rack with cooking spray. Place chicken on grill rack over drip pan. Spread legs out to form a tripod for support. Cover chicken and grill 2 hours or until a thermometer registers 180°. Add remaining wood chips after 1 hour; add charcoal as needed.

6. Lift chicken slightly using tongs; place spatula under can. Carefully lift chicken and can; place on a cutting board. Let stand 5 minutes. Gently lift chicken using tongs or insulated rubber gloves; carefully twist can to remove from cavity. Discard skin and can.

7. To prepare sauce, combine cola and remaining ingredients in a saucepan; bring to a boil. Reduce heat; simmer 6 minutes. Cool. Serve with chicken. Yield: 6 servings (serving size: 3 ounces chicken and about 2 tablespoons sauce).

CALORIES 215 (20% from fat); FAT 4.7g (sat 1.1g, mono 1.4g, poly 1.3g); PROTEIN 31.8g; CARB 10g; FIBER 0.5g; CHOL 100mg; IRON 2.2mg; SODIUM 741mg; CALC 29mg

Garlic-Rosemary Roasted Chicken

The beauty of roasted chicken is its versatility. For another serving suggestion, try rubbing it with paprika, and add some fresh tomatoes 20 minutes before the chicken is done.

1 (5- to 6-pound) roasting chicken
1 tablespoon chopped fresh or 1 teaspoon dried rosemary
8 garlic cloves, crushed
8 medium red onions
2 whole garlic heads
2 teaspoons olive oil
Rosemary sprigs (optional)

1. Preheat oven to 450°.

2. Remove the giblets and neck from the roasting chicken, and discard. Rinse the chicken under cold water, and pat dry. Trim the excess fat from chicken. Starting at the neck cavity, loosen the skin from the chicken breast and drumsticks by inserting fingers and gently pushing between the skin and meat. Place the chopped fresh rosemary and crushed garlic cloves beneath the skin on the breasts and drumsticks. Lift the wing tips up and over back, and tuck under the chicken.

3. Place the chicken, breast side up, on a broiler pan. Cut a thin slice from the end of each onion. Remove the white papery skins from the garlic heads (do not peel or separate the garlic cloves). Cut the tops off of the garlic cloves, leaving the root ends intact.

4. Brush the red onions and garlic cloves with the olive oil. Arrange the onions and garlic cloves around the chicken. Insert a meat thermometer into meaty part of thigh, making sure not to touch the bone. Bake the chicken at 450° for 30 minutes. Reduce oven temperature to 350° (do not remove the pan from the oven), and bake for an additional 1 hour and 15 minutes or until the meat thermometer registers 180°. Discard the chicken skin. Garnish the roasted chicken with rosemary sprigs, if desired. Yield: 8 servings (serving size: 3 ounces chicken and 1 onion).

NOTE: You can spread the roasted garlic on French bread, if desired.

CALORIES 231 (30% from fat); FAT 7.7g (sat 1.9g, mono 3.1g, poly 1.6g); PROTEIN 26.5g; CARB 13.5g; FIBER 2.7g; CHOL 76mg; IRON 1.4mg; SODIUM 133mg; CALC 50mg

Roast Chicken Provençale

2 tablespoons dried herbes de Provence
2 tablespoons fresh lemon juice
2 teaspoons kosher salt
½ teaspoon black pepper
3 garlic cloves, minced
1 (7-pound) roasting chicken
1 small onion, quartered
Cooking spray
⅓ cup Sauvignon Blanc or other dry white wine
⅔ cup fat-free, less-sodium chicken broth
1 tablespoon chilled butter, cut into small pieces

1. Preheat oven to 400°.

2. Combine the first 5 ingredients in a small bowl; mash to a paste consistency.

3. Remove and discard the giblets and neck from chicken. Rinse chicken with cold water; pat dry. Trim excess fat. Starting at neck cavity, loosen skin from breast and drumsticks by inserting fingers, gently pushing between skin and meat.

4. Rub seasoning mixture under loosened skin. Place onion in body cavity. Lift wing tips up and over back; tuck under chicken. Tie legs together with string.

5. Place chicken, breast side up, on a broiler pan coated with cooking spray. Insert a meat thermometer into breast, making sure not to touch bone. Bake at 400° for 1 hour and 20 minutes or until thermometer registers 180°. Remove chicken from pan. Cover with foil; let stand 10 minutes. Discard skin.

6. Place a zip-top plastic bag inside a 2-cup glass measure. Pour pan drippings into bag; let stand 5 minutes (the fat will rise to the top). Seal bag, and carefully snip off 1 bottom corner of bag. Drain drippings into pan, stopping before fat layer reaches opening; discard fat.

7. Place pan over medium-high heat. Stir in wine, scraping pan to loosen browned bits. Add broth, and bring to a boil. Cook until mixture is reduced to ⅔ cup (about 3 minutes). Remove pan from heat, and add butter, stirring with a whisk until well blended. Serve sauce with chicken. Yield: 12 servings (serving size: about 4 ounces chicken and about 1 tablespoon sauce).

CALORIES 204 (37% from fat); FAT 8.4g (sat 2.6g, mono 3.1g, poly 1.7g); PROTEIN 28.2g; CARB 1g; FIBER 0.3g; CHOL 86mg; IRON 1.7mg; SODIUM 433mg; CALC 25mg

Duck with Grape Demi-Glace

Look for veal and duck demi-glace in the frozen foods section or at the butcher's counter.

1 teaspoon olive oil
⅓ cup chopped fennel bulb
⅓ cup chopped shallots
⅔ cup coarsely chopped seedless red grapes
½ cup red wine
½ cup ruby port
5 juniper berries, crushed
1 (2-inch) thyme sprig
1 (1-inch) rosemary sprig
Cooking spray
1½ pounds skinless, boneless duck breasts, trimmed
1 teaspoon water
½ teaspoon cornstarch
2 tablespoons veal and duck demi-glace (such as D'Artagnan)
½ cup seedless red grapes, halved
1 teaspoon balsamic vinegar
1 teaspoon butter
⅛ teaspoon freshly ground black pepper

1. Heat oil in a medium saucepan over medium-low heat. Add fennel and shallots; cover and cook 3 minutes or until tender. Add ⅔ cup grapes and next 5 ingredients; bring to a boil. Reduce heat; simmer until liquid is reduced to ¾ cup (about 10 minutes). Strain wine mixture through a fine sieve; discard solids. Return wine mixture to pan.

2. Heat a large skillet coated with cooking spray over medium heat. Add duck; cook 8 minutes on each side or until done. Let stand 5 minutes; cut into ¼-inch-thick slices.

3. Combine water and cornstarch. Add cornstarch mixture and demi-glace to wine mixture, stirring constantly with a whisk. Bring to a boil, and cook 1 minute. Add ½ cup grapes; cook 30 seconds. Remove from heat; stir in balsamic vinegar, butter, and pepper. Yield: 6 servings (serving size: 3 ounces duck breast and about 2½ tablespoons sauce).

CALORIES 232 (26% from fat); FAT 6.6g (sat 2.1g, mono 2.2g, poly 0.8g); PROTEIN 23.3g; CARB 11.1g; FIBER 0.6g; CHOL 89mg; IRON 5.6mg; SODIUM 120mg; CALC 17mg

Cooking Light's Ultimate Roasted Turkey

Cooking Light's Ultimate Roasted Turkey

¾ cup apple cider
5 tablespoons dark corn syrup, divided
1 (12-pound) fresh or frozen turkey, thawed
1 tablespoon poultry seasoning
1 tablespoon dried rubbed sage
1 teaspoon salt
¼ teaspoon black pepper
4 garlic cloves, sliced
2 onions, quartered
2 Golden Delicious apples, cored, quartered
Cooking spray
1 teaspoon butter
1 (14½-ounce) can fat-free, less-sodium chicken broth
1 tablespoon cornstarch

1. Preheat oven to 375°.
2. Combine cider and 4 tablespoons corn syrup in a saucepan; bring to a boil. Remove from heat; set aside.
3. Remove giblets and neck from turkey; reserve. Rinse turkey with cold water; pat dry. Trim excess fat. Lift wing tips up and over back; tuck under turkey. Combine poultry seasoning, sage, salt, and pepper. Rub seasoning mixture into skin and body cavity. Place half of garlic, onion quarters, and apple quarters into body cavity. Place turkey, breast side up, in a shallow roasting pan coated with cooking spray. Arrange remaining garlic, onion, and apple around turkey in pan. Insert a meat thermometer into meaty part of thigh, making sure not to touch bone. Bake at 375° for 45 minutes. Baste turkey with cider syrup; cover with foil. Bake at 375° an additional 2 hours and 15 minutes or until thermometer registers 180°, basting with cider syrup 4 times at regular intervals. Let stand 10 minutes. Discard skin. Remove turkey from pan, reserving drippings for sauce. Place turkey on a platter; keep warm.
4. Strain drippings through a colander into a bowl; discard solids. Place a zip-top plastic bag inside a 2-cup glass measure. Pour drippings into bag; let stand 10 minutes (fat will rise to the top). Seal bag; carefully snip off 1 bottom corner of bag. Drain drippings into a bowl, stopping before fat layer reaches opening; discard fat.
5. While turkey bakes, melt butter in a medium saucepan over medium-high heat. Add reserved giblets and neck; sauté 2 minutes on each side or until browned. Add broth; bring to a boil. Cover, reduce heat, and simmer 45 minutes. Strain mixture through a colander into a bowl, discarding solids. Reserve ¼ cup broth mixture. Combine drippings and remaining broth mixture in roasting pan on stovetop over medium heat; scrape pan to loosen browned bits. Combine ¼ cup reserved broth mixture and cornstarch; add to roasting pan. Add 1 tablespoon corn syrup; stir with a whisk. Bring to a boil; cook 1 minute. Serve with turkey (gravy will be dark and thin). Yield: 12 servings (serving size: 6 ounces turkey and about 3 tablespoons gravy).

CALORIES 331 (24% from fat); FAT 8.8g (sat 3g, mono 1.9g, poly 2.5g); PROTEIN 50.4g; CARB 9.4g; FIBER 0.1g; CHOL 130mg; IRON 3.2mg; SODIUM 396mg; CALC 52mg

Smokey Turkey Almond Mole

½ cup roasted almonds
½ teaspoon vegetable oil
2 dried Anaheim chiles, stemmed, seeded, and chopped
1 cup chopped onion
1 garlic clove, crushed
1 (7-ounce) can chipotle chiles in adobo sauce
1½ cups fire-roasted crushed tomatoes
1 tablespoon sugar
½ teaspoon ground cumin
¼ teaspoon salt
⅛ teaspoon ground cloves
2 (6-inch) corn tortillas, torn into small pieces
1 (14½-ounce) can vegetable broth
1 tablespoon white wine vinegar
3 cups chopped cooked turkey breast

1. Place almonds in a food processor; process until smooth (about 2½ minutes), scraping sides of bowl once. Set aside.
2. Heat oil in a large nonstick skillet over medium-high heat. Add Anaheim chiles; sauté 1 minute or until softened. Add onion and garlic; sauté 4 minutes or until onion is lightly browned.
3. Remove 1 chipotle chile from can; cut in half. Add 1 chile half to onion mixture. Reserve remaining chiles and adobo sauce for another use. Add tomatoes and next 6 ingredients; bring to a boil. Reduce heat; simmer 15 minutes, stirring occasionally.
4. Spoon mixture into food processor; process until smooth. Return mixture to pan. Stir in almond butter and vinegar, and cook 1 minute. Stir in turkey. Yield: 4 servings (serving size: 1 cup).

CALORIES 366 (30% from fat); FAT 12.1g (sat 1.3g, mono 6.2g, poly 3g); PROTEIN 40.7g; CARB 25.9g; FIBER 6.2g; CHOL 94mg; IRON 4.2mg; SODIUM 737mg; CALC 117mg

Turkey Cutlets with Rosemary-Tomato Sauce

    4 teaspoons olive oil, divided
    8 (2-ounce) turkey cutlets
    ¾ teaspoon salt, divided
    ½ teaspoon black pepper, divided
    1 tablespoon chopped fresh rosemary
    1 teaspoon bottled minced garlic
 1½ cups chopped tomato
    1 tablespoon white wine vinegar

1. Heat 2 teaspoons oil in a large nonstick skillet over medium-high heat. Sprinkle turkey with ¼ teaspoon salt and ¼ teaspoon pepper. Add turkey to pan; cook 2 minutes on each side or until done. Remove from pan; keep warm.

2. Add 2 teaspoons oil, rosemary, and garlic to pan; sauté 1 minute. Add tomato; cook 1 minute, stirring frequently. Stir in ½ teaspoon salt, ¼ teaspoon pepper, and vinegar. Serve over turkey. Yield: 4 servings (serving size: 2 turkey cutlets and ¼ cup sauce).

CALORIES 182 (27% from fat); FAT 5.5g (sat 0.9g, mono 3.5g, poly 0.7g); PROTEIN 28.6g; CARB 3.6g; FIBER 0.9g; CHOL 70mg; IRON 1.8mg; SODIUM 498mg; CALC 19mg

Turkey Alfredo Pizza

    1 cup shredded cooked turkey breast
    1 cup frozen chopped collard greens or spinach, thawed, drained, and squeezed dry
    2 teaspoons lemon juice
    ½ teaspoon salt
    ¼ teaspoon black pepper
    1 garlic clove, halved
    1 (10-ounce) Italian cheese-flavored thin pizza crust (such as Boboli)
    ½ cup light Alfredo sauce (such as Contadina)
    ¾ cup (3 ounces) shredded fontina cheese
    ½ teaspoon crushed red pepper

1. Preheat oven to 450°.

2. Combine first 5 ingredients; toss. Rub cut sides of garlic over crust; discard garlic. Spread Alfredo sauce evenly over crust; top with turkey mixture. Sprinkle with cheese and red pepper. Bake at 450° for 12 minutes or until crust is crisp. Cut into 6 wedges. Yield: 6 servings (serving size: 1 wedge).

CALORIES 316 (29% from fat); FAT 10.3g (sat 5.2g, mono 3.5g, poly 1.1g); PROTEIN 19.2g; CARB 35.6g; FIBER 0.6g; CHOL 39mg; IRON 2.5mg; SODIUM 837mg; CALC 351mg

Turkey Alfredo Pizza

Chicago-Style Pizza

　2　(10-ounce) cans refrigerated pizza crust
　　　dough
　Cooking spray
　¾　cup (3 ounces) shredded part-skim
　　　mozzarella cheese
1¼　cups cooked Atsa Spicy Pizza Sausage
　3　tablespoons thinly sliced fresh basil
　1　(14.5-ounce) can no-salt-added diced
　　　tomatoes, drained
　½　cup (2 ounces) grated fresh Parmesan cheese
　⅛　teaspoon black pepper

1. Preheat oven to 450°.
2. Unroll dough portions onto a large baking sheet coated with cooking spray, slightly overlapping the edges. Pinch edges together to seal. Pat the dough into a 15 x 12-inch rectangle. Sprinkle mozzarella cheese over dough, leaving a ½-inch border, and top with sausage, basil, and tomatoes. Sprinkle with Parmesan cheese and pepper. Bake at 450° for 2 minutes. Reduce oven temperature to 425° (do not remove pizza from oven), and bake an additional 12 minutes or until cheese melts. Yield: 8 servings (serving size: 1 piece).

CALORIES 313 (30% from fat); FAT 10.3g (sat 4.2g, mono 3.7g, poly 1.8g); PROTEIN 17.2g; CARB 36.5g; FIBER 0.7g; CHOL 32mg; IRON 2.5mg; SODIUM 743mg; CALC 180mg

ATSA SPICY PIZZA SAUSAGE:

　1　pound ground turkey
　1　pound ground pork
　½　cup dry red wine
　⅓　cup minced fresh parsley
　2　tablespoons grated Parmesan cheese
　1　tablespoon fennel seeds
1½　teaspoons crushed red pepper
　1　teaspoon salt
　¼　teaspoon dried thyme
　¼　teaspoon freshly ground black pepper
　4　garlic cloves, crushed

1. Combine all ingredients in a large bowl. Cook sausage in a large nonstick skillet over medium heat until browned, stirring to crumble. Drain. Yield: 5 cups (serving size: ½ cup).
NOTE: The sausage can be frozen in a zip-top plastic bags for up to 3 months.

CALORIES 203 (61% from fat); FAT 13.7g (sat 4.6g, mono 5.8g, poly 2.1g); PROTEIN 17.6g; CARB 1.2g; FIBER 0.3g; CHOL 68mg; IRON 1.5mg; SODIUM 319mg; CALC 42mg

Southwestern Breakfast Casserole

You can assemble parts of or this entire dish up to a week ahead. Bake the corn muffin mix ahead; store in an airtight container in the freezer. Assemble the casserole according to directions; cover and freeze. A day in advance, take it out of the freezer and thaw in the refrigerator (about 24 hours). To serve, let stand 30 minutes at room temperature, uncover, and bake as directed.

　1　(8½-ounce) package corn muffin mix
　3　cups (½-inch) cubed white bread
　8　ounces hot turkey Italian sausage
　1　cup chopped onion
2½　cups fat-free milk
　1　teaspoon ground cumin
　⅛　teaspoon black pepper
　1　(10-ounce) can diced tomatoes and
　　　green chiles, undrained
　1　(8-ounce) carton egg substitute
　Cooking spray
　1　cup (4 ounces) shredded reduced-fat
　　　Monterey Jack or mild cheddar cheese,
　　　divided

1. Prepare corn muffin mix according to package directions; cool. Crumble muffins into a large bowl; stir in bread. Set aside.
2. Remove casings from sausage. Cook sausage and onion in a large nonstick skillet over medium heat until browned, stirring to crumble. Drain.
3. Combine next 5 ingredients, and stir with a whisk until well blended. Add sausage mixture; stir well. Stir into bread mixture. Spoon half of bread mixture into an 11 x 7-inch baking dish coated with cooking spray. Top with ½ cup cheese. Spoon remaining bread mixture over cheese. Cover and refrigerate for 8 hours or overnight. Uncover and let stand for 30 minutes at room temperature.
4. Preheat oven to 350°.
5. Bake, uncovered, at 350° for 20 minutes or until almost set. Top with ½ cup cheese; bake an additional 20 minutes or until set. Let stand 10 minutes before serving. Yield: 8 servings.

CALORIES 271 (25% from fat); FAT 7.6g (sat 2.7g, mono 2.6g, poly 1.7g); PROTEIN 14.7g; CARB 33.9g; FIBER 1.6g; CHOL 22mg; IRON 2.1mg; SODIUM 700mg; CALC 290mg

Salads

Pear, Walnut, and Blue Cheese Salad
with Cranberry Vinaigrette, page 239

Strawberry-Kiwi Salad with Basil

- ¼ cup half-and-half
- 2 tablespoons white balsamic vinegar
- 1 tablespoon sugar
- ¼ teaspoon salt
- 3 peeled kiwifruit, each cut into 6 wedges
- 2 cups quartered strawberries (about 1 pint)
- 2 tablespoons finely chopped fresh basil

1. Combine first 4 ingredients in a bowl. Add the kiwifruit and strawberries; toss well. Cover and chill 1 hour. Stir in basil just before serving. Yield: 4 servings (serving size: ¾ cup).

CALORIES 90 (23% from fat); FAT 2.3g (sat 1.1g, mono 0.6g, poly 0.4g); PROTEIN 1.6g; CARB 17.8g; FIBER 3.8g; CHOL 6mg; IRON 0.7mg; SODIUM 157mg; CALC 46mg

The Simplest Green Salad

This recipe begins with the Italian tradition of putting salt directly on the greens, before adding the olive oil or anything else. You'll be surprised by how much flavor that just ¼ teaspoon additive-free, coarse-grained kosher salt can impart when tossed with greens in this way.

- 10 cups mixed salad greens
- ¼ teaspoon kosher salt
- 5 teaspoons extravirgin olive oil
- 2 teaspoons fresh lemon juice
- ⅛ teaspoon freshly ground black pepper

1. Place greens in a large bowl; sprinkle with salt, tossing gently. Add remaining ingredients, tossing to coat. Serve immediately. Yield: 5 servings (serving size: 2 cups).
NOTE: You can find mixed salad greens packaged or loose in the produce section of supermarkets, or be creative and make your own mix.

CALORIES 58 (73% from fat); FAT 4.7g (sat 0.6g, mono 3.3g, poly 0.5g); PROTEIN 1.8g; CARB 2.9g; FIBER 1.9g; CHOL 0mg; IRON 1.3mg; SODIUM 65mg; CALC 41mg

Endive, Sweet Lettuce, and Cashew Salad

Walnut oil adds subtle and delicate flavor. If you can't find it, use light olive oil. Cashews lend a crunchy texture and slightly sweet flavor.

- 2 tablespoons minced shallots
- 1 tablespoon sherry vinegar
- 2 tablespoons honey
- 2 teaspoons walnut oil
- ½ teaspoon salt
- 8 cups torn green leaf lettuce
- 4 cups sliced Belgian endive (about 3 heads)
- 2 tablespoons roasted unsalted cashews, chopped

1. Combine first 5 ingredients in a large bowl, stirring with a whisk. Add lettuce, endive, and cashews, tossing gently to coat. Serve immediately. Yield: 8 servings (serving size: about 1¼ cups).

CALORIES 55 (35% from fat); FAT 2.1g (sat 0.3g, mono 0.8g, poly 0.9g); PROTEIN 1.3g; CARB 9.2g; FIBER 2g; CHOL 0mg; IRON 0.4mg; SODIUM 173mg; CALC 40mg

Mixed Apple Salad over Greens

Harmonious flavors converge in this simple salad: sour lemon juice and Granny Smith apple, sweet honey and Cameo apple, smoky bacon, and pungent cheese.

DRESSING:
- ¼ cup fresh lemon juice
- 2 tablespoons honey
- 1 teaspoon olive oil
- Dash of salt
- Dash of freshly ground black pepper

SALAD:
- 2 cups chopped Granny Smith apple
- 2 cups chopped Cameo or Braeburn apple
- ¼ cup (1 ounce) crumbled blue cheese
- 2 bacon slices, cooked and crumbled
- 4 cups mixed salad greens

1. To prepare dressing, combine first 5 ingredients in a small bowl, stirring well with a whisk.
2. To prepare salad, combine apples, cheese, and bacon. Drizzle dressing over apple mixture; toss gently to coat. Serve dressed apple mixture over salad greens. Yield: 4 servings (serving size: about 1 cup apple mixture and 1 cup greens).

CALORIES 163 (29% from fat); FAT 5.3g (sat 2.1g, mono 2.2g, poly 0.5g); PROTEIN 3.7g; CARB 28.7g; FIBER 4.3g; CHOL 8mg; IRON 1.1mg; SODIUM 201mg; CALC 78mg

Mixed Apple Salad
over Greens

Fig-and-Arugula Salad with Parmesan

  2 tablespoons minced shallots
1½ tablespoons balsamic vinegar
  1 tablespoon extravirgin olive oil
 ¼ teaspoon salt
16 fresh figs, each cut in half lengthwise
  6 cups trimmed arugula (about 6 ounces)
 ¼ teaspoon freshly ground black pepper
 ¼ cup (1 ounce) shaved fresh Parmesan cheese

1. Combine first 4 ingredients in a large bowl, stirring well with a whisk. Add figs; cover and let stand 20 minutes. Add arugula and pepper; toss well. Top with cheese. Serve immediately. Yield: 4 servings (serving size: 1½ cups).

CALORIES 156 (33% from fat); FAT 5.8g (sat 1.7g, mono 3.1g, poly 0.5g); PROTEIN 4.6g; CARB 25.1g; FIBER 4.9g; CHOL 5mg; IRON 1.1mg; SODIUM 273mg; CALC 194mg

Fig-and-Arugula Salad with Parmesan

Arugula, Fig, and Blue Cheese Salad

Use your favorite blue in this recipe. Or, if you're not a fan of blue, use Parmesan shavings.

  2 cups torn red leaf lettuce
1¼ cups fresh figs, quartered
  1 cup trimmed arugula
  2 tablespoons fresh lemon juice
  2 teaspoons olive oil
 ¼ teaspoon salt
 ¼ teaspoon freshly ground
     black pepper
  3 tablespoons crumbled blue cheese

1. Combine first 3 ingredients in a large bowl. Combine lemon juice, oil, salt, and pepper; stir well with a whisk. Gently toss lettuce mixture with lemon juice mixture. Sprinkle with blue cheese. Yield: 4 servings (serving size: 1 cup).

CALORIES 74 (35% from fat); FAT 2.9g (sat 1.1g, mono 0.9g, poly 0.2g); PROTEIN 2g; CARB 11.6g; FIBER 2.3g; CHOL 4mg; IRON 0.7mg; SODIUM 224mg; CALC 74mg

Bitter Greens with Tarragon Vinaigrette and Pine Nuts

Look for loose bitter greens in bins in the produce section of your supermarket, or create your own mix with watercress, endive, arugula, and radicchio. Though just about any nut will work nicely in this salad, we preferred pine nuts or hazelnuts.

  2 tablespoons white wine vinegar
  2 tablespoons plain fat-free yogurt
  1 tablespoon chopped fresh or 1 teaspoon
     dried tarragon
  2 teaspoons Dijon mustard
  2 teaspoons honey
  1 teaspoon olive oil
 ⅛ teaspoon salt
 ⅛ teaspoon black pepper
  5 cups mixed bitter greens
  1 tablespoon pine nuts, toasted

1. Combine first 8 ingredients in a small bowl; stir well with a whisk. Place greens and pine nuts in a large bowl, and drizzle with vinaigrette. Yield: 2 servings (serving size: 2 cups).

CALORIES 74 (36% from fat); FAT 3g (sat 0.4g, mono 1g, poly 01.1g); PROTEIN 4g; CARB 9.2g; FIBER 2.2g; CHOL 0mg; IRON 0.8mg; SODIUM 337mg; CALC 136mg

Orange, Date, and Endive Salad with Lemon-Cardamom Dressing

This refreshing, North African-inspired salad is excellent with turkey, chicken, and duck. It's also good with feta and other fresh cheeses. The cardamom seeds are toasted lightly and develop a citrusy fragrance.

DRESSING:

- ½ teaspoon cardamom seeds, toasted
- ¼ cup low-fat buttermilk
- 1 tablespoon extravirgin olive oil
- 2 teaspoons chopped fresh mint
- 1 teaspoon grated lemon rind
- ¼ teaspoon salt
- ¼ teaspoon freshly ground black pepper

SALAD:

- 12 Belgian endive leaves
- 3 cups blood or navel orange sections
- 1 cup thinly sliced radishes
- 1 cup thinly vertically sliced red onion
- ½ cup thinly sliced pitted dates (about 5 whole)
- 4 teaspoons chopped fresh mint

1. Place cardamom in a spice or coffee grinder; process until finely ground. Combine cardamom, buttermilk and next 5 ingredients; stir with a whisk.
2. Arrange 3 endive leaves on each of 4 salad plates. Top each with ¾ cup oranges, ¼ cup radishes, ¼ cup onion, 2 tablespoons dates, and 1 teaspoon mint. Drizzle each serving with 1 tablespoon dressing. Yield: 4 servings.

CALORIES 187 (20% from fat); FAT 4.1g (sat 0.7g, mono 2.8g, poly 0.4g); PROTEIN 3.2g; CARB 38.2g; FIBER 7g; CHOL 1mg; IRON 1mg; SODIUM 179mg; CALC 112mg

Grapefruit, Beet, and Blue Cheese Salad

- ¾ pound beets (about 2 medium)
- 3 pink grapefruit
- ¼ cup (1 ounce) crumbled blue cheese
- 2 tablespoons white balsamic vinegar
- 2 teaspoons olive oil
- 2 teaspoons Dijon mustard
- ⅛ teaspoon salt
- ⅛ teaspoon freshly ground black pepper
- 6 cups torn romaine lettuce

1. Leave root and 1 inch stem on beets; scrub with a brush. Place in a medium saucepan; cover with water. Bring to a boil; cover, reduce heat, and simmer 35 minutes or until tender. Drain and rinse with cold water; let cool. Trim off beet roots; rub off skins. Cut beets into ½-inch cubes.
2. Peel and section grapefruit over a bowl; squeeze membranes to extract juice. Set 1½ cups sections aside; reserve 2 tablespoons juice. Discard grapefruit membranes.
3. Place cheese in a small bowl; mash with a fork until smooth. Add reserved grapefruit juice, vinegar, and next 4 ingredients; stir well with a whisk.
4. Pour dressing over lettuce, tossing gently to coat. Divide lettuce mixture evenly among 6 plates. Top each serving with ¼ cup beets and ¼ cup grapefruit sections. Yield: 6 servings.

CALORIES 106 (28% from fat); FAT 3.3g (sat 1.1g, mono 1.6g, poly 0.3g); PROTEIN 3.6g; CARB 17.4g; FIBER 2.8g; CHOL 4mg; IRON 1.3mg; SODIUM 191mg; CALC 70mg

Pear, Walnut, and Blue Cheese Salad with Cranberry Vinaigrette

(pictured on page 234)

You can make and refrigerate the vinaigrette up to a week ahead.

VINAIGRETTE:

- ½ cup canned whole-berry cranberry sauce
- ¼ cup fresh orange juice (about 1 orange)
- 1 tablespoon olive oil
- 2 tablespoons balsamic vinegar
- 1 teaspoon sugar
- 1 teaspoon minced peeled fresh ginger
- ¼ teaspoon salt

SALAD:

- 18 Boston lettuce leaves (about 2 heads)
- 2 cups sliced peeled pear (about 2 pears)
- 1 cup (⅛-inch-thick) slices red onion, separated into rings
- ⅓ cup (2 ounces) crumbled blue cheese
- 6 teaspoons coarsely chopped walnuts, toasted

1. To prepare vinaigrette, place first 7 ingredients in a medium bowl; stir well with a whisk.
2. To prepare salads, divide the lettuce leaves evenly among 6 salad plates. Divide sliced pear and onion evenly among leaves. Top each serving with about 1 tablespoon cheese and 1 teaspoon walnuts. Drizzle each serving with about 2½ tablespoons vinaigrette. Yield: 6 servings.

CALORIES 148 (38% from fat); FAT 6.3g (sat 1.8g, mono 2.5g, poly 1.5g); PROTEIN 2.7g; CARB 22.3g; FIBER 2.4g; CHOL 5mg; IRON 0.4mg; SODIUM 205mg; CALC 60mg

239

Field Salad with Roasted Leeks,
Mushrooms, and Feta

Field Salad with Roasted Leeks, Mushrooms, and Feta

- 1 cup thinly sliced leek
- 1 teaspoon olive oil
Cooking spray
- 3 cups trimmed arugula (about 3 ounces)
- 3 cups fresh spinach leaves
- 1 cup sliced mushrooms
- ¼ cup (1 ounce) crumbled feta cheese
- 3 tablespoons bottled light dill-mustard dressing

1. Preheat oven to 450°.
2. Combine sliced leek and olive oil. Spread leek mixture into a jelly roll pan coated with cooking spray. Bake leek mixture at 450° for 10 minutes or until browned. Combine the leek mixture, arugula, spinach, sliced mushrooms, and crumbled feta cheese in a large bowl. Drizzle with the dill-mustard dressing, and toss gently to coat. Yield: 4 servings (serving size: 1¾ cups).

CALORIES 88 (51% from fat); FAT 5g (sat 1.6g, mono 1.7g, poly 1.4g); PROTEIN 2.6g; CARB 8.6g; FIBER 1.4g; CHOL 6mg; IRON 1.4mg; SODIUM 197mg; CALC 103mg

Spinach and Pear Salad

Flat-leaf or baby spinach works best in this salad, but you can also use red-leaf lettuce.

- 2 tablespoons water
- 1½ tablespoons red wine vinegar
- 1 tablespoon olive oil
- 1 tablespoon honey
- 2 teaspoons Dijon mustard
- ¼ teaspoon black pepper
- 1 Bosc or Anjou pear, cut lengthwise into 15 slices
- 8 cups torn spinach
- ¼ cup thinly sliced red onion

1. Combine first 6 ingredients in a small bowl, stirring with a whisk.
2. Place pear slices in a large bowl. Spoon 1 tablespoon dressing over pears; toss to coat. Add remaining dressing, spinach, and onion; toss to coat. Yield: 5 servings (serving size: about 1½ cups).

CALORIES 72 (41% from fat); FAT 3.3g (sat 0.4g, mono 2.1g, poly 0.4g); PROTEIN 1.8g; CARB 11g; FIBER 2.3g; CHOL 0mg; IRON 1.4mg; SODIUM 89mg; CALC 56mg

Spinach Salad with Nectarines and Spicy Pecans

PECANS:
¼ cup powdered sugar
½ teaspoon salt
¼ teaspoon ground allspice
⅛ teaspoon ground nutmeg
⅛ teaspoon ground red pepper
⅓ cup pecan halves
Cooking spray

VINAIGRETTE:
3 tablespoons finely chopped shallots
3 tablespoons balsamic vinegar
1 teaspoon sugar
2 teaspoons fresh lemon juice
2 teaspoons extravirgin olive oil
1 teaspoon Dijon mustard
¾ teaspoon salt
½ teaspoon freshly ground black pepper

SALAD:
¾ cup very thin slices prosciutto, coarsely chopped (about 2 ounces)
2 (6-ounce) packages fresh baby spinach (about 12 cups)
2 nectarines, each cut into ¼-inch wedges (about ¾ pound)

1. Preheat oven to 350°.
2. To prepare pecans, combine first 5 ingredients in a small bowl. Rinse pecans with cold water; drain (do not allow pecans to dry). Add pecans to sugar mixture, and toss well to coat. Arrange pecan mixture on a jelly roll pan coated with cooking spray. Bake at 350° for 10 minutes, stirring occasionally. Coarsely chop pecans. Set aside.
3. To prepare vinaigrette, combine shallots and next 7 ingredients in a small bowl, stirring with a whisk until blended.
4. To prepare salad, heat a small nonstick skillet coated with cooking spray over medium-high heat. Add prosciutto; sauté 5 minutes or until crisp. Finely chop. Combine spinach, nectarines, and vinaigrette in a bowl, tossing to coat. Sprinkle with pecans and prosciutto. Yield: 12 servings (serving size: 1 cup salad, 1 tablespoon prosciutto, and about 1½ teaspoons pecans).

CALORIES 75 (48% from fat); FAT 4g (sat 0.6g, mono 2g, poly 0.8g); PROTEIN 2.7g; CARB 8.2g; FIBER 1.5g; CHOL 4mg; IRON 1.1mg; SODIUM 369mg; CALC 36mg

Iceberg Salad with Ginger Dressing

Make the dressing up to two days ahead, if desired.

DRESSING:
¼ cup coarsely chopped onion
1 tablespoon grated peeled fresh ginger
1 tablespoon finely chopped celery
3 tablespoons rice vinegar
2 tablespoons water
1 tablespoon toasted peanut oil
1 tablespoon low-sodium soy sauce
2 teaspoons sugar
1 teaspoon fresh lemon juice
1 teaspoon miso (soybean paste)
¼ teaspoon salt
⅛ teaspoon black pepper

SALAD:
9 cups chopped iceberg lettuce
1½ cups cucumber, halved lengthwise and thinly sliced
¾ cup shredded carrot
¾ cup chopped celery
⅓ cup chopped onion
12 cherry tomatoes, halved

1. To prepare dressing, combine the first 12 ingredients in a blender; process until smooth.
2. To prepare salad, combine lettuce and remaining ingredients in a medium bowl. Drizzle dressing over salad; toss gently to coat. Yield: 6 servings (serving size: 1½ cups).

CALORIES 66 (37% from fat); FAT 2.7g (sat 0.5g, mono 1.1g, poly 0.9g); PROTEIN 2.1g; CARB 9.8g; FIBER 2.9g; CHOL 0mg; IRON 0.9mg; SODIUM 259mg; CALC 37mg

Greek Salad with
Feta and Olives

Greek Salad with Feta and Olives

    8 cups torn romaine lettuce
    4 cups torn escarole
1½ cups thinly sliced red onion, separated into
      rings
1½ cups thinly sliced green bell pepper rings
1½ cups thinly sliced red bell pepper rings
    ½ cup thinly sliced radishes
    ¼ cup pitted kalamata olives
    2 tomatoes, each cut into 8 wedges
      Oregano Vinaigrette
    ½ cup (2 ounces) crumbled feta cheese

1. Combine first 8 ingredients in a bowl. Pour vinaigrette over salad; toss well. Sprinkle salad with cheese. Yield: 10 servings (serving size: about 1⅔ cups).

CALORIES 78 (49% from fat); FAT 4.3g (sat 1.2g; mono 2.3g; poly 0.5g); PROTEIN 2.6g; CARB 8.1g; FIBER 2.4g; CHOL 5mg; IRON 1.4mg; SODIUM 208mg; CALC 68mg

OREGANO VINAIGRETTE:

    ¼ cup dry white wine
    ¼ cup fresh lemon juice
    1 tablespoon chopped fresh oregano
    1 tablespoon extravirgin olive oil
    ¼ teaspoon salt
    ¼ teaspoon black pepper
    4 garlic cloves, minced

1. Combine all of the ingredients in a jar; cover tightly, and shake vigorously. Yield: about ⅔ cup.

CALORIES 197 (67% from fat); FAT 13.7g (sat 1.9g; mono 10g; poly 1.3g); PROTEIN 1.3g; CARB 10.9g; FIBER 0.8g; CHOL 0mg; IRON 1.4mg; SODIUM 591mg; CALC 58mg

Kaleidoscope Tomato Salad with Balsamic-Olive Vinaigrette

Any combination of tomatoes will work in this salad. Olive pâté comes in tubes or jars and can be found with the condiments or in the ethnic-foods section of your supermarket.

VINAIGRETTE:

    3 tablespoons balsamic vinegar
    2 tablespoons water
    1 tablespoon extravirgin olive oil
    1 tablespoon olive pâté (such as Alessi)
    ¼ teaspoon salt
    ⅛ teaspoon black pepper
    1 garlic clove, crushed

SALAD:

    6 cups gourmet salad greens
    ½ cup chopped red onion
    ¼ cup chopped fresh basil
   12 (¼-inch-thick) slices green tomato, halved
   12 (¼-inch-thick) slices yellow tomato, halved
   12 (¼-inch-thick) slices red tomato, halved

1. To prepare vinaigrette, combine first 7 ingredients in a small bowl; stir well with a whisk.

2. To prepare salad, place greens on a platter. Sprinkle half of onion and half of basil evenly over greens. Arrange tomato slice halves over basil. Top with remaining onion and basil. Drizzle salad evenly with vinaigrette. Yield: 6 servings (serving size: 1 cup greens, 12 tomato slice halves, and about 1½ tablespoons vinaigrette).

CALORIES 62 (51% from fat); FAT 3.5g (sat 0.5g; mono 2.3g; poly 0.5g); PROTEIN 1.9g; CARB 7.1g; FIBER 2.3g; CHOL 0mg; IRON 1.2mg; SODIUM 119mg; CALC 32mg

Heartthrob Salad

Hearts of palm, which taste similar to artichoke hearts, come from the cabbage palm tree. Look for bottles of hearts of palm near the artichoke hearts in your supermarket.

1½ cups chopped plum tomato
    2 tablespoons minced fresh parsley
    1 tablespoon chopped pitted kalamata olives
    1 tablespoon white wine vinegar
    1 teaspoon Dijon mustard
    ½ teaspoon olive oil
    ⅛ teaspoon salt
    ⅛ teaspoon black pepper
    1 small garlic clove, minced
    1 (14.8-ounce) bottle hearts of palm
1½ cups thinly sliced Bibb lettuce leaves
    1 teaspoon grated fresh Parmesan cheese

1. Place first 9 ingredients in a medium bowl; toss gently to combine. Remove 3 hearts of palm from bottle; reserve remaining hearts of palm for another use. Dice 1 heart of palm; add to tomato mixture. Cover and chill at least 2 hours.

2. Cut 2 hearts of palm in half lengthwise. Arrange 2 hearts of palm halves, ¾ cup lettuce, and ¾ cup tomato mixture on each of 2 salad plates. Top each serving with ½ teaspoon cheese. Yield: 2 servings.

CALORIES 66 (40% from fat); FAT 2.9g (sat 0.4g; mono 1.5g; poly 0.5g); PROTEIN 2.8g; CARB 9.7g; FIBER 2.8g; CHOL 0mg; IRON 2mg; SODIUM 378mg; CALC 56mg

Tea-Crusted Tofu over Greens

Strong steeped green tea is the base for the vinaigrette. Loose tea leaves season the tofu slices.

VINAIGRETTE:

- ½ cup boiling water
- 2 green tea bags or 2 teaspoons loose green tea
- 2 tablespoons minced green onions
- 2 tablespoons fresh lime juice
- 1 tablespoon honey
- 2 teaspoons fish sauce
- 2 garlic cloves, chopped

SALAD:

- 1 (12.3-ounce) package reduced-fat extrafirm tofu, drained
- 1 tablespoon olive oil
- 2 teaspoons loose green tea or 2 green tea bags, opened
- 1½ teaspoons sesame seeds
- ⅛ teaspoon salt
- 4 cups gourmet salad greens
- 2 cups cubed Asian pear or ripe pear (about 2 pears)
- 1 cup halved cherry tomatoes (about 8 ounces)

1. To prepare vinaigrette, pour boiling water over tea bags in a medium bowl. Steep for 3 minutes; discard tea bags or strain tea leaves. Combine tea, onions, and next 4 ingredients; set aside.

2. To prepare salad, cut tofu into 8 squares. Heat oil in a large nonstick skillet over medium-high heat. Add 2 teaspoons tea leaves, sesame seeds, and salt; stir-fry 30 seconds or until fragrant. Arrange tofu on tea leaf mixture; sauté 6 minutes or until golden, turning after 3 minutes. Place tofu on a paper towel.

3. Combine greens, pear, and tomatoes in a large bowl. Drizzle with vinaigrette; toss well. Arrange 1¼ cups salad on each of 4 plates. Top each serving with 2 tofu squares. Yield: 4 servings.

CALORIES 166 (30% from fat); FAT 5.6g (sat 0.8g, mono 3g, poly 1.4g); PROTEIN 8.6g; CARB 23.7g; FIBER 3.7g; CHOL 0mg; IRON 2.2mg; SODIUM 401mg; CALC 92mg

White Bean Salad Niçoise

The dressing combines contrasting flavors: Dijon mustard, black pepper, and garlic provide hot sensations, while lemon juice offers sour notes. Salty olives and bitter greens round out the tastes of this salad. Haricots verts—thin French green beans—work well here. If you can't find them, use regular green beans. The dressing is versatile and livens up even the simplest mix of fresh greens.

SALAD:

- 4 ounces haricots verts, trimmed and cut in half crosswise
- ¼ cup kalamata olives, pitted and sliced
- ¼ cup thinly sliced green onions
- 4 ounces trimmed arugula
- 1 (16-ounce) can cannellini beans or other white beans, rinsed and drained
- 1 (7-ounce) bag fresh baby spinach

DRESSING:

- ¼ cup fresh lemon juice
- 2 tablespoons chopped fresh flat-leaf parsley
- 2 tablespoons chopped fresh basil
- 1 tablespoon Dijon mustard
- 2 teaspoons extravirgin olive oil
- ¼ teaspoon salt
- ¼ teaspoon freshly ground black pepper
- 2 garlic cloves, minced

1. Cook haricots verts in boiling water 2 minutes or until crisp-tender. Drain and plunge into ice water; drain. Place haricots verts in a large bowl. Add olives and next 4 ingredients; toss gently to combine.

2. Combine juice and remaining ingredients, stirring with a whisk. Drizzle dressing over the salad; toss to coat. Yield: 6 servings (serving size: 2 cups).

CALORIES 86 (30% from fat); FAT 2.9g (sat 0.3g, mono 1.7g, poly 0.6g); PROTEIN 3.9g; CARB 12.1g; FIBER 4g; CHOL 0mg; IRON 2.3mg; SODIUM 338mg; CALC 94mg

Spinach, White Bean, and Bacon Salad with Maple-Mustard Dressing

- ¼ cup maple syrup
- 3 tablespoons cider vinegar
- 1 tablespoon extravirgin olive oil
- 1 tablespoon Dijon mustard
- ¼ teaspoon salt
- ¼ teaspoon freshly ground black pepper
- 1 (15.5-ounce) can Great Northern beans, rinsed and drained
- ½ cup thinly sliced green onions
- ½ cup finely chopped red bell pepper
- 5 bacon slices, cooked and crumbled
- 2 (7-ounce) packages fresh baby spinach

1. Combine the first 6 ingredients in a small microwave-safe bowl, stirring mixture with a whisk, and microwave at HIGH 1 minute or until hot. Place beans in a 2-cup glass measure; microwave at HIGH 1 minute or until hot.

2. Combine green onions, bell pepper, bacon, and spinach in a large bowl. Add the syrup mixture and beans; toss well to combine. Serve immediately. Yield: 8 servings (serving size: about 1¾ cups).

CALORIES 124 (30% from fat); FAT 4.2g (sat 1g, mono 2.3g, poly 0.5g); PROTEIN 5.5g; CARB 17.6g; FIBER 2.7g; CHOL 3mg; IRON 2.2mg; SODIUM 227mg; CALC 79mg

Spinach, White Bean, and Bacon Salad with Maple-Mustard Dressing

Roasted Corn, Black Bean,
and Mango Salad

Roasted Corn, Black Bean, and Mango Salad

Browning corn in a skillet gives it a nutty, caramelized flavor that contrasts with the tart lime juice and the sweet mango. Black beans round out the contrast in color and flavor.

1   tablespoon vegetable oil
2   garlic cloves, minced
3   cups fresh corn kernels (about 6 ears)
2   cups diced peeled ripe mango (about 2 pounds)
1   cup chopped red onion
1   cup chopped red bell pepper
⅓   cup fresh lime juice
3   tablespoons chopped fresh cilantro
½   teaspoon salt
½   teaspoon ground cumin
1   drained canned chipotle chile in adobo sauce, chopped
2   (15-ounce) cans black beans, rinsed and drained
8   cups gourmet salad greens

1. Heat oil in a large nonstick skillet over medium-high heat. Add garlic; cook 30 seconds. Stir in corn; cook 8 minutes or until browned, stirring occasionally. Place corn mixture in a large bowl. Add mango and remaining ingredients except greens; stir well. Arrange 1 cup greens on each of 8 plates. Spoon 1 cup corn mixture over greens. Yield: 8 servings.

CALORIES 204 (15% from fat); FAT 3.3g (sat 0.6g, mono 0.8g, poly 1.5g); PROTEIN 9.2g; CARB 39g; FIBER 6.9g; CHOL 0mg; IRON 2.8mg; SODIUM 315mg; CALC 56mg

Grilled Corn and Black Bean Salad

Use a slotted spoon to serve this juicy salad over baked tortilla chips or chicken.

3   ears shucked corn
½   cup fresh lime juice (about 2 limes)
⅓   cup minced red onion
⅓   cup minced fresh cilantro
3   tablespoons white vinegar
2   teaspoons sugar
2   teaspoons ground cumin
2   teaspoons chili powder
1   (15-ounce) can black beans, drained
Lime wedges (optional)

1. Prepare grill.
2. Place corn on grill rack; grill 20 minutes or until corn is lightly browned, turning every 5 minutes. Cool. Cut kernels from corn; place in a bowl. Add juice and the remaining ingredients except lime wedges; stir gently. Cover and chill 1 hour. Garnish with lime wedges, if desired. Yield: 6 servings (serving size: ½ cup).

CALORIES 98 (8% from fat); FAT 0.8g (sat 0.1g, mono 0.2g, poly 0.3g); PROTEIN 4.7g; CARB 22.9; FIBER 5.4g; CHOL 0mg; IRON 1.6mg; SODIUM 238mg; CALC 36mg

Fingerling Potato and Prosciutto Salad

This salad, which also works with red-skinned potatoes, is best served immediately.

1   pound fingerling potatoes, halved lengthwise
1   tablespoon white wine vinegar
¼   cup finely chopped shallots
¼   cup chopped fresh flat-leaf parsley
3   tablespoons crème fraîche
1   teaspoon chopped fresh sage
½   teaspoon kosher salt
½   teaspoon freshly ground black pepper
3   ounces very thin slices prosciutto, finely chopped

1. Place potatoes in a medium saucepan; cover with water. Bring to a boil. Reduce heat, and simmer for 15 minutes or until tender. Drain. Stir in vinegar. Cover and chill.
2. Combine potato mixture and remaining ingredients in a large bowl; toss gently to coat. Yield: 4 servings (serving size: 1 cup).

CALORIES 109 (26% from fat); FAT 5.9g (sat 3.1g, mono 2.1g, poly 0.5g); PROTEIN 8.1g; CARB 31.9g; FIBER 3g; CHOL 21mg; IRON 2.3mg; SODIUM 574mg; CALC 45mg

Southwestern
Potato Salad

10 minutes or until tender. Drain and cool. Cut potatoes into ¼-inch cubes. Place potatoes in a large bowl.

3. Heat a large nonstick skillet coated with cooking spray over medium-high heat. Add corn; sauté 5 minutes or until lightly browned. Add corn, celery, and next 5 ingredients to potatoes; toss gently.

4. Combine 2 teaspoons chopped adobo chile, lime juice, oil, salt, and black pepper, stirring with a whisk. Drizzle the lime juice mixture over potato mixture; toss gently to coat. Cover and chill 1 to 24 hours. Yield: 8 servings (serving size: about 1 cup).

CALORIES 209 (25% from fat); FAT 5.8g (sat 0.4g, mono 3.1g, poly 1.8g); PROTEIN 5.1g; CARB 37.9g; FIBER 5.7g; CHOL 0mg; IRON 2.3mg; SODIUM 413mg; CALC 33mg

Two-Potato Salad with Crème Fraîche

Look for crème fraîche near the cheeses in gourmet markets; if you can't find it, substitute it with full-fat sour cream. You can prepare this dish a day ahead; stir gently before serving.

- 1½ pounds small red potatoes, halved
- 1½ pounds peeled sweet potatoes, cut into 1-inch pieces
- 3 tablespoons white vinegar
- ¾ cup crème fraîche
- ¼ cup chopped fresh chives
- ¾ teaspoon salt
- ¼ teaspoon freshly ground black pepper

1. Place potatoes in a large Dutch oven; cover with water. Bring to a boil; reduce heat, and simmer 18 minutes or until tender. Drain. Place potatoes in a large bowl. Drizzle with vinegar; toss gently to coat. Let cool to room temperature.

2. Combine the crème fraîche and remaining ingredients, stirring mixture with a whisk. Add to potatoes, tossing gently to coat. Yield: 8 servings (serving size: 1 cup).

CALORIES 253 (29% from fat); FAT 8.2g (sat 5g, mono 2.3g, poly 0.4g); PROTEIN 3.9g; CARB 41.3g; FIBER 3g; CHOL 18mg; IRON 1.2mg; SODIUM 255mg; CALC 70mg

Southwestern Potato Salad

Adjust the heat by increasing or decreasing the jalapeño and chipotle chile.

- 1 (7-ounce) can chipotle chiles in adobo sauce
- 2 pounds small red potatoes
- Cooking spray
- 1½ cups fresh corn kernels (about 3 ears)
- ½ cup chopped celery
- ½ cup finely chopped red onion
- ½ cup chopped red bell pepper
- ¼ cup chopped fresh cilantro
- 1 (15-ounce) can black beans, rinsed and drained
- 1 jalapeño pepper, seeded and finely chopped
- ¼ cup fresh lime juice
- 3 tablespoons canola oil
- ¾ teaspoon salt
- ¼ teaspoon freshly ground black pepper

1. Remove 1 chipotle chile from can. Chop chile to measure 2 teaspoons. Reserve remaining chiles and adobo sauce for another use.

2. Place potatoes in a saucepan, and cover with water. Bring to a boil. Reduce heat, and simmer for

Caesar Potato Salad

Pull a vegetable peeler firmly across the surface of Parmesan cheese to form shaved pieces.

1½ tablespoons extravirgin olive oil
2 garlic cloves, minced
2 (1-ounce) slices French bread
1½ pounds small red potatoes
3 tablespoons dry vermouth (optional)
¼ cup chopped green onions
3 tablespoons finely chopped fresh
flat-leaf parsley
2 tablespoons balsamic vinegar
1 tablespoon lemon juice
2 teaspoons Dijon mustard
2 teaspoons anchovy paste
¼ teaspoon salt
⅛ teaspoon black pepper
1 cup thinly sliced romaine lettuce
¼ cup (1 ounce) shaved fresh Parmesan cheese

1. Combine oil and garlic; let stand 30 minutes.
2. Preheat oven to 350°.

3. Brush 1½ teaspoons oil mixture over bread; cut into 1-inch cubes. Place the bread cubes in a single layer on a jelly roll pan. Bake at 350° for 9 minutes or until toasted.
4. Steam potatoes, covered, 18 minutes or until tender. Cool, and cut each into 6 wedges. Combine the potato wedges and vermouth, if desired; toss gently to coat.
5. Combine remaining oil mixture, onions, and next 7 ingredients in a bowl. Pour dressing over the potatoes; toss gently to coat. Cover and chill.
6. Add lettuce, and toss gently. Sprinkle potato mixture with cheese and croutons. Yield: 6 servings (serving size: ⅔ cup).
NOTE: Store anchovy paste (which comes in a tube) in the refrigerator for up to 2 months after using it in this recipe.

CALORIES 185 (26% from fat); FAT 5.4g (sat 1.3g, mono 3.1g, poly 0.6g); PROTEIN 5.5g; CARB 29.4g; FIBER 2.4g; CHOL 3mg; IRON 1mg; SODIUM 516mg; CALC 80mg

Sugar-Snap-Pea Salad with Sweet Ginger-Soy Dressing

DRESSING:
    2 teaspoons dark sesame oil
    1 tablespoon minced peeled fresh ginger
    1 tablespoon minced fresh garlic
    ¼ teaspoon crushed red pepper
    1 tablespoon oyster sauce
    1 tablespoon low-sodium soy sauce
    1 tablespoon sugar
    ⅛ teaspoon salt
SALAD:
    1 pound sugar snap peas, trimmed
    ½ cup julienne-cut carrot
    ½ cup drained, canned sliced water chestnuts
    ½ cup sliced mushrooms
    ½ cup julienne-cut red bell pepper
    2 teaspoons sesame seeds, toasted

1. To prepare dressing, heat oil in a small saucepan over medium heat. Add ginger; sauté 2 minutes. Add garlic and crushed red pepper; cook 1 minute. Stir in oyster sauce, soy sauce, sugar, and salt; bring to a simmer. Remove from heat; cool.

2. To prepare salad, cook peas in boiling water 30 seconds. Drain and rinse with cold water. Combine peas and remaining ingredients except sesame seeds. Drizzle dressing over salad; toss well. Sprinkle with sesame seeds. Yield: 5 servings (serving size: 1 cup).

CALORIES 107 (18% from fat); FAT 2.3g (sat 0.3g, mono 0.9g, poly 1g); PROTEIN 4g; CARB 18.9g; FIBER 4.3g; CHOL 0mg; IRON 1.1mg; SODIUM 289mg; CALC 77mg

Tomato, Lime, and Onion Salad

If you're unable to find good large tomatoes, substitute quartered cherry tomatoes.

    4 cups vertically sliced red onion
    ¼ cup fresh lime juice
    ½ teaspoon kosher salt
    1 cup chopped tomato
    ¼ cup chopped fresh cilantro
    2 teaspoons chopped fresh mint
    1 teaspoon grated lime rind

1. Combine first 3 ingredients in a medium bowl; let stand 1 hour. Stir in tomato and remaining ingredients. Yield: 8 servings (serving size: about ⅓ cup).

CALORIES 29 (6% from fat); FAT 0.2g (sat 0g, mono 0g, poly 0.1g); PROTEIN 0.9g; CARB 6.8g; FIBER 1.4g; CHOL 0mg; IRON 0.3mg; SODIUM 122mg; CALC 14mg

Tomato and Roasted Pepper Salad

Caperberries taste like capers but are about the size of olives and have stems. Look for them with olives at the grocery store.

    4 medium tomatoes (about 2 pounds), each cut into 4 slices
    2 tablespoons balsamic vinegar, divided
    1 tablespoon honey
    ¼ teaspoon salt
    ¼ teaspoon freshly ground black pepper
    1 large red bell pepper
    1 large yellow bell pepper
    1 tablespoon red wine vinegar
    2 teaspoons olive oil
    1 garlic clove, minced
    ½ cup bottled caperberries (about 20)

1. Preheat broiler.

2. Arrange tomato slices in a single layer on a platter. Combine 1 tablespoon balsamic vinegar and honey in a small bowl, stirring with a whisk. Drizzle mixture evenly over tomato slices. Sprinkle with salt and black pepper; marinate 15 minutes.

3. Cut bell peppers in half lengthwise; discard seeds and membranes. Place pepper halves, skin sides up, on a foil-lined baking sheet; flatten with hand. Broil 10 minutes or until bell peppers are blackened. Place in a zip-top plastic bag; seal. Let stand 10 minutes. Peel and cut into ¾-inch strips.

4. Combine 1 tablespoon balsamic vinegar, red wine vinegar, oil, and garlic in a medium bowl; stir well with a whisk. Add bell peppers and caperberries; toss gently to coat. Top tomato slices with bell pepper mixture. Yield: 8 servings (serving size: 2 tomato slices and about 2 tablespoons bell pepper mixture).

CALORIES 48 (28% from fat); FAT 1.5g (sat 0.2g, mono 0.9g, poly 0.2g); PROTEIN 1.1g; CARB 9g; FIBER 1.4g; CHOL 0mg; IRON 0.6mg; SODIUM 232mg; CALC 10mg

Green and Yellow Bean Salad with Chunky Tomato Dressing and Feta Cheese

Yellow wax beans contrast nicely with the green beans. If wax beans are unavailable, use extra green beans in their place.

¾ pound wax beans, trimmed
¾ pound green beans, trimmed
2 cups chopped tomato
1 tablespoon sherry vinegar
2 teaspoons extravirgin olive oil
½ teaspoon salt
¼ teaspoon freshly ground black pepper
½ cup thinly sliced fresh basil
½ cup (2 ounces) crumbled feta cheese

1. Cook beans in boiling water 5 minutes or until crisp-tender. Drain and rinse with cold water.
2. Combine tomato and next 4 ingredients in a bowl. Divide beans evenly among 8 plates. Spoon ¼ cup tomato mixture over beans. Sprinkle with 1 tablespoon sliced basil and 1 tablespoon cheese. Yield: 8 servings.

CALORIES 67 (39% from fat); FAT 2.9g (sat 1.3g, mono 1.2g, poly 0.3g); PROTEIN 3g; CARB 8.7g; FIBER 2.3g; CHOL 6mg; IRON 1.1mg; SODIUM 246mg; CALC 73mg

Spicy Cucumber Salad with Peanuts

Try this Thai-inspired salad with chicken or fish. The sugar in the dressing balances the heat of the crushed red pepper. Salting the cucumber slices draws out some of the moisture, making them especially crisp.

1½ pounds cucumber, peeled, halved lengthwise, and thinly sliced (about 4 cups)
2 teaspoons kosher salt
½ cup rice vinegar
½ cup water
3 tablespoons sugar
¼ teaspoon crushed red pepper
2 tablespoons minced red onion
1 tablespoon chopped dry-roasted peanuts

1. Place cucumber slices in a colander; sprinkle with salt, and toss well. Drain 1 hour. Place on several layers of paper towels; cover with additional paper towels. Let stand 5 minutes, pressing down occasionally. Rinse and pat dry.

2. Combine vinegar, water, sugar, and pepper in a small saucepan; bring to a boil. Reduce heat; cook until reduced to ⅓ cup (about 10 minutes). Remove vinegar reduction from heat; cool. Stir in onion. Combine cucumbers and vinegar reduction in a medium bowl; toss well. Sprinkle with peanuts. Yield: 4 servings (serving size: ¾ cup).

CALORIES 76 (17% from fat); FAT 1.4g (sat 0.2g, mono 0.6g, poly 0.5g); PROTEIN 1.6g; CARB 14.6g; FIBER 1.5g; CHOL 0mg; IRON 0.3mg; SODIUM 247mg; CALC 27mg

Bread Salad with Tomatoes, Herbs, and Ricotta Salata

  8 (1-ounce) slices sourdough bread
⅓ cup water
¼ cup red wine vinegar
  1 teaspoon extravirgin olive oil
¼ teaspoon salt
¼ teaspoon freshly ground black pepper
  1 cup (4 ounces) crumbled ricotta salata
  2 tablespoons chopped fresh basil
  2 tablespoons chopped fresh chives
  1 tablespoon chopped fresh mint
  1 teaspoon chopped fresh oregano
  1 teaspoon chopped fresh thyme
  4 cups cherry tomatoes, halved (about 2 pints)
  1 cup diced red onion

1. Sprinkle bread with water; let stand 2 minutes. Carefully squeeze moisture from bread. Tear into 1-inch pieces. Let stand on paper towels 20 minutes.
2. Combine vinegar, oil, salt, and pepper, stirring with a whisk. Combine ricotta and next 5 ingredients in a large bowl. Add bread, tomatoes, and onion to ricotta mixture. Drizzle with vinaigrette, and toss gently to coat. Yield: 6 servings (serving size: 1⅔ cups).

CALORIES 193 (29% from fat); FAT 6.3g (sat 3.2g, mono 2g, poly 0.6g); PROTEIN 7.3g; CARB 28.2g; FIBER 2.8g; CHOL 17mg; IRON 1.7mg; SODIUM 548mg; CALC 137mg

Crunchy Bok Choy Salad

DRESSING:
  2 tablespoons sugar
  3 tablespoons cider vinegar
  3 tablespoons low-sodium soy sauce
  2 teaspoons peanut butter
½ teaspoon curry powder
¼ teaspoon crushed red pepper
SALAD:
  1 (3-ounce) package ramen noodles
¼ cup unsalted dry-roasted peanuts
  3 cups thinly sliced bok choy
  1 cup very thin red bell pepper strips
½ cup shredded carrot
¼ cup diagonally cut green onions

1. To prepare dressing, combine first 6 ingredients in a large bowl; stir well with a whisk.
2. To prepare salad, crumble noodles, and discard seasoning packet. Heat a nonstick skillet over medium-high heat. Add peanuts, and sauté 4 minutes or until browned. Remove from heat. Combine crumbled noodles, peanuts, bok choy, and remaining ingredients in a large bowl. Drizzle dressing over salad; toss gently to coat. Serve immediately. Yield: 10 servings (serving size: ½ cup).

CALORIES 86 (39% from fat); FAT 3.7g (sat 1.9g, mono 1g, poly 0.7g); PROTEIN 2.6g; CARB 11.7g; FIBER 1.4g; CHOL 0mg; IRON 0.8mg; SODIUM 178mg; CALC 28mg

Asian Noodle Salad

Let the noodle mixture stand longer than 15 minutes if you prefer a less crunchy salad.

⅓ cup rice vinegar or cider vinegar
¼ cup sugar
2½ tablespoons vegetable oil
  2 tablespoons honey
  2 tablespoons low-sodium soy sauce
  1 tablespoon butter or stick margarine
¼ cup slivered almonds, toasted
  2 tablespoons sunflower seed kernels
  2 (5-ounce) packages Japanese curly noodles (*chuka soba*), uncooked and crumbled
  8 cups shredded napa (Chinese) cabbage
  2 cups shredded carrot
  1 cup thinly sliced green onions

1. Combine first 5 ingredients in a small saucepan. Bring to a boil, and cook for 1 minute, stirring constantly. Spoon mixture into a bowl; cover and chill.
2. Melt the butter in a large nonstick skillet over medium-high heat. Add almonds, sunflower kernels, and noodles; cook 3 minutes or until lightly toasted, tossing occasionally. Spoon mixture into a large bowl; cover and chill. Add vinegar mixture to noodle mixture; let stand 15 minutes. Add cabbage, carrot, and onions, tossing to coat. Yield: 12 servings (serving size: ¾ cup).
NOTE: You can quickly and easily shred the cabbage and carrot using the large slicing holes of a stand-up grater.

CALORIES 183 (30% from fat); FAT 6.1g (sat 1.4g, mono 2g, poly 2.4g); PROTEIN 4.4g; CARB 29g; FIBER 2g; CHOL 3mg; IRON 1.1mg; SODIUM 259mg; CALC 68mg

Sushi-Rice Salad

This refreshing side salad, which pairs well with seared tuna or soy-glazed salmon, has all the flavors of a cucumber roll, a popular sushi.

RICE:
- 2 cups uncooked sushi rice
- 2 cups water
- 1 teaspoon kosher salt

DRESSING:
- ½ cup rice vinegar
- 1 tablespoon vegetable oil
- 1 tablespoon dark sesame oil
- 1 tablespoon low-sodium soy sauce
- 1 teaspoon grated peeled fresh ginger
- 1 garlic clove, minced
- ¼ to ¾ teaspoon prepared wasabi (Japanese horseradish), optional

REMAINING INGREDIENTS:
- 1 cup (2-inch) julienne-cut peeled English cucumber
- ¼ cup minced red onion
- 1 tablespoon sesame seeds, toasted
- 1 sheet nori (seaweed), cut into 2-inch julienne strips

1. To prepare rice, rinse rice thoroughly in a sieve. Drain well. Bring 2 cups water to a boil in a medium saucepan, and add rice and salt. Cover, reduce heat, and simmer for 20 minutes or until liquid is absorbed. Remove from heat. Uncover and cool to room temperature.

2. To prepare dressing, combine rice vinegar and next 5 ingredients in a small bowl. Add wasabi, if desired. Combine cooled rice, dressing, cucumber, minced onion, and toasted sesame seeds in a large bowl. Sprinkle evenly with nori. Yield: 7 servings (serving size: 1 cup).

CALORIES 256 (15% from fat); FAT 4.3g (sat 0.5g, mono 2g, poly 1.5g); PROTEIN 4.2g; CARB 46.7g; FIBER 2g; CHOL 0mg; IRON 4.4mg; SODIUM 346mg; CALC 9mg

Wheat Berry Salad with Dried Fruit

This salad is best if made in advance so the flavors have time to mellow. It's high in fiber, filling, and easy to pack for a picnic or to take on a hike.

- 3 cups water
- 1 cup uncooked wheat berries
- ½ cup minced shallots
- ¼ cup cranberry juice
- 2 tablespoons vegetable oil
- 3 tablespoons raspberry or red wine vinegar
- 1 tablespoon balsamic vinegar
- 2 teaspoons Dijon mustard
- ½ teaspoon salt
- ½ cup coarsely chopped dried cranberries
- ½ cup coarsely chopped dried cherries
- ½ cup (2 ounces) diced Gouda cheese
- ⅓ cup chopped green onions
- ⅓ cup slivered almonds, toasted
- ¼ cup dried currants
- ¼ teaspoon freshly ground black pepper

1. Combine water and wheat berries in a medium saucepan; bring to a boil. Cover, reduce heat, and simmer 1 hour. Drain and rinse with cold water.

2. Combine minced shallots and the next 6 ingredients in a large bowl, and stir with a whisk. Let stand 30 minutes.

3. Add wheat berries, cranberries, and remaining ingredients to vinaigrette; toss to combine. Cover and chill at least 4 hours or overnight. Yield: 6 servings (serving size: 1 cup).

CALORIES 355 (30% from fat); FAT 11.7g (sat 2.7g, mono 4.4g, poly 3.8g); PROTEIN 9.4g; CARB 55.2g; FIBER 7.8g; CHOL 11mg; IRON 2.1mg; SODIUM 332mg; CALC 118mg

Sushi-Rice Salad

Fresh Mozzarella, Tomato, and Basil Couscous Salad

Part-skim mozzarella cheese can be substituted for the fresh mozzarella.

 2 cups diced tomato
¾ cup (3 ounces) diced fresh mozzarella cheese
 3 tablespoons minced shallots
 2 teaspoons extravirgin olive oil
½ teaspoon salt
½ teaspoon black pepper
 1 garlic clove, crushed
1¼ cups water
 1 cup uncooked couscous
¼ cup chopped fresh basil
 Basil leaves (optional)

1. Combine the first 7 ingredients in a large bowl; cover and marinate tomato mixture in refrigerator for 30 minutes.

2. Bring water to a boil in a medium saucepan; gradually stir in couscous. Remove from heat; cover and let stand 5 minutes. Fluff with a fork; cool. Add couscous and fresh basil to tomato mixture; toss gently. Garnish with basil leaves, if desired. Yield: 5 servings (serving size: 1 cup).

CALORIES 186 (29% from fat); FAT 6g (sat 2.5g, mono 2.5g, poly 0.4g); PROTEIN 7.9g; CARB 26.5g; FIBER 2.1g; CHOL 13mg; IRON 1.1mg; SODIUM 308mg; CALC 99mg

Salade
Niçoise

Salade Niçoise

All ingredients in the Salade Niçoise except tuna can be prepped a day ahead and stored separately.

    3 tablespoons fresh lemon juice
    1 pound tuna steaks (about 2 [8-ounce] steaks)
Freshly ground black pepper
Cooking spray
   10 small red potatoes (about 1 pound)
    ½ pound green beans, trimmed
    4 cups torn romaine lettuce
    4 cups trimmed watercress (about 1 bunch)
    3 medium tomatoes, each cut into 6 wedges
    3 hard-cooked large eggs, quartered lengthwise
    1 small green bell pepper, cut into strips
    ½ cup niçoise olives
    2 tablespoons capers
    6 canned anchovy fillets
Garlic-Basil Vinaigrette

1. Drizzle lemon juice over tuna; sprinkle with pepper. Marinate in refrigerator 15 minutes; discard lemon juice.
2. Prepare grill or broiler.
3. Place tuna on a grill rack or broiler pan coated with cooking spray; cook 4 minutes on each side or until desired degree of doneness.
4. Break tuna into chunks; set aside.
5. Steam potatoes, covered, 3 minutes. Add green beans, and steam, covered, 8 minutes or until vegetables are crisp-tender; cool.
6. Combine the lettuce and watercress on a large serving platter. Arrange the tuna, potatoes, green beans, tomatoes, egg quarters, and bell pepper strips over greens. Top with olives, capers, and anchovy fillets. Drizzle Garlic-Basil Vinaigrette over salad. Yield: 6 servings.

(Totals include Garlic-Basil Vinaigrette) CALORIES 290 (34% from fat); FAT 11.9g (sat 2.5g, mono 5.2g, poly 2.3g); PROTEIN 26.3g; CARB 22.5g; FIBER 4.6g; CHOL 139mg; IRON 3.9mg; SODIUM 471mg; CALC 105mg

GARLIC-BASIL VINAIGRETTE:

    ⅓ cup fat-free, less-sodium chicken broth
   1½ tablespoons chopped fresh or 1½ teaspoons
         dried basil
    1 tablespoon extravirgin olive oil
    1 tablespoon fresh lemon juice
    1 tablespoon red wine vinegar
    1 teaspoon Dijon mustard
    3 garlic cloves, halved
Freshly ground black pepper

1. Combine all of the ingredients in a blender, and process until smooth. Yield: 6 tablespoons (serving size: 1 tablespoon).
NOTE: Vinaigrette can be made ahead. Store in an airtight container for up to 1 week.

CALORIES 25 (83% from fat); FAT 2.3g (sat 0.3g, mono 1.7g, poly 0.2g); PROTEIN 0.3g; CARB 0.9g; FIBER 0g; CHOL 0mg; IRON 0mg; SODIUM 51mg; CALC 4mg

Lemon-Dill Bulgur Salad with Scallops

Watercress is a pungent green with a peppery bite. Generally sold in small bunches, its dark-green leaves are small and crisp. Wash watercress and shake it dry just before serving.

    2 cups water
    1 cup uncooked bulgur
Cooking spray
   1½ pounds sea scallops
    2 cups chopped seeded cucumber
   1½ cups chopped plum tomato
    1 cup frozen corn kernels, thawed
    ¼ cup chopped fresh or 1 tablespoon dried dill
    ¼ cup lemon juice
    2 tablespoons olive oil
   1½ teaspoons salt
    1 teaspoon sugar
    ¼ teaspoon freshly ground black pepper
    1 garlic clove, minced
    6 cups trimmed watercress (about 2 bunches) or
         baby spinach

1. Bring water to a boil in a medium saucepan. Add bulgur; partially cover, reduce heat, and simmer 5 minutes. Drain; cool.
2. While bulgur cooks, heat a medium nonstick skillet coated with cooking spray over medium-high heat. Add scallops; cook 3 minutes, turning once. Remove from heat, and place scallops in a large bowl.
3. Add bulgur, cucumber, and next 9 ingredients to scallops in bowl; toss well to coat. Place 1 cup watercress on each of 6 plates; top each serving with 1 cup scallop mixture. Yield: 6 servings.

CALORIES 275 (21% from fat); FAT 6.5g (sat 0.8g, mono 3.5g, poly 1g); PROTEIN 24.4g; CARB 32.4g; FIBER 6.9g; CHOL 37mg; IRON 1.7mg; SODIUM 795mg; CALC 103mg

Sizzling Salmon and Spinach Salad with Soy Vinaigrette

DRESSING:

- 3 tablespoons thinly sliced green onions
- 3 tablespoons rice vinegar
- 3 tablespoons low-sodium soy sauce
- 1 tablespoon water
- 1 teaspoon sesame seeds, toasted
- 1 teaspoon bottled minced garlic
- 1 teaspoon dark sesame oil
- ½ teaspoon chile paste with garlic or
- ¼ teaspoon crushed red pepper

SALAD:

- 2 teaspoons dark sesame oil, divided
- 4 cups thinly sliced shiitake or button mushroom caps (about 8 ounces)
- 1 cup (1-inch) sliced green onions
- 1 cup fresh or frozen corn kernels, thawed
- 4 (6-ounce) salmon fillets (about 1 inch thick)
- 8 cups baby spinach
- 1 cup fresh bean sprouts
- 1 cup red bell pepper strips

1. Preheat broiler.

2. To prepare dressing, combine first 8 ingredients in a small bowl; stir well with a whisk.

3. To prepare salad, heat 1 teaspoon oil in a large nonstick skillet over medium-high heat. Add mushrooms and 1 cup onions; sauté 8 minutes. Stir in corn; remove from heat.

4. Place fish on a foil-lined baking sheet; brush evenly with 1 teaspoon oil. Broil 8 minutes or until fish flakes easily when tested with a fork.

5. Place 2 cups spinach on each of 4 plates; top each serving with ¼ cup bean sprouts, ¼ cup red bell pepper, ½ cup mushroom mixture, and 1 fillet. Drizzle about 2 tablespoons dressing over each salad. Yield: 4 servings.

CALORIES 418 (40% from fat); FAT 18.8g (sat 3.2g, mono 8.3g, poly 5.1g); PROTEIN 42.9g; CARB 21.8g; FIBER 7.8g; CHOL 111mg; IRON 6.1mg; SODIUM 549mg; CALC 163mg

Flank Steak and Blue Cheese Quesadilla Salad

Because they're filled with steak, these quesadillas are a bit tricky to cut. Our solution: Let them stand a minute or so after cooking, then cut with kitchen shears.

VINAIGRETTE:

- 3 tablespoons Dijon-Lemon Vinaigrette
- 1½ tablespoons sugar
- 1½ tablespoons red wine vinegar
- ¼ teaspoon freshly ground black pepper
- ¼ teaspoon chopped fresh thyme (optional)

QUESADILLAS:

- ½ pound flank steak
- ¼ teaspoon salt
- ¼ teaspoon freshly ground black pepper

Cooking spray
- ½ cup (2 ounces) crumbled blue cheese
- 4 (8-inch) fat-free flour tortillas

REMAINING INGREDIENTS:

- 10 cups torn red leaf lettuce
- 1 cup vertically sliced red onion
- 2 large tomatoes, each cut into 8 wedges

1. Prepare grill.
2. To prepare vinaigrette, combine first 5 ingredients; set aside.
3. To prepare quesadillas, sprinkle steak with salt and ¼ teaspoon pepper. Place steak on grill rack coated with cooking spray; cook 4 minutes on each side or until done. Let stand 5 minutes. Cut steak diagonally across grain into thin slices. Sprinkle ¼ cup cheese evenly over each of 2 tortillas. Divide steak evenly over cheese, and top with the remaining tortillas.
4. Heat a large nonstick skillet coated with cooking spray over medium heat. Cook quesadillas 4 minutes on each side or until golden brown. Remove from pan, and cut each quesadilla into 8 wedges. Combine vinaigrette, lettuce, onion, and tomato in a large bowl, and toss well. Divide salad evenly among 4 plates, and top each serving with 4 quesadilla wedges. Yield: 4 servings.

CALORIES 338 (29% from fat); FAT 10.9g (sat 4.8g, mono 4.2g, poly 0.8g); PROTEIN 20.9g; CARB 39.5g; FIBER 4.8g; CHOL 11mg; IRON 4.3mg; SODIUM 809mg; CALC 142mg

DIJON-LEMON VINAIGRETTE:

- 3 tablespoons vegetable broth or water
- 2 tablespoons fresh lemon juice
- 2 tablespoons extravirgin olive oil
- 1½ tablespoons red wine vinegar
- 1 tablespoon Dijon mustard
- 2 teaspoons minced garlic
- 2 teaspoons Worcestershire sauce
- ½ teaspoon black pepper
- ¼ teaspoon salt

1. Combine all ingredients in a jar; cover tightly, and shake vigorously. Store in refrigerator. Yield: ⅔ cup (serving size: 1 tablespoon).

CALORIES 25 (86% from fat); FAT 2.4g (sat 0.3g, mono 1.7g, poly 0.2g); PROTEIN 0.1g; CARB 1g; FIBER 0g; CHOL 0mg; IRON 0.1mg; SODIUM 93mg; CALC 3mg

Thai Steak Salad

Thai Steak Salad

Flank steak is widely available and easy to recognize by its long, flat shape and distinctive longitudinal grain. Cutting across the grain breaks up the muscle fibers for more tender slices.

DRESSING:
⅓ cup fresh lime juice (about 3 limes)
1½ tablespoons brown sugar
1 tablespoon grated peeled fresh ginger
1 tablespoon Thai fish sauce
1 to 2 teaspoons chile paste with garlic

STEAK:
Cooking spray
1 (1½-pound) flank steak, trimmed
1 tablespoon cracked black pepper

SALAD:
3 cups trimmed watercress (about 2 bunches)
1 cup thinly sliced red cabbage
1 cup loosely packed fresh basil leaves
1 cup loosely packed fresh mint leaves
½ cup loosely packed fresh cilantro leaves
½ cup julienne-cut carrot
2 tablespoons finely chopped unsalted, dry-roasted peanuts

1. To prepare dressing, combine first 5 ingredients in a bowl; stir well with a whisk.

2. To prepare steak, heat a large nonstick skillet or grill pan coated with cooking spray over medium-high heat. Rub both sides of steak with pepper. Add steak to pan; cook 6 minutes on each side or until desired degree of doneness. Remove from pan; place on a cutting board. Cover loosely with foil; let stand 5 minutes. Cut steak diagonally across grain into thin slices. Place steak in a bowl. Drizzle with half of dressing; toss well.

3. To prepare salad, combine watercress and next 5 ingredients in a large bowl. Drizzle watercress mixture with remaining dressing, and toss well. Divide the salad evenly among 6 plates; arrange steak evenly over salad. Sprinkle each serving with 1 teaspoon peanuts. Yield: 6 servings.

CALORIES 230 (40% from fat); FAT 10.3g (sat 4g, mono 4.2g, poly 0.9g); PROTEIN 25.1g; CARB 9.5g; FIBER 2g; CHOL 57mg; IRON 3.3mg; SODIUM 327mg; CALC 68mg

Grilled Pork and Rice Noodle Salad

This Vietnamese dish, known as "bun," is replete with fresh herbs.

⅔ cup boiling water
¼ cup sugar
⅓ cup fresh lime juice
3 tablespoons fish sauce
2 teaspoons chile paste with garlic
1 garlic clove, minced
½ pound uncooked rice sticks (rice-flour noodles)
2 cups mixed salad greens
2 cups julienne-cut cucumber (about ¾ pound)
1½ cups julienne-cut carrot (about ½ pound)
1 cup fresh bean sprouts
½ cup chopped fresh mint
½ cup chopped fresh basil
4 Hoisin-Marinated Pork Chops, thinly sliced (recipe on page 186)
¼ cup chopped dry-roasted peanuts

1. Combine boiling water and sugar, stirring until sugar dissolves. Add juice, fish sauce, chile paste, and garlic. Cool.

2. Prepare noodles according to package directions; drain. Combine noodles, greens, and next 6 ingredients in a large bowl. Add juice mixture; toss well. Sprinkle with peanuts. Yield: 6 servings (serving size: 1½ cups).

(Totals include Hoisin-Marinated Pork Chops) CALORIES 370 (16% from fat); FAT 6.7g (sat 1.8g, mono 3g, poly 1.3g); PROTEIN 22.6g; CARB 55.4g; FIBER 3.6g; CHOL 42mg; IRON 2.6mg; SODIUM 947mg; CALC 82mg

Caesar Chicken-Pasta Salad

    3 cups hot cooked penne (about 6 ounces
       uncooked tube-shaped pasta)
    2 cups thinly sliced romaine lettuce
 1 ½ cups halved cherry tomatoes
    ½ cup thinly sliced fresh basil
    ½ cup chopped green onions
    ⅓ cup fat-free Caesar dressing
    ¼ cup chopped fresh parsley
    1 (4-ounce) package crumbled feta cheese
    1 garlic clove, minced
    4 roasted skinless, boneless chicken breast
       halves, sliced (about 12 ounces)

1. Combine first 9 ingredients in a bowl; toss well
to coat. Place 1¼ cups pasta mixture on each of 4
plates; top with a chicken breast. Yield: 4 servings.
NOTE: To lower the sodium in this dish, use plain
cooked chicken in place of the commercial roasted
variety, which is fairly high in sodium.

CALORIES 362 (22% from fat); FAT 8.8g (sat 5.2g, mono 1.4g, poly 0.6g); PROTEIN 19.4g;
CARB 40.4g; FIBER 3.5g; CHOL 78mg; IRON 2.6mg; SODIUM 951mg; CALC 206mg

Barbecue Chicken and Grape Salad

Chili-spiked spice rub gives the chicken color and flavor. Rinsing the onions takes away some of their bite.

    1 teaspoon onion powder
    1 teaspoon paprika
    1 teaspoon ancho chili powder
    ¾ teaspoon salt, divided
    1 pound skinless, boneless chicken breast halves
    1 teaspoon olive oil
    ¾ cup seedless green grapes, halved
    ¾ cup seedless red grapes, halved
    ⅔ cup coarsely chopped celery
    ½ cup thinly sliced red onion
    ¼ cup low-fat mayonnaise
    1 tablespoon red wine vinegar
    1 tablespoon fresh orange juice
    ¼ cup coarsely chopped walnuts, toasted

1. Preheat oven to 350°.
2. Combine onion powder, paprika, chili powder,
and ½ teaspoon salt; sprinkle over chicken.
3. Heat oil in a large nonstick skillet over medium-
high heat. Add chicken; sauté 2 minutes on each
side or until browned. Wrap handle of pan in foil;

bake at 350° for 10 minutes or until chicken is
done. Remove from pan; refrigerate until chilled.
Chop into bite-sized pieces.
4. Combine ¼ teaspoon salt, green grapes, and
next 6 ingredients in a large bowl. Add chopped
chicken; toss to coat. Sprinkle salad with walnuts.
Yield: 4 servings (serving size: about 1¼ cups).

CALORIES 266 (29% from fat); FAT 8.5g (sat 1.1g, mono 2.5g, poly 4.1g); PROTEIN 29.1g;
CARB 19.1g; FIBER 2g; CHOL 66mg; IRON 1.6mg; SODIUM 676mg; CALC 40mg

Asian Turkey Salad

This is a great use for leftover turkey, but you can substitute roasted ready-to-eat chicken, if you wish.

DRESSING:
    ¼ cup rice vinegar
    ¼ cup vegetable broth
    1 tablespoon low-sodium soy sauce
    2 teaspoons minced peeled fresh ginger
    2 teaspoons lime juice
    1 teaspoon peanut oil
    1 teaspoon dark sesame oil
    ½ teaspoon salt
    ½ teaspoon sugar
    1 serrano chile
    1 garlic clove
SALAD:
    4 cups thinly sliced napa (Chinese) cabbage
    3 cups shredded cooked turkey
    1 cup red bell pepper strips (about 1 small
       pepper)
    ½ cup thinly sliced red onion
    ½ cup chopped fresh cilantro
    ¼ cup sliced green onions
    1 tablespoon chopped dry-roasted peanuts

1. To prepare dressing, place first 11 ingredients in
a blender; process until smooth.
2. To prepare salad, combine cabbage and remaining ingredients in a large bowl; pour dressing over
salad, tossing to coat. Serve immediately. Yield: 4
servings (serving size: 1¾ cups).

CALORIES 250 (30% from fat); FAT 8.3g (sat 2.2g, mono 2.3g, poly 2.6g); PROTEIN 33.2g;
CARB 10.3g; FIBER 3.4g; CHOL 80mg; IRON 2.8mg; SODIUM 592mg; CALC 80mg

Grilled Thai Chicken Salad with Mango and Ginger

This recipe easily doubles, which makes it ideal for entertaining.

DRESSING:

¼ cup fresh lemon juice
3 tablespoons Thai fish sauce
2 tablespoons brown sugar
2 tablespoons minced seeded Thai, hot red, or serrano chiles

SALAD:

12 ounces skinless, boneless chicken breast
Cooking spray
2 cups sliced peeled mango (about 2 mangoes)
⅔ cup thinly sliced shallots
¼ cup matchstick-cut peeled fresh ginger
4 cups mixed salad greens
⅔ cup torn mint leaves

1. To prepare dressing, combine first 4 ingredients in a bowl; stir well with a whisk. Set dressing aside.

2. Prepare grill or broiler.

3. To prepare salad, combine 1 tablespoon dressing and chicken, and toss to coat. Place chicken on a grill rack or broiler pan coated with cooking spray, and cook for 6 minutes on each side or until chicken is done. Cut chicken diagonally across grain into thin slices. Combine chicken, sliced mango, shallots, and ginger. Toss with remaining dressing. Divide salad greens evenly among 3 plates. Top salad greens with chicken salad, and sprinkle with mint. Yield: 3 servings (serving size: 1 cup chicken salad, 1⅓ cups salad greens, and about 3 tablespoons mint).

NOTE: Thai fish sauce can be found in Asian markets or large supermarkets.

CALORIES 282 (7% from fat); FAT 2.2g (sat 0.5g, mono 0.5g, poly 0.5g); PROTEIN 30.2g; CARB 6.1g; FIBER 3.4g; CHOL 66mg; IRON 2.4mg; SODIUM 1,390mg; CALC 76mg

Sandwiches

Hot Browns, page 282

Catfish Po'boy with Hoisin-Peanut Sauce

A hoisin-peanut sauce stands in for the traditional rémoulade in this take on the New Orleans classic.

SAUCE:

- 1 teaspoon dark sesame oil
- 2 tablespoons chopped onion
- 1 teaspoon minced peeled fresh ginger
- 3 tablespoons hoisin sauce
- 1 tablespoon creamy peanut butter
- 1 tablespoon fresh lime juice
- ¼ teaspoon sugar

CATFISH:

- ¼ cup Thai chile sauce
- 2 garlic cloves, minced
- 4 (6-ounce) farm-raised catfish fillets
  Cooking spray

REMAINING INGREDIENTS:

- 4 (2½-ounce) hoagie rolls, split and lightly toasted
- 2 cups shredded napa (Chinese) cabbage

1. To prepare sauce, heat sesame oil in a small saucepan over medium heat. Add chopped onion and minced ginger, and cook 2 minutes, stirring frequently. Reduce heat to low. Add hoisin sauce, peanut butter, lime juice, and sugar, and cook for 3 minutes, stirring frequently. Remove sauce from heat, and set aside.

2. Prepare grill or broiler.

3. To prepare catfish, combine chile sauce and garlic in a large zip-top plastic bag. Add catfish; seal and marinate in refrigerator 30 minutes, turning bag occasionally.

4. Remove fish from marinade; discard marinade. Place fish on a grill rack or broiler pan coated with cooking spray. Cook 10 minutes or until fish flakes easily when tested with a fork.

5. Spread 1 tablespoon sauce over bottom half of each hoagie roll; top each serving with ½ cup cabbage, 1 fillet, and top half of roll. Serve immediately. Yield: 4 servings (serving size: 1 sandwich).

CALORIES 401 (27% from fat); FAT 12.1g (sat 4.1g, mono 3.5g, poly 3.2g); PROTEIN 30.1g; CARB 43.7g; FIBER 3.2g; CHOL 74mg; IRON 1.8mg; SODIUM 722mg; CALC 121mg

Cajun Catfish Wraps with Slaw

Crispy, spicy catfish meets its match with the vegetable crunch of our tangy cabbage slaw.

SLAW:

3½ cups thinly sliced red or green cabbage
¼ cup light mayonnaise
1½ tablespoons cider vinegar
½ teaspoon sugar

WRAPS:

1 tablespoon all-purpose flour
1 tablespoon paprika
1½ teaspoons dried thyme
1½ teaspoons dried oregano
1 teaspoon garlic powder
1 teaspoon black pepper
½ teaspoon salt
¼ teaspoon ground red pepper
4 (6-ounce) farm-raised catfish fillets
1 tablespoon butter or stick margarine
4 (8-inch) fat-free flour tortillas

1. To prepare slaw, combine first 4 ingredients in a bowl; cover and chill.

2. To prepare wraps, combine flour and next 7 ingredients in a shallow dish. Dredge fish fillets in flour mixture. Melt butter in a large nonstick skillet over medium-high heat. Add fillets; sauté 5 minutes. Turn fillets over; cook 4 minutes or until fish flakes easily when tested with a fork.

3. Warm tortillas according to package directions. Cut each fillet lengthwise into 4 pieces. Arrange 4 fillet pieces on each tortilla; top each serving with about ¾ cup slaw; roll up. Yield: 4 servings (serving size: 1 wrap).

CALORIES 397 (27% from fat); FAT 11.7g (sat 3.7g, mono 3.9g, poly 2.7g); PROTEIN 35.6g; CARB 36.6g; FIBER 3g; CHOL 106mg; IRON 4.7mg; SODIUM 918mg; CALC 126mg

Baked Cornmeal-Crusted Grouper Sandwich with Tartar Sauce

Cod, halibut, or sole are good substitutes for grouper.

GROUPER:

½ cup yellow cornmeal
½ teaspoon salt
¼ teaspoon ground red pepper
¼ cup 2% reduced-fat milk
4 (6-ounce) grouper fillets
Cooking spray

Cajun Catfish Wraps with Slaw

TARTAR SAUCE:

½ cup low-fat mayonnaise
2 tablespoons chopped green onions
1 tablespoon sweet pickle relish
1½ teaspoons capers
1½ teaspoons fresh lemon juice
½ teaspoon Worcestershire sauce

ADDITIONAL INGREDIENT:

4 (1½-ounce) hamburger buns, split

1. Preheat oven to 450°.

2. To prepare grouper, combine cornmeal, salt, and red pepper in a shallow dish, stirring well with a fork. Place milk in a shallow bowl.

3. Dip each fillet in milk, and dredge in cornmeal mixture. Place fish on a baking sheet coated with cooking spray. Bake at 450° for 10 minutes or until fish is done, turning once.

4. To prepare tartar sauce, combine the mayonnaise and next 5 ingredients, stirring with a whisk.

5. Spread 2 tablespoons tartar sauce over cut sides of each bun, and place one grouper fillet on bottom half of bun. Top with remaining bun halves. Yield: 4 servings (serving size: 1 sandwich).

CALORIES 443 (29% from fat); FAT 14.3g (sat 2.6g, mono 4.5g, poly 6.6g); PROTEIN 38.5g; CARB 38.3g; FIBER 2.5g; CHOL 75mg; IRON 3.2mg; SODIUM 961mg; CALC 110mg

Arugula-Cheese Grinder with Basil Mayonnaise

This vegetarian sandwich can be made with almost any combination of cheese or bread; we particularly like creamy Havarti cheese and crusty French bread.

```
 3  tablespoons light mayonnaise
 1  tablespoon minced fresh basil
¼  teaspoon salt
⅛  teaspoon black pepper
 4  (3-ounce) loaves French bread
 8  (½-inch-thick) slices tomato
¾  cup alfalfa sprouts
 4  (½-ounce) slices reduced-fat Havarti cheese
20  arugula leaves
```

1. Combine first 4 ingredients. Cut bread loaves in half horizontally; spread mayonnaise mixture evenly over cut sides of bread. Arrange 2 tomato slices over bottom half of each loaf, and top with 3 tablespoons alfalfa sprouts, 1 cheese slice, and 5 arugula leaves. Top with remaining bread halves, and serve immediately. Yield: 4 servings (serving size: 1 sandwich).

CALORIES 315 (27% from fat); FAT 9.3g (sat 2.9g, mono 3.3g, poly 2.4g); PROTEIN 12g; CARB 45.3g; FIBER 3.3g; CHOL 9mg; IRON 2.6mg; SODIUM 832mg; CALC 188mg

Arugula-Cheese Grinder with Basil Mayonnaise

Hummus Club Sandwiches

```
 3  tablespoons plain fat-free yogurt
 2  tablespoons water
 1  tablespoon lemon juice
 1  tablespoon tahini (sesame-seed paste)
½  teaspoon ground cumin
¼  teaspoon salt
 2  garlic cloves, peeled
 1  (15½-ounce) can chickpeas, drained
12  (1-ounce) slices whole-wheat bread
 2  cups shredded Bibb lettuce
 8  (¼-inch-thick) slices tomato
 4  (¼-inch-thick) slices red onion
 1  cup (⅛-inch-thick) slices cucumber
 4  cups alfalfa sprouts (4 ounces)
```

1. Combine first 8 ingredients in a food processor or blender; process until smooth.
2. Spread 2 tablespoons hummus over each of 4 bread slices. Top each slice with ½ cup lettuce, 2 tomato slices, 1 onion slice, 1 bread slice, ¼ cup cucumber, and 1 cup sprouts. Spread 2 tablespoons hummus over remaining bread slices; place on top of sandwiches. Cut sandwiches diagonally into quarters; secure with wooden picks. Yield: 4 servings (serving size: 1 sandwich).

CALORIES 398 (18% from fat); FAT 7.8g (sat 1.3g, mono 2.7g, poly 2.7g); PROTEIN 17.6g; CARB 67.3g; FIBER 8.3g; CHOL 0mg; IRON 5.9mg; SODIUM 760mg; CALC 185mg

Garden Grilled Cheese

```
 8  teaspoons Dijon mustard
 8  (1-ounce) slices sourdough bread
 1  cup (4 ounces) shredded reduced-fat
     sharp cheddar cheese
½  cup drained canned artichoke hearts, sliced
1⅓  cups sliced bottled roasted red bell peppers
Cooking spray
```

1. Spread 2 teaspoons mustard on 1 bread slice; top with ¼ cup cheese, 2 tablespoons artichokes, ⅓ cup bell peppers, and 1 bread slice. Repeat procedure with remaining mustard, bread, cheese, artichokes, and bell peppers.
2. Heat a large nonstick skillet coated with cooking spray over medium heat. Add sandwiches to pan; cook 2 minutes on each side or until golden brown. Yield: 4 servings (serving size: 1 sandwich).

CALORIES 264 (26% from fat); FAT 7.6g (sat 3.2g, mono 1.5g, poly 0.3g); PROTEIN 14.8g; CARB 34.7g; FIBER 0.9g; CHOL 19mg; IRON 2.9mg; SODIUM 951mg; CALC 321mg

Piadini with Cherry Tomatoes and Smoked Mozzarella

For these sandwiches, you can use any small sweet tomatoes, such as cherry, grape, or pear. In a pinch, you can substitute store-bought flatbread for the crust. If you do, heat the bread and melt the cheese before filling the sandwiches so they will stay together.

CRUST:
2¼ cups bread flour, divided
1 package dry yeast (about 2¼ teaspoons)
1 cup plus 2 tablespoons warm water (100° to 110°), divided
½ teaspoon salt
Cooking spray
¾ cup (3 ounces) shredded smoked mozzarella cheese, divided

FILLING:
1½ cups yellow cherry tomatoes, halved
1½ cups red cherry tomatoes, halved
½ cup thinly sliced fresh basil
3 tablespoons balsamic vinegar
1 tablespoon extravirgin olive oil
¼ teaspoon salt
¼ teaspoon freshly ground black pepper
1 garlic clove, minced

1. To prepare crust, lightly spoon flour into dry measuring cups; level with a knife. Dissolve yeast in ½ cup warm water in a large bowl; stir in ½ cup flour. Let stand 30 minutes. Add ½ cup plus 2 tablespoons warm water, 1½ cups flour, and salt, stirring to form a soft dough. Turn dough out onto a floured surface. Knead until smooth and elastic (about 8 minutes); add enough of remaining flour, 1 tablespoon at a time, to prevent dough from sticking to hands.
2. Place dough in a large bowl coated with cooking spray, turning to coat top. Cover the dough and let rise in a warm place (85°), free from drafts, for 45 minutes or until doubled in size. (Gently press two fingers into dough. If indentation remains, dough has risen enough.) Punch dough down; cover and let rest 5 minutes.
3. Divide dough into 4 equal portions. Working with one portion at a time (cover remaining dough to prevent drying), roll each into a 7-inch circle on a lightly floured surface. Heat a large nonstick skillet coated with cooking spray over medium-high heat. Place one dough circle in pan. Sprinkle with 3 tablespoons mozzarella cheese. Cook 3 minutes or until cheese melts and dough is browned on the bottom. Repeat procedure with remaining dough circles and cheese.
4. To prepare filling, combine cherry tomatoes and remaining ingredients; toss gently to coat. Spoon ¾ cup tomato mixture onto each crust; fold over. Yield: 4 servings (serving size: 1 piadini).

CALORIES 359 (21% from fat); FAT 8.5g (sat 3.6g, mono 2.6g, poly 0.5g); PROTEIN 14.9g; CARB 59g; FIBER 3.7g; CHOL 17mg; IRON 4.6mg; SODIUM 485mg; CALC 143mg

Black Bean Burgers with Spicy Cucumber and Red Pepper Relish

The cucumber releases some liquid while chilling, so serve the relish with a slotted spoon.

RELISH:
⅔ cup finely chopped peeled cucumber
½ cup finely chopped red bell pepper
¼ cup finely chopped red onion
1 tablespoon fresh lime juice
1 tablespoon honey
1 teaspoon finely chopped dill
⅛ teaspoon salt
Dash of ground red pepper

BURGERS:
1 (15-ounce) can black beans, rinsed and drained
½ cup dry breadcrumbs
¼ cup minced red onion
½ teaspoon dried oregano
¼ teaspoon ground cumin
⅛ teaspoon black pepper
1 large egg
Cooking spray
¼ cup light mayonnaise
4 (1½-ounce) hamburger buns

1. To prepare relish, combine first 8 ingredients in a medium bowl. Cover and chill 2 hours.
2. To prepare burgers, place beans in a large bowl; partially mash with a fork. Stir in breadcrumbs and next 5 ingredients. Divide bean mixture into 4 equal portions, shaping each into a ½-inch-thick patty.
3. Prepare grill.
4. Place patties on grill rack coated with cooking spray; grill 5 minutes on each side or until thoroughly heated. Spread 1 tablespoon mayonnaise on the bottom half of each bun; top each with a patty, ¼ cup relish, and top half of bun. Yield: 4 servings (serving size: 1 burger).

CALORIES 375 (23% from fat); FAT 9.5g (sat 1.9g, mono 2.4g, poly 3.7g); PROTEIN 14.6g; CARB 59.2g; FIBER 5.7g; CHOL 60mg; IRON 4.7mg; SODIUM 767mg; CALC 136mg

Grilled Tomato
Sandwiches

Grilled Tomato Sandwiches

12 (¾-inch-thick) slices tomato
½ teaspoon salt, divided
12 (1-ounce) slices sourdough bread, toasted
Cooking spray
1 tablespoon balsamic vinegar
¼ teaspoon freshly ground black pepper
6 tablespoons low-fat mayonnaise
1 teaspoon fresh lemon juice
1 garlic clove, minced
3 cups trimmed arugula

1. Prepare grill.
2. Sprinkle tomato slices with ⅛ teaspoon salt. Place tomato slices, salted sides down, on paper towels. Let stand 10 minutes. Repeat procedure on other side of tomato slices.
3. Place tomato slices and bread slices on grill rack coated with cooking spray; grill 2 minutes, turning once. Sprinkle tomato slices with ¼ teaspoon salt, vinegar, and pepper.
4. Combine mayonnaise, juice, and garlic in a bowl. Spread 1 tablespoon mayonnaise mixture on each of 6 bread slices; top each with 2 tomato slices, ½ cup arugula, and 1 bread slice. Serve sandwiches immediately. Yield: 6 servings (serving size: 1 sandwich).

CALORIES 215 (14% from fat); FAT 3.3g (sat 0.6g, mono 1g, poly 1.2g); PROTEIN 6.5g; CARB 41.1g; FIBER 3.5g; CHOL 0mg; IRON 2.3mg; SODIUM 697mg; CALC 68mg

Falafel-Stuffed Pitas

The patties will seem small when you're forming them, but they fit perfectly in the pita halves.

FALAFEL:
¼ cup dry breadcrumbs
¼ cup chopped fresh cilantro
1½ teaspoons ground cumin
½ teaspoon salt
¼ teaspoon ground red pepper
2 garlic cloves, crushed
1 large egg
1 (15-ounce) can chickpeas, drained
1 tablespoon olive oil
SAUCE:
½ cup plain low-fat yogurt
2 tablespoons fresh lemon juice
2 tablespoons tahini (sesame-seed paste)
1 garlic clove, minced
REMAINING INGREDIENTS:
4 (6-inch) whole-wheat pitas, cut in half
8 curly leaf lettuce leaves
16 (¼-inch-thick) slices tomato

1. To prepare falafel, place first 8 ingredients in a food processor; process until smooth. Divide mixture into 16 equal portions; shape each portion into a ¼-inch-thick patty. Heat oil in a large nonstick skillet over medium-high heat. Add patties; cook 5 minutes on each side or until patties are browned.
2. To prepare sauce, combine yogurt, juice, tahini, and 1 garlic clove, stirring mixture with a whisk. Spread about 1½ tablespoons sauce into each pita half. Fill each pita half with 1 lettuce leaf, 2 tomato slices, and 2 patties. Yield: 4 servings (serving size: 2 stuffed pita halves).

CALORIES 403 (28% from fat); FAT 12.6g (sat 1.9g, mono 5.6g, poly 3.9g); PROTEIN 15g; CARB 59g; FIBER 6.8g; CHOL 56mg; IRON 4.4mg; SODIUM 901mg; CALC 188mg

Greek-Style Burgers with Feta Aïoli

We've topped this Greek-flavored burger with our low-fat version of the garlicky French mayonnaise aïoli (ay-OH-lee) to which we've added feta cheese.

AÏOLI:
- ½ cup (2 ounces) crumbled feta cheese
- 2 tablespoons light mayonnaise
- 2 tablespoons plain fat-free yogurt
- ¼ teaspoon coarsely ground black pepper
- 1 garlic clove, minced

BURGERS:
- 1 (1-ounce) slice white bread
- 5 (½-inch-thick) slices red onion
- Cooking spray
- 1 pound ground round
- ⅓ cup chopped bottled roasted red bell peppers
- ¼ cup chopped fresh parsley
- 1 teaspoon dried oregano
- ¼ teaspoon salt
- ¼ teaspoon coarsely ground black pepper
- 1 (10-ounce) package frozen chopped spinach, thawed, drained, and squeezed dry
- 1 large egg, lightly beaten
- 2 garlic cloves, crushed
- 5 (1½-ounce) sourdough sandwich buns
- 5 lettuce leaves
- 5 tomato slices

1. Combine first 5 ingredients in a blender or food processor, and process 1 minute or until smooth. Cover and chill.

2. Prepare grill or broiler.

3. To prepare burgers, place 1 bread slice in blender or food processor; process until coarse crumbs form to measure ⅔ cup. Set aside. Place onion slices on a grill rack or broiler pan coated with cooking spray, and cook 2 minutes on each side. Set aside.

4. Combine breadcrumbs, beef, and next 8 ingredients in a large bowl. Divide beef mixture into 5 equal portions, shaping each portion into a ½-inch-thick patty. Place patties on grill rack or broiler pan coated with cooking spray, and cook for 6 minutes on each side or until burgers are done. Spread 1½ tablespoons aïoli over bottom half of each bun. Place the patties on bottom halves of buns, and top each with 1 onion slice, 1 lettuce leaf, 1 tomato slice, and top half of bun. Yield: 5 servings (serving size: 1 burger).

CALORIES 385 (28% from fat); FAT 12.1g (sat 4.4g, mono 4.4g, poly 1.8g); PROTEIN 30.5g; CARB 38g; FIBER 4.3g; CHOL 110mg; IRON 5.7mg; SODIUM 712mg; CALC 225mg

Meat Loaf Burgers with Caramelized Onions

The beef patties are delicate, so take extra care when turning them. Serve with corn on the cob. The caramelized onions also pair well with a grilled steak.

ONIONS:
- 1 teaspoon olive oil
- 4½ cups vertically sliced red onion (about 2 medium onions)
- ¼ teaspoon salt
- 1 tablespoon sugar
- 2 tablespoons balsamic vinegar

BURGERS:
- Cooking spray
- 1 cup finely chopped green bell pepper
- 1 cup finely chopped celery
- 1 cup crushed whole-wheat crackers (about 20 crackers)
- ⅓ cup ketchup, divided
- ½ teaspoon dried thyme
- ¼ teaspoon salt
- 1 pound ground sirloin
- 1 large egg
- 12 (1¼-ounce) slices rye bread, toasted

1. Prepare grill or broiler.

2. To prepare onions, heat olive oil in a large non-stick skillet over medium-high heat. Add onion and ¼ teaspoon salt; sauté 12 minutes or until golden brown. Stir in sugar and vinegar; cook 30 seconds. Remove from pan.

3. To prepare burgers, heat pan coated with cooking spray over medium-high heat. Add bell pepper and celery; sauté 3 minutes or until tender.

4. Combine bell pepper mixture, crackers, ¼ cup ketchup, thyme, ¼ teaspoon salt, beef, and egg in a large bowl. Divide mixture into 6 equal portions, shaping each into a ½-inch-thick patty.

5. Place patties on a grill rack or broiler pan coated with cooking spray; cook 5 minutes. Carefully turn patties over; brush with remaining ketchup. Cook 5 minutes or until done.

6. Place 1 burger on each of 6 toasted rye bread slices. Top each burger with ¼ cup caramelized onions and 1 bread slice. Yield: 6 servings (serving size: 1 burger).

CALORIES 419 (29% from fat); FAT 13.4g (sat 4.3g, mono 6g, poly 1.3g); PROTEIN 23.1g; CARB 51.8g; FIBER 6.6g; CHOL 86mg; IRON 4.2mg; SODIUM 906mg; CALC 92mg

Smothered Burgers

This robust open-faced burger is topped with onion, mushrooms, and Swiss. Serve with baked potato wedges.

Cooking spray
2 cups vertically sliced onion
2 teaspoons sugar
¾ teaspoon salt, divided
½ teaspoon freshly ground black pepper, divided
1 (8-ounce) package presliced mushrooms
2 tablespoons Worcestershire sauce
1 pound ground round
4 (1-ounce) slices Texas toast
½ cup (2 ounces) shredded Swiss cheese

1. Prepare grill or broiler.

2. Heat a medium nonstick skillet coated with cooking spray over medium heat. Add sliced onion; cover and cook for 5 minutes, stirring occasionally. Add sugar, ¼ teaspoon salt, and ¼ teaspoon pepper, and cook, uncovered, for 5 minutes or until tender, stirring frequently. Remove onion from pan, and keep warm.

3. Heat the pan coated with cooking spray over medium-high heat. Add mushrooms and ¼ teaspoon salt; sauté 5 minutes or until tender.

4. Combine ¼ teaspoon salt, ¼ teaspoon pepper, Worcestershire sauce, and beef. Divide the mixture into 4 equal portions, shaping each into a ½-inch-thick patty.

5. Preheat broiler.

6. Place patties on a grill rack or broiler pan coated with cooking spray; grill 5 minutes on each side or until done. Remove patties from pan. Place bread on grill rack or broiler pan; grill 1 minute on each side or until toasted.

7. Arrange bread on a baking sheet. Top each bread slice with 1 patty, ¼ cup onion, ¼ cup mushrooms, and 2 tablespoons cheese, and broil for 2 minutes or until cheese melts. Yield: 4 servings (serving size: 1 burger).

CALORIES 393 (40% from fat); FAT 17.5g (sat 7.5g, mono 6.7g, poly 1.4g); PROTEIN 31.1g; CARB 27.1g; FIBER 2.5g; CHOL 91mg; IRON 4.4mg; SODIUM 786mg; CALC 204mg

Deluxe Roast Beef Sandwich

A great sandwich can be easy. The three-ingredient sauce makes the difference.

 1 tablespoon light mayonnaise
 2 teaspoons prepared horseradish
 2 teaspoons bottled chili sauce
 2 (1-ounce) slices rye bread
 1 romaine lettuce leaf
 3 ounces thinly sliced deli roast beef
 2 (¼-inch-thick) slices tomato
 1 (⅛-inch-thick) slice red onion,
     separated into rings

1. Combine first 3 ingredients. Spread mayonnaise mixture on one bread slice. Top with lettuce leaf, sliced roast beef, tomato slices, onion slice, and remaining bread slice. Yield: 1 serving (serving size: 1 sandwich).

CALORIES 412 (28% from fat); FAT 12.7g (sat 4.4g, mono 5.3g, poly 2.9g); PROTEIN 25g; CARB 51.2g; FIBER 5.6g; CHOL 5mg; IRON 4.2mg; SODIUM 1,122mg; CALC 86mg

Slow-Cooker Barbecue-Beef Sandwiches

Store the barbecued beef in an airtight container in the refrigerator for up to five days.

 5 tablespoons dark brown sugar, divided
 ¾ teaspoon black pepper
 2 (1-pound) flank steaks
 1 cup chopped onion
 1 cup tomato paste
 3 tablespoons Worcestershire sauce
 3 tablespoons molasses
 3 tablespoons cider vinegar
 1 tablespoon chili powder
 1 teaspoon garlic powder
 1 teaspoon dry mustard
 1 teaspoon ground cumin
 ½ teaspoon salt
 10 (2½-ounce) submarine rolls, halved
    Red onion slices (optional)
    Dill pickle slices (optional)

1. Combine 1 tablespoon brown sugar and pepper, and rub over both sides of steaks. Combine ¼ cup brown sugar, chopped onion, and next 9 ingredients in an electric slow cooker. Add steaks; turn to coat. Cover with lid; cook on high-heat setting for

1 hour. Reduce heat setting to low; cook for 7 hours. Remove steaks; reserve sauce. Shred steaks with 2 forks. Return shredded steak to cooker; stir into sauce. Spoon ½ cup steak mixture onto bottom half of each roll; top with onion slices and pickles, if desired. Cover with tops of rolls. Yield: 10 servings (serving size: 1 sandwich).

CALORIES 435 (22% from fat); FAT 10.4g (sat 4.2g, mono 4.2g, poly 1.2g); PROTEIN 26g; CARB 57.2g; FIBER 3.1g; CHOL 47mg; IRON 4.9mg; SODIUM 668mg; CALC 77mg

Blue Cheese-Pepper Steak Wraps

 12 ounces boned top round steak
  2 teaspoons dry mustard
  ½ teaspoon black pepper
  ¼ teaspoon garlic powder
  ¼ teaspoon salt
     Cooking spray
  2 cups sliced mushrooms
  1 onion, cut into ¼-inch-thick wedges
  1 medium red bell pepper, seeded and cut into
     ¼-inch strips
  2 tablespoons water
 1½ tablespoons red wine vinegar
  ½ cup (2 ounces) crumbled blue cheese or feta
     cheese
  4 (8-inch) fat-free flour tortillas
  2 cups chopped romaine lettuce

1. Trim the fat from the beef, and slice into ¼-inch strips. Set aside.
2. Combine mustard, black pepper, garlic, and salt in a large bowl. Add beef, tossing to coat.
3. Heat a large nonstick skillet coated with cooking spray over medium-high heat. Add the beef mixture; sauté 4 minutes or until done. Remove from pan; keep warm. Add mushrooms, onion, and bell pepper to pan; sauté 2 minutes. Add water; cover and cook 5 minutes, stirring occasionally. Stir in beef mixture and vinegar. Remove from heat; stir in cheese.
4. Warm the tortillas according to package instructions. Spoon 1 cup mixture onto each tortilla; top each serving with ½ cup lettuce, and roll up. Yield: 4 servings (serving size: 1 wrap).

CALORIES 310 (24% from fat); FAT 8.1g (sat 3.9g, mono 2.5g, poly 0.5g); PROTEIN 26.3g; CARB 32.4g; FIBER 3.3g; CHOL 56mg; IRON 4.1mg; SODIUM 732mg; CALC 103mg

Barbecue Pork-and-Coleslaw Hoagies

 1 (1-pound) pork tenderloin
½ cup spicy barbecue sauce (such as Kraft Spicy Cajun), divided
 Cooking spray
2½ cups packaged cabbage-and-carrot coleslaw
2½ tablespoons low-fat sour cream
1½ tablespoons light mayonnaise
1½ teaspoons sugar
2½ teaspoons prepared horseradish
 4 (2½-ounce) hoagie rolls with sesame seeds
 Dill pickle slices (optional)

1. Prepare grill or broiler.
2. Trim fat from pork; cut pork in half lengthwise. Brush the pork with 3 tablespoons barbecue sauce. Insert a meat thermometer into the thickest portion of pork. Place the pork on a grill rack or broiler pan coated with cooking spray. Cook the pork for 15 minutes or until meat thermometer registers 155° (slightly pink), turning pork occasionally. Cover pork with foil and let stand 10 minutes. Cut into ¼-inch-thick slices.
3. Combine the coleslaw and next 4 ingredients in a medium bowl, and set aside.
4. Combine the pork and 3 tablespoons barbecue sauce. Brush cut sides of bread with 2 tablespoons barbecue sauce. Divide pork evenly among bottom halves of rolls. Top each roll half with about ½ cup coleslaw and pickles, if desired; cover with roll tops. Yield: 4 servings (serving size: 1 sandwich).

CALORIES 398 (23% from fat); FAT 10.2g (sat 3.6g, mono 4g, poly 1.7g); PROTEIN 34g; CARB 45g; FIBER 3.4g; CHOL 88mg; IRON 4.6mg; SODIUM 717mg; CALC 106mg

Our American Hero

½ cup light mayonnaise
¼ cup thinly sliced fresh basil
½ teaspoon coarsely ground black pepper
 1 (16-ounce) loaf Italian or French bread
 1 pound thinly sliced lean deli roast beef
 1 large tomato, cored and thinly sliced
 1 cup thinly sliced red onion
 1 large yellow bell pepper, seeded and thinly sliced into rings
 1 cup trimmed arugula, watercress, or gourmet salad greens
⅛ teaspoon salt
⅛ teaspoon black pepper

1. Combine mayonnaise, basil, and ground pepper; chill 15 minutes.
2. Cut bread loaf in half horizontally, and spread mayonnaise mixture over bottom half of bread. Top bread with sliced roast beef, remaining ingredients, and top half of bread. Cut loaf into 6 pieces. Yield: 6 servings (serving size: 1 sandwich).

CALORIES 400 (28% from fat); FAT 12.6g (sat 3.5g, mono 4.5g, poly 3.2g); PROTEIN 22.6g; CARB 48.5g; FIBER 3.2g; CHOL 7mg; IRON 4mg; SODIUM 1,104mg; CALC 29mg

Our American Hero

Open-Faced Bacon, Lettuce,
and Fried Green Tomato Sandwiches

Open-Faced Bacon, Lettuce, and Fried Green Tomato Sandwiches

Double-breading the tomato slices gives them a crunchy coating. Soaking the tomatoes in hot water draws out their moisture, which helps keep them crisp when cooked. On their own, the fried green tomatoes in this recipe are a classic Southern side dish.

     2 medium green tomatoes, cut into 12
          (¼-inch-thick) slices (about 1 pound)
     2 tablespoons fat-free milk
     4 large egg whites, lightly beaten
  1½ cups yellow cornmeal
     ¾ teaspoon salt
     ¼ teaspoon freshly ground black pepper
     2 tablespoons olive oil, divided
     5 tablespoons light mayonnaise
     1 teaspoon fresh lemon juice
     ¼ teaspoon hot sauce
     6 (1½-ounce) slices white bread, toasted
     6 Bibb lettuce leaves
     9 bacon slices, cooked and cut in half
     2 tablespoons chopped fresh chives

1. Place tomato slices in a large bowl; cover with hot water. Let stand 15 minutes. Drain and pat dry with paper towels. Combine milk and egg whites, stirring with a whisk. Combine cornmeal, salt, and pepper in a shallow dish, stirring with a whisk. Dip each tomato slice in milk mixture; dredge in cornmeal mixture. Return tomato slices, one at a time, to milk mixture; dredge in cornmeal mixture.
2. Heat 1 tablespoon oil in a large nonstick skillet over medium-high heat. Add half of tomato slices; cook 4 minutes on each side or until crisp and golden. Repeat procedure with remaining oil and tomato slices.
3. Combine mayonnaise, juice, and hot sauce, stirring with a whisk. Spread about 1 tablespoon mayonnaise mixture onto each bread slice, and top with 1 lettuce leaf, 3 bacon pieces, and 2 tomato slices. Sprinkle each sandwich with 1 teaspoon chopped chives. Serve immediately. Yield: 6 servings (serving size: 1 sandwich).

CALORIES 386 (30% from fat); FAT 12.8g (sat 2.8g, mono 4.5g, poly 2.6g); PROTEIN 12.2g; CARB 56.2g; FIBER 3.9g; CHOL 16mg; IRON 2.2mg; SODIUM 834mg; CALC 44mg

Grilled Cuban Sandwiches

     2 tablespoons Dijon mustard
     1 (8-ounce) loaf French bread, cut in half
          horizontally
     6 ounces reduced-fat Swiss cheese, thinly sliced
          (such as Alpine Lace)
     6 ounces deli-sliced ham (such as Hillshire
          Farms)
     8 sandwich-sliced dill pickles
  Cooking spray

1. Spread mustard evenly over cut sides of bread. Arrange half of cheese and half of ham on bottom half of loaf; top with pickle slices. Repeat layers with remaining cheese and ham; cover with top half of loaf. Cut into quarters.
2. Heat a large heavy skillet coated with cooking spray over medium-high heat. Add sandwiches; press with a heavy skillet (such as cast iron). Cook 2 minutes on each side. Yield: 4 servings (serving size: 1 sandwich).

CALORIES 335 (30% from fat); FAT 11g (sat 5.3g, mono 2.1g, poly 0.9g); PROTEIN 23.1g; CARB 36g; FIBER 3g; CHOL 43mg; IRON 2.8mg; SODIUM 1,301mg; CALC 318mg

Prosciutto-and-Fontina Panini

     1 (5.25-ounce) package focaccia (Italian flat-
          bread) or 1 (8-ounce) package Italian cheese-
          flavored pizza crust (such as Boboli)
     8 very thin slices prosciutto (about 2 ounces)
     ¼ cup (1 ounce) shredded fontina cheese
     1 cup trimmed arugula or watercress
     2 (⅛-inch-thick) red onion slices, separated
          into rings
     2 teaspoons balsamic vinegar
     ⅛ teaspoon black pepper

1. Preheat oven to 300°.
2. Slice each bread round in half horizontally. Divide prosciutto slices between bottom halves of bread, and top each bread half with fontina cheese, arugula, and red onion slices. Drizzle balsamic vinegar over sandwiches, and sprinkle with pepper; cover each sandwich with top half of bread. Wrap sandwiches tightly in foil, and bake at 300° for 15 minutes. Yield: 2 servings (serving size: 1 sandwich).

CALORIES 330 (31% from fat); FAT 11.5g (sat 5.6g, mono 2.5g, poly 0.6g); PROTEIN 20.2g; CARB 40.3g; FIBER 4.3g; CHOL 33mg; IRON 0.9mg; SODIUM 846mg; CALC 220mg

Croque Monsieur

Similar to a Monte Cristo, a croque monsieur is a French-style grilled ham and cheese sandwich that is dipped in egg batter and then cooked in a skillet. Our version is more like stuffed French toast than a sandwich, though. Keep the finished ones warm in a 200° oven while you're cooking the others.

4 (1½-ounce) slices French bread
4 teaspoons honey mustard
6 ounces reduced-fat deli ham, thinly sliced
4 (1-ounce) slices reduced-fat Swiss cheese
½ cup fat-free milk
3 large egg whites
Cooking spray

1. Cut a slit in each bread slice to form a pocket. Spread 1 teaspoon honey mustard into each bread pocket. Divide ham and cheese evenly among bread pockets.
2. Combine milk and egg whites in a shallow bowl, stirring with a whisk. Dip sandwiches, 1 at a time, in milk mixture, turning to coat.
3. Heat a large nonstick skillet coated with cooking spray over medium-high heat. Add 2 sandwiches, and cook 3 minutes on each side or until sandwiches are golden brown. Repeat the procedure with the remaining sandwiches. Yield: 4 servings (serving size: 1 sandwich).

CALORIES 293 (30% from fat); FAT 9.8g (sat 5.2g, mono 0.8g, poly 0.8g); PROTEIN 22.3g; CARB 27.9g; FIBER 1.3g; CHOL 40mg; IRON 1.6mg; SODIUM 649mg; CALC 475mg

Monte Cristo Sandwiches

Raspberry jam puts a nontraditional yet delicious spin on these quick-to-prepare sandwiches.

3 tablespoons honey mustard
8 (1-ounce) slices white bread
4 (1-ounce) slices Swiss cheese
¼ pound thinly sliced smoked ham
⅓ cup fat-free milk
2 large egg whites
Cooking spray
2 teaspoons powdered sugar
¼ cup seedless raspberry jam

1. Spread about 1 teaspoon mustard over each bread slice. Place 1 cheese slice on each of 4 bread slices. Divide the ham evenly over cheese. Cover with remaining bread slices, mustard sides down. Combine milk and egg whites in a shallow dish. Dip both sides of each sandwich into milk mixture.
2. Heat a large nonstick skillet coated with cooking spray over medium heat. Cook the sandwiches for 3 minutes on each side or until lightly browned. Sprinkle each sandwich with ½ teaspoon sugar; top each with 1 tablespoon jam. Yield: 4 servings (serving size: 1 sandwich).

CALORIES 387 (27% from fat); FAT 11.5g (sat 6g, mono 3.7g, poly 0.9g); PROTEIN 20.7g; CARB 49.1g; FIBER 1.6g; CHOL 40mg; IRON 2.1mg; SODIUM 840mg; CALC 366mg

Monte Cristo Sandwiches

Ginger-Peanut Chicken-Salad Wraps

You can substitute slices of breast meat from prepackaged rotisserie chicken, which makes the preparation easier, but the dish will be a little higher in fat and sodium. You can find it with the other deli items in the meat section.

    1   teaspoon olive oil
    6   (4-ounce) skinned, boned chicken breast
        halves
    1   cup chopped seeded peeled cucumber
    ¾   cup chopped red bell pepper
  1½   tablespoons sugar
    1   tablespoon minced peeled fresh ginger
    3   tablespoons fresh lime juice
    1   tablespoon low-sodium soy sauce
    ¼   teaspoon salt
    ¼   teaspoon ground red pepper
    1   garlic clove, crushed
    ¼   cup creamy peanut butter
    2   tablespoons water
    3   tablespoons chopped fresh cilantro
    8   (8-inch) fat-free flour tortillas
    4   cups chopped romaine lettuce

1. Heat oil in a large nonstick skillet over medium-high heat. Add chicken; cook 5 minutes on each side or until done. Remove chicken from pan; cool. Shred chicken into bite-size pieces. Place chicken, cucumber, and bell pepper in a large bowl; set aside.
2. Place the sugar and the next 6 ingredients in a blender, and process mixture until smooth. Add peanut butter and water; process until smooth, scraping sides. Add the peanut butter mixture to chicken mixture; stir well. Add cilantro; toss well. Warm tortillas according to package directions. Spoon ½ cup chicken mixture onto each tortilla; top each serving with ½ cup lettuce; roll up. Yield: 8 servings (serving size: 1 wrap).

CALORIES 280 (19% from fat); FAT 5.9g (sat 1.1g, mono 2.7g, poly 1.6g); PROTEIN 25.8g; CARB 30.5g; FIBER 2.4g; CHOL 49mg; IRON 2.5mg; SODIUM 572mg; CALC 29mg

Turkey Pesto Sandwiches

    ¼   cup fat-free mayonnaise
    1   tablespoon commercial pesto
    1   teaspoon fresh lemon juice
    ½   teaspoon dried oregano
    ⅛   teaspoon black pepper
    4   (2-ounce) French bread rolls
    2   cups trimmed arugula
    8   ounces thinly sliced cooked turkey breast
    8   (¼-inch-thick) slices tomato
    4   (1-ounce) slices part-skim mozzarella cheese

1. Preheat broiler.
2. Combine first 5 ingredients.
3. Cut rolls in half horizontally; spread mayonnaise mixture evenly over cut sides of rolls. Divide arugula, turkey, and tomato slices evenly among bottom halves of rolls; top each with 1 cheese slice. Place bottom halves of rolls on a baking sheet. Broil 2 minutes or until cheese melts. Cover with top halves of rolls. Yield: 4 servings.

CALORIES 358 (26% from fat); FAT 10.5g (sat 4.8g, mono 4g, poly 0.8g); PROTEIN 31.2g; CARB 34.1g; FIBER 0.8g; CHOL 65mg; IRON 2.9mg; SODIUM 705mg; CALC 309mg

Turkey-Havarti Grinder

    ⅓   cup mango chutney
    2   tablespoons chopped unsalted, dry-roasted
        peanuts
    2   tablespoons light mayonnaise
  Dash of ground red pepper
    1   (16-ounce) loaf French bread
    1   pound very thinly sliced deli turkey breast
    6   curly leaf lettuce leaves
    2   ounces thinly sliced reduced-fat Havarti
        cheese
    6   sandwich-cut bread-and-butter pickles
    1   medium Red Delicious apple, cored and sliced
        into rings

1. Combine first 4 ingredients in a bowl. Cut bread loaf in half horizontally. Spread chutney mixture over bottom half of bread; top with turkey, lettuce, cheese, pickles, apple, and top half of bread. Cut loaf into 8 pieces. Yield: 8 servings (serving size: 1 sandwich).

CALORIES 308 (19% from fat); FAT 6.5g (sat 1.9g, mono 2.3g, poly 1.8g); PROTEIN 19g; CARB 41.2g; FIBER 2.7g; CHOL 6mg; IRON 2mg; SODIUM 937mg; CALC 114mg

Chicken and Brie Sandwich with Roasted Cherry Tomatoes

A good balsamic vinegar makes all the difference in the roasted cherry tomatoes, whose heat will immediately melt the soft Brie. The rind on the cheese is edible, so be sure to leave it on.

1 teaspoon olive oil
2 cups halved cherry tomatoes (about 1 pound)
2 tablespoons balsamic vinegar
1 tablespoon chopped fresh thyme
¼ teaspoon kosher salt
⅛ teaspoon black pepper
¼ cup low-fat mayonnaise
1 tablespoon whole-grain Dijon mustard
1 garlic clove, minced
1 (16-ounce) loaf French bread, cut in half horizontally
3 ounces Brie cheese, sliced
3 cups shredded cooked chicken breast (about 1 pound)
2 teaspoons extravirgin olive oil
1 teaspoon balsamic vinegar
⅛ teaspoon kosher salt
2 cups fresh spinach

1. Preheat oven to 300°.

2. Heat 1 teaspoon oil in a large nonstick skillet over medium-high heat. Add tomatoes, and cook 4 minutes, stirring once. Remove from heat, and stir in 2 tablespoons vinegar. Sprinkle the tomatoes with thyme, ¼ teaspoon salt, and pepper. Wrap handle of pan with foil, and bake at 300° for 15 minutes. Keep warm.

3. Combine mayonnaise, mustard, and garlic in a small bowl. Spread mayonnaise mixture evenly over top half of bread loaf. Spoon cherry tomatoes evenly over bottom half of loaf. Arrange Brie over tomatoes; top with chicken. Combine 2 teaspoons oil, 1 teaspoon vinegar, and ⅛ teaspoon salt in a medium bowl, stirring with a whisk. Add spinach, tossing gently to coat. Top chicken with spinach mixture; replace top half of bread. Cut loaf into 6 pieces. Yield: 6 servings (serving size: 1 sandwich).

CALORIES 440 (25% from fat); FAT 12.3g (sat 4.2g, mono 4.9g, poly 1.9g); PROTEIN 34.3g; CARB 46.7g; FIBER 3.9g; CHOL 78mg; IRON 3.7mg; SODIUM 826mg; CALC 119mg

Hot Browns

(pictured on page 264)

Sliced tomato, crumbled bacon, and savory cheddar cheese sauce smother shredded turkey in this open-faced sandwich. You can also use leftover chicken in place of the turkey. Broiling the sandwiches browns and melts the Parmesan cheese that tops them.

SAUCE:
1½ tablespoons butter
2 tablespoons all-purpose flour
¼ teaspoon salt
⅛ teaspoon paprika
⅛ teaspoon black pepper
1 cup 2% reduced-fat milk
½ cup (2 ounces) shredded reduced-fat extrasharp cheddar cheese
½ teaspoon Worcestershire sauce
⅛ teaspoon dry mustard

REMAINING INGREDIENTS:
12 (1-ounce) slices white bread, toasted
3 cups shredded cooked turkey (about 6 ounces)
12 (¼-inch-thick) slices tomato
5 bacon slices, cooked and crumbled
¼ cup (1 ounce) grated fresh Parmesan cheese

1. Preheat broiler.

2. To prepare sauce, melt butter in a saucepan over medium heat; stir in flour, salt, paprika, and pepper. Cook mixture 30 seconds, stirring constantly. Gradually add milk, stirring with a whisk. Cook 3 minutes or until thick, stirring constantly. Remove from heat. Add cheddar, Worcestershire, and mustard; stir with a whisk until smooth. Keep warm.

3. Arrange toast on a large baking sheet. Arrange turkey evenly over toast. Drizzle the sauce evenly over turkey; top each toast slice with 1 tomato slice. Sprinkle evenly with bacon and Parmesan. Broil 7 minutes or until thoroughly heated and lightly browned. Serve immediately. Yield: 6 servings (serving size: 2 open-faced sandwiches).

CALORIES 440 (30% from fat); FAT 14.9g (sat 6.2g, mono 4g, poly 1.6g); PROTEIN 34.6g; CARB 44.3g; FIBER 4.5g; CHOL 79mg; IRON 3.2mg; SODIUM 815mg; CALC 255mg

Turkey Sandwich with Red Pepper–Pine Nut Pesto and Caramelized Onions

Ciabatta is crunchy on the outside and soft in the middle. Since it is a thin loaf, focaccia would be a good substitute.

¼ cup chopped fresh basil
2 tablespoons grated fresh Parmesan cheese
1 tablespoon pine nuts, toasted
1 tablespoon water
2 garlic cloves, halved
1 (7-ounce) bottle roasted red bell peppers, drained
2 teaspoons olive oil
2 cups vertically sliced onion
2 teaspoons sugar
1 (8-ounce) loaf ciabatta
12 (1-ounce) slices cooked turkey breast
2 (1-ounce) slices fontina cheese
2 cups trimmed watercress

1. Place first 6 ingredients in a blender, and process until smooth.

2. Heat oil in a large nonstick skillet over medium-high heat. Add onion and sugar; cook 8 minutes or until onion is browned, stirring occasionally.

3. Cut bread loaf in half horizontally; spread pepper mixture evenly over cut sides of bread. Layer turkey, fontina cheese, onion, and watercress over bottom half of loaf; top with remaining loaf half. Cut loaf into 4 pieces. Serve immediately. Yield: 4 servings (serving size: 1 sandwich).

CALORIES 416 (25% from fat); FAT 11.5g (sat. 4.4g, mono 4.5g, poly 1.6g) PROTEIN 37.5g; CARB 39.9g; FIBER 3.6g; CHOL 90mg; IRON 3.4mg; SODIUM 572mg; CALC 217mg

Turkey Sandwich with Red
Pepper-Pine Nut Pesto and
Caramelized Onions

Grilled Tomato, Smoked
Turkey, and Muenster
Sandwich

Grilled Tomato, Smoked Turkey, and Muenster Sandwich

1 tablespoon minced red onion
3 tablespoons fat-free sour cream
1 tablespoon Dijon mustard
¼ teaspoon dried thyme
4 teaspoons butter, softened
4 (1½-ounce) slices sourdough bread
6 (1-ounce) slices smoked turkey breast
4 (½-inch-thick) slices tomato
2 (½-ounce) slices Muenster cheese

1. Combine first 4 ingredients in a bowl. Spread 1 teaspoon butter on 1 side of each bread slice. Spread 2 tablespoons sour cream mixture over the unbuttered side of each of 2 bread slices, and top each slice with 3 smoked turkey slices, 2 tomato slices, 1 cheese slice, and 1 bread slice (with buttered side up).
2. Heat a large nonstick skillet over medium heat. Add sandwiches; cover and cook 3 minutes on each side or until golden brown. Yield: 2 servings (serving size: 1 sandwich).

CALORIES 451 (28% from fat); FAT 14.2g (sat 8g, mono 4.5g, poly 0.9g); PROTEIN 27.9g; CARB 48.7g; FIBER 1.8g; CHOL 65mg; IRON 2.4mg; SODIUM 913mg; CALC 238mg

Smoked Turkey, Brie, Green Apple, and Watercress Sandwich

1½ tablespoons honey
1½ tablespoons mustard
1 (8-ounce) French bread baguette
6 ounces thinly sliced smoked turkey breast
¼ pound Brie cheese, thinly sliced
1 cup trimmed watercress
1 cup thinly sliced peeled Granny Smith apple
⅛ teaspoon freshly ground black pepper

1. Preheat oven to 350°.
2. Combine honey and mustard in a small bowl. Cut bread in half lengthwise, and place on a baking sheet. Spread honey mixture on bottom half of loaf, and top with smoked turkey slices and cheese. Bake at 350° for 5 minutes or until the cheese begins to melt.
3. Arrange watercress and apple slices over melted cheese; sprinkle with pepper. Cover with top half of loaf; cut into 4 portions. Yield: 4 servings (serving size: 1 sandwich).

CALORIES 337 (29% from fat); FAT 10.7g (sat 5.3g, mono 3.1g, poly 0.7g); PROTEIN 19.4g; CARB 40.8g; FIBER 2.5g; CHOL 45mg; IRON 3.5mg; SODIUM 926mg; CALC 114mg

Open-Faced Turkey Sandwich with Apple and Havarti

The flavors of fall meet in this sandwich. Tangy Havarti cheese provides a pleasing contrast to the sweet apples and spicy arugula. Substitute nutty fontina or mild Muenster for the Havarti, if you prefer.

4 (2-ounce) slices country or peasant bread
4 teaspoons low-fat mayonnaise
4 teaspoons Dijon mustard
1 cup trimmed arugula
4 (⅛-inch-thick) slices red onion
12 ounces thinly sliced deli turkey
2 Pink Lady or Cameo apples, each cored and cut crosswise into 8 (¼-inch-thick) slices
½ cup (2 ounces) grated Havarti cheese
Coarsely ground black pepper (optional)

1. Preheat broiler with oven rack in middle position.
2. Spread each bread slice with 1 teaspoon mayonnaise and 1 teaspoon mustard. Layer each slice with ¼ cup arugula, 1 onion slice, 3 ounces turkey, 4 apple slices, and 2 tablespoons cheese.
3. Place sandwiches on a baking sheet; broil 4 minutes or until cheese is bubbly. Remove from heat; sprinkle with pepper, if desired. Serve immediately. Yield: 4 servings (serving size: 1 sandwich).

CALORIES 427 (30% from fat); FAT 14.1g (sat 6.2g, mono 4.5g, poly 1.6g); PROTEIN 29.9g; CARB 44.2g; FIBER 5.7g; CHOL 69mg; IRON 4.8mg; SODIUM 634mg; CALC 141mg

Brussels Sprouts with
Crisp Prosciutto, page 291

Sides

Grilled Asparagus Rafts

Pinning asparagus spears together with skewers makes them easier to flip and grill evenly on both sides. This recipe was adapted from Steven Raichlen's books *How to Grill* (Workman, 2001) and *BBQ USA* (Workman, 2003).

- 16 thick asparagus spears (about 1 pound)
- 1 tablespoon low-sodium soy sauce
- 1 teaspoon dark sesame oil
- 1 garlic clove, minced
- 2 teaspoons sesame seeds, toasted
- ¼ teaspoon black pepper
- Dash of salt

1. Prepare grill to high heat.
2. Snap off tough ends of the asparagus. Arrange 4 asparagus spears on a flat surface. Thread 2 (3-inch) skewers or toothpicks horizontally through spears 1 inch from each end to form a "raft." Repeat procedure with remaining asparagus spears.
3. Combine soy sauce, sesame oil, and minced garlic; brush evenly over asparagus rafts. Grill 3 minutes on each side or until crisp-tender. Remove from heat. Sprinkle evenly with sesame seeds, black pepper, and dash of salt. Yield: 4 servings (serving size: 1 asparagus raft).

CALORIES 50 (38% from fat); FAT 2.1g (sat 0.2g, mono 0.5g, poly 0.6g); PROTEIN 3.2g; CARB 6.1g; FIBER 2.4g; CHOL 0mg; IRON 3mg; SODIUM 190mg; CALC 26mg

Grilled Asparagus

- 1 pound asparagus
- 3 tablespoons balsamic vinegar
- 2 tablespoons fresh lemon juice
- 1 tablespoon olive oil
- 1 tablespoon low-sodium soy sauce
- ⅛ teaspoon black pepper
- Cooking spray

1. Prepare grill.
2. Snap off tough ends of asparagus. Combine all ingredients except cooking spray in a large zip-top plastic bag; seal bag and marinate for 30 minutes. Remove asparagus from bag, and discard marinade. Place asparagus on grill rack coated with cooking spray; grill 5 minutes on each side or until asparagus is done. Yield: 4 servings.

CALORIES 36 (50% from fat); FAT 2g (sat 0.3g, mono 1.3g, poly 0.3g); PROTEIN 1.8g; CARB 4g; FIBER 1.6g; CHOL 0mg; IRON 0.8mg; SODIUM 62mg; CALC 17mg

Grilled Asparagus Rafts

Roasted Asparagus with
Balsamic-Shallot Butter

Roasted Asparagus with Balsamic-Shallot Butter

Melt the butter and add the shallots and other flavorings ahead of time, if you like. Roast the asparagus
and toss it with the butter just before serving.

    3 tablespoons finely chopped shallots
    2 tablespoons butter, melted
    2 tablespoons balsamic vinegar
    1 teaspoon chopped fresh thyme
    ¾ teaspoon salt
    ½ teaspoon grated lemon rind
    2 pounds asparagus spears
Cooking spray

1. Combine shallots, butter, vinegar, thyme, salt,
and rind, stirring well with a whisk.
2. Preheat oven to 450°.
3. Snap off tough ends of the asparagus. Arrange
asparagus in a single layer on a jelly roll pan coated
with cooking spray. Cover with foil; bake at 450°
for 5 minutes.
4. Uncover and bake an additional 10 minutes or
until asparagus is crisp-tender. Pour butter mixture
over asparagus; toss gently to coat. Serve immediately. Yield: 8 servings.

CALORIES 56 (50% from fat); FAT 3.1g (sat 1.9g, mono 0.9g, poly 0.2g); PROTEIN 2.7g;
CARB 6.2g; FIBER 1.8g; CHOL 8mg; IRON 1.1mg; SODIUM 253mg; CALC 28mg

Ginger-Infused Black Beans

Serve with grilled fish and sautéed bok choy.

    1 (6-ounce) bottle pickled ginger
    1 teaspoon olive oil
    ½ cup chopped onion
    2 garlic cloves, minced
    ¼ teaspoon salt
    2 (15-ounce) cans black beans, undrained

1. Drain ginger in a colander over a bowl, reserving
¼ cup ginger juice. Reserve ginger and remaining
juice for another use; store in refrigerator.
2. Heat oil in a medium nonstick saucepan over
medium heat. Add onion; sauté 5 minutes. Add garlic; sauté 1 minute. Stir in salt and beans. Bring to a
boil; reduce heat, and simmer 15 minutes, stirring
occasionally. Stir in reserved ¼ cup ginger juice.
Yield: 6 servings (serving size: ½ cup).

CALORIES 219 (7% from fat); FAT 1.8g (sat 0.3g, mono 0.6g, poly 0.4g); PROTEIN 12.7g;
CARB 39.7g; FIBER 6.3g; CHOL 0mg; IRON 3.1mg; SODIUM 527mg; CALC 71mg

Roasted Sweet-and-Sour Beets, Carrots, and Parsnips

Steam the vegetables first to speed roasting. The vinegar provides fruity, acidic zip and enough liquid to prevent the sugary maple syrup from burning. Serve with ham or roast chicken.

1 pound small beets, trimmed, peeled, and cut into wedges
1 pound parsnips, cut into (2-inch-thick) slices
1 pound carrots, cut into (2-inch-thick) slices
Cooking spray
¼ cup maple syrup
3 tablespoons cider vinegar
1 lemon
2 tablespoons olive oil
2 teaspoons coriander seeds, crushed
2 teaspoons chopped fresh or ½ teaspoon dried tarragon
12 fresh thyme sprigs
½ teaspoon salt
½ teaspoon freshly ground black pepper
Fresh thyme sprigs (optional)

1. Preheat oven to 400°.

2. Steam beets, parsnips, and carrots, covered, for 5 minutes. Place in a shallow roasting pan coated with cooking spray.

3. Combine syrup and vinegar; set aside.

4. Squeeze juice from lemon; add lemon halves to beet mixture. Combine juice, oil, coriander, tarragon, and 12 thyme sprigs. Pour over beet mixture; toss well. Sprinkle with salt and pepper. Bake at 400° for 30 minutes. Pour syrup mixture over beet mixture; stir well to coat. Bake an additional 30 minutes or until beets are tender. Discard lemon halves. Garnish with thyme sprigs, if desired. Yield: 7 servings (serving size: about 1 cup).

CALORIES 157 (25% from fat); FAT 4.4g (sat 0.6g, mono 3g, poly 0.5g); PROTEIN 2.2g; CARB 29.9g; FIBER 6.3g; CHOL 0mg; IRON 1.4mg; SODIUM 232mg; CALC 62mg

Green Beans Provençale

2 pounds green beans, cut into 1½-inch pieces
24 small cherry tomatoes, halved
½ cup chopped red onion
¾ cup chopped fresh parsley
¼ cup water
¼ cup white wine vinegar
2 tablespoons grated Parmesan cheese
2 tablespoons olive oil
½ teaspoon dried thyme
½ teaspoon black pepper
2 garlic cloves, minced

1. Steam beans, covered, 8 minutes or until crisp-tender. Drain beans; plunge into cold water, and drain. Combine beans, tomatoes, and onion in a medium bowl.
2. Combine the parsley and remaining ingredients in a bowl and stir well. Pour parsley mixture over the vegetables, tossing gently to coat. Serve at room temperature. Yield: 12 servings (serving size: 1 cup).

CALORIES 56 (43% from fat); FAT 2.6g (sat 0.5g, mono 1.7g, poly 0.3g); PROTEIN 2g; CARB 7.2g; FIBER 2.1g; CHOL 0mg; IRON 1.2mg; SODIUM 25mg; CALC 48mg

Fiery Chipotle Baked Beans

Molasses sweetens the beans, vinegar adds tang, and the chipotle chile powder makes them spicy.

4 ounces chorizo, thinly sliced
2½ cups chopped onion
1 cup fat-free, less-sodium chicken broth
⅓ cup packed brown sugar
⅓ cup cider vinegar
⅓ cup bottled chili sauce
⅓ cup dark molasses
2 teaspoons dry mustard
2 teaspoons chipotle chile powder
¼ teaspoon salt
¼ teaspoon ground cloves
¼ teaspoon ground allspice
1 (15-ounce) can black beans, rinsed and drained
1 (15-ounce) can kidney beans, rinsed and drained
1 (15-ounce) can pinto beans, rinsed and drained

1. Preheat oven to 325°.
2. Heat a Dutch oven over medium-high heat. Add chorizo; sauté 2 minutes. Add onion; sauté 5 minutes, stirring occasionally. Stir in broth and remaining

Fiery Chipotle Baked Beans

ingredients; bake uncovered at 325° for 1 hour. Yield: 10 servings (serving size: ½ cup).

CALORIES 245 (20% from fat); FAT 5.4g (sat 1.8g, mono 2.2g, poly 0.6g); PROTEIN 10.3g; CARB 40g; FIBER 8g; CHOL 10mg; IRON 3.6mg; SODIUM 639mg; CALC 135mg

Brussels Sprouts with Crisp Prosciutto

(pictured on page 286)

3 cups trimmed halved Brussels sprouts (about 1½ pounds)
¼ cup chopped prosciutto (about 1½ ounces)
Cooking spray
1 tablespoon butter
½ teaspoon salt
¼ teaspoon freshly ground black pepper
1 tablespoon fresh lemon juice

1. Cook Brussels sprouts in boiling water 3 minutes or until crisp-tender; drain.
2. Heat a large nonstick skillet over medium heat; add prosciutto. Cook 6 minutes or until crisp, stirring occasionally. Remove from pan; set aside.
3. Heat pan coated with cooking spray over medium-high heat. Add Brussels sprouts, and sauté for 3 minutes or until lightly browned. Add butter, salt, and pepper, stirring until butter melts. Remove from heat, and drizzle with juice. Add prosciutto, and toss to combine. Yield: 6 servings (serving size: about ¾ cup).

CALORIES 79 (33% from fat); FAT 2.9g (sat 1.5g, mono 0.9g, poly 0.3g); PROTEIN 5.5g; CARB 10.4g; FIBER 4.3g; CHOL 9mg; IRON 1.7mg; SODIUM 350mg; CALC 50mg

Roasted Brussels Sprouts
with Ham and Garlic

Roasted Brussels Sprouts with Ham and Garlic

Don't trim too much from the stem ends of the sprouts since they may fall apart.

    1 (1-ounce) slice white bread
    3 pounds Brussels sprouts, trimmed and halved
   ¼ cup finely chopped country ham (about 1 ounce)
    2 tablespoons fresh lemon juice
    1 teaspoon olive oil
   ½ teaspoon salt
    3 garlic cloves, thinly sliced
       Cooking spray
    2 tablespoons grated fresh Parmesan cheese

1. Preheat oven to 425°.
2. Place bread in a food processor; pulse 2 times or until crumbly. Sprinkle crumbs on a baking sheet; bake at 425° for 5 minutes or until golden. Reduce oven temperature to 375°. Set aside 3 tablespoons toasted breadcrumbs, reserving remaining breadcrumbs for another use.
3. Combine sprouts and next 5 ingredients in a 3-quart baking dish coated with cooking spray, tossing to coat. Bake at 375° for 30 minutes or until sprouts are tender and lightly browned on edges, stirring twice.
4. Combine 3 tablespoons breadcrumbs and Parmesan cheese; sprinkle over sprouts. Serve immediately. Yield: 12 servings (serving size: ¾ cup).

CALORIES 58 (19% from fat); FAT 1.2g (sat 0.4g, mono 0.5g, poly 0.2g); PROTEIN 4.4g; CARB 9.6g; FIBER 3.6g; CHOL 2mg; IRON 1.4mg; SODIUM 211mg; CALC 57mg

Cauliflower and Potato Sabzi with Spices

    1 head cauliflower (about 1½ pounds)
    2 tablespoons vegetable oil, divided
    2 baking potatoes, peeled, halved lengthwise, and sliced (about 1¾ pounds)
    2 teaspoons cumin seeds
    4 garlic cloves, minced
   ⅓ cup water
   ⅓ cup tomato puree
    3 tablespoons chopped peeled fresh ginger
  1½ teaspoons salt
   ¾ teaspoon ground turmeric
   ½ teaspoon ground red pepper
   ⅓ cup chopped fresh cilantro
    1 teaspoon Garam Masala

1. Separate cauliflower into florets to measure 4 cups, reserving stems. Cut stems into thin slices to measure 1 cup. Heat 1½ tablespoons oil in a Dutch oven over medium-high heat. Add potatoes, cumin seeds, and garlic; stir-fry 6 minutes or until potatoes are crisp-tender. Stir in water and next 5 ingredients. Add cauliflower florets and stems, stirring well; cover, reduce heat, and simmer 20 minutes or until vegetables are tender. Uncover; drizzle with 1½ teaspoons oil, cilantro, and Garam Masala, tossing well. Yield: 6 servings (serving size: 1 cup).

CALORIES 200 (23% from fat); FAT 5.2g (sat 0.8g, mono 1.2g, poly 2.8g); PROTEIN 4.9g; CARB 36.2g; FIBER 4.8g; CHOL 0mg; IRON 1.8mg; SODIUM 676mg; CALC 43mg

GARAM MASALA:

This homemade spice mixture is much darker and more flavorful than commercial varieties. Toasting the spices is a crucial step that gives the masala a deep, roasted flavor. Cardamom pods are available at Middle Eastern and Indian markets.

    1 tablespoon cumin seeds
    1 tablespoon coriander seeds
    2 teaspoons black peppercorns
   12 cardamom pods
    8 whole cloves
    1 (2-inch) cinnamon stick, broken into pieces
   ½ teaspoon ground nutmeg

1. Place first 6 ingredients in a large skillet over medium-high heat. Cook until spices smoke, become fragrant, and turn dark; shake pan constantly (about 5 minutes). Stir in nutmeg. Remove from heat; cool completely. Place spice mixture in a spice or coffee grinder; process until finely ground. Store in an airtight container. Yield: ¼ cup.

CALORIES 69 (46% from fat); FAT 3.5g (sat 0.5g, mono 1.6g, poly 0.3g); PROTEIN 2.5g; CARB 11.7g; FIBER 5.9g; CHOL 0mg; IRON 6.3mg; SODIUM 19mg; CALC 149mg

Spring Giardiniera

Giardiniera is great to prepare ahead and have on hand. The marinated vegetables
make a fabulous side or snack.

1½ cups cider vinegar
½ cup water
2 tablespoons sugar
1 tablespoon salt
1 teaspoon black peppercorns
½ teaspoon mustard seeds
½ teaspoon dried dill
2 bay leaves
2 cups small cauliflower florets
2 cups (3-inch) diagonally cut asparagus
1½ cups green beans, trimmed (about 8 ounces)
1 cup (¼-inch) diagonally cut carrot
1 cup red bell pepper strips
6 green onion bottoms, trimmed
4 garlic cloves, halved

1. Combine first 8 ingredients in a large Dutch oven;
bring to a boil. Reduce heat; simmer 3 minutes.
2. Arrange cauliflower and remaining ingredients in a
large heavy-duty zip-top plastic bag. Carefully pour
vinegar mixture over cauliflower mixture. Seal bag;
refrigerate 8 hours or overnight, turning occasionally.
3. Remove vegetables from bag with a slotted
spoon. Discard bay leaves. Yield: 6 servings (serving size: 1 cup).

CALORIES 57 (5% from fat); FAT 0.3g (sat 0.1g, mono 0g, poly 0.2g); PROTEIN 3.2g;
CARB 12.8g; FIBER 4.7g; CHOL 0mg; IRON 1.5mg; SODIUM 141mg; CALC 55mg

Grilled Mexican Corn with Crema

On the streets of Mexico, people line up at vendor carts to buy giant ears of roasted corn dunked in rich *crema Mexicana* and sprinkled with chile powder and lime juice. *Crema Mexicana* is similar to sour cream and can be found in many large supermarkets. If you can't find it, use low-fat sour cream.

    1   teaspoon chipotle chile powder
    ½   teaspoon salt
    ⅛   teaspoon freshly ground black pepper
    6   ears corn
Cooking spray
    ¼   cup crema Mexicana
    6   lime wedges

1. Prepare grill.
2. Combine first 3 ingredients.
3. Place corn on a grill rack coated with cooking spray, and cook 12 minutes or until corn is lightly browned, turning frequently. Place corn on a platter; drizzle with crema. Sprinkle with chipotle mixture. Garnish with lime wedges. Yield: 6 servings (serving size: 1 ear).

CALORIES 160 (29% from fat); FAT 5.2g (sat 2.5g, mono 1.5g, poly 1g); PROTEIN 5g; CARB 28.2g; FIBER 4g; CHOL 8mg; IRON 0.8mg; SODIUM 228mg; CALC 24mg

Chili-Roasted Corn on the Cob

If you choose to broil the corn, place pan on the second rack level from top of oven. You can adjust the measurements for the chili powder and cumin to suit your own taste buds.

    6   ears corn with husks
    2   teaspoons chili powder
    ½   teaspoon salt
    ½   teaspoon ground cumin
    1   tablespoon butter or stick margarine, melted

1. Place corn with husks in cold water, and soak for 30 minutes. Pull husks back, and scrub the silks from the corn.
2. Combine chili powder, salt, cumin, and butter in a small bowl. Brush chili powder mixture over corn. Wrap husks around corn.
3. Prepare grill or broiler.
4. Place the corn on a grill rack or broiler pan, and cook 20 minutes or until corn is lightly browned, turning every 5 minutes. Yield: 6 servings (serving size: 1 ear of corn).

CALORIES 101 (27% from fat); FAT 3g (sat 1.4g, mono 0.9g, poly 0.6g); PROTEIN 2.6g; CARB 19.4g; FIBER 3.1g; CHOL 5mg; IRON 0.7mg; SODIUM 236mg; CALC 6mg

Creamed Corn with Bacon and Leeks

 6 ears fresh corn
 2 cups 1% low-fat milk
 1 tablespoon cornstarch
 1 teaspoon sugar
 ½ teaspoon salt
 ¼ teaspoon freshly ground black pepper
 4 slices bacon
 1 cup chopped leek

1. Cut kernels from ears of corn to measure 3 cups; using the dull side of a knife blade, scrape milk and remaining pulp from cobs into a bowl. Place 1½ cups kernels, low-fat milk, cornstarch, sugar, salt, and pepper in a food processor. Process corn mixture until smooth; set aside.

2. Cook bacon in a cast-iron or large nonstick skillet over medium heat until crisp. Remove bacon from pan; reserve 1 teaspoon drippings in pan. Crumble bacon. Add leek to pan; cook 2 minutes, stirring constantly. Add pureed corn mixture, 1½ cups corn kernels, and corn milk mixture to pan. Bring to a boil. Reduce heat; simmer 3 minutes or until slightly thick. Sprinkle with bacon just before serving. Yield: 6 servings (serving size: ⅔ cup).

CALORIES 151 (27% from fat); FAT 4.6g (sat 1.7g, mono 1.9g, poly 0.8g); PROTEIN 7g; CARB 23.1g; FIBER 2.4g; CHOL 9mg; IRON 0.8mg; SODIUM 325mg; CALC 111mg

Fresh Corn Custards

 3 cups fresh corn kernels (about 6 ears), divided
 2 cups 2% reduced-fat milk
 ½ teaspoon salt
 ¼ teaspoon black pepper
 4 large eggs, lightly beaten
Cooking spray
Fresh chives (optional)

1. Preheat oven to 350°.

2. Bring 2 cups corn and milk to a simmer in a large saucepan over medium heat. Cook 20 minutes; cool. Pour corn mixture into a blender or food processor; process until smooth. Strain mixture through a sieve over a large bowl. Discard solids. Add salt, pepper, and eggs to corn mixture; stir well with a whisk.

3. Divide remaining 1 cup corn evenly among 6 (6-ounce) ramekins generously coated with cooking spray; top each with ⅓ cup corn mixture.

4. Place the ramekins in a 13 x 9-inch baking pan, and add hot water to pan to a depth of 1 inch. Bake at 350° for 30 minutes or until center barely moves when the ramekin is touched.

5. Remove ramekins from pan; cool 5 minutes on a wire rack. Invert custards. Garnish with fresh chives, if desired. Yield: 6 servings (serving size: 1 custard).

CALORIES 181 (30% from fat); FAT 6.1g (sat 2.2g, mono 2.1g, poly 1.0g); PROTEIN 9.6g; CARB 25g; FIBER 1g; CHOL 147mg; IRON 1mg; SODIUM 291mg; CALC 118mg

Creamed Corn with Bacon and Leeks

Cucumber Pickle Spears

Cucumber Pickle Spears will last for up to six weeks in the refrigerator.

    4   large pickling cucumbers (about 1 pound),
        each cut lengthwise into 6 spears
    2   teaspoons salt
    3   large dill sprigs
    1   garlic clove, halved
    1   cup white vinegar
    1   cup water
  ¼   cup sugar

1. Place cucumber spears in a large bowl. Sprinkle the spears with salt, and toss gently to coat. Cover and chill for 2 hours.

2. Drain cucumber spears in a colander. Rinse spears under cold water, and drain well. Pack cucumber spears into a hot, sterilized wide-mouth 1-quart jar. Add dill and garlic to jar; set aside.

3. Combine vinegar, water, and sugar in a small saucepan, and bring to a boil, stirring until sugar dissolves. Pour hot liquid over cucumber spears. Cover jar with metal lid, and screw on band. Cool pickles completely. Cover pickles and marinate in refrigerator 5 days before serving. Yield: 24 spears (serving size: 1 spear).

NOTE: If you can't make the pickles right away, store the cucumbers, unwashed and unwrapped, in the refrigerator or in a cool, ventilated area. They will deteriorate at room temperature.

CALORIES 13 (7% from fat); FAT 0.1g (sat 0g, mono 0g, poly 0g); PROTEIN 0.4g; CARB 3g; FIBER 0.6g; CHOL 0mg; IRON 0.2mg; SODIUM 99mg; CALC 10mg

Cucumber Pickle Spears

Edamame with Mustard Vinaigrette

Blanching the onion and celery mellows their flavors, so they don't overpower the nutty edamame and tangy Dijon vinaigrette.

  1½   tablespoons red wine vinegar
    1   tablespoon Dijon mustard
  ½   teaspoon sea salt
    1   teaspoon extravirgin olive oil
    1   pound frozen shelled edamame, thawed
    1   cup thinly sliced red onion
  ½   cup finely chopped celery
    1   tablespoon chopped fresh parsley

1. Combine first 3 ingredients in a large bowl, stirring with a whisk. Add oil, stirring with a whisk until well combined.

2. Cook edamame in boiling water 4 minutes. Add onion and celery, and cook 1 minute. Drain well. Add edamame mixture to vinaigrette; toss well to coat. Stir in parsley. Chill 1 hour. Yield: 6 servings (serving size: about ½ cup).

CALORIES 124 (30% from fat); FAT 4.1g (sat 0.5g, mono 1.2g, poly 1.6g); PROTEIN 8.6g; CARB 12.4g; FIBER 0.7g; CHOL 0mg; IRON 1.9mg; SODIUM 295mg; CALC 44mg

Sautéed Green Beans and
Onions with Bacon

Green Beans with Crushed Walnuts

This simple dish relies on freshly ground nutmeg. Look for whole nutmeg in the spice aisle, and store it in the freezer for up to one year.

1¼ pounds green beans, trimmed
  2 teaspoons butter
  2 tablespoons finely crushed walnuts
  ½ teaspoon salt
  ¼ teaspoon freshly ground whole nutmeg

1. Place beans in a large saucepan of boiling water; cook 5 minutes. Drain.
2. Heat butter in a large nonstick skillet over medium-high heat. Add walnuts; sauté 1 minute, stirring constantly. Add beans, salt, and nutmeg; cook 1 minute. Yield: 6 servings (serving size: ⅔ cup).

CALORIES 52 (52% from fat); FAT 3g (sat 1g, mono 0.6g, poly 1.3g); PROTEIN 1.8g; CARB 5.8g; FIBER 2.8g; CHOL 3mg; IRON 0.9mg; SODIUM 213mg; CALC 31mg

Sautéed Green Beans and Onions with Bacon

  1 pound green beans, trimmed and halved crosswise
  4 bacon slices
  1 (16-ounce) bottle cocktail onions, drained
  2 teaspoons sugar
  ½ teaspoon dried thyme
1½ tablespoons cider vinegar
  ¾ teaspoon salt
  ¼ teaspoon black pepper

1. Cook green beans in boiling water for 4 minutes or until crisp-tender. Rinse with cold water, and drain and pat dry.
2. Cook bacon in a large nonstick skillet over medium-high heat until crisp. Remove bacon from pan, reserving 2 tablespoons drippings in pan; crumble bacon, and set aside. Add onions to drippings in pan; cook 3 minutes, stirring occasionally. Add sugar and thyme; cook for 3 minutes or until onions are golden brown, stirring occasionally. Add the beans, and cook 2 minutes or until thoroughly heated. Add vinegar, salt, and pepper; toss to coat. Stir in crumbled bacon just before serving. Yield: 8 servings (serving size: ½ cup).

CALORIES 59 (46% from fat); FAT 3.0g (sat 1.1g, mono 1.4g, poly 0.4g); PROTEIN 2.2g; CARB 6.5g; FIBER 1.2g; CHOL 4mg; IRON 0.8mg; SODIUM 621mg; CALC 24mg

Eggplant and Tomato Gratin

Japanese eggplant is longer and narrower than the more readily available globe eggplant, so the slices are more manageable in this dish.

  1 pound Japanese eggplant, cut diagonally into ¼-inch-thick slices
Cooking spray
  ¼ teaspoon salt
  ½ cup (2 ounces) grated fresh Parmesan cheese
  2 teaspoons chopped fresh or ½ teaspoon dried oregano
  ¼ teaspoon freshly ground black pepper
  4 garlic cloves, minced
  6 plum tomatoes, cut into ¼-inch-thick slices
  2 medium zucchini, cut into ¼-inch-thick slices

1. Preheat oven to 375°.
2. Arrange eggplant slices in a single layer on a baking sheet coated with cooking spray. Coat slices with cooking spray; sprinkle with salt. Bake at 375° for 16 minutes, turning eggplant over after 8 minutes. Combine cheese, oregano, pepper, and minced garlic in a bowl.
3. Arrange half of eggplant slices in an 8-inch square baking dish coated with cooking spray. Arrange half of tomato slices over eggplant slices. Top with half of zucchini slices; sprinkle with half of cheese mixture. Repeat procedure with remaining eggplant slices, tomato slices, zucchini slices, and cheese mixture.
4. Bake, covered, at 375° for 1 hour. Uncover and bake an additional 10 minutes or until vegetables are tender and cheese is golden brown. Yield: 8 servings.

CALORIES 87 (29% from fat); FAT 2.8g (sat 1.6g, mono 0.8g, poly 0.2g); PROTEIN 5.5g; CARB 11.2g; FIBER 4g; CHOL 6mg; IRON 0.9mg; SODIUM 257mg; CALC 140mg

Ragout of Cipollini Onions with Tomato, Cinnamon, and Cumin

This recipe, full of North African flavors, is good either served as part of a mixed hors d'oeuvre, such as tapas, or over basmati rice to catch all the sauce. Roasting the tomatoes yields a deeper, richer, slightly sweeter flavor than you'd get by cooking them on the stovetop the entire time.

2 garlic cloves, chopped
Cooking spray
1¼ pounds tomatoes, cut in half crosswise (about 3 large)
½ teaspoon salt, divided
¼ teaspoon freshly ground black pepper, divided
2 pounds cipollini onions, peeled
1 teaspoon ground coriander
¼ teaspoon ground cumin
1 (2-inch) cinnamon stick
1 cup vegetable broth
¼ cup dried currants
3 thyme sprigs
2 bay leaves
1 (3-inch) orange rind strip
2 tablespoons fresh orange juice
1 teaspoon brown sugar
2 tablespoons chopped fresh cilantro

1. Preheat oven to 375°.
2. Sprinkle garlic evenly in bottom of a 13 x 9-inch baking dish coated with cooking spray. Arrange tomato halves, cut sides down, over garlic. Sprinkle with ¼ teaspoon salt and ⅛ teaspoon pepper; lightly spray tomato halves with cooking spray. Bake at 375° for 55 minutes or until tender. Remove from oven; cool in dish.
3. Place tomato mixture in a blender or food processor, reserving liquid in baking dish. Process tomato mixture until smooth; strain through a sieve into a large bowl. Discard solids. Add the reserved liquid to bowl.
4. Heat a large nonstick skillet coated with cooking spray over medium-high heat. Add onions, and sauté for 8 minutes. Remove onions from pan. Add coriander, cumin, and cinnamon to pan, and sauté 1 minute. Add onions, pureed tomato mixture, ¼ teaspoon salt, ⅛ teaspoon pepper, broth, and next 4 ingredients to pan. Bring to a simmer over medium heat, and cook for 30 minutes or until onions are tender and sauce is thick, stirring occasionally. Remove from heat, and stir in orange juice and sugar. Remove the cinnamon stick, bay leaves, and orange rind. Sprinkle with chopped cilantro. Yield: 6 servings (serving size: ⅔ cup).

CALORIES 143 (5% from fat); FAT 0.8g (sat 0g, mono 0.1g, poly 0.1g); PROTEIN 3.4g; CARB 32.2g; FIBER 2.3g; CHOL 0mg; IRON 1.4mg; SODIUM 397mg; CALC 55mg

Caramelized Onion and Horseradish Mashed Potatoes

Horseradish and Dijon mustard perk up these potatoes. Pair them with steak or tuna.

¼ cup butter, divided
4 cups chopped onion
2 teaspoons brown sugar
1 tablespoon white balsamic vinegar (optional)
2½ pounds cubed peeled baking potato
½ cup whole milk
¼ cup Dijon mustard
2 tablespoons prepared horseradish
1 tablespoon fresh lemon juice
1 tablespoon light mayonnaise
½ teaspoon salt

1. Melt 1 tablespoon butter in a medium nonstick skillet over medium-high heat. Add onion and sugar, and sauté 10 minutes or until caramelized. Remove from heat; stir in vinegar, if desired.

2. Place potato in a saucepan; cover with water. Bring to a boil. Reduce heat; simmer 15 minutes or until tender.

3. Drain and return potato to pan. Add 3 tablespoons butter and milk, and mash to desired consistency. Cook for 2 minutes or until thoroughly heated, stirring constantly.

4. Combine Dijon mustard and remaining ingredients in a small bowl, stirring mixture with a whisk until blended. Add Dijon mustard mixture and caramelized onion mixture to potato mixture, stirring to combine. Yield: 10 servings (serving size: about ¾ cup).

CALORIES 186 (30% from fat); FAT 6.3g (sat 3.3g, mono 1.7g, poly 0.4g); PROTEIN 3.9g; CARB 30.4g; FIBER 2.9g; CHOL 15mg; IRON 1.3mg; SODIUM 353mg; CALC 45mg

Rosemary-Glazed Vidalia Onions

1 cup dry red wine
2 tablespoons sugar
1 tablespoon chopped fresh or 1 teaspoon dried rosemary
1 tablespoon fresh lemon juice
⅛ teaspoon ground cloves
⅛ teaspoon black pepper
2 medium Vidalia or other sweet onions, unpeeled (about 1¼ pounds)
Cooking spray
2 teaspoons olive oil

1. Preheat oven to 400°.

2. Combine first 6 ingredients in a small saucepan; bring to a boil. Reduce heat to medium, and cook, uncovered, until reduced to ½ cup (about 10 minutes). Set aside.

3. Cut onions in half lengthwise. Place onions, cut sides down, in a small baking dish coated with cooking spray. Drizzle oil over onions. Cover onions and bake at 400° for 25 minutes. Uncover; bake an additional 20 minutes. Remove onions from oven. Turn onions over; pour wine mixture over onions. Bake for an additional 20 minutes or until onions are tender, basting every 5 minutes. Serve onions with wine mixture. Yield: 4 servings (serving size: 1 onion half and about 1 tablespoon glaze).

CALORIES 105 (23% from fat); FAT 2.7g (sat 0.4g, mono 1.7g, poly 0.4g); PROTEIN 1.8g; CARB 19.9g; FIBER 2.8g; CHOL 0mg; IRON 0.7mg; SODIUM 9mg; CALC 37mg

Rosemary-Glazed Vidalia Onions

Black-Eyed Peas with Ham and Pickled Onions

PICKLED ONIONS:

1½ tablespoons cider vinegar
1 teaspoon sugar
Dash of ground red pepper
½ cup finely chopped onion

PEAS:

1 teaspoon vegetable oil
1 cup finely chopped onion
2 garlic cloves, minced
3 cups frozen black-eyed peas (about 1 pound)
½ teaspoon salt
½ teaspoon dried thyme
½ teaspoon black pepper
⅛ teaspoon ground red pepper
1 (14½-ounce) can fat-free, less-sodium chicken broth
½ pound diced ham (about ¼ inch thick)

1. Combine the vinegar, sugar, and red pepper in a microwave-safe bowl. Microwave at HIGH 25 seconds; stir until sugar dissolves. Stir in ½ cup onion; cover and refrigerate overnight.
2. Heat oil in a saucepan over medium-high heat. Add 1 cup onion and garlic; cook 2 minutes, stirring frequently. Stir in the peas and remaining ingredients; bring to a boil. Cover, reduce heat, and simmer 20 minutes. Partially mash the peas with a potato masher; cook, uncovered, 5 minutes. Serve with pickled onions. Yield: 8 servings (serving size: ½ cup peas and 1 tablespoon pickled onions).

CALORIES 141 (17% from fat); FAT 2.6g (sat 0.7g, mono 0.9g, poly 0.7g); PROTEIN 11.9g; CARB 17.6g; FIBER 4.3g; CHOL 15mg; IRON 1.8mg; SODIUM 603mg; CALC 24mg

Rosemary Potatoes

These microwaved potatoes taste as if they were roasted in the oven.

1 tablespoon butter
1 teaspoon bottled minced garlic
1 teaspoon dried rosemary
½ teaspoon kosher salt
¼ teaspoon black pepper
1½ pounds red potatoes, quartered (about 4 cups)

1. Place butter and garlic in an 8-inch square baking dish. Microwave at MEDIUM-HIGH (70% power) 45 seconds or until butter melts. Add rosemary, salt, pepper, and potatoes, and toss well. Cover and microwave at HIGH 15 minutes or until potatoes are tender. Yield: 4 servings (serving size: ¾ cup).

CALORIES 155 (18% from fat); FAT 3.1g (sat 1.9g, mono 0.8g, poly 0.2g); PROTEIN 3.9g; CARB 29g; FIBER 3.2g; CHOL 8mg; IRON 2.4mg; SODIUM 182mg; CALC 30mg

Mashed Potatoes with Blue Cheese and Parsley

2 pounds red potatoes, cut into 2-inch chunks
2 garlic cloves, peeled
1 cup (4 ounces) crumbled blue cheese
½ cup 1% low-fat milk
2 tablespoons chopped fresh parsley
¼ teaspoon freshly ground black pepper

1. Place potatoes and garlic in a large saucepan, and cover with water. Bring to a boil, and cook 15 minutes or until tender. Drain. Place the potato mixture and remaining ingredients in a large bowl, and mash to the desired consistency. Yield: 4 servings (serving size: 1 cup).

CALORIES 284 (28% from fat); FAT 8.7g (sat 5.6g, mono 2.3g, poly 0.3g); PROTEIN 12.2g; CARB 40.5g; FIBER 4.2g; CHOL 22mg; IRON 3.2mg; SODIUM 428mg; CALC 223mg

Garlic Fries

3 pounds peeled baking potatoes, cut into ¼-inch-thick strips
4 teaspoons vegetable oil
¾ teaspoon salt
Cooking spray
2 tablespoons butter
8 garlic cloves, minced (about 5 teaspoons)
2 tablespoons finely chopped fresh parsley
2 tablespoons freshly grated Parmesan cheese

1. Preheat oven to 400°.
2. Combine first 3 ingredients in a large zip-top plastic bag, tossing to coat.
3. Arrange potatoes in a single layer on a baking sheet coated with cooking spray. Bake at 400° for 50 minutes or until potatoes are tender and golden brown, turning after 20 minutes.
4. Place butter and garlic in a large nonstick skillet; cook over low heat 2 minutes, stirring constantly. Add potatoes, parsley, and cheese to pan; toss to coat. Serve immediately. Yield: 6 servings.

CALORIES 256 (27% from fat); FAT 7.7g (sat 3.3g, mono 2g, poly 2g); PROTEIN 5.9g; CARB 42.3g; FIBER 3.5g; CHOL 12mg; IRON 1.9mg; SODIUM 386mg; CALC 55mg

Garlic Fries

Cider Scalloped Potatoes

Potatoes and cider pair up for a slightly sweet twist on a traditional favorite.

  3   tablespoons all-purpose flour
  1   cup 1% low-fat milk
  1   cup apple cider
 ½ cup fat-free, less-sodium chicken broth
 ½ teaspoon salt
 ¼ teaspoon black pepper
 ⅛ teaspoon ground nutmeg
 ½ cup (2 ounces) shredded smoked
     Gouda cheese
 ½ cup (2 ounces) shredded reduced-fat
     Jarlsberg cheese
  2   pounds Yukon gold or red potatoes, peeled
     and thinly sliced

1. Preheat oven to 425°.
2. Place flour in a medium saucepan. Gradually add milk, stirring with a whisk until blended. Stir in cider, broth, salt, pepper, and nutmeg; bring to a boil over medium heat, stirring constantly. Remove from heat. Combine cheeses in a small bowl. Arrange half of the potato slices in a 3-quart casserole dish, and sprinkle with ½ cup cheese mixture. Arrange remaining potato slices on top. Pour the cider mixture over potatoes, and bake at 425° for 25 minutes. Remove from oven; press potatoes with a spatula. Sprinkle potatoes with the remaining cheese mixture, and bake at 425° for an additional 20 minutes or until potatoes are tender. Let stand for 10 minutes. Yield: 8 servings (serving size: about ¾ cup).

CALORIES 140 (18% from fat); FAT 2.8g (sat 1.7g, mono 0.8g, poly 0.1g); PROTEIN 6.7g; CARB 22.1g; FIBER 1.5g; CHOL 10mg; IRON 0.9mg; SODIUM 274mg; CALC 146mg

Llapingachos Ecuatorianos
(Ecuadorean Potato and Cheese Patties)

1½ teaspoons kosher salt
  2   medium peeled baking potatoes, quartered
     (about 1¼ pounds)
  6   tablespoons (1½ ounces) shredded queso
     fresco or Monterey Jack cheese
  2   tablespoons minced green onions
 ¼ teaspoon kosher salt
 ¼ teaspoon freshly ground black pepper
  1   tablespoon olive oil
 ¾ cup diced tomato
 ½ cup julienne-cut red onion

1. Place 1½ teaspoons salt and potatoes in a saucepan; cover with water. Bring to a boil; reduce heat, and simmer 15 minutes or until tender. Drain; mash with a potato masher until smooth. Cool.
2. Add cheese, green onions, ¼ teaspoon salt, and pepper to potato mixture, stirring well. Divide the potato mixture into 6 balls (about ½ cup per ball). Flatten balls into ½-inch-thick patties (about 3 inches each in diameter). Place on a baking sheet; cover and refrigerate 20 minutes or until firm.
3. Heat oil in a large nonstick skillet over medium heat. Place patties in pan; cook 5 minutes or until bottoms are browned. Turn patties; cook 3 minutes. Top patties with tomato and red onion. Yield: 6 servings (serving size: 1 patty).

CALORIES 157 (26% from fat); FAT 4.6g (sat 1.8g, mono 1.3g, poly 1.2g); PROTEIN 4.2g; CARB 24.9g; FIBER 2.1g; CHOL 6mg; IRON 0.6mg; SODIUM 279mg; CALC 64mg

Grilled Bacon and Herb Grit Cakes

Chilling the grits helps them hold their shape and makes them firm enough to cut when grilled.

  4   cups hot cooked instant grits
 ½ cup (2 ounces) shredded white cheddar
     cheese
  1   tablespoon minced fresh or 1 teaspoon dried
     thyme
  2   teaspoons chopped fresh parsley
 ½ teaspoon garlic powder
 ½ teaspoon black pepper
  3   bacon slices, cooked and crumbled
Cooking spray

1. Combine first 7 ingredients in a large bowl; stir well. Pour grits into a 10-inch square baking dish coated with cooking spray, spreading evenly. Cover and chill 1 hour or until completely cool.
2. Prepare grill.
3. Invert the grits onto a cutting board, and cut them into 4 squares. Cut each grits square diagonally into 2 triangles.
4. Place grits triangles on grill rack coated with cooking spray; grill 5 minutes on each side or until lightly browned and thoroughly heated. Yield: 4 servings (serving size: 2 triangles).

CALORIES 255 (30% from fat); FAT 8.5g (sat 4g, mono 2.7g, poly 0.5g); PROTEIN 9.3g; CARB 38.8g; FIBER 2.4g; CHOL 20mg; IRON 15.2mg; SODIUM 695mg; CALC 123mg

Potato-Gorgonzola Gratin

To easily create uniformly thin potato slices, use a mandoline or the slicing blade of a food processor.
Substitute fontina or Monterey Jack for the blue cheese, if you like.

2 tablespoons butter
2½ tablespoons all-purpose flour
1 teaspoon chopped fresh or ¼ teaspoon dried thyme
2½ cups fat-free milk
¾ cup (3 ounces) crumbled Gorgonzola or other blue cheese
1½ teaspoons salt
¼ teaspoon freshly ground black pepper
3 pounds baking potatoes, peeled and cut into ⅛-inch-thick slices
Cooking spray
⅓ cup (1½ ounces) grated Parmigiano-Reggiano cheese

1. Preheat oven to 375°.
2. Melt butter in a small saucepan over medium-high heat. Add flour, and cook 2 minutes, stirring constantly with a whisk. Stir in thyme. Gradually add milk, stirring with a whisk; cook over medium heat until slightly thick (about 3 minutes), stirring constantly. Stir in Gorgonzola; cook 3 minutes or until cheese melts, stirring constantly. Stir in salt and pepper. Remove from heat.
3. Arrange one-fourth of potatoes in bottom of a 13 x 9-inch baking dish coated with cooking spray, and spoon about ¾ cup sauce over potatoes. Repeat layers twice, and arrange remaining potato slices over sauce. Sprinkle with Parmigiano-Reggiano. Cover and bake at 375° for 30 minutes. Uncover and bake an additional 40 minutes or until potatoes are tender. Remove from oven, and let stand 10 minutes before serving. Yield: 8 servings (serving size: about 1 cup).

CALORIES 254 (28% from fat); FAT 7.9g (sat 5g, mono 2g, poly 0.2g); PROTEIN 10.6g; CARB 36.8g; FIBER 2.8g; CHOL 22mg; IRON 1.5mg; SODIUM 751mg; CALC 228mg

Brûléed Mashed
Sweet Potatoes

Brûléed Mashed Sweet Potatoes

Borrowing from the classic dessert, crème brûlée, this dish has a hard candy topping, a crisp contrast to the creamy sweet potatoes.

    6   cups hot mashed sweet potatoes (about
        4 pounds)
    ¾   cup whole milk
    3   tablespoons butter, softened
    ½   teaspoon salt
    ¼   teaspoon ground cinnamon
    ⅛   teaspoon ground nutmeg
    Cooking spray
    ½   cup packed brown sugar

1. Preheat broiler.
2. Combine first 6 ingredients in a bowl. Spoon the potato mixture into an 11 x 7-inch baking dish coated with cooking spray. Sprinkle ½ cup brown sugar evenly over top. Broil mixture 2 minutes or until sugar melts. Let stand until melted sugar hardens (about 5 minutes). Yield: 14 servings (serving size: about ½ cup).

CALORIES 207 (14% from fat); FAT 3.3g (sat 1.9g, mono 0.9g, poly 0.3g); PROTEIN 2.8g; CARB 42.4g; FIBER 2.6g; CHOL 8mg; IRON 1mg; SODIUM 137mg; CALC 53mg

Chipotle-Maple Sweet Potatoes

    1   pound coarsely chopped peeled sweet potato
    2   tablespoons maple syrup
    2   tablespoons fat-free milk
    1   tablespoon butter
    ¼   teaspoon salt
    ⅛   teaspoon black pepper
    1   can chipotle chiles in adobo sauce

1. Place sweet potato in a saucepan, and cover with water; bring to a boil. Reduce heat; simmer 15 minutes or until tender. Drain. Return to pan. Add syrup and next 4 ingredients; set mixture aside.
2. Remove 1 chile and 1½ teaspoons adobo sauce from can. Cut chile in half lengthwise; mince.
3. Add minced chile and adobo sauce to potato in pan; beat with a mixer at medium speed until smooth. Yield: 4 servings (serving size: ½ cup).

CALORIES 177 (17% from fat); FAT 3.4g (sat 1.9g, mono 0.9g, poly 0.3g); PROTEIN 2.1g; CARB 35.2g; FIBER 3.4g; CHOL 8mg; IRON 0.8mg; SODIUM 195mg; CALC 42mg

Sweet Potato Casserole

    3   cups mashed peeled cooked sweet potato
        (about 2¼ pounds)
    ⅓   cup packed brown sugar
    ⅓   cup fat-free milk
    2   tablespoons reduced-calorie stick margarine,
        melted
    1   teaspoon vanilla extract
    ½   teaspoon salt
    2   large egg whites, lightly beaten
    Cooking spray
    ½   cup packed brown sugar
    ¼   cup all-purpose flour
    2   tablespoons chilled reduced-calorie
        stick margarine
    ⅓   cup chopped pecans

1. Preheat oven to 350°.
2. Combine first 7 ingredients in a bowl. Spoon sweet potato mixture into an 8-inch square baking dish coated with cooking spray.
3. Combine ½ cup brown sugar and flour; cut in 2 tablespoons margarine with a pastry blender or 2 knives until mixture resembles coarse meal. Stir in pecans; sprinkle over potato mixture. Bake at 350° for 30 minutes. Yield: 8 servings (serving size: ½ cup).

CALORIES 273 (24% from fat); FAT 7.4g (sat 0.9g, mono 3.5g, poly 2.5g); PROTEIN 3.5g; CARB 49.8g; FIBER 3.3g; CHOL 0mg; IRON 1.3mg; SODIUM 242mg; CALC 56mg

Roasted Butternut Squash with Herbes de Provence

If you're roasting in a stainless pan, use a metal spatula to turn the squash so you can scrape up the flavorful browned edges on every single cube. These roasted vegetables are good with other savory dried herbs, too.

    6   cups (1½-inch) cubed peeled butternut
        squash (about 2½ pounds)
    1   tablespoon olive oil
 1½   teaspoons dried herbes de Provence
    ¾   teaspoon kosher salt
    ½   teaspoon freshly ground black pepper
    2   medium onions, each cut into 8 wedges
        (about ¾ pound)
  Cooking spray

1. Preheat oven to 425°.
2. Place the first 6 ingredients in a shallow roasting pan coated with cooking spray, and toss well. Bake at 425° for 30 minutes or until tender and lightly browned, stirring occasionally. Yield: 4 servings (serving size: 1 cup).

CALORIES 125 (27% from fat); FAT 3.8g (sat 0.5g, mono 2.5g, poly 0.5g); PROTEIN 3.6g; CARB 22.5g; FIBER 4.2g; CHOL 0mg; IRON 1.3mg; SODIUM 362mg; CALC 75mg

Mashed Roots

    4   cups cubed peeled baking potato
        (about 1½ pounds)
    2   cups sliced peeled parsnip (about 12 ounces)
    2   cups cubed peeled turnip (about 12 ounces)
    2   bay leaves
    5   tablespoons reduced-calorie stick margarine
    ¼   cup fat-free milk
    ½   teaspoon salt
    ¼   teaspoon black pepper

1. Place first 4 ingredients in a large saucepan; cover with water, and bring to a boil. Cook 20 minutes or until vegetables are very tender. Drain well; discard bay leaves. Return vegetables to pan, and add margarine, milk, salt, and pepper. Beat at medium speed of a mixer until smooth. Yield: 6 servings (serving size: 1 cup).

CALORIES 221 (26% from fat); FAT 6.4g (sat 1.3g, mono 2.7g, poly 2g); PROTEIN 3.7g; CARB 38.7g; FIBER 3.9g; CHOL 0mg; IRON 0.9mg; SODIUM 342mg; CALC 56mg

Parsnip-Potato Latkes with Horseradish Cream

Pressing the patties firmly between your hands when shaping helps bind the ingredients together.

    ½   cup fat-free sour cream
    ¼   teaspoon prepared horseradish
 2½   cups shredded peeled baking potato (about
        1 pound)
 2½   cups shredded peeled parsnip
    1   cup grated carrot
    1   teaspoon salt, divided
    ½   cup chopped red onion
    ¼   cup all-purpose flour
    ¼   teaspoon freshly ground black pepper
    2   tablespoons vegetable oil

1. Combine sour cream and horseradish in a custard cup; cover and chill.
2. Combine potato, parsnip, and carrot; spread evenly onto several layers of paper towels. Sprinkle with ¾ teaspoon salt, and let stand 30 minutes. Cover with additional paper towels; press down to absorb liquid. Place parsnip mixture in a large bowl. Add onion, flour, and pepper; toss to combine.
3. Preheat oven to 400°.
4. Divide parsnip mixture into 10 equal portions (about ¼ cup per portion), shaping each into a ½-inch-thick patty.
5. Heat 1 tablespoon oil in a large nonstick skillet over medium heat. Add 5 patties; cook 2 minutes on each side or until golden brown. Place cooked patties on a baking sheet. Repeat procedure with remaining 1 tablespoon oil and 5 uncooked patties. Bake latkes at 400° for 20 minutes, turning after 10 minutes. Sprinkle evenly with ¼ teaspoon salt. Serve with horseradish cream. Yield: 5 servings (serving size: 2 latkes and about 1½ tablespoons horseradish cream).

CALORIES 201 (17% from fat); FAT 3.9g (sat 0.9g, mono 1.9g, poly 0.9g); PROTEIN 3.9g; CARB 37.6g; FIBER 5.3g; CHOL 5mg; IRON 1.1mg; SODIUM 571mg; CALC 71mg

Fried Green Tomatoes

Fried Green Tomatoes

8 (½-inch-thick) slices green tomato (about 4
    tomatoes)
½ teaspoon salt
¼ teaspoon black pepper
½ cup yellow cornmeal
1 tablespoon vegetable oil

1. Sprinkle 1 side of each tomato slice evenly with
salt and pepper. Dredge seasoned sides in cornmeal.
2. Heat oil in a large skillet over medium-high heat.
Add the tomato slices, coated sides down; cook 6
minutes, turning after 3 minutes. Serve immediately. Yield: 4 servings (serving size: 2 slices).

CALORIES 123 (29% from fat); FAT 3.9g (sat 0.6g, mono 0.9g, poly 2.2g); PROTEIN 3g;
CARB 19.8g; FIBER 2.7g; CHOL 0mg; IRON 0.9mg; SODIUM 310mg; CALC 18mg

Squash-Rice Casserole

8 cups sliced zucchini (about 2½ pounds)
1 cup chopped onion
½ cup fat-free, less-sodium chicken broth
2 cups cooked rice
1 cup fat-free sour cream
1 cup (4 ounces) shredded reduced-fat sharp
    cheddar cheese
¼ cup (1 ounce) grated fresh Parmesan cheese,
    divided
¼ cup Italian-seasoned breadcrumbs
1 teaspoon salt
¼ teaspoon black pepper
2 large eggs, lightly beaten
Cooking spray

1. Preheat oven to 350°.
2. Combine first 3 ingredients in a Dutch oven;
bring to a boil. Cover, reduce heat, and simmer 20
minutes or until tender. Drain; partially mash with
a potato masher. Combine zucchini mixture, rice,
sour cream, cheddar cheese, 2 tablespoons Parmesan, breadcrumbs, salt, pepper, and eggs in a bowl;
stir gently. Spoon zucchini mixture into a 13 x 9-
inch baking dish coated with cooking spray; sprinkle
with 2 tablespoons Parmesan. Bake at 350° for 30
minutes or until bubbly and golden.
3. Preheat broiler.
4. Broil 1 minute or until lightly browned. Yield: 8
servings (serving size: 1 cup).

CALORIES 197 (25% from fat); FAT 5.5g (sat 2.7g, mono 1.5g, poly 0.4g); PROTEIN 12.7g;
CARB 24g; FIBER 1.4g; CHOL 65mg; IRON 1.5mg; SODIUM 623mg; CALC 209mg

Chile-Vinegar Turnip Greens

1½ teaspoons olive oil
2 garlic cloves, minced
1 (1-pound) bag turnip greens, chopped
1 cup fat-free, less-sodium chicken broth
¼ cup rice vinegar
2 teaspoons chile paste with garlic
½ teaspoon freshly ground black pepper

1. Heat oil in a stockpot over medium-high heat.
Add garlic; sauté 30 seconds or until lightly
browned. Add greens; sauté 5 minutes or until
wilted. Add remaining ingredients. Bring to a boil;
cover, reduce heat, and cook 45 minutes. Yield: 4
servings (serving size: 1 cup).

CALORIES 56 (32% from fat); FAT 2g (sat 0.3g, mono 1.3g, poly 0.3g); PROTEIN 2g;
CARB 7.4g; FIBER 2.8g; CHOL 0mg; IRON 1.4mg; SODIUM 202mg; CALC 219mg

Baked Garlic-Cheese Grits

A touch of hot pepper sauce is added to enhance the
sharp flavor of the cheese.

4 cups water
1¼ teaspoons salt
1 cup uncooked quick-cooking grits
1½ cups (6 ounces) shredded reduced-fat
    extrasharp cheddar cheese, divided
1 tablespoon butter
¾ cup 2% reduced-fat milk
2 teaspoons garlic powder
½ teaspoon hot pepper sauce (such as Tabasco)
2 large eggs
Cooking spray

1. Preheat oven to 350°.
2. Bring water and salt to a boil in a saucepan. Gradually add grits; stir constantly. Cover, and simmer 8
minutes until thick. Stir frequently. Remove from heat.
Add 1 cup cheese and butter; stir until cheese melts.
3. Combine milk and next 3 ingredients, stirring
with a whisk. Stir milk mixture into grits mixture.
Pour into an 8-inch square baking dish coated with
cooking spray. Bake, uncovered, at 350° for 45
minutes. Sprinkle with ½ cup cheese, and bake an
additional 15 minutes or until cheese melts. Let
grits stand 10 minutes before serving. Yield: 8 servings (serving size: ¾ cup).

CALORIES 162 (27% from fat); FAT 4.9g (sat 2.3g, mono 1.5g, poly 0.3g); PROTEIN 6.7g;
CARB 23g; FIBER 1.3g; CHOL 66mg; IRON 0.9mg; SODIUM 560mg; CALC 223mg

Peanutty Noodles

Break the pasta in half before cooking it to make serving easier. These noodles become their own main dish when you add cooked shrimp or chicken. If stovetop space is a problem, this dish cooks up beautifully in an electric skillet.

2   carrots, peeled
1   tablespoon vegetable oil, divided
2   teaspoons grated peeled fresh ginger
3   garlic cloves, minced
1   cup fat-free, less-sodium chicken
    broth
½   cup natural-style peanut butter
¼   cup low-sodium soy sauce
3   tablespoons rice vinegar or white
    wine vinegar
1   teaspoon chili garlic sauce
¼   teaspoon salt
Cooking spray
2   cups red bell pepper strips
1   pound snow peas, trimmed
8   cups hot cooked linguine (about
    1 pound uncooked pasta)
½   cup chopped fresh cilantro

1. Shave carrots lengthwise into thin strips using a vegetable peeler; set aside.

2. Heat 1 teaspoon oil in a small saucepan over medium heat. Add ginger and garlic; sauté for 30 seconds. Add broth and next 5 ingredients, and stir until well blended. Reduce heat, and simmer for 7 minutes, stirring occasionally. Remove from heat, and keep warm.

3. Heat 2 teaspoons oil in a large nonstick skillet coated with cooking spray over medium-high heat. Add bell peppers and snow peas; sauté 5 minutes or until tender. Remove from heat. Combine carrot, peanut butter mixture, bell pepper mixture, and linguine in a large bowl, and toss well. Sprinkle with cilantro. Serve warm or at room temperature. Yield: 10 servings (serving size: 1 cup).

CALORIES 296 (27% from fat); FAT 8.8g (sat 1.7g, mono 3.8g, poly 2.7g); PROTEIN 11.7g; CARB 43.1g; FIBER 3.4g; CHOL 1mg; IRON 3.6mg; SODIUM 400mg; CALC 44mg

Creamy Polenta with Warm Tomato Compote

You can keep the polenta warm over very low heat for up to 30 minutes before serving; stir in a little water or milk if it gets too thick.

  6 cups cherry tomatoes (about 2 pounds)
Cooking spray
  1 tablespoon olive oil
¼ cup sliced shallots (about 3 medium)
1½ tablespoons sugar
¾ cup dry white wine
1½ teaspoons salt, divided
¼ teaspoon black pepper
  2 cups 1% low-fat milk
  2 cups water
  1 cup dry polenta
½ cup (2 ounces) shaved fresh Parmesan cheese

1. Preheat oven to 425°.
2. Cut several slits in bottom of each tomato; place, stem sides down, in a shallow roasting pan coated with cooking spray. Bake at 425° for 20 minutes. Reduce oven temperature to 375° (do not remove tomatoes from oven), and bake for 45 minutes or until tomatoes are browned. Cover and let stand for 10 minutes.
3. Heat oil in a large nonstick skillet over medium-high heat. Add shallots; sauté 5 minutes or until browned. Add sugar; sauté 5 minutes. Add wine; reduce heat, and simmer for 5 minutes. Add ½ teaspoon salt and pepper. Remove from heat; stir in tomatoes. Cover; set aside.
4. Combine milk and water in a large saucepan; bring to a boil. Remove from heat, and gradually add polenta, stirring constantly with a whisk. Cover and cook over medium-low heat 2 minutes. Add 1 teaspoon salt; cover and let stand for 5 minutes or until thick, stirring occasionally. Top with tomato compote and Parmesan. Yield: 8 servings (serving size: ½ cup polenta, ⅓ cup tomato compote, and 1 tablespoon Parmesan).

CALORIES 153 (28% from fat); FAT 4.8g (sat 1.9g, mono 2g, poly 0.4g); PROTEIN 6.8g; CARB 21.6g; FIBER 1.7g; CHOL 7mg; IRON 0.9mg; SODIUM 597mg; CALC 169mg

Herbed Basmati Rice

  2 teaspoons butter or stick margarine
  1 garlic clove, minced
½ cup uncooked basmati rice
  1 cup water
¼ teaspoon salt
  2 tablespoons thinly sliced green onion tops
  2 teaspoons minced fresh or ½ teaspoon dried basil
  1 teaspoon minced fresh or ¼ teaspoon dried thyme
  2 tablespoons (½ ounce) grated fresh Parmesan cheese
Thyme sprigs (optional)

1. Melt butter in a small saucepan over medium heat. Add garlic; sauté 1 minute. Add rice, and stir well. Add water and salt, and bring to a boil. Cover, reduce heat, and simmer 20 minutes or until liquid is absorbed. Stir in onions, basil, and minced thyme. Sprinkle with cheese; garnish with thyme sprigs, if desired. Yield: 4 servings (serving size: ½ cup).

CALORIES 115 (22% from fat); FAT 2.8g (sat 0.9g, mono 1.1g, poly 0.7g); PROTEIN 2.8g; CARB 19.2g; FIBER 0.3g; CHOL 2mg; IRON 1.5mg; SODIUM 217mg; CALC 52mg

Herbed Basmati Rice

Wild Rice Cakes with Bacon

2 teaspoons butter
1 cup uncooked brown and wild rice blend
(such as Uncle Ben's)
1½ teaspoons salt
1 (14-ounce) can fat-free, less-sodium chicken
broth
1 large egg
1 large egg white
½ cup all-purpose flour
½ teaspoon baking powder
1 cup thinly sliced green onions
½ cup slivered almonds, toasted
2 teaspoons fresh thyme leaves
1 teaspoon fresh lemon juice
2 bacon slices, cooked and crumbled
Cooking spray

1. Melt butter in a large saucepan over medium-high heat. Add rice, and cook 1 minute, stirring constantly. Add salt and broth, and bring to a boil. Cover, reduce heat, and simmer for 40 minutes or until rice is tender and liquid is absorbed. Drain any excess liquid. Cool slightly.
2. Place egg and egg white in a large bowl. Lightly spoon flour into a dry measuring cup, and level with a knife. Add flour and baking powder to egg mixture, stirring with a whisk. Add rice, green onions, and next 4 ingredients, stirring with a rubber spatula until well blended.
3. Heat a large nonstick skillet coated with cooking spray over medium-high heat. Spoon 3 (¼-cup) mounds rice mixture into skillet; flatten slightly with spatula. Cook 2 minutes on each side or until golden brown and thoroughly heated. Repeat the procedure with remaining rice mixture. Serve immediately. Yield: 12 servings (serving size: 1 cake).

CALORIES 128 (30% from fat); FAT 4.2g (sat 0.9g, mono 2.1g, poly 0.8g); PROTEIN 4.7g; CARB 17.7g; FIBER 1.6g; CHOL 20mg; IRON 0.8mg; SODIUM 412mg; CALC 28mg

Champagne-Feta Risotto

Use that little bit of leftover Champagne from last night's dinner party in this recipe.

⅓ cup water
½ teaspoon dried basil
2 (15.75-ounce) cans fat-free, less-sodium
chicken broth
1 tablespoon olive oil
1 cup chopped onion
1 cup uncooked Arborio rice or other
short-grain rice
½ cup Champagne or white wine
⅔ cup (about 2½ ounces) crumbled feta cheese
¼ cup (1 ounce) grated fresh Parmesan cheese

1. Bring first 3 ingredients to a simmer in a medium saucepan (do not boil). Keep warm over low heat.
2. Heat oil in a large saucepan over medium-high heat. Add onion, and sauté 3 minutes. Add rice; sauté 2 minutes. Stir in Champagne; cook 1 minute or until the liquid is absorbed. Stir in 1 cup broth mixture, and cook for 5 minutes or until liquid is nearly absorbed, stirring constantly. Reduce heat to medium. Add remaining broth mixture, ½ cup at a time, stirring constantly until each portion of broth is absorbed before adding the next (about 25 minutes total). Stir in feta. Sprinkle each serving with Parmesan. Yield: 4 servings (serving size: 1 cup risotto and 1 tablespoon Parmesan).

CALORIES 331 (27% from fat); FAT 10.1g (sat 4.9g, mono 4.1g, poly 0.6g); PROTEIN 12.4g; CARB 45.8g; FIBER 1.5g; CHOL 24mg; IRON 2.6mg; SODIUM 835mg; CALC 204mg

Corn Bread, Cherry, and Bacon Stuffing

Make the corn bread croutons a day ahead (place them in an airtight container)
or up to a week in advance (keep them in the freezer).

⅔ cup fat-free milk
2 large eggs
2 (8½-ounce) packages corn muffin mix
Cooking spray
6 bacon slices
2 cups chopped onion
2 cups diced carrot
2 cups diced celery
½ cup dried tart cherries
1 (15.75-ounce) can fat-free, less-sodium
    chicken broth
1 cup chopped fresh parsley
1 teaspoon dried thyme
½ teaspoon salt
¼ teaspoon black pepper

1. Preheat oven to 400°.

2. Combine milk and eggs in a bowl; stir well with a whisk. Stir in muffin mix; let stand 2 minutes. Pour corn bread mixture into a 13 x 9-inch baking dish coated with cooking spray. Bake at 400° for 20 minutes or until a wooden pick inserted in center comes out clean. Cool and cut into ½-inch cubes. Place cubes on a baking sheet; bake at 400° for 10 minutes or until golden brown.

3. Cook the bacon in a large nonstick skillet over medium heat until crisp. Remove bacon from pan, reserving 1 teaspoon drippings in pan. Crumble the bacon, and set aside. Add the onion, carrot, and celery to pan, and sauté for 5 minutes over medium-high heat. Stir in the cherries and chicken broth, and cook for 5 minutes.

4. Combine the corn bread cubes, crumbled bacon, onion mixture, chopped parsley, dried thyme, salt, and pepper in a large bowl, and stir until well blended. Spoon corn bread mixture into a 13 x 9-inch baking dish coated with cooking spray. Bake at 400° for 20 minutes or until thoroughly heated, stirring after 10 minutes. Yield: 12 servings (serving size: ¾ cup).

CALORIES 248 (28% from fat); FAT 7.6g (sat 2g, mono 3g, poly 2.1g); PROTEIN 5.7g; CARB 39g; FIBER 2.9g; CHOL 41mg; IRON 2.1mg; SODIUM 524mg; CALC 113mg

Soups

Gazpacho with Avocado and
Cumin Chips, page 318

Yellow Pepper Soup with Cilantro Puree

Peas add body and sweetness to the puree. If you can't find crème fraîche, substitute sour cream.

SOUP:

1 teaspoon butter
1½ cups chopped onion
1 cup chopped fennel bulb
1 teaspoon curry powder
1 teaspoon grated peeled fresh ginger
2 garlic cloves, chopped
⅓ cup dry white wine
3¼ cups coarsely chopped yellow bell pepper (about 1¼ pounds)
3 cups fat-free, less-sodium chicken broth
1½ cups chopped peeled Granny Smith apple (about ½ pound)
1 cup cubed peeled Yukon gold or red potato
¼ teaspoon salt
2 tablespoons fresh lemon juice

PUREE:

⅓ cup frozen green peas, thawed
⅓ cup fresh cilantro leaves
3 tablespoons fat-free, less-sodium chicken broth
1 tablespoon mirin (sweet rice wine)
1 teaspoon vegetable oil
Dash of salt

REMAINING INGREDIENT:

2 tablespoons crème fraîche

1. To prepare soup, melt butter in a Dutch oven over medium-high heat. Add chopped onion and fennel, and sauté 3 minutes. Add curry, grated ginger, and garlic, and sauté 1 minute. Stir in wine, and cook 1 minute or until liquid almost evaporates. Add chopped bell pepper, broth, apple, potato, and ¼ teaspoon salt; bring to a boil. Reduce heat; simmer 20 minutes. Cool.

2. Place half of soup in a blender, and process until smooth. Pour into a bowl. Repeat the procedure with remaining soup. Chill for at least 2 hours; stir in lemon juice.

3. To prepare the puree, place peas and the next 5 ingredients in a blender, and process until smooth.

4. Pour ¾ cup soup into each of 6 bowls. Make 3 dollops with 1 teaspoon each of puree. Using the tip of a knife, swirl each dollop into a "V" shape. Dollop 1 teaspoon crème fraîche in center of each serving. Yield: 6 servings.

CALORIES 138 (18% from fat); FAT 2.7g (sat 1.1g, mono 0.7g, poly 0.7g); PROTEIN 4.2g; CARB 23g; FIBER 4.5g; CHOL 4mg; IRON 1mg; SODIUM 392mg; CALC 40mg

Gazpacho with Roasted Peppers

3 cups chopped seeded peeled tomato
  (about 1½ pounds)
⅓ cup finely chopped red onion
3 large basil leaves
1 garlic clove, minced
1 cup finely chopped peeled cucumber, divided
1½ cups tomato juice
½ cup finely chopped Roasted Bell Peppers or
  bottled roasted bell peppers
2 tablespoons red wine vinegar
1 teaspoon Worcestershire sauce
1 teaspoon extravirgin olive oil
½ teaspoon salt
¼ teaspoon black pepper
4 teaspoons chopped fresh flat-leaf parsley

1. Combine first 4 ingredients in a food processor, and add ¾ cup cucumber. Pulse 5 times or until coarsely pureed. (Mixture will not be smooth.)
2. Combine pureed tomato mixture, juice, and next 6 ingredients; stir well. Cover and refrigerate 3 hours or until chilled.
3. Sprinkle soup with ¼ cup cucumber and parsley. Yield: 4 servings (serving size: about 1 cup).
NOTE: Store soup in refrigerator up to 2 days. Stir and sprinkle with parsley before serving.

(Totals include Roasted Bell Peppers) CALORIES 72 (23% from fat); FAT 1.8g (sat 0.3g, mono 0.9g, poly 0.4g); PROTEIN 2.5g; CARB 14.2g; FIBER 2.8g; CHOL 0mg; IRON 1.6mg; SODIUM 651mg; CALC 31mg

ROASTED BELL PEPPERS:
When making substitutions, keep in mind that green peppers aren't as sweet as red, yellow, and orange bell peppers, which are interchangeable.

4 large bell peppers (about 2 pounds)

1. Preheat broiler.
2. Cut bell peppers in half lengthwise; discard seeds and membranes. Place pepper halves, skin sides up, on a foil-lined baking sheet; flatten with hand. Broil 20 minutes or until skin sides are thoroughly blackened.
3. Immediately place peppers in a large zip-top plastic bag; seal. Let stand 20 minutes. Peel peppers, and discard skins. Chop peppers according to recipe directions or store in an airtight container in refrigerator. Yield: 4 servings (serving size: 1 pepper).

CALORIES 44 (6% from fat); FAT 0.3g (sat 0.1g, mono 0g, poly 0.2g); PROTEIN 1.5g; CARB 10.6g; FIBER 3.1g; CHOL 0mg; IRON 0.8mg; SODIUM 3.3mg; CALC 15mg

Gazpacho with Avocado and Cumin Chips

(pictured on page 314)

1½ cups bottled Bloody Mary mix
1½ cups finely diced tomato
1 cup finely diced yellow bell pepper
¾ cup chopped seeded peeled cucumber
¾ cup finely diced red onion
2 tablespoons fresh lime juice
1 teaspoon red wine vinegar
1 teaspoon Worcestershire sauce
½ teaspoon freshly ground black pepper
2 garlic cloves, crushed
1 (5.5-ounce) can low-sodium vegetable juice
1 (5.5-ounce) can tomato juice
¾ cup diced peeled avocado
¾ cup chopped green onions
Cumin Chips

1. Combine first 12 ingredients in a large nonaluminum bowl. Cover; chill. Serve with avocado, green onions, and Cumin Chips. Yield: 6 servings (serving size: 1 cup soup, 2 tablespoons avocado, 2 tablespoons green onions, and 4 cumin chips).

(Totals include Cumin Chips) CALORIES 129 (27% from fat); FAT 3.8g (sat 0.6g, mono 2g, poly 0.7g); PROTEIN 3g; CARB 22.8g; FIBER 3.4g; CHOL 0mg; IRON 2mg; SODIUM 571mg; CALC 75mg

CUMIN CHIPS:

4 (6-inch) corn tortillas, each cut into 6 wedges
Cooking spray
½ teaspoon ground cumin

1. Preheat oven to 350°.
2. Place tortilla wedges on a large baking sheet. Lightly coat wedges with cooking spray, and sprinkle with cumin. Bake at 350° for 10 minutes or until chips are lightly browned and crisp. Yield: 2 dozen (serving size: 4 chips)

Carrot-Ginger Soup

Ginger juice—squeezed from minced fresh ginger—provides flavor in this recipe without altering the puree's creamy smoothness. The juice is added at the end so the flavor stays strong.

2 tablespoons coriander seeds
1 tablespoon black peppercorns
3 garlic cloves, peeled
2 star anise
2 (3-inch) cinnamon sticks
1 tablespoon olive oil
3 cups chopped onion
3 garlic cloves, minced
2½ cups chopped carrot (about 1 pound)
2 cups water
2 (14½-ounce) cans vegetable broth
⅓ cup chopped peeled fresh ginger
1 tablespoon water
½ cup 2% reduced-fat milk
2 tablespoons honey
Fresh chives (optional)

1. Place first 5 ingredients on a double layer of cheesecloth. Gather edges of cheesecloth together; tie securely.
2. Heat oil in a Dutch oven over medium-high heat. Add onion; sauté 5 minutes or until tender. Add minced garlic; sauté 1 minute. Add cheesecloth bag, carrot, 2 cups water, and broth; bring to a boil. Cover, reduce heat, and cook 1 hour or until carrot is tender. Discard cheesecloth bag.
3. Place ginger and 1 tablespoon water in a food processor; process until finely minced, scraping sides of bowl occasionally. Place ginger mixture on a double layer of cheesecloth. Gather edges of cheesecloth together; squeeze to extract juice to equal 2 tablespoons. Add ginger juice, milk, and honey to carrot mixture. Place half of carrot mixture in food processor; process until smooth. Pour pureed carrot mixture into a large bowl. Repeat procedure with remaining carrot mixture. Garnish with chives, if desired. Yield: 6 servings (serving size: 1 cup).

CALORIES 125 (26% from fat); FAT 3.6g (sat 0.6g, mono 1.8g, poly 0.3g); PROTEIN 2.5g; CARB 24.3g; FIBER 4g; CHOL 2mg; IRON 0.6mg; SODIUM 706mg; CALC 65mg

Butternut Squash Soup with Sautéed Radicchio

A topping of sautéed radicchio provides a slightly bitter, sharp contrast to the creamy, sweet soup.

3 pounds butternut squash (about 2 medium)
Cooking spray
5 teaspoons olive oil, divided
5½ cups finely chopped onion (about 2 large)
¼ cup chopped fresh parsley
2 tablespoons chopped fresh or 1½ teaspoons dried sage
½ teaspoon chopped fresh or ⅛ teaspoon dried thyme
4½ cups water
1½ teaspoons sea salt, divided
½ teaspoon coarsely ground black pepper, divided
2 garlic cloves, minced
6 cups thinly sliced radicchio (about 1¼ pounds)
1 tablespoon balsamic vinegar
6 tablespoons (1½ ounces) grated fresh Parmesan cheese

1. Preheat oven to 375°.
2. Cut squash in half lengthwise, and remove seeds. Place squash halves, cut sides down, on a foil-lined baking sheet coated with cooking spray. Bake at 375° for 30 minutes or until tender. Scoop out pulp; set aside. Discard skins.

3. Heat 2 teaspoons olive oil in a large Dutch oven over medium heat. Add finely chopped onion, parsley, sage, and thyme; cook for 15 minutes or until lightly browned, stirring frequently. Add squash, water, 1¼ teaspoons salt, ¼ teaspoon pepper, and minced garlic, and bring to a boil. Partially cover, reduce heat, and simmer 25 minutes. Place about 2½ cups squash mixture in a blender, and process until smooth. Pour pureed soup into a large bowl. Repeat the procedure with remaining squash mixture, 2½ cups at a time.

4. Heat 1 tablespoon oil in a large nonstick skillet over medium-high heat. Add radicchio, ¼ teaspoon salt, and ¼ teaspoon pepper, and sauté 5 minutes or until lightly browned. Remove from heat; drizzle with vinegar, tossing to coat. Ladle 1⅓ cups soup into each of 6 bowls. Top each serving with ⅓ cup radicchio and 1 tablespoon cheese. Yield: 6 servings.

CALORIES 217 (26% from fat); FAT 6.2g (sat 1.8g, mono 3.4g, poly 0.6g); PROTEIN 6.9g; CARB 38.1g; FIBER 9.6g; CHOL 5mg; IRON 2.2mg; SODIUM 712mg; CALC 224mg

Tomato-Basil Soup

Tomato-Basil Soup

    4   cups chopped seeded peeled tomato
    4   cups low-sodium tomato juice
    ⅓   cup fresh basil leaves
    1   cup 1% low-fat milk
    ¼   teaspoon salt
    ¼   teaspoon cracked black pepper
    ½   cup (4 ounces) ⅓-less-fat cream cheese,
        softened
        Basil leaves, thinly sliced (optional)
    8   (½-inch-thick) slices diagonally cut French
        bread baguette

1. Bring tomato and juice to a boil in a large saucepan. Reduce heat; simmer 30 minutes.
2. Place tomato mixture and ⅓ cup basil in a blender or food processor; process until smooth. Return pureed mixture to pan; stir in milk, salt, and pepper. Add the cream cheese, stirring well with a whisk, and cook over medium heat until thick (about 5 minutes). Ladle soup into each of 8 bowls; garnish with sliced basil, if desired. Serve with bread. Yield: 8 servings (serving size: 1 cup soup and 1 bread slice).
NOTE: Refrigerate remaining soup in an airtight container for up to 1 week.

CALORIES 133 (30% from fat); FAT 4.4g (sat 2.4g, mono 1.3g, poly 0.4g); PROTEIN 5.4g; CARB 18.7g; FIBER 1.9g; CHOL 12mg; IRON 1.5mg; SODIUM 310mg; CALC 77mg

Vegetarian West African Soup

This hearty, one-dish meal is high in dietary fiber and can be ready in less than an hour.

    ⅔   cup roasted peanuts
    2   teaspoons vegetable oil
    2   cups chopped onion
    6   cups (1-inch) cubed peeled sweet potato
    1   tablespoon ground cumin
    ½   teaspoon black pepper
    ¼   teaspoon salt
    2   (15½-ounce) cans chickpeas (garbanzo
        beans), drained
    2   (14½-ounce) cans vegetable broth
    1   (28-ounce) can diced tomatoes, undrained

1. Place peanuts in a food processor; process until smooth, scraping sides of bowl once.
2. Heat oil in a Dutch oven over medium-high heat. Add onion; sauté 7 minutes or until lightly browned.

3. Add peanut butter, potato, and remaining ingredients; bring to a boil. Reduce heat; simmer, uncovered, 30 minutes or until potato is tender. Yield: 8 servings (serving size: 1½ cups).

CALORIES 477 (18% from fat); FAT 9.4g (sat 1.3g, mono 3.5g, poly 3.3g); PROTEIN 13g; CARB 89.7g; FIBER 13.1g; CHOL 0mg; IRON 3.2mg; SODIUM 904mg; CALC 110mg

Vegetarian Minestrone

This earthy, elegant soup is probably also one of our most economical, using familiar ingredients that are on hand in most kitchens.

    2   teaspoons olive oil
    ¾   cup chopped onion
    3   cups water
    2   cups diced zucchini
    1   cup diced carrot
    1   cup drained canned cannellini beans or
        other white beans
    ¾   cup diced celery
    ½   teaspoon dried basil
    ¼   teaspoon salt
    ¼   teaspoon dried oregano
    ⅛   teaspoon coarsely ground black pepper
    1   (14.5-ounce) can diced tomatoes, undrained
    1   garlic clove, minced
    ¼   cup uncooked ditalini (very short tube-shaped
        macaroni) or elbow macaroni
    4   teaspoons grated Parmesan cheese

1. Heat oil in a large saucepan over medium-high heat. Add onion, and sauté for 4 minutes or until lightly browned. Add water and next 10 ingredients, and bring to a boil. Cover, reduce heat to medium-low, and cook for 25 minutes. Add pasta; cover and cook for 10 minutes. Ladle into each of 4 bowls, and sprinkle with cheese. Yield: 4 servings (serving size: 1½ cups soup and 1 teaspoon cheese).

CALORIES 176 (17% from fat); FAT 3.3g (sat 0.7g, mono 1.9g, poly 0.5g); PROTEIN 8.8g; CARB 30.2g; FIBER 4.4g; CHOL 1mg; IRON 2.9mg; SODIUM 699mg; CALC 112mg

Chunky Potato-Crab Chowder

This easy New England-style chowder lets the red-skinned potatoes shine. Cream-style corn is a surprise ingredient that adds a little sweetness and contributes to the creamy texture.

2 tablespoons butter
1 cup chopped onion
¾ cup chopped celery
1 garlic clove, minced
3½ cups (1-inch) cubed red potato (about 1 pound)
3 tablespoons all-purpose flour
2½ cups 2% reduced-fat milk
½ teaspoon dried thyme
½ teaspoon freshly ground black pepper
¼ teaspoon grated whole nutmeg
1 (14¾-ounce) can cream-style corn
1 (14-ounce) can fat-free, less-sodium chicken broth
8 ounces lump crabmeat, shell pieces removed
3 tablespoons chopped fresh parsley
1 teaspoon salt

1. Melt butter in a large saucepan over medium-high heat. Add onion, celery, and garlic; sauté 4 minutes. Add potato; sauté 1 minute. Sprinkle with flour, and cook 1 minute, stirring constantly. Stir in milk, thyme, pepper, nutmeg, corn, and broth. Bring to a simmer over medium heat, stirring frequently. Cover, reduce heat, and simmer 20 minutes or until potato is tender, stirring occasionally. Stir in crab, parsley, and salt; cook 5 minutes, stirring occasionally. Yield: 6 servings (serving size: 1½ cups).

CALORIES 265 (23% from fat); FAT 6.8g (sat 3.8g, mono 1.9g, poly 0.6g); PROTEIN 16.3g; CARB 36.5g; FIBER 3.1g; CHOL 47mg; IRON 1.5mg; SODIUM 968mg; CALC 176mg

Thai Shrimp Bisque

A bisque is a rich, thickened soup that usually contains seafood. For this dish, we've combined the strong accents of traditional Thai flavorings—lime, cilantro, ginger, and coconut milk to produce a bold and creamy main-dish soup.

MARINADE:

1½ pounds medium shrimp
1½ tablespoons grated lime rind
⅓ cup fresh lime juice
1½ tablespoons ground coriander
1 tablespoon minced fresh cilantro
1 tablespoon minced peeled fresh ginger
1½ teaspoons sugar
¼ teaspoon ground red pepper
2 garlic cloves, crushed

SHRIMP STOCK:

2 cups water
¼ cup dry white wine
1 tablespoon tomato paste

SOUP:

1 teaspoon olive oil
½ cup chopped onion
⅓ cup chopped celery
1 (14-ounce) can light coconut milk
1 tablespoon tomato paste
¼ cup all-purpose flour
1 cup 2% reduced-fat milk
1 tablespoon grated lime rind
1 tablespoon minced fresh cilantro
½ teaspoon salt

1. To prepare the marinade, peel shrimp, reserving shells. Combine the shrimp and the next 8 ingredients in a large zip-top plastic bag; seal and marinate in refrigerator 30 minutes.

2. To prepare the shrimp stock, combine reserved shrimp shells, water, wine, and 1 tablespoon tomato paste in a large Dutch oven. Bring mixture to a boil. Reduce heat; simmer until liquid is reduced to 1 cup (about 10 minutes). Strain mixture through a sieve over a bowl, and discard solids.

3. To prepare soup, heat oil in a large Dutch oven over medium heat. Add onion and celery, and sauté for 8 minutes or until browned. Add 1 cup shrimp stock, coconut milk, and 1 tablespoon tomato paste, scraping pan to loosen browned bits. Bring mixture to a boil. Lightly spoon flour into a dry measuring cup, and level with a knife. Combine the flour and reduced-fat milk in a small bowl, stirring with a whisk. Add to pan; reduce heat, and simmer until thick (about 5 minutes). Add shrimp and marinade, and cook 5 minutes. Stir in 1 tablespoon lime rind, 1 tablespoon cilantro, and salt. Yield: 6 servings (serving size: 1½ cups).

CALORIES 201 (30% from fat); FAT 6.7g (sat 3.2g, mono 1.7g, poly 1.2g); PROTEIN 19.9g; CARB 15.2g; FIBER 0.9g; CHOL 133mg; IRON 3.3mg; SODIUM 380mg; CALC 117mg

Pork Cassoulet

Pork Cassoulet

1 pound dried Great Northern beans
2 bacon slices, cut into 1-inch pieces
3 pounds boneless pork loin, cut into 1-inch cubes
1 pound turkey kielbasa, cut into ½-inch pieces
2½ cups chopped onion
1 cup sliced celery
1 cup (¼-inch-thick) slices carrot
4 garlic cloves, minced
2 teaspoons dried thyme
¼ cup water
2 tablespoons tomato paste
1 (14½-ounce) can fat-free, less-sodium chicken broth
1 (14.5-ounce) can no-salt-added diced tomatoes, undrained
½ cup dry white wine
½ teaspoon salt
¼ teaspoon black pepper
1 cup (¼-inch-thick) red bell pepper rings
1½ cups (1-inch) cubed French bread
⅓ cup (about 1½ ounces) grated fresh Parmesan cheese

1. Sort and wash beans; place in a large Dutch oven. Cover with water to 2 inches above beans; bring to a boil, and cook for 2 minutes. Remove from heat; cover and let stand 1 hour. Drain; return beans to pan. Cover beans with water; bring to a boil. Cover, reduce heat, and simmer for 20 minutes; drain. Set aside.
2. Preheat oven to 300°.
3. Add bacon to pan; cook over medium heat until crisp. Remove bacon with a slotted spoon. Increase heat to medium-high. Add pork to drippings in pan, and cook 5 minutes or until browned, stirring occasionally. Remove pork with a slotted spoon. Add the kielbasa; cook 5 minutes or until browned, stirring occasionally. Remove kielbasa with a slotted spoon. Add onion, celery, carrot, garlic, and thyme; sauté 4 minutes or until tender. Stir in ¼ cup water, tomato paste, broth, and tomatoes.
4. Return beans, bacon, pork, and kielbasa to pan; bring to a boil. Cover; bake at 300° for 1 hour. Remove 1 cup of beans and vegetables with a slotted spoon. Place in a blender or food processor; process until smooth. Return to pan. Stir in wine, salt, and black pepper. Arrange bell pepper rings evenly over top.
5. Place the bread in a food processor; pulse 10 times or until coarse crumbs form to measure 1½ cups. Combine with cheese. Sprinkle cassoulet with the breadcrumb mixture. Return the cassoulet to the oven, and bake, uncovered, an additional 45 minutes. Yield: 10 servings (serving size: about 1½ cups).

CALORIES 526 (30% from fat); FAT 17.6g (sat 6.5g, mono 7.3g, poly 2.5g); PROTEIN 50.7g; CARB 40.8g; FIBER 11.5g; CHOL 117mg; IRON 5.1mg; SODIUM 808mg; CALC 193mg

New England Pork Bowl

Perciatelli is thick spaghetti with a hole in the center. We've found it's heartier than regular spaghetti and stands up well to the ingredients in this dish.

¼ cup bourbon
¼ cup maple syrup
1 tablespoon Dijon mustard
½ teaspoon salt
½ teaspoon black pepper
5 garlic cloves, minced
1 pound boned pork loin, cut into thin strips
3 bacon slices, cut into ½-inch pieces
2 cups vertically sliced onion
1 cup thinly sliced leek (about 1 large)
2 cups (1-inch) cubed peeled sweet potato
2 cups water
3 (16-ounce) cans fat-free, less-sodium chicken broth
3 cups chopped spinach
4 cups hot cooked perciatelli (about 8 ounces uncooked tube-shaped spaghetti)
¾ cup (3 ounces) finely shredded white cheddar cheese
6 tablespoons chopped green onions

1. Combine first 7 ingredients in a large zip-top plastic bag. Seal and marinate in refrigerator 4 to 24 hours, turning bag occasionally. Remove pork from bag, reserving marinade.
2. Cook the bacon in a Dutch oven over medium-high heat until bacon is crisp. Remove bacon from pan; set aside. Add half of pork to drippings in pan; sauté 5 minutes, and remove pork from pan. Repeat procedure with remaining pork. Add onion and leek to pan; sauté for 5 minutes. Add reserved marinade, pork, and next 3 ingredients; bring to a boil. Reduce heat, and simmer 10 minutes. Stir in bacon and spinach; cook for 1 minute. Place pasta into each of 6 bowls; top with broth mixture, cheese, and green onions. Yield: 6 servings (serving size: ⅔ cup pasta, 2 cups broth mixture, 2 tablespoons cheese, and 1 tablespoon green onions).

CALORIES 478 (25% from fat); FAT 13.4g (sat 5.8g, mono 4.9g, poly 1.4g); PROTEIN 30.7g; CARB 57.3g; FIBER 4.5g; CHOL 63mg; IRON 4.1mg; SODIUM 983mg; CALC 189mg

Beef-Barley Pho

Beef and barley soup is a staple American comfort food; pho—beef and rice noodle soup—is the Vietnamese equivalent. Barley adds an interesting twist, as well as heartiness, to this anise-flavored soup. Charring the onion and ginger in a dry skillet gives the broth a deep flavor.

    2 cups sliced onion
    4 (⅛-inch) slices unpeeled fresh ginger
    5 cups low-salt beef broth
    2 tablespoons sugar
    2 tablespoons fish sauce
    5 star anise
    3 whole cloves
    4 cups water
    ½ cup uncooked pearl barley
Cooking spray
    3 (4-ounce) beef tenderloin steaks, trimmed
    1 cup fresh bean sprouts
    ½ cup vertically sliced onion
    ½ cup chopped green onions
   12 fresh basil leaves
    4 lime wedges
Chopped seeded serrano chiles (optional)

1. Combine 2 cups sliced onion and ginger slices in a heavy skillet over high heat. Cook for 4 minutes or until charred, stirring often. Remove from heat. Combine onion mixture, broth, and next 4 ingredients in a large saucepan, and bring to a boil. Cover, reduce heat, and simmer for 30 minutes. Drain the broth mixture through a sieve into a large bowl, reserving liquid, and discard solids. Return broth to pan, and set aside.

2. Bring water to a boil in a large saucepan. Add barley. Cover, reduce heat, and simmer 35 minutes or until done. Drain.

3. Heat a large nonstick skillet coated with cooking spray over medium-high heat. Add steaks; cook 4 minutes on each side or until desired degree of doneness. Remove from pan; cut steaks diagonally across grain into thin slices.

4. Bring broth to a boil. Spoon ½ cup barley into each of 4 bowls; ladle ⅔ cup boiling broth over barley. Divide beef, bean sprouts, ½ cup onion, green onions, and basil evenly among individual serving bowls. Serve with lime wedges and chiles, if desired. Yield: 4 servings.

CALORIES 315 (23% from fat); FAT 8.2g (sat 2.9g, mono 3.2g, poly 0.8g); PROTEIN 28g; CARB 31.2g; FIBER 5.2g; CHOL 54mg; IRON 3.9mg; SODIUM 787mg; CALC 32mg

French Onion-Beef Bowl

   1½ pounds boned sirloin steak, thinly sliced
    ½ cup chopped fresh parsley
    2 tablespoons balsamic vinegar
    2 teaspoons chopped fresh or ½ teaspoon dried thyme
    4 garlic cloves, crushed
    1 tablespoon butter or stick margarine
    6 cups vertically sliced onion (about 3 onions)
    1 teaspoon sugar
    3 tablespoons all-purpose flour
    3 cups water
    1 cup dry white wine
    1 (16-ounce) can fat-free, less-sodium chicken broth
    1 (10½-ounce) can beef consommé
    1 tablespoon Worcestershire sauce
    ½ teaspoon black pepper
    ¼ teaspoon salt
    4 cups hot cooked soba noodles (about 8 ounces uncooked buckwheat noodles)
    2 cups garlic-flavored croutons
    ½ cup (2 ounces) shredded Gruyère or Jarlsberg cheese
Chopped fresh parsley (optional)

1. Combine first 5 ingredients in a large zip-top plastic bag. Seal and marinate in refrigerator 1 to 4 hours. Remove steak from bag.

2. Melt butter in a large Dutch oven over medium-high heat. Add onion and sugar, and cook for 10 minutes or until golden brown, stirring frequently. Reduce heat to medium. Cover and cook for 10 minutes, stirring frequently. Stir flour into onion mixture, and cook, uncovered, 2 minutes. Add water, wine, broth, and consommé, stirring with a whisk. Bring to a boil; partially cover, reduce heat, and simmer 20 minutes. Add the beef mixture, Worcestershire, pepper, and salt; cook, uncovered, 5 minutes. Place noodles into each of 6 large bowls, and top with broth mixture, croutons, and cheese. Sprinkle with parsley, if desired. Yield: 6 servings (serving size: ⅔ cup noodles, about 1⅔ cups broth mixture, ⅓ cup croutons, and about 1 tablespoon cheese).

CALORIES 526 (25% from fat); FAT 14.9g (sat 6.1g, mono 5.4g, poly 2g); PROTEIN 37.7g; CARB 56.1g; FIBER 2.6g; CHOL 94mg; IRON 5.2mg; SODIUM 733mg; CALC 159mg

French Onion-Beef Bowl

Baked Potato Soup

Baked Potato Soup

All the flavors of a loaded baked potato come together in this rich, creamy soup.

    4   baking potatoes (about 2½ pounds)
    ⅔   cup all-purpose flour
    6   cups 2% reduced-fat milk
    1   cup (4 ounces) reduced-fat shredded
        extrasharp cheddar cheese, divided
    1   teaspoon salt
    ½   teaspoon black pepper
    1   cup reduced-fat sour cream
    ¾   cup chopped green onions, divided
    6   bacon slices, cooked and crumbled

1. Preheat oven to 400°.
2. Pierce potatoes with a fork; bake at 400° for 1 hour or until tender. Cool. Peel potatoes; coarsely mash. Discard skins.
3. Lightly spoon flour into a dry measuring cup; level with a knife. Place flour in a large Dutch oven; gradually add milk, stirring with a whisk until blended. Cook over medium heat until thick and bubbly (about 8 minutes). Add mashed potatoes, ¾ cup cheese, salt, and pepper, stirring until cheese melts. Remove from heat.
4. Stir in sour cream and ½ cup onions. Cook over low heat 10 minutes or until thoroughly heated (do not boil); ladle about 1½ cups soup into each of 8 bowls. Sprinkle each serving with 1½ teaspoons cheese, 1½ teaspoons onions, and about 1 tablespoon bacon. Yield: 8 servings.

CALORIES 329 (30% from fat); FAT 10.8g (sat 5.9g, mono 3.5g, poly 0.7g); PROTEIN 13.6g; CARB 44.5g; FIBER 2.8g; CHOL 38mg; IRON 1.1mg; SODIUM 587mg; CALC 407mg

Bean and Bacon Soup

    3   bacon slices, chopped
    1   cup chopped onion
    1   tablespoon chili powder
   1½   teaspoons dry mustard
   1½   cups water
    1   tablespoon dark molasses
    1   tablespoon red wine vinegar
    2   (15-ounce) cans cannellini beans or other
        white beans, drained
    1   (14½-ounce) can diced tomatoes with garlic
        and onions, undrained

1. Cook bacon in a saucepan over medium-high heat until crisp. Remove bacon from pan, reserving 2 teaspoons drippings in pan.
2. Add onion, chili powder, and mustard to drippings in pan; sauté 3 minutes. Stir in cooked bacon, water, and remaining ingredients; bring to a boil. Reduce heat; simmer 7 minutes.
3. Remove pan from heat. Partially mash the beans with a potato masher. Yield: 4 servings (serving size: 1¼ cups).

CALORIES 361 (28% from fat); FAT 11.2g (sat 3.8g, mono 4.6g, poly 1.7g); PROTEIN 20g; CARB 47.9g; FIBER 2.2g; CHOL 15mg; IRON 6.8mg; SODIUM 804mg; CALC 132mg

Avgolemono
(Greek Lemon Soup)

This quick-and-easy soup can be on your table in no time flat. Make sure to cook the rice first.

    4   large eggs, lightly beaten
    2   teaspoons grated lemon rind
    ⅓   cup fresh lemon juice
    ½   teaspoon kosher salt
    ¼   teaspoon ground red pepper
    1   (15.75-ounce) can fat-free, less-sodium
        chicken broth
    3   cups hot cooked long-grain rice
    ¼   cup chopped fresh parsley
   Thin lemon slices (optional)

1. Combine the eggs, lemon rind, lemon juice, salt, and red pepper in a small bowl, and set aside. Place the chicken broth in a large saucepan over medium-high heat, and bring to a boil. Reduce heat to medium, and whisk in the egg mixture. Cook mixture until thick (about 5 minutes), stirring constantly (do not boil). Serve over rice; sprinkle with parsley, and garnish with lemon slices, if desired. Yield: 4 servings (serving size: ¾ cup soup, ¾ cup rice, and 1 tablespoon parsley).

CALORIES 263 (19% from fat); FAT 5.6g (sat 1.7g, mono 2.1g, poly 0.8g); PROTEIN 11.5g; CARB 40.3g; FIBER 0.9g; CHOL 221mg; IRON 3mg; SODIUM 550mg; CALC 47mg

Spicy Mulligatawny

The name of this highly seasoned Indian soup means "pepper water." It gets quite a kick from the combination of curry powder, ground ginger, and crushed red pepper, but you can halve those ingredients if you don't like spicy foods.

1   tablespoon vegetable oil, divided
½   pound skinless, boneless chicken breast, cut into bite-sized pieces
1   cup chopped peeled Gala or Braeburn apple
¾   cup chopped onion
½   cup chopped carrot
½   cup chopped celery
½   cup chopped green bell pepper
2   tablespoons all-purpose flour
1   tablespoon curry powder
1   teaspoon ground ginger
½   teaspoon crushed red pepper
¼   teaspoon salt
2   (14½-ounce) cans fat-free, less-sodium chicken broth
⅓   cup mango chutney
¼   cup tomato paste
Chopped fresh parsley (optional)

1. Heat 1 teaspoon oil in a Dutch oven over medium-high heat. Add chicken; sauté 3 minutes. Remove from pan; set aside.

2. Heat 2 teaspoons oil in pan. Add apple and next 4 ingredients, and sauté 5 minutes, stirring frequently. Stir in flour and next 4 ingredients, and cook 1 minute. Stir in broth, chutney, and tomato paste, and bring to a boil.

3. Reduce heat; simmer 8 minutes. Return chicken to pan; cook 2 minutes or until mixture is thoroughly heated. Sprinkle with parsley, if desired. Yield: 4 servings (serving size: 1¼ cups).

CALORIES 236 (18% from fat); FAT 4.8g (sat 0.8g, mono 1.1g, poly 2.3g); PROTEIN 18g; CARB 31g; FIBER 4.9g; CHOL 33mg; IRON 1.9mg; SODIUM 599mg; CALC 42mg

Vietnamese Chicken Noodle Soup

Vietnamese recipes often call for adding herbs and sauces to a dish at the end of cooking. These ingredients allow you to easily tailor the soup to your taste. However, additional chili oil and fish sauce will increase the fat and sodium content.

    4   cups water
    ½   cup sliced shallots
    ¼   cup minced peeled fresh ginger
    5   teaspoons minced garlic (about 2 large cloves)
    1   tablespoon Thai fish sauce
    ½   teaspoon salt
    ½   teaspoon black pepper
    2   (14½-ounce) cans fat-free, less-sodium
        chicken broth
 1½   pounds skinless, boneless chicken thighs
    ¼   pound uncooked rice sticks (rice flour
        noodles) or vermicelli
    1   cup fresh bean sprouts
    2   tablespoons thinly sliced green onions
    2   tablespoons chopped fresh cilantro
    2   tablespoons thinly sliced fresh basil
    2   tablespoons thinly sliced fresh mint
    4   lime wedges
        Chopped hot red or Thai chile (optional)
        Fish sauce (optional)
        Chili oil (optional)

1. Combine first 9 ingredients in a large Dutch oven; bring to a boil. Reduce heat, and simmer 15 minutes or until chicken is done. Remove chicken from pan; cool slightly. Cut into bite-sized pieces.

2. Cook the rice sticks in boiling water for 5 minutes, and drain.

3. Divide chicken and noodles evenly among 4 large bowls. Ladle 2 cups soup into each bowl. Top each serving with ¼ cup bean sprouts and 1½ teaspoons each of onions, cilantro, basil, and mint. Serve with lime wedges; garnish with chopped chile, fish sauce, or chili oil, if desired. Yield: 4 servings.

CALORIES 346 (18% from fat); FAT 7.1g (sat 1.7g, mono 2.1g, poly 1.7g); PROTEIN 40.4g; CARB 29.1g; FIBER 1.1g; CHOL 141mg; IRON 2.6mg; SODIUM 1,279mg; CALC 61mg

Sausage and Chicken Gumbo

    1   (3½-ounce) bag boil-in-bag rice
    2   tablespoons all-purpose flour
    1   tablespoon vegetable oil
    1   cup frozen chopped onion
    1   cup frozen chopped green bell pepper
    1   cup frozen cut okra
    1   cup chopped celery
    1   teaspoon bottled minced garlic
    ½   teaspoon dried thyme
    ¼   teaspoon ground red pepper
    2   cups chopped roasted skinless, boneless
        chicken breasts (about 2 breasts)
    8   ounces turkey kielbasa, cut into 1-inch pieces
    1   (14½-ounce) can diced tomatoes with
        peppers and onion
    1   (14½-ounce) can fat-free, less-sodium
        chicken broth

1. Cook rice according to package directions, omitting salt and fat.

2. While the rice cooks, combine the flour and oil in a Dutch oven; sauté over medium-high heat for 3 minutes. Add onion and next 6 ingredients, and cook 3 minutes or until vegetables are tender, stirring frequently.

3. Stir in chicken, kielbasa, tomatoes, and broth; cook 6 minutes or until thoroughly heated, stirring occasionally. Serve over rice. Yield: 4 servings (serving size: 1½ cups gumbo and ½ cup rice).

CALORIES 369 (28% from fat); FAT 11.3g (sat 2.7g, mono 4.8g, poly 3g); PROTEIN 29.4g; CARB 37g; FIBER 3g; CHOL 77mg; IRON 2.2mg; SODIUM 949mg; CALC 92mg

Quick Chicken Corn
Chowder

Quick Chicken Corn Chowder

You can have this soup ready in less than 30 minutes.

2 tablespoons butter
¼ cup chopped onion
¼ cup chopped celery
1 jalapeño pepper, seeded and minced
2 tablespoons all-purpose flour
3 cups 2% reduced-fat milk
2 cups chopped roasted skinless, boneless chicken breasts (about 2 breast halves)
1 (14¾-ounce) can cream-style corn
1½ cups fresh or frozen corn kernels (about 3 ears)
1 teaspoon chopped fresh or ¼ teaspoon dried thyme
¼ teaspoon ground red pepper
⅛ teaspoon salt

1. Melt butter in a large Dutch oven over medium heat. Add onion, celery, and jalapeño; cook 3 minutes or until tender, stirring frequently. Add flour; cook 1 minute, stirring constantly. Stir in milk and remaining ingredients. Bring to a boil; cook until thick (about 5 minutes). Yield: 6 servings (serving size: about 1 cup).

CALORIES 257 (28% from fat); FAT 8.1g (sat 4.4g, mono 2.4g, poly 0.8g); PROTEIN 19.1g; CARB 28.6g; FIBER 1.9g; CHOL 52mg; IRON 0.4mg; SODIUM 668mg; CALC 165mg

Sopa Ranchera

SOUP:

1 teaspoon vegetable oil
1 cup chopped onion
½ teaspoon dried oregano
½ teaspoon ground cumin
1 garlic clove, minced
6 cups Chicken Stock or 3 (16-ounce) cans fat-free, less-sodium chicken broth
1¾ cups cubed peeled baking potato
1 (15-ounce) can chickpeas (garbanzo beans), drained
2 cups shredded cooked chicken breast (about 8 ounces)
1 cup frozen whole-kernel corn, thawed
¾ teaspoon salt
1 zucchini, quartered lengthwise and sliced (about 1½ cups)
1 cup diced tomato
⅓ cup chopped fresh cilantro

TOPPINGS:

⅔ cup finely chopped onion
⅔ cup chopped fresh cilantro
⅔ cup low-fat sour cream
⅔ cup (2½ ounces) shredded queso quesadilla cheese or reduced-fat Monterey Jack cheese
10 lime wedges

1. To prepare soup, heat oil in a large Dutch oven over medium-high heat. Add 1 cup onion; sauté 3 minutes. Add oregano, cumin, and garlic, and sauté 1 minute. Add Chicken Stock, potato, and chickpeas; bring mixture to a boil, and cook 5 minutes. Add chicken, corn, salt, and zucchini, and cook 5 minutes. Stir in tomato and ⅓ cup cilantro, and cook 2 minutes.

2. Ladle 1 cup soup into each of 10 bowls, and top with 1 tablespoon finely chopped onion, 1 tablespoon fresh cilantro, 1 tablespoon sour cream, and 1 tablespoon shredded cheese. Serve with lime wedges. Yield: 10 servings.

NOTE: Use reserved chicken from stock for soup.

(Totals include Chicken Stock) CALORIES 208 (31% from fat); FAT 7.2g (sat 2.9g, mono 2.2g, poly 1.3g); PROTEIN 16.1g; CARB 21.2g; FIBER 3g; CHOL 39mg; IRON 2.2mg; SODIUM 498mg; CALC 119mg

CHICKEN STOCK:

8 cups water
1 teaspoon salt
1 (3½-pound) chicken
1 medium onion, unpeeled and sliced
1 medium tomato, sliced
6 garlic cloves, sliced
3 bay leaves
1 tablespoon cider vinegar

1. Combine the first 7 ingredients in a large Dutch oven; cover and bring mixture to a boil over medium heat. Reduce heat, and simmer for 40 minutes or until chicken is done. Remove chicken from cooking liquid; cool. Remove chicken from bones, and reserve meat for another use. Return bones and skin to cooking liquid, and stir in cider vinegar. Cover and simmer 1 hour. Strain broth through a sieve into a large bowl, and discard solids. Cover and chill broth 8 hours. Skim solidified fat from surface of broth, and discard. Yield: 8 cups (serving size: 1 cup).

NOTE: The Chicken Stock may be frozen for up to 2 months.

CALORIES 26 (35% from fat); FAT 1g (sat 0.3g, mono 0.3g, poly 0.2g); PROTEIN 4g; CARB 0.1g; FIBER 0g; CHOL 12mg; IRON 0.2mg; SODIUM 304mg; CALC 2mg

Chocolate Chunk Bread
Puddings, page 381

Desserts

Buttermilk-Apple
Coffee Cake

Buttermilk-Apple Coffee Cake

CAKE:

1½ cups thinly sliced peeled Granny Smith apple
3 tablespoons brown sugar
1 tablespoon lemon juice
½ teaspoon ground cinnamon
1 cup all-purpose flour
½ teaspoon baking soda
⅛ teaspoon salt
⅓ cup granulated sugar
2 tablespoons butter, softened
1 large egg
1 teaspoon vanilla extract
½ teaspoon almond extract
½ cup low-fat buttermilk
Cooking spray
2 tablespoons sliced almonds

GLAZE:

¼ cup sifted powdered sugar
1 teaspoon low-fat buttermilk
¼ teaspoon vanilla extract

1. Preheat oven to 350°.

2. To prepare the cake, combine the first 4 ingredients in a small saucepan over medium-high heat. Cook for 5 minutes or until syrupy, stirring frequently, and cool.

3. Lightly spoon flour into a dry measuring cup; level with a knife. Combine flour, baking soda, and salt in a small bowl, stirring well with a whisk. Combine granulated sugar and butter in a large bowl; beat with a mixer at medium speed until well blended. Add egg, 1 teaspoon vanilla extract, and almond extracts, beating well. Add flour mixture to sugar mixture alternately with buttermilk, beginning and ending with flour mixture; beat well after each addition.

4. Spoon the batter into an 8-inch round cake pan coated with cooking spray. Arrange apple mixture over cake; top with almonds. Bake at 350° for 25 minutes or until cake begins to pull away from sides of pan. Cool in pan on a wire rack for 10 minutes. Quickly invert cake onto wire rack. Then invert onto a serving plate.

5. To prepare glaze, combine powdered sugar, 1 teaspoon buttermilk, and ¼ teaspoon vanilla in a small bowl; stir with a whisk. Drizzle glaze over cake. Serve warm or at room temperature. Yield: 8 servings (serving size: 1 wedge).

CALORIES 185 (24% from fat); FAT 5g (sat 2.3g, mono 1.7g, poly 0.6g); PROTEIN 3.4g; CARB 31.8g; FIBER 1g; CHOL 35mg; IRON 1mg; SODIUM 162mg; CALC 36mg

Blueberry-Pecan Cake

Cooking spray
2 teaspoons all-purpose flour
5 tablespoons butter
¾ cup granulated sugar
2 large eggs
⅔ cup low-fat buttermilk
2 teaspoons grated orange rind
1 teaspoon baking powder
½ teaspoon salt
1½ teaspoons vanilla extract
½ teaspoon almond extract
¼ teaspoon baking soda
1½ cups all-purpose flour
2 cups fresh or frozen blueberries
⅓ cup finely chopped pecans
2 tablespoons sifted powdered sugar

1. Preheat oven to 350°.

2. Coat a 9-inch round springform pan with cooking spray; dust with 2 teaspoons flour.

3. Place butter in a large microwave-safe bowl. Cover and microwave at HIGH 1 minute or until butter melts. Add granulated sugar, stirring with a whisk. Add eggs; stir well. Stir in buttermilk and next 6 ingredients; stir well. Lightly spoon 1½ cups flour into dry measuring cups; level with a knife. Add flour to batter, stirring just until blended (do not overstir). Stir in blueberries and pecans. Spoon into prepared pan, spreading evenly.

4. Bake at 350° for 45 minutes or until lightly browned and a wooden pick inserted in center comes out clean. Cool 10 minutes in pan on a wire rack. Sprinkle with powdered sugar. Cut into wedges. Yield: 10 servings (serving size: 1 wedge).

CALORIES 253 (36% from fat); FAT 10.1g (sat 4.3g, mono 3.8g, poly 1.3g); PROTEIN 4.5g; CARB 36.9g; FIBER 1.7g; CHOL 59mg; IRON 1.3mg; SODIUM 287mg; CALC 60mg

Espresso-Walnut Cake

Cooking spray
2 teaspoons all-purpose flour
¼ cup packed brown sugar
3 tablespoons finely chopped walnuts
1 teaspoon ground cinnamon
1 tablespoon instant espresso or 2 tablespoons instant coffee granules, divided
5 tablespoons butter
1 cup granulated sugar
2 large eggs
⅔ cup plain fat-free yogurt
2 teaspoons vanilla extract
½ teaspoon baking soda
¼ teaspoon salt
1⅓ cups all-purpose flour

1. Preheat oven to 350°.
2. Coat an 8-inch square baking pan with cooking spray; dust with 2 teaspoons flour.
3. Combine brown sugar, walnuts, cinnamon, and 1 teaspoon espresso granules in a small bowl.
4. Place butter in a large microwave-safe bowl. Cover and microwave at HIGH 1 minute or until butter melts. Add granulated sugar, stirring with a whisk. Add eggs; stir well. Stir in yogurt, vanilla, baking soda, and salt. Lightly spoon 1⅓ cups flour into dry measuring cups; level with a knife. Add flour and 2 teaspoons espresso granules, stirring just until blended. Spread half of batter into pan; sprinkle with half of brown sugar mixture. Carefully spread remaining batter over brown sugar mixture; sprinkle with remaining brown sugar mixture.
5. Bake at 350° for 25 minutes or until a wooden pick inserted in center comes out clean. Cool 10 minutes in pan on a wire rack. Cut into squares. Yield: 9 servings (serving size: 1 cake square).

CALORIES 284 (30% from fat); FAT 9.4g (sat 4.5g, mono 2.6g, poly 1.7g); PROTEIN 5g; CARB 45.4g; FIBER 0.8g; CHOL 65mg; IRON 1.4mg; SODIUM 231mg; CALC 58mg

Gingerbread Cake with Blueberry Sauce

2 cups all-purpose flour
⅓ cup chopped crystallized ginger (optional)
1½ teaspoons ground ginger
1½ teaspoons ground cinnamon
1 teaspoon baking powder
1 teaspoon baking soda
½ teaspoon salt
⅛ teaspoon ground cloves
¾ cup low-fat buttermilk
½ cup sugar
½ cup molasses
¼ cup 1% low-fat milk
¼ cup vegetable oil
2 large eggs
1½ cups frozen blueberries, thawed
Cooking spray
Blueberry Sauce
¾ cup frozen reduced-calorie whipped topping, thawed

1. Preheat oven to 350°.
2. Lightly spoon flour into dry measuring cups; level with a knife. Combine flour and next 7 ingredients in a large bowl, stirring well with a whisk; make a well in center of the flour mixture.
3. Combine buttermilk and next 5 ingredients; stir well with a whisk. Add buttermilk mixture to flour mixture, stirring just until moist. Fold in blueberries. Spoon batter into an 11 x 7-inch baking dish or 9-inch square baking pan coated with cooking spray. Bake at 350° for 45 minutes or until a wooden pick inserted in center of cake comes out clean. Cool in dish 10 minutes on a wire rack; remove from pan. Cool completely on wire rack, and cut into squares.
4. Spoon Blueberry Sauce over each square; dollop with whipped topping. Yield: 12 servings (serving size: 1 cake square, about 2 tablespoons sauce, and 1 tablespoon whipped topping).

(Totals include Blueberry Sauce) CALORIES 284 (22% from fat); FAT 7g (sat 1.8g, mono 1.8g, poly 2.6g); PROTEIN 4.4g; CARB 52.4g; FIBER 1.9g; CHOL 38mg; IRON 3mg; SODIUM 277mg; CALC 105mg

BLUEBERRY SAUCE:

½ cup orange juice
⅓ cup sugar
2 tablespoons chopped crystallized ginger or 1 teaspoon ground ginger
2 cups frozen blueberries, thawed

1. Combine first 3 ingredients in a medium saucepan. Bring to a boil; add blueberries. Return to a boil; cook 1 minute. Cool. Yield: 1⅔ cups (serving size: about 2 tablespoons).

CALORIES 44 (4% from fat); FAT 0.2g (sat 0g, mono 0g, poly 0.1g); PROTEIN 0.2g; CARB 11g; FIBER 0.7g; CHOL 3mg; IRON 0.3mg; SODIUM 1mg; CALC 6mg

Cinnamon-Apple Cake

Cinnamon-Apple Cake is a great make-ahead dish. It will keep up to three days stored in an airtight container.

1¾ cups sugar, divided
¾ cup (6 ounces) block-style fat-free cream cheese, softened
½ cup butter or stick margarine, softened
1 teaspoon vanilla extract
2 large eggs
1½ cups all-purpose flour
1½ teaspoons baking powder
¼ teaspoon salt
2 teaspoons ground cinnamon
3 cups chopped peeled Rome apple (about 2 large)
Cooking spray

1. Preheat oven to 350°.
2. Beat 1½ cups sugar, cream cheese, butter, and vanilla at medium speed of a mixer until well blended (about 4 minutes). Add eggs, 1 at a time, beating well after each addition. Lightly spoon flour into dry measuring cups, and level with a knife. Combine flour, baking powder, and salt. Add flour mixture to creamed mixture, beating at low speed until blended.
3. Combine ¼ cup sugar and cinnamon. Combine 2 tablespoons cinnamon mixture and chopped apple in a bowl, and stir the apple mixture into batter. Pour batter into an 8-inch springform pan coated with cooking spray, and sprinkle with the remaining cinnamon mixture.
4. Bake at 350° for 1 hour and 15 minutes or until cake pulls away from the sides of the pan. Cool completely on a wire rack, and cut using a serrated knife. Yield: 12 servings.
NOTE: You can also make this cake in a 9-inch square cake pan or a 9-inch springform pan; just reduce the cooking time by 5 minutes.

CALORIES 281 (28% from fat); FAT 8.7g (sat 1.8g, mono 3.7g, poly 2.6g); PROTEIN 4.8g; CARB 46.3g; FIBER 1.2g; CHOL 39mg; IRON 1.1mg; SODIUM 234mg; CALC 89mg

Warm Gingerbread with Lemon Glaze

Glazing the gingerbread with a lemon syrup balances the sweet molasses in this old-fashioned favorite.

⅓ cup butter, cut into small pieces
⅔ cup hot water
1 cup light or dark molasses
1 large egg
2¾ cups all-purpose flour
1½ teaspoons baking soda
1½ teaspoons ground ginger
1 teaspoon ground cinnamon
½ teaspoon salt
¼ teaspoon ground cloves
Cooking spray
1½ cups powdered sugar
6 tablespoons fresh lemon juice
1 cup frozen reduced-fat whipped topping, thawed
Ground cinnamon (optional)
Lemon slices (optional)

1. Preheat oven to 350°.
2. Combine butter and hot water in a large bowl, and stir with a whisk until butter melts. Add molasses and egg, and stir with a whisk until blended. Lightly spoon flour into dry measuring cups, and level with a knife. Combine flour, baking soda, ginger, 1 teaspoon ground cinnamon, salt, and cloves. Add the flour mixture to molasses mixture, and stir just until the batter is moist.

3. Spoon batter into a 9-inch cake pan coated with cooking spray. Bake at 350° for 30 minutes or until a wooden pick inserted in center comes out clean. Cool gingerbread in pan on a wire rack 15 minutes.

4. Combine sugar and lemon juice, stirring until mixture is well blended. Pierce top of gingerbread liberally with a wooden skewer. Pour glaze over gingerbread.

5. Top each serving with dollop of whipped topping. Sprinkle with cinnamon and garnish with lemon slices, if desired. Yield: 12 servings (serving size: 1 gingerbread piece and about 1½ tablespoons whipped topping).

CALORIES 296 (20% from fat); FAT 6.5g (sat 3.7g, mono 1.7g, poly 0.4g); PROTEIN 3.6g; CARB 57.3g; FIBER 1g; CHOL 35mg; IRON 2.8mg; SODIUM 322mg; CALC 68mg

Orange Tea Cake

This not-too-sweet cake is great for breakfast, brunch, or a dessert buffet.

CAKE:
- 1 cup granulated sugar
- 7 tablespoons butter, softened
- 1 large egg
- 1⅔ cups sifted cake flour
- 1 teaspoon baking powder
- ½ teaspoon salt
- ½ cup 2% reduced-fat milk
- 1 tablespoon grated orange rind
- ½ teaspoon almond extract
- 2 large egg whites
- Cooking spray

GLAZE:
- 1 cup powdered sugar
- 1 tablespoon Cointreau (orange-flavored liqueur) or orange juice
- 2 teaspoons orange juice

1. Preheat oven to 350°.

2. To prepare cake, place granulated sugar and butter in a large bowl, and beat with a mixer at high speed until well blended. Add egg, beating well. Combine cake flour, baking powder, and salt in a bowl, stirring well with a whisk. Add flour mixture to sugar mixture alternately with milk, beginning and ending with flour mixture. Stir in orange rind and almond extract.

3. Beat egg whites with a mixer at high speed until stiff peaks form using clean, dry beaters (do not overbeat). Fold egg whites into batter; pour batter into an 8 x 4-inch loaf pan coated with cooking spray. Bake at 350° for 50 minutes or until a wooden pick inserted in center comes out clean. Cool in pan 10 minutes on a wire rack; remove from pan. Cool completely on wire rack.

4. To prepare the glaze, combine powdered sugar, liqueur, and orange juice in a small bowl. Poke holes in the top of cake using a skewer, and drizzle the glaze over cake. Yield: 10 servings (serving size: 1 [¾-inch] slice).

CALORIES 287 (29% from fat); FAT 9.2g (sat 5.4g, mono 2.7g, poly 0.6g); PROTEIN 3.3g; CARB 47.9g; FIBER 0g; CHOL 45mg; IRON 1.5mg; SODIUM 272mg; CALC 51mg

Chocolate Sheet Cake

Chocolate Sheet Cake

CAKE:

Cooking spray
2   teaspoons all-purpose flour
2   cups all-purpose flour
2   cups granulated sugar
1   teaspoon baking soda
1   teaspoon ground cinnamon (optional)
¼   teaspoon salt
¾   cup water
½   cup butter or stick margarine
¼   cup unsweetened cocoa
½   cup low-fat buttermilk
1   teaspoon vanilla extract
2   large eggs

ICING:

6   tablespoons butter or stick margarine
⅓   cup fat-free milk
¼   cup unsweetened cocoa
3   cups powdered sugar
¼   cup chopped pecans, toasted
2   teaspoons vanilla extract

1. Preheat oven to 375°.

2. To prepare cake, coat a 15 x 10-inch jelly roll pan with cooking spray, and dust with 2 teaspoons flour. Set aside.

3. Lightly spoon 2 cups flour into dry measuring cups; level with a knife. Combine 2 cups flour and next 4 ingredients in a large bowl; stir well with a whisk. Combine water, ½ cup butter, and ¼ cup cocoa in a small saucepan; bring to a boil, stirring frequently. Remove from heat; pour into flour mixture. Beat with a mixer at medium speed until well blended. Add buttermilk, 1 teaspoon vanilla, and eggs; beat well. Pour batter into prepared pan; bake at 375° for 17 minutes or until a wooden pick inserted in center comes out clean. Place on a wire rack.

4. To prepare icing, combine 6 tablespoons butter, milk, and ¼ cup cocoa in a medium saucepan; bring to a boil, stirring constantly. Remove from heat, and gradually stir in powdered sugar, pecans, and 2 teaspoons vanilla. Spread over hot cake. Cool completely on wire rack. Yield: 20 servings (serving size: 1 slice).

NOTE: You can also make this recipe in a 13 x 9-inch baking pan. Bake at 375° for 22 minutes.

CALORIES 298 (30% from fat); FAT 10g (sat 5.5g, mono 3.2g, poly 0.7g); PROTEIN 3.1g; CARB 49.8g; FIBER 0.5g; CHOL 44mg; IRON 1.1mg; SODIUM 188mg; CALC 25mg

Orange Marmalade Layer Cake

Cooking spray
3   cups sifted cake flour
1½ teaspoons baking soda
¾   teaspoon salt
9   tablespoons butter, softened
2   cups sugar, divided
1   tablespoon grated orange rind
1   tablespoon vanilla extract
4   large egg whites
1¼ cups low-fat buttermilk
1   cup fat-free milk
½   cup fresh orange juice (about 1½ oranges)
1   (12-ounce) jar orange marmalade, melted and cooled
¼   cup low-fat sour cream
1½ cups frozen reduced-calorie whipped topping, thawed

1. Preheat oven to 350°.

2. Coat 2 (9-inch) round cake pans with cooking spray; line bottoms of pans with wax paper.

3. Lightly spoon sifted cake flour into dry measuring cups; level with a knife. Combine sifted flour, baking soda, and salt, stirring with a whisk. Place butter in a large bowl; beat with a mixer at medium speed until light and fluffy (about 2 minutes). Gradually add 1¾ cups sugar, 1 tablespoon at a time, beating until well blended. Beat in orange rind and vanilla. Add egg whites, 1 at a time, beating well after each addition.

4. Combine buttermilk and milk. Add flour mixture and buttermilk mixture alternately to the butter mixture, beginning and ending with flour mixture. Pour batter into prepared pans; sharply tap pans once on counter to remove air bubbles. Bake at 350° for 25 minutes or until a wooden pick inserted in center comes out clean. Cool in pans 20 minutes on a wire rack; remove from pans. Cool completely on wire rack.

5. Combine juice and ¼ cup sugar; stir until sugar dissolves. Pierce cake layers liberally with a wooden pick. Slowly drizzle juice mixture over cake layers.

6. Carefully place 1 layer on a plate; spread with ⅓ cup marmalade. Top with remaining layer, and spread remaining marmalade on top of cake. Fold sour cream into whipped topping; spread over sides of cake. Store cake loosely covered in refrigerator at least 2 hours. Yield: 16 servings (serving size: 1 slice).

CALORIES 309 (23% from fat); FAT 7.8g (sat 4.7g, mono 1.9g, poly 0.3g); PROTEIN 3.9g; CARB 57.7g; FIBER 0.4g; CHOL 23mg; IRON 1.5mg; SODIUM 350mg; CALC 61mg

Double-Caramel Turtle Cake

This decadent cake, which plays off the popular Turtle candies, boasts chocolate layers and a nutty caramel glaze.

CAKE:

Cooking spray
- 1 tablespoon all-purpose flour
- 1½ cups boiling water
- ¾ cup unsweetened cocoa
- 1½ cups granulated sugar
- 6 tablespoons butter, softened
- 1 teaspoon vanilla extract
- 2 large eggs
- 1⅔ cups all-purpose flour
- 1 teaspoon baking soda
- ¾ teaspoon baking powder
- ¼ teaspoon salt

FROSTING:
- 2 tablespoons butter
- ¼ cup packed dark brown sugar
- 2 to 3 tablespoons fat-free milk
- 2 teaspoons vanilla extract
- 2 cups sifted powdered sugar

TOPPING:
- ⅔ cup fat-free caramel apple dip (such as T. Marzetti's)
- ¼ cup finely chopped pecans, toasted

1. Preheat oven to 350°.

2. To prepare cake, coat bottoms of 2 (8-inch) round cake pans with cooking spray (do not coat sides of pans); line bottoms with wax paper. Coat wax paper with cooking spray; dust with 1 tablespoon flour.

3. Combine boiling water and cocoa, stirring well with a whisk. Cool completely.

4. Place granulated sugar, 6 tablespoons butter, and vanilla in a large bowl; beat with a mixer at medium speed until well blended (about 5 minutes). Add eggs, 1 at a time, beating well after each addition. Lightly spoon 1⅔ cups flour into dry measuring cups; level with a knife. Combine 1⅔ cups flour, baking soda, baking powder, and salt, stirring well with a whisk. Add flour mixture and cocoa mixture alternately to sugar mixture, beginning and ending with flour mixture.

5. Pour batter into prepared pans; sharply tap pans once on counter to remove air bubbles. Bake at 350° for 30 minutes or until a wooden pick inserted in center comes out clean. Cool in pans 10 minutes on wire rack, and remove from pans. Cool completely on wire rack.

6. To prepare frosting, melt 2 tablespoons butter in a small saucepan over medium heat. Add brown sugar and 2 tablespoons milk, and cook 1 minute or until sugar melts. Remove from heat; cool slightly. Combine butter mixture and 2 teaspoons vanilla in a large bowl. Gradually add powdered sugar; beat with a mixer at medium speed until smooth. Add additional milk, 1 teaspoon at a time, beating until spreading consistency.

7. Place 1 cake layer on a plate, and spread top with half of frosting. Place caramel dip in a small zip-top plastic bag. (If dip is too thick, place bag in microwave for 20 seconds.) Snip a small hole in 1 corner of bag, and drizzle half of caramel dip over frosting. Top with other cake layer. Spread remaining frosting over top of cake, and drizzle with remaining caramel dip. Sprinkle with pecans. Yield: 16 servings.

CALORIES 309 (24% from fat); FAT 8.4g (sat 4.3g, mono 2.9g, poly 0.8g); PROTEIN 3.7g; CARB 56.7g; FIBER 1.9g; CHOL 42mg; IRON 1.5mg; SODIUM 249mg; CALC 41mg

Beet Cake with Cream Cheese Frosting

If you like carrot cake, you'll love this. The batter is bright red but bakes to a golden brown. Wear an apron while grating the beets.

CAKE:

    1   pound beets (about 2 medium)
    Cooking spray
    ⅔   cup granulated sugar
    ⅔   cup packed dark brown sugar
    ½   cup vegetable oil
    2   large eggs
    2½   cups all-purpose flour
    2   teaspoons baking powder
    1   teaspoon ground ginger
    1   teaspoon ground cinnamon
    ½   teaspoon baking soda
    ¼   teaspoon salt
    ½   cup 1% low-fat milk

FROSTING:

    2   teaspoons grated orange
         rind
    1   teaspoon vanilla extract
    1   (8-ounce) block ⅓-less-fat
         cream cheese, chilled
    3   cups sifted powdered sugar
    2   tablespoons finely chopped
         walnuts, toasted

1. Preheat oven to 350°.

2. To prepare cake, peel the beets using a vegetable peeler. Grate beets, using the large holes of a grater, to measure 2 cups.

3. Coat 2 (9-inch) round cake pans with cooking spray; line bottoms with wax paper. Coat wax paper with cooking spray.

4. Combine the granulated sugar, brown sugar, oil, and eggs in a large bowl, and beat with a mixer at medium speed until well blended. Add beets, and beat well. Lightly spoon flour into dry measuring cups, and level with a knife. Combine flour and next 5 ingredients in a large bowl, stirring well with a whisk. Add flour mixture to sugar mixture alternately with milk, beginning and ending with flour mixture. Pour the batter into prepared pans, and sharply tap pans once on counter to remove air bubbles.

5. Bake at 350° for 30 minutes or until a wooden pick inserted in center comes out clean. Cool in pans 10 minutes on wire racks; remove from pans. Carefully peel off wax paper, and cool completely on wire racks.

6. To prepare frosting, beat rind, vanilla, and cream cheese with a mixer at high speed until fluffy. Add powdered sugar, and beat at low speed just until blended (do not overbeat).

7. Place 1 cake layer on a plate. Spread with ½ cup frosting, and top with remaining cake layer. Spread the remaining frosting over top and sides of cake. Sprinkle the walnuts over top of cake. Store the cake loosely covered in refrigerator. Yield: 18 servings (serving size: 1 piece).

CALORIES 312 (30% from fat); FAT 10.5g (sat 3.3g, mono 3g, poly 3.6g); PROTEIN 4.5g; CARB 51.2g; FIBER 0.7g; CHOL 34mg; IRON 1.4mg; SODIUM 198mg; CALC 65mg

Double-Coconut Cake

Coconut milk, available in the Asian-foods sections of most supermarkets, makes this cake moist and rich.

Cooking spray
  1 tablespoon cake flour
2¼ cups sifted cake flour
2¼ teaspoons baking powder
  ½ teaspoon salt
1⅔ cups sugar
  ⅓ cup butter, softened
  2 large eggs
  1 (14-ounce) can light coconut milk
  1 tablespoon vanilla extract
Fluffy Coconut Frosting
  ⅔ cup flaked sweetened coconut, divided

1. Preheat oven to 350°.
2. Coat 2 (9-inch) round cake pans with cooking spray; dust with 1 tablespoon flour.
3. Combine 2¼ cups flour, baking powder, and salt, stirring with a whisk. Place sugar and butter in a large bowl, and beat with a mixer at medium speed until well blended (about 5 minutes). Add eggs, 1 at a time, beating well after each addition. Add flour mixture and milk alternately to sugar mixture, beginning and ending with the flour mixture. Stir in vanilla.
4. Pour batter into prepared pans. Sharply tap pans once on countertop to remove air bubbles. Bake at 350° for 30 minutes or until a wooden pick inserted in center comes out clean. Cool in pans for 10 minutes on wire racks, and remove from pans. Cool completely on wire racks.
5. Place 1 layer on a plate; spread with 1 cup Fluffy Coconut Frosting. Sprinkle with ⅓ cup coconut. Top with remaining layer. Spread with ½ cup frosting. Spread remaining frosting over sides of cake. Sprinkle top with ⅓ cup coconut. Store cake loosely covered in refrigerator. Yield: 14 servings.

(Totals include Fluffy Coconut Frosting) CALORIES 298 (24% from fat); FAT 7.9g (sat 5g, mono 1.7g, poly 0.3g); PROTEIN 3.4g; CARB 53.8g; FIBER 0.4g; CHOL 42mg; IRON 1.6mg; SODIUM 273mg; CALC 52mg

FLUFFY COCONUT FROSTING:

  4 large egg whites
  ½ teaspoon cream of tartar
Dash of salt
  1 cup sugar
  ¼ cup water
  ½ teaspoon vanilla extract
  ¼ teaspoon coconut extract

1. Place egg whites, cream of tartar, and salt in a large bowl; beat with a mixer at high speed until stiff peaks form. Combine sugar and water in a saucepan; bring to a boil. Cook, without stirring, until candy thermometer registers 238°. Pour hot sugar syrup in a thin stream over egg whites, beating at high speed. Stir in extracts. Yield: about 4 cups (serving size: about ¼ cup).

CALORIES 54 (0% from fat); FAT 0g (sat 0g, mono 0g, ploy 0g); PROTEIN 0.9g; CARB 12.7g; FIBER 0g; CHOL 0mg; IRON 0mg; SODIUM 32mg; CALC 1mg

Brown Sugar Pound Cake

The brown sugar gives this flavorful pound cake its rich, caramel-like flavor.

Cooking spray
  3 tablespoons dry breadcrumbs
  3 cups all-purpose flour
  1 teaspoon baking powder
  ¼ teaspoon salt
  ¾ cup butter or stick margarine, softened
  2 cups packed light brown sugar
  1 tablespoon vanilla extract
  3 large eggs
  1 cup fat-free milk
  1 tablespoon powdered sugar

1. Preheat oven to 350°.
2. Coat a 10-inch tube pan with cooking spray, and dust with breadcrumbs.
3. Lightly spoon flour into dry measuring cups, and level with a knife. Combine the flour, baking powder, and salt in a bowl, and stir mixture well with a whisk. Beat butter in a large bowl with a mixer at medium speed until butter is light and fluffy. Gradually add brown sugar and vanilla, beating until well blended. Add eggs, 1 at a time, beating well after each addition. Add the flour mixture to the sugar mixture alternately with milk, beating at low speed, beginning and ending with flour mixture.
4. Spoon batter into prepared pan. Bake at 350° for 1 hour and 5 minutes or until a wooden pick inserted in center of cake comes out clean. Cool cake in pan for 10 minutes on a wire rack, and remove from pan. Cool completely on wire rack. Sift powdered sugar over top of cake. Yield: 18 servings (serving size: 1 slice).

CALORIES 265 (30% from fat); FAT 8.9g (sat 5.1g, mono 2.6g, poly 0.5g); PROTEIN 3.9g; CARB 42.6g; FIBER 0.6g; CHOL 58mg; IRON 1.7mg; SODIUM 176mg; CALC 65mg

Italian Cream Cake

Our version of Italian Cream Cake is a favorite because it tastes delicious and freezes well.

Cooking spray
  2 cups sugar
 ½ cup light butter
  2 large egg yolks
  2 cups all-purpose flour
  1 teaspoon baking soda
  1 cup low-fat buttermilk
 ½ cup chopped pecans
  1 teaspoon butter extract
  1 teaspoon coconut extract
  1 teaspoon vanilla extract
  6 large egg whites
Cream Cheese Frosting
Lemon rind (optional)

1. Preheat oven to 350°.

2. Coat bottoms of 3 (9-inch) round cake pans with cooking spray (do not coat sides of pans), and line bottoms of pans with wax paper. Coat wax paper with cooking spray. Dust with flour; set aside.

3. Combine sugar and butter in a large bowl, and beat at medium speed of a mixer until well blended. Add egg yolks, 1 at a time, beating well after each addition. Lightly spoon flour into dry measuring cups, and level with a knife. Combine flour and baking soda. Add the flour mixture to the creamed mixture alternately with buttermilk, beginning and ending with the flour mixture. Stir in chopped pecans and extracts.

4. Beat egg whites at high speed of a mixer using clean, dry beaters until stiff peaks form (do not overbeat). Fold egg whites into batter, and pour batter into prepared pans. Bake at 350° for 23 minutes. Cool in pans 5 minutes on a wire rack. Loosen cake layers from sides of pans using a narrow metal spatula, and turn out onto wire racks. Peel off wax paper; cool completely.

5. Place 1 cake layer on a plate. Spread with ⅔ cup Cream Cheese Frosting, and top with another cake layer. Repeat with ⅔ cup frosting and the remaining layer, ending with a cake layer. Spread the remaining frosting over sides and top of the cake. Garnish with lemon rind, if desired. Yield: 20 servings (serving size: 1 slice).

(Totals include Cream Cheese Frosting) CALORIES 290 (24% from fat); FAT 7.6g (sat 3.3g, mono 2.9g, poly 0.8g); PROTEIN 4.1g; CARB 52.3g; FIBER 0.5g; CHOL 37mg; IRON 0.8mg; SODIUM 172mg; CALC 38mg

CREAM CHEESE FROSTING:
 ½ cup (4 ounces) block-style fat-free
      cream cheese, chilled
 ¼ cup butter or stick margarine, softened
  1 teaspoon grated lemon rind
  1 teaspoon vanilla extract
3½ cups powdered sugar

1. Beat first 4 ingredients at medium speed of a mixer until smooth. Lightly spoon sugar into dry measuring cups, and level with a knife. Gradually add sugar to butter mixture, and beat at low speed just until blended (do not overbeat). Yield: 2 cups (serving size: 1 tablespoon).

NOTE: Light butter is OK to bake with. Store the cake in refrigerator, and bring to room temperature before serving.

CALORIES 68 (20% from fat); FAT 1.5g (sat 0.9g, mono 0.4g, poly 0.1g); PROTEIN 0.5g; CARB 13.4g; FIBER 0g; CHOL 5mg; IRON 0mg; SODIUM 36mg; CALC 11mg

Sour Cream-Lemon Pound Cake

Sour Cream-Lemon Pound Cake

Cooking spray
  3 tablespoons dry breadcrumbs
3¼ cups all-purpose flour
  ½ teaspoon baking soda
  ¼ teaspoon salt
  ¾ cup butter or stick margarine, softened
2½ cups granulated sugar
  2 teaspoons lemon extract
  3 large eggs
1½ tablespoons grated lemon rind (about 2 lemons)
  ¼ cup fresh lemon juice, divided
  1 (8-ounce) carton low-fat sour cream
  1 cup powdered sugar

1. Preheat oven to 350°.
2. Coat a 10-inch tube pan with cooking spray, and dust with breadcrumbs.
3. Lightly spoon the flour into dry measuring cups; level with a knife. Combine flour, baking soda, and salt in a bowl; stir well with a whisk. Beat butter in a large bowl with a mixer at medium speed until light and fluffy. Gradually add the granulated sugar and lemon extract, beating until well blended. Add the eggs, 1 at a time, beating well after each addition. Add rind and 2 tablespoons lemon juice, and beat 30 seconds. Add flour mixture to sugar mixture alternately with sour cream, beating at low speed, beginning and ending with flour mixture.
4. Spoon batter into the prepared pan. Bake at 350° for 1 hour and 10 minutes or until a wooden pick inserted in center of cake comes out clean. Cool cake in pan 10 minutes on a wire rack, and remove from pan. Cool completely on wire rack. Combine 2 tablespoons lemon juice and powdered sugar. Drizzle glaze over top of cake. Yield: 18 servings (serving size: 1 slice).

CALORIES 323 (29% from fat); FAT 10.4g (sat 6g, mono 3g, poly 0.6g); PROTEIN 4g; CARB 53.4g; FIBER 0.7g; CHOL 62mg; IRON 1.3mg; SODIUM 172mg; CALC 27mg

Black-and-White Pound Cake

The chocolate batter bakes into the vanilla batter, resulting in a contrasting swirl of colors.

Cooking spray
  3 tablespoons dry breadcrumbs
  3 cups all-purpose flour
  1 teaspoon baking powder
  ¼ teaspoon salt
  ¾ cup butter or stick margarine, softened
  2 cups sugar
  2 teaspoons vanilla extract
  3 large eggs
  1 cup 2% reduced-fat milk
  ¾ cup chocolate syrup
  ¼ teaspoon baking soda
  1 tablespoon unsweetened cocoa

1. Preheat oven to 350°.
2. Coat a 10-inch tube pan with cooking spray, and dust with breadcrumbs.
3. Lightly spoon flour into dry measuring cups, and level with a knife. Combine flour, baking powder, and salt in a bowl, stirring well with a whisk. Beat butter in a large bowl with a mixer at medium speed until light and fluffy. Gradually add sugar and vanilla, beating until well blended. Add eggs, 1 at a time, beating well after each addition. Add flour mixture to sugar mixture alternately with milk, beating at low speed, beginning and ending with flour mixture.
4. Spoon two-thirds of batter (about 4 cups) into prepared pan. Add syrup and baking soda to the remaining batter in bowl, stirring just until blended; spoon on top of batter in pan.
5. Bake at 350° for 1 hour and 15 minutes or until cake pulls away from sides of pan. Cool in pan 10 minutes on a wire rack; remove cake from pan. Cool completely on wire rack. Sift the cocoa over top of cake. Yield: 18 servings (serving size: 1 slice).

CALORIES 289 (29% from fat); FAT 9.3g (sat 5.4g, mono 2.7g, poly 0.5g); PROTEIN 4.4g; CARB 47.3g; FIBER 0.6g; CHOL 59mg; IRON 1.5mg; SODIUM 192mg; CALC 46mg

Blueberry Pound
Cake

Blueberry Pound Cake

Tossing the blueberries with flour helps to suspend them in the cake.

  2 cups granulated sugar
  ½ cup light butter
  ½ cup (4 ounces) ⅓-less-fat cream cheese, softened
  3 large eggs
  1 large egg white
  3 cups all-purpose flour, divided
  2 cups fresh or frozen blueberries
  1 teaspoon baking powder
  ½ teaspoon baking soda
  ½ teaspoon salt
  1 (8-ounce) carton lemon low-fat yogurt
  2 teaspoons vanilla extract
Cooking spray
  ½ cup powdered sugar
  4 teaspoons lemon juice

1. Preheat oven to 350°.
2. Beat first 3 ingredients at medium speed of a mixer until well blended (about 5 minutes). Add eggs and egg white, 1 at a time, beating well after each addition. Lightly spoon flour into dry measuring cups; level with a knife. Combine 2 tablespoons flour and blueberries in a small bowl, and toss well. Combine remaining flour, baking powder, baking soda, and salt. Add the flour mixture to sugar mixture alternately with yogurt, beginning and ending with flour mixture. Fold in blueberry mixture and vanilla; pour cake batter into a 10-inch tube pan coated with cooking spray. Bake at 350° for 1 hour and 10 minutes or until a wooden pick inserted in center comes out clean.
3. Cool cake in pan 10 minutes, and remove from pan. Lightly spoon powdered sugar into a dry measuring cup, and level with a knife. Combine with lemon juice in a bowl, and drizzle over warm cake. Cut with a serrated knife. Yield: 16 servings (serving size: 1 slice).

CALORIES 287 (19% from fat); FAT 6.1g (sat 3.4g, mono 1.8g, poly 0.4g); PROTEIN 5.7g; CARB 53.9g; FIBER 1.5g; CHOL 57mg; IRON 1.3mg; SODIUM 227mg; CALC 50mg

Blueberry Angel Food Cake

CAKE:
1½ cups sugar, divided
  1 cup sifted cake flour
 12 large egg whites (about 1½ cups)
1¼ teaspoons cream of tartar
  ½ teaspoon salt
  1 teaspoon vanilla extract
1½ cups fresh or frozen blueberries
  2 tablespoons sifted cake flour
  1 tablespoon grated lemon rind
GLAZE:
  1 cup powdered sugar
  3 tablespoons fresh lemon juice

1. Preheat oven to 375°.
2. Sift together ½ cup sugar and 1 cup flour.
3. In a large bowl, beat egg whites with a mixer at high speed until foamy. Add cream of tartar and salt; beat until soft peaks form. Add 1 cup sugar, 2 tablespoons at a time, beating until stiff peaks form.
4. Sift flour mixture over egg white mixture, ¼ cup at a time; fold in. Fold in vanilla and blueberries.
5. Combine 2 tablespoons flour and rind; toss to coat. Sprinkle over egg white mixture; fold in.
6. Spoon batter into an ungreased 10-inch tube pan, spreading evenly. Break air pockets by cutting through batter with a knife. Bake at 375° for 40 minutes or until cake springs back when lightly touched. Invert pan, and cool completely. Loosen cake from sides of pan using a narrow metal spatula. Invert cake onto plate.
7. To prepare glaze, combine powdered sugar and juice in a small bowl; stir well with a whisk. Drizzle over cooled cake. Yield: 8 servings.

CALORIES 297 (1% from fat); FAT 0.2g (sat 0g, mono 0.1g, poly 0.1g); PROTEIN 6.6g; CARB 68.2g; FIBER 1g; CHOL 0mg; IRON 1.1mg; SODIUM 232mg; CALC 8mg

Café au Lait Angel Food Cake

The custard, a versatile dessert sauce that's also great with fresh fruit, makes use of some of the extra egg yolks. For a fitting garnish, you can arrange a few chocolate-covered coffee beans around the cake.

CAKE:
- 1 cup sifted cake flour
- 1½ cups sugar, divided
- ¼ teaspoon ground cinnamon
- 2 tablespoons instant espresso granules or 2 tablespoons instant coffee granules
- 2 tablespoons hot water
- 12 large egg whites
- 1 teaspoon cream of tartar
- ¼ teaspoon salt
- 1½ teaspoons vanilla extract

SAUCE:
- 3 large egg yolks, lightly beaten
- ½ cup sugar
- 1 tablespoon cornstarch
- ⅛ teaspoon salt
- 3 cups 2% reduced-fat milk, divided
- 1 vanilla bean, split lengthwise
- 3 tablespoons Frangelico (hazelnut-flavored liqueur)

REMAINING INGREDIENT:
- ½ cup chopped hazelnuts, toasted

1. Preheat oven to 350°.

2. To prepare cake, lightly spoon flour into a dry measuring cup; level with a knife. Combine flour, ¾ cup sugar, and cinnamon, stirring with a whisk; set aside. Combine espresso and hot water, stirring until espresso dissolves; set aside.

3. Place egg whites in a large bowl; beat with a mixer at high speed until foamy. Add cream of tartar and ¼ teaspoon salt; beat until soft peaks form. Add ¾ cup sugar, 2 tablespoons at a time, beating until stiff peaks form.

4. Beat in espresso mixture and vanilla extract. Sift ¼ cup flour mixture over egg white mixture; fold in. Repeat procedure with remaining flour mixture, ¼ cup at a time.

5. Spoon batter into an ungreased 10-inch tube pan, spreading evenly. Break air pockets by cutting through batter with a knife. Bake at 350° for 50 minutes or until cake springs back when lightly touched. Invert pan, and cool completely. Loosen cake from sides of pan using a narrow metal spatula. Invert cake onto plate.

6. To prepare sauce, place egg yolks in a large bowl; set aside. Combine ½ cup sugar, cornstarch, and ⅛ teaspoon salt in a medium saucepan. Gradually add ½ cup milk, stirring with a whisk until smooth. Stir in remaining milk. Scrape seeds from vanilla bean into milk mixture; add bean to mixture. Heat milk mixture over medium heat to a boil. Remove from heat; gradually add hot milk mixture to egg yolks, stirring constantly with a whisk.

7. Return milk mixture to pan. Cook mixture over medium heat until thick and bubbly (about 4 minutes), stirring constantly. Remove from heat. Spoon milk mixture into a bowl; place bowl in a large ice-filled bowl for 10 minutes or until milk mixture comes to room temperature, stirring occasionally. Remove bowl from ice; stir in liqueur. Cover and chill completely.

8. Remove and discard vanilla bean. Serve cake with sauce; sprinkle with hazelnuts. Yield: 12 servings (serving size: 1 cake slice, about 3 tablespoons sauce, and 2 teaspoons hazelnuts).

CALORIES 271 (18% from fat); FAT 5.5g (sat 1.4g, mono 3g, poly 0.6g); PROTEIN 7.7g; CARB 46.8g; FIBER 0.6g; CHOL 58mg; IRON 1.1mg; SODIUM 162mg; CALC 90mg

Cornmeal Pound Cake

Cooking spray
1 tablespoon stone-ground white cornmeal
2 cups sugar, divided
⅔ cup butter, softened
1 teaspoon grated lemon rind
1 teaspoon vanilla extract
5 large egg yolks
1 cup low-fat sour cream
2 cups all-purpose flour
½ cup stone-ground white cornmeal
½ cup stone-ground white grits
½ teaspoon salt
½ teaspoon baking soda
5 large egg whites

1. Preheat oven to 325°.
2. Coat a 10-inch tube pan with cooking spray; dust with 1 tablespoon cornmeal.
3. Place 1¾ cups sugar, butter, grated lemon rind, and vanilla extract in a large bowl; beat with a mixer at medium speed until light and fluffy. Add egg yolks, 1 at a time, beating well after each addition. Beat in sour cream.
4. Lightly spoon flour into dry measuring cups; level with a knife. Combine flour, ½ cup cornmeal, grits, salt, and baking soda in a medium bowl; stir well with a whisk. Add flour mixture to sugar mixture, stirring to combine.
5. Beat egg whites with a mixer at high speed until foamy. Gradually add ¼ cup sugar, 1 tablespoon at a time, beating until stiff peaks form. Gently stir one-fourth of egg white mixture into batter; gently fold in remaining egg white mixture. Spoon batter into prepared pan.
6. Bake at 325° for 50 minutes or until a wooden pick inserted in center comes out clean. Cool in pan 15 minutes on a wire rack; remove from pan. Cool completely on wire rack. Yield: 16 servings.

CALORIES 294 (30% from fat); FAT 9.9g (sat 6.6g, mono 0.6g, poly 0.2g); PROTEIN 4.7g; CARB 47g; FIBER 0.6g; CHOL 91mg; IRON 1.2mg; SODIUM 203mg; CALC 28mg

Cornmeal Pound Cake

Double-Chocolate Cupcakes

1 (18.25-ounce) package light devil's food cake mix
1 cup water
3 large eggs
Cooking spray
¼ cup semisweet chocolate chips
¼ cup fat-free milk
3 tablespoons unsweetened cocoa
2 cups sifted powdered sugar
2 teaspoons vanilla extract
2 tablespoons powdered sugar

1. Preheat oven to 350°.
2. Combine cake mix, water, and eggs in a bowl, and beat at medium speed of a mixer 2 minutes.
3. Divide the batter evenly among 24 muffin cups coated with cooking spray. Bake at 350° for 20 minutes or until a wooden pick inserted in center comes out clean. Cool 10 minutes; remove from pans, and cool on a wire rack.
4. Split each cupcake in half horizontally using string or a serrated knife.
5. Combine the chocolate chips, milk, and cocoa in the top of a double boiler. Cook mixture over simmering water until the chocolate melts, stirring the mixture occasionally. Remove from heat, and stir in 2 cups powdered sugar and vanilla extract. Spread 2 teaspoons chocolate mixture over bottom half of each cupcake, and top with top halves. Sift 2 tablespoons powdered sugar over the tops of the cupcakes. Yield: 2 dozen (serving size: 1 cupcake).

CALORIES 155 (17% from fat); FAT 2.9g (sat 1.1g, mono 1g, poly 0.1g); PROTEIN 2.1g; CARB 30.2g; FIBER 0g; CHOL 27mg; IRON 0.3mg; SODIUM 175mg; CALC 8mg

Chocolate Lava Cakes with
Pistachio Cream

Chocolate Lava Cakes with Pistachio Cream

These flourless chocolate cakes are as rich as a restaurant dessert, but they're made with a fraction of the fat and no dairy butter. When these cakes bake, the gooey filling causes the center to sink in.

 1 cup shelled dry-roasted pistachios
1¾ cups sugar, divided
 ¼ cup unsweetened cocoa
 2 large eggs
 5 large egg whites
 2 ounces bittersweet chocolate, coarsely chopped
 ½ teaspoon baking powder
 ½ teaspoon vanilla extract
Cooking spray
 1 cup 2% reduced-fat milk
Dash of salt
Powdered sugar (optional)

1. Place pistachios in a food processor, and process until a crumbly paste forms (about 3½ minutes), scraping sides of bowl once.

2. Place ¼ cup pistachio butter, 1¼ cups sugar, cocoa, eggs, and egg whites in top of a double boiler; stir well with a whisk. Add chocolate; cook over simmering water until chocolate melts and sugar dissolves (about 3 minutes). Remove from heat; add baking powder and vanilla. Stir with a whisk until smooth. Spoon batter into 12 muffin cups coated with cooking spray. Chill 2 hours.

3. Place remaining ¼ cup pistachio butter and ½ cup sugar in food processor; pulse 4 times or until combined. Add milk and salt; process until smooth. Strain mixture through a sieve into a small saucepan; discard solids. Bring to a boil. Reduce heat, and simmer 4 minutes or until thick. Remove from heat; pour into a bowl. Cover and chill.

4. Preheat oven to 450°.

5. Bake the cakes at 450° for 9 minutes or until almost set (centers will not be firm). Let cool in pan for 5 minutes.

6. Invert each cake onto a dessert plate; drizzle about 2 teaspoons sauce over each serving. Garnish with powdered sugar, if desired. Yield: 12 servings.

CALORIES 232 (30% from fat); FAT 7.7g (sat 2.2g, mono 3.1g, poly 1.5g); PROTEIN 6.1g; CARB 37.2g; FIBER 2g; CHOL 37mg; IRON 0.9mg; SODIUM 73mg; CALC 51mg

Blackberry-Lemon Pudding Cake

As this dessert bakes, a light, spongy cake forms over a delicate bottom layer of custard. The water bath cooks the pudding cake with gentle, even heat.

 ¼ cup all-purpose flour
 ⅔ cup granulated sugar
 ⅛ teaspoon salt
 ⅛ teaspoon ground nutmeg
 1 cup low-fat buttermilk
 1 teaspoon grated lemon rind
 ¼ cup fresh lemon juice
 2 tablespoons butter or stick margarine, melted
 2 large egg yolks
 3 large egg whites
 ¼ cup granulated sugar
1½ cups blackberries, blueberries, or raspberries
Cooking spray
 ¾ teaspoon powdered sugar

1. Preheat oven to 350°.

2. Lightly spoon flour into a dry measuring cup; level with a knife. Combine flour, ⅔ cup granulated sugar, salt, and nutmeg in a large bowl; add buttermilk, rind, juice, butter, and egg yolks, stirring with a whisk until smooth.

3. Beat egg whites at high speed of a mixer until foamy. Add ¼ cup granulated sugar, 1 tablespoon at a time, beating until stiff peaks form. Gently stir one-fourth of egg white mixture into buttermilk mixture; gently fold in remaining egg white mixture. Fold in blackberries.

4. Pour batter into an 8-inch square baking pan coated with cooking spray. Place in a larger baking pan; add hot water to larger pan to depth of 1 inch. Bake at 350° for 35 minutes or until cake springs back when touched lightly in center. Sprinkle cake with powdered sugar. Serve warm. Yield: 5 servings (serving size: 1 cup).

CALORIES 285 (23% from fat); FAT 7.2g (sat 1.7g, mono 2.8g, poly 1.8g); PROTEIN 6g; CARB 51.2g; FIBER 3.3g; CHOL 89mg; IRON 0.8mg; SODIUM 198mg; CALC 86mg

Fudgy Soufflé Cake with Warm Turtle Sauce

Butter-flavored cooking spray
¼ teaspoon sugar
½ cup unsweetened cocoa
6 tablespoons hot water
2 tablespoons butter or stick margarine
3 tablespoons all-purpose flour
¾ cup 1% low-fat milk
¼ cup sugar
⅛ teaspoon salt
4 large egg whites
3 tablespoons sugar
Warm Turtle Sauce

1. Preheat oven to 375°.
2. Coat a 1½-quart soufflé dish with cooking spray; sprinkle with ¼ teaspoon sugar. Set aside.
3. Combine the cocoa and the hot water in a bowl, and set mixture aside.
4. Melt the butter in a small, heavy saucepan over medium heat. Add flour; cook 1 minute, stirring constantly with a whisk. Add milk, ¼ cup sugar, and salt; cook 3 minutes or until thick, stirring constantly. Remove from heat. Add cocoa mixture; stir well. Spoon into a large bowl; cool slightly.
5. Beat egg whites at high speed of a mixer until foamy. Add 3 tablespoons sugar, 1 tablespoon at a time, beating until stiff peaks form. Gently fold 1 cup egg white mixture into cocoa mixture; gently fold in remaining egg white mixture. Spoon into prepared soufflé dish.
6. Bake at 375° for 35 minutes or until puffy and set. Remove from oven, and serve warm, at room temperature, or chilled with Warm Turtle Sauce. Yield: 6 servings (serving size: 1 wedge and about 1 tablespoon sauce).

(Totals include Warm Turtle Sauce) CALORIES 241 (29% from fat); FAT 7.8g (sat 1.7g, mono 3.3g, poly 1.9g); PROTEIN 6.1g; CARB 58.6g; FIBER 0.4g; CHOL 2mg; IRON 1.6mg; SODIUM 182mg; CALC 54mg

WARM TURTLE SAUCE:

6 tablespoons fat-free caramel-flavored sundae syrup
3 tablespoons chopped pecans, toasted

1. Place caramel syrup in a small bowl; microwave at high 30 seconds or until warm. Stir in pecans. Yield: ½ cup (serving size: about 1½ tablespoons).

CALORIES 79 (28% from fat); FAT 2.5g (sat 0.2g, mono 1.5g, poly 0.6g); PROTEIN 0.2g; CARB 35.6g; FIBER 0.2g; CHOL 0mg; IRON 0.1mg; SODIUM 35mg; CALC 1mg

German Chocolate Cheesecake

CRUST:
⅔ cup all-purpose flour
2 tablespoons sugar
2 tablespoons chilled butter or stick margarine, cut into small pieces
1 tablespoon ice water
Cooking spray

FILLING:
½ cup Dutch process cocoa
½ cup fat-free hot fudge topping
¼ cup 2% reduced-fat milk
2 (8-ounce) blocks fat-free cream cheese, softened
1½ cups (12 ounces) ⅓-less-fat cream cheese, softened
1½ cups sugar
3 tablespoons all-purpose flour
2 teaspoons vanilla extract
¼ teaspoon coconut extract
2 large eggs
2 large egg whites

TOPPING:
⅔ cup fat-free caramel sundae topping
⅓ cup chopped pecans, toasted
⅓ cup flaked sweetened coconut, toasted

1. Preheat oven to 400°.
2. Lightly spoon flour into dry measuring cups; level with a knife. Place flour and 2 tablespoons sugar in a food processor; pulse until combined. Add butter; pulse 3 times or until it resembles coarse meal. With processor on, pour water through chute; process just until blended. Press into bottom of a 9-inch springform pan coated with cooking spray. Bake at 400° for 8 minutes or until lightly browned. Cool on a wire rack. Reduce oven temperature to 325°.
3. Combine cocoa, fudge topping, and milk. Beat cheeses with a mixer at high speed until smooth. Add 1½ cups sugar, 3 tablespoons flour, and extracts. Add eggs and whites, 1 at a time; beat well after each addition. Add chocolate mixture; beat well.
4. Pour mixture into the prepared pan. Bake at 325° for 1 hour and 5 minutes or until cheesecake center barely moves when pan is touched. Remove cheesecake from oven; run knife around outside edge. Cool to room temperature.
5. Combine sundae topping, pecans, and coconut; spread over cheesecake. Cover; chill at least 8 hours. Yield: 16 servings (serving size: 1 wedge).

CALORIES 314 (29% from fat); FAT 10g (sat 5.3g, mono 3.2g, poly 0.8g); PROTEIN 9.7g; CARB 46.1g; FIBER 1.1g; CHOL 53mg; IRON 1.2mg; SODIUM 352mg; CALC 128mg

Vanilla Cheesecake with Cherry Topping

We use the entire vanilla bean: The seeds flavor the cheesecake, and the bean halves flavor the topping.

CRUST:
- ¾ cup graham cracker crumbs
- ¼ cup sugar
- 2 tablespoons butter, melted
- 2 teaspoons water
- Cooking spray

FILLING:
- 3 (8-ounce) blocks fat-free cream cheese, softened
- 2 (8-ounce) blocks ⅓-less-fat cream cheese, softened
- 1 cup sugar
- 3 tablespoons all-purpose flour
- ¼ teaspoon salt
- 1 (8-ounce) carton fat-free sour cream
- 4 large eggs
- 2 teaspoons vanilla extract
- 1 vanilla bean, split lengthwise

TOPPING:
- ⅔ cup tawny port or other sweet red wine
- ½ cup sugar
- 2 (10-ounce) bags frozen pitted dark sweet cherries
- 2 tablespoons fresh lemon juice
- 4 teaspoons cornstarch
- 4 teaspoons water

1. Preheat oven to 400°.

2. To prepare crust, combine first 3 ingredients, tossing with a fork. Add 2 teaspoons water; toss with a fork until moist and crumbly. Gently press mixture into bottom and 1½ inches up sides of a 9-inch springform pan coated with cooking spray. Bake at 400° for 5 minutes; cool on a wire rack.

3. Reduce oven temperature to 325°.

4. To prepare filling, beat cheeses with a mixer at high speed until smooth. Combine 1 cup sugar, flour, and salt, stirring with a whisk. Add to cheese mixture; beat well. Add sour cream; beat well. Add eggs, 1 at a time, beating well after each addition. Stir in vanilla extract. Scrape seeds from vanilla bean; stir seeds into cheese mixture, reserving bean halves.

5. Pour cheese mixture into prepared pan; bake at 325° for 1 hour and 15 minutes or until cheesecake center barely moves when pan is touched. Remove cheesecake from oven; run a knife around outside edge. Cool to room temperature. Cover and chill at least 8 hours.

6. To prepare topping, combine port, ½ cup sugar, cherries, and reserved vanilla bean halves in a large saucepan; bring to a boil. Cook 5 minutes or until cherries are thawed and mixture is syrupy. Remove vanilla bean halves; discard.

7. Combine the lemon juice, cornstarch, and 4 teaspoons water, stirring with a whisk until well blended. Stir cornstarch mixture into cherry mixture, and bring to a boil. Reduce heat, and simmer 3 minutes or until mixture is slightly thickened and shiny. Remove from heat, and cool to room temperature. Cover and chill. Serve over cheesecake. Yield: 16 servings (serving size: 1 slice cheesecake and about 2 tablespoons topping).

CALORIES 324 (30% from fat); FAT 10.7g (sat 6.1g, mono 3.2g, poly 0.7g); PROTEIN 12.2g; CARB 42.8g; FIBER 1g; CHOL 83mg; IRON 0.8mg; SODIUM 458mg; CALC 134mg

desserts

Sour Cream Cheesecake

Fresh fruit isn't necessary but is a beautiful addition.

CRUST:
- 1 cup reduced-fat graham cracker crumbs (about 10 cookie sheets)
- ¼ cup sugar
- 2 tablespoons butter or stick margarine, melted
- Cooking spray

FILLING:
- 1 cup 2% low-fat cottage cheese
- 1½ tablespoons vanilla extract
- ½ teaspoon salt
- 1 (8-ounce) block ⅓-less-fat cream cheese
- 1 (8-ounce) block fat-free cream cheese
- 3 large eggs
- 1 large egg white
- 1 cup sugar

TOPPING:
- 3 tablespoons sugar
- 1 teaspoon vanilla extract
- 1 (8-ounce) carton low-fat sour cream
- 1 (8-ounce) carton fat-free sour cream

1. Preheat oven to 350°.

2. To prepare crust, combine the first 3 ingredients in a bowl. Firmly press the crumb mixture into the bottom and 2 inches up the sides of a 9-inch springform pan coated with cooking spray. Bake at 350° for 10 minutes, and cool on a wire rack.

3. To prepare filling, combine cottage cheese, 1½ tablespoons vanilla, salt, and cream cheeses in a food processor; process 1 minute or until smooth, scraping bowl once. Add eggs and egg white, 1 at a time, pulsing after each addition. Add 1 cup sugar; process just until blended.

4. Pour the cheese mixture into the prepared crust, and bake at 350° for 50 minutes or until the cheesecake is almost set. Remove the cheesecake from the oven, and let stand 10 minutes. Increase the oven temperature to 450°.

5. To prepare the topping, combine 3 tablespoons sugar and the remaining ingredients. Spread topping evenly over the cheesecake. Bake cheesecake at 450° for 5 minutes or until set. Cool completely on wire rack. Cover and chill 8 hours. Yield: 12 servings (serving size: 1 slice).

CALORIES 300 (29% from fat); FAT 9.6g (sat 5.5g, mono 2.9g, poly 0.6g); PROTEIN 11.8g; CARB 38.9g; FIBER 0.4g; CHOL 83mg; IRON 0.7mg; SODIUM 508mg; CALC 128mg

Banana-Split Cheesecake

CRUST:
- 1 cup packaged chocolate cookie crumbs (such as Oreo)
- 2 tablespoons sugar
- 1 tablespoon butter or stick margarine, melted
- Cooking spray

FILLING:
- 3 (8-ounce) blocks fat-free cream cheese, softened
- 1 (8-ounce) block ⅓-less-fat cream cheese, softened
- 1 (8-ounce) carton low-fat sour cream
- 1½ cups sugar
- 1½ cups mashed ripe banana
- 3 tablespoons all-purpose flour
- 2 teaspoons vanilla extract
- 4 large eggs

TOPPINGS:
- ⅓ cup canned crushed pineapple in juice, drained
- ⅓ cup strawberry sundae syrup
- ⅓ cup chocolate syrup
- ¼ cup chopped pecans, toasted
- 16 maraschino cherries, drained

1. Preheat oven to 325°.

2. To prepare the crust, combine first 3 ingredients in a bowl, and toss with a fork until moist. Press into the bottom of a 9-inch springform pan coated with cooking spray.

3. To prepare the filling, beat cream cheeses and sour cream with a mixer at high speed until smooth. Add 1½ cups sugar, banana, flour, and vanilla, and beat well. Add eggs, 1 at a time, and beat well after each addition.

4. Pour cheese mixture into prepared pan, and bake at 325° for 1 hour and 10 minutes or until almost set. Cheesecake is done when the center barely moves when pan is touched. Remove the cheesecake from oven, and run a knife around outside edge. Cool cheesecake to room temperature. Cover and chill for at least 8 hours. Top each serving with 1 teaspoon pineapple, 1 teaspoon strawberry syrup, 1 teaspoon chocolate syrup, ¾ teaspoon pecans, and 1 cherry. Yield: 16 servings (serving size: 1 wedge with toppings).

CALORIES 317 (30% from fat); FAT 10.6g (sat 4.6g, mono 3.7g, poly 1.5g); PROTEIN 10.7g; CARB 45g; FIBER 1g; CHOL 81mg; IRON 1.2mg; SODIUM 393mg; CALC 158mg

Warm Apple-Buttermilk Custard Pie

CRUST:
½ (15-ounce) package refrigerated pie dough (such as Pillsbury)
Cooking spray

STREUSEL:
⅓ cup all-purpose flour
⅓ cup packed brown sugar
½ teaspoon ground cinnamon
2½ tablespoons chilled butter, cut into small pieces

FILLING:
5 cups sliced peeled Granny Smith apple (about 2 pounds)
1 cup granulated sugar, divided
½ teaspoon ground cinnamon
2 tablespoons all-purpose flour
¼ teaspoon salt
3 large eggs
1¾ cups fat-free buttermilk
1 teaspoon vanilla extract

1. Preheat oven to 325°.
2. To prepare crust, roll dough into a 14-inch circle, and fit into a 9-inch deep-dish pie plate coated with cooking spray. Fold edges under, and flute.

Place pie plate in refrigerator until ready to use.
3. To prepare streusel, lightly spoon ⅓ cup flour into a dry measuring cup, and level with a knife. Combine ⅓ cup flour, brown sugar, and ½ teaspoon ground cinnamon in a medium bowl, and cut in butter with a pastry blender or 2 knives until the mixture resembles coarse meal. Place streusel in the refrigerator.
4. To prepare filling, heat a large nonstick skillet coated with cooking spray over medium heat. Add sliced apple, ¼ cup granulated sugar, and ½ teaspoon cinnamon; cook 10 minutes or until apple is tender, stirring mixture occasionally. Spoon apple mixture into prepared crust.
5. Combine remaining ¾ cup granulated sugar, 2 tablespoons flour, salt, and eggs, stirring with a whisk. Stir in buttermilk and vanilla. Pour over the apple mixture. Bake at 325° for 30 minutes. Reduce the oven temperature to 300° (do not remove pie from oven); sprinkle streusel over pie. Bake at 300° for 40 minutes or until set. Let stand 1 hour before serving. Yield: 10 servings (serving size: 1 wedge).

CALORIES 317 (29% from fat); FAT 10.1g (sat 4.6g, mono 3g, poly 1.2g); PROTEIN 5g; CARB 52.6g; FIBER 1.3g; CHOL 76mg; IRON 0.8mg; SODIUM 230mg; CALC 73mg

Cheddar-Crusted Apple Pie

Granny Smith apples are good for baking, and their tartness contrasts with the sharp cheddar flavor in the pie's crust.

CRUST:

2¼ cups all-purpose flour, divided
¾ cup (3 ounces) shredded extrasharp cheddar cheese
½ cup ice water
½ teaspoon salt
¼ cup chilled butter, cut into small pieces

FILLING:

10 cups very thinly sliced peeled Granny Smith apple (about 2¾ pounds)
2 tablespoons fresh lemon juice
⅓ cup packed brown sugar
¼ cup granulated sugar
¼ teaspoon ground cinnamon
¼ teaspoon ground nutmeg
¼ teaspoon ground ginger
Dash of salt
Cooking spray
1 large egg white, lightly beaten
1 tablespoon water

1. Preheat oven to 400°.

2. To prepare crust, lightly spoon flour into dry measuring cups, and level with a knife. Combine 1 tablespoon flour and cheese in a small bowl; toss well. Place mixture in freezer for 10 minutes.

3. Combine ¼ cup flour and ½ cup ice water in a small bowl, stirring with a whisk until well blended to form a slurry. Combine 1¾ cups flour and ½ teaspoon salt in a large bowl, and cut in butter with a pastry blender or 2 knives until mixture resembles coarse meal. Stir in cheese mixture. Add slurry, and toss with a fork. Sprinkle the surface with up to 1 tablespoon ice water, tossing with a fork until moist and crumbly (do not form a ball). Mixture will seem slightly dry.

4. Divide dough in half. Gently press each half into a 4-inch circle on 2 sheets of overlapping heavy-duty plastic wrap; cover with 2 additional sheets of overlapping plastic wrap. Roll each dough half, still covered, into a 12-inch circle. Chill 30 minutes or until plastic wrap can be easily removed.

5. To prepare filling, combine apple and lemon juice in a large bowl. Combine 3 tablespoons flour, brown sugar, and next 5 ingredients in a small bowl. Sprinkle brown sugar mixture over apples; toss well.

6. To assemble pie, remove top sheets of plastic wrap from 1 dough circle; fit dough, plastic wrap side up, into a 10-inch deep-dish pie plate coated with cooking spray, letting dough extend over edge of plate. Remove remaining plastic wrap. Spoon filling into crust. Brush edges of crust lightly with water. Remove top sheets of plastic wrap from the remaining dough circle; place, plastic wrap side up, on apple mixture. Remove remaining plastic wrap. Press edges of dough together. Fold edges under, and flute. Cut 3 (1-inch) slits in top of pastry using a sharp knife.

7. Combine egg white and 1 tablespoon water. Brush egg mixture over top and edges of pie. Place pie on a baking sheet, and bake at 400° for 45 minutes or until golden. Cool the pie on a wire rack. Yield: 10 servings.

CALORIES 285 (24% from fat); FAT 7.7g (sat 4.5g, mono 1.4g, poly 0.3g); PROTEIN 5.4g; CARB 52g; FIBER 3.1g; CHOL 22mg; IRON 1.6mg; SODIUM 242mg; CALC 75mg

Winter-Fruit Tart with Caramel Ice Cream

With an electric ice-cream maker and a food processor, you can make this decadent duet in a snap.

FRUIT MIXTURE:
1½ cups sliced dried apricots (about 8 ounces)
1½ cups water
1¼ cups coarsely chopped dried apple (about 4 ounces)
½ cup golden raisins
½ cup amaretto (almond-flavored liqueur) or apple juice
⅓ cup packed brown sugar
1 tablespoon butter or stick margarine
2 teaspoons vanilla extract

CRUST:
1¾ cups all-purpose flour
1 tablespoon granulated sugar
½ teaspoon ground cinnamon
¼ teaspoon salt
6 tablespoons chilled butter or stick margarine, cut into small pieces
4 to 5 tablespoons ice water
Cooking spray
Caramel Ice Cream

1. To prepare the fruit mixture, combine the first 6 ingredients in a medium saucepan. Bring to a boil, and cook for 1 minute. Remove from heat. Stir in 1 tablespoon butter and vanilla; cover the mixture and let stand 10 minutes.

2. Preheat oven to 375°.

3. To prepare the crust, lightly spoon the flour into dry measuring cups, and level with a knife. Place the flour, granulated sugar, cinnamon, and salt in a food processor, and pulse 3 times or until combined. Add the chilled butter, and pulse 10 times or until the mixture resembles coarse meal. With food processor on, add ice water through food chute, processing just until combined (do not form a ball). Gently press the mixture into a 4-inch circle on heavy-duty plastic wrap, and cover dough with additional plastic wrap. Roll the dough, still covered, into a 14-inch circle, and freeze 5 minutes or until the plastic wrap can be easily removed. Remove 1 sheet of plastic wrap, and fit the dough into a 10-inch pie plate or quiche dish coated with cooking spray, allowing the dough to extend over the edge of the dish. Remove the top sheet of plastic wrap. Spoon the fruit mixture into the crust.

Fold dough over the fruit mixture, pressing gently to seal (pastry will partially cover the fruit mixture). Coat the dough with cooking spray.

4. Bake at 375° for 50 minutes or until the crust is crisp (shield the fruit mixture with foil if it begins to burn). Serve tart warm with Caramel Ice Cream. Yield: 12 servings.

(Totals include Caramel Ice Cream) CALORIES 317 (23% from fat); FAT 8.1g (sat 2g, mono 3.3g, poly 2.2g); PROTEIN 4.6g; CARB 58.1g; FIBER 2.5g; CHOL 5mg; IRON 2.1mg; SODIUM 188mg; CALC 86mg

CARAMEL ICE CREAM:

4 cups 2% reduced-fat milk
2 teaspoons vanilla extract
1 (10-ounce) jar caramel topping

1. Combine all ingredients in a large bowl, and stir until well blended.

2. Pour mixture into the freezer can of an ice-cream freezer, and freeze according to the manufacturer's instructions. Spoon the ice cream into a freezer-safe container; cover and freeze 1 hour or until firm. Yield: 6 cups (serving size: ¼ cup).

CALORIES 59 (17% from fat); FAT 1.1g (sat 0.6g, mono 0.3g, poly 0g); PROTEIN 1.6g; CARB 10.2g; FIBER 0g; CHOL 5mg; IRON 0mg; SODIUM 48mg; CALC 61mg

Fresh-Fruit Pizza with
Lemon Curd

Fresh-Fruit Pizza with Lemon Curd

The Lemon Curd not only holds the fruit in place, it serves as an exquisite anchor for all the flavors. This pizza is best served the day it's made. Be creative and choose different fruit combinations.

  1 (18-ounce) package refrigerated sugar cookie dough
  Cooking spray
  2 tablespoons seedless raspberry jam, melted
  ¾ cup Lemon Curd
  2 cups fresh raspberries
  2 cups fresh blackberries
  1 cup sliced strawberries
  1 plum, sliced
  2 teaspoons sugar

1. Preheat oven to 350°.
2. Press dough into a 12-inch pizza pan coated with cooking spray. Bake at 350° for 12 minutes or until golden brown. Cool completely on a wire rack.
3. Preheat broiler.
4. Spread jam over crust. Spread Lemon Curd over jam, and arrange fruit on top. Sprinkle sugar over fruit, and broil 3 minutes. Yield: 12 servings (serving size: 1 wedge).

CALORIES 261 (30% from fat); FAT 8.6g (sat 2.3g, mono 2.8g, poly 3g); PROTEIN 2.5g; CARB 43.1g; FIBER 3.1g; CHOL 37mg; IRON 1.4mg; SODIUM 173mg; CALC 19mg

Lemon Curd

Remember to stir this constantly while cooking. For a lime-curd variation, substitute lime rind and juice for the lemon rind and juice.

  ¾ cup sugar
  1 tablespoon grated lemon rind
  2 large eggs
  ⅔ cup fresh lemon juice (about 3 large lemons)
  2 tablespoons butter or stick margarine

1. Combine first 3 ingredients in a saucepan over medium heat, stirring with a whisk. Cook until the sugar dissolves and mixture is light in color (about 3 minutes). Stir in lemon juice and butter; cook for 5 minutes or until mixture thinly coats the back of a spoon, stirring constantly with a whisk. Cool. Cover and chill (mixture will thicken as it cools). Yield: 1⅓ cups (serving size: 1 tablespoon).

NOTE: Lemon Curd can be stored in the refrigerator for up to 1 week. You can easily double the recipe and freeze half of it in a heavy-duty zip-top plastic bag. Thaw in the refrigerator, and use within 1 week of thawing.

CALORIES 47 (31% from fat); FAT 1.6g (sat 0.8g, mono 0.5g, poly 0.1g); PROTEIN 0.7g; CARB 7.9g; FIBER 0g; CHOL 24mg; IRON 0.1mg; SODIUM 18mg; CALC 4mg

Brown Sugar-Peach Pie with Coconut Streusel

Peel peaches with a potato peeler if they're not too ripe. If they are ripe, plunge them in boiling water for about 30 seconds; that makes the skin a cinch to remove with a paring knife.

  ½ (15-ounce) package refrigerated pie dough (such as Pillsbury)
  ⅔ cup packed brown sugar, divided
  ¼ cup uncooked quick-cooking tapioca
  ½ teaspoon ground cinnamon
  6 cups sliced peeled ripe peaches, divided (about 3 pounds)
  ⅓ cup regular oats
  ¼ cup flaked sweetened coconut
  1½ tablespoons butter or stick margarine, melted

1. Preheat oven to 425°.
2. Fit the dough into a 9-inch pie plate. Fold edges under; flute. Line the dough with a piece of foil, and arrange pie weights or dried beans on foil. Bake at 425° for 12 minutes. Remove pie weights and foil. Cool crust on a wire rack.
3. Combine ⅓ cup sugar, tapioca, and cinnamon in a bowl; sprinkle over 4½ cups peaches. Toss gently, and let stand 15 minutes. Spoon into the prepared crust. Top with 1½ cups peaches. Place the pie in a 425° oven. Immediately reduce oven temperature to 350° (do not remove pie from oven); bake 30 minutes. Combine ⅓ cup sugar, oats, coconut, and butter; sprinkle over peach mixture. Shield edges of crust with foil. Bake an additional 30 minutes or until golden. Cool on a wire rack. Yield: 8 servings.

CALORIES 307 (31% from fat); FAT 10.5g (sat 5g, mono 3.9g, poly 1g); PROTEIN 2.1g; CARB 52.7g; FIBER 3.1g; CHOL 11mg; IRON 0.8mg; SODIUM137mg; CALC 27mg

Rustic Grape Tart

Rustic Grape Tart

This free-form dessert is a simple but elegant coda to a dinner for company. Cornmeal adds a little texture.

CRUST:
1 cup all-purpose flour
¼ cup yellow cornmeal
3 tablespoons granulated sugar
½ teaspoon baking powder
½ teaspoon salt
¼ cup chilled butter, cut into small pieces
3 tablespoons orange juice
1 teaspoon all-purpose flour

FILLING:
2¼ cups seedless red grapes
2¼ cups seedless black grapes
2 tablespoons granulated sugar
1 tablespoon cornstarch
¾ teaspoon vanilla extract
¼ teaspoon ground cinnamon

REMAINING INGREDIENTS:
1 teaspoon water
1 large egg yolk
1 teaspoon turbinado sugar (optional)

1. Preheat oven to 400°.
2. To prepare crust, lightly spoon 1 cup flour into a dry measuring cup; level with a knife. Combine 1 cup flour, cornmeal, 3 tablespoons granulated sugar, baking powder, and salt in a food processor; pulse 4 times or until blended. Add chilled butter, and pulse 6 times or until mixture resembles coarse meal. With processor on, slowly pour orange juice through food chute, processing just until blended (do not allow dough to form a ball).
3. Press mixture gently into a 4-inch circle on plastic wrap; cover. Chill 15 minutes. Slightly overlap 2 sheets of plastic wrap on a slightly damp surface. Unwrap and place chilled dough on plastic wrap. Cover dough with 2 additional sheets of overlapping plastic wrap. Roll dough, still covered, into an 11-inch circle. Remove top sheets of plastic wrap; place dough, plastic wrap side up, on a baking sheet lined with parchment paper. Remove plastic wrap. Sprinkle dough with 1 teaspoon flour.
4. To prepare filling, combine grapes, 2 tablespoons granulated sugar, cornstarch, vanilla, and cinnamon. Spoon into center of dough, leaving a 2-inch border. Fold edges of dough toward center, pressing gently to seal (dough will only partially cover grape mixture). Combine water and egg yolk; brush over edges of dough. Sprinkle turbinado sugar over grape mixture and dough, if desired. Bake at 400° for 25 minutes or until crust is brown. Serve warm or at room temperature. Yield: 8 servings.

CALORIES 231 (26% from fat); FAT 6.7g (sat 4.4g, mono 0.3g, poly 0.2g); PROTEIN 2.9g; CARB 40.8g; FIBER 1.5g; CHOL 42mg; IRON 1.3mg; SODIUM 180mg; CALC 31mg

Easy Caramel-Banana Galette

The trick to making the caramel for this simple dessert is leaving it unstirred for 8 minutes; stirring can cause it to harden. Even easier, substitute bottled fat-free caramel sauce for the sugar and water. Heat the sauce in the microwave for 1 minute, then stir in the raisin mixture. The raisins should sit in the rum for at least 30 minutes. Slice the bananas immediately before arranging them on the tart so they don't discolor. To dress it up even more, serve this dessert warm with vanilla frozen yogurt.

¼ cup golden raisins
2 tablespoons dark rum
½ (15-ounce) package refrigerated pie dough (such as Pillsbury)
Cooking spray
3 cups (¼-inch-thick) diagonally sliced ripe banana (about 1½ pounds)
½ cup sugar
2 tablespoons water

1. Combine raisins and rum in a small bowl.
2. Preheat oven to 425°.
3. Roll dough into a 10½-inch circle, and place on a foil-lined baking sheet coated with cooking spray. Arrange the banana slices in concentric circles on crust, leaving a 1-inch border. Fold a 2-inch dough border over banana slices, pressing gently to seal (dough will partially cover slices). Bake at 425° for 30 minutes.
4. Combine sugar and water in a small saucepan; cook over medium heat until golden (about 8 minutes). Remove from heat, and carefully stir in raisin mixture until combined. Cool slightly. Pour over banana slices. Cut into 6 wedges. Yield: 6 servings (serving size: 1 wedge).

CALORIES 318 (27% from fat); FAT 9.7g (sat 2.4g, mono 4g, poly 2.5g); PROTEIN 3.3g; CARB 57.3g; FIBER 2.5g; CHOL 0mg; IRON 0.9mg; SODIUM 160mg; CALC 35mg

Blueberry-Peach Galettes

This dessert is ideal for entertaining. The refrigerated pie dough makes preparation simple.

- 1 (15-ounce) package refrigerated pie dough (such as Pillsbury)
- 6 cups fresh or frozen sliced peeled peaches, thawed
- 1 cup fresh or frozen blueberries, thawed
- ¼ cup granulated sugar
- 2 tablespoons apricot preserves, melted and divided
- 1 tablespoon turbinado or granulated sugar

1. Preheat oven to 425°.
2. Line a baking sheet with foil or parchment paper. Roll 1 dough portion into a 12-inch circle; place on foil. Combine peaches, blueberries, and ¼ cup granulated sugar. Arrange half of peach mixture in center of dough, leaving a 3-inch border. Fold edges of dough toward center, pressing gently to seal (dough will only partially cover peach mixture). Brush half of melted apricot preserves over peach mixture and edges of dough.
3. Bake at 425° for 10 minutes. Reduce oven temperature to 350° (do not remove galette from oven), and bake an additional 20 minutes or until lightly browned. Repeat procedure with remaining dough, peach mixture, and apricot preserves. Sprinkle with 1 tablespoon sugar. Serve warm or at room temperature. Cut each galette into 8 wedges. Yield: 2 galettes, 16 servings (serving size: 1 wedge).

CALORIES 232 (29% from fat); FAT 7.6g (sat 1.9g, mono 3.3g, poly 2g); PROTEIN 2.1g; CARB 40.6g; FIBER 2.8g; CHOL 0mg; IRON 1mg; SODIUM 124mg; CALC 6mg

Pecan and Date Pie

CRUST:
- 1 cup all-purpose flour, divided
- 3 tablespoons ice water
- 1 teaspoon fresh lemon juice
- 2 tablespoons powdered sugar
- ¼ teaspoon salt
- ¼ cup vegetable shortening
- Cooking spray

FILLING:
- ½ cup whole pitted dates, chopped
- ⅓ cup chopped pecans
- 1 cup dark corn syrup
- ½ cup packed brown sugar
- 3 tablespoons all-purpose flour
- 1 teaspoon vanilla extract
- ¼ teaspoon salt
- 4 large eggs
- Reduced-calorie whipped topping, thawed (optional)

1. Preheat oven to 325°.
2. To prepare crust, lightly spoon 1 cup flour into a dry measuring cup, and level with a knife. Combine ¼ cup flour, water, and juice, stirring with a whisk until well blended to form a slurry.
3. Combine ¾ cup flour, powdered sugar, and ¼ teaspoon salt; cut in shortening with a pastry blender or 2 knives until mixture resembles coarse meal. Add slurry; toss with a fork until mixture is moist. Gently press mixture into a 4-inch circle on 2 sheets of heavy-duty plastic wrap that overlap; cover with 2 additional sheets of overlapping plastic wrap. Roll dough, still covered, into a 12-inch circle; freeze 10 minutes.
4. Remove top 2 sheets of plastic wrap; let dough stand 1 minute or until pliable. Fit dough, plastic-wrap side up, into a 9-inch pie plate coated with cooking spray. Remove remaining plastic wrap. Press dough into bottom and up sides of pan. Fold edges under; flute.
5. To prepare filling, sprinkle dates and pecans evenly over bottom of crust. Combine corn syrup and remaining ingredients in a large bowl; beat with a mixer at medium speed until well blended. Pour mixture into prepared crust. Bake at 325° for 55 minutes or until a knife inserted 1 inch from the edge comes out clean. Cool on a wire rack. When serving, dollop each slice with whipped topping, if desired. Yield: 10 servings.

CALORIES 321 (29% from fat); FAT 10.2g (sat 2.2g, mono 4.7g, poly 2.5g); PROTEIN 4.6g; CARB 55.8g; FIBER 1.5g; CHOL 85mg; IRON 1.5mg; SODIUM 198mg; CALC 33mg

Pecan and Date Pie

Pecan Tassies in Cream Cheese Pastry

Pecan Tassies in Cream Cheese Pastry

PASTRY:

1 cup all-purpose flour
1 tablespoon granulated sugar
Dash of salt
¼ cup (2 ounces) ⅓-less-fat cream cheese, softened
2 tablespoons butter or stick margarine, softened
2 tablespoons fat-free milk
Cooking spray

FILLING:

⅓ cup finely chopped pecans
½ cup packed brown sugar
⅓ cup light-colored corn syrup
1 teaspoon vanilla extract
⅛ teaspoon salt
1 large egg
1 large egg white

1. Preheat oven to 350°.

2. To prepare pastry, lightly spoon flour into a dry measuring cup, and level with a knife. Combine flour, granulated sugar, and dash of salt in a small bowl. Combine cream cheese, softened butter, and milk in a large bowl, and beat with a mixer at medium speed until mixture is well blended. Add flour mixture to cheese mixture; beat at low speed just until blended (mixture will be crumbly). Press flour mixture into a ball.

3. Turn dough out onto a lightly floured surface, and knead lightly 3 to 4 times. Divide dough into 24 portions. Place 1 dough portion into each of 24 miniature muffin cups coated with cooking spray. Press dough into bottom and up sides of cups, using lightly floured fingers.

4. To prepare filling, divide pecans evenly among muffin cups. Combine brown sugar and remaining ingredients; spoon about 2 teaspoons filling over pecans in each muffin cup.

5. Bake at 350° for 20 minutes or until pastry is lightly browned and filling is puffy. Cool in cups for 10 minutes on a wire rack. Run a knife around the outside edge of each tassie; remove from pan. Cool completely on a wire rack. Yield: 2 dozen tassies (serving size: 1 tassie).

NOTE: Tassies may be frozen for up to 1 month in an airtight container.

CALORIES 77 (35% from fat); FAT 3g (sat 1.1g, mono 1.2g, poly 0.4g); PROTEIN 1.4g; CARB 11.3g; FIBER 0.2g; CHOL 14mg; IRON 0.4mg; SODIUM 50mg; CALC 9mg

Gingered Pumpkin Pie

A gingersnap streusel topping adds crunch to traditional pumpkin pie.

½ (15-ounce) package refrigerated pie dough (such as Pillsbury)
10 gingersnaps
2 tablespoons sugar
1 tablespoon all-purpose flour
2 tablespoons chilled butter, cut into small pieces
¾ cup sugar
1½ teaspoons ground cinnamon
½ teaspoon ground ginger
¼ teaspoon salt
¼ teaspoon ground nutmeg
1 (15-ounce) can pumpkin
1 (12-ounce) can evaporated fat-free milk
1 large egg
3 large egg whites

1. Preheat oven to 350°.

2. Roll dough into a 12-inch circle, and fit into a 10-inch deep-dish pie plate. Fold edges under; flute. Freeze 30 minutes.

3. Place cookies, 2 tablespoons sugar, and flour in a food processor; process until cookies are ground. Add butter; pulse until crumbly.

4. Combine ¾ cup sugar and remaining ingredients; pour into prepared crust. Bake at 350° for 35 minutes. Sprinkle crumb mixture over pie; bake an additional 20 minutes or until center is set. Cool to room temperature on a wire rack. Yield: 8 servings (serving size: 1 wedge).

CALORIES 338 (31% from fat); FAT 11.5g (sat 5.1g, mono 4.7g, poly 1.1g); PROTEIN 7.2g; CARB 51.7g; FIBER 2.6g; CHOL 41mg; IRON 1.2mg; SODIUM 340mg; CALC 157mg

Blueberry Crisp à la Mode

Blueberry Crisp à la Mode

You can use almost any combination of fresh berries in this dessert. Try cherries or blackberries.

  6 cups blueberries
  2 tablespoons brown sugar
  1 tablespoon all-purpose flour
  1 tablespoon fresh lemon juice
 ⅔ cup all-purpose flour
 ½ cup packed brown sugar
 ½ cup regular oats
 ¾ teaspoon ground cinnamon
4½ tablespoons chilled butter or stick
     margarine, cut into small pieces
  2 cups vanilla low-fat frozen yogurt

1. Preheat oven to 375°.
2. Combine first 4 ingredients in a medium bowl, and spoon into an 11 x 7-inch baking dish. Lightly spoon ⅔ cup flour into a dry measuring cup, and level with a knife. Combine ⅔ cup flour, ½ cup brown sugar, oats, and cinnamon; cut in butter with a pastry blender or 2 knives until the mixture resembles coarse meal. Sprinkle over the blueberry mixture. Bake at 375° for 30 minutes or until bubbly. Top each serving with ¼ cup frozen yogurt. Yield: 8 servings.
NOTE: The topping may also be made in the food processor. Place ⅔ cup flour, ½ cup brown sugar, oats, and cinnamon in a food processor, and pulse 2 times or until combined. Add the chilled butter, and pulse 4 times or until the mixture resembles coarse meal.

CALORIES 288 (26% from fat); FAT 8.3g (sat 4.8g, mono 2g, poly 0.9g); PROTEIN 4.2g; CARB 52g; FIBER 3.8g; CHOL 22mg; IRON 1.3mg; SODIUM 96mg; CALC 77mg

Strawberry-Almond Cream Tart

Cover Recipe

CRUST:
36 honey graham crackers (about 9 sheets)
 2 tablespoons sugar
 2 tablespoons butter, melted
 4 teaspoons water
   Cooking spray
FILLING:
⅔ cup light cream cheese
¼ cup sugar
½ teaspoon vanilla extract
¼ teaspoon almond extract
TOPPING:
6 cups small fresh strawberries, divided
⅔ cup sugar
1 tablespoon cornstarch
1 tablespoon fresh lemon juice
2 tablespoons sliced almonds, toasted

1. Preheat oven to 350°.
2. Place crackers in a food processor, and process until crumbly. Add 2 tablespoons sugar, butter, and water; pulse just until moist. Place the mixture in a 12 x 8-inch rectangular pan coated with cooking spray, pressing into bottom and up sides of pan to ¾ inch. Bake at 350° for 10 minutes or until lightly browned. Cool completely on a wire rack.
3. Combine the cream cheese, ¼ cup sugar, and extracts in a medium bowl; stir until smooth. Spread filling mixture evenly over bottom of crust.
4. Place 2 cups strawberries in food processor; process until pureed. Combine puree, ⅔ cup sugar, and cornstarch in a small saucepan over medium heat, stirring with a whisk. Bring to a boil; stir constantly. Reduce heat to low; cook 1 minute. Remove from heat; cool to room temperature, stirring occasionally.
5. Combine 4 cups strawberries and juice; toss to coat. Arrange berries, bottoms up, in 5 straight lines over filling. Spoon half of glaze evenly over berries (reserve remaining glaze for another use). Arrange nuts around edge. Cover and chill 3 hours. Yield: 10 servings (serving size: 1 piece).
NOTE: Use a 9-inch round removable-bottom tart pan, a 9-inch springform pan, or a 10-inch pie plate.

CALORIES 289 (28% from fat); FAT 8.9g (sat 4.2g, mono 1.7g, poly 0.5g); PROTEIN 4.5g; CARB 48.7g; FIBER 3g; CHOL 15mg; IRON 1.3mg; SODIUM 242mg; CALC 59mg

French Toast-Peach Cobbler

The sturdier the bread, the better for this simple dessert. Turbinado or raw sugar crystals have a coarse texture and add a nice crunch to the topping, but granulated sugar can be used instead.

12   large ripe peaches
1/3 cup all-purpose flour
 1   cup granulated sugar, divided
Cooking spray
 1   teaspoon grated orange rind
1/3 cup fresh orange juice
1/4 cup butter or stick margarine, melted
1/4 teaspoon ground cinnamon
 3   large egg whites
 8   (1.5-ounce) slices hearty white bread
     (such as Pepperidge Farm)
 2   tablespoons turbinado sugar or
     granulated sugar

1. Cut an "X" on the bottoms of peaches, carefully cutting just through the skin. Fill a large Dutch oven with water, and bring to a boil. Immerse the peaches for 20 seconds, remove with a slotted spoon, and plunge into ice water. Slip the skins off peaches using a paring knife (skins will be very loose). Cut peaches in half, and remove pits. Slice peaches to yield 12 cups.
2. Preheat oven to 350°.
3. Lightly spoon flour into a dry measuring cup; level with a knife. Combine peaches, 3/4 cup granulated sugar, and flour in a 13 x 9-inch baking dish coated with cooking spray, and let stand 30 minutes, stirring occasionally.
4. Combine 1/4 cup granulated sugar, orange rind, orange juice, butter, cinnamon, and egg whites in a shallow bowl, stirring with a whisk. Trim the crusts from bread; cut each slice into 2 triangles. Dip bread triangles in the orange juice mixture; arrange on top of peach mixture. Sprinkle turbinado sugar over bread. Bake at 350° for 45 minutes or until golden. Yield: 10 servings.

CALORIES 289 (17% from fat); FAT 5.6g (sat 3g, mono 1.7g, poly 0.4g); PROTEIN 4.5g; CARB 58.5g; FIBER 4.6g; CHOL 13mg; IRON 1mg; SODIUM 162mg; CALC 35mg

Peanut Brittle-Apple Crisp

1/2 cup all-purpose flour
1/4 cup granulated sugar
1/4 cup packed brown sugar
1/8 teaspoon salt
1/4 cup chilled butter or stick margarine,
     cut into small pieces
1/2 cup coarsely broken peanut brittle
     (about 2 ounces)
 7   cups peeled sliced Granny Smith apple
     (about 2 pounds)
 3   tablespoons orange marmalade
 2   cups low-fat vanilla frozen yogurt

1. Preheat oven to 375°.
2. Lightly spoon flour into a dry measuring cup, and level with a knife. Combine flour, sugars, and salt in a bowl; cut in butter with a pastry blender or 2 knives until mixture resembles coarse meal. Add peanut brittle, stirring to combine.
3. Arrange apple in an 8-inch square baking dish; spoon marmalade over apple. Sprinkle flour mixture over marmalade. Bake at 375° for 40 minutes. Serve warm. Top with yogurt. Yield: 8 servings (serving size: 1/3 cup crisp and 1/4 cup yogurt).

CALORIES 281 (25% from fat); FAT 7.8g (sat 2g, mono 2.9g, poly 2.4g); PROTEIN 2.9g; CARB 53g; FIBER 3.2g; CHOL 5mg; IRON 0.8mg; SODIUM 131mg; CALC 69mg

Black Bottom
Banana-Cream Pie

- 1 (9-inch) Pastry Crust
- 3 tablespoons cornstarch, divided
- 2 tablespoons sugar
- 2 tablespoons unsweetened cocoa
- Dash of salt
- 1⅓ cups 1% low-fat milk, divided
- 1 ounce semisweet chocolate, chopped
- ½ cup sugar
- ¼ teaspoon salt
- 2 large eggs
- 1 tablespoon butter or stick margarine
- 2 teaspoons vanilla extract
- ¼ cup (2 ounces) block-style fat-free cream cheese, softened
- 2 cups sliced ripe banana (about 2 large bananas)
- 1½ cups frozen fat-free whipped topping, thawed
- Chocolate curls (optional)

1. Prepare and bake Pastry Crust in a 9-inch pie plate. Cool completely on a wire rack.

2. Combine 1 tablespoon cornstarch, 2 tablespoons sugar, cocoa, and dash of salt in a small, heavy saucepan; gradually add ⅓ cup milk, stirring with a whisk. Cook 2 minutes over medium-low heat. Stir in chopped chocolate, and bring to a boil over medium heat. Reduce heat to low, and cook for 1 minute, stirring constantly. Spread chocolate mixture into bottom of prepared crust.

3. Combine 2 tablespoons cornstarch, 1 cup milk, ½ cup sugar, ¼ teaspoon salt, eggs, and butter in a heavy saucepan over medium heat, stirring constantly with a whisk. Bring to a boil. Reduce heat to low, and cook for 1 minute or until thick. Remove from heat. Add the vanilla. Beat cream cheese until light (about 30 seconds). Add ¼ cup hot custard to cream cheese, and beat just until blended. Stir in the remaining custard.

4. Arrange the banana slices on top of chocolate layer, and spoon custard over bananas. Press plastic wrap onto surface of custard, and chill for 4 hours. Remove the plastic wrap. Spread whipped topping evenly over custard. Garnish with chocolate curls, if desired. Chill until ready to serve. Yield: 8 servings (serving size: 1 wedge).

(Totals include Pastry Crust) CALORIES 315 (29% from fat); FAT 10.1g (sat 4.8g, mono 3.4g, poly 2.4g); PROTEIN 6.9g; CARB 49.6g; FIBER 1.6g; CHOL 58mg; IRON 1.4mg; SODIUM 253mg; CALC 94mg

PASTRY CRUST:

- 1 cup all-purpose flour, divided
- 3 tablespoons ice water
- ½ teaspoon cider vinegar
- 1 tablespoon powdered sugar
- ¼ teaspoon salt
- ¼ cup vegetable shortening, chilled

1. Preheat oven to 400°.

2. Lightly spoon flour into dry measuring cups; level with a knife. Combine ¼ cup flour, ice water, and vinegar, stirring with a whisk until blended.

3. Combine ¾ cup flour, sugar, and salt in a bowl; cut in shortening with a pastry blender or 2 knives until mixture resembles coarse meal. Add slurry; toss with a fork until flour mixture is moist. Gently press mixture into a 4-inch circle on heavy-duty plastic wrap; cover with additional plastic wrap. Roll dough, still covered, into a 12-inch circle, and freeze 10 minutes. Remove 1 sheet of plastic wrap, and let stand 1 minute or until pliable. Fit dough, plastic-wrap side up, into a 9-inch pie plate. Remove plastic wrap. Press the dough against bottom and sides of pan. Fold edges under or flute decoratively. Line bottom of dough with a piece of foil, and arrange pie weights on foil. Bake at 400° for 20 minutes or until edge is lightly browned. Remove pie weights and foil, and cool on a wire rack. Yield: 1 (9-inch) crust.

Double-Chocolate Cream Pie

Grate the chocolate with a handheld grater or zester, or use the smallest holes on a box grater.

CRUST:
- 1 cup reduced-calorie vanilla wafer crumbs (about 30 cookies)
- 2 tablespoons butter, melted and cooled
- 1 large egg white, lightly beaten
- Cooking spray

FILLING:
- ¾ cup sugar
- ¼ cup unsweetened cocoa
- 3 tablespoons cornstarch
- ⅛ teaspoon salt
- 2 cups 1% low-fat milk
- 1 large egg, lightly beaten
- 1½ ounces semisweet chocolate, grated
- 1 teaspoon vanilla extract
- 1½ cups frozen fat-free whipped topping, thawed

1. Preheat oven to 350°.

2. To prepare crust, combine first 3 ingredients in a bowl, tossing with a fork until moist. Press into bottom and up sides of a 9-inch pie plate coated with cooking spray. Bake at 350° for 12 minutes; cool crust on a wire rack.

3. To prepare filling, combine sugar, cocoa, cornstarch, salt, and milk in a medium saucepan; stir well with a whisk. Cook, stirring constantly, for 1 minute until mixture comes to a full boil. Gradually add ⅓ cup hot milk mixture to egg; stir well. Return egg mixture to pan. Cook 2 minutes or until the mixture thickens, stirring constantly. Remove from heat; add grated chocolate, stirring until chocolate melts and mixture is smooth. Stir in vanilla. Spoon mixture into pastry crust. Cover surface of filling with plastic wrap. Chill until set (about 2 hours). Remove the plastic wrap; spread whipped topping evenly over filling. Yield: 8 servings.

CALORIES 265 (25% from fat); FAT 7.3g (sat 3.9g, mono 2.2g, poly 0.3g); PROTEIN 4.8g; CARB 44.8g; FIBER 0.3g; CHOL 38mg; IRON 1.2mg; SODIUM 237mg; CALC 95mg

Banana-Split Ice-Cream Pie

Make this simple recipe up to three days ahead, and keep it frozen until you're ready to serve it.

- 1¼ cups chocolate wafer crumbs (about 25 cookies; such as Nabisco's Famous Chocolate Wafers)
- 2 tablespoons butter, melted
- ¾ cup fat-free chocolate sundae syrup, divided
- 4 cups sliced firm banana (about 5 bananas)
- 1 (1.75-quart) container vanilla low-fat ice cream, softened
- 1 (18-ounce) jar strawberry sundae topping
- 1 cup coarsely chopped pineapple
- 5 tablespoons chopped dry-roasted peanuts
- 16 maraschino cherries with stems (optional)

1. Combine crumbs and butter, stirring with a fork until moist. Press crumb mixture into bottom and ½ inch up sides of a 10-inch springform pan. Spread ½ cup chocolate syrup evenly over crust, and top with banana. Spread ice cream evenly over banana. Cover and freeze 3 hours or until firm.

2. Spread strawberry sundae topping evenly over ice cream. Cover and freeze 1 hour.

3. Let stand at room temperature 5 minutes. Cut into 16 wedges. Drizzle each serving with about ¾ teaspoon chocolate sundae syrup; top each with 1 tablespoon chopped pineapple, about 1 teaspoon chopped peanuts, and 1 maraschino cherry, if desired. Serve immediately. Yield: 16 servings.

CALORIES 313 (18% from fat); FAT 6.1g (sat 2.5g, mono 1.6g, poly 0.7g); PROTEIN 4.6g; CARB 61.6g; FIBER 2.7g; CHOL 9mg; IRON 0.6mg; SODIUM 156mg; CALC 94mg

Crisp Plum Ravioli with Lemon-Thyme Honey and Yogurt Cheese

Drain the yogurt, make the plum filling, infuse the honey, and assemble the raviolis ahead of time.
Bake this special dessert just before you're ready to eat, since it's best straight from the oven.

  1 (16-ounce) carton vanilla yogurt
  4 cups chopped plums (about 2 pounds)
  3 tablespoons honey
  ¾ teaspoon ground cinnamon
  ⅛ teaspoon ground nutmeg
1½ tablespoons butter
 60 won ton wrappers
    Cooking spray
  ½ cup honey
  1 teaspoon grated lemon rind
  ½ teaspoon chopped fresh thyme

1. Place colander in a medium bowl. Line colander with 4 layers of cheesecloth, allowing cheesecloth to extend over outside edges. Spoon yogurt into colander. Cover loosely with plastic wrap; refrigerate 12 hours. Spoon yogurt cheese into a bowl, and discard liquid. Cover and refrigerate.

2. Combine plums, 3 tablespoons honey, cinnamon, and nutmeg in a large saucepan; bring to a boil over medium-high heat. Reduce heat, and simmer 45 minutes, stirring occasionally. Remove from heat. Cool 5 minutes; stir in butter. Cool completely.

3. Preheat oven to 400°.

4. Working with 1 won ton wrapper at a time (cover remaining wrappers with a damp towel to prevent them from drying), spoon about 1 tablespoon plum mixture into center of wrapper. Moisten edges of dough with water, and top with another wrapper. Press 4 edges together to seal. Place ravioli on a large baking sheet coated with cooking spray (cover ravioli with a damp towel to prevent drying). Repeat procedure with remaining wrappers and plum mixture. Bake at 400° for 14 minutes or until golden.

5. While raviolis bake, combine ½ cup honey, grated lemon rind, and chopped thyme in a small saucepan over low heat. Cook for 20 minutes (do not boil). Place 3 raviolis on each of 10 plates. Drizzle 2 teaspoons honey mixture over each serving, and top with about 1 tablespoon yogurt cheese. Yield: 10 servings.

CALORIES 328 (13% from fat); FAT 4.7g (sat 2.4g, mono 1.4g, poly 0.5g); PROTEIN 7.8g; CARB 65.7g; FIBER 2.2g; CHOL 14mg; IRON 1.9mg; SODIUM 328mg; CALC 116mg

Fresh Strawberry Pie

Make this recipe when you have a bucket of freshly picked berries. The berries used to make the glaze can be any size, as they're macerated and pureed. But the berries piled in the pie itself should be small—the smaller the better.

CRUST:
50   reduced-calorie vanilla wafers
¼   cup butter or stick margarine, melted
2   tablespoons sugar
1   teaspoon grated orange rind
Cooking spray

FILLING:
2   cups ripe strawberries
½   cup water
⅔   cup sugar
2   tablespoons cornstarch
1   tablespoon fresh lemon juice
6   cups small ripe strawberries
½   cup frozen reduced-calorie whipped topping, thawed and divided

1. Preheat oven to 350°.
2. To prepare the crust, place the wafers in a food processor, and process until finely ground. Add butter, 2 tablespoons sugar, and orange rind, and pulse 10 times or just until wafers are moist. Press mixture into bottom and up sides of a 9-inch pie plate coated with cooking spray. Bake crust at 350°

for 15 minutes, and cool on a wire rack.
3. To prepare filling, mash 2 cups strawberries with a potato masher. Combine mashed strawberries and water in a small saucepan; bring to a boil, and cook for 5 minutes, stirring occasionally. Press strawberry mixture through a sieve into a bowl; reserve 1 cup strawberry liquid (add enough water to measure 1 cup, if necessary). Discard pulp.
4. Combine ⅔ cup sugar and cornstarch in a pan; add strawberry liquid, stirring well with a whisk. Bring to a boil; cook 1 minute, stirring constantly. Reduce heat, and cook for 2 minutes. Remove from heat; stir in lemon juice.
5. Arrange a layer of the small strawberries, stem sides down, in the crust. Spoon about one-third of the sauce over the strawberries. Arrange remaining small strawberries on top, and spoon the remaining sauce over strawberries. Chill the pie for at least 3 hours. Serve pie with whipped topping. Yield: 8 servings (serving size: 1 wedge and 1 tablespoon whipped topping).

CALORIES 285 (27% from fat); FAT 8.5g (sat 4.6g, mono 2.5g, poly 0.9g); PROTEIN 1.9g; CARB 52.2g; FIBER 3.5g; CHOL 16mg; IRON 1.2mg; SODIUM 146mg; CALC 42mg

Outrageous Warm Double-Chocolate Pudding

If you are a fan of dark chocolate, this two-layer pudding will satisfy your cravings.

CUSTARD LAYER:
¼ cup sugar
¼ cup egg substitute
1 cup plus 2 tablespoons evaporated fat-free milk
1½ ounces semisweet baking chocolate, chopped
Cooking spray

CAKE LAYER:
3 ounces dark-chocolate candy bar, chopped
⅓ cup sugar
⅓ cup egg substitute
¼ cup applesauce
6 tablespoons frozen fat-free whipped topping, thawed

1. Preheat oven to 325°.

2. To prepare custard layer, combine ¼ cup sugar and ¼ cup egg substitute; stir well with a whisk. Cook milk in a small, heavy saucepan over medium-high heat to 180° or until tiny bubbles form around edge (do not boil). Remove from heat; add semisweet chocolate, stirring until chocolate melts. Gradually add hot milk mixture to sugar mixture, stirring constantly with a whisk.

3. Pour hot milk mixture into 6 (4-ounce) ramekins or custard cups coated with cooking spray. Place the ramekins in a baking pan, and add hot water to pan to a depth of 1 inch. Bake at 325° for 30 minutes or until almost set. Remove from oven, and cool in pan 30 minutes. Remove ramekins from pan; drain water.

4. To prepare cake layer, place dark chocolate in a small glass bowl; microwave at HIGH 2 minutes or until almost melted, stirring after 1 minute. Set aside. Beat ⅓ cup sugar and ⅓ cup egg substitute with a mixer at medium speed until well blended (about 5 minutes). Add dark chocolate and applesauce; beat until well blended. Pour evenly over custard layer. Place ramekins in baking pan; add hot water to pan to a depth of 1 inch. Bake at 325° for 20 minutes. Remove ramekins from pan. Top each serving with 1 tablespoon whipped topping. Serve immediately. Yield: 6 servings.

CALORIES 257 (26% from fat); FAT 7.5g (sat 4.3g, mono 1.8g, poly 0.5g); PROTEIN 6.9g; CARB 41.1g; FIBER 1.8g; CHOL 4mg; IRON 1.1mg; SODIUM 104mg; CALC 131mg

Bittersweet Chocolate Pudding

Adding cornstarch to this homey pudding lessens the possibility of its curdling. To prevent the custard from tipping and taking on ice water, make sure the bowl you use for the ice bath is only slightly larger than the custard bowl.

½ cup granulated sugar
⅓ cup unsweetened cocoa
3 tablespoons cornstarch
3 tablespoons dark brown sugar
⅛ teaspoon salt
4 cups 2% reduced-fat milk
3 large egg yolks, lightly beaten
2 ounces bittersweet chocolate, chopped
1 teaspoon vanilla extract

1. Combine first 5 ingredients in a large saucepan. Gradually add milk, stirring with a whisk. Bring to a boil over medium heat, stirring constantly. Cook 1 minute, stirring constantly.

2. Place egg yolks in a bowl. Gradually add hot milk mixture to egg yolks, stirring constantly. Return milk mixture to pan. Cook over medium heat 5 minutes or until thick, stirring constantly. Remove from heat, and add chopped chocolate and vanilla extract, stirring until the chocolate melts. Spoon pudding into a small bowl. Place bowl in a large ice-filled bowl for 15 minutes or until the pudding is cool, stirring occasionally. Remove bowl from ice; cover and chill. Yield: 6 servings (serving size: ¾ cup).

CALORIES 282 (30% from fat); FAT 9.5g (sat 5.1g, mono 2.4g, poly 0.5g); PROTEIN 8.4g; CARB 43g; FIBER 2.4g; CHOL 119mg; IRON 1.2mg; SODIUM 138mg; CALC 222mg

379

Banana Pudding

Banana Pudding

This pudding has a mile-high meringue and will easily feed a crowd. Although we think using a vanilla bean infuses superior flavor, you can substitute ½ teaspoon of vanilla extract; stir it into the cooked custard.

⅔ cup all-purpose flour
1¼ cups sugar
½ teaspoon salt
4 cups 2% reduced-fat milk
1 (4-inch) vanilla bean, split lengthwise
2 large eggs, lightly beaten
4 large egg whites
6 tablespoons sugar
80 vanilla wafers (about 1 box)
5 cups sliced banana (about 6 bananas)

1. Preheat oven to 325°.
2. Lightly spoon flour into a dry measuring cup; level with a knife. Combine flour, 1¼ cups sugar, and salt in a large saucepan, stirring with a whisk. Gradually add milk, stirring until smooth. Scrape seeds from vanilla bean, and add seeds and bean to milk mixture.
3. Cook over medium heat 12 minutes or until thick and bubbly, stirring constantly.
4. Place eggs in a large bowl; gradually add hot milk mixture, stirring constantly. Place mixture in pan; cook over medium heat 2 minutes or until thick and bubbly, stirring constantly. Discard vanilla bean.
5. Place the egg whites in a clean large bowl, and beat with a mixer at high speed until egg whites are foamy. Add 6 tablespoons sugar, 1 tablespoon at a time, beating until stiff peaks form.
6. Arrange 33 vanilla wafers in bottom of a 3-quart round baking dish. Arrange half of banana slices over wafers. Pour half of custard over banana. Repeat procedure with 33 vanilla wafers, banana, and custard.
7. Top with meringue, spreading evenly to edges of dish. Arrange remaining vanilla wafers around edge of meringue.
8. Bake at 325° for 20 minutes or until lightly browned. Serve pudding warm or chilled. Yield: 16 servings (serving size: about ¾ cup).

CALORIES 277 (16% from fat); FAT 5.4g (sat 1.7g, mono 1.5g, poly 0.2g); PROTEIN 5.4g; CARB 54.3g; FIBER 1.6g; CHOL 33mg; IRON 1.2mg; SODIUM 191mg; CALC 95mg

Chocolate Chunk Bread Puddings

(pictured on page 334)

Chop the chocolate so you'll have good-sized chunks to bite into. Hawaiian bread is a soft, sweet bread found in the bakery section of most grocery stores. This recipe can be doubled easily.

1¾ cups (½-inch) cubed Hawaiian sweet bread
⅔ cup 2% reduced-fat milk
2 tablespoons sugar
1½ tablespoons unsweetened cocoa
1 tablespoon Kahlúa (coffee-flavored liqueur)
½ teaspoon vanilla extract
1 large egg, lightly beaten
Cooking spray
1 ounce semisweet chocolate, coarsely chopped
2 tablespoons fat-free whipped topping

1. Preheat oven to 350°.
2. Arrange bread cubes in a single layer on a baking sheet. Bake at 350° for 5 minutes or until toasted. Remove bread from oven; decrease oven temperature to 325°.
3. Combine milk and the next 5 ingredients in a medium bowl, stirring well with a whisk. Add bread, tossing gently to coat. Cover and chill 30 minutes or up to 4 hours.
4. Divide half of bread mixture evenly between 2 (6-ounce) ramekins or custard cups coated with cooking spray; sprinkle evenly with half of chocolate. Divide remaining bread mixture between ramekins; top with remaining chocolate.
5. Place ramekins in an 8-inch square baking pan; add hot water to pan to a depth of 1 inch. Bake at 325° for 35 minutes or until set. Serve warm with 1 tablespoon whipped topping per pudding. Yield: 2 servings.

CALORIES 319 (30% from fat); FAT 10.6g (sat 5.2g, mono 3.6g, poly 0.8g); PROTEIN 9.8g; CARB 45.3g; FIBER 2.1g; CHOL 121mg; IRON 1.8mg; SODIUM 141mg; CALC 125mg

New Orleans Bread Pudding with Bourbon Sauce

Raisin-studded bread pudding and buttery, bourbon-spiked sauce combine in this classic dessert.

BREAD PUDDING:

¼ cup raisins
2 tablespoons bourbon
1¼ cups 2% reduced-fat milk
½ cup sugar
1 tablespoon vanilla extract
½ teaspoon ground cinnamon
¼ teaspoon ground nutmeg
Dash of salt
3 large eggs, lightly beaten
4½ cups (½-inch) cubed French bread
    (about 8 ounces)
Cooking spray

SAUCE:

½ cup sugar
¼ cup light-colored corn syrup
¼ cup butter
¼ cup bourbon

1. To prepare the bread pudding, combine raisins and 2 tablespoons bourbon in a bowl. Let stand 30 minutes. Drain mixture in a sieve over a small bowl, reserving liquid. Set aside raisins.

2. Combine the reserved liquid, milk, and the next 6 ingredients in a large bowl, stirring well with a whisk. Add bread, tossing gently to coat.

3. Spoon bread mixture into an 8-inch square baking dish coated with cooking spray. Sprinkle evenly with reserved raisins, pressing gently into bread mixture. Cover with foil, and chill for 30 minutes or up to 4 hours.

4. Preheat oven to 350°.

5. Place dish in a 13 x 9-inch baking pan; add hot water to pan to a depth of 1 inch. Bake, covered, at 350° for 20 minutes. Uncover and bake an additional 10 minutes or until a knife inserted in center comes out clean.

6. To prepare sauce, combine ½ cup sugar, corn syrup, and butter in a small saucepan over medium heat. Bring mixture to a simmer, and cook for 1 minute, stirring constantly. Remove mixture from heat, and stir in ¼ cup bourbon. Drizzle about 1 tablespoon sauce over each serving, and serve warm. Yield: 9 servings.

CALORIES 309 (24% from fat); FAT 8.2g (sat 4.3g, mono 2.7g, poly 0.6g); PROTEIN 5.6g; CARB 47.6g; FIBER 1g; CHOL 87mg; IRON 1.1mg; SODIUM 272mg; CALC 74mg

Irish Bread Pudding with Caramel-Whiskey Sauce

¼ cup light butter, melted
1 (10-ounce) French bread baguette, cut into 1-inch-thick slices
½ cup raisins
¼ cup Irish whiskey
1¾ cups 1% low-fat milk
1 cup sugar
1 tablespoon vanilla extract
1 (12-ounce) can evaporated fat-free milk
2 large eggs, lightly beaten
Cooking spray
1 tablespoon sugar
1 teaspoon ground cinnamon
Caramel-Whiskey Sauce

1. Preheat oven to 350°.
2. Brush the melted butter on one side of French bread slices, and place bread, buttered sides up, on a baking sheet. Bake bread at 350° for 10 minutes or until lightly toasted. Cut bread into ½-inch cubes, and set aside.
3. While bread is toasting, combine raisins and whiskey in a small bowl; cover and let stand 10 minutes or until soft (do not drain).
4. Combine 1% milk and the next 4 ingredients in a large bowl, and stir well with a whisk. Add bread cubes and raisin mixture, pressing gently to moisten, and let bread mixture stand for 15 minutes. Spoon the bread mixture into a 13 x 9-inch baking dish coated with cooking spray. Combine 1 tablespoon sugar and ground cinnamon, and sprinkle over pudding. Bake at 350° for 35 minutes or until pudding is set. Serve warm with Caramel-Whiskey Sauce. Yield: 12 servings (serving size: 1 [3-inch] square and 2 tablespoons sauce).
NOTE: Substitute ¼ cup apple juice for the Irish whiskey, if desired.

(Totals include Caramel-Whiskey Sauce) CALORIES 362 (17% from fat); FAT 6.7g (sat 4g, mono 2.1g, poly 0.6g); PROTEIN 8.1g; CARB 66.7g; FIBER 0.9g; CHOL 57mg; IRON 1mg; SODIUM 269mg; CALC 155mg

CARAMEL-WHISKEY SAUCE:

1½ cups sugar
⅔ cup water
¼ cup light butter
¼ cup (2 ounces) ⅓-less-fat cream cheese
¼ cup Irish whiskey
¼ cup 1% low-fat milk

1. Combine the sugar and water in a small, heavy saucepan over medium-high heat; cook until sugar dissolves, stirring constantly. Cook an additional 15 minutes or until golden (do not stir). Remove from heat. Carefully add butter and cream cheese, stirring constantly with a whisk (mixture will be hot and bubble vigorously). Cool slightly, and stir in whiskey and milk. Yield: 1½ cups (serving size: 2 tablespoons).
NOTE: You can substitute 1 tablespoon imitation rum extract and 3 tablespoons water for the Irish whiskey, if desired.

CALORIES 136 (20% from fat); FAT 3g (sat 2g, mono 0.9g, poly 0.1g); PROTEIN 1g; CARB 25.9g; FIBER 0g; CHOL 10mg; IRON 0mg; SODIUM 46mg; CALC 28mg

Rice Pudding with Pomegranate Syrup

PUDDING:
3½ cups 2% reduced-fat milk, divided
½ cup uncooked Arborio rice or other short-grain rice
⅓ cup sugar
1 tablespoon butter
1 large egg
1 teaspoon vanilla extract

SYRUP:
2 large pomegranates, halved crosswise
¼ cup sugar
6 tablespoons pomegranate seeds

1. Combine 3 cups milk, rice, ⅓ cup sugar, and butter in a medium saucepan; bring to a boil. Reduce heat, and simmer, uncovered, for 10 minutes, stirring occasionally. Remove from heat.
2. Combine ½ cup milk and egg; stir with a whisk. Stir about one-fourth of warm rice mixture into egg mixture; add to pan, stirring constantly. Simmer, uncovered, 30 minutes or until rice is tender, stirring occasionally. Remove from heat; stir in vanilla.
3. Squeeze juice from pomegranate halves using a citrus reamer or juicer to measure 1 cup. Combine juice and ¼ cup sugar in a small saucepan, and bring to a boil. Reduce heat; simmer until reduced to ⅓ cup (about 20 minutes), stirring frequently.
4. Drizzle syrup evenly over pudding; sprinkle with seeds. Yield: 6 servings (serving size: ½ cup pudding, about 1 tablespoon syrup, and 1 tablespoon seeds).

CALORIES 296 (18% from fat); FAT 5.9g (sat 3.2g, mono 1.8g, poly 0.2g); PROTEIN 7.7g; CARB 53.1g; FIBER 0.7g; CHOL 52mg; IRON 0.5mg; SODIUM 131mg; CALC 171mg

Rhubarb Custard Bars

Rhubarb, which looks like crimson celery, has a short season. It freezes beautifully; just store in a heavy-duty zip-top plastic bag.

CRUST:

1½ cups all-purpose flour

½ cup sugar

⅛ teaspoon salt

9 tablespoons chilled butter, cut into small pieces

Cooking spray

FILLING:

⅓ cup all-purpose flour

1½ cups sugar

1½ cups 1% low-fat milk

3 large eggs

5 cups (½-inch) sliced fresh or frozen rhubarb (unthawed)

TOPPING:

½ cup sugar

½ cup (4 ounces) block-style fat-free cream cheese

½ cup (4 ounces) block-style ⅓-less-fat cream cheese

½ teaspoon vanilla extract

1 cup frozen fat-free whipped topping, thawed

Mint sprigs (optional)

1. Preheat oven to 350°.

2. To prepare crust, lightly spoon 1½ cups flour into dry measuring cups; level with a knife. Combine 1½ cups flour, ½ cup sugar, and salt in a bowl. Cut in butter with a pastry blender or 2 knives until mixture resembles coarse meal. Press mixture into a 13 x 9-inch baking dish coated with cooking spray. Bake at 350° for 15 minutes or until crust is golden brown.

3. To prepare filling, lightly spoon ⅓ cup flour into a dry measuring cup; level with a knife. Combine ⅓ cup flour and 1½ cups sugar in a large bowl; add milk and eggs, stirring with a whisk until well blended. Stir in rhubarb. Pour rhubarb mixture over crust. Bake at 350° for 40 minutes or until set. Cool to room temperature.

4. To prepare topping, place ½ cup sugar, cheeses, and vanilla in a bowl; beat with a mixer at medium speed until smooth. Gently fold in whipped topping, and spread evenly over baked custard. Cover and chill at least 1 hour. Garnish with mint sprigs, if desired. Yield: 3 dozen bars (serving size: 1 bar).

CALORIES 131 (29% from fat); FAT 4.2g (sat 2.5g, mono 1.3g, poly 0.2g); PROTEIN 2.5g; CARB 21g; FIBER 0.5g; CHOL 29mg; IRON 0.4mg; SODIUM 78mg; CALC 42mg

Mandarin Cream Delight

CRUST:

9 tablespoons butter or stick margarine, softened

½ cup sugar

1 teaspoon vanilla extract

1½ cups all-purpose flour

⅛ teaspoon salt

Cooking spray

FILLING:

2 (11-ounce) cans mandarin oranges in light syrup, undrained

¼ cup sugar

1 (16-ounce) carton fat-free sour cream

1 (8-ounce) carton low-fat sour cream

2 (3.4-ounce) packages vanilla instant pudding mix or 2 (1.4-ounce) packages sugar-free vanilla instant pudding mix

1 (8-ounce) container frozen reduced-calorie whipped topping, thawed

1. To prepare crust, combine first 3 ingredients in a large bowl. Beat with a mixer at medium speed until light and fluffy (about 2 minutes). Lightly spoon flour into dry measuring cups, and level with a knife. Add flour and salt to butter mixture, beating at low speed until well blended.

2. Preheat oven to 400°.

3. Pat dough into a 13 x 9-inch baking dish coated with cooking spray; pierce bottom of dough with a fork. Bake at 400° for 12 minutes or until lightly browned. Cool crust on a wire rack.

4. To prepare filling, drain mandarin oranges over a large bowl, reserving ½ cup juice. Combine juice, ¼ cup sugar, sour creams, and pudding mix. Stir in orange segments. Spoon orange mixture over crust, spreading evenly. Top with whipped topping. Chill 1 hour. Yield: 16 servings (serving size: 1 piece).

CALORIES 276 (30% from fat); FAT 9.3g (sat 6.4g, mono 2g, poly 0.4g); PROTEIN 4.2g; CARB 43g; FIBER 0.3g; CHOL 18mg; IRON 0.7mg; SODIUM 212mg; CALC 44mg

Raspberries with Butterscotch-Amaretto Custard Sauce

This custard sauce has a subtle flavor that pairs well with raspberries (or any kind of berry).

1 tablespoon butter
½ cup packed light brown sugar
1 cup evaporated fat-free milk, divided
1⅔ cups 2% reduced-fat milk
2 tablespoons granulated sugar
2 tablespoons cornstarch
⅛ teaspoon salt
3 large egg yolks
1 tablespoon amaretto (almond-flavored liqueur) or a drop of almond extract
6 cups fresh raspberries or other berries

1. Melt butter in a medium saucepan over medium heat. Add the brown sugar, and cook 2 minutes, stirring constantly with a whisk. Stir in ¼ cup evaporated milk. Bring to a boil, and cook for 30 seconds, stirring constantly. Remove from heat.

2. Heat 2% milk in a heavy saucepan over medium-high heat to 180° or until tiny bubbles form around edge (do not boil). Remove milk from heat.
3. Combine granulated sugar, cornstarch, salt, and egg yolks in a medium bowl, stirring with a whisk until smooth. Stir in hot 2% milk and ¾ cup evaporated milk. Add milk mixture to the brown sugar mixture. Bring to a boil over medium heat; cook for 2 minutes or until thick, stirring constantly with a whisk. Remove from heat; cool to room temperature. Stir in amaretto. Pour the sauce into a bowl; cover and chill. Spoon sauce over raspberries. Yield: 6 servings (serving size: 1 cup raspberries and ½ cup sauce).

CALORIES 273 (22% from fat); FAT 6.6g (sat 2.9g, mono 2g, poly 0.9g); PROTEIN 8g; CARB 47.2g; FIBER 8.4g; CHOL 121mg; IRON 1.5mg; SODIUM 162mg; CALC 262mg

Brown Sugar Pavlovas

A pavlova is a crisp meringue shell piled high with whipped cream and fruit. We used brown sugar to add a butterscotch flavor. The meringues freeze for up to two months; remove them from the freezer before you assemble the pavlovas—no reheating required.

    4 large egg whites
    2 teaspoons cornstarch
 ¼ teaspoon salt
 ¾ cup granulated sugar
 ¼ cup packed brown sugar
    1 teaspoon vanilla extract
 ¾ cup whipping cream
    2 tablespoons powdered sugar
 ¼ teaspoon ground cinnamon
    3 cups chopped fresh pineapple
 ¾ cup chopped peeled kiwifruit
 ¾ cup fresh blackberries or raspberries
    3 tablespoons fat-free caramel sundae syrup

1. Preheat oven to 350°.
2. Cover a large baking sheet with parchment paper. Draw 6 (4-inch) circles on paper. Turn paper over; secure with masking tape.
3. Beat egg whites, cornstarch, and salt with a mixer at high speed until foamy. Add granulated sugar and brown sugar, 1 tablespoon at a time, beating until thick and glossy. Add vanilla, beating well. Divide egg white mixture evenly among 6 drawn circles. Shape meringues into nests with 1-inch sides using the back of a spoon. Place meringues in oven. Immediately reduce oven temperature to 300°; bake for 1 hour. Turn oven off; cool meringues in closed oven at least 4 hours or until completely dry. (Meringues are done when the surface is dry and meringues can be removed from paper without sticking to your fingers.) Carefully remove meringue nests from paper.
4. Beat whipping cream, powdered sugar, and cinnamon with a mixer at high speed until stiff peaks form. Dollop ¼ cup whipping cream into each meringue nest. Top each with ½ cup pineapple, 2 tablespoons kiwi, and 2 tablespoons blackberries. Drizzle 1½ teaspoons caramel syrup over each serving. Serve immediately. Yield: 6 servings.
NOTE: Whipping cream whips better when bowl and beaters are chilled.

CALORIES 356 (29% from fat); FAT 11.5g (sat 6.9g, mono 3.2g, poly 0.6g); PROTEIN 3.5g; CARB 61.9g; FIBER 2.8g; CHOL 41mg; IRON 0.7mg; SODIUM 178mg; CALC 53mg

Fresh-Berry Pavlovas

Crème fraîche is cultured cream that has a texture and consistency similar to that of sour cream, which you could substitute in a pinch. Use the most beautiful—and flavorful—fruit you can find.

    4 large egg whites
 ¼ teaspoon cream of tartar
 1¼ cups sugar, divided
    1 (8-ounce) carton plain fat-free yogurt
 ¾ cup commercial crème fraîche
    1 cup sliced strawberries
    1 cup blackberries
    1 cup blueberries

1. Preheat oven to 250°.
2. Cover a baking sheet with parchment paper. Draw 8 (3-inch) circles on paper. Turn paper over, and secure with masking tape. Beat egg whites and cream of tartar with a mixer at high speed until soft peaks form. Gradually add ¾ cup sugar, 1 tablespoon at a time, beating until stiff peaks form (do not underbeat). Divide egg white mixture evenly among 8 drawn circles on baking sheet. Shape meringues into nests with 1-inch sides using the back of a spoon. Bake at 250° for 1 hour. Turn oven off; cool meringues in closed oven at least 2 hours or until completely dry. Carefully remove meringues from paper.
3. Spoon yogurt onto several layers of heavy-duty paper towels; spread to ½-inch thickness. Cover with additional paper towels; let stand 5 minutes. Scrape into a bowl using a rubber spatula. Combine ½ cup sugar, drained yogurt, and crème fraîche. Spoon yogurt mixture evenly into meringues. Top each serving with 2 tablespoons each of strawberries, blackberries, and blueberries. Yield: 8 servings.

CALORIES 249 (29% from fat); FAT 8.1g (sat 5g, mono 2.3g, poly 0.4g); PROTEIN 4.5g; CARB 40.7g; FIBER 1.9g; CHOL 18mg; IRON 0.3mg; SODIUM 65mg; CALC 110mg

Fresh-Berry Pavlovas

Coconut Crème Caramel with
Pineapple Concassé

Coconut Crème Caramel with Pineapple Concassé

This is a great make-ahead dessert, because both the crème caramel and the concassé (a coarsely chopped mixture) need to chill at least 4 hours.

⅓ cup sugar
3 tablespoons water
Cooking spray
3 large eggs
1 large egg white
1⅔ cups 2% reduced-fat milk
½ cup sugar
⅓ cup cream of coconut
2 teaspoons vanilla extract
⅛ teaspoon salt
Pineapple Concassé

1. Preheat oven to 325°.
2. Combine ⅓ cup sugar and water in a small, heavy saucepan over medium-high heat, and cook until sugar dissolves, stirring frequently. Continue cooking until golden (about 10 minutes). Immediately pour into 6 (6-ounce) ramekins or custard cups coated with cooking spray, tilting each ramekin quickly until caramelized sugar coats bottom of cup.
3. Place eggs and egg white in a medium bowl, and stir well with a whisk. Add milk and next 4 ingredients, stirring until well blended. Divide egg mixture evenly among prepared ramekins. Place ramekins in a 13 x 9-inch baking pan, and add hot water to pan to a depth of 1 inch. Bake at 325° for 50 minutes or until a knife inserted in center comes out clean. Remove ramekins from pan. Cover and chill at least 4 hours.
4. Loosen edges of custards with a knife or rubber spatula. Place dessert plate, upside down, on top of each ramekin; invert onto plate. Serve with about ¼ cup Pineapple Concassé. Yield: 6 servings.

(Totals include Pineapple Concassé) CALORIES 239 (26% from fat); FAT 6.9g (sat 4.2g, mono 1.5g, poly 0.5g); PROTEIN 6.6g; CARB 38.5g; FIBER 0.9g; CHOL 111mg; IRON 0.7mg; SODIUM 132mg; CALC 99mg

PINEAPPLE CONCASSÉ:

Basil adds an interesting, fresh flavor to the concassé, but it can be omitted.

1½ cups finely chopped pineapple
1 tablespoon thinly sliced fresh basil
1 teaspoon sugar
1 teaspoon fresh lime juice

1. Combine all ingredients in a small bowl. Cover and chill at least 4 hours. Yield: 6 servings (serving size: ¼ cup).

CALORIES 22 (8% from fat); FAT 0.2g (sat 0g, mono 0g, poly 0.1g); PROTEIN 0.2g; CARB 5.6g; FIBER 0.5g; CHOL 0mg; IRON 0.2mg; SODIUM 0mg; CALC 3mg

French Vanilla Summer Trifle

2½ cups finely chopped peeled ripe peaches
2 tablespoons brown sugar
¼ teaspoon ground cinnamon
⅔ cup granulated sugar
2 tablespoons cornstarch
⅛ teaspoon salt
3 large egg yolks
1⅔ cups 2% reduced-fat milk
1 cup evaporated fat-free milk
½ teaspoon vanilla extract
15 cakelike ladyfingers, halved lengthwise

1. Combine peaches, brown sugar, and cinnamon, tossing well to combine; let stand at room temperature 30 minutes.
2. Combine granulated sugar, cornstarch, salt, and egg yolks in a medium bowl, stirring with a whisk until smooth.
3. Heat the milks in a medium, heavy saucepan over medium-high heat to 180° or until tiny bubbles form around edge (do not boil). Gradually add the hot milk mixture to sugar mixture, stirring constantly with a whisk.
4. Return milk mixture to saucepan. Cook over medium heat 2 minutes or until thick and bubbly, stirring constantly. Remove from heat, and stir in vanilla extract.
5. Spoon custard into a small bowl. Place bowl in a large ice-filled bowl for 15 minutes or until custard is cool, stirring occasionally. Remove bowl from ice.
6. Arrange 10 ladyfinger halves, cut sides up, in a single layer on the bottom of a 1½-quart soufflé or trifle dish. Spoon half of peach mixture over the ladyfingers. Spread half of custard over the peach mixture. Arrange 10 ladyfinger halves, standing upright, around side of dish. Arrange remaining 10 ladyfinger halves, cut sides up, on top of custard. Spoon remaining peach mixture over ladyfingers. Spread remaining custard over peach mixture. Cover and refrigerate 4 hours or overnight. Yield: 6 servings (serving size: about 1 cup).

CALORIES 300 (15% from fat); FAT 4.9g (sat 2g, mono 1.5g, poly 0.8g); PROTEIN 8.8g; CARB 56.7g; FIBER 1.7g; CHOL 144mg; IRON 1mg; SODIUM 265mg; CALC 246mg

Vanilla Bean Crème Brûlée

Crème brûlée, French for "burned cream," is a custard whose brown sugar topping is melted and crystallized under a broiler. Melting the topping in the microwave instead and pouring it over each chilled dessert keeps the custard cold so it can be served in the classic tradition. Vanilla beans, found in the spice section at the supermarket, are worth the extra expense. Nonfat dry milk thickens the custard.

    4   large egg yolks
    1   teaspoon granulated sugar
  ⅛   teaspoon salt
    2   cups 2% reduced-fat milk
    1   (3-inch) piece vanilla bean, split lengthwise, or 1 teaspoon vanilla extract
    3   tablespoons granulated sugar
  ¾   cup nonfat dry milk
  ¼   cup packed light brown sugar
1½   teaspoons water

1. Preheat oven to 300°.
2. Combine first 3 ingredients in a medium bowl; stir well with a whisk. Set aside.
3. Pour 2% milk into a medium saucepan. Scrape seeds from vanilla bean; add seeds, bean, 3 tablespoons granulated sugar, and dry milk to pan. Heat over medium heat to 180° or until tiny bubbles form around the edge (do not boil), stirring occasionally with a whisk. Discard bean.
4. Gradually add hot milk mixture to egg mixture, stirring constantly with a whisk. Divide milk mixture evenly among 6 (4-ounce) ramekins or custard cups. Place ramekins in a 13 x 9-inch baking pan; add hot water to pan to a depth of 1 inch. Bake at 300° for 1 hour or until center barely moves when ramekin is touched. Remove ramekins from pan; cool completely on a wire rack. Cover and chill at least 4 hours or overnight.
5. Combine brown sugar and water in a 1-cup glass measure. Microwave at HIGH 30 seconds; stir until sugar dissolves. Microwave at HIGH 60 seconds; pour evenly over each dessert, quickly tipping ramekins to coat tops of brûlées (there will be a thin layer of melted sugar). Let sugar mixture harden. Yield: 6 servings (serving size: 1 custard).

CALORIES 185 (25% from fat); FAT 5.2g (sat 2.1g, mono 1.8g, poly 0.5g); PROTEIN 10g; CARB 24.7g; FIBER 0g; CHOL 155mg; IRON 0.6mg; SODIUM 177mg; CALC 309mg

Chocolate Mousse

Even our food staff was surprised that a dessert made with tofu could taste so sinfully delicious.

  ¾   cup semisweet chocolate chips
    1   (12.3-ounce) package reduced-fat extrafirm silken tofu (such as Mori-Nu)
  ¼   teaspoon salt
    3   large egg whites
  ½   cup sugar
  ¼   cup water
Fat-free whipped topping, thawed (optional)
Grated chocolate (optional)

1. Place chocolate chips in a small glass bowl, and microwave at HIGH 1½ minutes or until almost melted, stirring after 1 minute. Place chocolate and tofu in a food processor or blender; process 2 minutes or until smooth.
2. Place salt and egg whites in a medium bowl; beat with a mixer at high speed until stiff peaks form. Combine sugar and water in a small saucepan; bring to a boil. Cook, without stirring, until candy thermometer registers 238°. Pour hot sugar syrup in a thin stream over egg whites, beating at high speed. Gently stir one-fourth of meringue into tofu mixture; gently fold in remaining meringue. Spoon ½ cup mousse into each of 8 (6-ounce) custard cups. Cover and chill at least 4 hours. Garnish with whipped topping and grated chocolate, if desired. Yield: 8 servings.

CALORIES 147 (34% from fat); FAT 5.6g (sat 3.3g, mono 1.8g, poly 0.5g); PROTEIN 5.2g; CARB 22.5g; FIBER 0.2g; CHOL 0mg; IRON 0.9mg; SODIUM 134mg; CALC 26mg

Hot Grand Marnier Soufflés

Cooking spray
- ¾ cup granulated sugar, divided
- 4 large egg yolks
- 3 tablespoons Grand Marnier
- ¾ teaspoon vanilla extract
- 6 large egg whites
- ¼ teaspoon cream of tartar
- ⅛ teaspoon salt
- 1 teaspoon powdered sugar

1. Preheat oven to 400°; place a heavy baking sheet on middle rack.

2. Coat 6 (8-ounce) ramekins with cooking spray; sprinkle each dish with 2 teaspoons granulated sugar.

3. Place egg yolks in a large bowl; beat with a mixer at medium-high speed 5 minutes or until thick and pale. Gradually add ¼ cup granulated sugar; beat 2 minutes. Beat in liqueur and vanilla.

4. Place egg whites in a large bowl; beat with a mixer at high speed 1 minute or until foamy. Add cream of tartar and salt, and beat until soft peaks form. Gradually add ¼ cup granulated sugar, 1 tablespoon at a time, beating until stiff peaks form. Gently stir one-fourth of egg white mixture into liqueur mixture; gently fold in remaining egg white mixture. Divide evenly among prepared ramekins.

5. Place soufflé dishes on baking sheet in oven; bake at 400° for 10 minutes or until tall and golden brown (soufflés will rise 1½ to 2 inches above dish rim). Quickly dust soufflés with powdered sugar. Serve immediately. Yield: 6 servings.

CALORIES 167 (18% from fat); FAT 3.4g (sat 1.1g, mono 1.3g, poly 0.5g); PROTEIN 5.4g; CARB 27.2g; FIBER 0g; CHOL 142mg; IRON 0.4mg; SODIUM 109mg; CALC 18mg

Bittersweet Chocolate Soufflés

Cooking spray
- 2 tablespoons granulated sugar
- ¾ cup granulated sugar, divided
- ½ cup Dutch process cocoa
- 2 tablespoons all-purpose flour
- ⅛ teaspoon salt
- ½ cup 1% low-fat milk
- 1 teaspoon vanilla extract
- 2 large egg yolks
- 4 large egg whites
- ⅛ teaspoon cream of tartar
- 3 ounces bittersweet chocolate, finely chopped
- 1 tablespoon powdered sugar

Hot Grand Marnier Soufflés

1. Preheat oven to 350°.

2. Coat 8 (4-ounce) ramekins with cooking spray; sprinkle with 2 tablespoons granulated sugar.

3. Combine ½ cup granulated sugar, cocoa, flour, and salt in a small saucepan. Gradually add milk, stirring with a whisk until blended. Bring to a boil over medium heat; cook until thick (about 3 minutes), stirring constantly. Remove from heat; let stand 3 minutes. Gradually stir in vanilla and egg yolks. Spoon chocolate mixture into a large bowl; cool.

4. Place egg whites in a large bowl; beat with a mixer at high speed until foamy. Gradually add ¼ cup granulated sugar and cream of tartar, beating mixture until stiff peaks form. Gently stir one-fourth of egg white mixture into chocolate mixture; gently fold in remaining egg white mixture and chopped chocolate. Spoon into prepared ramekins.

5. Bake at 350° for 15 minutes or until puffy and set. Sprinkle with powdered sugar. Yield: 8 servings.

CALORIES 206 (24% from fat); FAT 5.5g (sat 3g, mono 1g, poly 0.3g); PROTEIN 5.2g; CARB 34.1g; FIBER 2.3g; CHOL 55mg; IRON 1mg; SODIUM 75mg; CALC 33mg

Tiramisu Anacapri

This tiramisu was a hit with our Test Kitchens staff, who agreed that it's one of the best they've tried.
Ladyfingers can be found in the bakery or the frozen-food section of the supermarket. We used
soft ladyfingers, which are made to be split.

1   cup cold water
1   (14-ounce) can fat-free sweetened
    condensed milk
1   (1.4-ounce) package sugar-free vanilla
    instant pudding mix
1   (8-ounce) block ⅓-less-fat cream cheese,
    softened
1   (8-ounce) tub frozen reduced-calorie
    whipped topping, thawed
1   cup hot water
½   cup Kahlúa (coffee-flavored liqueur)
1   tablespoon instant espresso or 2 tablespoons
    instant coffee granules
24 ladyfingers (2 [3-ounce] packages)
3   tablespoons unsweetened cocoa,
    divided

1. Combine first 3 ingredients in a large bowl; stir
well with a whisk. Cover surface with plastic wrap;
chill 30 minutes or until firm.
2. Remove the plastic wrap, and add cream cheese.
Beat mixture with a mixer at medium speed until
well blended. Gently fold in whipped topping.
3. Combine hot water, Kahlúa, and espresso. Split
ladyfingers in half lengthwise. Arrange 16 ladyfinger
halves, flat sides down, in a trifle bowl or large glass
bowl. Drizzle with ½ cup Kahlúa mixture. Spread
one-third of pudding mixture evenly over ladyfingers, and sprinkle with 1 tablespoon cocoa. Repeat
layers, ending with cocoa. Cover; chill at least 8
hours. Yield: 12 servings (serving size: about ⅔ cup).

CALORIES 310 (26% from fat); FAT 9.1g (sat 6g, mono 2.1g, poly 0.3g); PROTEIN 7.8g;
CARB 44g; FIBER 0.2g; CHOL 95mg; IRON 1.1mg; SODIUM 265mg; CALC 124mg

White Russian Tiramisu

This creamy tiramisu uses mascarpone cheese—a soft triple-cream cheese that comes in small tubs. Use regular cream cheese in its place, if you prefer.

½ cup ground coffee beans
1¾ cups cold water
¼ cup Kahlúa (coffee-flavored liqueur), divided
½ cup (3½ ounces) mascarpone cheese
1 (8-ounce) block fat-free cream cheese, softened
⅓ cup packed brown sugar
¼ cup granulated sugar
24 ladyfingers (2 [3-ounce] packages)
2 teaspoons unsweetened cocoa, divided

1. Assemble drip coffee maker according to manufacturer's directions. Place the ground coffee in the coffee filter or filter basket. Add cold water to coffee maker and brew to make 1½ cups. Combine the brewed coffee and 2 tablespoons Kahlúa in a shallow dish, and cool.
2. Combine cheeses in a large bowl. Beat at high speed of a mixer until smooth. Add the sugars and 2 tablespoons Kahlúa, and beat until well blended.
3. Split ladyfingers in half lengthwise.
4. Quickly dip 24 ladyfinger halves, flat sides down, into coffee mixture; place, dipped sides down, in the bottom of an 8-inch square baking dish, slightly overlapping ladyfinger halves. Spread half of cheese mixture over ladyfingers, and sprinkle with 1 teaspoon cocoa. Repeat procedure with remaining ladyfinger halves, coffee mixture, cheese mixture, and 1 teaspoon cocoa.
5. Place 1 toothpick in each corner and 1 in the center of tiramisu (to prevent plastic wrap from sticking to cheese mixture); cover with plastic wrap. Chill 2 hours. Yield: 12 servings.

CALORIES 134 (30% from fat); FAT 4.5g (sat 2.2g, mono 1.5g, poly 0.4g); PROTEIN 3.3g; CARB 21.7g; FIBER 0g; CHOL 31mg; IRON 0.3mg; SODIUM 139mg; CALC 77mg

Cranberry Ice

8 cups water
4 cups fresh cranberries
3 cups sugar

1. Combine all ingredients in a Dutch oven, and bring to a boil. Reduce heat, and cook 15 minutes or until all cranberries pop. Strain the cranberry mixture through a fine sieve over a bowl, discarding solids. Cover and chill.
2. Pour the cranberry mixture into the freezer can of an ice-cream freezer, and freeze according to the manufacturer's instructions. Spoon the cranberry ice into a freezer-safe container; cover and freeze for 1 hour or until ready to serve. Yield: 10 cups (serving size: ½ cup).

CALORIES 125 (0% from fat); FAT 0g (sat 0g, mono 0g, poly 0g); PROTEIN 0.1g; CARB 32.4g; FIBER 0.2g; CHOL 0mg; IRON 0.1mg; SODIUM 0mg; CALC 2mg

Chambord Granita

Chambord is an expensive liqueur that is made with black raspberries, honey, and herbs. It's the essential ingredient that gives the granita its distinctive flavor. Chambord is also nice as an after-dinner cordial.

3 cups water, divided
1 cup sugar
4 cups fresh raspberries (about 1½ pounds)
1 cup Chambord (raspberry-flavored liqueur)

1. Combine 1 cup water and sugar in a saucepan, and bring to a boil, stirring until sugar dissolves. Remove from heat; cool completely.
2. Place raspberries in a blender; process until smooth. Press raspberry puree through a sieve into a medium bowl; discard seeds. Stir in sugar syrup, 2 cups water, and liqueur. Pour into an 11 x 7-inch baking dish. Cover and freeze 8 hours or until firm. Remove from freezer; let stand 10 minutes. Scrape entire mixture with a fork until fluffy. Yield: 2 quarts (serving size: ½ cup).

CALORIES 105 (2% from fat); FAT 0.2g (sat 0g, mono 0g, poly 0.1g); PROTEIN 0.3g; CARB 21.3g; FIBER 0g; CHOL 0mg; IRON 0.2mg; SODIUM 0mg; CALC 7mg

Peach and Muscat Granita

Rich, sweet Muscat is a match for ripe peaches in this refreshing, elegant dessert.

4 cups sliced peaches (about 2 pounds)
1 (375-milliliter) bottle Muscat wine
3 cups water, divided
¾ cup sugar

1. Combine sliced peaches and wine in a food processor or blender, and process until smooth. Strain peach mixture through a sieve into a large bowl, and discard solids.
2. Combine 1 cup water and ¾ cup sugar in a small saucepan; bring to a boil, stirring until sugar dissolves. Remove from heat; stir in 2 cups water.
3. Combine peach mixture and sugar mixture in a 13 x 9-inch baking dish, stirring with a whisk. Freeze 6 hours or until firm, stirring twice during first 2 hours. Yield: 8 servings (serving size: 1 cup).

CALORIES 181 (0% from fat); FAT 0.1g (sat 0g, mono 0g, poly 0.1g); PROTEIN 0.7g; CARB 33.7g; FIBER 1.7g; CHOL 0mg; IRON 0.2mg; SODIUM 4mg; CALC 8mg

Raspberry Sorbet and Meringue Sandwiches

Crisp meringues encase fruity sorbet in this refreshing frozen treat. Any flavor of sorbet will work.

MERINGUES:
1 cup sugar
2 teaspoons cornstarch
¼ teaspoon salt
½ teaspoon cream of tartar
5 large egg whites
2 teaspoons white vinegar
½ teaspoon vanilla extract
FILLING:
1 quart raspberry sorbet, softened

1. Preheat oven to 250°.
2. To prepare meringues, cover a large baking sheet with parchment paper. Draw 2 (8 x 12-inch) rectangles on paper. Turn paper over, and secure with masking tape.
3. Combine the first 3 ingredients, stirring mixture with a whisk. Place the cream of tartar and egg whites in a large bowl, and beat with a mixer at high speed until foamy. Gradually add sugar mixture, 1 tablespoon at a time, beating until stiff peaks form

(do not underbeat). Add the white vinegar and vanilla extract, and beat until combined. Divide egg white mixture evenly between drawn rectangles, and spread egg white mixture to outside edges of each rectangle.
4. Bake at 250° for 2 hours or until dry. Turn oven off; partially open oven door. Cool meringues in oven 1 hour. Remove from oven. Carefully remove meringues from paper.
5. To prepare sandwiches, spread sorbet over flat side of 1 meringue, and top with remaining meringue, flat side down, pressing gently. Wrap sandwich tightly in plastic wrap, and freeze for 4 hours or until firm. Unwrap and cut sandwich in half lengthwise. Cut each half crosswise into 6 (4 x 2-inch) pieces. Cut each piece in half diagonally to form 24 sandwiches. Wrap each sandwich tightly in plastic wrap; store in freezer. Yield: 12 servings (serving size: 2 sandwiches).

CALORIES 143 (0% from fat); FAT 0g (sat 0g, mono 0g, poly 0g); PROTEIN 1.5g; CARB 34.6g; FIBER 1.3g; CHOL 0mg; IRON 0mg; SODIUM 73mg; CALC 1mg

Lemon-Basil Sorbet

Basil's faint licorice flavor is nothing short of fabulous in this tart sorbet. Don't stuff the basil leaves into the measuring cup; pack them loosely, instead. Then tear them in half.

3 cups loosely packed fresh basil leaves, torn
1½ cups sugar
1½ cups water
½ cup light-colored corn syrup
2 cups fresh lemon juice (about 2 pounds lemons)

1. Combine first 4 ingredients in a saucepan. Bring to a boil; cook 3 minutes or until sugar dissolves. Remove from heat, and chill. Strain basil mixture through a sieve into a bowl, pressing basil with the back of a spoon to remove as much liquid as possible. Discard basil. Combine the sugar mixture and lemon juice.
2. Pour mixture into the freezer can of an ice-cream freezer; freeze according to manufacturer's instructions. Spoon sorbet into a freezer-safe container. Cover and freeze 1 hour or until firm. Remove sorbet from freezer 10 minutes before serving. Yield: 10 servings (serving size: ½ cup).

CALORIES 175 (0% from fat); FAT 0g (sat 0g, mono 0g, poly 0g); PROTEIN 0.2g; CARB 46.7g; FIBER 0.2g; CHOL 0mg; IRON 0mg; SODIUM 21mg; CALC 4mg

Fresh Orange Sorbet

This is great to serve on a hot day or as a palate cleanser during a fine meal. To make orange rind strips for the Fresh Orange Sorbet, remove rind with a vegetable peeler. Then cut rind into thin strips.

2½ cups water
 1 cup sugar
    Orange rind strips from 2 oranges
2⅔ cups fresh orange juice (about 6 oranges)
 ⅓ cup fresh lemon juice (about 2 lemons)
    Orange rind strips (optional)

1. Combine water and sugar in a saucepan, and bring mixture to a boil. Add orange rind strips; reduce heat, and simmer for 5 minutes. Discard the orange rind strips; remove the liquid from heat, and cool completely.

2. Add the orange juice and lemon juice, and stir mixture well. Pour the mixture into the freezer can of an ice-cream freezer, and freeze according to manufacturer's instructions. Cover and freeze for 1 hour or until sorbet is firm. Garnish sorbet with orange rind, if desired. Yield: 12 servings (serving size: ½ cup).

CALORIES 91 (0% from fat); FAT 0g; PROTEIN 0.4g; CARB 23.2g; FIBER 0.1g; CHOL 0mg; IRON 0.1mg; SODIUM 1mg; CALC 6mg

Strawberry-Buttermilk Gelato

Pureed strawberries create the "juice" that flavors this creamy gelato.

2 cups sugar
2 cups water
5 cups quartered strawberries (about 4 pints)
2 cups low-fat buttermilk

1. Combine sugar and water in a large saucepan; bring to a boil, stirring until sugar dissolves. Pour into a large bowl; cool completely.

2. Place strawberries in a blender; process until smooth. Add strawberry puree and buttermilk to sugar syrup; stir to combine.

3. Pour the strawberry mixture into the freezer can of an ice-cream freezer, and freeze according to manufacturer's instructions. Yield: 8 cups (serving size: ½ cup).

CALORIES 134 (5% from fat); FAT 0.8g (sat 0.3g, mono 0.2g, poly 0.1g); PROTEIN 1.6g; CARB 31.7g; FIBER 1.7g; CHOL 1mg; IRON 0.3mg; SODIUM 17mg; CALC 48mg

Cookies-and-Cream Ice Cream

Garnish each serving with a whole cookie, if you wish.

 1 (12.3-ounce) package reduced-fat firm tofu, drained
 ½ cup sugar
 ½ cup half-and-half
 1 teaspoon vanilla extract
 ¼ teaspoon salt
 2 cups frozen fat-free whipped topping, thawed
10 cream-filled chocolate sandwich cookies (such as Oreos), crushed

1. Combine first 5 ingredients in a food processor or blender; process until smooth. Place tofu mixture in a large bowl. Fold in whipped topping. Pour mixture into the freezer can of an ice-cream freezer; freeze according to manufacturer's instructions. Stir in crushed cookies during last 5 minutes of freezing. Spoon ice cream into a freezer-safe container; cover and freeze 1 hour or until firm. Yield: 8 servings (serving size: ½ cup).

CALORIES 184 (25% from fat); FAT 5.2g (sat 1.8g, mono 1.9g, poly 0.6g); PROTEIN 3.8g; CARB 29.3g; FIBER 0.4g; CHOL 6mg; IRON 0.7mg; SODIUM 307mg; CALC 31mg

Cookies-and-Cream Ice Cream

Peaches-and-Cream Ice Cream

5 cups 1% low-fat milk, divided
4 large egg yolks
4 cups mashed peeled ripe peaches
   (about 8 medium peaches)
2 tablespoons fresh lemon juice
2 tablespoons vanilla extract
½ teaspoon ground ginger
½ teaspoon almond extract
2 (14-ounce) cans fat-free sweetened
   condensed milk
Mint sprigs (optional)

1. Combine 2½ cups 1% milk and egg yolks in a large, heavy saucepan, and stir well with a whisk. Cook over medium heat 10 minutes or until mixture thickens and coats a spoon, and stir constantly (do not boil). Combine egg yolk mixture, 2½ cups 1% milk, peaches, and the remaining ingredients except mint sprigs in a large bowl. Cover and chill completely.

2. Pour mixture into the freezer can of an ice-cream freezer; freeze according to manufacturer's instructions. Spoon the ice cream into a large freezer-safe container; cover and freeze 1 hour or until firm. Garnish with mint sprigs, if desired. Yield: 24 servings (serving size: ½ cup).

CALORIES 140 (9% from fat); FAT 1.4g (sat 0.6g, mono 0.5g, poly 0.2g); PROTEIN 4.9g; CARB 26.2g; FIBER 0.5g; CHOL 40mg; IRON 0.2mg; SODIUM 60mg; CALC 135mg

Lemon-Buttermilk Ice Cream

Three different kinds of milk provide a rich, creamy consistency. The ice cream is at its peak served as soon as it's become firm in the freezer. Let it stand at room temperature for 30 minutes so that it will be soft enough to scoop.

1½ cups sugar
1 cup fresh lemon juice (about 10 lemons)
2 cups half-and-half
2 cups whole milk
2 cups fat-free buttermilk

1. Combine sugar and lemon juice in a large bowl, stirring with a whisk until sugar dissolves. Add half-and-half, whole milk, and buttermilk. Pour mixture into freezer can of an ice-cream freezer, and freeze according to manufacturer's instructions. Spoon

into a freezer-safe container. Cover and freeze 1 hour or until firm. Yield: 18 servings (serving size: ½ cup).

CALORIES 130 (25% from fat); FAT 3.6g (sat 2.3g, mono 1.2g, poly 0g); PROTEIN 2.8g; CARB 21.4g; FIBER 0.1g; CHOL 18mg; IRON 0mg; SODIUM 54mg; CALC 93mg

Banana-Maple Ice Cream

It's important to make sure eggs are safe, which means bringing them to a temperature of at least 160°. Do this slowly over medium heat so you don't curdle the yolks. Using your heaviest saucepan will control and disperse the heat much better than a thinner pan. The dry milk gives this ice cream a smooth consistency.

1½ cups 2% reduced-fat milk, divided
¼ cup sugar
2 large egg yolks
¼ cup nonfat dry milk
1 teaspoon vanilla extract
1 cup mashed ripe banana (about 2 medium)
½ cup maple syrup

1. Combine 1 cup 2% milk, sugar, and egg yolks in a small, heavy saucepan; stir well with a whisk. Place over medium heat, stirring constantly. Cook for 8 minutes or until mixture reaches 180° and is slightly thick (do not boil). Remove from heat. Pour custard into a cool bowl; place bowl over ice water to cool completely. Combine ½ cup 2% milk, dry milk, and vanilla extract. Stir in custard, banana, and syrup. Cover and chill.

2. Pour mixture into the freezer can of an ice-cream freezer, and freeze according to manufacturer's instructions. Spoon the ice cream into a freezer-safe container; cover and freeze 1 hour or until firm. Yield: 3½ cups (serving size: ½ cup).

CALORIES 177 (14% from fat); FAT 2.7g (sat 1.2g, mono 0.9g, poly 0.3g); PROTEIN 4.4g; CARB 34.7g; FIBER 0.8g; CHOL 67mg; IRON 0.6mg; SODIUM 54mg; CALC 141mg

Peppermint Ice Cream

This is a great make-ahead dessert; if it's frozen solid, remove it from the freezer 30 minutes before serving to soften.

2½ cups 2% reduced-fat milk, divided
2 large egg yolks
2 teaspoons vanilla extract
1 (14-ounce) can fat-free sweetened condensed milk
⅔ cup crushed peppermint candies (about 25 candies)

1. Combine 1¼ cups 2% milk and yolks in a heavy saucepan over medium heat. Cook until mixture is slightly thick and coats the back of a spoon; stir constantly (do not boil). Cool slightly.
2. Combine the egg mixture, 1¼ cups 2% milk, vanilla, and condensed milk in a large bowl. Cover and chill completely. Stir in crushed candies. Pour mixture into the freezer can of an ice-cream freezer; freeze according to manufacturer's instructions. Spoon ice cream into a freezer-safe container; cover and freeze 1 hour or until firm. Yield: 8 servings (serving size: ½ cup).

CALORIES 268 (10% from fat); FAT 2.9g (sat 1.3g, mono 0.9g, poly 0.2g); PROTEIN 7.6g; CARB 52.2g; FIBER 0g; CHOL 62mg; IRON 0.3mg; SODIUM 99mg; CALC 238mg

Peppermint Patties

The peppermint candies should be coarsely crushed in a large zip-top plastic bag by lightly tapping with a rolling pin or heavy skillet (a food processor would just pulverize them). You can substitute regular unsweetened cocoa powder in the cookies.

COOKIES:
1½ cups all-purpose flour
⅓ cup Dutch process cocoa
½ teaspoon baking soda
¼ teaspoon salt
½ cup granulated sugar
½ cup packed brown sugar
½ cup butter, softened
1 teaspoon vanilla extract
1 large egg
Cooking spray
FILLING:
30 hard peppermint candies, crushed (about 1 cup)
3 cups vanilla low-fat ice cream, softened

1. To prepare cookies, lightly spoon flour into dry measuring cups; level with a knife. Combine flour, cocoa, baking soda, and salt, stirring with a whisk. Combine sugars and butter in a large bowl; beat with a mixer at medium speed until well blended. Add vanilla and egg; beat well. Add flour mixture to sugar mixture; beat at low speed until well blended.
2. Lightly coat hands with cooking spray. Divide dough in half. Shape each half into a 6-inch log. Wrap logs individually in plastic wrap; freeze 1 hour or until firm.
3. Preheat oven to 350°.
4. Cut each dough log into 24 (¼-inch) slices; place cookies 1 inch apart on baking sheets coated with cooking spray. Bake at 350° for 11 minutes or until set. Cool completely on wire racks.
5. To prepare filling, place candies in a shallow bowl. Spread 2 tablespoons ice cream onto flat side of each of 24 cookies. Top with remaining cookies, flat sides down, pressing gently. Lightly roll the sides of each sandwich in candy. Wrap each sandwich tightly in plastic wrap; freeze 4 hours or until firm. Yield: 12 servings (serving size: 2 sandwiches).

CALORIES 321 (30% from fat); FAT 10.6g (sat 6.2g, mono 2.4g, poly 0.4g); PROTEIN 4.3g; CARB 51.6g; FIBER 1.1g; CHOL 56mg; IRON 1.3mg; SODIUM 216mg; CALC 69mg

Peppermint Patties

Anzac Biscuits

Of Australian origin, these "biscuits" could possibly be the best cookies we've ever made. The cane syrup imparts a chewy, slightly sticky texture that gives them a wonderful richness.

 1 cup all-purpose flour
 1 cup regular oats
 1 cup packed brown sugar
 ½ cup shredded sweetened coconut
 ½ teaspoon baking soda
 ¼ cup butter or stick margarine, melted
 3 tablespoons water
 2 tablespoons golden cane syrup (such as Lyle's) or light-colored corn syrup
 Cooking spray

1. Preheat oven to 325°.
2. Lightly spoon flour into a dry measuring cup; and level with a knife. Combine flour and next 4 ingredients in a bowl. Add butter, water, and syrup, stirring well. Drop dough by level tablespoons, 2 inches apart, onto baking sheets coated with cooking spray. Bake at 325° for 12 minutes or until almost set. Remove from oven; let stand 2 to 3 minutes or until firm. Remove cookies from baking sheets. Place on wire racks; cool completely. Yield: 2 dozen (serving size: 1 cookie).
NOTE: We found that these cookies were much better when they were made with golden cane syrup such as Lyle's. Cane syrup is thicker and sweeter than corn syrup and can be found in cans next to the jellies and syrups, or in stores specializing in Caribbean and Creole goods.

CALORIES 98 (27% from fat); FAT 2.9g (sat 1g, mono 0.9g, poly 0.7g); PROTEIN 1.2g; CARB 17.3g; FIBER 0.6g; CHOL 0mg; IRON 0.6mg; SODIUM 59mg; CALC 11mg

Coconut-Macadamia Nut Cookies

 1 cup all-purpose flour
 1 cup regular oats
 1 cup packed brown sugar
 ⅓ cup golden raisins
 ⅓ cup flaked sweetened coconut
 ¼ cup chopped macadamia nuts
 ½ teaspoon baking soda
 ¼ cup butter or stick margarine, melted
 3 tablespoons water
 2 tablespoons honey
 Cooking spray

1. Preheat oven to 325°.
2. Lightly spoon the flour into a dry measuring cup; level with a knife. Combine flour and the next 6 ingredients; stir well with a whisk. Combine butter, water, and honey, stirring well to combine. Add butter mixture to flour mixture, stirring until well blended. Drop by level tablespoons 2 inches apart onto baking sheets coated with cooking spray. Bake at 325° for 10 minutes or until almost set. Cool on pan 2 to 3 minutes or until firm. Remove cookies from pan, and cool on wire racks. Yield: 2½ dozen (serving size: 1 cookie).

CALORIES 90 (30% from fat); FAT 3g (sat 1.5g, mono 1.2g, poly 0.2g); PROTEIN 1.1g; CARB 15.4g; FIBER 0.5g; CHOL 4mg; IRON 0.5mg; SODIUM 43mg; CALC 10mg

Spicy Oatmeal Crisps

Pepper may seem like an odd ingredient for a cookie, but it complements the other spices well (although you can omit it if you prefer).

 ¾ cup all-purpose flour
 1 teaspoon ground cinnamon
 ½ teaspoon baking soda
 ½ teaspoon ground allspice
 ½ teaspoon grated whole nutmeg
 ¼ teaspoon salt
 ¼ teaspoon ground cloves
 ¼ teaspoon black pepper (optional)
 1 cup packed brown sugar
 5 tablespoons butter or stick margarine, softened
 1 teaspoon vanilla extract
 1 large egg
 ½ cup regular oats
 Cooking spray

1. Preheat oven to 350°.
2. Lightly spoon the flour into dry measuring cups; level with a knife. Combine flour and next 7 ingredients in a medium bowl, stirring with a whisk. Beat sugar, butter, and vanilla in a large bowl with a mixer at medium speed until light and fluffy. Add egg; beat well. Stir in flour mixture and oats.
3. Drop mixture by level tablespoons 2 inches apart onto baking sheets coated with cooking spray. Bake at 350° for 12 minutes or until crisp. Cool on pan for 2 to 3 minutes or until firm. Remove cookies from pan, and cool on wire racks. Yield: 2 dozen (serving size: 1 cookie).

CALORIES 81 (34% from fat); FAT 3.1g (sat 1.7g, mono 0.9g, poly 0.3g); PROTEIN 1.5g; CARB 12.2g; FIBER 0.7g; CHOL 15mg; IRON 0.6mg; SODIUM 71mg; CALC 12mg

Macadamia Butter Cookies with Dried Cranberries

Dried cranberries provide a slightly tart counterpoint to the rich macadamia nuts. The dough is somewhat sticky; chilling it briefly makes handling easier.

- ⅔ cup macadamia nuts
- ½ cup granulated sugar
- ½ cup packed light brown sugar
- 1 teaspoon vanilla extract
- 1 large egg
- 1¼ cups all-purpose flour
- ½ teaspoon baking soda
- ¼ teaspoon salt
- ⅛ teaspoon ground nutmeg
- ½ cup sweetened dried cranberries, chopped
- 1 tablespoon granulated sugar

1. Preheat oven to 375°.

2. Place nuts in a food processor; process until smooth (about 2 minutes), scraping sides of bowl once. Combine macadamia butter, ½ cup granulated sugar, and brown sugar in a large bowl; beat with a mixer at medium speed. Add vanilla and egg, and beat well.

3. Lightly spoon flour into dry measuring cups; level with a knife. Combine flour, baking soda, salt, and nutmeg, stirring with a whisk. Add flour mixture to sugar mixture; beat at low speed just until combined (mixture will be very thick). Stir in cranberries. Chill 10 minutes.

4. Divide chilled dough into 30 equal portions; roll each portion into a ball. Place 1 tablespoon granulated sugar in a small bowl. Lightly press each ball into sugar; place each ball, sugar side up, on a baking sheet covered with parchment paper.

5. Gently press top of each cookie with a fork. Dip fork in water; gently press top of each cookie again to form a crisscross pattern. Place 15 cookies on each of 2 baking sheets.

6. Bake cookies, 1 baking sheet at a time, at 375° for 9 minutes or until golden. Remove from pan, and cool on a wire rack. Repeat the procedure with remaining cookies. Yield: 30 servings (serving size: 1 cookie).

CALORIES 76 (30% from fat); FAT 2.5g (sat 0.4g, mono 1.8g, poly 0.1g); PROTEIN 1g; CARB 13.2g; FIBER 0.6g; CHOL 7mg; IRON 0.5mg; SODIUM 44mg; CALC 7mg

Macadamia Butter Cookies
with Dried Cranberries

Crisp Pecan Cookies

- 1 cup all-purpose flour
- ½ teaspoon baking powder
- ¼ teaspoon salt
- 1 cup packed brown sugar
- 5 tablespoons butter, softened
- 1 teaspoon vanilla extract
- 1 large egg white
- 3 tablespoons pecans, toasted and finely chopped
- ⅓ cup powdered sugar, divided
- Cooking spray

1. Lightly spoon flour into a dry measuring cup; level with a knife. Combine flour, baking powder, and salt, stirring with a whisk.

2. Combine brown sugar and butter in a bowl; beat with a mixer at high speed until light and fluffy. Add vanilla and egg white; beat for 1 minute. Stir in the flour mixture and chopped pecans, and refrigerate for 30 minutes.

3. Preheat oven to 350°.

4. Place ¼ cup powdered sugar in a small bowl. With moist hands, shape dough into 30 (½-inch) balls. Roll balls in ¼ cup powdered sugar. Place 2 inches apart on baking sheets coated with cooking spray. Place pans in freezer 10 minutes.

5. Bake at 350° for 12 minutes or until golden. Cool on pans 2 minutes. Remove from pans; cool completely on wire racks. Using a fine sieve, dust cookies with the remaining powdered sugar. Yield: 30 cookies (serving size: 1 cookie).

CALORIES 69 (33% from fat); FAT 2.5g (sat 1.2g, mono 0.9g, poly 0.2g); PROTEIN 0.6g; CARB 11.6g; FIBER 0.2g; CHOL 5mg; IRON 0.4mg; SODIUM 50mg; CALC 10mg

Double Chocolate Cookies,
Black-and-White Cake Cookies,
Cocoa Fudge Cookies

Double Chocolate Cookies

1¼ cups all-purpose flour
½ teaspoon baking powder
¼ teaspoon salt
5 tablespoons butter, softened
½ cup granulated sugar
½ cup packed brown sugar
1½ teaspoons vanilla extract
1 large egg white
⅓ cup dried tart cherries
¼ cup semisweet chocolate chunks
2½ tablespoons premium white chocolate chips
Cooking spray

1. Preheat oven to 350°.

2. Lightly spoon the flour into dry measuring cups, and level with a knife. Combine the flour, baking powder, and salt, stirring with a whisk.

3. Combine butter, granulated sugar, and brown sugar in a large bowl; beat with a mixer at medium speed until well blended. Add vanilla and egg white; beat 1 minute. Stir in flour mixture, cherries, and chocolates.

4. Drop the mixture by level tablespoons 2 inches apart onto baking sheets coated with cooking spray. Place the pans in the freezer for 5 minutes. Bake at 350° for 10 minutes or until cookies are lightly browned. Cool cookies on pans 2 minutes. Remove the cookies from pans, and cool completely on wire racks. Yield: 2 dozen cookies (serving size: 1 cookie).

CALORIES 98 (30% from fat); FAT 3.3g (sat 2g, mono 1g, poly 0.1g); PROTEIN 1g; CARB 16.6g; FIBER 0.4g; CHOL 7mg; IRON 0.5mg; SODIUM 63mg; CALC 12mg

Cocoa Fudge Cookies

You can mix these incredibly easy, fudgy cookies right in the saucepan. Just out of the oven, they have crisp edges and chewy centers. You can make them with either Dutch process or unsweetened cocoa; we opted for the latter.

    1   cup all-purpose flour
 ¼   teaspoon baking soda
 ⅛   teaspoon salt
    5   tablespoons butter
    7   tablespoons unsweetened cocoa
 ⅔   cup granulated sugar
 ⅓   cup packed brown sugar
 ⅓   cup plain low-fat yogurt
    1   teaspoon vanilla extract
Cooking spray

1. Preheat oven to 350°.
2. Lightly spoon flour into a dry measuring cup; level with a knife. Combine flour, baking soda, and salt. Melt butter in a large saucepan over medium heat. Remove from heat; stir in cocoa and sugars (mixture will resemble coarse sand). Add yogurt and vanilla, stirring to combine. Add flour mixture, stirring until moist. Drop by level tablespoons 2 inches apart onto baking sheets coated with cooking spray.
3. Bake at 350° for 8 to 10 minutes or until cookies are almost set. Cool cookies on pans 2 to 3 minutes or until firm. Remove cookies from pans, and cool on wire racks. Yield: 2 dozen cookies (serving size: 1 cookie).

CALORIES 78 (31% from fat); FAT 2.7g (sat 1.6g, mono 0.8g, poly 0.1g); PROTEIN 1g; CARB 13.4g; FIBER 0.5g; CHOL 7mg; IRON 0.5mg; SODIUM 54mg; CALC 12mg

Black-and-White Cake Cookies

COOKIES:
 1½   cups all-purpose flour
 1½   teaspoons baking powder
 ½   teaspoon salt
 ⅔   cup applesauce
    1   cup granulated sugar
 ¼   cup butter, softened
 1½   teaspoons vanilla extract
    2   large egg whites
FROSTING:
 1½   cups powdered sugar, divided
    3   tablespoons 2% reduced-fat milk, divided
 ¼   teaspoon almond extract
    2   tablespoons unsweetened cocoa

1. Preheat oven to 375°.
2. To prepare cookies, lightly spoon flour into dry measuring cups; level with a knife. Combine flour, baking powder, and salt, stirring with a whisk.
3. Place applesauce in a fine sieve, and let stand for 15 minutes.
4. Combine drained applesauce, granulated sugar, and butter in a large bowl; beat with a mixer at medium speed 2 minutes or until well blended. Beat in vanilla and egg whites. Add flour mixture, and beat at low speed until blended.
5. Drop dough by level tablespoons 2 inches apart onto parchment-lined baking sheets. Bake at 375° for 10 minutes or until set (not browned). Cool on pans 2 minutes or until firm. Remove from pans; cool completely on wire racks.
6. To prepare frosting, combine ¾ cup powdered sugar, 1 tablespoon milk, and almond extract in a bowl, stirring well with a whisk until smooth. Working with 1 cookie at a time, hold cookie over bowl and spread about 1 teaspoon white frosting over half of cookie (scrape excess frosting from edges). Let stand 10 minutes or until frosting is set.
7. Combine ¾ cup powdered sugar and cocoa in a bowl. Gradually add 2 tablespoons milk, stirring with a whisk until smooth. Working with 1 cookie at a time, hold cookie over bowl and spread about 1 teaspoon chocolate frosting over other half of cookie (scrape excess frosting from edges). Let stand 10 minutes or until frosting is set. Yield: 2 dozen cookies (serving size: 1 cookie).

CALORIES 106 (17% from fat); FAT 2g (sat 1.2g, mono 0.6g, poly 0.1g); PROTEIN 1.3g; CARB 21.4g; FIBER 0.4g; CHOL 5mg; IRON 0.4mg; SODIUM 100mg; CALC 14mg

401

Double-Ginger Cookies

mixture, stirring just until moist; cover and chill dough at least 1 hour.

2. Preheat oven to 350°.

3. Lightly coat hands with flour. Shape dough into 24 balls (about 2 tablespoons each; dough will be sticky). Roll balls in ¼ cup sugar. Place balls 2 inches apart on baking sheets coated with cooking spray. Bake at 350° for 15 minutes or until lightly browned. Cool 1 minute on pan. Remove from pan; cool completely on wire racks. Yield: 2 dozen (serving size: 1 cookie).

NOTE: These freeze well. Place cooled cookies in a heavy-duty zip-top plastic bag; store in freezer for up to 1 month. Thaw at room temperature.

CALORIES 123 (18% from fat); FAT 2.5g (sat 0.5g, mono 0.7g, poly 1.2g); PROTEIN 1.5g; CARB 24.2g; FIBER 0.9g; CHOL 0mg; IRON 1.4mg; SODIUM 98mg; CALC 24mg

Heavenly Apricot Cobbler Bars

These cookies can be made several days ahead; store in an airtight container with wax paper between layers to prevent them from sticking together.

  5   tablespoons butter or stick margarine, softened
 ¼   cup powdered sugar
 ¼   cup packed brown sugar
 ¼   teaspoon salt
 ⅛   teaspoon almond extract
1¼   cups all-purpose flour
 ¾   cup apricot preserves
 ½   cup low-fat granola without raisins, crushed

1. Preheat oven to 350°.

2. Beat butter with a mixer at medium speed until light and fluffy. Add sugars, salt, and extract, beating well. Lightly spoon the flour into dry measuring cups; level with a knife. Gradually add the flour to butter mixture, beating until moist. Remove ⅓ cup flour mixture; set aside.

3. Press remaining flour mixture into bottom of an 8-inch square baking dish. Bake at 350° for 15 minutes or until lightly golden. Gently spread preserves over warm shortbread. Combine ⅓ cup flour mixture and granola; sprinkle over preserves. Bake at 350° for an additional 20 minutes or until golden brown. Cool. Yield: 2 dozen bars (serving size: 1 piece).

CALORIES 91 (26% from fat); FAT 2.6g (sat 1.5g, mono 0.8g, poly 0.1g); PROTEIN 0.9g; CARB 16.5g; FIBER 0.4g; CHOL 6mg; IRON 0.5mg; SODIUM 59mg; CALC 7mg

Double-Ginger Cookies

Small chunks of crystallized ginger add spark to these cookies. The dough can be chilled for up to 24 hours before shaping and baking.

1½   cups all-purpose flour
  1   cup whole-wheat or all-purpose flour
 ¾   cup chopped crystallized ginger
  1   teaspoon baking powder
 ½   teaspoon baking soda
 ½   teaspoon salt
 ½   teaspoon ground ginger
1¼   cups sugar, divided
 ½   cup applesauce
 ¼   cup vegetable oil
  1   teaspoon grated lemon rind
  1   tablespoon lemon juice
 ¼   teaspoon vanilla extract
Cooking spray

1. Lightly spoon flours into dry measuring cups, and level with a knife. Combine flours and next 5 ingredients, and stir well with a whisk. Make a well in center of mixture. Combine 1 cup sugar, apple-sauce, and the next 4 ingredients. Add to the flour

Easy Lemon Squares

CRUST:
- ¼ cup granulated sugar
- 3 tablespoons butter or stick margarine, softened
- 1 cup all-purpose flour
- Cooking spray

TOPPING:
- 3 large eggs
- ¾ cup granulated sugar
- 2 teaspoons grated lemon rind
- ⅓ cup fresh lemon juice
- 3 tablespoons all-purpose flour
- ½ teaspoon baking powder
- ⅛ teaspoon salt
- 2 teaspoons powdered sugar

1. Preheat oven to 350°.

2. To prepare the crust, beat ¼ cup granulated sugar and butter at medium speed of a mixer until creamy. Lightly spoon 1 cup flour into a dry measuring cup; level with a knife. Gradually add 1 cup flour to sugar mixture, beating at low speed until mixture resembles fine crumbs. Gently press mixture into bottom of an 8-inch square baking pan coated with cooking spray. Bake at 350° for 15 minutes; cool on a wire rack.

3. To prepare the topping, beat eggs at medium speed until foamy. Add ¾ cup granulated sugar and the next 5 ingredients, and beat until well blended. Pour the mixture over the partially baked crust. Bake at 350° for 20 to 25 minutes or until set. Cool on wire rack. Sift the powdered sugar evenly over the top. Yield: 16 servings (serving size: 1 square).

CALORIES 118 (24% from fat); FAT 3.2g (sat 1.7g, mono 1g, poly 0.3g); PROTEIN 2.2g; CARB 20.5g; FIBER 0.3g; CHOL 47mg; IRON 0.6mg; SODIUM 68mg; CALC 16mg

Raspberry Strippers

You're not limited to raspberry preserves for the filling. Try apricot preserves as well.

- ⅓ cup granulated sugar
- 5 tablespoons butter or stick margarine, softened
- 1½ teaspoons vanilla extract
- 1 large egg white
- 1 cup all-purpose flour
- 2 tablespoons cornstarch
- ¼ teaspoon baking powder
- ¼ teaspoon salt
- Cooking spray
- ⅓ cup raspberry or apricot preserves
- ½ cup powdered sugar
- 2 teaspoons fresh lemon juice
- ¼ teaspoon almond or vanilla extract

1. Preheat oven to 375°.

2. Beat granulated sugar and butter with a mixer at medium speed until well blended (about 5 minutes). Add 1½ teaspoons vanilla and egg white, and beat well. Lightly spoon flour into a dry measuring cup; level with a knife. Combine flour, cornstarch, baking powder, and salt; stir well with a whisk. Add flour mixture to sugar mixture, stirring until well blended. (Dough will be stiff.)

3. Turn dough out onto a lightly floured surface. Divide in half. Roll each portion into a 12-inch log. Place logs 3 inches apart on a baking sheet coated with cooking spray. Form a ½-inch-deep indentation down the length of each log using an index finger or end of a wooden spoon. Spoon preserves into the center. Bake at 375° for 20 minutes or until lightly browned. Remove logs to a cutting board.

4. Combine the powdered sugar, lemon juice, and almond extract; stir well with a whisk. Drizzle sugar mixture over warm logs. Immediately cut each log diagonally into 12 slices. (Do not separate slices.) Cool 10 minutes; separate slices. Transfer slices to wire racks. Cool completely. Yield: 2 dozen (serving size: 1 cookie).

CALORIES 75 (30% from fat); FAT 2.5g (sat 1.5g, mono 0.7g, poly 0.2g); PROTEIN 0.7g; CARB 12.4g; FIBER 0.2g; CHOL 6mg; IRON 0.3mg; SODIUM 56mg; CALC 4mg

Easy Chocolate-Caramel Brownies

Use a cake mix that contains pudding; the recipe won't work otherwise. Cut the brownies after they've cooled. To make ahead, cool completely, wrap tightly in heavy-duty plastic wrap, and freeze.

   2 tablespoons fat-free milk
  27 small soft caramel candies (about 8 ounces)
  ½ cup fat-free sweetened condensed milk
   1 (18.25-ounce) package devil's food cake mix with pudding (such as Pillsbury)
   7 tablespoons reduced-calorie stick margarine, melted
   1 large egg white, lightly beaten
Cooking spray
   1 teaspoon all-purpose flour
  ½ cup reduced-fat chocolate baking chips

1. Preheat oven to 350°.
2. Combine fat-free milk and candies in a bowl. Microwave at HIGH 1½ to 2 minutes or until the caramels melt and mixture is smooth, stirring with a whisk after every minute. Set aside.
3. Combine sweetened condensed milk, cake mix, margarine, and egg white in a bowl (batter will be very stiff). Coat bottom only of a 13 x 9-inch baking pan with cooking spray; dust lightly with flour. Press two-thirds of batter into prepared pan using floured hands; pat evenly (layer will be thin).
4. Bake at 350° for 10 minutes. Remove from oven; sprinkle with chocolate chips. Drizzle caramel mixture over chips; carefully drop remaining batter by spoonfuls over caramel mixture. Bake at 350° for 25 minutes. Cool in pan on a wire rack. Yield: 3 dozen (serving size: 1 brownie).
NOTE: For a gooey serving, microwave a brownie at high 10 seconds to soften caramel and chips.

CALORIES 122 (30% from fat); FAT 4g (sat 1.6g, mono 1.3g, poly 0.6g); PROTEIN 1.6g; CARB 20.4g; FIBER 0.4g; CHOL 1mg; IRON 0.5mg; SODIUM 224mg; CALC 34mg

Ooey-Gooey Peanut Butter-Chocolate Brownies

  ¾ cup fat-free sweetened condensed milk, divided
  ¼ cup butter or stick margarine, melted and cooled
  ¼ cup fat-free milk
   1 (18.25-ounce) package devil's food cake mix
   1 large egg white, lightly beaten
Cooking spray
   1 (7-ounce) jar marshmallow creme
  ½ cup peanut butter chips

1. Preheat oven to 350°.
2. Combine ¼ cup condensed milk, butter, and next 3 ingredients (batter will be very stiff). Coat bottom of a 13 x 9-inch baking pan with cooking spray. Press two-thirds of batter into prepared pan using floured hands; pat evenly (layer will be thin).
3. Bake at 350° for 10 minutes. Combine ½ cup condensed milk and marshmallow creme in a bowl; stir in chips. Spread marshmallow mixture evenly over brownie layer. Carefully drop remaining batter by spoonfuls over marshmallow mixture. Bake at 350° for 30 minutes. Cool completely in pan on a wire rack. Yield: 2 dozen (serving size: 1 brownie).

CALORIES 176 (25% from fat); FAT 5g (sat 2.1g, mono 1.6g, poly 1.1g); PROTEIN 2.6g; CARB 29.9g; FIBER 0.8g; CHOL 6mg; IRON 0.8mg; SODIUM 212mg; CALC 30mg

Buttermilk Pralines

1½ cups sugar
  ½ cup whole buttermilk
1½ tablespoons light-colored corn syrup
  ½ teaspoon baking soda
Dash of salt
  ⅔ cup chopped pecans, toasted
1½ teaspoons butter
   1 tablespoon vanilla extract

1. Combine first 5 ingredients in a saucepan. Cook over low heat until sugar dissolves; stir constantly. Continue cooking over low heat until a candy thermometer registers 234° (about 10 minutes); stir occasionally. Remove from heat; let stand 5 minutes.
2. Stir in pecans, butter, and vanilla; beat with a wooden spoon until mixture begins to lose its shine (about 6 minutes). Drop by teaspoonfuls onto wax paper. Let stand 20 minutes or until set. Yield: 30 servings (serving size: 1 praline).

CALORIES 65 (30% from fat); FAT 2.2g (sat 0.4g, mono 1.2g, poly 0.6g); PROTEIN 0.4g; CARB 11.4g; FIBER 0.3g; CHOL 1mg; IRON 0.1mg; SODIUM 36mg; CALC 7mg

Ooey-Gooey Peanut Butter-
Chocolate Brownies

Chocolate-Cherry Biscotti

A serrated knife works best for cutting the rolls after the first baking.

     2 cups all-purpose flour
     1 cup whole-wheat flour
    ¼ teaspoon salt
     1 cup sugar
     3 large eggs
     2 tablespoons vegetable oil
     2 teaspoons vanilla extract
    1½ teaspoons almond extract
    ⅔ cup dried tart cherries or dried cranberries
    ½ cup semisweet chocolate chips
       Cooking spray

1. Preheat oven to 350º.
2. Lightly spoon flours into dry measuring cups; level with a knife. Combine flours and salt in a bowl; stir well with a whisk.
3. Beat sugar and eggs with a mixer at high speed until thick and pale (about 4 minutes). Add oil and extracts, beating until well blended. Add flour mixture, beating at low speed just until blended. Stir in cherries and chocolate chips.
4. Divide dough in half; turn out onto a baking sheet coated with cooking spray. Shape each portion into a 10-inch-long roll; flatten to 1-inch thickness. Bake at 350º for 25 minutes or until lightly browned. Remove rolls from baking sheet; cool 10 minutes on a wire rack. Reduce oven temperature to 325º.
5. Cut each roll diagonally into 20 (½-inch) slices. Place slices, cut sides down, on baking sheet. Bake at 325º for 10 minutes. Turn cookies over; bake an additional 10 minutes (cookies will be slightly soft in center but will harden as they cool). Remove from baking sheet; cool completely on wire racks. Yield: 40 biscotti (serving size: 1 biscotto).

CALORIES 81 (22% from fat); FAT 2g (sat 0.7g, mono 0.6g, poly 0.5g); PROTEIN 1.6g; CARB 14.6g; FIBER 0.6g; CHOL 17mg; IRON 0.5mg; SODIUM 20mg; CALC 6mg

Cranberry-Chocolate Chip Biscotti

    2¾ cups all-purpose flour
     1 cup sugar
    ½ cup dried cranberries
    ⅓ cup semisweet chocolate chips
     2 teaspoons baking powder
    ⅛ teaspoon salt
     1 tablespoon vegetable oil
     1 teaspoon almond extract
     1 teaspoon vanilla extract
     3 large eggs
       Cooking spray

1. Preheat oven to 350º.
2. Lightly spoon flour into dry measuring cups, and level with a knife. Combine flour and next 5 ingredients in a large bowl, stirring with a whisk. Combine oil, extracts, and eggs; add to flour mixture, stirring until well blended (dough will be dry and crumbly). Turn the dough out onto a lightly floured surface; knead lightly 7 to 8 times. Divide dough in half. Shape each portion into an 8-inch-long roll. Place rolls 6 inches apart on a baking sheet coated with cooking spray; flatten each roll to 1-inch thickness.
3. Bake at 350º for 35 minutes. Remove rolls from baking sheet; cool 10 minutes on a wire rack. Cut each roll diagonally into 15 (½-inch) slices. Place the slices, cut sides down, on baking sheet. Reduce oven temperature to 325º, and bake for 10 minutes. Turn cookies over; bake an additional 10 minutes (the cookies will be slightly soft in center but will harden as they cool). Remove from baking sheet, and cool completely on wire rack. Yield: 2½ dozen (serving size: 1 biscotto).

CALORIES 98 (17% from fat); FAT 1.8g (sat 0.7g, mono 0.6g, poly 0.4g); PROTEIN 2g; CARB 18.6g; FIBER 0.4g; CHOL 22mg; IRON 0.7mg; SODIUM 50mg; CALC 24mg

Coffee-Hazelnut Biscotti

2 tablespoons Frangelico (hazelnut-flavored liqueur)
2 tablespoons unsweetened cocoa
1 teaspoon instant espresso or 2 teaspoons instant coffee granules
1 teaspoon vegetable oil
2 large egg whites
1 large egg
1 1/3 cups all-purpose flour
1/2 cup whole-wheat flour
1/2 cup granulated sugar
1/2 cup packed brown sugar
1/2 cup coarsely chopped toasted hazelnuts, divided
1 teaspoon baking soda
1/8 teaspoon salt
2 teaspoons ground coffee beans
Cooking spray

1. Preheat oven to 300°.

2. Place the liqueur in a small bowl. Microwave at HIGH 10 seconds. Stir in cocoa and espresso until smooth. Add oil, egg whites, and egg, stirring with a whisk until blended.

3. Lightly spoon flours into dry measuring cups, and level with a knife. Place flours, sugars, 2 tablespoons chopped hazelnuts, baking soda, and salt in a food processor, and process until the hazelnuts are ground. Add ground coffee, and pulse 2 times or until mixture is blended. With processor on, slowly add liqueur mixture through food chute, and process until dough forms a ball. Add 6 tablespoons hazelnuts, and pulse 5 times or until blended (dough will be sticky). Turn dough out onto a floured surface, kneading lightly 4 to 5 times. Divide the dough into 3 equal portions, shaping each portion into a 10-inch-long roll. Place rolls 3 inches apart on a large baking sheet coated with cooking spray. Bake at 300° for 28 minutes. Remove rolls from baking sheet, and cool for 10 minutes on a wire rack.

4. Cut each roll diagonally into 20 (1/2-inch) slices. Place the slices, cut sides down, on baking sheets. Bake at 300° for 20 minutes. Turn the cookies over, and bake for an additional 10 minutes (the cookies will be slightly soft in center but will harden as they cool). Remove cookies from baking sheets; cool completely on wire racks. Yield: 5 dozen (serving size: 1 biscotto).

NOTE: To toast the hazelnuts, place on a baking sheet, and bake at 350° for 15 minutes, stirring once. Turn the nuts out onto a towel; roll up the towel, and rub off the skins (some skin will remain on the nuts). Chop nuts.

CALORIES 38 (24% from fat); FAT 1g (sat 0.1g, mono 0.6g, poly 0.1g); PROTEIN 0.8g; CARB 6.9g; FIBER 0.2g; CHOL 4mg; IRON 0.3mg; SODIUM 30mg; CALC 5mg

HOW TO USE IT AND WHY Glance at the end of any *Cooking Light* recipe, and you'll see how committed we are to helping you make the best of today's light cooking. With chefs, registered dietitians, home economists, and a computer system that analyzes every ingredient we use, *Cooking Light* gives you authoritative dietary detail like no other magazine. We go to such lengths so you can see how our recipes fit into your healthful eating plan. If you're trying to lose weight, the calorie and fat figures will probably help most. But if you're keeping a close eye on the sodium, cholesterol, and saturated fat in your diet, we provide those numbers, too. And because many women don't get enough iron or calcium, we can also help there, as well. Finally, there's a fiber analysis for those of us who don't get enough roughage.

Here's a helpful guide to put our nutrition analysis numbers into perspective. Remember, one size doesn't fit all, so take your lifestyle, age, and circumstances into consideration when determining your nutrition needs. For example, pregnant or breast-feeding women need more protein, calories, and calcium. And men over 50 need 1,200mg of calcium daily, 200mg more than the amount recommended for younger men.

IN OUR NUTRITIONAL ANALYSIS, WE USE THESE ABBREVIATIONS:

sat	saturated fat	**CHOL**	cholesterol
mono	monounsaturated fat	**CALC**	calcium
poly	polyunsaturated fat	**g**	gram
CARB	carbohydrates	**mg**	milligram

Your Daily Nutrition Guide

	WOMEN AGES 25 TO 50	WOMEN OVER 50	MEN OVER 24
Calories	2,000	2,000 or less	2,700
Protein	50g	50g or less	63g
Fat	65g or less	65g or less	88g or less
Saturated Fat	20g or less	20g or less	27g or less
Carbohydrates	304g	304g	410g
Fiber	25g to 35g	25g to 35g	25g to 35g
Cholesterol	300mg or less	300mg or less	300mg or less
Iron	18mg	8mg	8mg
Sodium	2,400mg or less	2,400mg or less	2,400mg or less
Calcium	1,000mg	1,200mg	1,000mg

The nutritional values used in our calculations either come from The Food Processor, Version 7.5 (ESHA Research), or are provided by food manufacturers.

index

index

index

index